COLLEGE MATHEMATICS II

Custom Edition

Robert Blitzer

Edited by Brian K. Saltzer

Taken from
Algebra and Trigonometry, Second Edition
by Robert Blitzer

PEARSON
Custom
Publishing

PEARSON
Prentice
Hall

Cover Art: *Roof*, by Barry Cronin.

Taken from:

Algebra and Trigonometry, Second Edition
by Robert Blitzer
Copyright © 2004, 2001 by Pearson Education, Inc.
Published by Prentice-Hall
Upper Saddle River, New Jersey 07458

This special edition published in cooperation with Pearson Custom Publishing.

Printed in the United States of America

10 9 8 7 6 5 4 3

ISBN 0-536-81126-1

BA 999146

JP

Please visit our web site at *www.pearsoncustom.com*

PEARSON CUSTOM PUBLISHING
75 Arlington Street, Suite 300, Boston, MA 02116
A Pearson Education Company

Contents

Chapter 3

Exponential and Logarithmic Functions   158

3.1 Exponential Functions 159
3.2 Logarithmic Functions 170
3.3 Properties of Logarithms 183
3.4 Exponential and Logarithmic Equations 192
3.5 Modeling with Exponential and Logarithmic Functions 203
Summary 217
Review Exercises 218
Chapter 3 Test 222

Chapter 4

Sequences and Probability   223

4.1 Sequences and Summation Notation 224
4.2 Arithmetic Sequences 235
4.3 Geometric Sequences 244
4.4 Counting Principles, Permutations, and Combinations 258
4.5 Probability 270
Summary 283
Review Exercises 285
Chapter 4 Test 288

Answers to Selected Exercises AA1
Subject Index I1
Photo Credits P1

Preface

'*ve written **Algebra and Trigonometry, Second Edition, Vols I and II** to help diverse students, with different backgrounds and future goals to succeed. These books have three fundamental goals:

1. To help students acquire a solid foundation in algebra and trigonometry, preparing them for other courses such as calculus, business calculus, and finite mathematics.
2. To show students how algebra and trigonometry can model and solve authentic real-world problems.
3. To enable students to develop problem-solving skills, while fostering critical thinking, within an interesting setting.

One major obstacle in the way of achieving these goals is the fact that very few students actually read their textbook. This has been a regular source of frustration for me and my colleagues in the classroom. Anectodal evidence gathered over years highlights two basic reasons that students do not take advantage of their textbook:

- "I'll never use this information."
- "I can't follow the explanations."

As a result, I've written every page of these books with the intent of eliminating these two objections.

A Brief Note on Technology

Technology, and specifically the use of a graphing utility, is covered thoroughly, although its coverage by an instructor is optional. If you require the use of a graphing utility in the course, you will find support for this approach, particularly in the wide selection of clearly designated technology exercises in each exercise set. If you wish to minimize or eliminate the discussion or use of a graphing utility, these books are written to enable you to do so. Regardless of the role technology plays in your course, the technology boxes with TI-83 screens that appear throughout the books should allow your students to understand what graphing utilities can do, enabling them to visualize, verify, or explore what they have already graphed or manipulated by hand. The books' technology coverage is intended to reinforce, but never replace, algebraic solutions.

Acknowledgments

I wish to express my appreciation to all of the reviewers of my precalculus series for their helpful criticisms and suggestions, frequently transmitted with wit, humor, and intelligence. In particular, I would like to thank the following for reviewing **College Algebra**, **Algebra and Trigonometry,** and **Precalculus.**

Reviewers for the Previous Editions

Kayoko Yates Barnhill, *Clark College*
Lloyd Best, *Pacific Union College*
Diana Colt, *University of Minnesota-Duluth*
Yvelyne Germain-McCarthy, *University of New Orleans*
Cynthia Glickman, *Community College of Southern Nevada*
Sudhir Kumar Goel, *Valdosta State University*
Donald Gordon, *Manatee Community College*
David L. Gross, *University of Connecticut*
Joel K. Haack, *University of Northern Iowa*
Mike Hall, *Univeristy of Mississippi*
Christopher N. Hay-Jahans, *University of South Dakota*
Celeste Hernandez, *Richland College*
Winfield A. Ihlow, *SUNY College at Oswego*
Nancy Raye Johnson, *Manatee Community College*
James Miller, *West Virginia University*
Debra A. Pharo, *Northwestern Michigan College*
Gloria Phoenix, *North Carolina Agricultural and Technical State University*
Juha Pohjanpelto, *Oregon State University*
Richard E. Van Lommel, *California State University-Sacramento*
Dan Van Peursem, *University of South Dakota*
David White, *The Victoria College*

Reviewers for the Current Edition

Timothy Beaver, *Isothermal Community College*
Bill Burgin, *Gaston College*
Jimmy Chang, *St. Petersburg College*
Donna Densmore, *Bossier Parish Community College*
Disa Enegren, *Rose State College*
Nancy Fisher, *University of Alabama*
Jeremy Haefner, *University of Colorado*
Joyce Hague, *University of Wisconsin at River Falls*
Mary Leesburg, *Manatee Community College*
Christine Heinecke Lehmann, *Purdue University North Central*
Alexander Levichev, *Boston University*
Zongzhu Lin, *Kansas State University*
Benjamin Marlin, *Northwestern Oklahoma State University*
Marilyn Massey, *Collin County Community College*
David Platt, *Front Range Community College*
Janice Rech, *University of Nebraska at Omaha*
Judith Salmon, *Fitchburg State College*
Cynthia Schultz, *Illinois Valley Community College*
Chris Stump, *Bethel College*
Pamela Trim, *Southwest Tennessee Community College*
Chris Turner, *Arkansas State University*
Philip Van Veldhuizen, *University of Nevada at Reno*
Tracy Wienckowski, *Univesity of Buffalo*

To the Student

I've written these two volumes so that you can learn about the power of algebra and trigonometry and how it relates directly to your life outside the classroom. All concepts are carefully explained, important definitions and procedures are set off in boxes, and worked-out examples that present solutions in a step-by-step manner appear in every section. Each example is followed by a similar matched problem, called a Check Point, for you to try so that you can actively participate in the learning process as you read the books. (Answers to all Check Points appear in the back of each book.) Study Tips offer hints and suggestions and often point out common errors to avoid. A great deal of attention has been given to applying algebra and trigonometry to your life to make your learning experience both interesting and relevant.

As you begin your studies, I would like to offer some specific suggestions for using these books and for being successful in this course:

1. **Attend all lectures.** No book is intended to be a substitute for valuable insights and interactions that occur in the classroom. In addition to arriving for lectures on time and being prepared, you will find it useful to read the section before it is covered in the lecture. This will give you a clear idea of the new material that will be discussed.

2. **Read the book.** Read each section with pen (or pencil) in hand. Move through the illustrative examples with great care. These worked-out examples provide a model for doing exercises in the exercise sets. As you proceed through the reading, do not give up if you do not understand every single word. Things will become clearer as you read on and see how various procedures are applied to specific worked-out examples.

3. **Work problems every day and check your answers.** The way to learn mathematics is by doing mathematics, which means working the Check Points and assigned exercises in the exercise sets. The more exercises you work, the better you will understand the material.

4. **Prepare for chapter exams.** After completing a chapter, study the summary, work the exercises in the Chapter Review, and work the exercises in the Chapter Test. Answers to all these exercises are given in the back of each book.

5. **Use the supplements available with this book.** A solutions manual containing worked-out solutions to each book's odd-numbered exercises, all review exercises, and all Check Points; a dynamic web page; and videotapes and CD-ROMs created for every section of the books are among the supplements created to help you tap into the power of mathematics. Ask your instructor or bookstore which supplements are available and where you can find them.

I wrote this book in beautiful and pristine Point Reyes National Seashore, north of San Francisco. It was my hope to convey the beauty of mathematics using nature as a source of inspiration and creativity. Enjoy the pages that follow as you empower yourself with the algebra and trigonometry needed to succeed in college, your career, and your life.

Regards,
Bob
Robert Blitzer

About the Author

Bob Blitzer is a native of Manhattan and received a Bachelor of Arts degree with dual majors in mathematics and psychology (minor: English literature) from the City College of New York. His unusual combination of academic interests led him toward a Master of Arts in mathematics from the University of Miami and a doctorate in behavioral sciences from Nova University. Bob is most energized by teaching mathematics and has taught a variety of mathematics courses at Miami-Dade Community College for nearly 30 years. He has received numerous teaching awards, including Innovator of the Year from the League for Innovations in the Community College, and was among the first group of recipients at Miami-Dade Community College for an endowed chair based on excellence in the classroom. In addition to *Algebra and Trigonometry*, Bob has written *Introductory Algebra for College Students*, *Intermediate Algebra for College Students*, *Introductory and Intermediate Algebra for College Students*, *Algebra for College Students*, *Thinking Mathematically*, *College Algebra*, and *Precalculus*, all published by Prentice Hall.

Finally, Bob loves to spend time with his pal, Harley, pictured to the right. He's so cute (Harley, not Bob) that we couldn't resist including him.

TUTORIAL

Blitzer M@thP@k

An Integrated Learning Environment

Today's textbooks offer a wide variety of ancillary materials to students, from solutions manuals to tutorial software to text-specific Websites. Making the most of all of these resources can be difficult. Blitzer **M@thP@k** helps students get it together. **M@thP@k** seamlessly integrates the following key products into **an integrated learning environment:**

MathPro 5

MathPro 5 is online, customizable tutorial software integrated with the text at the Learning Objective level. MathPro 5's "watch" feature integrates lecture videos into the algorithmic tutorial environment. The easy-to-use course management system enables instructors to track and assess student performance on tutorial work, quizzes, and tests. A robust reports wizard provides a grade book, individual student reports, and class summaries. The customizable syllabus allows instructors to remove and reorganize chapters, sections, and objectives. MathPro 5's messaging system enhances communication between students and instructors. The combination of MathPro 5's richly integrated tutorial, testing, and robust course management tools provides an unparalleled tutorial experience for students, and new assessment and time-saving tools for instructors.

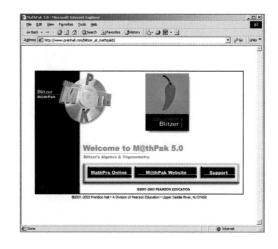

The Blitzer M@thP@k Website

This robust passcode-protected site features quizzes, homework starters, live animated examples, graphing calculator manuals, and much more. It offers the student many ways to test and reinforce their understanding of the course material.

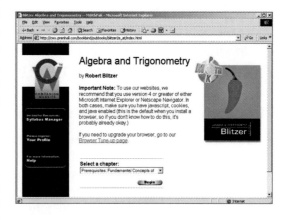

Student Solutions Manual

The *Student Solutions Manual* offers thorough, accurate solutions that are consistent with the precise mathematics found in the text.

Blitzer M@thP@k.
Helping Students Get it Together.

Problem Solving for Students.
Solving Problems for You.

Students need to practice solving problems—The more they practice, the better problem solvers they become. Professors want relief from the tedium of grading.

That's why we created **PH GradeAssist**. It's...

✓ online—available anytime, anywhere.
✓ text-specific—tied directly to your Prentice Hall Precalculus or Calculus text.
✓ algorithmic—contains unlimited questions and assignments for practice and assessment.
✓ customizable—completely unique to your course—edit questions and add yours.

How does PH GradeAssist work for the instructor?

- You create quizzes or homework assignments from question banks specific to your text. Choose the problems you prefer, edit them, or add your own.
- Your students go online and work the assignments that you have created.
- The problems let students work with real math, not just multiple choice.
- Many problems are algorithmically generated, so each student gets a slightly different problem with a different answer.
- PH GradeAssist scores these assignments for you, using a sophisticated math parser, which recognizes algebraic, numeric, and unit equivalents.
- Results can be easily accessed in a central gradebook.

**For a demonstration, contact your local Prentice Hall representative
or visit us online at www.prenhall.com/phga**

Applications Index

Trigonometric Functions

Have you had days where your physical, intellectual, and emotional potentials were all at their peak? Then there are those other days when we feel we should not even bother getting out of bed. Do our potentials run in oscillating cycles like the tides? Can they be described mathematically? In this chapter you will encounter functions that enable us to model phenomena that occur in cycles.

What a day! It started when you added two miles to your morning run. You've experienced a feeling of peak physical well-being ever since. College was wonderful: You actually enjoyed two difficult lectures and breezed through a math test that had you worried. Now you're having dinner with an old group of friends. You experience the warmth from bonds of friendship filling the room.

SECTION 1.1 *Angles and Their Measure*

Objectives

1. Recognize and use the vocabulary of angles.
2. Use degree measure.
3. Draw angles in standard position.
4. Find coterminal angles.
5. Find complements and supplements.
6. Use radian measure.
7. Convert between degrees and radians.
8. Find the length of a circular arc.
9. Use linear and angular speed to describe motion on a circular path.

The San Francisco Museum of Modern Art was constructed in 1995 to illustrate how art and architecture can enrich one another. The exterior involves geometric shapes, symmetry, and unusual facades. Although there are no windows, natural light streams in through a truncated cylindrical skylight that crowns the building. The architect worked with a scale model of the museum at the site and observed how light hit it during different times of the day. These observations were used to cut the cylindrical skylight at an angle that maximizes sunlight entering the interior.

Angles play a critical role in creating modern architecture. They are also fundamental in trigonometry. In this section, we begin our study of trigonometry by looking at angles and methods for measuring them.

1 Recognize and use the vocabulary of angles.

Figure 1.1 Clock with hands forming an angle

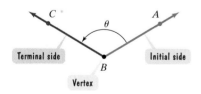

Figure 1.2 An angle; two rays with a common endpoint

Angles

The hour hand of a clock suggests a **ray,** a part of a line that has only one endpoint and extends forever in the opposite direction. An **angle** is formed by two rays that have a common endpoint. One ray is called the **initial side** and the other the **terminal side.**

A rotating ray is often a useful way to think about angles. The ray in Figure 1.1 rotates from 12 to 2. The ray pointing to 12 is the **initial side** and the ray pointing to 2 is the **terminal side.** The common endpoint of an angle's initial side and terminal side is the **vertex** of the angle.

Figure 1.2 shows an angle. The arrow near the vertex shows the direction and the amount of rotation from the initial side to the terminal side. Several methods can be used to name an angle. Lowercase Greek letters, such as α (alpha), β (beta), γ (gamma), and θ (theta), are often used.

An angle is in **standard position** if

- its vertex is at the origin of a rectangular coordinate system

and

- its initial side lies along the positive *x*-axis.

The angles in Figure 1.3 are both in standard position.

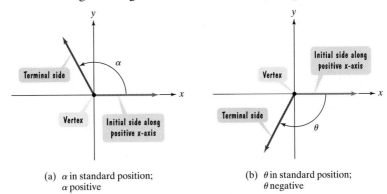

(a) α in standard position; α positive

(b) θ in standard position; θ negative

Figure 1.3 Two angles in standard position

When we see an initial side and a terminal side in place, there are two kinds of rotation that could have generated it. The arrow in Figure 1.3(a) indicates that the rotation from the initial side to the terminal side is in the counterclockwise direction. **Positive angles** are generated by counterclockwise rotation. Thus, angle α is positive. By contrast, the arrow in Figure 1.3(b) shows that the rotation from the initial side to the terminal side is in the clockwise direction. **Negative angles** are generated by clockwise rotation. Thus, angle θ is negative.

When an angle is in standard position, its terminal side can lie in a quadrant. We say that the angle **lies in that quadrant.** For example, in Figure 1.3(a), the terminal side of angle α lies in quadrant II. Thus, angle α lies in quadrant II. By contrast, in Figure 1.3(b), the terminal side of angle θ lies in quadrant III. Thus, angle θ lies in quadrant III.

Must all angles in standard position lie in a quadrant? The answer is no. The terminal side can lie on the x-axis or the y-axis. For example, angle β in Figure 1.4 has a terminal side that lies on the negative y-axis. An angle is called a **quadrantal angle** if its terminal side lies on the x-axis or the y-axis. Angle β in Figure 1.4 is an example of a quadrantal angle.

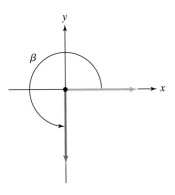

Figure 1.4 β is a quadrantal angle.

2 Use degree measure.

Measuring Angles Using Degrees

Angles are measured by determining the amount of rotation from the initial side to the terminal side. One way to measure angles is in **degrees,** symbolized by a small, raised circle °. Think of the hour hand of a clock. From 12 noon to 12 midnight, the hour hand moves around in a complete circle. By definition, the ray has rotated through 360 degrees, or 360°. Using 360° as the amount of rotation of a ray back onto itself, a degree, 1°, is $\frac{1}{360}$ of a complete rotation.

Figure 1.5 shows angles classified by their degree measurement. An **acute angle** measures less than 90° [see Figure 1.5(a)]. A **right angle,** one quarter of a complete rotation, measures 90° [Figure 1.5(b)]. Examine the right angle—do you see a small square at the vertex? This symbol is used to indicate a right angle. An **obtuse angle** measures more than 90°, but less than 180° [Figure 1.5(c)]. Finally, a **straight angle,** one-half a complete rotation, measures 180° [Figure 1.5(d)].

A complete 360° rotation

Figure 1.5 Classifying angles by their degree measurement

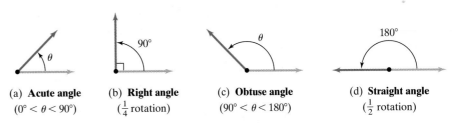

(a) **Acute angle** $(0° < \theta < 90°)$

(b) **Right angle** ($\frac{1}{4}$ rotation)

(c) **Obtuse angle** $(90° < \theta < 180°)$

(d) **Straight angle** ($\frac{1}{2}$ rotation)

3 Draw angles in standard position.

We will be using notation such as $\theta = 60°$ to refer to an angle θ whose measure is 60°. We also refer to *an angle of 60°* or a *60° angle*, rather than using the more precise (but cumbersome) phrase *an angle whose measure is 60°*.

EXAMPLE 1 Drawing Angles in Standard Position

Draw each angle in standard position:

a. a 45° angle   **b.** a 225° angle   **c.** a −135° angle   **d.** a 405° angle.

Solution Because we are drawing angles in standard position, each vertex is at the origin and each initial side lies along the positive *x*-axis.

a. A 45° angle is half of a right angle. The angle lies in quadrant I and is shown in Figure 1.6(a).

b. A 225° angle is a positive angle. It has a counterclockwise rotation of 180° followed by a counterclockwise rotation of 45°. The angle lies in quadrant III and is shown in Figure 1.6(b).

c. A −135° angle is negative angle. It has a clockwise rotation of 90° followed by a clockwise rotation of 45°. The angle lies in quadrant III and is shown in Figure 1.6(c).

d. A 405° angle is a positive angle. It has a counterclockwise rotation of 360°, one complete rotation, followed by a counterclockwise rotation of 45°. The angle lies in quadrant I and is shown in Figure 1.6(d).

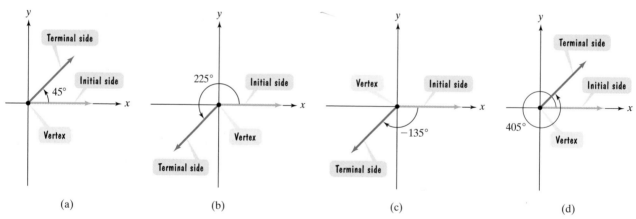

(a)   (b)   (c)   (d)

Figure 1.6 Four angles in standard position

4 Find coterminal angles.

Check Point 1 Draw each angle in standard position:

a. a 30° angle   **b.** a 210° angle
c. a −120° angle   **d.** a 390° angle.

Look at Figure 1.6 again. The 45° and 405° angles in parts (a) and (d) have the same initial and terminal sides. Similarly, the 225° and −135° angles in parts (b) and (c) have the same initial and terminal sides. Two angles with the same initial and terminal sides are called **coterminal angles.**

Every angle has infinitely many coterminal angles. Why? Think of an angle in standard position. One or more complete rotations of 360°, clockwise or counterclockwise, result in angles with the same initial and terminal sides as the original angle.

> **Coterminal Angles**
> An angle of $x°$ is coterminal with angles of
> $$x° + k \cdot 360°$$
> where k is an integer.

Two coterminal angles for an angle of $x°$ can be found by adding 360° to $x°$ and subtracting 360° from $x°$.

EXAMPLE 2   Finding Coterminal Angles

Assume the following angles are in standard position. Find a positive angle less than 360° that is coterminal with:

a. a 420° angle   **b.** a −120° angle.

Solution   We obtain the coterminal angle by adding or subtracting 360°. The requirement to obtain a positive angle less than 360° determines whether we should add or subtract.

a. For a 420° angle, subtract 360° to find a positive coterminal angle.
$$420° - 360° = 60°$$

A 60° angle is coterminal with a 420° angle. Figure 1.7(a) illustrates that these angles have the same initial and terminal sides.

b. For a −120° angle, add 360° to find a positive coterminal angle.
$$-120° + 360° = 240°$$

A 240° angle is coterminal with a −120° angle. Figure 1.7(b) illustrates that these angles have the same initial and terminal sides.

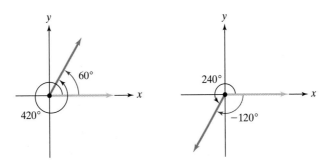

(a) Angles of 420° and 60° are coterminal.

(b) Angles of −120° and 240° are coterminal.

Figure 1.7 Pairs of coterminal angles

Check Point 2 Find a positive angle less than 360° that is coterminal with:
a. a 400° angle   **b.** a −135° angle.

5 Find complements and supplements.

Two positive angles are **complements** if their sum is 90°. For example, angles of 70° and 20° are complements because 70° + 20° = 90°.

Two positive angles are **supplements** if their sum is 180°. For example, angles of 130° and 50° are supplements because 130° + 50° = 180°.

Finding Complements and Supplements

- For an $x°$ angle, the complement is a $90° − x°$ angle. Thus, the complement's measure is found by subtracting the angle's measure from 90°.
- For an $x°$ angle, the supplement is a $180° − x°$ angle. Thus, the supplement's measure is found by subtracting the angle's measure from 180°.

Because we use only positive angles for complements and supplements, some angles do not have complements and supplements.

EXAMPLE 3   Complements and Supplements

If possible, find the complement and the supplement of the given angle:

a. $\theta = 62°$ **b.** $\alpha = 123°$.

Solution   We find the complement by subtracting the angle's measure from 90°. We find the supplement by subtracting the angle's measure from 180°.

a. We begin with $\theta = 62°$.

$$\text{complement} = 90° − 62° = 28°$$
$$\text{supplement} = 180° − 62° = 118°$$

For a 62° angle, the complement is a 28° angle and the supplement is a 118° angle.

b. Now we turn to $\alpha = 123°$. For the angle's complement, we consider subtracting 123° from 90°. The difference is negative. Because we use only positive angles for complements, a 123° angle has no complement. It does, however, have a supplement.

$$\text{supplement} = 180° − 123° = 57°$$

The supplement of a 123° angle is a 57° angle.

Check Point 3 If possible, find the complement and the supplement of the given angle:
a. $\theta = 78°$ **b.** $\alpha = 150°$.

6 Use radian measure.

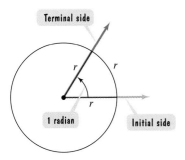

Figure 1.8 For a 1-radian angle, the intercepted arc and the radius are equal.

Measuring Angles Using Radians

Another way to measure angles is in *radians*. Let's first define an angle measuring **1 radian.** We use a circle of radius r. In Figure 1.8, we've constructed an angle whose vertex is at the center of the circle. Such an angle is called a **central angle.** Notice that this central angle intercepts an arc along the circle measuring r units. The radius of the circle is also r units. The measure of such an angle is 1 radian.

Definition of a Radian

One radian is the measure of the central angle of a circle that intercepts an arc equal in length to the radius of the circle.

The **radian measure** of any central angle is the length of the intercepted arc divided by the circle's radius. In Figure 1.9(a), the length of the arc intercepted by angle β is double the radius, r. We find the measure of angle β in radians by dividing the length of the intercepted arc by the radius.

$$\beta = \frac{\text{length of the intercepted arc}}{\text{radius}} = \frac{2r}{r} = 2$$

Thus, angle β measures 2 radians.

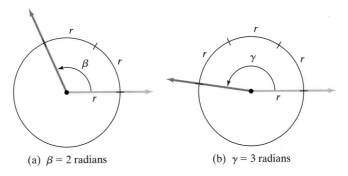

(a) $\beta = 2$ radians   (b) $\gamma = 3$ radians

Figure 1.9 Two central angles measured in radians

In Figure 1.9(b), the length of the intercepted arc is triple the radius, r. Let us find the measure of angle γ:

$$\gamma = \frac{\text{length of the intercepted arc}}{\text{radius}} = \frac{3r}{r} = 3.$$

Thus, angle γ measures 3 radians.

Radian Measure

Consider an arc of length s on a circle of radius r. The measure of the central angle, θ, that intercepts the arc is

$$\theta = \frac{s}{r} \text{ radians.}$$

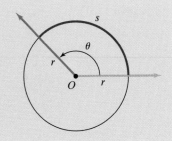

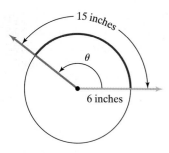

Figure 1.10

EXAMPLE 4 Computing Radian Measure

A central angle, θ, in a circle of radius 6 inches intercepts an arc of length 15 inches. What is the radian measure of θ?

Solution Angle θ is shown in Figure 1.10. The radian measure of a central angle is the length of the intercepted arc, s, divided by the circle's radius, r. The length of the intercepted arc is 15 inches: $s = 15$ inches. The circle's radius is 6 inches: $r = 6$ inches. Now we use the formula for radian measure to find the radian measure of θ.

$$\theta = \frac{s}{r} = \frac{15 \text{ inches}}{6 \text{ inches}} = 2.5$$

Thus, the radian measure of θ is 2.5.

Study Tip

Before applying the formula for radian measure, be sure that the same unit of length is used for the intercepted arc, s, and the radius, r.

In Example 4, notice that the units (inches) cancel when we use the formula for radian measure. We are left with a number with no units. Thus, if an angle θ has a measure of 2.5 radians, we can write $\theta = 2.5$ radians or $\theta = 2.5$. We will often include the word *radians* simply for emphasis. There should be no confusion as to whether radian or degree measure is being used. Why is this so? If θ has a degree measure of, say, $2.5°$, we must include the degree symbol and write $\theta = 2.5°$, and *not* $\theta = 2.5$.

Check Point 4 A central angle, θ, in a circle of radius 12 feet intercepts an arc of length 42 feet. What is the radian measure of θ?

7 Convert between degrees and radians.

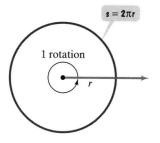

Figure 1.11 A complete rotation

Relationship between Degrees and Radians

How can we obtain a relationship between degrees and radians? We compare the number of degrees and the number of radians in one complete rotation, shown in Figure 1.11. We know that $360°$ is the amount of rotation of a ray back onto itself. The length of the intercepted arc is equal to the circumference of the circle. Thus, the radian measure of this central angle is the circumference of the circle divided by the circle's radius, r. The circumference of a circle of radius r is $2\pi r$. We use the formula for radian measure to find the radian measure of the $360°$ angle.

$$\theta = \frac{s}{r} = \frac{\text{the circle's circumference}}{r} = \frac{2\pi r}{r} = 2\pi$$

Because one complete rotation measures $360°$ and 2π radians,

$$360° = 2\pi \text{ radians.}$$

Dividing both sides by 2, we have

$$180° = \pi \text{ radians.}$$

Dividing this last equation by $180°$ or π gives the conversion rules that appear on the next page.

Study Tip

The unit you are converting *to* appears in the *numerator* of the conversion factor.

Conversion between Degrees and Radians

Using the basic relationship π radians $= 180°$,

1. To convert degrees to radians, multiply degrees by $\dfrac{\pi \text{ radians}}{180°}$.

2. To convert radians to degrees, multiply radians by $\dfrac{180°}{\pi \text{ radians}}$.

Angles that are fractions of a complete rotation are usually expressed in radian measure as fractional multiples of π, rather than as decimal approximations. For example, we write $\theta = \dfrac{\pi}{2}$ rather than using the decimal approximation $\theta \approx 1.57$.

EXAMPLE 5   Converting from Degrees to Radians

Convert each angle in degrees to radians:

  a. $30°$ **b.** $90°$ **c.** $-135°$.

Solution   To convert degrees to radians, multiply by $\dfrac{\pi \text{ radians}}{180°}$. Observe how the degree units cancel.

  a. $30° = 30° \cdot \dfrac{\pi \text{ radians}}{180°} = \dfrac{30\pi}{180} \text{ radians} = \dfrac{\pi}{6} \text{ radians}$

  b. $90° = 90° \cdot \dfrac{\pi \text{ radians}}{180°} = \dfrac{90\pi}{180} \text{ radians} = \dfrac{\pi}{2} \text{ radians}$

  c. $-135° = -135° \cdot \dfrac{\pi \text{ radians}}{180°} = -\dfrac{135\pi}{180} \text{ radians} = -\dfrac{3\pi}{4} \text{ radians}$

Divide the numerator and denominator by 45.

Check Point 5   Convert each angle in degrees to radians:

  a. $60°$ **b.** $270°$ **c.** $-300°$.

EXAMPLE 6   Converting from Radians to Degrees

Convert each angle in radians to degrees:

  a. $\dfrac{\pi}{3}$ radians   **b.** $-\dfrac{5\pi}{3}$ radians   **c.** 1 radian.

Solution   To convert radians to degrees, multiply by $\dfrac{180°}{\pi \text{ radians}}$. Observe how the radian units cancel.

Study Tip

In Example 6(c), we see that 1 radian is approximately 57°. Keep in mind that a radian is much larger than a degree.

a. $\dfrac{\pi}{3}$ radians $= \dfrac{\pi \text{ radians}}{3} \cdot \dfrac{180°}{\pi \text{ radians}} = \dfrac{180°}{3} = 60°$

b. $-\dfrac{5\pi}{3}$ radians $= -\dfrac{5\pi \text{ radians}}{3} \cdot \dfrac{180°}{\pi \text{ radians}} = -\dfrac{5 \cdot 180°}{3} = -300°$

c. 1 radian $= 1 \text{ radian} \cdot \dfrac{180°}{\pi \text{ radians}} = \dfrac{180°}{\pi} \approx 57.3°$

Check Point 6 Convert each angle in radians to degrees:

a. $\dfrac{\pi}{4}$ radians **b.** $-\dfrac{4\pi}{3}$ radians **c.** 6 radians.

Figure 1.12 illustrates the degree and radian measures of angles that you will commonly see in trigonometry. Each angle is in standard position, so that the initial side lies along the positive x-axis. We will be using both degree and radian measure for these angles.

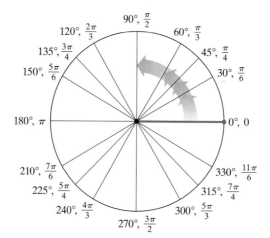

Figure 1.12 Degree and radian measures of selected angles

8 Find the length of a circular arc.

The Length of a Circular Arc

We can use the radian measure formula, $\theta = \dfrac{s}{r}$, to find the length of the arc of a circle. How do we do this? Remember that s represents the length of the arc intercepted by the central angle θ. Thus, by solving the formula for s, we have an equation for arc length.

The Length of a Circular Arc

Let r be the radius of a circle and θ the nonnegative radian measure of a central angle of the circle. The length of the arc intercepted by the central angle is

$$s = r\theta.$$

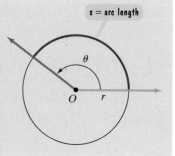

EXAMPLE 7 Finding the Length of a Circular Arc

A circle has a radius of 10 inches. Find the length of the arc intercepted by a central angle of 120°.

Study Tip

The unit used to describe the length of a circular arc is the same unit that is given in the circle's radius.

Solution   The formula $s = r\theta$ can be used only when θ is expressed in radians. Thus, we begin by converting 120° to radians. Multiply by $\dfrac{\pi \text{ radians}}{180°}$.

$$120° = 120° \cdot \frac{\pi \text{ radians}}{180°} = \frac{120\pi}{180} \text{ radians} = \frac{2\pi}{3} \text{ radians}$$

Now we can use the formula $s = r\theta$ to find the length of the arc. The circle's radius is 10 inches: $r = 10$ inches. The measure of the central angle, in radians, is $\dfrac{2\pi}{3}$: $\theta = \dfrac{2\pi}{3}$. The length of the arc intercepted by this central angle is

$$s = r\theta = (10 \text{ inches})\left(\frac{2\pi}{3}\right) = \frac{20\pi}{3} \text{ inches} \approx 20.94 \text{ inches}.$$

> **Check Point 7**
> A circle has a radius of 6 inches. Find the length of the arc intercepted by a central angle of 45°. Express arc length in terms of π. Then round your answer to two decimal places.

9 Use linear and angular speed to describe motion on a circular path.

Linear and Angular Speed

A carousel contains four circular rows of animals. As the carousel revolves, the animals in the outer row travel a greater distance per unit of time than those in the inner rows. These animals have a greater *linear speed* than those in the inner rows. By contrast, all animals, regardless of the row, complete the same number of revolutions per unit of time. All animals in the four circular rows travel at the same *angular speed*.

Using v for linear speed and ω (omega) for angular speed, we define these two kinds of speeds along a circular path as follows:

Definitions of Linear and Angular Speed

If a point is in motion on a circle of radius r through an angle of θ radians in time t, then its **linear speed** is

$$v = \frac{s}{t}$$

where s is the arc length given by $s = r\theta$, and its **angular speed** is

$$\omega = \frac{\theta}{t}.$$

The hard drive in a computer rotates at 3600 revolutions per minute. This angular speed, expressed in revolutions per minute, can also be expressed in revolutions per second, radians per minute, and radians per second. Using 2π radians $= 1$ revolution, we express the angular speed of a hard drive in radians per minute as follows:

3600 revolutions per minute

$$= \frac{3600 \text{ revolutions}}{1 \text{ minute}} \cdot \frac{2\pi \text{ radians}}{1 \text{ revolution}} = \frac{7200\pi \text{ radians}}{1 \text{ minute}}$$

$= 7200\pi$ radians per minute.

We can establish a relationship between the two kinds of speed by dividing both sides of the arc length formula, $s = r\theta$, by t:

$$\frac{s}{t} = \frac{r\theta}{t} = r\frac{\theta}{t}.$$

This expression defines linear speed.

This expression defines angular speed.

Thus, linear speed is the product of the radius and the angular speed.

> **Linear Speed in Terms of Angular Speed**
>
> The linear speed, v, of a point a distance r from the center of rotation is given by
>
> $$v = r\omega$$
>
> where ω is the angular speed in radians per unit of time.

EXAMPLE 8   Finding Linear Speed

A wind machine used to generate electricity has blades that are 10 feet in length (see Figure 1.13). The propeller is rotating at four revolutions per second. Find the linear speed, in feet per second, of the tips of the blades.

10 feet

Figure 1.13

Figure 1.13, repeated

Solution   We are given ω, the angular speed.

$$\omega = 4 \text{ revolutions per second}$$

We use the formula $v = r\omega$ to find v, the linear speed. Before applying the formula, we must express ω in radians per second.

$$\omega = \frac{4 \text{ revolutions}}{1 \text{ second}} \cdot \frac{2\pi \text{ radians}}{1 \text{ revolution}} = \frac{8\pi \text{ radians}}{1 \text{ second}} \quad \text{or} \quad \frac{8\pi}{1 \text{ second}}$$

The angular speed of the propeller is 8π radians per second. The linear speed is

$$v = r\omega = 10 \text{ feet} \cdot \frac{8\pi}{1 \text{ second}} = \frac{80\pi \text{ feet}}{\text{second}}.$$

The linear speed of the tips of the blades is 80π feet per second, which is approximately 251 feet per second.

Check Point 8   A 45-rpm record has an angular speed of 45 revolutions per minute. Find the linear speed, in inches per minute, at the point where the needle is 1.5 inches from the record's center.

EXERCISE SET 1.1

Practice Exercises

In Exercises 1–6, each angle is in standard position. Determine the quadrant in which the angle lies.

1. 145°   **2.** 285°

3. −100°   **4.** −110°

5. 362°   **6.** 364°

In Exercises 7–10, classify the angle as acute, right, straight, or obtuse.

7.

8.

9.

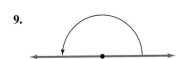

10.

In Exercises 11–18, draw each angle in standard position.

11. 135°   **12.** 120°

13. −150°   **14.** −240°

15. 420°   **16.** 450°

17. −90°   **18.** −270°

In Exercises 19–24, find a positive angle less than 360° that is coterminal with the given angle.

19. 395°   **20.** 415°

21. −150°   **22.** −160°

23. −45°   **24.** −40°

In Exercises 25–30, if possible, find the complement and the supplement of the given angle.

25. 52°   **26.** 85°

27. 37.4°   **28.** 47.6°

29. 111°   **30.** 95°

In Exercises 31–36, find the radian measure of the central angle of a circle of radius r that intercepts an arc of length s.

Radius, r	Arc length, s
31. 10 inches	40 inches
32. 5 feet	30 feet
33. 6 yards	8 yards
34. 8 yards	18 yards
35. 1 meter	400 centimeters
36. 1 meter	600 centimeters

In Exercises 37–44, convert each angle in degrees to radians. Express your answer as a multiple of π.

37. $45°$ **38.** $18°$

39. $135°$ **40.** $150°$

41. $300°$ **42.** $330°$

43. $-225°$ **44.** $-270°$

In Exercises 45–52, convert each angle in radians to degrees.

45. $\dfrac{\pi}{2}$ **46.** $\dfrac{\pi}{9}$

47. $\dfrac{2\pi}{3}$ **48.** $\dfrac{3\pi}{4}$

49. $\dfrac{7\pi}{6}$ **50.** $\dfrac{11\pi}{6}$

51. -3π **52.** -4π

In Exercises 53–58, convert each angle in degrees to radians. Round to two decimal places.

53. $18°$ **54.** $76°$

55. $-40°$ **56.** $-50°$

57. $200°$ **58.** $250°$

In Exercises 59–64, convert each angle in radians to degrees. Round to two decimal places.

59. 2 radians   **60.** 3 radians

61. $\dfrac{\pi}{13}$ radians   **62.** $\dfrac{\pi}{17}$ radians

63. -4.8 radians   **64.** -5.2 radians

In Exercises 65–68, find the length of the arc on a circle of radius r intercepted by a central angle θ. Express arc length in terms of π. Then round your answer to two decimal places.

Radius, r	Central angle, θ
65. 12 inches	$\theta = 45°$
66. 16 inches	$\theta = 60°$
67. 8 feet	$\theta = 225°$
68. 9 yards	$\theta = 315°$

In Exercises 69–70, express each angular speed in radians per second.

69. 6 revolutions per second

70. 20 revolutions per second

Application Exercises

71. The minute hand of a clock moves from 12 to 2 o'clock, or $\frac{1}{6}$ of a complete revolution. Through how many degrees does it move? Through how many radians does it move?

72. The minute hand of a clock moves from 12 to 4 o'clock, or $\frac{1}{3}$ of a complete revolution. Through how many degrees does it move? Through how many radians does it move?

73. The minute hand of a clock is 8 inches long and moves from 12 to 2 o'clock. How far does the tip of the minute hand move? Express your answer in terms of π and then round to two decimal places.

74. The minute hand of a clock is 6 inches long and moves from 12 to 4 o'clock. How far does the tip of the minute hand move? Express your answer in terms of π and then round to two decimal places.

75. The figure shows a highway sign that warns of a railway crossing. The lines that form the cross pass through the circle's center and intersect at right angles. If the radius of the circle is 24 inches, find the length of each of the four arcs formed by the cross. Express your answer in terms of π and then round to two decimal places.

76. The radius of a wheel is 80 centimeters. If the wheel rotates through an angle of $60°$, how many centimeters does it move? Express your answer in terms of π and then round to two decimal places.

How do we measure the distance between two points, A and B, on Earth? We measure along a circle with a center, C, at the center of Earth. The radius of the circle is equal to the distance from C to the surface. Use the fact that Earth is a sphere of radius equal to approximately 4000 miles to solve Exercises 77–80.

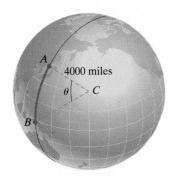

77. If two points, *A* and *B*, are 8000 miles apart, express angle θ in radians and in degrees.

78. If two points, *A* and *B*, are 10,000 miles apart, express angle θ in radians and in degrees.

79. If $\theta = 30°$, find the distance between *A* and *B* to the nearest mile.

80. If $\theta = 10°$, find the distance between *A* and *B* to the nearest mile.

81. The angular speed of a point on Earth is $\frac{\pi}{12}$ radians per hour. The Equator lies on a circle of radius approximately 4000 miles. Find the linear velocity, in miles per hour, of a point on the Equator.

82. A ferris wheel has a radius of 25 feet. The wheel is rotating at three revolutions per minute. Find the linear speed, in feet per minute, of this ferris wheel.

83. A water wheel has a radius of 12 feet. The wheel is rotating at 20 revolutions per minute. Find the linear speed, in feet per minute, of the water.

84. On a carousel, the outer row of animals is 20 feet from the center. The inner row of animals is 10 feet from the center. The carousel is rotating at 2.5 revolutions per minute. What is the difference, in feet per minute, in the linear speeds of the animals in the outer and inner rows? Round to the nearest foot per minute.

Writing in Mathematics

85. What is an angle?

86. What determines the size of an angle?

87. Describe an angle in standard position.

88. Explain the difference between positive and negative angles. What are coterminal angles?

89. Explain what is meant by one radian.

90. Explain how to find the radian measure of a central angle.

91. Describe how to convert an angle in degrees to radians.

92. Explain how to convert an angle in radians to degrees.

93. Explain how to find the length of a circular arc.

94. If a carousel is rotating at 2.5 revolutions per minute, explain how to find the linear speed of a child seated on one of the animals.

95. The angular velocity of a point on Earth is $\frac{\pi}{12}$ radians per hour. Describe what happens every 24 hours.

96. Have you ever noticed that we use the vocabulary of angles in everyday speech? Here is an example:

> My opinion about art museums took a 180° turn after visiting the San Francisco Museum of Modern Art.

Explain what this means. Then give another example of the vocabulary of angles in everyday use.

Technology Exercises

In Exercises 97–100, use the keys on your calculator or graphing utility for converting an angle in degrees, minutes, and seconds ($D°M'S''$) into decimal form, and vice versa.

In Exercises 97–98, convert each angle to a decimal in degrees. Round your answer to two decimal places.

97. $30°15'10''$ **98.** $65°45'20''$

In Exercises 99–100, convert each angle to $D°M'S''$ form. Round your answer to the nearest second.

99. $30.42°$ **100.** $50.42°$

Critical Thinking Exercises

101. If $\theta = \frac{3}{2}$, is this angle larger or smaller than a right angle?

102. A railroad curve is laid out on a circle. What radius should be used if the track is to change direction by 20° in a distance of 100 miles? Round your answer to the nearest mile.

103. Assuming Earth to be a sphere of radius 4000 miles, how many miles north of the Equator is Miami, Florida, if it is 26° north from the Equator? Round your answer to the nearest mile.

SECTION 1.2 *Right Triangle Trigonometry*

Objectives

1. Use right triangles to evaluate trigonometric functions.
2. Find function values for $30° \left(\dfrac{\pi}{6} \right)$, $45° \left(\dfrac{\pi}{4} \right)$, and $60° \left(\dfrac{\pi}{3} \right)$.
3. Recognize and use fundamental identities.
4. Use equal cofunctions of complements.
5. Evaluate trigonometric functions with a calculator.
6. Use right triangle trigonometry to solve applied problems.

In the last century, Ang Rita Sherpa climbed Mount Everest ten times, all without the use of bottled oxygen.

Mountain climbers have forever been fascinated by reaching the top of Mount Everest, sometimes with tragic results. The mountain, on Asia's Tibet-Nepal border, is Earth's highest, peaking at an incredible 29,035 feet. The heights of mountains can be found using **trigonometry.** The word *trigonometry* means *measurement of triangles*. Trigonometry is used in navigation, building, and engineering. For centuries, Muslims used trigonometry and the stars to navigate across the Arabian desert to Mecca, the birthplace of the prophet Muhammad, the founder of Islam. The ancient Greeks used trigonometry to record the locations of thousands of stars and worked out the motion of the Moon relative to Earth. Today, trigonometry is used to study the structure of DNA, the master molecule that determines how we grow from a single cell to a complex, fully developed adult.

1 Use right triangles to evaluate trigonometric functions.

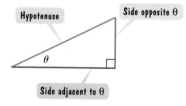

Figure 1.14 Naming a right triangle's sides from the point of view of an acute angle θ

The Six Trigonometric Functions

We begin the study of trigonometry by defining six functions, the six *trigonometric functions*. The inputs for these functions are measures of acute angles in right triangles. The outputs are the ratios of the lengths of the sides of right triangles.

Figure 1.14 shows a right triangle with one of its acute angles labeled θ. The side opposite the right angle is known as the **hypotenuse.** The other sides of the triangle are described by their position relative to the acute angle θ. One side is opposite θ and one is adjacent to θ.

The trigonometric functions have names that are words, rather than single letters such as f, g, and h. For example, the **sine of** θ is the length of the side opposite θ divided by the length of the hypotenuse:

$$\sin \theta = \frac{\text{length of side opposite } \theta}{\text{length of hypotenuse}}.$$

Input is the measure of an acute angle.

Output is the ratio of the lengths of the sides.

The ratio of lengths depends on angle θ and thus is a function of θ. The expression $\sin \theta$ really means $\sin(\theta)$, where sine is the name of the function and θ, the measure of an acute angle, is an input.

Here are the names of the six trigonometric functions, along with their abbreviations:

Name	Abbreviation	Name	Abbreviation
sine	sin	cosecant	csc
cosine	cos	secant	sec
tangent	tan	cotangent	cot

Now, let θ be an acute angle in a right triangle, shown in Figure 1.15. The length of the side opposite θ is a, the length of the side adjacent to θ is b, and the length of the hypotenuse is c.

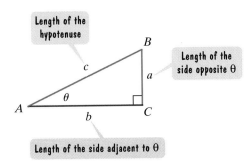

Length of the hypotenuse

Length of the side opposite θ

Length of the side adjacent to θ

Figure 1.15

Right Triangle Definitions of Trigonometric Functions

See Figure 1.15. The six **trigonometric functions of the acute angle θ** are defined as follows:

$$\sin \theta = \frac{\text{length of side opposite angle } \theta}{\text{length of hypotenuse}} = \frac{a}{c} \qquad \csc \theta = \frac{\text{length of hypotenuse}}{\text{length of side opposite angle } \theta} = \frac{c}{a}$$

$$\cos \theta = \frac{\text{length of side adjacent to angle } \theta}{\text{length of hypotenuse}} = \frac{b}{c} \qquad \sec \theta = \frac{\text{length of hypotenuse}}{\text{length of side adjacent to angle } \theta} = \frac{c}{b}$$

$$\tan \theta = \frac{\text{length of side opposite angle } \theta}{\text{length of side adjacent to angle } \theta} = \frac{a}{b} \qquad \cot \theta = \frac{\text{length of side adjacent to angle } \theta}{\text{length of side opposite angle } \theta} = \frac{b}{a}$$

Each of the trigonometric functions of the acute angle θ is positive. Observe that the functions in the second column in the box are the reciprocals of the corresponding functions in the first column.

Figure 1.16 on the next page shows four right triangles of varying sizes. In each of the triangles, θ is the same acute angle, measuring approximately 56.3°. All four of these similar triangles have the same shape and the lengths of corresponding sides are in the same ratio. In each triangle, the tangent function has the same value: $\tan \theta = \frac{3}{2}$.

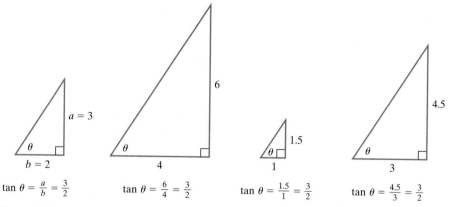

$$\tan \theta = \frac{a}{b} = \frac{3}{2} \qquad \tan \theta = \frac{6}{4} = \frac{3}{2} \qquad \tan \theta = \frac{1.5}{1} = \frac{3}{2} \qquad \tan \theta = \frac{4.5}{3} = \frac{3}{2}$$

Figure 1.16 A particular acute angle always gives the same ratio of opposite to adjacent sides.

In general, **the trigonometric function values of θ depend only on the size of angle θ, and not on the size of the triangle.**

Figure 1.17

EXAMPLE 1   Evaluating Trigonometric Functions

Find the value of each of the six trigonometric functions of θ in Figure 1.17.

Solution   We need to find the values of the six trigonometric functions of θ. However, we must know the lengths of all three sides of the triangle (a, b, and c) to evaluate all six functions. The values of a and b are given. We can use the Pythagorean Theorem, $c^2 = a^2 + b^2$, to find c.

$a = 5$ $b = 12$

$$c^2 = a^2 + b^2 = 5^2 + 12^2 = 25 + 144 = 169$$

$$c = \sqrt{169} = 13$$

Now that we know the lengths of the three sides of the triangle, we apply the definitions of the six trigonometric functions of θ. Referring to these lengths as opposite, adjacent, and hypotenuse, we have

$$\sin \theta = \frac{\text{opposite}}{\text{hypotenuse}} = \frac{5}{13} \qquad \csc \theta = \frac{\text{hypotenuse}}{\text{opposite}} = \frac{13}{5}$$

$$\cos \theta = \frac{\text{adjacent}}{\text{hypotenuse}} = \frac{12}{13} \qquad \sec \theta = \frac{\text{hypotenuse}}{\text{adjacent}} = \frac{13}{12}$$

$$\tan \theta = \frac{\text{opposite}}{\text{adjacent}} = \frac{5}{12} \qquad \cot \theta = \frac{\text{adjacent}}{\text{opposite}} = \frac{12}{5}.$$

Study Tip

The functions in the second column are reciprocals of those in the first column. You can obtain their values by exchanging the numerator and denominator of the corresponding ratios in the first column.

Check Point 1   Find the value of each of the six trigonometric functions of θ in the figure.

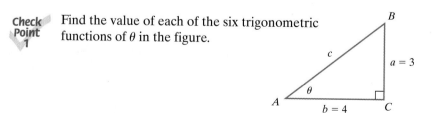

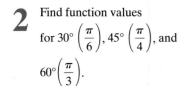

2 Find function values for 30° $\left(\frac{\pi}{6}\right)$, 45° $\left(\frac{\pi}{4}\right)$, and 60° $\left(\frac{\pi}{3}\right)$.

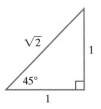

Figure 1.18 An isosceles right triangle

Function Values for Some Special Angles

A 45°, or $\frac{\pi}{4}$ radian, angle occurs frequently in trigonometry. How do we find the values of the trigonometric functions of 45°? We construct a right triangle with a 45° angle, shown in Figure 1.18. The triangle actually has two 45° angles. Thus, the triangle is isosceles—that is, it has two sides of the same length. Assume that each leg of the triangle has a length equal to 1. We can find the length of the hypotenuse using the Pythagorean Theorem.

$$(\text{length of hypotenuse})^2 = 1^2 + 1^2 = 2$$
$$\text{length of hypotenuse} = \sqrt{2}$$

With Figure 1.18, we can determine the trigonometric function values for 45°.

EXAMPLE 2   Evaluating Trigonometric Functions of 45°

Use Figure 1.18 to find sin 45°, cos 45°, and tan 45°.

Solution   We apply the definitions of these three trigonometric functions.

$$\sin 45° = \frac{\text{length of side opposite 45°}}{\text{length of hypotenuse}} = \frac{1}{\sqrt{2}}$$

$$\cos 45° = \frac{\text{length of side adjacent to 45°}}{\text{length of hypotenuse}} = \frac{1}{\sqrt{2}}$$

$$\tan 45° = \frac{\text{length of side opposite 45°}}{\text{length of side adjacent to 45°}} = \frac{1}{1} = 1$$

Check Point 2   Use Figure 1.18 to find csc 45°, sec 45°, and cot 45°.

When you worked Check Point 2, did you actually use Figure 1.18 or did you use reciprocals to find the values?

$$\csc 45° = \sqrt{2} \qquad \sec 45° = \sqrt{2} \qquad \cot 45° = 1$$

Take the reciprocal of sin 45° = $\frac{1}{\sqrt{2}}$. Take the reciprocal of cos 45° = $\frac{1}{\sqrt{2}}$. Take the reciprocal of tan 45° = $\frac{1}{1}$.

We found that sin 45° = $\frac{1}{\sqrt{2}}$ and cos 45° = $\frac{1}{\sqrt{2}}$. This value is often expressed by rationalizing the denominator:

$$\frac{1}{\sqrt{2}} = \frac{1}{\sqrt{2}} \cdot \frac{\sqrt{2}}{\sqrt{2}} = \frac{\sqrt{2}}{2}.$$

We are multiplying by 1 and not changing the value of $\frac{1}{\sqrt{2}}$.

Thus, sin 45° = $\frac{\sqrt{2}}{2}$ and cos 45° = $\frac{\sqrt{2}}{2}$.

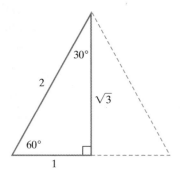

Figure 1.19 30°–60°–90° triangle

Two other angles that occur frequently in trigonometry are 30°, or $\frac{\pi}{6}$ radian, and 60°, or $\frac{\pi}{3}$ radian, angles. We can find the values of the trigonometric functions of 30° and 60° by using a right triangle. To form this right triangle, draw an equilateral triangle—that is a triangle with all sides the same length. Assume that each side has a length equal to 2. Now take half of the equilateral triangle. We obtain the right triangle in Figure 1.19. This right triangle has a hypotenuse of length 2 and a leg of length 1. The other leg has length a, which can be found using the Pythagorean Theorem.

$$a^2 + 1^2 = 2^2$$
$$a^2 + 1 = 4$$
$$a^2 = 3$$
$$a = \sqrt{3}$$

With the right triangle in Figure 1.19, we can determine the trigonometric functions for 30° and 60°.

EXAMPLE 3   Evaluating Trigonometric Functions of 30° and 60°

Use Figure 1.19 to find $\sin 60°$, $\cos 60°$, $\sin 30°$, and $\cos 30°$.

Solution   We begin with 60°. Use the angle on the lower left in Figure 1.19.

$$\sin 60° = \frac{\text{length of side opposite } 60°}{\text{length of hypotenuse}} = \frac{\sqrt{3}}{2}$$

$$\cos 60° = \frac{\text{length of side adjacent to } 60°}{\text{length of hypotenuse}} = \frac{1}{2}$$

To find $\sin 30°$ and $\cos 30°$, use the angle on the upper right in Figure 1.19.

$$\sin 30° = \frac{\text{length of side opposite } 30°}{\text{length of hypotenuse}} = \frac{1}{2}$$

$$\cos 30° = \frac{\text{length of side adjacent to } 30°}{\text{length of hypotenuse}} = \frac{\sqrt{3}}{2}$$

Check Point 3   Use Figure 1.19 to find $\tan 60°$ and $\tan 30°$. If a radical appears in a denominator, rationalize the denominator.

Because we will often use the function values of 30°, 45°, and 60°, you should learn to construct the right triangles shown in Figures 1.18 and 1.19. With sufficient practice, you will memorize the values in the box on the next page.

Sines, Cosines, and Tangents of Special Angles

$$\sin 30° = \sin \frac{\pi}{6} = \frac{1}{2} \qquad \cos 30° = \cos \frac{\pi}{6} = \frac{\sqrt{3}}{2} \qquad \tan 30° = \tan \frac{\pi}{6} = \frac{\sqrt{3}}{3}$$

$$\sin 45° = \sin \frac{\pi}{4} = \frac{\sqrt{2}}{2} \qquad \cos 45° = \cos \frac{\pi}{4} = \frac{\sqrt{2}}{2} \qquad \tan 45° = \tan \frac{\pi}{4} = 1$$

$$\sin 60° = \sin \frac{\pi}{3} = \frac{\sqrt{3}}{2} \qquad \cos 60° = \cos \frac{\pi}{3} = \frac{1}{2} \qquad \tan 60° = \tan \frac{\pi}{3} = \sqrt{3}$$

3 Recognize and use fundamental identities.

Fundamental Identities

Many relationships exist among the six trigonometric functions. These relationships are described using **trigonometric identities.** For example, $\csc \theta$ is defined as the reciprocal of $\sin \theta$. This relationship can be expressed by the identity

$$\csc \theta = \frac{1}{\sin \theta}.$$

This identity is one of six **reciprocal identities.**

Reciprocal Identities

$$\sin \theta = \frac{1}{\csc \theta} \qquad \cos \theta = \frac{1}{\sec \theta} \qquad \tan \theta = \frac{1}{\cot \theta}$$

$$\csc \theta = \frac{1}{\sin \theta} \qquad \sec \theta = \frac{1}{\cos \theta} \qquad \cot \theta = \frac{1}{\tan \theta}$$

Two other relationships that follow from the definitions of the trigonometric functions are called the **quotient identities.**

Quotient Identities

$$\tan \theta = \frac{\sin \theta}{\cos \theta} \qquad \cot \theta = \frac{\cos \theta}{\sin \theta}$$

If $\sin \theta$ and $\cos \theta$ are known, a quotient identity and three reciprocal identities make it possible to find the value of each of the four remaining trigonometric functions.

EXAMPLE 4   Using Quotient and Reciprocal Identities

Given $\sin\theta = \dfrac{1}{2}$ and $\cos\theta = \dfrac{\sqrt{3}}{2}$, find the value of each of the four remaining trigonometric functions.

Solution   We can find $\tan\theta$ by using the quotient identity that describes $\tan\theta$ as the quotient of $\sin\theta$ and $\cos\theta$.

$$\tan\theta = \frac{\sin\theta}{\cos\theta} = \frac{\dfrac{1}{2}}{\dfrac{\sqrt{3}}{2}} = \frac{1}{2}\cdot\frac{2}{\sqrt{3}} = \frac{1}{\sqrt{3}} = \frac{1}{\sqrt{3}}\cdot\frac{\sqrt{3}}{\sqrt{3}} = \frac{\sqrt{3}}{3}$$

Rationalize the denominator.

We use the reciprocal identities to find the value of each of the remaining three functions.

$$\csc\theta = \frac{1}{\sin\theta} = \frac{1}{\dfrac{1}{2}} = 2$$

$$\sec\theta = \frac{1}{\cos\theta} = \frac{1}{\dfrac{\sqrt{3}}{2}} = \frac{2}{\sqrt{3}} = \frac{2}{\sqrt{3}}\cdot\frac{\sqrt{3}}{\sqrt{3}} = \frac{2\sqrt{3}}{3}$$

Rationalize the denominator.

$$\cot\theta = \frac{1}{\tan\theta} = \frac{1}{\dfrac{1}{\sqrt{3}}} = \sqrt{3}$$ We found $\tan\theta = \dfrac{1}{\sqrt{3}}$. We could use $\tan\theta = \dfrac{\sqrt{3}}{3}$, but then we would have to rationalize the denominator.

Check Point 4   Given $\sin\theta = \dfrac{2}{3}$ and $\cos\theta = \dfrac{\sqrt{5}}{3}$, find the value of each of the four remaining trigonometric functions.

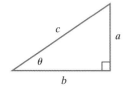

Figure 1.20

Other relationships among trigonometric functions follow from the Pythagorean Theorem. Using Figure 1.20, the Pythagorean Theorem states that

$$a^2 + b^2 = c^2.$$

To obtain ratios that correspond to trigonometric functions, divide both sides of this equation by c^2.

$$\frac{a^2}{c^2} + \frac{b^2}{c^2} = 1 \quad \text{or} \quad \left(\frac{a}{c}\right)^2 + \left(\frac{b}{c}\right)^2 = 1$$

In Figure 1.20, $\sin\theta = \dfrac{a}{c}$, so this is $(\sin\theta)^2$.

In Figure 1.20, $\cos\theta = \dfrac{b}{c}$, so this is $(\cos\theta)^2$.

Based on the observations in the voice balloons, we see that

$$(\sin\theta)^2 + (\cos\theta)^2 = 1.$$

We will use the notation $\sin^2\theta$ for $(\sin\theta)^2$ and $\cos^2\theta$ for $(\cos\theta)^2$. With this notation, we can write the identity as

$$\sin^2\theta + \cos^2\theta = 1.$$

Two additional identities can be obtained from $a^2 + b^2 = c^2$ by dividing both sides by b^2 and a^2, respectively. The three identities are called the **Pythagorean identities.**

Pythagorean Identities

$$\sin^2\theta + \cos^2\theta = 1 \qquad 1 + \tan^2\theta = \sec^2\theta \qquad 1 + \cot^2\theta = \csc^2\theta$$

EXAMPLE 5 Using a Pythagorean Identity

Given that $\sin\theta = \frac{3}{5}$ and θ is an acute angle, find the value of $\cos\theta$ using a trigonometric identity.

Solution   We can find the value of $\cos\theta$ by using the Pythagorean identity

$$\sin^2\theta + \cos^2\theta = 1.$$

$$\left(\frac{3}{5}\right)^2 + \cos^2\theta = 1 \qquad \text{We are given that } \sin\theta = \frac{3}{5}.$$

$$\frac{9}{25} + \cos^2\theta = 1 \qquad \text{Square } \frac{3}{5}: \left(\frac{3}{5}\right)^2 = \frac{3^2}{5^2} = \frac{9}{25}.$$

$$\cos^2\theta = 1 - \frac{9}{25} \qquad \text{Subtract } \frac{9}{25} \text{ from both sides.}$$

$$\cos^2\theta = \frac{16}{25} \qquad \text{Simplify: } 1 - \frac{9}{25} = \frac{25}{25} - \frac{9}{25} = \frac{16}{25}.$$

$$\cos\theta = \sqrt{\frac{16}{25}} = \frac{4}{5} \qquad \text{Because } \theta \text{ is an acute angle, } \cos\theta \text{ is positive.}$$

Thus, $\cos\theta = \frac{4}{5}$.

Check Point 5   Given that $\sin\theta = \frac{1}{2}$ and θ is an acute angle, find the value of $\cos\theta$ using a trigonometric identity.

4   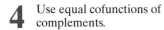 Use equal cofunctions of complements.

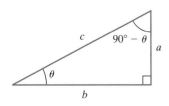

Figure 1.21

Trigonometric Functions and Complements

Another relationship among trigonometric functions is based on angles that are complements. Refer to Figure 1.21. Because the sum of the angles of any triangle is 180°, in a right triangle the sum of the acute angles is 90°. Thus, the acute angles are complements. If the degree measure of one acute angle is θ, then the degree measure of the other acute angle is $(90° - \theta)$. This angle is shown on the upper right in Figure 1.21.

Let's use Figure 1.21 to compare $\sin\theta$ and $\cos(90° - \theta)$.

$$\sin\theta = \frac{\text{length of side opposite } \theta}{\text{length of hypotenuse}} = \frac{a}{c}$$

$$\cos(90° - \theta) = \frac{\text{length of side adjacent to } (90° - \theta)}{\text{length of hypotenuse}} = \frac{a}{c}$$

Thus, $\sin\theta = \cos(90° - \theta)$. If two angles are complements, the sine of one equals the cosine of the other. Because of this relationship, the sine and cosine are called *cofunctions* of each other. The name *cosine* is a shortened form of the phrase *complement's sine.*

Any pair of trigonometric functions f and g for which

$$f(\theta) = g(90° - \theta) \quad \text{and} \quad g(\theta) = f(90° - \theta)$$

are called **cofunctions.** Using Figure 1.21, we can show that the tangent and cotangent are also cofunctions of each other. So are the secant and cosecant.

Cofunction Identities

The value of a trigonometric function of θ is equal to the cofunction of the complement of θ.

$$\sin \theta = \cos(90° - \theta) \qquad \cos \theta = \sin(90° - \theta)$$

$$\tan \theta = \cot(90° - \theta) \qquad \cot \theta = \tan(90° - \theta)$$

$$\sec \theta = \csc(90° - \theta) \qquad \csc \theta = \sec(90° - \theta)$$

If θ is in radians, replace 90° with $\dfrac{\pi}{2}$.

EXAMPLE 6

Find a cofunction with the same value as the given expression:

$$\textbf{a. } \sin 72° \qquad \textbf{b. } \csc \frac{\pi}{3}.$$

Solution   Because the value of a trigonometric function of θ is equal to the cofunction of the complement of θ, we need to find the complement of each angle. We do this by subtracting the angle's measure from 90° or its radian equivalent, $\dfrac{\pi}{2}$.

a. $\sin 72° = \cos(90° - 72°) = \cos 18°$

> We have a function and its cofunction.

b. $\csc \dfrac{\pi}{3} = \sec\left(\dfrac{\pi}{2} - \dfrac{\pi}{3}\right) = \sec\left(\dfrac{3\pi}{6} - \dfrac{2\pi}{6}\right) = \sec \dfrac{\pi}{6}$

> We have a cofunction and its function.

> Perform the subtraction using the least common denominator, 6.

Check Point 6   Find a cofunction with the same value as the given expression:

$$\textbf{a. } \sin 46° \quad \textbf{b. } \cot \frac{\pi}{12}.$$

5 Evaluate trigonometric functions with a calculator.

Using a Calculator to Evaluate Trigonometric Functions

The values of the trigonometric functions obtained with the special triangles are exact values. For most angles other than 30°, 45°, and 60°, we approximate the value of each of the trigonometric functions using a calculator. The first step is to set the calculator to the correct *mode*, degrees or radians, depending on how the acute angle is measured.

Most calculators have keys marked $\boxed{\text{SIN}}$, $\boxed{\text{COS}}$, and $\boxed{\text{TAN}}$. For example, to find the value of sin 30°, set the calculator to the degree mode and enter 30 $\boxed{\text{SIN}}$ on most scientific calculators and $\boxed{\text{SIN}}$ 30 $\boxed{\text{ENTER}}$ on most graphing calculators. Consult the manual for your calculator.

To evaluate the cosecant, secant, and cotangent functions, use the key for the respective reciprocal function, $\boxed{\text{SIN}}$, $\boxed{\text{COS}}$, or $\boxed{\text{TAN}}$, and then use the reciprocal key. The reciprocal key is $\boxed{1/x}$ on many scientific calculators and $\boxed{x^{-1}}$ on many graphing calculators. For example, we can evaluate $\sec \dfrac{\pi}{12}$ using the following reciprocal relationship:

$$\sec \frac{\pi}{12} = \frac{1}{\cos \dfrac{\pi}{12}}.$$

Using the radian mode, enter one of the following keystroke sequences:

Many Scientific Calculators

$$\boxed{\pi}\ \boxed{\div}\ \boxed{12}\ \boxed{=}\ \boxed{\text{COS}}\ \boxed{1/x}$$

Many Graphing Calculators

$$\boxed{(}\ \boxed{\text{COS}}\ \boxed{(}\ \boxed{\pi}\ \boxed{\div}\ \boxed{12}\ \boxed{)}\ \boxed{)}\ \boxed{x^{-1}}\ \boxed{\text{ENTER}}.$$

Rounding the display to four decimal places, we obtain $\sec \dfrac{\pi}{12} = 1.0353$.

> **EXAMPLE 7** **Evaluating Trigonometric Functions with a Calculator**

Use a calculator to find the value to four decimal places:

    a. $\cos 48.2°$ **b.** $\cot 1.2$.

Solution

Scientific Calculator Solution

Function	Mode	Keystrokes	Display, rounded to four decimal places
a. $\cos 48.2°$	Degree	48.2 $\boxed{\text{COS}}$	0.6665
b. $\cot 1.2$	Radian	1.2 $\boxed{\text{TAN}}\boxed{1/x}$	0.3888

Graphing Calculator Solution

Function	Mode	Keystrokes	Display, rounded to four decimal places
a. $\cos 48.2°$	Degree	$\boxed{\text{COS}}$ 48.2 $\boxed{\text{ENTER}}$	0.6665
b. $\cot 1.2$	Radian	$\boxed{(}\ \boxed{\text{TAN}}\ 1.2\ \boxed{)}\ \boxed{x^{-1}}\ \boxed{\text{ENTER}}$	0.3888

Check Point 7

Use a calculator to find the value to four decimal places:
a. sin 72.8°   **b.** csc 1.5.

6 Use right triangle trigonometry to solve applied problems.

Applications

Many applications of right triangle trigonometry involve the angle made with an imaginary horizontal line. As shown in Figure 1.22, an angle formed by a horizontal line and the line of sight to an object that is above the horizontal line is called the **angle of elevation.** The angle formed by a horizontal line and the line of sight to an object that is below the horizontal line is called the **angle of depression.** Transits and sextants are instruments used to measure such angles.

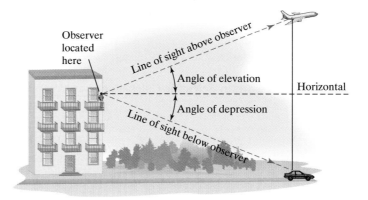

Figure 1.22

EXAMPLE 8 Problem Solving Using an Angle of Elevation

Sighting the top of a building, a surveyor measured the angle of elevation to be 22°. The transit is 5 feet above the ground and 300 feet from the building. Find the building's height.

Solution The situation is illustrated in Figure 1.23. Let a be the height of the portion of the building that lies above the transit. The height of the building is the transit's height, 5 feet, plus a. Thus, we need to identify a trigonometric function that will make it possible to find a. In terms of the 22° angle, we are looking for the side opposite the angle. The transit is 300 feet from the building, so the side adjacent to the 22° angle is 300 feet. Because we have a known angle, an unknown opposite side, and a known adjacent side, we select the tangent function.

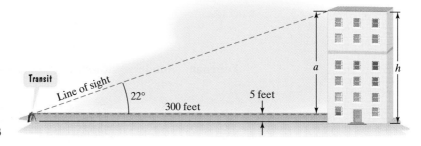

Figure 1.23

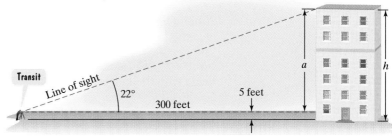

Figure 1.23, repeated

$$\tan 22° = \frac{a}{300}$$

Length of side opposite the 22° angle

Length of side adjacent to the 22° angle

$$a = 300 \tan 22°$$ Multiply both sides of the equation by 300.

$$a \approx 300(0.4040) \approx 121$$ Find tan 22° with a calculator in the degree mode.

The height of the part of the building above the transit is approximately 121 feet. Thus, the height of the building is determined by adding the transit's height, 5 feet, to 121 feet.

$$h \approx 5 + 121 = 126$$

The building's height is approximately 126 feet.

Check Point 8

The irregular blue shape in Figure 1.24 represents a lake. The distance across the lake, a, is unknown. To find this distance, a surveyor took the measurements shown in the figure. What is the distance across the lake?

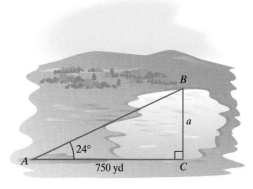

Figure 1.24

If two sides of a right triangle are known, an appropriate trigonometric function can be used to find an acute angle θ in the triangle. You will also need to use the *inverse key* on a calculator. This key uses a function value to display the acute angle θ. For example, suppose that $\sin \theta = 0.866$. We can find θ in the degree mode by using the secondary *inverse sine* key, usually labeled $\boxed{\text{SIN}^{-1}}$.

Study Tip

$\boxed{\text{SIN}^{-1}}$ is not a button you will actually press. It is the secondary function for the button labeled $\boxed{\text{SIN}}$.

Many Scientific Calculators:

$.866 \boxed{\text{2nd}} \boxed{\text{SIN}^{-1}}$

Many Graphing Calculators:

$\boxed{\text{2nd}} \boxed{\text{SIN}^{-1}} .866 \boxed{\text{ENTER}}$

The display should show approximately 59.99, which can be rounded to 60. Thus, if $\sin \theta = 0.866$, then $\theta \approx 60°$.

EXAMPLE 9 Determining the Angle of Elevation

A building that is 21 meters tall casts a shadow 25 meters long. Find the angle of elevation of the sun to the nearest degree.

Solution   The situation is illustrated in Figure 1.25. We are asked to find θ. We begin with the tangent function.

$$\tan \theta = \frac{\text{side opposite } \theta}{\text{side adjacent to } \theta} = \frac{21}{25}$$

We use a calculator in the degree mode to find θ.

Many Scientific Calculators:

$(\;21\;\div\;25\;)\;\boxed{\text{2nd}}\;\boxed{\text{TAN}^{-1}}$

Many Graphing Calculators:

$\boxed{\text{2nd}}\;\boxed{\text{TAN}^{-1}}\;(\;21\;\div\;25\;)\;\boxed{\text{ENTER}}$

The display should show approximately 40. Thus, the angle of elevation of the sun is approximately 40°.

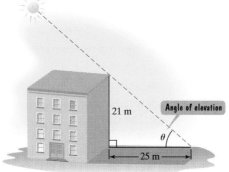

21 m

Angle of elevation

θ

25 m

Figure 1.25

Check Point 9   A flagpole that is 14 meters tall casts a shadow 10 meters long. Find the angle of elevation of the sun to the nearest degree.

The Mountain Man

In the 1930s, a *National Geographic* team headed by Brad Washburn used trigonometry to create a map of the 5000-square-mile region of the Yukon, near the Canadian border. The team started with aerial photography. By drawing a network of angles on the photographs, the approximate locations of the major mountains and their rough heights were determined. The expedition then spent three months on foot to find the exact heights. Team members established two base points a known distance apart, one directly under the mountain's peak. By measuring the angle of elevation from one of the base points to the peak, the tangent function was used to determine the peak's height. The Yukon expedition was a major advance in the way maps are made.

EXERCISE SET 1.2

Practice Exercises

In Exercises 1–8, use the Pythagorean Theorem to find the length of the missing side of each right triangle. Then find the value of each of the six trigonometric functions of θ.

1.

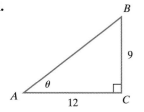

2.

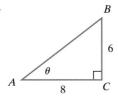

3.

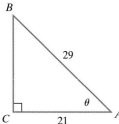

4.

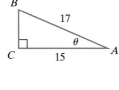

5.

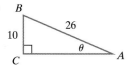

6.

7.

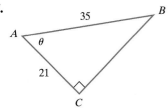

8.

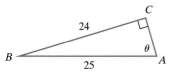

In Exercises 9–16, use the given triangles to evaluate each expression. If necessary, express the value without a square root in the denominator by rationalizing the denominator.

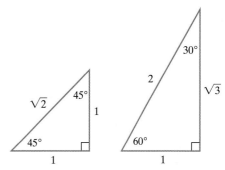

9. $\cos 30°$

10. $\tan 30°$

11. $\sec 45°$

12. $\csc 45°$

13. $\tan \dfrac{\pi}{3}$

14. $\cot \dfrac{\pi}{3}$

15. $\sin \dfrac{\pi}{4} - \cos \dfrac{\pi}{4}$

16. $\tan \dfrac{\pi}{4} + \csc \dfrac{\pi}{6}$

In Exercises 17–20, θ is an acute angle and $\sin\theta$ and $\cos\theta$ are given. Use identities to find $\tan\theta$, $\csc\theta$, $\sec\theta$, and $\cot\theta$. Where necessary, rationalize denominators.

17. $\sin\theta = \dfrac{8}{17}, \quad \cos\theta = \dfrac{15}{17}$

18. $\sin\theta = \dfrac{3}{5}, \quad \cos\theta = \dfrac{4}{5}$

19. $\sin\theta = \dfrac{1}{3}, \quad \cos\theta = \dfrac{2\sqrt{2}}{3}$

20. $\sin\theta = \dfrac{2}{3}, \quad \cos\theta = \dfrac{\sqrt{5}}{3}$

In Exercises 21–24, θ is an acute angle and $\sin\theta$ is given. Use the Pythagorean identity $\sin^2\theta + \cos^2\theta = 1$ to find $\cos\theta$.

21. $\sin\theta = \dfrac{6}{7}$

22. $\sin\theta = \dfrac{7}{8}$

23. $\sin\theta = \dfrac{\sqrt{39}}{8}$

24. $\sin\theta = \dfrac{\sqrt{21}}{5}$

In Exercises 25–30, use an identity to find the value of each expression. Do not use a calculator.

25. $\sin 37° \csc 37°$

26. $\cos 53° \sec 53°$

27. $\sin^2 \dfrac{\pi}{9} + \cos^2 \dfrac{\pi}{9}$

28. $\sin^2 \dfrac{\pi}{10} + \cos^2 \dfrac{\pi}{10}$

29. $\sec^2 23° - \tan^2 23°$

30. $\csc^2 63° - \cot^2 63°$

In Exercises 31–38, find a cofunction with the same value as the given expression.

31. $\sin 7°$

32. $\sin 19°$

33. $\csc 25°$

34. $\csc 35°$

35. $\tan \dfrac{\pi}{9}$

36. $\tan \dfrac{\pi}{7}$

37. $\cos \dfrac{2\pi}{5}$

38. $\cos \dfrac{3\pi}{8}$

In Exercises 39–48, use a calculator to find the value of the trigonometric function to four decimal places.

39. $\sin 38°$

40. $\cos 21°$

41. $\tan 32.7°$

42. $\tan 52.6°$

43. $\csc 17°$

44. $\sec 55°$

45. $\cos \dfrac{\pi}{10}$

46. $\sin \dfrac{3\pi}{10}$

47. $\cot \dfrac{\pi}{12}$

48. $\cot \dfrac{\pi}{18}$

In Exercises 49–54, find the measure of the side of the right triangle whose length is designated by a lowercase letter. Round answers to the nearest whole number.

49.

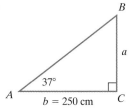

50.

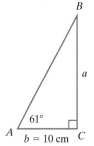

51.

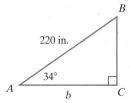

52.

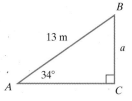

53.

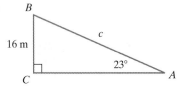

54.

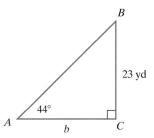

In Exercises 55–58, use a calculator to find the value of the acute angle θ to the nearest degree.

55. $\sin \theta = 0.2974$

56. $\cos \theta = 0.8771$

57. $\tan \theta = 4.6252$

58. $\tan \theta = 26.0307$

In Exercises 59–62, use a calculator to find the value of the acute angle θ in radians, rounded to three decimal places.

59. $\cos \theta = 0.4112$

60. $\sin \theta = 0.9499$

61. $\tan \theta = 0.4169$

62. $\tan \theta = 0.5117$

 Application Exercises

63. To find the distance across a lake, a surveyor took the measurements in the figure shown. Use these measurements to determine how far it is across the lake. Round to the nearest yard.

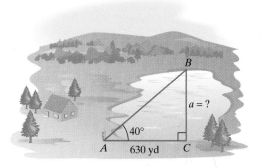

64. At a certain time of day, the angle of elevation of the sun is 40°. To the nearest foot, find the height of a tree whose shadow is 35 feet long.

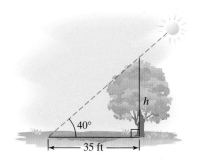

65. A tower that is 125 feet tall casts a shadow 172 feet long. Find the angle of elevation of the sun to the nearest degree.

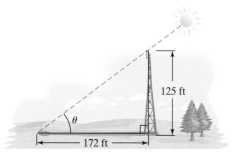

66. The Washington Monument is 555 feet high. If you stand one quarter of a mile, or 1320 feet, from the base of the monument and look to the top, find the angle of elevation to the nearest degree.

Washington Monument

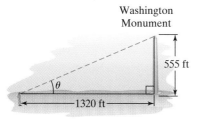

67. A plane rises from take-off and flies at an angle of 10° with the horizontal runway. When it has gained 500 feet, find the distance, to the nearest foot, the plane has flown.

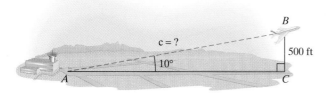

68. A road is inclined at an angle of 5°. After driving 5000 feet along this road, find the driver's increase in altitude. Round to the nearest foot.

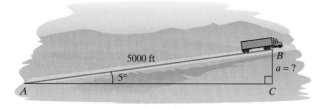

69. A telephone pole, shown at the top of the next column, is 60 feet tall. A guy wire 75 feet long is attached from the ground to the top of the pole. Find the angle between the wire and the pole to the nearest degree.

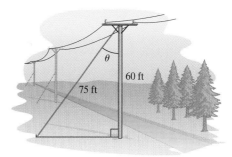

70. A telephone pole is 55 feet tall. A guy wire 80 feet long is attached from the ground to the top of the pole. Find the angle between the wire and the pole to the nearest degree.

Writing in Mathematics

71. If you are given the lengths of the sides of a right triangle, describe how to find the sine of either acute angle.

72. Describe one similarity and one difference between the definitions of $\sin\theta$ and $\cos\theta$, where θ is an acute angle of a right triangle.

73. Describe the triangle used to find the trigonometric functions of 45°.

74. Describe the triangle used to find the trigonometric functions of 30° and 60°.

75. What is a trigonometric identity?

76. Use words (not an equation) to describe one of the reciprocal identities.

77. Use words (not an equation) to describe one of the quotient identities.

78. Use words (not an equation) to describe one of the Pythagorean identities.

79. Describe a relationship among trigonometric functions that is based on angles that are complements.

80. Describe what is meant by an angle of elevation and an angle of depression.

81. Stonehenge, the famous "stone circle" in England, was built between 2750 B.C. and 1300 B.C. using solid stone blocks weighing over 99,000 pounds each. It required 550 people to pull a single stone up a ramp inclined at a 9° angle. Describe how right triangle trigonometry can be used to determine the distance the 550 workers had to drag a stone in order to raise it to a height of 30 feet.

Technology Exercises

82. Use a calculator in the radian mode to fill in the values in the following table. Then draw a conclusion about $\dfrac{\sin\theta}{\theta}$ as θ approaches 0.

θ	0.4	0.3	0.2	0.1	0.01	0.001	0.0001	0.00001
$\sin\theta$								
$\dfrac{\sin\theta}{\theta}$								

83. Use a calculator in the radian mode to fill in the values in the following table. Then draw a conclusion about $\dfrac{\cos\theta - 1}{\theta}$ as θ approaches 0.

θ	0.4	0.3	0.2	0.1	0.01	0.001	0.0001	0.00001
$\cos\theta$								
$\dfrac{\cos\theta - 1}{\theta}$								

Critical Thinking Exercises

84. Which one of the following is true?

a. $\dfrac{\tan 45°}{\tan 15°} = \tan 3°$

b. $\tan^2 15° - \sec^2 15° = -1$

c. $\sin 45° + \cos 45° = 1$

d. $\tan^2 5° = \tan 25°$

85. Explain why the sine or cosine of an acute angle cannot be greater than or equal to 1.

86. Describe what happens to the tangent of an acute angle as the angle gets close to 90°. What happens at 90°?

87. From the top of a 250-foot lighthouse, a plane is sighted overhead and a ship is observed directly below the plane. The angle of elevation of the plane is 22° and the angle of depression of the ship is 35°. Find **a.** the distance of the ship from the lighthouse; **b.** the plane's height above the water. Round to the nearest foot.

SECTION 1.3 *Trigonometric Functions of Any Angle*

Objectives

1. Use the definitions of trigonometric functions of any angle.
2. Use the signs of the trigonometric functions.
3. Find reference angles.
4. Use reference angles to evaluate trigonometric functions.

There is something comforting in the repetition of some of nature's patterns. The ocean level at a beach varies between high and low tide approximately every 12 hours. The number of hours of daylight oscillates from a maximum on the summer solstice, June 21, to a minimum on the winter solstice, December 21. Then it increases to the same maximum the following June 21. Some believe that cycles, called biorhythms, represent physical, emotional, and intellectual aspects of our lives. Throughout the remainder of this chapter, we will see how the trigonometric functions are used to model phenomena that occur again and again. To do this, we need to move beyond right triangles.

1 Use the definitions of trigonometric functions of any angle.

Trigonometric Functions of Any Angle

In the last section, we evaluated trigonometric functions of acute angles, such as that shown in Figure 1.26(a). Note that this angle is in standard position. The point $P = (x, y)$ is a point r units from the origin on the terminal side of θ. A right triangle is formed by drawing a perpendicular from $P = (x, y)$ to the x-axis. Note that y is the length of the side opposite θ and x is the length of the side adjacent to θ.

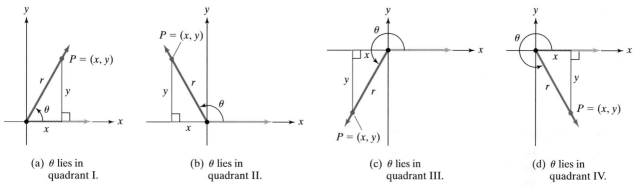

(a) θ lies in quadrant I.

(b) θ lies in quadrant II.

(c) θ lies in quadrant III.

(d) θ lies in quadrant IV.

Figure 1.26

Figures 1.26(b), (c), and (d) show angles in standard position, but they are not acute. We can extend our definitions of the six trigonometric functions to include such angles, as well as quadrantal angles. (Recall that a quadrantal angle has its terminal side on the x-axis or y-axis; such angles are *not* shown in Figure 1.26.) The point $P = (x, y)$ may be any point on the terminal side of the angle θ other than the origin, $(0, 0)$.

Study Tip

If θ is acute, we have the right triangle shown in Figure 1.26(a). In this situation, the definitions in the box are the right triangle definitions of the trigonometric functions. This should make it easier for you to remember the six definitions.

Definitions of Trigonometric Functions of Any Angle

Let θ be any angle in standard position, and let $P = (x, y)$ be a point on the terminal side of θ. If $r = \sqrt{x^2 + y^2}$ is the distance from $(0, 0)$ to (x, y), as shown in Figure 1.26, the **six trigonometric functions of θ** are defined by the following ratios:

$$\sin \theta = \frac{y}{r} \qquad \cos \theta = \frac{x}{r} \qquad \tan \theta = \frac{y}{x}, x \neq 0$$

$$\csc \theta = \frac{r}{y}, y \neq 0 \qquad \sec \theta = \frac{r}{x}, x \neq 0 \qquad \cot \theta = \frac{x}{y}, y \neq 0.$$

Because the point $P = (x, y)$ is any point on the terminal side of θ other than the origin, $(0, 0), r = \sqrt{x^2 + y^2}$ cannot be zero. Examine the six trigonometric functions defined previously. Note that the denominator of the sine and cosine functions is r. Because $r \neq 0$, the sine and cosine functions are defined for any real value of the angle θ. This is not true for the other four trigonometric functions. Note that the denominator of the tangent and secant functions is x. These functions are not defined if $x = 0$. If the point $P = (x, y)$ is on the y-axis, then $x = 0$. Thus, the tangent and secant functions are undefined for all quadrantal angles with terminal sides on the positive or negative y-axis. Likewise, if $P = (x, y)$ is on the x-axis, then $y = 0$, and the cotangent and cosecant functions are undefined. The cotangent and cosecant functions are undefined for all quadrantal angles with terminal sides on the positive or negative x-axis.

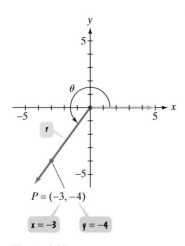

$x = -3$ $y = -4$

Figure 1.27

EXAMPLE 1   Evaluating Trigonometric Functions

Let $P = (-3, -4)$ be a point on the terminal side of θ. Find each of the six trigonometric functions of θ.

Solution   The situation is shown in Figure 1.27. We need values for x, y, and r to evaluate all six trigonometric functions. We are given the values of x and y. Because $P = (-3, -4)$ is a point on the terminal side of θ, $x = -3$ and $y = -4$. Furthermore,

$$r = \sqrt{x^2 + y^2} = \sqrt{(-3)^2 + (-4)^2} = \sqrt{9 + 16} = \sqrt{25} = 5.$$

Now that we know x, y, and r, we can find the six trigonometric functions of θ.

$$\sin\theta = \frac{y}{r} = \frac{-4}{5} = -\frac{4}{5}, \quad \cos\theta = \frac{x}{r} = \frac{-3}{5} = -\frac{3}{5}, \quad \tan\theta = \frac{y}{x} = \frac{-4}{-3} = \frac{4}{3}$$

$$\csc\theta = \frac{r}{y} = \frac{5}{-4} = -\frac{5}{4}, \quad \sec\theta = \frac{r}{x} = \frac{5}{-3} = -\frac{5}{3}, \quad \cot\theta = \frac{x}{y} = \frac{-3}{-4} = \frac{3}{4}$$

These ratios are the reciprocals of those shown directly above.

Check Point 1   Let $P = (4, -3)$ be a point on the terminal side of θ. Find each of the six trigonometric functions of θ.

How do we find the values of the trigonometric functions for a quadrantal angle? First, draw the angle in standard position. Second, choose a point P on the angle's terminal side. The trigonometric function values of θ depend only on the size of θ and not on the distance of point P from the origin. Thus, we choose a point that is 1 unit from the origin. Finally, apply the definition of the appropriate trigonometric function.

EXAMPLE 2   Trigonometric Functions of Quadrantal Angles

Evaluate, if possible, the sine function and the tangent function at the following four quadrantal angles:

a. $\theta = 0° = 0$ **b.** $\theta = 90° = \dfrac{\pi}{2}$ **c.** $\theta = 180° = \pi$ **d.** $\theta = 270° = \dfrac{3\pi}{2}$.

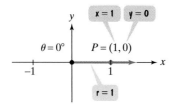

$x = 1$ $y = 0$

$r = 1$

Solution

a. If $\theta = 0° = 0$ radians, then the terminal side of the angle is on the positive x-axis. Let us select the point $P = (1, 0)$ with $x = 1$ and $y = 0$. This point is 1 unit from the origin, so $r = 1$. Now that we know x, y, and r, we can apply the definitions of the sine and tangent functions. (The figure on the left is repeated at the top of the next page.)

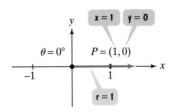

$$\sin 0° = \sin 0 = \frac{y}{r} = \frac{0}{1} = 0$$

$$\tan 0° = \tan 0 = \frac{y}{x} = \frac{0}{1} = 0$$

b. If $\theta = 90° = \dfrac{\pi}{2}$ radians, then the terminal side of the angle is on the positive
y-axis. Let us select the point $P = (0, 1)$ with $x = 0$ and $y = 1$. This point
is 1 unit from the origin, so $r = 1$. Now that we know x, y, and r, we can
apply the definitions of the sine and tangent functions.

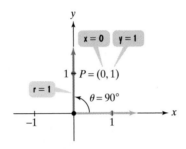

$$\sin 90° = \sin \frac{\pi}{2} = \frac{y}{r} = \frac{1}{1} = 1$$

$$\tan 90° = \tan \frac{\pi}{2} = \frac{y}{x} = \frac{1}{0}$$

Because division by 0 is undefined, $\tan 90°$ is undefined.

c. If $\theta = 180° = \pi$ radians, then the terminal side of the angle is on the
negative x-axis. Let us select the point $P = (-1, 0)$ with $x = -1$ and $y = 0$.
This point is 1 unit from the origin, so $r = 1$. Now that we know x, y, and r,
we can apply the definitions of the sine and tangent functions.

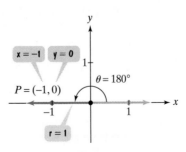

$$\sin 180° = \sin \pi = \frac{y}{r} = \frac{0}{1} = 0$$

$$\tan 180° = \tan \pi = \frac{y}{x} = \frac{0}{-1} = 0$$

Discovery

Try finding tan 90° and tan 270° with your calculator. Describe what occurs.

d. If $\theta = 270° = \dfrac{3\pi}{2}$ radians, then the terminal side of the angle is on the negative y-axis. Let us select the point $P = (0, -1)$ with $x = 0$ and $y = -1$. This point is 1 unit from the origin, so $r = 1$. Now that we know x, y, and r, we can apply the definitions of the sine and tangent functions.

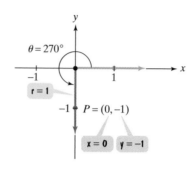

$$\sin 270° = \sin \frac{3\pi}{2} = \frac{y}{r} = \frac{-1}{1} = -1$$

$$\tan 270° = \tan \frac{3\pi}{2} = \frac{y}{x} = \frac{-1}{0}$$

Because division by 0 is undefined, $\tan 270°$ is undefined.

Check Point 2 Evaluate, if possible, the cosine function and the cosecant function at the following four quadrantal angles:

a. $\theta = 0° = 0$ **b.** $\theta = 90° = \dfrac{\pi}{2}$

c. $\theta = 180° = \pi$ **d.** $\theta = 270° = \dfrac{3\pi}{2}$.

2   Use the signs of the trigonometric functions.

The Signs of the Trigonometric Functions

In Example 2, we evaluated trigonometric functions of quadrantal angles. However, we will now return to the trigonometric functions of nonquadrantal angles. **If θ is not a quadrantal angle, the sign of a trigonometric function depends on the quadrant in which θ lies.** In all four quadrants, r is positive. However, x and y can be positive or negative. For example, if θ lies in quadrant II, x is negative and y is positive. Thus, the only positive ratios in this quadrant are $\dfrac{y}{r}$ and its reciprocal, $\dfrac{r}{y}$. These ratios are the function values for the sine and cosecant, respectively. In short, if θ lies in quadrant II, $\sin \theta$ and $\csc \theta$ are positive. The other four trigonometric functions are negative.

Figure 1.28 summarizes the signs of the trigonometric functions. If θ lies in quadrant I, all six functions are positive. If θ lies in quadrant II, only $\sin \theta$ and $\csc \theta$ are positive. If θ lies in quadrant III, only $\tan \theta$ and $\cot \theta$ are positive. Finally, if θ lies in quadrant IV, only $\cos \theta$ and $\sec \theta$ are positive. Observe that the positive functions in each quadrant occur in reciprocal pairs.

Quadrant II	Quadrant I
sine and cosecant positive	All functions positive

Quadrant III	Quadrant IV
tangent and cotangent positive	cosine and secant positive

Figure 1.28 The signs of the trigonometric functions

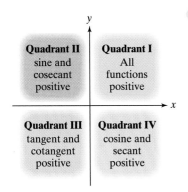

Figure 1.28 The signs of the trigonometric functions, repeated

EXAMPLE 3   Finding the Quadrant in Which an Angle Lies

If $\tan \theta < 0$ and $\cos \theta > 0$, name the quadrant in which angle θ lies.

Solution   Because $\tan \theta < 0$, θ cannot lie in quadrant I; all the functions are positive in quadrant I. Furthermore, θ cannot lie in quadrant III; $\tan \theta$ is positive in quadrant III. Thus, with $\tan \theta < 0$, θ lies in quadrant II or quadrant IV. We are also given that $\cos \theta > 0$. Because quadrant IV is the only quadrant in which the cosine is positive and the tangent is negative, we conclude that θ lies in quadrant IV.

> **Check Point 3**   If $\sin \theta < 0$ and $\cos \theta < 0$, name the quadrant in which angle θ lies.

EXAMPLE 4   Evaluating Trigonometric Functions

Given $\tan \theta = -\frac{2}{3}$ and $\cos \theta > 0$, find $\cos \theta$ and $\csc \theta$.

Solution   Because the tangent is negative and the cosine is positive, θ lies in quadrant IV. This will help us to determine whether the negative sign in $\tan \theta = -\frac{2}{3}$ should be associated with the numerator or the denominator. Keep in mind that in quadrant IV, x is positive and y is negative. Thus,

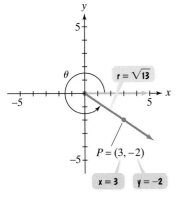

Figure 1.29 $\tan \theta = -\frac{2}{3}$ and $\cos \theta > 0$

In quadrant IV, y is negative.

$$\tan \theta = -\frac{2}{3} = \frac{y}{x} = \frac{-2}{3}.$$

(See Figure 1.29.) Thus, $x = 3$ and $y = -2$. Furthermore,

$$r = \sqrt{x^2 + y^2} = \sqrt{3^2 + (-2)^2} = \sqrt{9 + 4} = \sqrt{13}.$$

Now that we know x, y, and r, we can find $\cos \theta$ and $\csc \theta$.

$$\cos \theta = \frac{x}{r} = \frac{3}{\sqrt{13}} = \frac{3}{\sqrt{13}} \cdot \frac{\sqrt{13}}{\sqrt{13}} = \frac{3\sqrt{13}}{13} \qquad \csc \theta = \frac{r}{y} = \frac{\sqrt{13}}{-2} = -\frac{\sqrt{13}}{2}$$

> **Check Point 4**   Given $\tan \theta = -\frac{1}{3}$ and $\cos \theta < 0$, find $\sin \theta$ and $\sec \theta$.

3   Find reference angles.

Reference Angles

We will often evaluate trigonometric functions of positive angles greater than 90° and all negative angles by making use of a positive acute angle. This positive acute angle is called a *reference angle*.

Definition of a Reference Angle

Let θ be a nonacute angle in standard position that lies in a quadrant. Its **reference angle** is the positive acute angle θ' formed by the terminal side of θ and the x-axis.

Figure 1.30 shows the reference angle for θ lying in quadrants II, III, and IV. Notice that the formula used to find θ', the reference angle, varies according to the quadrant in which θ lies. You may find it easier to find the reference angle for a given angle by making a figure that shows the angle in standard position. The acute angle formed by the terminal side of this angle and the x-axis is the reference angle.

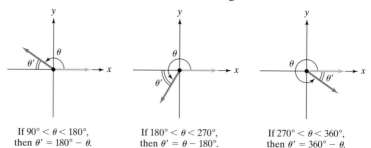

Figure 1.30 Reference angles, θ', for positive angles, θ, in quadrants II, III, and IV

If $90° < \theta < 180°$, then $\theta' = 180° - \theta$.

If $180° < \theta < 270°$, then $\theta' = \theta - 180°$.

If $270° < \theta < 360°$, then $\theta' = 360° - \theta$.

EXAMPLE 5 Finding Reference Angles

Find the reference angle, θ', for each of the following angles:

a. $\theta = 345°$ **b.** $\theta = \dfrac{5\pi}{6}$ **c.** $\theta = -135°$ **d.** $\theta = 2.5$.

Solution

a. A 345° angle in standard position is shown in Figure 1.31. Because 345° lies in quadrant IV, the reference angle is

$$\theta' = 360° - 345° = 15°.$$

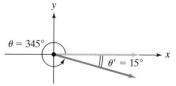

Figure 1.31

b. Because $\dfrac{5\pi}{6}$ lies between $\dfrac{\pi}{2} = \dfrac{3\pi}{6}$ and $\pi = \dfrac{6\pi}{6}$, $\theta = \dfrac{5\pi}{6}$ lies in quadrant II. The angle is shown in Figure 1.32. The reference angle is

$$\theta' = \pi - \frac{5\pi}{6} = \frac{6\pi}{6} - \frac{5\pi}{6} = \frac{\pi}{6}.$$

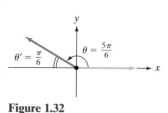

Figure 1.32

c. A −135° angle in standard position is shown in Figure 1.33. The figure indicates that the positive acute angle formed by the terminal side of θ and the x-axis is 45°. The reference angle is

$$\theta' = 45°.$$

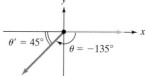

Figure 1.33

d. The angle $\theta = 2.5$ lies between $\dfrac{\pi}{2} \approx 1.57$ and $\pi \approx 3.14$. This means that $\theta = 2.5$ is in quadrant II, shown in Figure 1.34. The reference angle is

$$\theta' = \pi - 2.5 \approx 0.64.$$

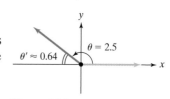

Figure 1.34

Check Point 5

Find the reference angle, θ', for each of the following angles:

a. $\theta = 210°$ **b.** $\theta = \dfrac{7\pi}{4}$ **c.** $\theta = -240°$ **d.** $\theta = 3.6$

The way that reference angles are defined makes them useful in evaluating trigonometric functions.

4 Use reference angles to evaluate trigonometric functions.

Using Reference Angles to Evaluate Trigonometric Functions

The values of the trigonometric functions of a given angle, θ, are the same as the values of the trigonometric functions of the reference angle, θ', except possibly for the sign. A function value of the acute reference angle, θ', is always positive. However, the same function value for θ may be positive or negative.

For example, we can use a reference angle, θ', to obtain an exact value for $\tan 120°$. The reference angle for $\theta = 120°$ is $\theta' = 180° - 120° = 60°$. We know the exact value of the tangent function of the reference angle: $\tan 60° = \sqrt{3}$. We also know that the value of a trigonometric function of a given angle, θ, is the same as that of its reference angle, θ', except possibly for the sign. Thus, we can conclude that $\tan 120°$ equals $-\sqrt{3}$ or $\sqrt{3}$.

What sign should we attach to $\sqrt{3}$? A $120°$ angle lies in quadrant II, where only the sine and cosecant are positive. Thus, the tangent function is negative for a $120°$ angle. Therefore,

> Prefix by a negative sign to show tangent is negative in quadrant II.

$$\tan 120° = -\tan 60° = -\sqrt{3}.$$

> The reference angle for $120°$ is $60°$.

In the previous section, we used two right triangles to find exact trigonometric values of $30°, 45°,$ and $60°$. Using a procedure similar to finding $\tan 120°$, we can now find the function values of all angles for which $30°, 45°,$ or $60°$ are reference angles.

A Procedure for Using Reference Angles to Evaluate Trigonometric Functions

The value of a trigonometric function of any angle θ is found as follows:

1. Find the associated reference angle, θ', and the function value for θ'.
2. Use the quadrant in which θ lies to prefix the appropriate sign to the function value in step 1.

Discovery

Draw the two right triangles involving $30°, 45°,$ and $60°$. Indicate the length of each side. Use these lengths to verify the function values for the reference angles in the solution to Example 6.

EXAMPLE 6   Using Reference Angles to Evaluate Trigonometric Functions

Use reference angles to find the exact value of each of the following trigonometric functions:

a. $\sin 135°$ **b.** $\cos \dfrac{4\pi}{3}$ **c.** $\cot\left(-\dfrac{\pi}{3}\right)$.

Solution

a. We use our two-step procedure to find $\sin 135°$.

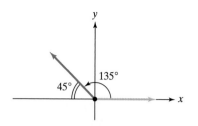

Figure 1.35 Reference angle for 135°

Step 1   Find the reference angle, θ', and $\sin \theta'$. Figure 1.35 shows 135° lies in quadrant II. The reference angle is

$$\theta' = 180° - 135° = 45°.$$

The function value for the reference angle is $\sin 45° = \dfrac{\sqrt{2}}{2}$.

Step 2   Use the quadrant in which θ lies to prefix the appropriate sign to the function value in step 1. The angle $\theta = 135°$ lies in quadrant II. Because the sine is positive in quadrant II, we put a $+$ sign before the function value of the reference angle. Thus,

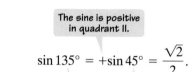

The sine is positive in quadrant II.

$$\sin 135° = +\sin 45° = \dfrac{\sqrt{2}}{2}.$$

The reference angle for 135° is 45°.

b. We use our two-step procedure to find $\cos \dfrac{4\pi}{3}$.

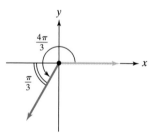

Figure 1.36 Reference angle for $\dfrac{4\pi}{3}$

Step 1   Find the reference angle, θ', and $\cos \theta'$. Figure 1.36 shows that $\theta = \dfrac{4\pi}{3}$ lies in quadrant III. The reference angle is

$$\theta' = \dfrac{4\pi}{3} - \pi = \dfrac{4\pi}{3} - \dfrac{3\pi}{3} = \dfrac{\pi}{3}.$$

The function value for the reference angle is

$$\cos \dfrac{\pi}{3} = \dfrac{1}{2}.$$

Step 2   Use the quadrant in which θ lies to prefix the appropriate sign to the function value in step 1. The angle $\theta = \dfrac{4\pi}{3}$ lies in quadrant III. Because only the tangent and cotangent are positive in quadrant III, the cosine is negative in this quadrant. We put a $-$ sign before the function value of the reference angle. Thus,

The cosine is negative in quadrant III.

$$\cos \dfrac{4\pi}{3} = -\cos \dfrac{\pi}{3} = -\dfrac{1}{2}.$$

The reference angle for $\dfrac{4\pi}{3}$ is $\dfrac{\pi}{3}$.

c. We use our two-step procedure to find $\cot\left(-\dfrac{\pi}{3}\right)$.

Step 1 Find the reference angle, θ', and $\cot\theta'$. Figure 1.37 shows that $\theta = -\dfrac{\pi}{3}$ lies in quadrant IV. The reference angle is $\theta' = \dfrac{\pi}{3}$. The function value for the reference angle is $\cot\dfrac{\pi}{3} = \dfrac{\sqrt{3}}{3}$.

Figure 1.37 Reference angle for $-\dfrac{\pi}{3}$

Step 2 Use the quadrant in which θ lies to prefix the appropriate sign to the function value in step 1. The angle $\theta = -\dfrac{\pi}{3}$ lies in quadrant IV. Because only the cosine and secant are positive in quadrant IV, the cotangent is negative in this quadrant. We put a $-$ sign before the function value of the reference angle. Thus,

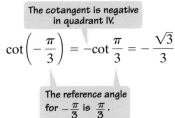

The cotangent is negative in quadrant IV.

$$\cot\left(-\frac{\pi}{3}\right) = -\cot\frac{\pi}{3} = -\frac{\sqrt{3}}{3}.$$

The reference angle for $-\dfrac{\pi}{3}$ is $\dfrac{\pi}{3}$.

Check Point 6 Use reference angles to find the exact value of the following trigonometric functions:

a. $\sin 300°$ **b.** $\tan\dfrac{5\pi}{4}$ **c.** $\sec\left(-\dfrac{\pi}{6}\right)$.

EXERCISE SET 1.3

Practice Exercises

In Exercises 1–8, a point on the terminal side of angle θ is given. Find the exact value of each of the six trigonometric functions of θ.

1. $(-4, 3)$ **2.** $(-12, 5)$
3. $(2, 3)$ **4.** $(3, 7)$
5. $(3, -3)$ **6.** $(5, -5)$
7. $(-2, -5)$ **8.** $(-1, -3)$

In Exercises 9–16, evaluate the trigonometric function at the quadrantal angle, or state that the expression is undefined.

9. $\cos\pi$ **10.** $\tan\pi$
11. $\sec\pi$ **12.** $\csc\pi$
13. $\tan\dfrac{3\pi}{2}$ **14.** $\cos\dfrac{3\pi}{2}$
15. $\cot\dfrac{\pi}{2}$ **16.** $\tan\dfrac{\pi}{2}$

In Exercises 17–22, let θ be an angle in standard position. Name the quadrant in which θ lies.

17. $\sin\theta > 0, \quad \cos\theta > 0$
18. $\sin\theta < 0, \quad \cos\theta > 0$
19. $\sin\theta < 0, \quad \cos\theta < 0$
20. $\tan\theta < 0, \quad \sin\theta < 0$
21. $\tan\theta < 0, \quad \cos\theta < 0$
22. $\cot\theta > 0, \quad \sec\theta < 0$

In Exercises 23–34, find the exact value of each of the remaining trigonometric functions of θ.

23. $\cos\theta = -\dfrac{3}{5}, \quad \theta$ in quadrant III
24. $\sin\theta = -\dfrac{12}{13}, \quad \theta$ in quadrant III
25. $\sin\theta = \dfrac{5}{13}, \quad \theta$ in quadrant II
26. $\cos\theta = \dfrac{4}{5}, \quad \theta$ in quadrant IV
27. $\cos\theta = \dfrac{8}{17}, \quad 270° < \theta < 360°$
28. $\cos\theta = \dfrac{1}{3}, \quad 270° < \theta < 360°$
29. $\tan\theta = -\dfrac{2}{3}, \quad \sin\theta > 0$
30. $\tan\theta = -\dfrac{1}{3}, \quad \sin\theta > 0$
31. $\tan\theta = \dfrac{4}{3}, \quad \cos\theta < 0$
32. $\tan\theta = \dfrac{5}{12}, \quad \cos\theta < 0$
33. $\sec\theta = -3, \quad \tan\theta > 0$
34. $\csc\theta = -4, \quad \tan\theta > 0$

In Exercises 35–50, find the reference angle for each angle.

35. $160°$

36. $170°$

37. $205°$

38. $210°$

39. $355°$

40. $351°$

41. $\dfrac{7\pi}{4}$

42. $\dfrac{5\pi}{4}$

43. $\dfrac{5\pi}{6}$

44. $\dfrac{5\pi}{7}$

45. $-150°$

46. $-250°$

47. $-335°$

48. $-359°$

49. 4.7

50. 5.5

In Exercises 51–66, use reference angles to find the exact value of each expression. Do not use a calculator.

51. $\cos 225°$

52. $\sin 300°$

53. $\tan 210°$

54. $\sec 240°$

55. $\tan 420°$

56. $\tan 405°$

57. $\sin \dfrac{2\pi}{3}$

58. $\cos \dfrac{3\pi}{4}$

59. $\csc \dfrac{7\pi}{6}$

60. $\cot \dfrac{7\pi}{4}$

61. $\tan \dfrac{9\pi}{4}$

62. $\tan \dfrac{9\pi}{2}$

63. $\sin(-240°)$

64. $\sin(-225°)$

65. $\tan\left(-\dfrac{\pi}{4}\right)$

66. $\tan\left(-\dfrac{\pi}{6}\right)$

Writing in Mathematics

67. If you are given a point on the terminal side of angle θ, explain how to find $\sin \theta$.

68. Explain why $\tan 90°$ is undefined.

69. If $\cos \theta > 0$ and $\tan \theta < 0$, explain how to find the quadrant in which θ lies.

70. What is a reference angle? Give an example with your description.

71. Explain how reference angles are used to evaluate trigonometric functions. Give an example with your description.

SECTION 1.4 Trigonometric Functions of Real Numbers; Periodic Functions

Objectives

1. Use a unit circle to define trigonometric functions of real numbers.
2. Recognize the domain and range of sine and cosine functions.
3. Use even and odd trigonometric functions.
4. Use periodic properties.

Cycles govern many aspects of life—heartbeats, sleep patterns, seasons, and tides all follow regular, predictable cycles. In this section, we will see why trigonometric functions are used to model phenomena that occur in cycles. To do this, we need to move beyond angles and consider trigonometric functions of real numbers.

1 Use a unit circle to define trigonometric functions of real numbers.

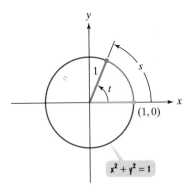

Figure 1.38 Unit circle with a central angle measuring t radians

Trigonometric Functions of Real Numbers

Thus far, we have considered trigonometric functions of angles measured in degrees or radians. To define trigonometric functions of real numbers, rather than angles, we use a unit circle. A **unit circle** is a circle of radius 1, with its center at the origin of a rectangular coordinate system. The equation of this unit circle is $x^2 + y^2 = 1$. Figure 1.38 shows a unit circle in which the central angle measures t radians. We can use the formula for the length of a circular arc, $s = r\theta$, to find the length of the intercepted arc.

$$s = r\theta = 1 \cdot t = t$$

| The radius of a unit circle is 1. | The radian measure of the central angle is t. |

Thus, the length of the intercepted arc is t. This is also the radian measure of the central angle. Thus, **in a unit circle, the radian measure of the angle is equal to the measure of the intercepted arc.** Both are given by the same *real number t*.

In Figure 1.39, the radian measure of the angle and the length of the intercepted arc are both shown by t. Let $P = (x, y)$ denote the point on the unit circle that has arc length t from $(1, 0)$. Figure 1.39(a) shows that if t is positive, point P is reached by moving counterclockwise along the unit circle from $(1, 0)$. Figure 1.39(b) shows that if t is negative, point P is reached by moving clockwise along the unit circle from $(1, 0)$. For each real number t, there corresponds a point $P = (x, y)$ on the unit circle.

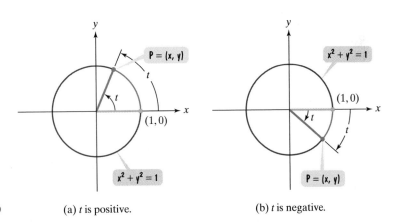

Figure 1.39

(a) t is positive.

(b) t is negative.

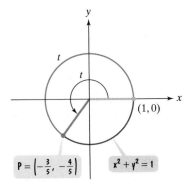

Figure 1.40

Using Figure 1.39, we define the cosine function at t as the x-coordinate of P and the sine function at t as the y-coordinate of P. Thus,

$$x = \cos t \quad \text{and} \quad y = \sin t.$$

For example, a point $P = (x, y)$ on the unit circle corresponding to a real number t is shown in Figure 1.40 for $\pi < t < \dfrac{3\pi}{2}$. We see that the coordinates of $P = (x, y)$ are $x = -\frac{3}{5}$ and $y = -\frac{4}{5}$. Because the cosine function is the x-coordinate of P and the sine function is the y-coordinate of P, the values of these trigonometric functions at the real number t are

$$\cos t = -\frac{3}{5} \quad \text{and} \quad \sin t = -\frac{4}{5}.$$

Definitions of the Trigonometric Functions in Terms of a Unit Circle

If t is a real number and $P = (x, y)$ is a point on the unit circle that corresponds to t, then

$$\sin t = y \qquad\qquad \cos t = x \qquad\qquad \tan t = \frac{y}{x}, x \neq 0$$

$$\csc t = \frac{1}{y}, y \neq 0 \qquad\qquad \sec t = \frac{1}{x}, x \neq 0 \qquad\qquad \cot t = \frac{x}{y}, y \neq 0.$$

Because this definition expresses function values in terms of coordinates of a point on a unit circle, the trigonometric functions are sometimes called the **circular functions.**

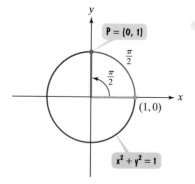

Figure 1.41

EXAMPLE 1 Finding Values of the Trigonometric Functions

Use Figure 1.41 to find the values of the trigonometric functions at $t = \dfrac{\pi}{2}$.

Solution The point P on the unit circle that corresponds to $t = \dfrac{\pi}{2}$ has coordinates $(0, 1)$. We use $x = 0$ and $y = 1$ to find the values of the trigonometric functions.

$$\sin\frac{\pi}{2} = y = 1 \qquad\qquad \cos\frac{\pi}{2} = x = 0$$

$$\csc\frac{\pi}{2} = \frac{1}{y} = \frac{1}{1} = 1 \qquad\qquad \cot\frac{\pi}{2} = \frac{x}{y} = \frac{0}{1} = 0$$

By definition, $\tan t = \dfrac{y}{x}$ and $\sec t = \dfrac{1}{x}$. Because $x = 0$, $\tan\dfrac{\pi}{2}$ and $\sec\dfrac{\pi}{2}$, are undefined.

Check Point 1 Use the figure on the right to find the values of the trigonometric functions at $t = \pi$.

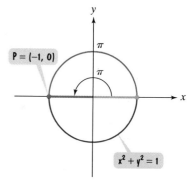

2 Recognize the domain and range of sine and cosine functions.

Domain and Range of Sine and Cosine Functions

The value of a trigonometric function at the real number t is its value at an angle of t radians. However, using real number domains, we can observe properties of trigonometric functions that are not as apparent using the angle approach. For example, the domain and range of each trigonometric function can be found from the unit circle definition. At this point, let's look only at the sine and cosine functions,

$$\sin t = y \quad \text{and} \quad \cos t = x.$$

Because t can be the radian measure of any angle or, equivalently, the measure of any intercepted arc, the domain of the sine function and the cosine function is the set of all real numbers. Because the radius of the unit circle is 1, we have

$$-1 \le x \le 1 \quad \text{and} \quad -1 \le y \le 1.$$

Therefore, with $x = \cos t$ and $y = \sin t$, we obtain

$$-1 \le \cos t \le 1 \quad \text{and} \quad -1 \le \sin t \le 1.$$

The range of the cosine and sine functions is $[-1, 1]$.

The Domain and Range of the Sine and Cosine Functions

The domain of the sine function and the cosine function is the set of all real numbers. The range of these functions is the set of all real numbers from -1 to 1, inclusive.

3 Use even and odd trigonometric functions.

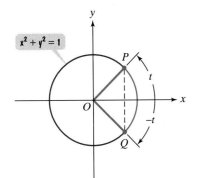

Figure 1.42

Even and Odd Trigonometric Functions

In Chapter 2, we saw that a function is even if $f(-t) = f(t)$ and odd if $f(-t) = -f(t)$. We can use Figure 1.42 to show that the cosine function is an even function and the sine function is an odd function. By definition, the coordinates of the points P and Q in Figure 1.42 are as follows:

$$P: (\cos t, \sin t)$$

$$Q: (\cos(-t), \sin(-t)).$$

In Figure 1.42, the x-coordinates of P and Q are the same. Thus,

$$\cos(-t) = \cos t.$$

This shows that the cosine function is an even function. By contrast, the y-coordinates of P and Q are negatives of each other. Thus,

$$\sin(-t) = -\sin t.$$

This shows that the sine function is an odd function.

This argument is valid regardless of the length of t. Thus, the arc may terminate in any of the four quadrants or on any axis. Using the unit circle definition of the trigonometric functions, we obtain the following results:

Even and Odd Trigonometric Functions

The cosine and secant functions are *even*.

$$\cos(-t) = \cos t \qquad \sec(-t) = \sec t$$

The sine, cosecant, tangent, and cotangent functions are *odd*.

$$\sin(-t) = -\sin t \qquad \csc(-t) = -\csc t$$

$$\tan(-t) = -\tan t \qquad \cot(-t) = -\cot t$$

EXAMPLE 2 **Using Even and Odd Functions to Find Exact Values**

Find the exact value of:

    a. $\cos(-45°)$ **b.** $\tan\left(-\dfrac{\pi}{3}\right)$.

Solution

    a. $\cos(-45°) = \cos 45° = \dfrac{\sqrt{2}}{2}$ **b.** $\tan\left(-\dfrac{\pi}{3}\right) = -\tan\dfrac{\pi}{3} = -\sqrt{3}$

Check
Point
2

Find the exact value of:

    a. $\cos(-60°)$ **b.** $\tan\left(-\dfrac{\pi}{6}\right)$.

4 Use periodic properties.

Periodic Functions

Certain patterns in nature repeat again and again. For example, the ocean level at a beach varies from low tide to high tide and then back to low tide approximately every 12 hours. If low tide occurs at noon, then high tide will be around 6 P.M. and low tide will occur again around midnight, and so on infinitely. If $f(t)$ represents the ocean level at the beach at any time t, then the level is the same 12 hours later. Thus,

$$f(t + 12) = f(t).$$

The word *periodic* means that this tidal behavior repeats infinitely. The *period*, 12 hours, is the time it takes to complete one full cycle.

Definition of a Periodic Function

A function f is **periodic** if there exists a positive number p such that

$$f(t + p) = f(t)$$

for all t in the domain of f. The smallest number p for which f is periodic is called the **period** of f.

    The trigonometric functions are used to model periodic phenomena. Why? If we begin at any point P on the unit circle and travel a distance of 2π units along the perimeter, we will return to the same point P. Because the trigonometric functions are defined in terms of the coordinates of that point P, we obtain the following results:

Periodic Properties of the Sine and Cosine Functions

$$\sin(t + 2\pi) = \sin t \quad \text{and} \quad \cos(t + 2\pi) = \cos t$$

The sine and cosine functions are periodic functions and have period 2π.

EXAMPLE 3   Using Periodic Properties to Find Exact Values

Find the exact value of: **a.** $\tan 420°$ **b.** $\sin \dfrac{9\pi}{4}$.

Solution

a. $\tan 420° = \tan(60° + 360°) = \tan 60° = \sqrt{3}$

b. $\sin \dfrac{9\pi}{4} = \sin\left(\dfrac{\pi}{4} + 2\pi\right) = \sin \dfrac{\pi}{4} = \dfrac{\sqrt{2}}{2}$

Check
Point
3

Find the exact value of:

a. $\cos 405°$ **b.** $\tan \dfrac{7\pi}{3}$.

Like the sine and cosine functions, the secant and cosecant functions have period 2π. However, the tangent and cotangent functions have a smaller period. If we begin at any point $P(x, y)$ on the unit circle and travel a distance of π units along the perimeter, we arrive at the point $(-x, -y)$. The tangent function, defined in terms of the coordinates of a point, is the same at (x, y) and $(-x, -y)$.

Tangent function
at (x, y) $\dfrac{y}{x} = \dfrac{-y}{-x}$ Tangent function
π radians later

We see that $\tan(t + \pi) = \tan t$. The same observations apply to the cotangent function.

Periodic Properties of the Tangent and Cotangent Functions

$$\tan(t + \pi) = \tan t \quad \text{and} \quad \cot(t + \pi) = \cot t$$

The tangent and cotangent functions are periodic functions and have period π.

Why do the trigonometric functions model phenomena that repeat *indefinitely?* By starting at point P on the unit circle and traveling a distance of 2π units, 4π units, 6π units, and so on, we return to the starting point P. Because the trigonometric functions are defined in terms of the coordinates of that point P, if we add (or subtract) multiples of 2π, the trigonometric values do not change. Furthermore, the trigonometric values for the tangent and cotangent functions do not change if we add (or subtract) multiples of π.

Repetitive Behavior of the Sine, Cosine, and Tangent Functions

For any integer n and real number t,

$$\sin(t + 2\pi n) = \sin t, \quad \cos(t + 2\pi n) = \cos t, \quad \text{and} \quad \tan(t + \pi n) = \tan t.$$

EXERCISE SET 1.4

Practice Exercises

In Exercises 1–4, a point $P(x, y)$ is shown on the unit circle corresponding to a real number t. Find the values of the trigonometric functions at t.

1.

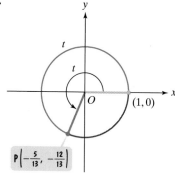

2.

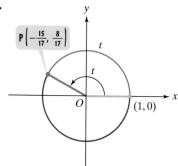

3.

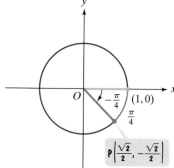

4.

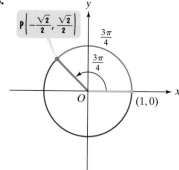

In Exercises 5–8, use even and odd properties of the trigonometric functions to find the exact value of each expression.

5. $\sin(-45°)$

6. $\tan(-45°)$

7. $\sec\left(-\dfrac{\pi}{3}\right)$

8. $\sec\left(-\dfrac{\pi}{6}\right)$

In Exercises 9–12, use periodic properties to find the exact value of each expression.

9. $\cos 585°$

10. $\cos 570°$

11. $\cot \dfrac{7\pi}{3}$

12. $\cot \dfrac{9\pi}{4}$

 Application Exercises

13. The number of hours of daylight, H, on day t of any given year (on January 1, $t = 1$) in Fairbanks, Alaska, can be modeled by the function

$$H(t) = 12 + 8.3 \sin\left[\dfrac{2\pi}{365}(t - 80)\right].$$

a. March 21, the 80th day of the year, is the spring equinox. Find the number of hours of daylight in Fairbanks on this day.

b. June 21, the 172nd day of the year, is the summer solstice, the day with the maximum number of hours of daylight. To the nearest tenth of an hour, find the number of hours of daylight in Fairbanks on this day.

c. December 21, the 355th day of the year, is the winter solstice, the day with the minimum number of hours of daylight. Find, to the nearest tenth of an hour, the number of hours of daylight in Fairbanks on this day.

14. The number of hours of daylight, H, on day t of any given year (on January 1, $t = 1$) in San Diego, California, can be modeled by the function

$$H(t) = 12 + 2.4 \sin\left[\dfrac{2\pi}{365}(t - 80)\right].$$

a. March 21, the 80th day of the year, is the spring equinox. Find the number of hours of daylight in San Diego on this day.

b. June 21, the 172nd day of the year, is the summer solstice, the day with the maximum number of hours of daylight. Find, to the nearest tenth of an hour, the number of hours of daylight in San Diego on this day.

c. December 21, the 355th day of the year, is the winter solstice, the day with the minimum number of hours of daylight. To the nearest tenth of an hour, find the number of hours of daylight in San Diego on this day.

15. People who believe in biorhythms claim that there are three cycles that rule our behavior—the physical, emotional, and mental. Each is a sine function of a certain period. The function for our emotional fluctuations is

$$E = \sin \dfrac{\pi}{14} t$$

where t is measured in days starting at birth. Emotional fluctuations, E, are measured from -1 to 1, inclusive, with 1 representing peak emotional well-being, -1 representing the low for emotional well-being, and 0 representing feeling neither emotionally high nor low.

a. Find E corresponding to $t = 7, 14, 21, 28,$ and 35. Describe what you observe.

b. What is the period of the emotional cycle?

16. The height of the water, H, in feet, at a boat dock t hours after 6 A.M. is given by

$$H = 10 + 4 \sin \dfrac{\pi}{6} t.$$

a. Find the height of the water at the dock at 6 A.M., 9 A.M., noon, 6 P.M., midnight, and 3 A.M.

b. When is low tide and when is high tide?

c. What is the period of this function and what does this mean about the tides?

 Writing in Mathematics

17. Why are the trigonometric functions sometimes called circular functions?

18. What is the range of the sine function? Use the unit circle to explain where this range comes from.

19. What do we mean by even trigonometric functions? Which of the six functions fall into this category?

20. What is a periodic function? Why are the sine and cosine functions periodic?

21. Explain how you can use the function for emotional fluctuations in Exercise 15 to determine good days for having dinner with your moody boss.

22. Describe a phenomenon that repeats infinitely. What is its period?

 Critical Thinking Exercises

23. Find the exact value of $\cos 0° + \cos 1° + \cos 2° + \cos 3° + \cdots + \cos 179° + \cos 180°$.

24. If $f(x) = \sin x$ and $f(a) = \frac{1}{4}$, find the value of

$$f(a) + f(a + 2\pi) + f(a + 4\pi) + f(a + 6\pi).$$

25. If $f(x) = \sin x$ and $f(a) = \frac{1}{4}$, find the value of $f(a) + 2f(-a)$.

26. The seats of a ferris wheel are 40 feet from the wheel's center. When you get on the ride, your seat is 5 feet above the ground. How far above the ground are you after rotating through an angle of 765°? Round to the nearest foot.

SECTION 1.5 *Graphs of Sine and Cosine Functions*

Objectives

1. Understand the graph of $y = \sin x$.
2. Graph variations of $y = \sin x$.
3. Understand the graph of $y = \cos x$.
4. Graph variations of $y = \cos x$.
5. Use vertical shifts of sine and cosine curves.
6. Model periodic behavior.

Take a deep breath and relax. Many relaxation exercises involve slowing down our breathing. Some people suggest that the way we breathe affects every part of our lives. Did you know that graphs of trigonometric functions can be used to analyze the breathing cycle, which is our closest link to both life and death?

In this section, we use graphs of sine and cosine functions to visualize their properties. We use the traditional symbol x, rather than θ or t, to represent the independent variable. We use the symbol y for the dependent variable, or the function's value at x. Thus, we will be graphing $y = \sin x$ and $y = \cos x$ in rectangular coordinates. In all graphs of trigonometric functions, the independent variable, x, is measured in radians.

1 Understand the graph of $y = \sin x$.

The Graph of $y = \sin x$

The trigonometric functions can be graphed in a rectangular coordinate system by plotting points whose coordinates satisfy the function. Thus, we graph $y = \sin x$ by listing some points on the graph. Because the period of the sine function is 2π, we will graph the function on the interval $[0, 2\pi]$. The rest of the graph is made up of repetitions of this portion.

Table 1.1 lists some values of (x, y) on the graph of $y = \sin x, 0 \le x \le 2\pi$.

Table 1.1 Values of (x, y) on $y = \sin x$

x	0	$\dfrac{\pi}{6}$	$\dfrac{\pi}{3}$	$\dfrac{\pi}{2}$	$\dfrac{2\pi}{3}$	$\dfrac{5\pi}{6}$	π	$\dfrac{7\pi}{6}$	$\dfrac{4\pi}{3}$	$\dfrac{3\pi}{2}$	$\dfrac{5\pi}{3}$	$\dfrac{11\pi}{6}$	2π
$y = \sin x$	0	$\dfrac{1}{2}$	$\dfrac{\sqrt{3}}{2}$	1	$\dfrac{\sqrt{3}}{2}$	$\dfrac{1}{2}$	0	$-\dfrac{1}{2}$	$-\dfrac{\sqrt{3}}{2}$	-1	$-\dfrac{\sqrt{3}}{2}$	$-\dfrac{1}{2}$	0

As x increases from 0 to $\frac{\pi}{2}$, y increases from 0 to 1.

As x increases from $\frac{\pi}{2}$ to π, y decreases from 1 to 0.

As x increases from π to $\frac{3\pi}{2}$, y decreases from 0 to -1.

As x increases from $\frac{3\pi}{2}$ to 2π, y increases from -1 to 0.

In plotting the points obtained in Table 1.1, we will use the approximation $\dfrac{\sqrt{3}}{2} \approx 0.87$. Rather than approximating π, we will mark off units on the x-axis in terms of π. If we connect these points with a smooth curve, we obtain the graph shown in Figure 1.43 on the next page. The figure shows one period of the graph of $y = \sin x$.

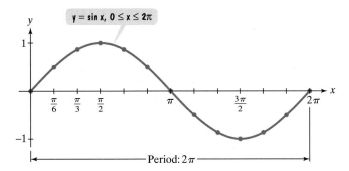

Figure 1.43 One period of the graph of $y = \sin x$

We can obtain a more complete graph of $y = \sin x$ by continuing the portion shown in Figure 1.43 to the left and to the right. The graph of the sine function, called a **sine curve,** is shown in Figure 1.44. Any part of the graph that corresponds to one period (2π) is one cycle of the graph of $y = \sin x$.

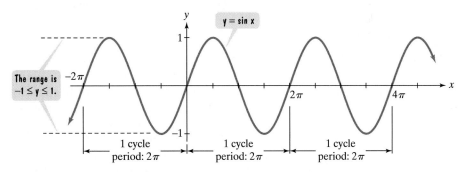

Figure 1.44 The graph of $y = \sin x$

The graph of $y = \sin x$ allows us to visualize some of the properties of the sine function.

- The domain is the set of all real numbers. The graph extends indefinitely to the left and to the right with no gaps or holes.
- The range consists of all numbers between -1 and 1, inclusive. The graph never rises above 1 or falls below -1.
- The period is 2π. The graph's pattern repeats in every interval of length 2π.
- The function is an odd function: $\sin(-x) = -\sin x$. This can be seen by observing that the graph is symmetric with respect to the origin.

2 Graph variations of $y = \sin x$.

Graphing Variations of $y = \sin x$

To graph variations of $y = \sin x$ by hand, it is helpful to find x-intercepts, maximum points, and minimum points. One complete cycle of the sine curve includes three x-intercepts, one maximum point, and one minimum point. The graph of $y = \sin x$ has x-intercepts at the beginning, middle, and end of its full period, shown in Figure 1.45. The curve reaches its maximum point $\frac{1}{4}$ of the way through the period. It reaches its minimum point $\frac{3}{4}$ of the way through the period. Thus, key points in graphing sine functions are

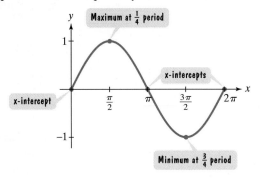

Figure 1.45 Key points in graphing the sine function

obtained by dividing the period into four equal parts. The x-coordinates of the five key points are as follows:

$$x_1 = \text{value of } x \text{ where the cycle begins}$$

$$x_2 = x_1 + \frac{\text{period}}{4}$$

$$x_3 = x_2 + \frac{\text{period}}{4}$$

Add "quarter-periods" to find successive value of x.

$$x_4 = x_3 + \frac{\text{period}}{4}$$

$$x_5 = x_4 + \frac{\text{period}}{4}.$$

The y-coordinates of the five key points are obtained by evaluating the given function at each of these values of x.

The graph of $y = \sin x$ forms the basis for graphing functions of the form

$$y = A \sin x.$$

For example, consider $y = 2 \sin x$, in which $A = 2$. We can obtain the graph of $y = 2 \sin x$ from that of $y = \sin x$ if we multiply each y-coordinate on the graph of $y = \sin x$ by 2. Figure 1.46 shows the graphs. The basic sine curve is *stretched* and ranges between -2 and 2, rather than between -1 and 1. However, both $y = \sin x$ and $y = 2 \sin x$ have a period of 2π.

In general, the graph of $y = A \sin x$ ranges between $-|A|$ and $|A|$. Thus, the range of the function is $-|A| \le y \le |A|$. If $|A| > 1$, the basic sine curve is *stretched*, as in Figure 1.46. If $|A| < 1$, the basic sine curve is *shrunk*. We call $|A|$ the **amplitude** of $y = A \sin x$. The maximum value of y on the graph of $y = A \sin x$ is $|A|$, the amplitude.

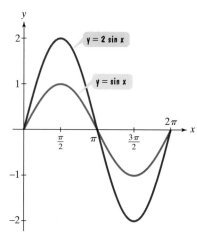

Figure 1.46 Comparing the graphs of $y = \sin x$ and $y = 2 \sin x$

Graphing Variations of $y = \sin x$

1. Identify the amplitude and the period.
2. Find the values of x for the five key points—the three x-intercepts, the maximum point, and the minimum point. Start with the value of x where the cycle begins and add quarter-periods—that is, $\dfrac{\text{period}}{4}$ —to find successive values of x.
3. Find the values of y for the five key points by evaluating the function at each value of x from step 2.
4. Connect the five key points with a smooth curve and graph one complete cycle of the given function.
5. Extend the graph in step 4 to the left or right as desired.

EXAMPLE 1   Graphing a Variation of $y = \sin x$

Determine the amplitude of $y = \frac{1}{2} \sin x$. Then graph $y = \sin x$ and $y = \frac{1}{2} \sin x$ for $0 \le x \le 2\pi$.

Solution

Step 1   Identify the amplitude and the period.   The equation $y = \frac{1}{2} \sin x$ is of the form $y = A \sin x$ with $A = \frac{1}{2}$. Thus, the amplitude is $|A| = \frac{1}{2}$. This means that the maximum value of y is $\frac{1}{2}$ and the minimum value of y is $-\frac{1}{2}$. The period for both $y = \frac{1}{2} \sin x$ and $y = \sin x$ is 2π.

Step 2   Find the values of x for the five key points.   We need to find the three x-intercepts, the maximum point, and the minimum point on the interval $[0, 2\pi]$. To do so, we begin by dividing the period, 2π, by 4.

$$\frac{\text{period}}{4} = \frac{2\pi}{4} = \frac{\pi}{2}$$

We start with the value of x where the cycle begins: $x = 0$. Now we add quarter-periods, $\dfrac{\pi}{2}$, to generate x-values for each of the key points. The five x-values are

$$x = 0, \quad x = 0 + \frac{\pi}{2} = \frac{\pi}{2}, \quad x = \frac{\pi}{2} + \frac{\pi}{2} = \pi,$$

$$x = \pi + \frac{\pi}{2} = \frac{3\pi}{2}, \quad x = \frac{3\pi}{2} + \frac{\pi}{2} = 2\pi.$$

Step 3   Find the values of y for the five key points.   We evaluate the function at each value of x from step 2.

Value of x	Value of y: $y = \frac{1}{2}\sin x$	Coordinates of key point	
0	$y = \dfrac{1}{2}\sin 0 = \dfrac{1}{2} \cdot 0 = 0$	$(0, 0)$	
$\dfrac{\pi}{2}$	$y = \dfrac{1}{2}\sin\dfrac{\pi}{2} = \dfrac{1}{2} \cdot 1 = \dfrac{1}{2}$	$\left(\dfrac{\pi}{2}, \dfrac{1}{2}\right)$	maximum point
π	$y = \dfrac{1}{2}\sin \pi = \dfrac{1}{2} \cdot 0 = 0$	$(\pi, 0)$	
$\dfrac{3\pi}{2}$	$y = \dfrac{1}{2}\sin\dfrac{3\pi}{2} = \dfrac{1}{2}(-1) = -\dfrac{1}{2}$	$\left(\dfrac{3\pi}{2}, -\dfrac{1}{2}\right)$	minimum point
2π	$y = \dfrac{1}{2}\sin 2\pi = \dfrac{1}{2} \cdot 0 = 0$	$(2\pi, 0)$	

There are x-intercepts at 0, π, and 2π. The maximum and minimum points are indicated by the voice balloons.

Step 4   Connect the five key points with a smooth curve and graph one complete cycle of the given function.   The five key points for $y = \frac{1}{2}\sin x$ are shown in Figure 1.47. By connecting the points with a smooth curve, the figure shows one complete cycle of $y = \frac{1}{2}\sin x$. Also shown is the graph of $y = \sin x$. The graph of $y = \frac{1}{2}\sin x$ shrinks the graph of $y = \sin x$.

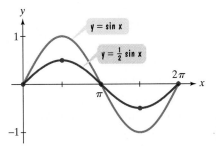

Figure 1.47 The graphs of $y = \sin x$ and $y = \frac{1}{2}\sin x$, $0 \le x \le 2\pi$

Check Point 1 Determine the amplitude of $y = 3 \sin x$. Then graph $y = \sin x$ and $y = 3 \sin x$ for $0 \le x \le 2\pi$.

EXAMPLE 2   Graphing a Variation of $y = \sin x$

Determine the amplitude of $y = -2 \sin x$. Then graph $y = \sin x$ and $y = -2 \sin x$ for $-\pi \le x \le 3\pi$.

Solution

Step 1   Identify the amplitude and the period.   The equation $y = -2 \sin x$ is of the form $y = A \sin x$ with $A = -2$. Thus, the amplitude is $|A| = |-2| = 2$. This means that the maximum value of y is 2 and the minimum value of y is -2. Both $y = \sin x$ and $y = -2 \sin x$ have a period of 2π.

Step 2   Find the x-values for the five key points.   Begin by dividing the period, 2π, by 4.

$$\frac{\text{period}}{4} = \frac{2\pi}{4} = \frac{\pi}{2}$$

Start with the value of x where the cycle begins: $x = 0$. Adding quarter-periods, $\frac{\pi}{2}$, the five x-values for the key points are

$$x = 0, \quad x = 0 + \frac{\pi}{2} = \frac{\pi}{2}, \quad x = \frac{\pi}{2} + \frac{\pi}{2} = \pi,$$

$$x = \pi + \frac{\pi}{2} = \frac{3\pi}{2}, \quad x = \frac{3\pi}{2} + \frac{\pi}{2} = 2\pi.$$

Step 3   Find the values of y for the five key points.   We evaluate the function at each value of x from step 2.

Value of x	Value of y: $y = -2 \sin x$	Coordinates of key point	
0	$y = -2 \sin 0 = -2 \cdot 0 = 0$	$(0, 0)$	
$\dfrac{\pi}{2}$	$y = -2 \sin \dfrac{\pi}{2} = -2 \cdot 1 = -2$	$\left(\dfrac{\pi}{2}, -2 \right)$	minimum point
π	$y = -2 \sin \pi = -2 \cdot 0 = 0$	$(\pi, 0)$	
$\dfrac{3\pi}{2}$	$y = -2 \sin \dfrac{3\pi}{2} = -2(-1) = 2$	$\left(\dfrac{3\pi}{2}, 2 \right)$	maximum point
2π	$y = -2 \sin 2\pi = -2 \cdot 0 = 0$	$(2\pi, 0)$	

There are x-intercepts at 0, π, and 2π. The minimum and maximum points are indicated by the voice balloons.

Step 4   Connect the five key points with a smooth curve and graph one complete cycle of the given function.   The five key points for $y = -2 \sin x$ are shown in Figure 1.48. By connecting the points with a smooth curve, the dark red portion shows one complete cycle of $y = -2 \sin x$. Also shown in dark blue is one complete cycle of the graph of $y = \sin x$.

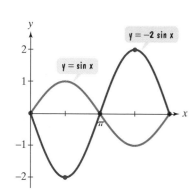

Figure 1.48 The graphs of $y = \sin x$ and $y = -2 \sin x$, $0 \le x \le 2\pi$

Step 5 Extend the graph in step 4 to the left or right as desired. The dark red and dark blue portions of the graphs in Figure 1.48 are from 0 to 2π. In order to graph for $-\pi \le x \le 3\pi$, continue the pattern of each graph to the left and to the right. These extensions are shown by the lighter colors in Figure 1.48.

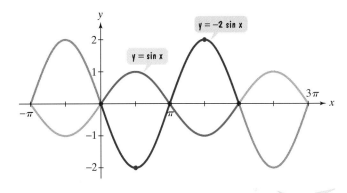

Figure 1.48, extended
The graphs of $y = \sin x$ and
$y = -2 \sin x, -\pi \le x \le 3\pi$

Check Point 2 Determine the amplitude of $y = -\frac{1}{2} \sin x$. Then graph $y = \sin x$ and $y = -\frac{1}{2} \sin x$ for $-\pi \le x \le 3\pi$.

Now let us examine the graphs of functions of the form $y = A \sin Bx$, where B is the coefficient of x. How do such graphs compare to those of functions of the form $y = A \sin x$? We know that $y = A \sin x$ completes one cycle from $x = 0$ to $x = 2\pi$. Thus, $y = A \sin Bx$ completes one cycle from $Bx = 0$ to $Bx = 2\pi$. Solve each of these equations for x.

$$Bx = 0 \qquad\qquad Bx = 2\pi$$
$$x = 0 \qquad\qquad x = \frac{2\pi}{B} \qquad \text{Divide both sides of each equation by } B.$$

This means that $y = A \sin Bx$ completes one cycle from 0 to $\dfrac{2\pi}{B}$. The period is $\dfrac{2\pi}{B}$.

Amplitudes and Periods

The graph of $y = A \sin Bx$ has

amplitude $= |A|$

period $= \dfrac{2\pi}{B}$.

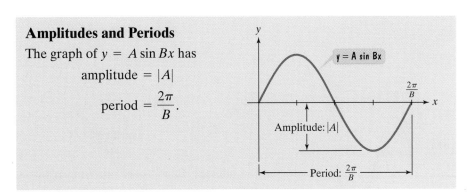

EXAMPLE 3 Graphing a Function of the Form $y = A \sin Bx$

Determine the amplitude and period of $y = 3 \sin 2x$. Then graph the function for $0 \le x \le 2\pi$.

Solution

Step 1 Identify the amplitude and the period. The equation $y = 3\sin 2x$ is of the form $y = A\sin Bx$ with $A = 3$ and $B = 2$.

$$\text{amplitude:} \quad |A| = |3| = 3$$

$$\text{period:} \quad \frac{2\pi}{B} = \frac{2\pi}{2} = \pi$$

The amplitude, 3, tells us that the maximum value of y is 3 and the minimum value of y is -3.

Step 2 Find the x-values for the five key points. Begin by dividing the period, π, by 4.

$$\frac{\text{period}}{4} = \frac{\pi}{4}$$

Start with the value of x where the cycle begins: $x = 0$. Adding quarter-periods, $\frac{\pi}{4}$, the five x-values for the key points are

$$x = 0, \quad x = 0 + \frac{\pi}{4} = \frac{\pi}{4}, \quad x = \frac{\pi}{4} + \frac{\pi}{4} = \frac{\pi}{2},$$

$$x = \frac{\pi}{2} + \frac{\pi}{4} = \frac{3\pi}{4}, \quad x = \frac{3\pi}{4} + \frac{\pi}{4} = \pi.$$

Step 3 Find the values of y for the five key points. We evaluate the function at each value of x from step 2.

Value of x	Value of y: $y = 3\sin 2x$	Coordinates of key point	
0	$y = 3\sin 2 \cdot 0$ $= 3\sin 0 = 3 \cdot 0 = 0$	$(0, 0)$	
$\frac{\pi}{4}$	$y = 3\sin 2 \cdot \frac{\pi}{4}$ $= 3\sin\frac{\pi}{2} = 3 \cdot 1 = 3$	$\left(\frac{\pi}{4}, 3\right)$	maximum point
$\frac{\pi}{2}$	$y = 3\sin 2 \cdot \frac{\pi}{2}$ $= 3\sin\pi = 3 \cdot 0 = 0$	$\left(\frac{\pi}{2}, 0\right)$	
$\frac{3\pi}{4}$	$y = 3\sin 2 \cdot \frac{3\pi}{4}$ $= 3\sin\frac{3\pi}{2} = 3(-1) = -3$	$\left(\frac{3\pi}{4}, -3\right)$	minimum point
π	$y = 3\sin 2 \cdot \pi$ $= 3\sin 2\pi = 3 \cdot 0 = 0$	$(\pi, 0)$	

In the interval $[0, \pi]$, there are x-intercepts at 0, $\frac{\pi}{2}$, and π. The maximum and minimum points are indicated by the voice balloons.

Step 4 Connect the five key points with a smooth curve and graph one complete cycle of the given function. The five key points for $y = 3\sin 2x$ are shown in Figure 1.49. By connecting the points with a smooth curve, the blue portion shows one complete cycle of $y = 3\sin 2x$ from 0 to π.

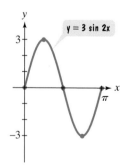

Figure 1.49 The graph of $y = 3\sin 2x, 0 \le x \le \pi$

Technology

The graph of $y = 3 \sin 2x$ in a $\left[0, 2\pi, \dfrac{\pi}{2}\right]$ by $[-4, 4, 1]$ viewing rectangle verifies our hand-drawn graph in Figure 1.49.

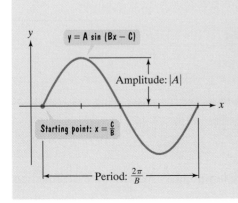

Step 5 Extend the graph in step 4 to the left or right as desired. The blue portion of the graph in Figure 1.49 is from 0 to π. In order to graph for $0 \le x \le 2\pi$, we continue this portion and extend the graph another full period to the right. This extension is shown in black in Figure 1.49.

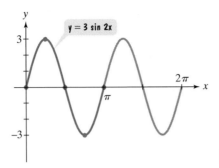

Figure 1.49, extended

Check Point 3 Determine the amplitude and period of $y = 2 \sin \frac{1}{2} x$. Then graph the function for $0 \le x \le 8\pi$.

Now let us examine the graphs of functions of the form $y = A \sin (Bx - C)$. How do such graphs compare to those of functions of the form $y = A \sin Bx$?

In both cases, the amplitude is $|A|$ and the period is $\dfrac{2\pi}{B}$. One complete cycle occurs if $Bx - C$ increases from 0 to 2π. This means that we can find an interval containing one cycle by solving the equations

$$Bx - C = 0 \quad \text{and} \quad Bx - C = 2\pi.$$

$$Bx = C \qquad\qquad Bx = C + 2\pi \qquad \text{Add } C \text{ to both sides in each equation.}$$

$$x = \frac{C}{B} \qquad\qquad x = \frac{C}{B} + \frac{2\pi}{B}. \qquad \text{Divide both sides by } B \text{ in each equation.}$$

This is the x-coordinate on the left where the cycle begins.

This is the x-coordinate on the right where the cycle ends. $\frac{2\pi}{B}$ is the period.

The voice balloon on the left indicates that $y = A \sin (Bx - C)$ shifts the graph of $y = A \sin Bx$ horizontally by $\dfrac{C}{B}$. Thus, the number $\dfrac{C}{B}$ is the **phase shift** associated with the graph.

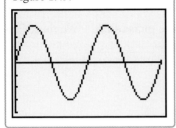

The Graph of $y = A \sin(Bx - C)$

The graph of $y = A \sin (Bx - C)$ is obtained by horizontally shifting the graph of $y = A \sin Bx$ so that the starting point of the cycle is shifted from $x = 0$ to $x = \dfrac{C}{B}$. If $\dfrac{C}{B} > 0$, the shift is to the right. If $\dfrac{C}{B} < 0$, the shift is to the left. The number $\dfrac{C}{B}$ is called the **phase shift.**

$$\text{amplitude} = |A|$$

$$\text{period} = \frac{2\pi}{B}$$

EXAMPLE 4 Graphing a Function of the Form $y = A \sin(Bx - C)$

Determine the amplitude, period, and phase shift of $y = 4 \sin\left(2x - \dfrac{2\pi}{3}\right)$. Then graph one period of the function.

Solution

Step 1 Identify the amplitude, the period, and the phase shift. We must first identify values for A, B, and C.

> This equation is of the form
> $y = A \sin(Bx - C)$.

$$y = 4 \sin\left(2x - \frac{2\pi}{3}\right)$$

Using the voice balloon, we see that $A = 4$, $B = 2$, and $C = \dfrac{2\pi}{3}$.

amplitude: $|A| = |4| = 4$ > The maximum y is 4 and the minimum is −4.

period: $\dfrac{2\pi}{B} = \dfrac{2\pi}{2} = \pi$ > Each cycle is completed in π radians.

phase shift: $\dfrac{C}{B} = \dfrac{\frac{2\pi}{3}}{2} = \dfrac{2\pi}{3} \cdot \dfrac{1}{2} = \dfrac{\pi}{3}$ > A cycle starts at $x = \frac{\pi}{3}$.

Step 2 Find the x-values for the five key points. Begin by dividing the period, π, by 4.

$$\frac{\text{period}}{4} = \frac{\pi}{4}$$

Study Tip

You can speed up the additions on the right by first writing the starting point, $\frac{\pi}{3}$, and the quarter-period, $\frac{\pi}{4}$, with a common denominator, 12.

starting point
$$= \frac{\pi}{3} = \frac{4\pi}{12}$$

quarter-period
$$= \frac{\pi}{4} = \frac{3\pi}{12}$$

Start with the value of x where the cycle begins: $x = \dfrac{\pi}{3}$. Adding quarter-periods, $\dfrac{\pi}{4}$, the five x-values for the key points are

$$x = \frac{\pi}{3}, \quad x = \frac{\pi}{3} + \frac{\pi}{4} = \frac{4\pi}{12} + \frac{3\pi}{12} = \frac{7\pi}{12},$$

$$x = \frac{7\pi}{12} + \frac{\pi}{4} = \frac{7\pi}{12} + \frac{3\pi}{12} = \frac{10\pi}{12} = \frac{5\pi}{6},$$

$$x = \frac{5\pi}{6} + \frac{\pi}{4} = \frac{10\pi}{12} + \frac{3\pi}{12} = \frac{13\pi}{12},$$

$$x = \frac{13\pi}{12} + \frac{\pi}{4} = \frac{13\pi}{12} + \frac{3\pi}{12} = \frac{16\pi}{12} = \frac{4\pi}{3}.$$

Step 3 Find the values of y for the five key points. We evaluate the function at each value of x from step 2.

Value of x	Value of y: $y = 4\sin\left(2x - \dfrac{2\pi}{3}\right)$	Coordinates of key point
$\dfrac{\pi}{3}$	$\begin{aligned} y &= 4\sin\left(2\cdot\dfrac{\pi}{3} - \dfrac{2\pi}{3}\right) \\ &= 4\sin 0 = 4\cdot 0 = 0 \end{aligned}$	$\left(\dfrac{\pi}{3},0\right)$
$\dfrac{7\pi}{12}$	$\begin{aligned} y &= 4\sin\left(2\cdot\dfrac{7\pi}{12} - \dfrac{2\pi}{3}\right) \\ &= 4\sin\left(\dfrac{7\pi}{6} - \dfrac{2\pi}{3}\right) \\ &= 4\sin\dfrac{3\pi}{6} = 4\sin\dfrac{\pi}{2} = 4\cdot 1 = 4 \end{aligned}$	$\left(\dfrac{7\pi}{12},4\right)$ ◁ maximum point
$\dfrac{5\pi}{6}$	$\begin{aligned} y &= 4\sin\left(2\cdot\dfrac{5\pi}{6} - \dfrac{2\pi}{3}\right) \\ &= 4\sin\left(\dfrac{5\pi}{3} - \dfrac{2\pi}{3}\right) \\ &= 4\sin\dfrac{3\pi}{3} = 4\sin\pi = 4\cdot 0 = 0 \end{aligned}$	$\left(\dfrac{5\pi}{6},0\right)$
$\dfrac{13\pi}{12}$	$\begin{aligned} y &= 4\sin\left(2\cdot\dfrac{13\pi}{12} - \dfrac{2\pi}{3}\right) \\ &= 4\sin\left(\dfrac{13\pi}{6} - \dfrac{4\pi}{6}\right) \\ &= 4\sin\dfrac{9\pi}{6} = 4\sin\dfrac{3\pi}{2} = 4(-1) = -4 \end{aligned}$	$\left(\dfrac{13\pi}{12},-4\right)$ ◁ minimum point
$\dfrac{4\pi}{3}$	$\begin{aligned} y &= 4\sin\left(2\cdot\dfrac{4\pi}{3} - \dfrac{2\pi}{3}\right) \\ &= 4\sin\dfrac{6\pi}{3} = 4\sin 2\pi = 4\cdot 0 = 0 \end{aligned}$	$\left(\dfrac{4\pi}{3},0\right)$

In the interval $\left[\dfrac{\pi}{3},\dfrac{4\pi}{3}\right]$, there are x-intercepts at $\dfrac{\pi}{3}$, $\dfrac{5\pi}{6}$, and $\dfrac{4\pi}{3}$. The maximum and minimum points are indicated by the voice balloons.

Step 4   Connect the five key points with a smooth curve and graph one complete cycle of the given function.   The key points and the graph of $y = 4\sin\left(2x - \dfrac{2\pi}{3}\right)$ are shown in Figure 1.50.

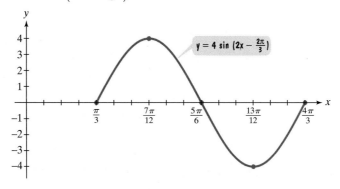

Figure 1.50

Check Point 4
Determine the amplitude, period, and phase shift of $y = 3 \sin\left(2x - \dfrac{\pi}{3}\right)$. Then graph one period of the function.

3 Understand the graph of $y = \cos x$.

The Graph of $y = \cos x$

We graph $y = \cos x$ by listing some points on the graph. Because the period of the cosine function is 2π, we will concentrate on the graph of the basic cosine curve on the interval $[0, 2\pi]$. The rest of the graph is made up of repetitions of this portion. Table 1.2 lists some values of (x, y) on the graph of $y = \cos x$.

Table 1.2 Values of (x, y) on $y = \cos x$

x	0	$\dfrac{\pi}{6}$	$\dfrac{\pi}{3}$	$\dfrac{\pi}{2}$	$\dfrac{2\pi}{3}$	$\dfrac{5\pi}{6}$	π	$\dfrac{7\pi}{6}$	$\dfrac{4\pi}{3}$	$\dfrac{3\pi}{2}$	$\dfrac{5\pi}{3}$	$\dfrac{11\pi}{6}$	2π
$y = \cos x$	1	$\dfrac{\sqrt{3}}{2}$	$\dfrac{1}{2}$	0	$-\dfrac{1}{2}$	$-\dfrac{\sqrt{3}}{2}$	-1	$-\dfrac{\sqrt{3}}{2}$	$-\dfrac{1}{2}$	0	$\dfrac{1}{2}$	$\dfrac{\sqrt{3}}{2}$	1

As x increases from 0 to $\dfrac{\pi}{2}$, y decreases from 1 to 0.

As x increases from $\dfrac{\pi}{2}$ to π, y decreases from 0 to -1.

As x increases from π to $\dfrac{3\pi}{2}$, y increases from -1 to 0.

As x increases from $\dfrac{3\pi}{2}$ to 2π, y increases from 0 to 1.

Plotting the points in Table 1.2 and connecting them with a smooth curve, we obtain the graph shown in Figure 1.51. The portion of the graph in dark blue shows one complete period. We can obtain a more complete graph of $y = \cos x$ by extending this dark blue portion to the left and to the right.

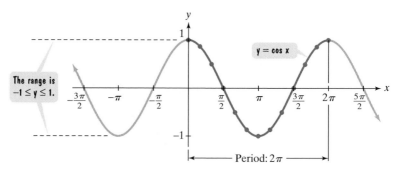

Figure 1.51 The graph of $y = \cos x$

The graph of $y = \cos x$ allows us to visualize some of the properties of the cosine function.

- The domain is the set of all real numbers. The graph extends indefinitely to the left and to the right with no gaps or holes.
- The range consists of all numbers between -1 and 1, inclusive. The graph never rises above 1 or falls below -1.
- The period is 2π. The graph's pattern repeats in every interval of length 2π.
- The function is an even function: $\cos(-x) = \cos x$. This can be seen by observing that the graph is symmetric with respect to the y-axis.

Turn back the page and take a second look at Figure 1.51. Can you see that the graph of $y = \cos x$ is the graph of $y = \sin x$ with a phase shift of $-\dfrac{\pi}{2}$ radians? If you trace along the curve from $x = -\dfrac{\pi}{2}$ to $x = \dfrac{3\pi}{2}$, you are tracing one complete cycle of the sine curve. This can be expressed as an identity:

$$\cos x = \sin\left(x + \frac{\pi}{2}\right).$$

Because of this similarity, the graphs of sine functions and cosine functions are called **sinusoidal graphs.**

4 Graph variations of $y = \cos x$.

Graphing Variations of $y = \cos x$

We use the same steps to graph variations of $y = \cos x$ as we did for graphing variations of $y = \sin x$. We will continue finding key points by dividing the period into four equal parts. Amplitudes, periods, and phase shifts play an important role when graphing by hand.

The Graph of $y = A\cos Bx$

The graph of $y = A\cos Bx$ has

$$\text{amplitude} = |A|$$

$$\text{period} = \frac{2\pi}{B}.$$

EXAMPLE 5   **Graphing a Function of the Form $y = A\cos Bx$**

Determine the amplitude and period of $y = -3\cos\dfrac{\pi}{2}x$. Then graph the function for $-4 \le x \le 4$.

Solution

Step 1   Identify the amplitude and the period.   The equation $y = -3\cos\dfrac{\pi}{2}x$ is of the form $y = A\cos Bx$ with $A = -3$ and $B = \dfrac{\pi}{2}$.

amplitude: $|A| = |-3| = 3$ [The maximum y is 3 and the minimum is −3.]

period: $\dfrac{2\pi}{B} = \dfrac{2\pi}{\dfrac{\pi}{2}} = 2\pi \cdot \dfrac{2}{\pi} = 4$ [Each cycle is completed in 4 radians.]

Step 2   Find the x-values for the five key points.   Begin by dividing the period, 4, by 4.

$$\frac{\text{period}}{4} = \frac{4}{4} = 1$$

Start with the value of x where the cycle begins: $x = 0$. Adding quarter-periods, 1, the five x-values for the key points are

$$x = 0, \quad x = 0 + 1 = 1, \quad x = 1 + 1 = 2, \quad x = 2 + 1 = 3, \quad x = 3 + 1 = 4$$

Step 3   Find the values of y for the five key points.   We evaluate the function at each value of x from step 2.

Value of x	Value of y: $y = -3 \cos \dfrac{\pi}{2} x$	Coordinates of key point	
0	$y = -3 \cos \dfrac{\pi}{2} \cdot 0$ $= -3 \cos 0 = -3 \cdot 1 = -3$	$(0, -3)$	minimum point
1	$y = -3 \cos \dfrac{\pi}{2} \cdot 1$ $= -3 \cos \dfrac{\pi}{2} = -3 \cdot 0 = 0$	$(1, 0)$	
2	$y = -3 \cos \dfrac{\pi}{2} \cdot 2$ $= -3 \cos \pi = -3(-1) = 3$	$(2, 3)$	maximum point
3	$y = -3 \cos \dfrac{\pi}{2} \cdot 3$ $= -3 \cos \dfrac{3\pi}{2} = -3(0) = 0$	$(3, 0)$	
4	$y = -3 \cos \dfrac{\pi}{2} \cdot 4$ $= -3 \cos 2\pi = -3(1) = -3$	$(4, -3)$	minimum point

In the interval $[0, 4]$, there are x-intercepts at 1 and 3. The minimum and maximum points are indicated by the voice balloons.

Step 4   Connect the five key points with a smooth curve and graph one complete cycle of the given function.   The five key points for $y = -3 \cos \dfrac{\pi}{2} x$ are shown in Figure 1.52. By connecting the points with a smooth curve, the blue portion shows one complete cycle of $y = -3 \cos \dfrac{\pi}{2} x$ from 0 to 4.

Technology

The graph of $y = -3 \cos \dfrac{\pi}{2} x$ in a $[-4, 4, 1]$ by $[-4, 4, 1]$ viewing rectangle verifies our hand-drawn graph in Figure 1.52.

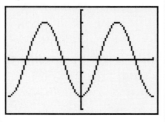

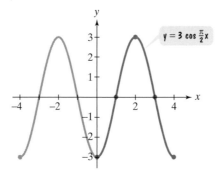

Figure 1.52

Step 5   Extend the graph in step 4 to the left or right as desired.   The blue portion of the graph in Figure 1.52 is for x from 0 to 4. In order to graph for $-4 \le x \le 4$, we continue this portion and extend the graph another full period to the left. This extension is shown in black in Figure 1.52.

Check Point 5 Determine the amplitude and period of $y = -4\cos \pi x$. Then graph the function for $-2 \leq x \leq 2$.

Finally, let us examine the graphs of functions of the form $y = A\cos(Bx - C)$.

Graphs of these functions shift the graph of $y = A\cos Bx$ horizontally by $\dfrac{C}{B}$.

The Graph of $y = A\cos(Bx - C)$

The graph of $y = A\cos(Bx - C)$ is obtained by horizontally shifting the graph of $y = A\cos Bx$ so that the starting point of the cycle is shifted from $x = 0$ to $x = \dfrac{C}{B}$. If $\dfrac{C}{B} > 0$, the shift is to the right. If $\dfrac{C}{B} < 0$, the shift is to the left. The number $\dfrac{C}{B}$ is called the **phase shift.**

$$\text{amplitude} = |A|$$
$$\text{period} = \frac{2\pi}{B}$$

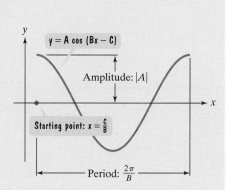

EXAMPLE 6   **Graphing a Function of the Form**
$$y = A\cos(Bx - C)$$

Determine the amplitude, period, and phase shift of $y = \frac{1}{2}\cos(4x + \pi)$. Then graph one period of the function.

Solution

Step 1   Identify the amplitude, the period, and the phase shift.   We must first identify values for A, B, and C. To do this, we need to express the equation in the form $y = A\cos(Bx - C)$. Thus, we write $y = \frac{1}{2}\cos(4x + \pi)$ as $y = \frac{1}{2}\cos[4x - (-\pi)]$. Now we can identify values for A, B, and C.

This equation is of the form
$y = A\cos(Bx - C)$.

$$y = \frac{1}{2}\cos[4x - (-\pi)]$$

Using the voice balloon, we see that $A = \frac{1}{2}$, $B = 4$, and $C = -\pi$.

amplitude: $|A| = \left|\dfrac{1}{2}\right| = \dfrac{1}{2}$ The maximum y is $\frac{1}{2}$ and the minimum is $-\frac{1}{2}$.

period: $\dfrac{2\pi}{B} = \dfrac{2\pi}{4} = \dfrac{\pi}{2}$ Each cycle is completed in $\frac{\pi}{2}$ radians.

phase shift: $\dfrac{C}{B} = -\dfrac{\pi}{4}$ A cycle starts at $x = -\frac{\pi}{4}$.

Step 2   Find the x-values for the five key points.   Begin by dividing the period, $\dfrac{\pi}{2}$, by 4.

$$\frac{\text{period}}{4} = \frac{\dfrac{\pi}{2}}{4} = \frac{\pi}{8}$$

Start with the value of x where the cycle begins: $x = -\dfrac{\pi}{4}$. Adding quarter-periods, $\dfrac{\pi}{8}$, the five x-values for the key points are

$$x = -\frac{\pi}{4}, \quad x = -\frac{\pi}{4} + \frac{\pi}{8} = -\frac{2\pi}{8} + \frac{\pi}{8} = -\frac{\pi}{8}, \quad x = -\frac{\pi}{8} + \frac{\pi}{8} = 0,$$

$$x = 0 + \frac{\pi}{8} = \frac{\pi}{8}, \quad x = \frac{\pi}{8} + \frac{\pi}{8} = \frac{2\pi}{8} = \frac{\pi}{4}.$$

Step 3   Find the values of y for the five key points.   Take a few minutes and use your calculator to evaluate the function at each value of x from step 2. Show that the key points are

$$\left(-\frac{\pi}{4}, \frac{1}{2}\right), \quad \left(-\frac{\pi}{8}, 0\right), \quad \left(0, -\frac{1}{2}\right), \quad \left(\frac{\pi}{8}, 0\right), \quad \text{and} \quad \left(\frac{\pi}{4}, \frac{1}{2}\right).$$

| maximum point | x-intercept at $-\dfrac{\pi}{8}$ | minimum point | x-intercept at $\dfrac{\pi}{8}$ | maximum point |

Technology

The graph of

$$y = \frac{1}{2}\cos(4x + \pi)$$

in a $\left[-\dfrac{\pi}{4}, \dfrac{\pi}{4}, \dfrac{\pi}{8}\right]$ by $[-1, 1, 1]$ viewing rectangle verifies our hand-drawn graph in Figure 1.53.

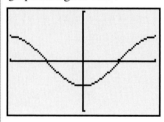

Step 4   Connect the five key points with a smooth curve and graph one complete cycle of the given function.   The key points and the graph of $y = \frac{1}{2}\cos(4x + \pi)$ are shown in Figure 1.53.

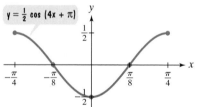

Figure 1.53

Check Point 6   Determine the amplitude, period, and phase shift of $y = \frac{3}{2}\cos(2x + \pi)$. Then graph one period of the function.

5 Use vertical shifts of sine and cosine curves.

Vertical Shifts of Sinusoidal Graphs

We now look at sinusoidal graphs of

$$y = A\sin(Bx - C) + D \quad \text{and} \quad y = A\cos(Bx - C) + D.$$

The constant D causes vertical shifts in the graphs of $y = A\sin(Bx - C)$ and $y = A\cos(Bx - C)$. If D is positive, the shift is D units upward. If D is negative, the shift is D units downward. These vertical shifts result in sinusoidal graphs oscillating about the horizontal line $y = D$ rather than about the x-axis. Thus, the maximum y is $D + |A|$ and the minimum y is $D - |A|$.

EXAMPLE 7   A Vertical Shift

Graph one period of the function $y = \frac{1}{2} \cos x - 1$.

Solution   The graph of $y = \frac{1}{2} \cos x - 1$ is the graph of $y = \frac{1}{2} \cos x$ shifted one unit downward. The period of $y = \frac{1}{2} \cos x$ is 2π, which is also the period for the vertically shifted graph. The key points on the interval $[0, 2\pi]$ for $y = \frac{1}{2} \cos x - 1$ are found by first determining their x-coordinates. The quarter-period is $\dfrac{2\pi}{4}$, or $\dfrac{\pi}{2}$.

The cycle begins at $x = 0$. As always, we add quarter-periods to generate x-values for each of the key points. The five x-values are

$$x = 0, \quad x = 0 + \frac{\pi}{2} = \frac{\pi}{2}, \quad x = \frac{\pi}{2} + \frac{\pi}{2} = \pi,$$

$$x = \pi + \frac{\pi}{2} = \frac{3\pi}{2}, \quad x = \frac{3\pi}{2} + \frac{\pi}{2} = 2\pi.$$

The values of y for the five key points and their coordinates are determined as follows.

Value of x	Value of y: $y = \dfrac{1}{2} \cos x - 1$	Coordinates of key point
0	$y = \dfrac{1}{2} \cos 0 - 1$ $= \dfrac{1}{2} \cdot 1 - 1 = -\dfrac{1}{2}$	$\left(0, -\dfrac{1}{2}\right)$
$\dfrac{\pi}{2}$	$y = \dfrac{1}{2} \cos \dfrac{\pi}{2} - 1$ $= \dfrac{1}{2} \cdot 0 - 1 = -1$	$\left(\dfrac{\pi}{2}, -1\right)$
π	$y = \dfrac{1}{2} \cos \pi - 1$ $= \dfrac{1}{2}(-1) - 1 = -\dfrac{3}{2}$	$\left(\pi, -\dfrac{3}{2}\right)$
$\dfrac{3\pi}{2}$	$y = \dfrac{1}{2} \cos \dfrac{3\pi}{2} - 1$ $= \dfrac{1}{2} \cdot 0 - 1 = -1$	$\left(\dfrac{3\pi}{2}, -1\right)$
2π	$y = \dfrac{1}{2} \cos 2\pi - 1$ $= \dfrac{1}{2} \cdot 1 - 1 = -\dfrac{1}{2}$	$\left(2\pi, -\dfrac{1}{2}\right)$

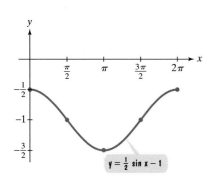

$y = \frac{1}{2} \sin x - 1$

Figure 1.54

The five key points for $y = \frac{1}{2} \cos x - 1$ are shown in Figure 1.54. By connecting the points with a smooth curve, we obtain one period of the graph.

Check Point 7   Graph one period of the function $y = 2 \cos x + 1$.

6 Model periodic behavior.

Modeling Periodic Behavior

Our breathing consists of alternating periods of inhaling and exhaling. Each complete pumping cycle of the human heart can be described using a sine function. Our brain waves during deep sleep are sinusoidal. Viewed in this way, trigonometry becomes an intimate experience.

Some graphing utilities have a SINe REGression feature. This feature gives the sine function in the form $y = A \sin(Bx + C) + D$ of best fit for wavelike data. At least four data points must be used. However, it is not always necessary to use technology. In our next example, we use our understanding of sinusoidal graphs to model the process of breathing.

EXAMPLE 8 A Trigonometric Breath of Life

The graph in Figure 1.55 shows one complete normal breathing cycle. The cycle consists of inhaling and exhaling. It takes place every 5 seconds. Velocity of air flow is positive when we inhale and negative when we exhale. It is measured in liters per second. If y represents velocity of air flow after x seconds, find a function of the form $y = A \sin Bx$ that models air flow in a normal breathing cycle.

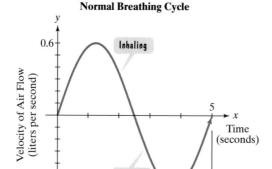

Velocity of Air Flow in a Normal Breathing Cycle

Figure 1.55

Solution We need to determine values for A and B in the equation $y = A \sin Bx$. A, the amplitude, is the maximum value of y. Figure 1.55 shows that this maximum value is 0.6. Thus, $A = 0.6$.

The value of B in $y = A \sin Bx$ can be found using the formula for the period: period $= \dfrac{2\pi}{B}$. The period of our breathing cycle is 5 seconds. Thus,

$$5 = \frac{2\pi}{B} \qquad \text{Our goal is to solve this equation for B.}$$

$$5B = 2\pi \qquad \text{Multiply both sides of the equation by B.}$$

$$B = \frac{2\pi}{5}. \qquad \text{Divide both sides of the equation by 5.}$$

We see that $A = 0.6$ and $B = \dfrac{2\pi}{5}$. Substitute these values into $y = A \sin Bx$. The breathing cycle is modeled by

$$y = 0.6 \sin \frac{2\pi}{5} x.$$

Check Point 8 Find an equation of the form $y = A \sin Bx$ that produces the graph shown in the figure on the right.

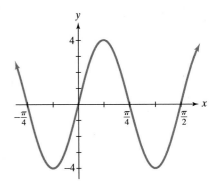

EXAMPLE 9 Modeling a Tidal Cycle

Figure 1.56 shows that the depth of water at a boat dock varies with the tides. The depth is 5 feet at low tide and 13 feet at high tide. On a certain day, low tide occurs at 4 A.M. and high tide at 10 A.M. If y represents the depth of the water, in feet, x hours after midnight, use a sine function of the form $y = A \sin(Bx - C) + D$ to model the water's depth.

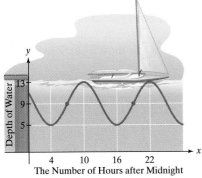

Figure 1.56

Solution We need to determine values for A, B, C, and D in the equation $y = A \sin(Bx - C) + D$. We can find these values using Figure 1.56. We begin with D.

To find D, we use the vertical shift. Because the water's depth ranges from a minimum of 5 feet to a maximum of 13 feet, the curve oscillates about the middle value, 9 feet. Thus, $D = 9$, which is the vertical shift.

At maximum depth, the water is 4 feet above 9 feet. Thus, A, the amplitude, is 4: $A = 4$.

To find B, we use the period. The blue portion of the graph shows that one complete tidal cycle occurs in $19 - 7$, or 12 hours. The period is 12. Thus,

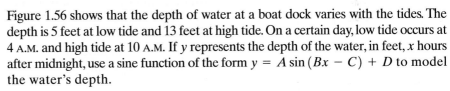

$$12 = \frac{2\pi}{B} \qquad \text{Our goal is to solve this equation for B.}$$

$$12B = 2\pi \qquad \text{Multiply both sides by B.}$$

$$B = \frac{2\pi}{12} = \frac{\pi}{6}. \qquad \text{Divide both sides by 12.}$$

To find C, we use the phase shift. The blue portion of the graph shows that the starting point of the cycle is shifted from 0 to 7. The phase shift, $\frac{C}{B}$, is 7.

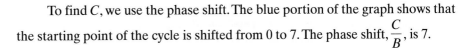

$$7 = \frac{C}{B} \qquad \text{The phase shift of } y = A \sin(Bx - C) \text{ is } \frac{C}{B}.$$

$$7 = \frac{C}{\frac{\pi}{6}} \qquad \text{From above, we have } B = \frac{\pi}{6}.$$

$$\frac{7\pi}{6} = C \qquad \text{Multiply both sides of the equation by } \frac{\pi}{6}.$$

Technology

We can use a graphing utility to verify that the model in Example 9

$$y = 4 \sin\left(\frac{\pi}{6} x - \frac{7\pi}{6}\right) + 9$$

is correct. The graph of the function is shown in a $[0, 28, 4]$ by $[0, 15, 5]$ viewing rectangle.

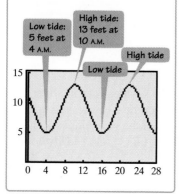

We see that $A = 4$, $B = \dfrac{\pi}{6}$, $C = \dfrac{7\pi}{6}$, and $D = 9$. Substitute these values into $y = A \sin(Bx - C) + D$. The water's depth, in feet, x hours after midnight is modeled by

$$y = 4 \sin\left(\frac{\pi}{6} x - \frac{7\pi}{6}\right) + 9.$$

Check Point 9

The figure shows the number of hours of daylight for a region that is 30° north of the equator. Hours of daylight are at a minimum of 10 hours in December. Hours of daylight are at a maximum of 14 hours in June. Let x represent the month of the year, with 1 for January, 2 for February, 3 for March, and 12 for December. If y represents the number of hours of daylight in month x, use a sine function of the form $y = A \sin(Bx - C) + D$ to model the hours of daylight.

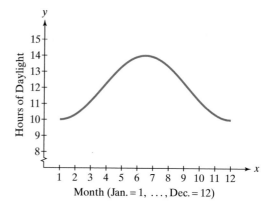

Month (Jan. = 1, ..., Dec. = 12)

EXERCISE SET 1.5

Practice Exercises

In Exercises 1–6, determine the amplitude of each function. Then graph the function and $y = \sin x$ in the same rectangular coordinate system for $0 \le x \le 2\pi$.

1. $y = 4 \sin x$

2. $y = 5 \sin x$

3. $y = \frac{1}{3} \sin x$

4. $y = \frac{1}{4} \sin x$

5. $y = -3 \sin x$

6. $y = -4 \sin x$

In Exercises 7–16, determine the amplitude and period of each function. Then graph one period of the function.

7. $y = \sin 2x$

8. $y = \sin 4x$

9. $y = 3 \sin \frac{1}{2} x$

10. $y = 2 \sin \frac{1}{4} x$

11. $y = 4 \sin \pi x$

12. $y = 3 \sin 2\pi x$

13. $y = -3 \sin 2\pi x$

14. $y = -2 \sin \pi x$

15. $y = -\sin \frac{2}{3} x$

16. $y = -\sin \frac{4}{3} x$

In Exercises 17–30, determine the amplitude, period, and phase shift of each function. Then graph one period of the function.

17. $y = \sin(x - \pi)$

18. $y = \sin\left(x - \frac{\pi}{2}\right)$

19. $y = \sin(2x - \pi)$

20. $y = \sin\left(2x - \frac{\pi}{2}\right)$

21. $y = 3 \sin(2x - \pi)$ **22.** $y = 3 \sin\left(2x - \dfrac{\pi}{2}\right)$

23. $y = \frac{1}{2} \sin\left(x + \dfrac{\pi}{2}\right)$ **24.** $y = \frac{1}{2} \sin(x + \pi)$

25. $y = -2 \sin\left(2x + \dfrac{\pi}{2}\right)$ **26.** $y = -3 \sin\left(2x + \dfrac{\pi}{2}\right)$

27. $y = 3 \sin(\pi x + 2)$ **28.** $y = 3 \sin(2\pi x + 4)$

29. $y = -2 \sin(2\pi x + 4\pi)$ **30.** $y = -3 \sin(2\pi x + 4\pi)$

In Exercises 31–34, determine the amplitude of each function. Then graph the function and $y = \cos x$ in the same rectangular coordinate system for $0 \le x \le 2\pi$.

31. $y = 2 \cos x$ **32.** $y = 3 \cos x$

33. $y = -2 \cos x$ **34.** $y = -3 \cos x$

In Exercises 35–42, determine the amplitude and period of each function. Then graph one period of the function.

35. $y = \cos 2x$ **36.** $y = \cos 4x$

37. $y = 4 \cos 2\pi x$ **38.** $y = 5 \cos 2\pi x$

39. $y = -4 \cos \frac{1}{2} x$ **40.** $y = -3 \cos \frac{1}{3} x$

41. $y = -\frac{1}{2} \cos \dfrac{\pi}{3} x$ **42.** $y = -\frac{1}{2} \cos \dfrac{\pi}{4} x$

In Exercises 43–50, determine the amplitude, period, and phase shift of each function. Then graph one period of the function.

43. $y = 3 \cos(2x - \pi)$ **44.** $y = 4 \cos(2x - \pi)$

45. $y = \frac{1}{2} \cos\left(3x + \dfrac{\pi}{2}\right)$ **46.** $y = \frac{1}{2} \cos(2x + \pi)$

47. $y = -3 \cos\left(2x - \dfrac{\pi}{2}\right)$ **48.** $y = -4 \cos\left(2x - \dfrac{\pi}{2}\right)$

49. $y = 2 \cos(2\pi x + 8\pi)$ **50.** $y = 3 \cos(2\pi x + 4\pi)$

In Exercises 51–58, use a vertical shift to graph one period of the function.

51. $y = \sin x + 2$ **52.** $y = \sin x - 2$

53. $y = \cos x - 3$ **54.** $y = \cos x + 3$

55. $y = 2 \sin \frac{1}{2} x + 1$ **56.** $y = 2 \cos \frac{1}{2} x + 1$

57. $y = -3 \cos 2\pi x + 2$ **58.** $y = -3 \sin 2\pi x + 2$

Application Exercises

In the theory of biorhythms, sine functions are used to measure a person's potential. You can obtain your biorhythm chart online by simply entering your date of birth, the date you want your biorhythm chart to begin, and the number of months you wish to be included in the plot. At the top of the next column is your author's chart, beginning January 25, 2003, when he was 21,093 days old. We all have cycles with the same amplitudes and periods as those shown here. Each of our three basic cycles begins at birth. Use the biorhythm chart shown to solve Exercises 59–66. The longer tick marks correspond to the dates shown.

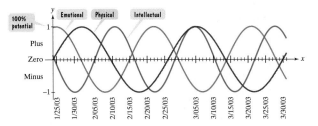

59. What is the period of the physical cycle?

60. What is the period of the emotional cycle?

61. What is the period of the intellectual cycle?

62. For the period shown, what is the worst day in February for your author to run in a marathon?

63. For the period shown, what is the best day in March for your author to meet an online friend for the first time?

64. For the period shown, what is the best day in February for your author to begin writing this trigonometry chapter?

65. If you extend these sinusoidal graphs to the end of the year, is there a day when your author should not even bother getting out of bed?

66. If you extend these sinusoidal graphs to the end of the year, are there any days where your author is at near-peak physical, emotional, and intellectual potential?

67. Rounded to the nearest hour, Los Angeles averages 14 hours of daylight in June, 10 hours in December, and 12 hours in March and September. Let x represent the number of months after June and y represent the number of hours of daylight in month x. Make a graph that displays the information from June of one year to June of the following year.

68. A clock with an hour hand that is 15 inches long is hanging on a wall. At noon, the distance between the tip of the hour hand and the ceiling is 23 inches. At 3 P.M., the distance is 38 inches; at 6 P.M., 53 inches; at 9 P.M., 38 inches; and at midnight the distance is again 23 inches. If y represents the distance between the tip of the hour hand and the ceiling x hours after noon, make a graph that displays the information for $0 \le x \le 24$.

69. The number of hours of daylight in Boston is given by

$$y = 3 \sin \frac{2\pi}{365} (x - 79) + 12$$

where x is the number of days after January 1.
  a. What is the amplitude of this function?
  b. What is the period of this function?

c. How many hours of daylight are there on the longest day of the year?

d. How many hours of daylight are there on the shortest day of the year?

e. Graph the function for one period, starting on January 1.

70. The average monthly temperature, y, in degrees Fahrenheit, for Juneau, Alaska, can be modeled by

$$y = 16 \sin\left(\frac{\pi}{6}x - \frac{2\pi}{3}\right) + 40,$$ where x is the month of

the year (January $= 1$, February $= 2$, ... December $= 12$). Graph the function for $1 \le x \le 12$. What is the highest average monthly temperature? In which month does this occur?

71. The figure shows the depth of water at the end of a boat dock. The depth is 6 feet at low tide and 12 feet at high tide. On a certain day, low tide occurs at 6 A.M. and high tide at noon. If y represents the depth of the water x hours after midnight, use a cosine function of the form $y = A \cos Bx + D$ to model the water's depth.

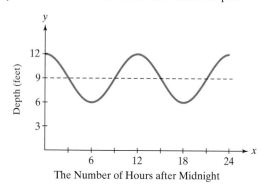
The Number of Hours after Midnight

72. The figure shows the depth of water at the end of a boat dock. The depth is 5 feet at high tide and 3 feet at low tide. On a certain day, high tide occurs at noon and low tide at 6 P.M. If y represents the depth of the water x hours after noon, use a cosine function of the form $y = A \cos Bx + D$ to model the water's depth.

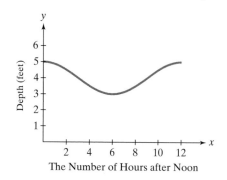
The Number of Hours after Noon

Writing in Mathematics

73. Without drawing a graph, describe the behavior of the basic sine curve.

74. What is the amplitude of the sine function? What does this tell you about the graph?

75. If you are given the equation of a sine function, how do you determine the period?

76. What does a phase shift indicate about the graph of a sine function? How do you determine the phase shift from the function's equation?

77. Describe a general procedure for obtaining the graph of $y = A \sin(Bx - C)$.

78. Without drawing a graph, describe the behavior of the basic cosine curve.

79. Describe a relationship between the graphs of $y = \sin x$ and $y = \cos x$.

80. Describe the relationship between the graphs of $y = A \cos(Bx - C)$ and $y = A \cos(Bx - C) + D$.

81. Biorhythm cycles provide interesting applications of sinusoidal graphs. But do you believe in the validity of biorhythms? Write a few sentences explaining why or why not.

Technology Exercises

82. Use a graphing utility to verify any five of the sine curves that you drew by hand in Exercises 7–30. The amplitude, period, and phase shift should help you to determine appropriate range settings.

83. Use a graphing utility to verify any five of the cosine curves that you drew by hand in Exercises 31–50.

84. Use a graphing utility to verify any two of the sinusoidal curves with vertical shifts that you drew in Exercises 51–58.

In Exercises 85–88, use a graphing utility to graph two periods of the function.

85. $y = 3 \sin(2x + \pi)$ **86.** $y = -2 \cos\left(2\pi x - \frac{\pi}{2}\right)$

87. $y = 0.2 \sin\left(\frac{\pi}{10}x + \pi\right)$ **88.** $y = 3 \sin(2x - \pi) + 5$

89. Use a graphing utility to graph $y = \sin x$ and $y = x - \frac{x^3}{6} + \frac{x^5}{120}$ in a $\left[-\pi, \pi, \frac{\pi}{2}\right]$ by $[-2, 2, 1]$ viewing rectangle. How do the graphs compare?

90. Use a graphing utility to graph $y = \cos x$ and $y = 1 - \dfrac{x^2}{2} + \dfrac{x^4}{24}$ in a $\left[-\pi, \pi, \dfrac{\pi}{2} \right]$ by $[-2, 2, 1]$ viewing rectangle. How do the graphs compare?

91. Use a graphing utility to graph

$$y = \sin x + \frac{\sin 2x}{2} + \frac{\sin 3x}{3} + \frac{\sin 4x}{4}$$

in a $\left[-2\pi, 2\pi, \dfrac{\pi}{2} \right]$ by $[-2, 2, 1]$ viewing rectangle. How do these waves compare to the smooth rolling waves of the basic sine curve?

92. Use a graphing utility to graph

$$y = \sin x - \frac{\sin 3x}{9} + \frac{\sin 5x}{25}$$

in a $\left[-2\pi, 2\pi, \dfrac{\pi}{2} \right]$ by $[-2, 2, 1]$ viewing rectangle. How do these waves compare to the smooth rolling waves of the basic sine curve?

93. The data show the average monthly temperatures for Washington, D.C.

   a. Use your graphing utility to draw a scatter plot of the data from $x = 1$ through $x = 12$.

   b. Use the SINe REGression feature to find the sinusoidal function of the form $y = A \sin (Bx + C) + D$ that best fits the data.

   c. Use your graphing utility to draw the sinusoidal function of best fit on the scatter plot.

x Month		Average Monthly Temperature, °F
1	(January)	34.6
2	(February)	37.5
3	(March)	47.2
4	(April)	56.5
5	(May)	66.4
6	(June)	75.6
7	(July)	80.0
8	(August)	78.5
9	(September)	71.3
10	(October)	59.7
11	(November)	49.8
12	(December)	39.4

Source: U.S. National Oceanic and Atmospheric Administration

94. Repeat Exercise 93 for data of your choice. The data can involve the average monthly temperatures for the region where you live or any data whose scatter plot takes the form of a sinusoidal function.

 Critical Thinking Exercises

Graph each function in Exercises 95–96 by hand.

95. $y = \sin x + \cos x$ for $0 \le x \le 2\pi$

96. $y = x + \cos x$ for $0 \le x \le \dfrac{5\pi}{2}$

97. Use the cosine function to find an equation of the graph in the figure shown.

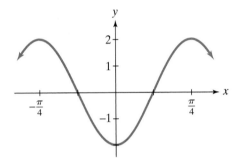

 Group Exercise

98. This exercise is intended to provide some fun with biorhythms, regardless of whether you believe they have any validity. We will use each member's chart to determine biorhythmic compatibility. Before meeting, each group member should go online and obtain his or her biorhythm chart. The date of the group meeting is the date on which your chart should begin. Include 12 months in the plot. At the meeting, compare differences and similarities among the intellectual sinusoidal curves. Using these comparisons, each person should find the one other person with whom he or she would be most intellectually compatible.

SECTION 1.6   *Graphs of Other Trigonometric Functions*

Objectives

1. Understand the graph of $y = \tan x$.
2. Graph variations of $y = \tan x$.
3. Understand the graph of $y = \cot x$.
4. Graph variations of $y = \cot x$.
5. Understand the graphs of $y = \csc x$ and $y = \sec x$.
6. Graph variations of $y = \csc x$ and $y = \sec x$.

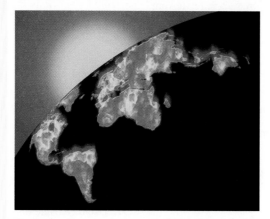

Recent advances in our understanding of climate have changed global warming from a subject for a disaster movie (the Statue of Liberty up to its chin in water) to a serious but manageable scientific and policy issue. Global warming is related to the burning of fossil fuels, which adds carbon dioxide to the atmosphere. In the new millennium, we will see whether our use of fossil fuels will add enough carbon dioxide to the atmosphere to change it (and our climate) in significant ways. In this section's exercise set, you will see how trigonometric graphs reveal interesting patterns in carbon dioxide concentration from 1990 through 2005. In the section itself, trigonometric graphs will reveal patterns involving the tangent, cotangent, secant, and cosecant functions.

1 Understand the graph of $y = \tan x$.

The Graph of $y = \tan x$

The properties of the tangent function discussed in Section 1.4 will help us determine its graph. Because the tangent function has properties that are different from sinusoidal functions, its graph differs significantly from those of sine and cosine. Properties of the tangent function include the following:

- The period is π. It is only necessary to graph $y = \tan x$ over an interval of length π. The remainder of the graph consists of repetitions of that graph at intervals of π.
- The tangent function is an odd function: $\tan(-x) = -\tan x$. The graph is symmetric with respect to the origin.
- The tangent function is undefined at $\frac{\pi}{2}$. The graph of $y = \tan x$ has a vertical asymptote at $x = \frac{\pi}{2}$.

We obtain the graph of $y = \tan x$ using some points on the graph and origin symmetry. Table 1.3 lists some values of (x, y) on the graph of $y = \tan x$ on the interval $\left[0, \frac{\pi}{2}\right)$.

Table 1.3   Values of (x, y) on $y = \tan x$

x	0	$\dfrac{\pi}{6}$	$\dfrac{\pi}{4}$	$\dfrac{\pi}{3}$	$\dfrac{5\pi}{12}$ (75°)	$\dfrac{17\pi}{36}$ (85°)	$\dfrac{89\pi}{180}$ (89°)	1.57	$\dfrac{\pi}{2}$
$y = \tan x$	0	$\dfrac{\sqrt{3}}{3} \approx 0.6$	1	$\sqrt{3} \approx 1.7$	3.7	11.4	57.3	1255.8	undefined

As x increases from 0 to $\frac{\pi}{2}$, y increases slowly at first, then more and more rapidly.

The graph in Figure 1.57(a) is based on our observation that as x increases from 0 to $\frac{\pi}{2}$, y increases slowly at first, then more and more rapidly. Notice that y increases without bound as x approaches $\frac{\pi}{2}$. As the figure shows, the graph of $y = \tan x$ has a vertical asymptote at $x = \frac{\pi}{2}$.

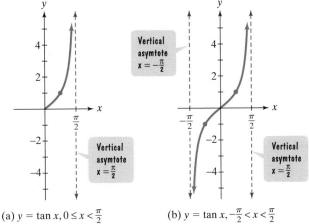

Figure 5.57 Graphing the tangent function

(a) $y = \tan x, 0 \le x < \frac{\pi}{2}$ (b) $y = \tan x, -\frac{\pi}{2} < x < \frac{\pi}{2}$

The graph of $y = \tan x$ can be completed on the interval $\left(-\frac{\pi}{2}, \frac{\pi}{2}\right)$ by using origin symmetry. Figure 1.57(b) shows the result of reflecting the graph in Figure 1.57(a) about the origin. The graph of $y = \tan x$ has another vertical asymptote at $x = -\frac{\pi}{2}$. Notice that y decreases without bound as x approaches $-\frac{\pi}{2}$.

Because the period of the tangent function is π radians, the graph in Figure 1.57(b) shows one complete period of $y = \tan x$. We obtain the complete graph of $y = \tan x$ by repeating the graph in Figure 1.57(b) to the left and right over intervals of π. The resulting graph and its main characteristics are shown in the following box:

The Tangent Curve: The Graph of $y = \tan x$ and Its Characteristics

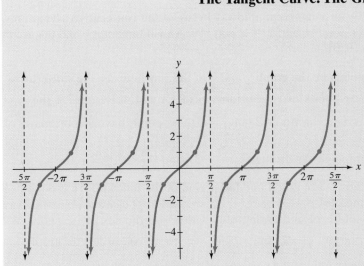

Characteristics

- **Period**: π
- **Domain**: All real numbers except odd multiples of $\frac{\pi}{2}$
- **Range**: All real numbers
- **Vertical asymptotes** at odd multiples of $\frac{\pi}{2}$
- **An x-intercept** occurs midway between each pair of consecutive asymptotes.
- **Odd function** with origin symmetry
- Points on the graph $\frac{1}{4}$ and $\frac{3}{4}$ of the way between consecutive asymptotes have y-coordinates of -1 and 1.

2 Graph variations of $y = \tan x$.

Graphing Variations of $y = \tan x$

We use the characteristics of the tangent curve to graph tangent functions of the form $y = A \tan(Bx - C)$.

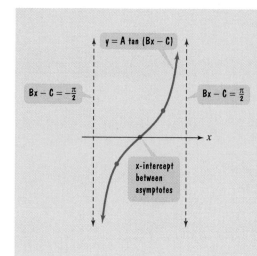

Graphing $y = A \tan(Bx - C)$

1. Find two consecutive asymptotes by setting the variable expression in the tangent equal to $-\dfrac{\pi}{2}$ and $\dfrac{\pi}{2}$ and solving

$$Bx - C = -\frac{\pi}{2} \quad \text{and} \quad Bx - C = \frac{\pi}{2}.$$

2. Identify an x-intercept, midway between the consecutive asymptotes.

3. Find the points on the graph $\dfrac{1}{4}$ and $\dfrac{3}{4}$ of the way between the consecutive asymptotes. These points have y-coordinates of $-A$ and A.

4. Use steps 1–3 to graph one full period of the function. Add additional cycles to the left or right as needed.

EXAMPLE 1   Graphing a Tangent Function

Graph $y = 2 \tan \dfrac{x}{2}$ for $-\pi < x < 3\pi$.

Solution   Refer to Figure 1.58 as you read each step.

Step 1   Find two consecutive asymptotes. We must solve the equations

$$\frac{x}{2} = -\frac{\pi}{2} \quad \text{and} \quad \frac{x}{2} = \frac{\pi}{2}. \quad \textit{Set the variable expression in the tangent equal to}$$
$$-\frac{\pi}{2} \textit{ and } \frac{\pi}{2}.$$
$$x = -\pi \qquad x = \pi \quad \textit{Multiply both sides of each equation by 2.}$$

Thus, two consecutive asymptotes occur at $x = -\pi$ and $x = \pi$.

Step 2   Identify an x-intercept, midway between the consecutive asymptotes. Midway between $x = -\pi$ and $x = \pi$ is $x = 0$. An x-intercept is 0 and the graph passes through $(0, 0)$.

Step 3   Find points on the graph $\dfrac{1}{4}$ and $\dfrac{3}{4}$ of the way between the consecutive asymptotes. These points have y-coordinates of $-A$ and A. Because A, the coefficient of the tangent in $y = 2 \tan \dfrac{x}{2}$ is 2, these points have y-coordinates of -2 and 2. The graph passes through $\left(-\dfrac{\pi}{2}, -2\right)$ and $\left(\dfrac{\pi}{2}, 2\right)$.

Step 4   Use steps 1–3 to graph one full period of the function. We use the two consecutive asymptotes, $x = -\pi$ and $x = \pi$, an x-intercept of 0, and points midway between the x-intercept and asymptotes with y-coordinates of -2 and 2. We graph one period of $y = 2 \tan \dfrac{x}{2}$ from $-\pi$ to π. In order to graph for $-\pi < x < 3\pi$, we continue the pattern and extend the graph another full period to the right. The graph is shown in Figure 1.58.

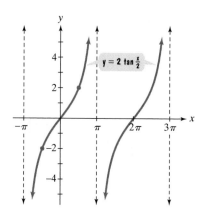

Figure 1.58 The graph is shown for two full periods.

Check Point 1   Graph $y = 3 \tan 2x$ for $-\dfrac{\pi}{4} < x < \dfrac{3\pi}{4}$.

EXAMPLE 2   Graphing a Tangent Function

Graph two full periods of $y = \tan\left(x + \dfrac{\pi}{4}\right)$.

Solution   The graph of $y = \tan\left(x + \dfrac{\pi}{4}\right)$ is the graph of $y = \tan x$ shifted horizontally to the left $\dfrac{\pi}{4}$ units. Refer to Figure 1.59 as you read each step.

Step 1   Find two consecutive asymptotes. We must solve the equations

$$x + \frac{\pi}{4} = -\frac{\pi}{2} \quad \text{and} \quad x + \frac{\pi}{4} = \frac{\pi}{2}.$$

Set the variable expression in the tangent equal to $-\dfrac{\pi}{2}$ *and* $\dfrac{\pi}{2}$.

$$x = -\frac{\pi}{4} - \frac{\pi}{2} \qquad\qquad x = -\frac{\pi}{4} + \frac{\pi}{2}$$

Subtract $\dfrac{\pi}{4}$ *from both sides in each equation.*

$$x = -\frac{3\pi}{4} \qquad\qquad x = \frac{\pi}{4}$$

Simplify.

Thus, two consecutive asymptotes occur at $x = -\dfrac{3\pi}{4}$ and $x = \dfrac{\pi}{4}$.

Step 2   Identify an x-intercept, midway between the consecutive asymptotes.

$$x\text{-intercept} = \frac{-\dfrac{3\pi}{4} + \dfrac{\pi}{4}}{2} = \frac{-\dfrac{2\pi}{4}}{2} = -\frac{2\pi}{8} = -\frac{\pi}{4}$$

An x-intercept is $-\dfrac{\pi}{4}$ and the graph passes through $\left(-\dfrac{\pi}{4}, 0\right)$.

Step 3   Find points on the graph $\dfrac{1}{4}$ and $\dfrac{3}{4}$ of the way between the consecutive asymptotes. These points have y-coordinates of $-A$ and A. Because A, the coefficient of the tangent in $y = \tan\left(x + \dfrac{\pi}{4}\right)$ is 1, these points have y-coordinates of -1 and 1. They are shown as blue dots in Figure 1.59.

Step 4   Use steps 1–3 to graph one full period of the function. We use the two consecutive asymptotes, $x = -\dfrac{3\pi}{4}$ and $x = \dfrac{\pi}{4}$, to graph one full period of $y = \tan\left(x + \dfrac{\pi}{4}\right)$ from $-\dfrac{3\pi}{4}$ to $\dfrac{\pi}{4}$. We graph two full periods by continuing the pattern and extending the graph another full period to the right. The graph is shown in Figure 1.59.

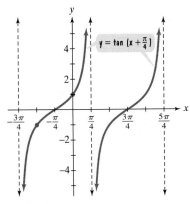

Figure 1.59 The graph is shown for two full periods.

Check Point 2   Graph two full periods of $y = \tan\left(x - \dfrac{\pi}{2}\right)$.

3 Understand the graph of $y = \cot x$.

The Graph of $y = \cot x$

Like the tangent function, the cotangent function, $y = \cot x$, has a period of π. The graph and its main characteristics are shown in the following box:

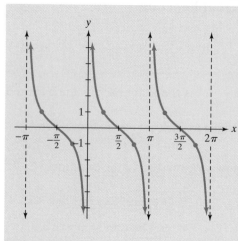

The Cotangent Curve: The Graph of $y = \cot x$ and Its Characteristics

Characteristics

- **Period:** π
- **Domain:** All real numbers except integral multiples of π
- **Range:** All real numbers
- **Vertical asymptotes** at integral multiples of π
- **An x-intercept** occurs midway between each pair of consecutive asymptotes.
- **Odd function** with origin symmetry
- Points on the graph $\frac{1}{4}$ and $\frac{3}{4}$ of the way between consecutive asymptotes have y-coordinates of 1 and -1.

4 Graph variations of $y = \cot x$.

Graphing Variations of $y = \cot x$

We use the characteristics of the cotangent curve to graph cotangent functions of the form $y = A \cot(Bx - C)$.

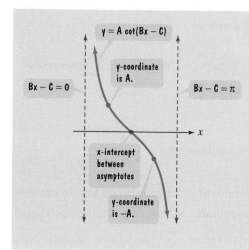

Graphing $y = A \cot(Bx - C)$

1. Find two consecutive asymptotes by setting the variable expression in the cotangent equal to 0 and π and solving
$$Bx - C = 0 \text{ and } Bx - C = \pi.$$

2. Identify an x-intercept, midway between the consecutive asymptotes.

3. Find the points on the graph $\frac{1}{4}$ and $\frac{3}{4}$ of the way between the consecutive asymptotes. These points have y-coordinates of A and $-A$.

4. Use steps 1–3 to graph one full period of the function. Add additional cycles to the left or right as needed.

EXAMPLE 3 Graphing a Cotangent Function

Graph $y = 3 \cot 2x$.

Solution Refer to Figure 1.60, shown on the next page, as you read each step.

Step 1 Find two consecutive asymptotes. We must solve the equations

$$2x = 0 \quad \text{and} \quad 2x = \pi. \quad \text{Set the variable expression in the cotangent equal to 0 and } \pi.$$

$$x = 0 \qquad x = \frac{\pi}{2} \quad \text{Divide both sides of each equation by 2.}$$

Two consecutive asymptotes occur at $x = 0$ and $x = \frac{\pi}{2}$.

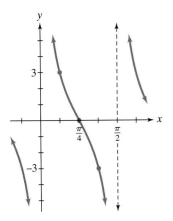

Figure 1.60 The graph of
$y = 3 \cot 2x$

Step 2   Identify an x-intercept, midway between the consecutive asymptotes. Midway between $x = 0$ and $x = \dfrac{\pi}{2}$ is $x = \dfrac{\pi}{4}$. An x-intercept is $\dfrac{\pi}{4}$ and the graph passes through $\left(\dfrac{\pi}{4}, 0 \right)$.

Step 3   Find points on the graph $\dfrac{1}{4}$ and $\dfrac{3}{4}$ of the way between consecutive asymptotes. These points have y-coordinates of A and $-A$. Because A, the coefficient of the cotangent in $y = 3 \cot 2x$ is 3, these points have y-coordinates of 3 and -3.

Step 4   Use steps 1–3 to graph one full period of the function. We use the two consecutive asymptotes, $x = 0$ and $x = \dfrac{\pi}{2}$, to graph one full period of $y = 3 \cot 2x$. This curve is repeated to the left and right, as shown in Figure 1.60.

Check Point 3   Graph $y = \dfrac{1}{2} \cot \dfrac{\pi}{2} x$.

5   Understand the graphs of $y = \csc x$ and $y = \sec x$.

The Graphs of $y = \csc x$ and $y = \sec x$

We obtain the graphs of the cosecant and secant curves by using the reciprocal identities

$$\csc x = \frac{1}{\sin x} \quad \text{and} \quad \sec x = \frac{1}{\cos x}.$$

The identity on the left tells us that the value of the cosecant function $y = \csc x$ at a given value of x equals the reciprocal of the corresponding value of the sine function, provided that the value of the sine function is not 0. If the value of $\sin x$ is 0, then at each of these values of x, the cosecant function is not defined. A vertical asymptote is associated with each of these values on the graph of $y = \csc x$.

   We obtain the graph of $y = \csc x$ by taking reciprocals of the y-values in the graph of $y = \sin x$. Vertical asymptotes of $y = \csc x$ occur at the x-intercepts of $y = \sin x$. Likewise, we obtain the graph of $y = \sec x$ by taking the reciprocal of $y = \cos x$. Vertical asymptotes of $y = \sec x$ occur at the x-intercepts of $y = \cos x$. The graphs of $y = \csc x$ and $y = \sec x$ and their key characteristics are shown in the following boxes. We have used dashed red lines to first graph $y = \sin x$ and $y = \cos x$, drawing vertical asymptotes through the x-intercepts.

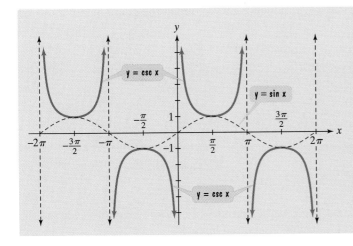

The Cosecant Curve: The Graph of $y = \csc x$ and Its Characteristics

Characteristics

- **Period:** 2π
- **Domain:** All real numbers except integral multiples of π
- **Range:** All real numbers y such that $y \leq -1$ or $y \geq 1$
- **Vertical asymptotes** at integral multiples of π
- **Odd function,** $\csc(-x) = -\csc x$, with origin symmetry

The Secant Curve: The Graph of $y = \sec x$ and Its Characteristics

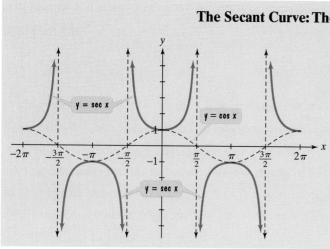

Characteristics
- **Period:** 2π
- **Domain:** All real numbers except odd multiples of $\dfrac{\pi}{2}$
- **Range:** All real numbers y such that $y \leq -1$ or $y \geq 1$
- **Vertical asymptotes** at odd multiples of $\dfrac{\pi}{2}$
- **Even function,** $\sec(-x) = \sec x$, with y-axis symmetry

6 Graph variations of $y = \csc x$ and $y = \sec x$.

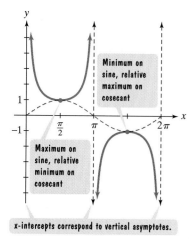

Minimum on sine, relative maximum on cosecant

Maximum on sine, relative minimum on cosecant

x-intercepts correspond to vertical asymptotes.

Figure 1.61

Graphing Variations of $y = \csc x$ and $y = \sec x$

We use graphs of reciprocal functions to obtain graphs of cosecant and secant functions. To graph a cosecant or secant curve, begin by graphing the reciprocal function. For example, to graph $y = 2\csc 2x$, we use the graph of $y = 2\sin 2x$. Likewise, to graph $y = -3\sec \dfrac{x}{2}$, we use the graph of $y = -3\cos \dfrac{x}{2}$.

Figure 1.61 illustrates how we use a sine curve to obtain a cosecant curve. Notice that

- x-intercepts on the red sine curve correspond to vertical asymptotes of the blue cosecant curve.
- A maximum point on the red sine curve corresponds to a minimum point on a continuous portion of the blue cosecant curve.
- A minimum point on the red sine curve corresponds to a maximum point on a continuous portion of the blue cosecant curve.

EXAMPLE 4 **Using a Sine Curve to Obtain a Cosecant Curve**

Use the graph of $y = 2\sin 2x$ in Figure 1.62 to obtain the graph of $y = 2\csc 2x$.

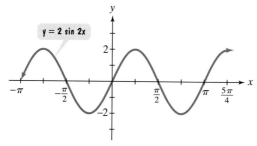

Figure 1.62

Solution On the next page, we begin our work by showing the given graph, the graph of $y = 2\sin 2x$, using dashed red lines.

The x-intercepts of $y = 2\sin 2x$ correspond to the vertical asymptotes of $y = 2\csc 2x$. Thus, we draw vertical asymptotes through the x-intercepts, shown in Figure 1.63. Using the asymptotes as guides, we sketch the graph of $y = 2\csc 2x$ in Figure 1.63.

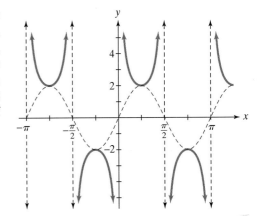

Figure 1.63 Using a sine curve to graph $y = 2\csc 2x$

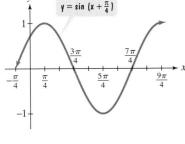

Check Point 4 Use the graph of $y = \sin\left(x + \dfrac{\pi}{4}\right)$, shown on the left, to obtain the graph of $y = \csc\left(x + \dfrac{\pi}{4}\right)$.

We use a cosine curve to obtain a secant curve in exactly the same way we used a sine curve to obtain a cosecant curve. Thus,

- x-intercepts on the cosine curve correspond to vertical asymptotes on the secant curve.
- A maximum point on the cosine curve corresponds to a minimum point on a continuous portion of the secant curve.
- A minimum point on the cosine curve corresponds to a maximum point on a continuous portion of the secant curve.

EXAMPLE 5   Graphing a Secant Function

Graph $y = -3\sec\dfrac{x}{2}$ for $-\pi < x < 5\pi$.

Solution   We begin by graphing the reciprocal cosine function, $y = -3\cos\dfrac{x}{2}$. This equation is of the form $y = A\cos Bx$ with $A = -3$ and $B = \frac{1}{2}$.

amplitude: $|A| = |-3| = 3$ *The maximum y is 3 and the minimum is −3.*

period: $\dfrac{2\pi}{B} = \dfrac{2\pi}{\frac{1}{2}} = 4\pi$ *Each cycle is completed in 4π radians.*

We use quarter-periods, $\dfrac{4\pi}{4}$, or π, to find the x-values for the five key points. Starting with $x = 0$, the x-values are $0, \pi, 2\pi, 3\pi$, and 4π. Evaluating the function at each of these values of x, the key points are

$$(0, -3), (\pi, 0), (2\pi, 3), (3\pi, 0), \text{ and } (4\pi, -3).$$

We use these key points to graph $y = -3\cos\dfrac{x}{2}$ from 0 to 4π. In order to graph for $-\pi \le x \le 5\pi$, extend the graph π units to the left and π units to the right. The graph is shown using a dashed red line in Figure 1.64. Now use this dashed red graph to obtain the graph of the reciprocal function. Draw vertical asymptotes through the x-intercepts. Using these asymptotes as guides, the graph of $y = -3\sec\dfrac{x}{2}$ is shown in blue in Figure 1.64.

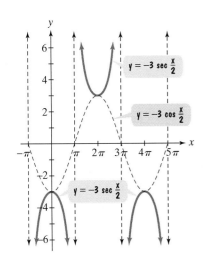

Figure 1.64 Using a cosine curve to graph $y = -3\sec\dfrac{x}{2}$

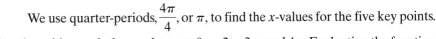

Check Point 5 Graph $y = 2 \sec 2x$ for $-\dfrac{3\pi}{4} < x < \dfrac{3\pi}{4}$.

The Six Curves of Trigonometry

Table 1.4 summarizes the graphs of the six trigonometric functions. Below each of the graphs is a description of the domain, range, and period of the function.

Table 1.4   Graphs of the Six Trigonometric Functions

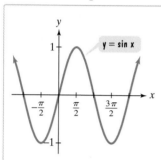

Domain: all real numbers

Range: $[-1, 1]$
Period: 2π

Domain: all real numbers

Range: $[-1, 1]$
Period: 2π

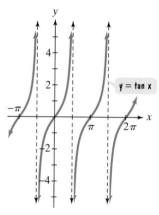

Domain: all real numbers
except odd multiples of $\dfrac{\pi}{2}$

Range: all real numbers
Period: π

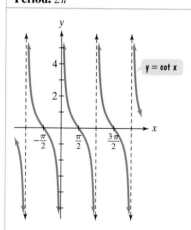

Domain: all real numbers
except integral multiples of π

Range: all real numbers
Period: π

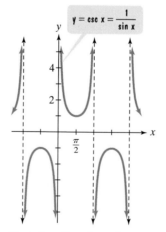

Domain: all real numbers
except integral multiples of π

Range: $(-\infty, -1]$ or $[1, \infty)$
Period: 2π

Domain: all real numbers
except odd multiples of $\dfrac{\pi}{2}$

Range: $(-\infty, -1]$ or $[1, \infty)$
Period: 2π

EXERCISE SET 1.6

Practice Exercises

In Exercises 1–4, the graph of a tangent function is given.
Select the equation for each graph from the following options:

$$y = \tan\left(x + \frac{\pi}{2}\right), \quad y = \tan(x + \pi), \quad y = -\tan x, \quad y = -\tan\left(x - \frac{\pi}{2}\right).$$

1.

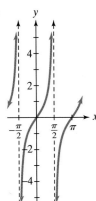

2.

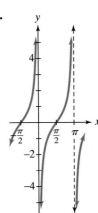

3.

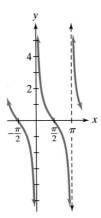

4.

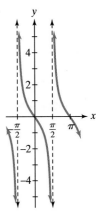

In Exercises 5–12, graph two periods of the given tangent function.

5. $y = 3\tan\dfrac{x}{4}$

6. $y = 2\tan\dfrac{x}{4}$

7. $y = \dfrac{1}{2}\tan 2x$

8. $y = 3\tan 2x$

9. $y = -2\tan\dfrac{1}{2}x$

10. $y = -3\tan\dfrac{1}{2}x$

11. $y = \tan(x - \pi)$

12. $y = \tan\left(x + \dfrac{\pi}{2}\right)$

In Exercises 13–16, the graph of a cotangent function is given. Select the equation for each graph from the following options:

$$y = \cot\left(x + \frac{\pi}{2}\right), \quad y = \cot(x + \pi), \quad y = -\cot x, \quad y = -\cot\left(x - \frac{\pi}{2}\right).$$

13.

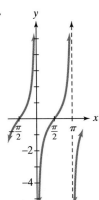

14.

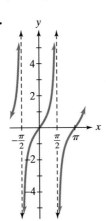

15.

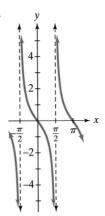

16.

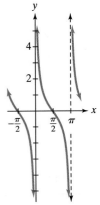

In Exercises 17–24, graph two periods of the given cotangent function.

17. $y = 2\cot x$

18. $y = \dfrac{1}{2}\cot x$

19. $y = \dfrac{1}{2}\cot 2x$

20. $y = 2\cot 2x$

21. $y = -3 \cot \dfrac{\pi}{2} x$ **22.** $y = -2 \cot \dfrac{\pi}{4} x$

23. $y = 3 \cot \left(x + \dfrac{\pi}{2} \right)$ **24.** $y = 3 \cot \left(x + \dfrac{\pi}{4} \right)$

In Exercises 25–28, use each graph to obtain the graph of the reciprocal function. Give the equation of the function for the graph that you obtain.

25.

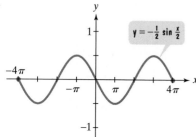

$y = -\frac{1}{2} \sin \frac{x}{2}$

26.

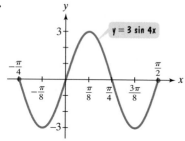

$y = 3 \sin 4x$

27.

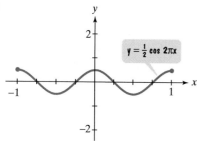

$y = \frac{1}{2} \cos 2\pi x$

28.

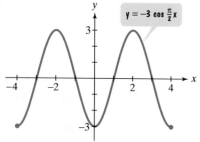

$y = -3 \cos \frac{\pi}{2} x$

In Exercises 29–44, graph two periods of the given cosecant or secant function.

29. $y = 3 \csc x$ **30.** $y = 2 \csc x$

31. $y = \dfrac{1}{2} \csc \dfrac{x}{2}$ **32.** $y = \dfrac{3}{2} \csc \dfrac{x}{4}$

33. $y = 2 \sec x$ **34.** $y = 3 \sec x$

35. $y = \sec \dfrac{x}{3}$ **36.** $y = \sec \dfrac{x}{2}$

37. $y = -2 \csc \pi x$ **38.** $y = -\dfrac{1}{2} \csc \pi x$

39. $y = -\dfrac{1}{2} \sec \pi x$ **40.** $y = -\dfrac{3}{2} \sec \pi x$

41. $y = \csc(x - \pi)$ **42.** $y = \csc \left(x - \dfrac{\pi}{2} \right)$

43. $y = 2 \sec(x + \pi)$ **44.** $y = 2 \sec \left(x + \dfrac{\pi}{2} \right)$

 Application Exercises

45. An ambulance with a rotating beacon of light is parked 12 feet from a building. The function

$$d = 12 \tan 2\pi t$$

describes the distance, d, in feet, of the rotating beacon from point C after t seconds.

a. Graph the function on the interval $[0, 2]$.

b. For what values of t in $[0, 2]$ is the function undefined? What does this mean in terms of the rotating beacon in the figure shown?

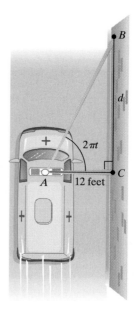

46. The angle of elevation from the top of a house to a jet flying 2 miles above the house is x radians. If d represents the horizontal distance, in miles, of the jet from the house, express d in terms of a trigonometric function of x. Then graph the function for $0 < x < \pi$.

47. Your best friend is marching with a band and has asked you to film her. The figure below shows that you have set yourself up 10 feet from the street where your friend will be passing from left to right. If d represents your distance, in feet, from your friend and x is the radian measure of the angle shown, express d in terms of a trigonometric function of x. Then graph the function for $-\dfrac{\pi}{2} < x < \dfrac{\pi}{2}$. Negative angles indicate that your marching buddy is on your left.

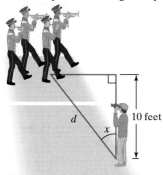

In Exercises 48–50, sketch a reasonable graph that models the given situation.

48. The number of hours of daylight per day in your hometown over a two-year period

49. The motion of a diving board vibrating 10 inches in each direction per second just after someone has dived off

50. The distance of a rotating beacon of light from a point on a wall (See the figure for Exercise 45.)

 Writing in Mathematics

51. Without drawing a graph, describe the behavior of the basic tangent curve.

52. If you are given the equation of a tangent function, how do you find consecutive asymptotes?

53. If you are given the equation of a tangent function, how do you identify an x-intercept?

54. Without drawing a graph, describe the behavior of the basic cotangent curve.

55. If you are given the equation of a cotangent function, how do you find consecutive asymptotes?

56. Explain how to determine the range of $y = \csc x$ from the graph. What is the range?

57. Explain how to use a sine curve to obtain a cosecant curve. Why can the same procedure be used to obtain a secant curve from a cosine curve?

58. Scientists record brain activity by attaching electrodes to the scalp and then connecting these electrodes to a machine. The record of brain activity recorded with this machine is shown in the three graphs at the top of the next column. Which trigonometric functions would be most appropriate for describing the oscillations in brain

activity? Describe similarities and differences among these functions when modeling brain activity when awake, during dreaming sleep, and during nondreaming sleep.

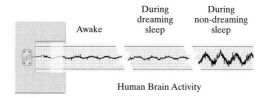

Human Brain Activity

Technology Exercises

In working Exercises 59–62, describe what happens at the asymptotes on the graphing utility. Compare the graphs in the connected and dot modes.

59. Use a graphing utility to verify any two of the tangent curves that you drew by hand in Exercises 5–12.

60. Use a graphing utility to verify any two of the cotangent curves that you drew by hand in Exercises 17–24.

61. Use a graphing utility to verify any two of the cosecant curves that you drew by hand in Exercises 29–44.

62. Use a graphing utility to verify any two of the secant curves that you drew by hand in Exercises 29–44.

In Exercises 63–68, use a graphing utility to graph each function. Use a range setting so that the graph is shown for at least two periods.

63. $y = \tan \dfrac{x}{4}$ **64.** $y = \tan 4x$

65. $y = \cot 2x$ **66.** $y = \cot \dfrac{x}{2}$

67. $y = \dfrac{1}{2} \tan \pi x$ **68.** $y = \dfrac{1}{2} \tan(\pi x + 1)$

In Exercises 69–72, use a graphing utility to graph each pair of functions in the same viewing rectangle. Use a range setting so that the graphs are shown for at least two periods.

69. $y = 0.8 \sin \dfrac{x}{2}$ and $y = 0.8 \csc \dfrac{x}{2}$

70. $y = -2.5 \sin \dfrac{\pi}{3} x$ and $y = -2.5 \csc \dfrac{\pi}{3} x$

71. $y = 4 \cos \left(2x - \dfrac{\pi}{6} \right)$ and $y = 4 \sec \left(2x - \dfrac{\pi}{6} \right)$

72. $y = -3.5 \cos \left(\pi x - \dfrac{\pi}{6} \right)$ and $y = -3.5 \sec \left(\pi x - \dfrac{\pi}{6} \right)$

73. Carbon dioxide particles in our atmosphere trap heat and raise the planet's temperature. The resultant gradually increasing temperature is called the greenhouse effect. Carbon dioxide accounts for about half of global warming. The function

$$y = 2.5 \sin 2\pi x + 0.0216x^2 + 0.654x + 316$$

models carbon dioxide concentration, y, in parts per million, where $x = 0$ represents January 1960; $x = \frac{1}{12}$, February 1960; $x = \frac{2}{12}$, March 1960; $\cdots$, $x = 1$, January 1961; $x = \frac{13}{12}$, February 1961; and so on. Use a graphing utility to graph the function in a [30, 45, 5] by [310, 420, 5] viewing rectangle. Describe what the graph reveals about carbon dioxide concentration from 1990 through 2005.

74. Graph $y = \sin \dfrac{1}{x}$ in a $[-0.2, 0.2, 0.01]$ by $[-1.2, 1.2, 0.01]$

viewing rectangle. What is happening as x approaches 0 from the left or the right? Explain this behavior.

 Critical Thinking Exercises

In Exercises 75–76, write an equation for each blue graph.

75.

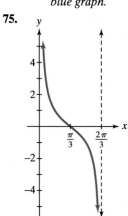

76.

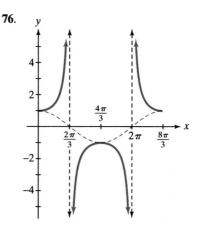

77. For $x > 0$, what effect does 2^{-x} in $y = 2^{-x} \sin x$ have on the graph of $y = \sin x$? What kind of behavior can be modeled by a function such as $y = 2^{-x} \sin x$?

Chapter Summary, Review, and Test

Summary

DEFINITIONS AND CONCEPTS	EXAMPLES

1.1 Angles and Their Measure

a. An angle consists of two rays with a common endpoint, the vertex.

b. An angle is in standard position if its vertex is at the origin and its initial side lies along the positive x-axis. Figure 1.3 on page 3 shows positive and negative angles in standard position.   *Ex. 1, p. 4*

c. A quadrantal angle is one with its terminal side on the x-axis or the y-axis.

d. Angles can be measured in degrees. $1°$ is $\frac{1}{360}$ of a complete rotation.

e. Acute angles measure less than $90°$, right angles $90°$, obtuse angles more than $90°$ but less than $180°$, and straight angles $180°$.

f. Two angles with the same initial and terminal sides are called coterminal angles.   *Ex. 2, p. 5*

g. Two angles are complements if their sum is $90°$ and supplements if their sum is $180°$. Only positive angles are used.   *Ex. 3, p. 6*

h. Angles can be measured in radians. One radian is the measure of the central angle when the intercepted arc and radius have the same length. In general, the radian measure of a central angle is the length of the intercepted arc divided by the circle's radius: $\theta = \dfrac{s}{r}$.   *Ex. 4, p. 8*

i. To convert from degrees to radians, multiply degrees by $\dfrac{\pi \text{ radians}}{180°}$. To convert from radians to degrees, multiply radians by $\dfrac{180°}{\pi \text{ radians}}$.   *Ex. 5, p. 9; Ex. 6, p. 9*

j. The arc length formula, $s = r\theta$, is described in the box on page 10.   *Ex. 7, p. 11*

DEFINITIONS AND CONCEPTS	EXAMPLES

k. The definitions of linear speed, $v = \dfrac{s}{t}$, and angular speed, $\omega = \dfrac{\theta}{t}$, are given in the box on page 11.

l. Linear speed is expressed in terms of angular speed by $v = r\omega$, where v is the linear speed of a point a distance r from the center of rotation and ω is the angular speed in radians per unit of time.   Ex. 8, p. 12

1.2 Right Triangle Trigonometry

a. The right triangle definitions of the six trigonometric functions are given in the box on page 17.   Ex. 1, p. 18

b. Function values for $30°, 45°,$ and $60°$ can be obtained using these special triangles.   Ex. 2, p. 19; Ex. 3, p. 20

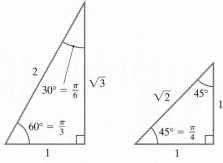

c. Fundamental Identities

1. Reciprocal Identities

$$\sin\theta = \frac{1}{\csc\theta} \quad \cos\theta = \frac{1}{\sec\theta} \quad \tan\theta = \frac{1}{\cot\theta}$$

$$\csc\theta = \frac{1}{\sin\theta} \quad \sec\theta = \frac{1}{\cos\theta} \quad \cot\theta = \frac{1}{\tan\theta}$$

Ex. 4, p. 22; Ex. 5, p. 23

2. Quotient Identities

$$\tan\theta = \frac{\sin\theta}{\cos\theta} \quad \cot\theta = \frac{\cos\theta}{\sin\theta}$$

3. Pythagorean Identities

$$\sin^2\theta + \cos^2\theta = 1$$
$$1 + \tan^2\theta = \sec^2\theta$$
$$1 + \cot^2\theta = \csc^2\theta$$

d. The value of a trigonometric function of θ is equal to the cofunction of the complement of θ. Cofunction identities are listed in the box on page 24.   Ex. 6, p. 24

1.3 Trigonometric Functions of Any Angle

a. Definitions of the trigonometric functions of any angle are given in the box on page 33.   Ex. 1, p. 34; Ex. 2, p. 34

b. Signs of the trigonometric functions: All functions are positive in quadrant I. If θ lies in quadrant II, $\sin\theta$ and $\csc\theta$ are positive. If θ lies in quadrant III, $\tan\theta$ and $\cot\theta$ are positive. If θ lies in quadrant IV, $\cos\theta$ and $\sec\theta$ are positive.   Ex. 3, p. 37; Ex. 4, p. 37

c. If θ is a nonacute angle in standard position that lies in a quadrant, its reference angle is the positive acute angle θ' formed by the terminal side of θ and the x-axis. The reference angle for a given angle can be found by making a sketch that shows the angle in standard position. Figure 1.30 on page 38 shows reference angles for θ in quadrants II, III, and IV.   Ex. 5, p. 38

DEFINITIONS AND CONCEPTS	EXAMPLES

d. The values of the trigonometric functions of a given angle are the same as the values of the functions of the reference angle, except possibly for the sign. A procedure for using reference angles to evaluate trigonometric functions is given in the box on page 39.
Ex. 6, p. 39

1.4 Trigonometric Functions of Real Numbers; Periodic Functions

a. Definitions of the trigonometric functions in terms of a unit circle are given in the box on page 44.
Ex. 1, p. 44

b. The cosine and secant functions are even:
Ex. 2, p. 46

$$\cos(-t) = \cos t, \quad \sec(-t) = \sec t.$$

The other trigonometric functions are odd:

$$\sin(-t) = -\sin t, \quad \csc(-t) = -\csc t,$$
$$\tan(-t) = -\tan t, \quad \cot(-t) = -\cot t.$$

c. If $f(t + p) = f(t)$, function f is periodic. The smallest p for which f is periodic is the period of f. The tangent and cotangent functions have period π. The other four trigonometric functions have period 2π.
Ex. 3, p. 47

1.5 and 1.6 Graphs of the Trigonometric Functions

a. Graphs of the six trigonometric functions, with a description of the domain, range, and period of each function, are given in Table 1.4 on page 80.

b. The graph of $y = A\sin(Bx - C)$ can be obtained using amplitude $= |A|$, period $= \dfrac{2\pi}{B}$ and phase shift $= \dfrac{C}{B}$. See the illustration in the box on page 57.
Ex. 1, p. 52; Ex. 2, p. 54; Ex. 3, p. 55; Ex. 4, p. 58

c. The graph of $y = A\cos(Bx - C)$ can be obtained using amplitude $= |A|$, period $= \dfrac{2\pi}{B}$, and phase shift $= \dfrac{C}{B}$. See the illustration in the box on page 63.
Ex. 5, p. 61; Ex. 6, p. 63

d. The constant D in $y = A\sin(Bx - C) + D$ and $y = A\cos(Bx - C) + D$ causes vertical shifts in the graphs in the preceding items (b) and (c). If $D > 0$, the shift is D units upward and if $D < 0$, the shift is D units downward. Oscillation is about $y = D$.
Ex. 7, p. 65

e. The graph of $y = A\tan(Bx - C)$ is obtained using the procedure in the box on page 74. Consecutive asymptotes $\left(\text{solve } Bx - C = -\dfrac{\pi}{2} \text{ and } Bx - C = \dfrac{\pi}{2}\right)$ and an x-intercept midway between them play a key role in the graphing process.
Ex. 1, p. 74; Ex. 2, p. 75

f. The graph of $y = A\cot(Bx - C)$ is obtained using the procedure in the box on page 76. Consecutive asymptotes (solve $Bx - C = 0$ and $Bx - C = \pi$) and an x-intercept midway between them play a key role in the graphing process.
Ex. 3, p. 76

g. To graph a cosecant curve, begin by graphing the reciprocal sine curve. Draw vertical asymptotes through x-intercepts, using asymptotes as guides to sketch the graph. To graph a secant curve, first graph the reciprocal cosine curve and use the same procedure.
Ex. 4, p. 78; Ex. 5, p. 79

Review Exercises

1.1

In Exercises 1–4, draw each angle in standard position.

1. 190°

2. −135°

3. $\dfrac{5\pi}{6}$

4. $-\dfrac{2\pi}{3}$

In Exercises 5–6, find a positive angle less than 360° that is coterminal with the given angle.

5. 400°

6. −85°

In Exercises 7–8, if possible, find the complement and the supplement of the given angle.

7. 73°

8. $\dfrac{2\pi}{3}$

9. Find the radian measure of the central angle of a circle of radius 6 centimeters that intercepts an arc of length 27 centimeters.

In Exercises 10–12, convert each angle in degrees to radians. Express your answer as a multiple of π.

10. $15°$ **11.** $120°$ **12.** $315°$

In Exercises 13–15, convert each angle in radians to degrees.

13. $\dfrac{5\pi}{3}$ **14.** $\dfrac{7\pi}{5}$ **15.** $-\dfrac{5\pi}{6}$

16. Find the length of the arc on a circle of radius 10 feet intercepted by a $135°$ central angle. Express arc length in terms of π. Then round your answer to two decimal places.

17. The angular speed of a propeller on a wind generator is 10.3 revolutions per minute. Express this angular speed in radians per minute.

18. The propeller of an airplane has a radius of 3 feet. The propeller is rotating at 2250 revolutions per minute. Find the linear speed, in feet per minute, of the tip of the propeller.

1.2

19. Use the triangle to find each of the six trigonometric functions of θ.

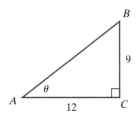

In Exercises 20–23, find the exact value of each expression. Do not use a calculator.

20. $\tan 60°$ **21.** $\cos \dfrac{\pi}{4}$

22. $\sec \dfrac{\pi}{6}$ **23.** $\sin^2 \dfrac{\pi}{5} + \cos^2 \dfrac{\pi}{5}$

24. If θ is an acute angle and $\sin\theta = \dfrac{2}{\sqrt{7}}$, use the identity $\sin^2\theta + \cos^2\theta = 1$ to find $\cos\theta$.

In Exercises 25–26, find a cofunction with the same value as the given expression.

25. $\sin 70°$ **26.** $\cos \dfrac{\pi}{2}$

In Exercises 27–29, find the measure of the side of the right triangle whose length is designated by a lowercase letter. Round answers to the nearest whole number.

27.

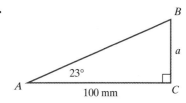

28.   **29.**

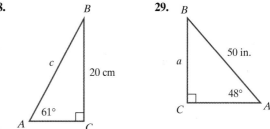

30. A hiker climbs for a half mile up a slope whose inclination is $17°$. How many feet of altitude, to the nearest foot, does the hiker gain?

31. To find the distance across a lake, a surveyor took the measurements in the figure shown. What is the distance across the lake? Round to the nearest meter.

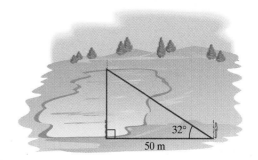

32. When a six-foot pole casts a four-foot shadow, what is the angle of elevation of the sun? Round to the nearest whole degree.

1.3 and 1.4

In Exercises 33–34, a point on the terminal side of angle θ is given. Find the exact value of each of the six trigonometric functions of θ, or state that the function is undefined.

33. $(-1, -5)$ **34.** $(0, -1)$

In Exercises 35–36, let θ be an angle in standard position. Name the quadrant in which θ lies.

35. $\tan\theta > 0$ and $\sec\theta > 0$

36. $\tan\theta > 0$ and $\cos\theta < 0$

In Exercises 37–38, find the exact value of each of the remaining trigonometric functions of θ.

37. $\cos\theta = \frac{2}{5}, \sin\theta < 0$ **38.** $\tan\theta = -\frac{1}{3}, \sin\theta > 0$

In Exercises 39–41, find the reference angle for each angle.

39. $265°$ **40.** $\dfrac{5\pi}{8}$ **41.** $-410°$

In Exercises 42–50, find the exact value of each expression. Do not use a calculator.

42. $\sin 240°$ **43.** $\tan 120°$ **44.** $\sec\dfrac{7\pi}{4}$

45. $\cos\dfrac{11\pi}{6}$ **46.** $\cot(-210°)$ **47.** $\csc\left(-\dfrac{2\pi}{3}\right)$

48. $\sin\left(-\dfrac{\pi}{3}\right)$ **49.** $\sin 495°$ **50.** $\tan\dfrac{13\pi}{4}$

1.5

In Exercises 51–56, determine the amplitude and period of each function. Then graph one period of the function.

51. $y = 3\sin 4x$ **52.** $y = -2\cos 2x$

53. $y = 2\cos\frac{1}{2}x$ **54.** $y = \frac{1}{2}\sin\frac{\pi}{3}x$

55. $y = -\sin\pi x$ **56.** $y = 3\cos\dfrac{x}{3}$

In Exercises 57–61, determine the amplitude, period, and phase shift of each function. Then graph one period of the function.

57. $y = 2\sin(x - \pi)$ **58.** $y = -3\cos(x + \pi)$

59. $y = \dfrac{3}{2}\cos\left(2x + \dfrac{\pi}{4}\right)$ **60.** $y = \dfrac{5}{2}\sin\left(2x + \dfrac{\pi}{2}\right)$

61. $y = -3\sin\left(\dfrac{\pi}{3}x - 3\pi\right)$

In Exercises 62–63, use a vertical shift to graph one period of the function.

62. $y = \sin 2x + 1$ **63.** $y = 2\cos\frac{1}{3}x - 2$

64. The equation

$$y = 98.6 + 0.3\sin\left(\dfrac{\pi}{12}x - \dfrac{11\pi}{12}\right)$$

models variation in body temperature, y, in °F, x hours after midnight.

a. What is body temperature at midnight?

b. What is the period of the body temperature cycle?

c. When is body temperature highest? What is the body temperature at this time?

d. When is body temperature lowest? What is the body temperature at this time?

e. Graph one period of the body temperature function.

1.6

In Exercises 65–71, graph two full periods of the given tangent or cotangent function.

65. $y = 4\tan 2x$ **66.** $y = -2\tan\dfrac{\pi}{4}x$

67. $y = \tan(x + \pi)$ **68.** $y = -\tan\left(x - \dfrac{\pi}{4}\right)$

69. $y = 2\cot 3x$ **70.** $y = -\dfrac{1}{2}\cot\dfrac{\pi}{2}x$

71. $y = 2\cot\left(x + \dfrac{\pi}{2}\right)$

In Exercises 72–75, graph two full periods of the given cosecant or secant function.

72. $y = 3\sec 2\pi x$ **73.** $y = -2\csc\pi x$

74. $y = 3\sec(x + \pi)$ **75.** $y = \frac{5}{2}\csc(x - \pi)$

Chapter 1 Test

1. Convert $135°$ to exact radian measure.

2. Find the supplement of the angle whose radian measure is $\dfrac{9\pi}{13}$. Express the answer in terms of π.

3. Find the length of the arc on a circle of radius 20 feet intercepted by a $75°$ central angle. Express arc length in terms of π. Then round your answer to two decimal places.

4. If $(-2, 5)$ is a point on the terminal side of angle θ, find the exact value of each of the six trigonometric functions of θ.

5. Determine the quadrant in which θ lies if $\cos\theta < 0$ and $\cot\theta > 0$.

6. If $\cos\theta = \frac{1}{3}$ and $\tan\theta < 0$, find the exact value of each of the remaining trigonometric functions of θ.

In Exercises 7–9, find the exact value of each expression. Do not use a calculator.

7. $\tan\dfrac{\pi}{6}\cos\dfrac{\pi}{3} - \cos\dfrac{\pi}{2}$ 8. $\tan 300°$

9. $\sin\dfrac{7\pi}{4}$

In Exercises 10–13, graph one period of each function.

10. $y = 3\sin 2x$ 11. $y = -2\cos\left(x - \dfrac{\pi}{2}\right)$

12. $y = 2\tan\dfrac{x}{2}$ 13. $y = -\frac{1}{2}\csc\pi x$

14. Find the exact value of $\tan\left[\cos^{-1}\left(-\frac{1}{2}\right)\right]$.

15. Solve the right triangle in the figure shown. Round lengths to one decimal place.

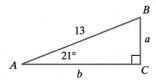

16. The angle of elevation of a building from a point on the ground 30 yards from its base is 37°. Find the height of the building to the nearest yard.

17. A 73-foot rope from the top of a circus tent pole is anchored to the flat ground 43 feet from the bottom of the pole. Find the angle, to the nearest tenth of a degree, that the rope makes with the pole.

Additional Topics in Trigonometry

Chapter 2

These days, computers and trigonometric functions are everywhere. Trigonometry plays a critical role in analyzing the forces that surround your every move. Using trigonometry to understand how forces are measured is one of the topics in this chapter that focuses on additional applications of trigonometry.

You enjoy running, although lately you experience discomfort at various points of impact. Your doctor suggests a computer analysis. By attaching sensors to your running shoes as you jog along a treadmill, the computer provides a printout of the magnitude and direction of the forces as your feet hit the ground. Based on this analysis, customized orthotics can be made to fit inside your shoes to minimize the impact.

SECTION 2.1 *The Law of Sines*

Objectives

1. Use the Law of Sines to solve oblique triangles.
2. Use the Law of Sines to solve, if possible, the triangle or triangles in the ambiguous case.
3. Find the area of an oblique triangle using the sine function.
4. Solve applied problems using the Law of Sines.

Point Reyes National Seashore, 40 miles north of San Francisco, consists of 75,000 acres with miles of pristine surf-pummeled beaches, forested ridges, and bays flanked by white cliffs. A few people, inspired by nature in the raw, live on private property adjoining the National Seashore. In 1995, a fire in the park burned 12,350 acres and destroyed 45 homes.

Fire is a necessary part of the life cycle in many wilderness areas. It is also an ongoing threat to those who choose to live surrounded by nature's unspoiled beauty. In this section, we see how trigonometry can be used to locate small wilderness fires before they become raging infernos. To do this, we begin by considering triangles other than right triangles.

The Law of Sines and Its Derivation

An **oblique triangle** is a triangle that does not contain a right angle. Figure 2.1 shows that an oblique triangle has either three acute angles or two acute angles and one obtuse angle. Notice that the angles are labeled A, B, and C. The sides opposite each angle are labeled as a, b, and c, respectively.

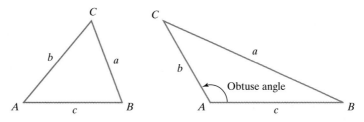

Figure 2.1 Oblique triangles

Many relationships exist among the sides and angles in an oblique triangle. One such relationship is called the **Law of Sines.**

Study Tip

The Law of Sines can be expressed with the sines in the numerator:

$$\frac{\sin A}{a} = \frac{\sin B}{b} = \frac{\sin C}{c}.$$

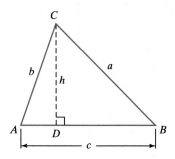

Figure 2.2 Drawing an altitude to prove the Law of Sines

The Law of Sines

If A, B, and C are the measures of the angles of a triangle, and a, b, and c are the lengths of the sides opposite these angles, then

$$\frac{a}{\sin A} = \frac{b}{\sin B} = \frac{c}{\sin C}.$$

The ratio of the length of the side of any triangle to the sine of the angle opposite that side is the same for all three sides of the triangle.

To prove the Law of Sines, we draw an altitude of length h from one of the vertices of the triangle. In Figure 2.2, the altitude is drawn from vertex C. Two smaller triangles are formed, triangles ACD and BCD. Note that both are right triangles. Thus, we can use the definition of the sine of an angle of a right triangle.

$$\sin B = \frac{h}{a} \qquad \sin A = \frac{h}{b} \qquad \sin \theta = \frac{opposite}{hypotenuse}$$

$$h = a \sin B \qquad h = b \sin A \qquad \text{Solve each equation for } h.$$

Because we have found two expressions for h, we can set these expressions equal to each other.

$$a \sin B = b \sin A \qquad \text{Equate the expressions for } h.$$

$$\frac{a \sin B}{\sin A \sin B} = \frac{b \sin A}{\sin A \sin B} \qquad \text{Divide both sides by } \sin A \sin B.$$

$$\frac{a}{\sin A} = \frac{b}{\sin B} \qquad \text{Simplify.}$$

This proves part of the Law of Sines. If we use the same process and draw an altitude of length h from vertex A, we obtain the following result:

$$\frac{b}{\sin B} = \frac{c}{\sin C}.$$

When this equation is combined with the previous equation, we obtain the Law of Sines. Because the sine of an angle is equal to the sine of 180° minus that angle, the Law of Sines is derived in a similar manner if the oblique triangle contains an obtuse angle.

1 Use the Law of Sines to solve oblique triangles.

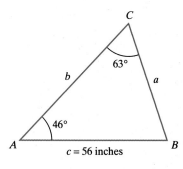

Figure 2.3 Solving an oblique SAA triangle

Solving Oblique Triangles

Solving an oblique triangle means finding the lengths of its sides and the measurement of its angles. The Law of Sines can be used to solve a triangle in which one side and two angles are known. The three known measurements can be abbreviated using SAA (a side and two angles are known) or ASA (two angles and the side between them are known).

EXAMPLE 1 Solving an SAA Triangle Using the Law of Sines

Solve the triangle shown in Figure 2.3 with $A = 46°$, $C = 63°$, and $c = 56$ inches.

Solution We begin by finding B, the third angle of the triangle. We do not need the Law of Sines to do this. Instead, we use the fact that the sum of the measures of the interior angles of a triangle is 180°.

$$A + B + C = 180°$$

$$46° + B + 63° = 180°$$ Substitute the given values: $A = 46°$ and $C = 63°$.

$$109° + B = 180°$$ Add.

$$B = 71°$$ Subtract 109° from both sides.

When we use the Law of Sines, we must be given one of the three ratios. In this example, we are given c and C: $c = 56$ and $C = 63°$. Thus, we use the ratio $\dfrac{c}{\sin C}$, or $\dfrac{56}{\sin 63°}$, to find the other two sides. Use the Law of Sines to find a.

$$\frac{a}{\sin A} = \frac{c}{\sin C}$$ The ratio of any side to the sine of its opposite angle equals the ratio of any other side to the sine of its opposite angle.

$$\frac{a}{\sin 46°} = \frac{56}{\sin 63°}$$ $A = 46°$, $c = 56$, and $C = 63°$.

$$a = \frac{56 \sin 46°}{\sin 63°}$$ Multiply both sides by $\sin 46°$ and solve for a.

$$a \approx 45 \text{ inches}$$ Use a calculator.

Use the Law of Sines again, this time to find b.

$$\frac{b}{\sin B} = \frac{c}{\sin C}$$ We use the given ratio, $\dfrac{c}{\sin C}$, to find b.

$$\frac{b}{\sin 71°} = \frac{56}{\sin 63°}$$ We found that $B = 71°$. We are given $c = 56$ and $C = 63°$.

$$b = \frac{56 \sin 71°}{\sin 63°}$$ Multiply both sides by $\sin 71°$ and solve for b.

$$b \approx 59 \text{ inches}$$ Use a calculator.

The solution is $B = 71°$, $a \approx 45$ inches, and $b \approx 59$ inches.

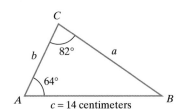

Figure 2.4

Check Point 1 Solve the triangle shown in Figure 2.4 with $A = 64°$, $C = 82°$, and $c = 14$ centimeters.

EXAMPLE 2 Solving an ASA Triangle Using the Law of Sines

Solve triangle ABC if $A = 50°$, $C = 33.5°$, and $b = 76$.

Solution We begin by drawing a picture of triangle ABC and labeling it with the given information. Figure 2.5 shows the triangle that we must solve. We begin by finding B.

$$A + B + C = 180°$$ The sum of the measures of a triangle's interior angles is 180°.

$$50° + B + 33.5° = 180°$$ $A = 50°$ and $C = 33.5°$.

$$83.5° + B = 180°$$ Add.

$$B = 96.5°$$ Subtract 83.5° from both sides.

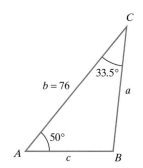

Figure 2.5 Solving an ASA triangle

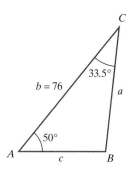

Figure 2.5, repeated

Keep in mind that we must be given one of the three ratios to apply the Law of Sines. In this example, we are given that $b = 76$ and we found that $B = 96.5°$. Thus, we use the ratio $\dfrac{b}{\sin B}$, or $\dfrac{76}{\sin 96.5°}$, to find the other two sides. Use the Law of Sines to find a and c.

Find a: **Find c:**

This is the known ratio.

$$\frac{a}{\sin A} = \frac{b}{\sin B} \qquad\qquad \frac{c}{\sin C} = \frac{b}{\sin B}$$

$$\frac{a}{\sin 50°} = \frac{76}{\sin 96.5°} \qquad\qquad \frac{c}{\sin 33.5°} = \frac{76}{\sin 96.5°}$$

$$a = \frac{76 \sin 50°}{\sin 96.5°} \approx 59 \qquad\qquad c = \frac{76 \sin 33.5°}{\sin 96.5°} \approx 42$$

The solution is $B = 96.5°$, $a \approx 59$, and $c \approx 42$.

2   Use the Law of Sines to solve, if possible, the triangle or triangles in the ambiguous case.

Check Point 2   Solve triangle ABC if $A = 40°$, $C = 22.5°$, and $b = 12$.

The Ambiguous Case (SSA)

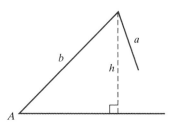

Figure 2.6 Given SSA, no triangle may result.

If we are given two sides and an angle opposite one of them (SSA), does this determine a unique triangle? Can we solve this case using the Law of Sines? Such a case is called the **ambiguous case** because the given information may result in one triangle, two triangles, or no triangle at all. For example, in Figure 2.6, we are given a, b, and A. Because a is shorter than h, it is not long enough to form a triangle. The number of possible triangles, if any, that can be formed in the SSA case depends on h, the length of the altitude, where $h = b \sin A$.

The Ambiguous Case (SSA)

Consider a triangle in which a, b, and A are given. This information may result in

No Triangle	**One Right Triangle**	**Two Triangles**	**One Triangle**
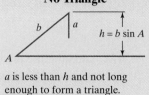		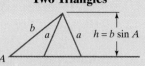	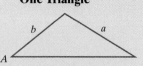
a is less than h and not long enough to form a triangle.	$a = h$ and just the right length to form a right triangle.	a is greater than h and a is less than b. Two distinct triangles are formed.	a is greater than h and a is greater than b. One triangle is formed.

In an SSA situation, it is not necessary to draw an accurate sketch like those shown in the box. The Law of Sines determines the number of triangles, if any, and gives the solution for each triangle.

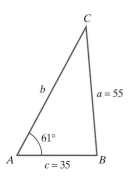

Figure 2.7 Solving an SSA triangle; the ambiguous case

EXAMPLE 3 Solving an SSA Triangle Using the Law of Sines (One Solution)

Solve triangle ABC if $A = 61°$, $a = 55$, and $c = 35$.

Solution   We begin with the sketch in Figure 2.7. The known ratio is $\dfrac{a}{\sin A}$, or $\dfrac{55}{\sin 61°}$. Because side c is given, we use the Law of Sines to find angle C.

$$\frac{a}{\sin A} = \frac{c}{\sin C} \qquad \text{Apply the Law of Sines.}$$

$$\frac{55}{\sin 61°} = \frac{35}{\sin C} \qquad A = 55, c = 35, \text{ and } A = 61°.$$

$$55 \sin C = 35 \sin 61° \qquad \text{Cross multiply: If } \frac{a}{b} = \frac{c}{d}, \text{ then } ad = bc.$$

$$\sin C = \frac{35 \sin 61°}{55} \qquad \text{Divide both sides by 55 and solve for } \sin C.$$

$$\sin C \approx 0.5566 \qquad \text{Use a calculator.}$$

There are two angles C between $0°$ and $180°$ for which $\sin C \approx 0.5566$.

$$C_1 \approx 34° \qquad\qquad C_2 \approx 180° - 34° \approx 146°$$

Obtain the acute angle with your calculator: $\sin^{-1} 0.5566$

The sine is positive in quadrant II.

Look at Figure 2.7. Given that $A = 61°$, can you see that $C_2 \approx 146°$ is impossible? By adding $146°$ to the given angle, $61°$, we exceed a $180°$ sum:

$$61° + 146° = 207°.$$

Thus, the only possibility is that $C_1 \approx 34°$. We find B using this approximation for C_1 and the measure that was given for $A: A = 61°$.

$$B = 180° - C_1 - A \approx 180° - 34° - 61° = 85°$$

Side b that lies opposite this $85°$ angle can now be found using the Law of Sines.

$$\frac{b}{\sin B} = \frac{a}{\sin A} \qquad \text{Apply the Law of Sines.}$$

$$\frac{b}{\sin 85°} = \frac{55}{\sin 61°} \qquad a = 55, B \approx 85°, \text{ and } A = 61°.$$

$$b = \frac{55 \sin 85°}{\sin 61°} \approx 63 \qquad \text{Multiply both sides by } \sin 85° \text{ and solve for } b.$$

There is one triangle and the solution is C_1 (or C) $\approx 34°$, $B \approx 85°$, and $b \approx 63$.

Check Point 3   Solve triangle ABC if $A = 123°$, $a = 47$, and $c = 23$.

EXAMPLE 4   Solving an SSA Triangle Using the Law of Sines (No Solution)

Solve triangle ABC if $A = 75°$, $a = 51$, and $b = 71$.

Solution   The known ratio is $\dfrac{a}{\sin A}$, or $\dfrac{51}{\sin 75°}$. Because side b is given, we use the Law of Sines to find angle B.

$$\frac{a}{\sin A} = \frac{b}{\sin B}$$ Use the Law of Sines.

$$\frac{51}{\sin 75°} = \frac{71}{\sin B}$$ Substitute the given values.

$$51 \sin B = 71 \sin 75°$$ Cross multiply: If $\dfrac{a}{b} = \dfrac{c}{d}$, then $ad = bc$.

$$\sin B = \frac{71 \sin 75°}{51} \approx 1.34$$ Divide by 51 and solve for sin B.

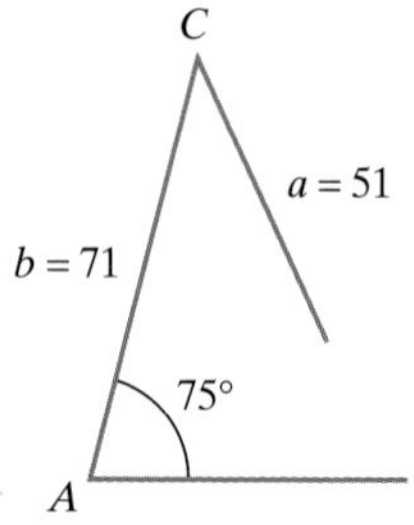

Figure 2.8 a is not long enough to form a triangle

Because the sine can never exceed 1, there is no angle B for which $\sin B \approx 1.34$. There is no triangle with the given measurements, as illustrated in Figure 2.8.

Check Point 4   Solve triangle ABC if $A = 50°$, $a = 10$, and $b = 20$.

EXAMPLE 5   Solving an SSA Triangle Using the Law of Sines (Two Solutions)

Solve triangle ABC if $A = 40°$, $a = 54$, and $b = 62$.

Solution   The known ratio is $\dfrac{a}{\sin A}$, or $\dfrac{54}{\sin 40°}$. We use the Law of Sines to find angle B.

$$\frac{a}{\sin A} = \frac{b}{\sin B}$$ Use the Law of Sines.

$$\frac{54}{\sin 40°} = \frac{62}{\sin B}$$ Substitute the given values.

$$54 \sin B = 62 \sin 40°$$ Cross multiply: If $\dfrac{a}{b} = \dfrac{c}{d}$, then $ad = bc$.

$$\sin B = \frac{62 \sin 40°}{54} \approx 0.7380$$ Divide by 54 and solve for sin B.

There are two angles B between $0°$ and $180°$ for which $\sin B \approx 0.7380$.

$$B_1 \approx 48° \qquad\qquad B_2 \approx 180° - 48° = 132°$$

Find $\sin^{-1} 0.7380$ with your calculator.

The sine is positive in quadrant II.

If you add either angle to the given angle, $40°$, the sum does not exceed $180°$. Thus, there are two triangles with the given conditions, shown in Figure 2.9(a). The triangles, AB_1C_1 and AB_2C_2, are shown separately in Figures 2.9(b) and (c).

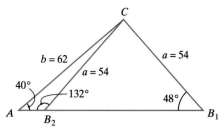

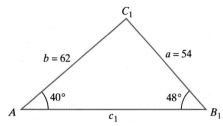

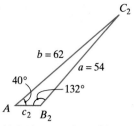

(a) Two triangles are possible with $A = 40°$, $a = 54$, and $b = 62$.

(b) In one possible triangle, $B_1 = 48°$.

(c) In the second possible triangle, $B_2 = 132°$.

Figure 2.9

Study Tip

The two triangles shown in Figure 2.9 are helpful in organizing the solutions. However, if you keep track of the two triangles, one with the given information and $B_1 = 48°$, and the other with the given information and $B_2 = 132°$, you do not have to draw the figure to solve the triangles.

We find angles C_1 and C_2 using a 180° angle sum in each of the two triangles.

$$C_1 = 180° - A - B_1$$
$$\approx 180° - 40° - 48°$$
$$= 92°$$

$$C_2 = 180° - A - B_2$$
$$\approx 180° - 40° - 132°$$
$$= 8°$$

We use the Law of Sines to find c_1 and c_2.

$$\frac{c_1}{\sin C_1} = \frac{a}{\sin A}$$

$$\frac{c_1}{\sin 92°} = \frac{54}{\sin 40°}$$

$$c_1 = \frac{54 \sin 92°}{\sin 40°} \approx 84$$

$$\frac{c_2}{\sin C_2} = \frac{a}{\sin A}$$

$$\frac{c_2}{\sin 8°} = \frac{54}{\sin 40°}$$

$$c_2 = \frac{54 \sin 8°}{\sin 40°} \approx 12$$

There are two triangles. In one triangle, the solution is $B_1 \approx 48°$, $C_1 \approx 92°$, and $c_1 \approx 84$. In the other triangle, $B_2 \approx 132°$, $C_2 \approx 8°$, and $c_2 \approx 12$.

Check Point 5 Solve triangle ABC if $A = 35°$, $a = 12$, and $b = 16$.

3 Find the area of an oblique triangle using the sine function.

The Area of an Oblique Triangle

A formula for the area of an oblique triangle can be obtained using the procedure for proving the Law of Sines. We draw an altitude of length h from one of the vertices of the triangle, as shown in Figure 2.10. We apply the definition of the sine of angle A, $\dfrac{\text{opposite}}{\text{hypotenuse}}$, in right triangle ACD:

$$\sin A = \frac{h}{b} \quad \text{or} \quad h = b \sin A.$$

The area of a triangle is $\frac{1}{2}$ the product of any side and the altitude drawn to that side. Using the altitude h in Figure 2.10, we have

$$\text{Area} = \tfrac{1}{2}ch = \tfrac{1}{2}cb \sin A.$$

Use the result from above: $h = b \sin A$.

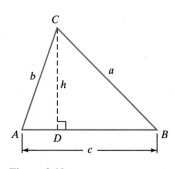

Figure 2.10

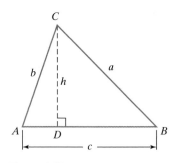

Figure 2.10, repeated

This result, Area $= \frac{1}{2} cb \sin A$, or $\frac{1}{2} bc \sin A$, indicates that the area of the triangle is one-half the product of b and c times the sine of their included angle. If we draw altitudes from the other two vertices, we can use any two sides to compute the area.

Area of An Oblique Triangle

The area of a triangle equals one-half the product of the lengths of two sides times the sine of their included angle. In Figure 2.10, this wording can be expressed by the formulas

$$\text{Area} = \tfrac{1}{2} bc \sin A = \tfrac{1}{2} ab \sin C = \tfrac{1}{2} ac \sin B.$$

EXAMPLE 6   Finding the Area of an Oblique Triangle

Find the area of a triangle having two sides of lengths 24 meters and 10 meters and an included angle of 62°.

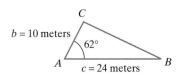

Figure 2.11 Finding the area of an SAS triangle

Solution   The triangle is shown in Figure 2.11. Its area is half the product of the lengths of the two sides times the sine of the included angle.

$$\text{Area} = \tfrac{1}{2}(24)(10)(\sin 62°) \approx 106$$

The area of the triangle is approximately 106 square meters.

> **Check Point 6**   Find the area of a triangle having two sides of lengths 8 meters and 12 meters and an included angle of 135°.

4 Solve applied problems using the Law of Sines.

Applications of the Law of Sines

We have seen how the trigonometry of right triangles can be used to solve many different kinds of applied problems. The Law of Sines enables us to work with triangles that are not right triangles. As a result, this law can be used to solve problems involving surveying, engineering, astronomy, navigation, and the environment. Example 7 illustrates the use of the Law of Sines in detecting potentially devastating fires.

EXAMPLE 7   An Application of the Law of Sines

Two fire-lookout stations are 20 miles apart, with station B directly east of station A. Both stations spot a fire on a mountain to the north. The bearing from station A to the fire is N50°E (50° east of north). The bearing from station B to the fire is N36°W (36° west of north). How far is the fire from station A?

Solution   Figure 2.12 at the top of the next page shows the information given in the problem. The distance from station A to the fire is represented by b. Notice that the angles describing the bearing from each station to the fire, 50° and 36°, are not interior angles of triangle ABC. Using a north-south line, the interior angles are found as follows:

$$A = 90° - 50° = 40° \qquad B = 90° - 36° = 54°.$$

To find b using the Law of Sines, we need a known side and an angle opposite that side. Because $c = 20$ miles, we find angle C using a 180° angle sum in the triangle. Thus,

$$C = 180° - A - B = 180° - 40° - 54° = 86°.$$

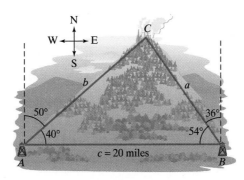

Figure 2.12

The ratio $\dfrac{c}{\sin C}$, or $\dfrac{20}{\sin 86°}$, is now known. We use this ratio and the Law of Sines to find b.

$$\frac{b}{\sin B} = \frac{c}{\sin C} \qquad \text{Use the Law of Sines.}$$

$$\frac{b}{\sin 54°} = \frac{20}{\sin 86°} \qquad c = 20,\ B = 54°,\ \text{and } C = 86°.$$

$$b = \frac{20 \sin 54°}{\sin 86°} \approx 16 \qquad \text{Multiply both sides by } \sin 54° \text{ and solve for } b.$$

The fire is approximately 16 miles from station A.

Check Point 7 Two fire-lookout stations are 13 miles apart, with station B directly east of station A. Both stations spot a fire. The bearing of the fire from station A is N35°E, and the bearing of the fire from station B is N49°W. How far, to the nearest mile, is the fire from station B?

EXERCISE SET 2.1

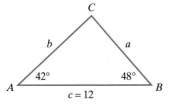

Practice Exercises

In Exercises 1–8, solve each triangle. Round lengths of sides to the nearest tenth and angle measures to the nearest degree.

1.

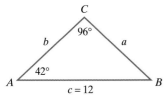

2.

3.

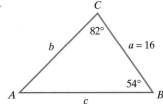

4.

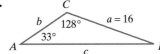

5.

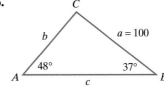

6.

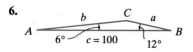

7.

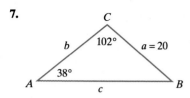

8.

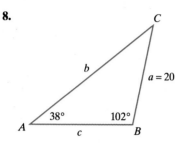

In Exercises 9–16, solve each triangle. Round lengths to the nearest tenth and angle measures to the nearest degree.

9. $A = 44°, B = 25°, a = 12$

10. $A = 56°, C = 24°, a = 22$

11. $B = 85°, C = 15°, b = 40$

12. $A = 85°, B = 35°, c = 30$

13. $A = 115°, C = 35°, c = 200$

14. $B = 5°, C = 125°, b = 200$

15. $A = 65°, B = 65°, c = 6$

16. $B = 80°, C = 10°, a = 8$

In Exercises 17–32, two sides and an angle (SSA) of a triangle are given. Determine whether the given measurements produce one triangle, two triangles, or no triangle at all. Solve each triangle that results. Round to the nearest tenth and the nearest degree for sides and angles, respectively.

17. $a = 20, b = 15, A = 40°$

18. $a = 30, b = 20, A = 50°$

19. $a = 10, c = 8.9, A = 63°$

20. $a = 57.5, c = 49.8, A = 136°$

21. $a = 42.1, c = 37, A = 112°$

22. $a = 6.1, b = 4, A = 162°$

23. $a = 10, b = 40, A = 30°$

24. $a = 10, b = 30, A = 150°$

25. $a = 16, b = 18, A = 60°$

26. $a = 30, b = 40, A = 20°$

27. $a = 12, b = 16.1, A = 37°$

28. $a = 7, b = 28, A = 12°$

29. $a = 22, c = 24.1, A = 58°$

30. $a = 95, c = 125, A = 49°$

31. $a = 9.3, b = 41, A = 18°$

32. $a = 1.4, b = 2.9, A = 142°$

In Exercises 33–38, find the area of the triangle having the given measurements. Round to the nearest square unit.

33. $A = 48°, b = 20$ feet, $c = 40$ feet

34. $A = 22°, b = 20$ feet, $c = 50$ feet

35. $B = 36°, a = 3$ yards, $c = 6$ yards

36. $B = 125°, a = 8$ yards, $c = 5$ yards

37. $C = 124°, a = 4$ meters, $b = 6$ meters

38. $C = 102°, a = 16$ meters, $b = 20$ meters

Application Exercises

39. Two fire-lookout stations are 10 miles apart, with station B directly east of station A. Both stations spot a fire. The bearing of the fire from station A is N25°E and the bearing of the fire from station B is N56°W. How far, to the nearest mile, is the fire from each lookout station?

40. The Federal Communications Commission is attempting to locate an illegal radio station. It sets up two monitoring stations, A and B, with station B 40 miles east of station A. Station A measures the illegal signal from the radio station as coming from a direction of 48° east of north. Station B measures the signal as coming from a point 34° west of north. How far is the illegal radio station from monitoring stations A and B?

41. The figure shows a 1200-yard-long sand beach and an oil platform in the ocean. The angle made with the platform from one end of the beach is 85° and from the other end is 76°. Find the distance of the oil platform, to the nearest yard, from each end of the beach.

42. A surveyor needs to determine the distance between two points that lie on opposite banks of a river. The figure shows that 300 yards are measured along one bank. The angles from each end of this line segment to a point on the opposite bank are 62° and 53°. Find the distance between A and B to the nearest foot.

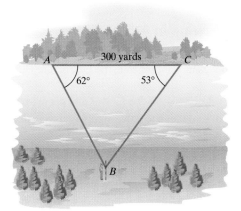

43. Closed to tourists since 1990, the Leaning Tower of Pisa in Italy leans at an angle of about 84.7°. The figure shows that 171 feet from the base of the tower, the angle of elevation to the top is 50°. Find the distance, to the nearest foot, from the base to the top of the tower.

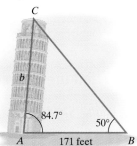

44. A pine tree growing on a hillside makes a 75° angle with the hill. From a point 80 feet up the hill, the angle of elevation to the top of the tree is 62° and the angle of depression to the bottom is 23°. Find, to the nearest foot, the height of the tree.

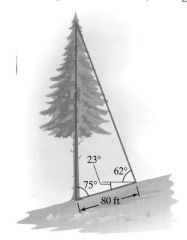

45. The figure shows a shot-put ring. The shot is tossed from A and lands at B. Using modern electronic equipment, the distance of the toss can be measured without the use of measuring tapes. When the shot lands at B, an electronic transmitter placed at B sends a signal to a device in the official's booth above the track. The device determines the angles at B and C. At a track meet, the distance from the official's booth to the shot-put ring is 562 feet. If $B = 85.3°$ and $C = 5.7°$, determine the length of the toss to the nearest foot.

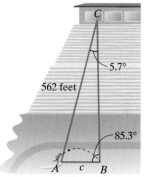

46. A pier forms an 85° angle with a straight shore. At a distance of 100 feet from the pier, the line of sight to the tip forms a 37° angle. Find the length of the pier to the nearest foot.

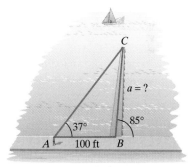

47. When the angle of elevation of the sun is 62°, a telephone pole that is tilted at an angle of 8° directly away from the sun casts a shadow 20 feet long. Determine the length of the pole to the nearest foot.

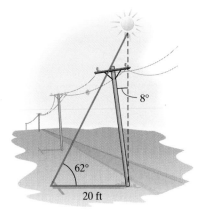

48. A leaning wall is inclined 6° from the vertical. At a distance of 40 feet from the wall, the angle of elevation to the top is 22°. Find the height of the wall to the nearest foot.

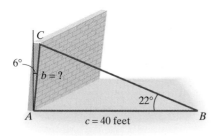

49. Redwood trees in California's Redwood National Park are hundreds of feet tall. The height of one of these trees is represented by *h* in the figure shown.

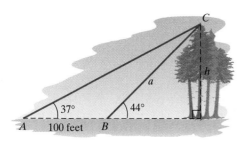

   a. Use the measurements shown to find *a*, to the nearest foot, in oblique triangle *ABC*.
   b. Use the right triangle shown to find the height, to the nearest foot, of a typical redwood tree in the park.

50. The figure shows a cable car that carries passengers from *A* to *C*. Point *A* is 1.6 miles from the base of the mountain. The angles of elevation from *A* and *B* to the mountain's peak are 22° and 66°, respectively.
   a. Determine, to the nearest foot, the distance covered by the cable car.
   b. Find *a*, to the nearest foot, in oblique triangle *ABC*.
   c. Use the right triangle to find the height of the mountain to the nearest foot.

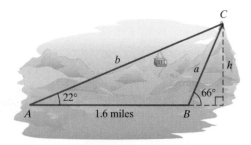

51. Lighthouse B is 7 miles west of lighthouse A. A boat leaves A and sails 5 miles. At this time, it is sighted from B. If the bearing of the boat from B is N62°E, how far from B is the boat? Round to the nearest tenth of a mile.

52. After a wind storm, you notice that your 16-foot flagpole may be leaning, but you are not sure. From a point on the ground 15 feet from the base of the flagpole, you find that the angle of elevation to the top is 48°. Is the flagpole leaning? If so, find the acute angle, to the nearest degree, that the flagpole makes with the ground.

Writing in Mathematics

53. What is an oblique triangle?
54. Without using symbols, state the Law of Sines in your own words.
55. Briefly describe how the Law of Sines is proved.
56. What does it mean to solve an oblique triangle?
57. What do the abbreviations SAA and ASA mean?
58. Why is SSA called the ambiguous case?
59. How is the sine function used to find the area of an oblique triangle?
60. Write an original problem that can be solved using the Law of Sines. Then solve the problem.
61. Use Exercise 45 to describe how the Law of Sines is used for throwing events at track and field meets. Why aren't tape measures used to determine tossing distance?
62. You are cruising in your boat parallel to the coast, looking at a lighthouse. Explain how you can use your boat's speed and a device for measuring angles to determine the distance at any instant from your boat to the lighthouse.

Critical Thinking Exercises

63. If you are given two sides of a triangle and their included angle, you can find the triangle's area. Can the Law of Sines be used to solve the triangle with this given information? Explain your answer.

64. Two buildings of equal height are 800 feet apart. An observer on the street between the buildings measures the angles of elevation to the tops of the buildings as 27° and 41°, respectively. How high, to the nearest foot, are the buildings?

65. The figure shows the design for the top of the wing of a jet fighter. The fuselage is 5 feet wide. Find the wing span *CC′* to the nearest foot.

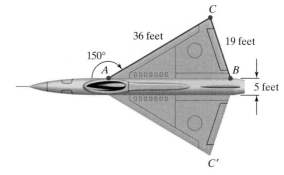

SECTION 2.2   *The Law of Cosines*

Objectives

1. Use the Law of Cosines to solve oblique triangles.
2. Solve applied problems using the Law of Cosines.
3. Use Heron's formula to find the area of a triangle.

Baseball was developed in the United States in the mid-1800s and became our national sport. Little League baseball is the largest youth sports program in the world. Three million boys and girls ages 5 to 18 play on 200,000 Little League teams in 90 countries. Although there are differences between Major League and Little League baseball diamonds, trigonometry can be used to find angles and distances in these fields of dreams. To see how this is done, we turn to the Law of Cosines.

The Law of Cosines and Its Derivation

We now look at another relationship that exists among the sides and angles in an oblique triangle. **The Law of Cosines** is used to solve triangles in which two sides and the included angle (SAS) are known, or those in which three sides (SSS) are known.

Discovery

What happens to the Law of Cosines

$$c^2 = a^2 + b^2 - 2ab \cos C$$

if $C = 90°$? What familiar theorem do you obtain?

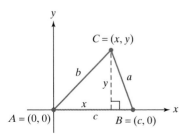

Figure 2.13

The Law of Cosines

If A, B, and C are the measures of the angles of a triangle, and $a, b,$ and c are the lengths of the sides opposite these angles, then

$$a^2 = b^2 + c^2 - 2bc \cos A$$
$$b^2 = a^2 + c^2 - 2ac \cos B$$
$$c^2 = a^2 + b^2 - 2ab \cos C.$$

The square of a side of a triangle equals the sum of the squares of the other two sides minus twice their product times the cosine of their included angle.

To prove the Law of Cosines, we place triangle ABC in a rectangular coordinate system. Figure 2.13 shows a triangle with three acute angles. The vertex A is at the origin and side c lies along the positive x-axis. The coordinates of C are (x, y). Using the right triangle that contains angle A, we apply the definitions of the cosine and the sine.

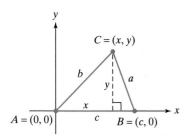

Figure 2.13, repeated

$$\cos A = \frac{x}{b} \qquad \sin A = \frac{y}{b}$$

$$x = b \cos A \qquad y = b \sin A \quad \text{Multiply both sides of each equation by } b \text{ and solve for } x \text{ and } y, \text{ respectively.}$$

Thus, the coordinates of C are $(x, y) = (b \cos A, b \sin A)$. Although triangle ABC in Figure 2.13 shows angle A as an acute angle, if A is obtuse, the coordinates of C are still $(b \cos A, b \sin A)$. This means that our proof applies to both kinds of oblique triangles.

We now apply the distance formula to the side of the triangle with length a. Notice that a is the distance from (x, y) to $(c, 0)$.

$$a = \sqrt{(x - c)^2 + (y - 0)^2} \qquad \text{Use the distance formula.}$$

$$a^2 = (x - c)^2 + y^2 \qquad \text{Square both sides of the equation.}$$

$$a^2 = (b \cos A - c)^2 + (b \sin A)^2 \qquad x = b \cos A \text{ and } y = b \sin A.$$

$$a^2 = b^2 \cos^2 A - 2bc \cos A + c^2 + b^2 \sin^2 A \qquad \text{Square the two expressions.}$$

$$a^2 = b^2 \sin^2 A + b^2 \cos^2 A + c^2 - 2bc \cos A \qquad \text{Rearrange terms.}$$

$$a^2 = b^2(\sin^2 A + \cos^2 A) + c^2 - 2bc \cos A \qquad \text{Factor } b^2 \text{ from the first two terms.}$$

$$a^2 = b^2 + c^2 - 2bc \cos A \qquad \sin^2 A + \cos^2 A = 1$$

The resulting equation is one of the three formulas for the Law of Cosines. The other two formulas are derived in a similar manner.

1 Use the Law of Cosines to solve oblique triangles.

Solving Oblique Triangles

If you are given two sides and an included angle (SAS) of an oblique triangle, none of the three ratios in the Law of Sines is known. This means that we do not begin solving the triangle using the Law of Sines. Instead, we apply the Law of Cosines and the following procedure:

Solving an SAS Triangle

1. Use the Law of Cosines to find the side opposite the given angle.

2. Use the Law of Sines to find the angle opposite the shorter of the two given sides. This angle is always acute.

3. Find the third angle by subtracting the measure of the given angle and the angle found in step 2 from 180°.

EXAMPLE 1   Solving an SAS Triangle

Solve the triangle in Figure 2.14 with $A = 60°$, $b = 20$, and $c = 30$.

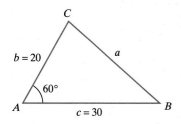

Figure 2.14 Solving an SAS triangle

Solution   We are given two sides and an included angle. Therefore, we apply the three-step procedure for solving an SAS triangle.

Step 1   Use the Law of Cosines to find the side opposite the given angle.   Thus, we will find a.

$$a^2 = b^2 + c^2 - 2bc \cos A$$ Apply the Law of Cosines to find a.

$$a^2 = 20^2 + 30^2 - 2(20)(30) \cos 60°$$ $b = 20$, $c = 30$, and $A = 60°$

$$= 400 + 900 - 1200(0.5)$$ Perform the indicated operations.

$$= 700$$

$$a = \sqrt{700} \approx 26$$ Take the square root of both sides and solve for a.

Step 2   Use the Law of Sines to find the angle opposite the shorter of the two given sides. This angle is always acute.   The shorter of the two given sides is $b = 20$. Thus, we will find acute angle B.

$$\frac{b}{\sin B} = \frac{a}{\sin A}$$ Apply the Law of Sines.

$$\frac{20}{\sin B} = \frac{\sqrt{700}}{\sin 60°}$$ We are given $b = 20$ and $A = 60°$. Use the exact value of a, $\sqrt{700}$, from step 1.

$$\sqrt{700} \sin B = 20 \sin 60°$$ Cross multiply: If $\frac{a}{b} = \frac{c}{d}$, then $ad = bc$.

$$\sin B = \frac{20 \sin 60°}{\sqrt{700}} \approx 0.6547$$ Divide by $\sqrt{700}$ and solve for sin B.

$$B \approx 41°$$ Find $\sin^{-1} 0.6547$ using a calculator.

Step 3   Find the third angle. Subtract the measure of the given angle and the angle found in step 2 from 180°.

$$C = 180° - A - B \approx 180° - 60° - 41° = 79°$$

The solution is $a \approx 26$, $B \approx 41°$, and $C \approx 79°$.

Check Point 1   Solve the triangle shown in Figure 2.15 with $A = 120°$, $b = 7$, and $c = 8$.

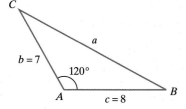

Figure 2.15

If you are given three sides of a triangle (SSS), solving the triangle involves finding the three angles. We use the following procedure:

Solving an SSS Triangle

1. Use the Law of Cosines to find the angle opposite the longest side.
2. Use the Law of Sines to find either of the two remaining acute angles.
3. Find the third angle by subtracting the measures of the angles found in steps 1 and 2 from 180°.

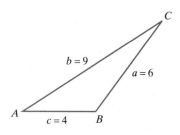

Figure 2.16 Solving an SSS triangle

EXAMPLE 2 Solving an SSS Triangle

Solve triangle ABC if $a = 6$, $b = 9$, and $c = 4$. Round to the nearest tenth of a degree.

Solution We are given three sides. Therefore, we apply the three-step procedure for solving an SSS triangle. The triangle is shown in Figure 2.16.

Step 1 Use the Law of Cosines to find the angle opposite the longest side. The longest side is $b = 9$. Thus, we will find angle B.

$$b^2 = a^2 + c^2 - 2ac \cos B \qquad \text{Apply the Law of Cosines to find B.}$$

$$2ac \cos B = a^2 + c^2 - b^2 \qquad \text{Solve for cos B.}$$

$$\cos B = \frac{a^2 + c^2 - b^2}{2ac}$$

$$\cos B = \frac{6^2 + 4^2 - 9^2}{2 \cdot 6 \cdot 4} = -\frac{29}{48} \qquad a = 6, b = 9, \text{ and } c = 4.$$

Using a calculator, $\cos^{-1}\left(\frac{29}{48}\right) \approx 52.8°$. Because $\cos B$ is negative, B is an obtuse angle. Thus,

$$B \approx 180° - 52.8° = 127.2°. \qquad \begin{array}{l}\text{Because the domain of } y = \cos^{-1}x \text{ is } [0,\pi], \text{ you}\\ \text{can use a calculator to find } \cos^{-1}(-\frac{29}{48}) \approx 127.2°.\end{array}$$

Step 2 Use the Law of Sines to find either of the two remaining acute angles. We will find angle A.

$$\frac{a}{\sin A} = \frac{b}{\sin B} \qquad \text{Apply the Law of Sines.}$$

$$\frac{6}{\sin A} = \frac{9}{\sin 127.2°} \qquad \begin{array}{l}\text{We are given } a = 6 \text{ and } b = 9. \text{ We found that}\\ B \approx 127.2°.\end{array}$$

$$9 \sin A = 6 \sin 127.2° \qquad \text{Cross multiply.}$$

$$\sin A = \frac{6 \sin 127.2°}{9} \approx 0.5310 \qquad \text{Divide by 9 and solve for sin A.}$$

$$A \approx 32.1° \qquad \text{Find } \sin^{-1} 0.5310 \text{ using a calculator.}$$

Step 3 Find the third angle. Subtract the measures of the angles found in steps 1 and 2 from 180°.

$$C = 180° - B - A \approx 180° - 127.2° - 32.1° = 20.7°$$

The solution is $B \approx 127.2°$, $A \approx 32.1°$, and $C \approx 20.7°$.

Check Point 2 Solve triangle ABC if $a = 8$, $b = 10$, and $c = 5$. Round to the nearest tenth of a degree.

2 Solve applied problems using the Law of Cosines.

Applications of the Law of Cosines

Applied problems involving SAS and SSS triangles can be solved using the Law of Cosines.

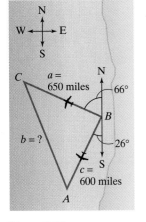

Figure 2.17

EXAMPLE 3   An Application of the Law of Cosines

Two airplanes leave an airport at the same time on different runways. One flies on a bearing of N66°W at 325 miles per hour. The other airplane flies on a bearing of S26°W at 300 miles per hour. How far apart will the airplanes be after two hours?

Solution   After two hours, the plane flying at 325 miles per hour travels $325 \cdot 2$ miles, or 650 miles. Similarly, the plane flying at 300 miles per hour travels 600 miles. The situation is illustrated in Figure 2.17.

Let b = the distance between the planes after two hours. We can use a north-south line to find angle B in triangle ABC. Thus,

$$B = 180° - 66° - 26° = 88°.$$

We now have $a = 650$, $c = 600$, and $B = 88°$. We use the Law of Cosines to find b in this SAS situation.

$$b^2 = a^2 + c^2 - 2ac \cos B \qquad \text{Apply the Law of Cosines.}$$

$$b^2 = 650^2 + 600^2 - 2(650)(600) \cos 88° \qquad \text{Substitute: } a = 650, c = 600, \text{ and } b = 88°.$$

$$\approx 755{,}278 \qquad \text{Use a calculator.}$$

$$b \approx \sqrt{755{,}278} \approx 869 \qquad \text{Take the square root and solve for } b.$$

After two hours, the planes are approximately 869 miles apart.

Check Point 3   Two airplanes leave an airport at the same time on different runways. One flies directly north at 400 miles per hour. The other airplane flies on a bearing of N75°E at 350 miles per hour. How far apart will the airplanes be after two hours?

3 Use Heron's formula to find the area of a triangle.

Heron's Formula

Approximately 2000 years ago, the Greek mathematician Heron of Alexandria derived a formula for the area of a triangle in terms of the lengths of its sides. A more modern derivation uses the Law of Cosines and can be found in the appendix.

> **Heron's Formula for the Area of a Triangle**
>
> The area of a triangle with sides a, b, and c is
>
> $$\text{Area} = \sqrt{s(s-a)(s-b)(s-c)}$$
>
> where s is one-half the perimeter: $s = \frac{1}{2}(a + b + c)$.

EXAMPLE 4 Using Heron's Formula

Find the area of the triangle with $a = 12$ yards, $b = 16$ yards, and $c = 24$ yards.

Solution Begin by calculating one-half the perimeter:
$$s = \tfrac{1}{2}(a + b + c) = \tfrac{1}{2}(12 + 16 + 24) = 26.$$

Use Heron's formula to find the area:
$$\text{Area} = \sqrt{s(s - a)(s - b)(s - c)}$$
$$= \sqrt{26(26 - 12)(26 - 16)(26 - 24)}$$
$$= \sqrt{7280} \approx 85.$$

The area of the triangle is approximately 85 square yards.

Check Point 4 Find the area of the triangle with $a = 6$ meters, $b = 16$ meters, and $c = 18$ meters. Round to the nearest square meter.

EXERCISE SET 2.2

Practice Exercises

In Exercises 1–8, solve each triangle. Round lengths of sides to the nearest tenth and angle measures to the nearest degree.

1.
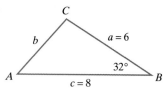

2.
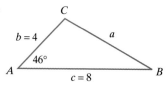

3.
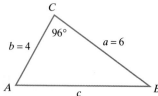

4.
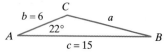

5.
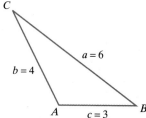

6.
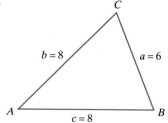

7.
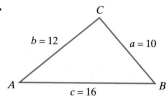

8.
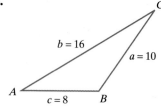

In Exercises 9–24, solve each triangle. Round lengths to the nearest tenth and angle measures to the nearest degree.

9. $a = 5, b = 7, C = 42°$ **10.** $a = 10, b = 3, C = 15°$

11. $b = 5, c = 3, A = 102°$ **12.** $b = 4, c = 1, A = 100°$

13. $a = 6, c = 5, B = 50°$ **14.** $a = 4, c = 7, B = 55°$

15. $a = 5, c = 2, B = 90°$ **16.** $a = 7, c = 3, B = 90°$

17. $a = 5, b = 7, c = 10$ **18.** $a = 4, b = 6, c = 9$

19. $a = 3, b = 9, c = 8$ **20.** $a = 4, b = 7, c = 6$

21. $a = 3, b = 3, c = 3$ **22.** $a = 5, b = 5, c = 5$

23. $a = 73, b = 22, c = 50$ **24.** $a = 66, b = 25, c = 45$

In Exercises 25–30, use Heron's formula to find the area of each triangle. Round to the nearest square unit.

25. $a = 4$ feet, $b = 4$ feet, $c = 2$ feet

26. $a = 5$ feet, $b = 5$ feet, $c = 4$ feet

27. $a = 14$ meters, $b = 12$ meters, $c = 4$ meters

28. $a = 16$ meters, $b = 10$ meters, $c = 8$ meters

29. $a = 11$ yards, $b = 9$ yards, $c = 7$ yards

30. $a = 13$ yards, $b = 9$ yards, $c = 5$ yards

 Application Exercises

31. Two ships leave a harbor at the same time. One ship travels on a bearing of S12°W at 14 miles per hour. The other ship travels on a bearing of N75°E at 10 miles per hour. How far apart will the ships be after three hours? Round to the nearest tenth of a mile.

32. A plane leaves airport A and travels 580 miles to airport B on a bearing of N34°E. The plane later leaves airport B and travels to airport C 400 miles away on a bearing of S74°E. Find the distance from airport A to airport C to the nearest tenth of a mile.

33. Find the distance across the lake from *A* to *C*, to the nearest yard, using the measurements shown in the figure.

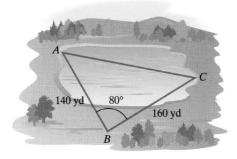

34. To find the distance across a protected cove at a lake, a surveyor makes the measurements shown in the figure at the top of the next column.

Use these measurements to find the distance from *A* to *B* to the nearest yard.

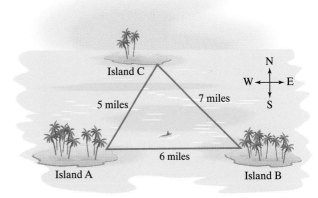

The diagram shows three islands in Florida Bay. You rent a boat and plan to visit each of these remote islands. Use the diagram to solve Exercises 35–36.

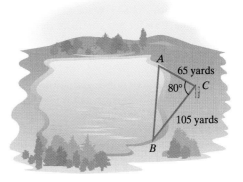

35. If you are on island A, on what bearing should you navigate to go to island C?

36. If you are on island B, on what bearing should you navigate to go to island C?

37. You are on a fishing boat that leaves its pier and heads east. After traveling for 25 miles, there is a report warning of rough seas directly south. The captain turns the boat and follows a bearing of S40°W for 13.5 miles.
  a. At this time, how far are you from the boat's pier? Round to the nearest tenth of a mile.
  b. What bearing could the boat have originally taken to arrive at this spot?

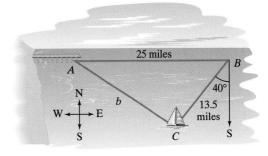

38. You are on a fishing boat that leaves its pier and heads east. After traveling for 30 miles, there is a report warning of rough seas directly south. The captain turns the boat and follows a bearing of S45°W for 12 miles.
   a. At this time, how far are you from the boat's pier? Round to the nearest tenth of a mile.
   b. What bearing could the boat have originally taken to arrive at this spot?

39. The figure shows a 400-foot tower on the side of a hill that forms 7° angle with the horizontal. Find the length of each of the two guy wires that are anchored 80 feet uphill and downhill from the tower's base and extend to the top of the tower. Round to the nearest tenth of a foot.

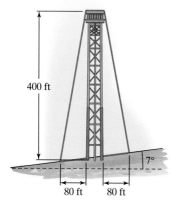

400 ft

7°

80 ft   80 ft

40. The figure shows a 200-foot tower on the side of a hill that forms a 5° angle with the horizontal. Find the length of each of the two guy wires that are anchored 150 feet uphill and downhill from the tower's base and extend to the top of the tower. Round to the nearest tenth of a foot.

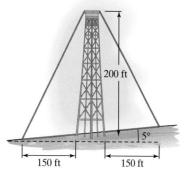

200 ft

5°

150 ft   150 ft

41. A Major League baseball diamond has four bases forming a square whose sides measure 90 feet each. The pitcher's mound is 60.5 feet from home plate on a line joining home plate and second base. Find the distance from the pitcher's mound to first base. Round to the nearest tenth of a foot.

42. A Little League baseball diamond has four bases forming a square whose sides measure 60 feet each. The pitcher's mound is 46 feet from home plate on a line joining home plate and second base. Find the distance from the pitcher's mound to third base. Round to the nearest tenth of a foot.

43. A commercial piece of real estate is priced at $3.50 per square foot. Find the cost, to the nearest dollar, of a triangular lot measuring 240 feet by 300 feet by 420 feet.

44. A commercial piece of real estate is priced at $4.50 per square foot. Find the cost, to the nearest dollar, of a triangular lot measuring 320 feet by 510 feet by 410 feet.

Writing in Mathematics

45. Without using symbols, state the Law of Cosines in your own words.

46. Why can't the Law of Sines be used in the first step to solve an SAS triangle?

47. Describe a strategy for solving an SAS triangle.

48. Describe a strategy for solving an SSS triangle.

49. Under what conditions would you use Heron's formula to find the area of a triangle?

50. Describe an applied problem that can be solved using the Law of Cosines, but not the Law of Sines.

51. The pitcher on your Little League team is studying angles in geometry and has a question. "Coach, suppose I'm on the pitcher's mound facing home plate. I catch a fly ball hit in my direction. If I turn to face first base and throw the ball, through how many degrees should I turn for a direct throw?" Use the information given in Exercise 42 and write an answer to your pitcher's question. Without getting too technical, describe to your pitcher how you obtained this angle.

Critical Thinking Exercises

52. The lengths of the diagonals of a parallelogram are 20 inches and 30 inches. The diagonals intersect at an angle of 35°. Find the lengths of the parallelogram's sides. (*Hint*: Diagonals of a parallelogram bisect one another.)

53. The vertices of a triangle are $A(4, -3)$, $B(2, 1)$, and $C(-2, 4)$. Find the triangle's largest angle to the nearest tenth of a degree.

54. The minute hand and the hour hand of a clock have lengths m inches and h inches, respectively. Determine the distance between the tips of the hands at 10:00 in terms of m and h.

Group Exercise

55. The group should design five original problems that can be solved using the Laws of Sines and Cosines. At least two problems should be solved using the Law of Sines and at least two problems should be solved using the Law of Cosines. At least one problem should be an application problem using the Law of Sines and at least one problem should involve an application using the Law of Cosines. The group should turn in both the problems and their solutions.

SECTION 2.3 *Polar Coordinates*

Objectives

1. Plot points in the polar coordinate system.
2. Find multiple sets of polar coordinates for a given point.
3. Convert a point from polar to rectangular coordinates.
4. Convert a point from rectangular to polar coordinates.
5. Convert an equation from rectangular to polar coordinates.
6. Convert an equation from polar to rectangular coordinates.

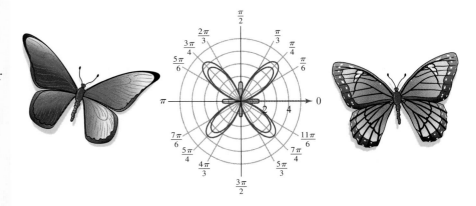

1 Plot points in the polar coordinate system.

Butterflies are among the most celebrated of all insects. It's hard not to notice their beautiful colors and graceful flight. Their symmetry can be explored with trigonometric functions and a system for plotting points called the **polar coordinate system.** In many cases, polar coordinates are simpler and easier to use than rectangular coordinates.

Plotting Points in the Polar Coordinate System

The foundation of the polar coordinate system is a horizontal ray that extends to the right. The ray is called the **polar axis** and is shown in Figure 2.18. The endpoint of the ray is called the **pole.**

A point P in the polar coordinate system is represented by an ordered pair of numbers (r, θ). Figure 2.19 shows $P = (r, \theta)$ in the polar coordinate system.

Figure 2.18

Figure 2.19 Representing a point in the polar coordinate system

- r is the directed distance from P to the pole. (We shall see that r can be positive, negative or zero.)
- θ is an angle from the polar axis to line segment OP. This angle can be measured in degrees or radians. Positive angles are measured counterclockwise from the polar axis. Negative angles are measured clockwise from the polar axis.

We refer to the ordered pair (r, θ) as the **polar coordinates** of P.

Let's look at a specific example. Suppose that the polar coordinates of a point P are $\left(3, \dfrac{\pi}{4}\right)$. Because θ is positive, we locate this point by drawing $\theta = \dfrac{\pi}{4}$ counterclockwise from the polar axis. Then we count out a distance of three units along the terminal side of the angle to reach the point P.

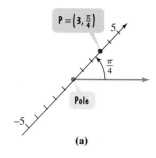

(a)

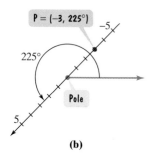

(b)

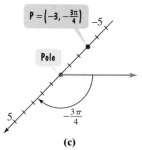

(c)

Figure 2.20 Locating points in polar coordinates

Figure 2.20(a) shows that $(r, \theta) = \left(3, \dfrac{\pi}{4}\right)$ lies three units from the pole on the terminal side of the angle $\theta = \dfrac{\pi}{4}$.

Figure 2.20 illustrates that in a polar coordinate system, a point can be represented in more than one way. In Figure 2.20(b), r is negative and θ is positive: $r = -3$ and $\theta = 225°$. Because θ is positive, we draw a 225° angle counterclockwise from the polar axis. Notice that the point P is not located on the terminal side of θ. Instead, it lies on the ray *opposite the terminal side of θ* at a distance of $|-3|$, or 3, units from the pole. In general, **when r in (r, θ) is negative, a point is located $|r|$ units along the ray opposite the terminal side of θ.**

In Figure 2.20(c), r and θ are both negative: $r = -3$ and $\theta = -\dfrac{3\pi}{4}$. Because θ is negative, we draw a $-\dfrac{3\pi}{4}$ (or $-135°$) angle clockwise from the polar axis.

Because r is negative, the point is located on the ray opposite the terminal side of θ.

Our observations indicate the importance of the sign of r in locating $P = (r, \theta)$ in polar coordinates.

The Sign of r and a Point's Location in Polar Coordinates

The point $P = (r, \theta)$ is located $|r|$ units from the pole. If $r > 0$, the point lies on the terminal side of θ. If $r < 0$, the point lies along the ray opposite the terminal side of θ. If $r = 0$, the point lies at the pole, regardless of the value of θ.

EXAMPLE 1   Plotting Points in a Polar Coordinate System

Plot the points with the following polar coordinates:

a. $(2, 135°)$ **b.** $\left(-3, \dfrac{3\pi}{2}\right)$ **c.** $\left(-1, -\dfrac{\pi}{4}\right)$.

Solution

a. To plot the point $(r, \theta) = (2, 135°)$, begin with the 135° angle. Because 135° is a positive angle, draw $\theta = 135°$ counterclockwise from the polar axis. Now consider $r = 2$. Because $r > 0$, plot the point by going out two units on the terminal side of θ. Figure 2.21(a) shows the point.

b. To plot the point $(r, \theta) = \left(-3, \dfrac{3\pi}{2}\right)$, begin with the $\dfrac{3\pi}{2}$ angle. Because $\dfrac{3\pi}{2}$ is a positive angle, we draw $\theta = \dfrac{3\pi}{2}$ counterclockwise from the polar axis. Now consider $r = -3$. Because $r < 0$, plot the point by going out three units along the ray *opposite* the terminal side of θ. Figure 2.21(b) shows the point.

c. To plot the point $(r, \theta) = \left(-1, -\dfrac{\pi}{4}\right)$, begin with the $-\dfrac{\pi}{4}$ angle. Because $-\dfrac{\pi}{4}$ is a negative angle, draw $\theta = -\dfrac{\pi}{4}$ clockwise from the polar axis.

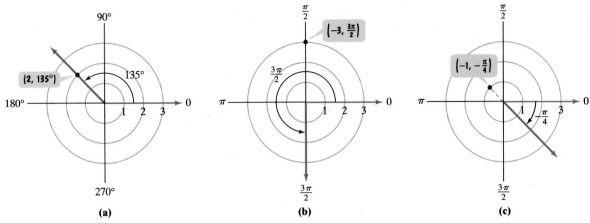

Figure 2.21 Plotting points

Now consider $r = -1$. Because $r < 0$, plot the point by going out one unit along the ray *opposite* the terminal side of θ. Figure 2.21(c) shows the point.

Check Point 1 Plot the points with the following polar coordinates:

a. $(3, 315°)$ **b.** $(-2, \pi)$ **c.** $\left(-1, -\dfrac{\pi}{2}\right)$.

2 Find multiple sets of polar coordinates for a given point.

Multiple Representation of Points in the Polar Coordinate System

In rectangular coordinates, each point (x, y) has exactly one representation. By contrast, any point in polar coordinates can be represented in infinitely many ways. For example,

$$(r, \theta) = (r, \theta + 2\pi) \qquad \text{and} \qquad (r, \theta) = (-r, \theta + \pi).$$

Adding 1 revolution, or 2π radians, to the angle does not change the point's location.

Adding $\frac{1}{2}$ revolution, or π radians, to the angle and replacing r with $-r$ does not change the point's location.

Discovery

Illustrate the statements in the voice balloons by plotting:

a. $\left(1, \dfrac{\pi}{2}\right)$ and $\left(1, \dfrac{5\pi}{2}\right)$.

b. $\left(3, \dfrac{\pi}{4}\right)$ and $\left(-3, \dfrac{5\pi}{4}\right)$.

Thus, to find two other representations for the point (r, θ),

- Add 2π to the angle and do not change r.
- Add π to the angle and replace r with $-r$.

Continually adding or subtracting 2π in either of these representations does not change the point's location.

> **Multiple Representation of Points**
> If n is any integer, the point (r, θ) can be represented as
> $$(r, \theta) = (r, \theta + 2n\pi) \quad \text{or} \quad (r, \theta) = (-r, \theta + \pi + 2n\pi).$$

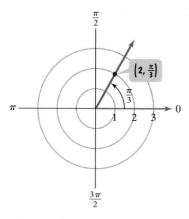

Figure 2.22 Finding other representations of a given point

EXAMPLE 2 Finding Other Polar Coordinates for a Given Point

The point $\left(2, \dfrac{\pi}{3}\right)$ is plotted in Figure 2.22. Find another representation of this point in which:

a. r is positive and $2\pi < \theta < 4\pi$.
b. r is negative and $0 < \theta < 2\pi$.
c. r is positive and $-2\pi < \theta < 0$.

Solution

a. Add 2π to the angle and do not change r.

$$\left(2, \frac{\pi}{3}\right) = \left(2, \frac{\pi}{3} + 2\pi\right) = \left(2, \frac{\pi}{3} + \frac{6\pi}{3}\right) = \left(2, \frac{7\pi}{3}\right)$$

b. Add π to the angle and replace r with $-r$.

$$\left(2, \frac{\pi}{3}\right) = \left(-2, \frac{\pi}{3} + \pi\right) = \left(-2, \frac{\pi}{3} + \frac{3\pi}{3}\right) = \left(-2, \frac{4\pi}{3}\right)$$

c. Subtract 2π from the angle and do not change r.

$$\left(2, \frac{\pi}{3}\right) = \left(2, \frac{\pi}{3} - 2\pi\right) = \left(2, \frac{\pi}{3} - \frac{6\pi}{3}\right) = \left(2, -\frac{5\pi}{3}\right)$$

Check Point 2 Find another representation of $\left(5, \dfrac{\pi}{4}\right)$ in which:

a. r is positive and $2\pi < \theta < 4\pi$.
b. r is negative and $0 < \theta < 2\pi$.
c. r is positive and $-2\pi < \theta < 0$.

Relations between Polar and Rectangular Coordinates

We now consider both polar and rectangular coordinates simultaneously. Figure 2.23 shows the two coordinate systems. The polar axis coincides with the positive x-axis and the pole coincides with the origin. A point P, other than the origin, has rectangular coordinates (x, y) and polar coordinates (r, θ), as indicated in the figure. We wish to find equations relating the two sets of coordinates. From the figure, we see that

$$x^2 + y^2 = r^2$$

$$\sin\theta = \frac{y}{r} \qquad \cos\theta = \frac{x}{r} \qquad \tan\theta = \frac{y}{x}.$$

These relationships hold when P is in any quadrant and when $r > 0$ or $r < 0$.

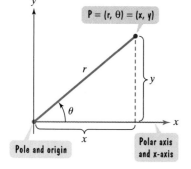

Figure 2.23 Polar and rectangular coordinate systems

Relations between Polar and Rectangular Coordinates

$$x = r\cos\theta$$
$$y = r\sin\theta$$
$$x^2 + y^2 = r^2$$
$$\tan\theta = \frac{y}{x}$$

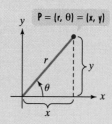

3 Convert a point from polar to rectangular coordinates.

Point Conversion from Polar to Rectangular Coordinates

To convert a point from polar coordinates (r, θ) to rectangular coordinates (x, y), use the formulas $x = r \cos \theta$ and $y = r \sin \theta$.

EXAMPLE 3 Polar-to-Rectangular Point Conversion

Find the rectangular coordinates of the points with the following polar coordinates:

a. $\left(2, \dfrac{3\pi}{2}\right)$ **b.** $\left(-8, \dfrac{\pi}{3}\right)$.

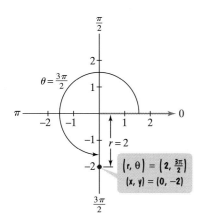

Figure 2.24 Converting $\left(2, \dfrac{3\pi}{2}\right)$ to rectangular coordinates

Solution We find (x, y) by substituting the given values for r and θ into $x = r \cos \theta$ and $y = r \sin \theta$.

a. We begin with the rectangular coordinates of the point $(r, \theta) = \left(2, \dfrac{3\pi}{2}\right)$.

$$x = r \cos \theta = 2 \cos \dfrac{3\pi}{2} = 2 \cdot 0 = 0$$

$$y = r \sin \theta = 2 \sin \dfrac{3\pi}{2} = 2(-1) = -2$$

The rectangular coordinates of $\left(2, \dfrac{3\pi}{2}\right)$ are $(0, -2)$. See Figure 2.24.

b. We now find the rectangular coordinates of the point $(r, \theta) = \left(-8, \dfrac{\pi}{3}\right)$.

$$x = r \cos \theta = -8 \cos \dfrac{\pi}{3} = -8 \left(\dfrac{1}{2}\right) = -4$$

$$y = r \sin \theta = -8 \sin \dfrac{\pi}{3} = -8 \left(\dfrac{\sqrt{3}}{2}\right) = -4\sqrt{3}$$

The rectangular coordinates of $\left(-8, \dfrac{\pi}{3}\right)$ are $\left(-4, -4\sqrt{3}\right)$.

Technology

Some graphing utilities can convert a point from polar coordinates to rectangular coordinates. Consult your manual. The screen on the right verifies the polar-rectangular conversion in Example 3(a). It shows that the rectangular coordinates of $(r, \theta) = \left(2, \dfrac{3\pi}{2}\right)$ are $(0, -2)$.

Notice that the x- and y-coordinates are displayed separately.

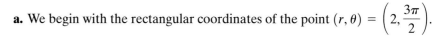

> **Check Point 3** Find the rectangular coordinates of the points with the following polar coordinates:
>
> **a.** $(3, \pi)$ **b.** $\left(-10, \dfrac{\pi}{6}\right)$.

4 Convert a point from rectangular to polar coordinates.

Point Conversion from Rectangular to Polar Coordinates

Conversion from rectangular coordinates (x, y) to polar coordinates (r, θ) is a bit more complicated. Keep in mind that there are infinitely many representations for a point in polar coordinates. If the point (x, y) lies in one of the four quadrants, we will use a representation in which

- r is positive, and
- θ is the smallest positive angle that lies in the same quadrant as (x, y).

These conventions provide the following procedure:

Converting a Point from Rectangular to Polar Coordinates
($r > 0$ and $0 \le \theta < 2\pi$)

1. Plot the point (x, y).

2. Find r by computing the distance from the origin to (x, y): $r = \sqrt{x^2 + y^2}$.

3. Find θ using $\tan\theta = \dfrac{y}{x}$ with θ lying in the same quadrant as (x, y).

EXAMPLE 4 Rectangular-to-Polar Point Conversion

Find polar coordinates of a point whose rectangular coordinates are $(-1, \sqrt{3})$.

Solution We begin with $(x, y) = (-1, \sqrt{3})$ and use our three-step procedure to find a set of polar coordinates (r, θ).

Step 1 Plot the point (x, y). The point $(-1, \sqrt{3})$ is plotted in quadrant II in Figure 2.25.

Step 2 Find r by computing the distance from the origin to (x, y).

$$r = \sqrt{x^2 + y^2} = \sqrt{(-1)^2 + (\sqrt{3})^2} = \sqrt{1 + 3} = \sqrt{4} = 2$$

Step 3 Find θ using $\tan\theta = \dfrac{y}{x}$ with θ lying in the same quadrant as (x, y).

$$\tan\theta = \frac{y}{x} = \frac{\sqrt{3}}{-1} = -\sqrt{3}$$

We know that $\tan\dfrac{\pi}{3} = \sqrt{3}$. Because θ lies in quadrant II,

$$\theta = \pi - \frac{\pi}{3} = \frac{3\pi}{3} - \frac{\pi}{3} = \frac{2\pi}{3}.$$

Polar coordinates of $(-1, \sqrt{3})$ are $(r, \theta) = \left(2, \dfrac{2\pi}{3}\right)$.

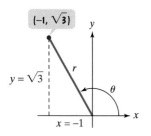

Figure 2.25 Converting $(-1, \sqrt{3})$ to polar coordinates

Technology

The screen shows the rectangular-polar conversion for $(-1, \sqrt{3})$ on a graphing utility. In Example 4, we showed that the polar coordinates of

$(x, y) = (-1, \sqrt{3})$ are $(r, \theta) = \left(2, \dfrac{2\pi}{3}\right)$. Using

$\dfrac{2\pi}{3} \approx 2.09439510239$ verifies that our

conversion is correct. Notice that the r- and (approximate) θ-coordinates are displayed separately.

```
R▶Pr(-1,√(3))
                    2
R▶Pθ(-1,√(3))
          2.094395102
```

Check Point 4   Find polar coordinates of a point whose rectangular coordinates are $(1, -\sqrt{3})$.

If a point (x, y) lies on a positive or negative axis, we use a representation in which

- r is positive, and
- θ is the smallest quadrantal angle that lies on the same positive or negative axis as (x, y).

In these cases, you can find r and θ by plotting (x, y) and inspecting the figure. Let's see how this is done.

EXAMPLE 5   Rectangular-to-Polar Point Conversion

Find polar coordinates of a point whose rectangular coordinates are $(-2, 0)$.

Solution   We begin with $(x, y) = (-2, 0)$ and find a set of polar coordinates (r, θ).

Step 1   **Plot the point (x, y).**   The point $(-2, 0)$ is plotted in Figure 2.26.

Step 2   **Find r, the distance from the origin to (x, y).**   Can you tell by looking at Figure 2.26 that this distance is 2?

$$r = \sqrt{x^2 + y^2} = \sqrt{(-2)^2 + 0^2} = \sqrt{4} = 2$$

Step 3   **Find θ with θ lying on the same positive or negative axis as (x, y).** The point $(-2, 0)$ is on the negative x-axis. Thus, θ lies on the negative x-axis and $\theta = \pi$. Polar coordinates of $(-2, 0)$ are $(2, \pi)$.

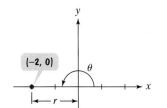

Figure 2.26 Converting $(-2, 0)$ to polar coordinates

Check Point 5   Find polar coordinates of a point whose rectangular coordinates are $(0, -4)$.

5   Convert an equation from rectangular to polar coordinates.

Equation Conversion from Rectangular to Polar Coordinates

A **polar equation** is an equation whose variables are r and θ. Two examples of polar equations are

$$r = \frac{5}{\cos\theta + \sin\theta} \qquad \text{and} \qquad r = \csc\theta.$$

To convert a rectangular equation in x and y to a polar equation in r and θ, replace x with $r \cos \theta$ and y with $r \sin \theta$.

EXAMPLE 6 Converting an Equation from Rectangular to Polar Coordinates

Convert $x + y = 5$ to a polar equation.

Solution   Our goal is to obtain an equation in which the variables are r and θ rather than x and y. We use $x = r \cos \theta$ and $y = r \sin \theta$.

$$x + y = 5 \quad \text{This is the given equation in rectangular coordinates.}$$

$$r \cos \theta + r \sin \theta = 5 \quad \text{Replace x with } r\cos\theta \text{ and y with } r\sin\theta.$$

Thus, the polar equation for $x + y = 5$ is $r \cos \theta + r \sin \theta = 5$. We can express this polar equation in a number of equivalent ways, including an equation that gives r in terms of θ.

$$r(\cos \theta + \sin \theta) = 5 \qquad \text{Factor out r.}$$

$$r = \frac{5}{\cos \theta + \sin \theta} \quad \text{Divide both sides of the equation by } \cos\theta + \sin\theta.$$

Check Point 6   Convert $3x - y = 6$ to a polar equation. Express the polar equation with r in terms of θ.

6 Convert an equation from polar to rectangular coordinates.

Equation Conversion from Polar to Rectangular Coordinates

When we convert an equation from polar to rectangular coordinates, our goal is to obtain an equation in which the variables are x and y rather than r and θ. We use one or more of the following equations:

$$r^2 = x^2 + y^2 \qquad r \cos \theta = x \qquad r \sin \theta = y \qquad \tan \theta = \frac{y}{x}.$$

To use these equations, it is sometimes necessary to do something to the given polar equation. This could include squaring both sides, using an identity, taking the tangent of both sides, or multiplying both sides by r.

EXAMPLE 7 Converting Equations from Polar to Rectangular Form

Convert each polar equation to a rectangular equation in x and y:

a. $r = 3$ **b.** $\theta = \dfrac{\pi}{4}$ **c.** $r = \csc \theta$.

Solution
   a. We use $r^2 = x^2 + y^2$ to convert the polar equation $r = 3$ to a rectangular equation.

$$r = 3 \qquad \text{This is the given polar equation.}$$

$$r^2 = 9 \qquad \text{Square both sides.}$$

$$x^2 + y^2 = 9 \qquad \text{Use } r^2 = x^2 + y^2 \text{ on the left side.}$$

The rectangular equation for $r = 3$ is $x^2 + y^2 = 9$.

b. We use $\tan\theta = \dfrac{y}{x}$ to convert the polar equation $\theta = \dfrac{\pi}{4}$ to a rectangular equation in x and y.

$$\theta = \frac{\pi}{4} \qquad \text{This is the given polar equation.}$$

$$\tan\theta = \tan\frac{\pi}{4} \qquad \text{Take the tangent of both sides.}$$

$$\tan\theta = 1 \qquad \tan\frac{\pi}{4} = 1$$

$$\frac{y}{x} = 1 \qquad \text{Use } \tan\theta = \frac{y}{x} \text{ on the left side.}$$

$$y = x \qquad \text{Multiply both sides by x.}$$

The rectangular equation for $\theta = \dfrac{\pi}{4}$ is $y = x$.

c. We use $r\sin\theta = y$ to convert the polar equation $r = \csc\theta$ to a rectangular equation. To do this, we express the cosecant in terms of the sine.

$$r = \csc\theta \qquad \text{This is the given polar equation.}$$

$$r = \frac{1}{\sin\theta} \qquad \csc\theta = \frac{1}{\sin\theta}$$

$$r\sin\theta = 1 \qquad \text{Multiply both sides by } \sin\theta.$$
$$y = 1 \qquad \text{Use } r\sin\theta = y \text{ on the left side.}$$

The rectangular equation for $r = \csc\theta$ is $y = 1$.

Converting a polar equation to a rectangular equation may be a useful way to develop or check a graph. For example, the graph of the polar equation $r = 3$ consists of all points that are three units from the pole. Thus, the graph is a circle centered at the pole with radius $= 3$. The rectangular equation for $r = 3$, namely $x^2 + y^2 = 9$, has precisely the same graph (see Figure 2.27). We will discuss graphs of polar equations in the next section.

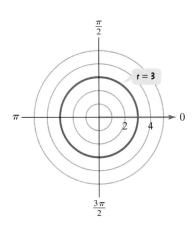

Figure 2.27 The equations $r = 3$ and $x^2 + y^2 = 9$ have the same graph

Check Point 7 Convert each polar equation to a rectangular equation in x and y:

a. $r = 4$ **b.** $\theta = \dfrac{3\pi}{4}$ **c.** $r = \sec\theta$.

EXERCISE SET 2.3

Practice Exercises

In Exercises 1–10, indicate if the point with the given polar coordinates is represented by A, B, C, or D on the graph.

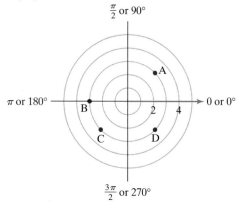

1. $(3, 225°)$ **2.** $(3, 315°)$

3. $\left(-3, \dfrac{5\pi}{4}\right)$ **4.** $\left(-3, \dfrac{\pi}{4}\right)$

5. $(3, \pi)$ **6.** $(-3, 0)$

7. $(3, -135°)$ **8.** $(3, -315°)$

9. $\left(-3, -\dfrac{3\pi}{4}\right)$ **10.** $\left(-3, -\dfrac{5\pi}{4}\right)$

In Exercises 11–20, use a polar coordinate system like the one shown for Exercises 1–10 to plot each point with the given polar coordinates.

11. $(2, 45°)$ **12.** $(1, 45°)$

13. $(3, 90°)$ **14.** $(2, 270°)$

15. $\left(3, \dfrac{4\pi}{3}\right)$ **16.** $\left(3, \dfrac{7\pi}{6}\right)$

17. $(-1, \pi)$ **18.** $\left(-1, \dfrac{3\pi}{2}\right)$

19. $\left(-2, -\dfrac{\pi}{2}\right)$ **20.** $(-3, -\pi)$

In Exercises 21–26, use a polar coordinate system like the one shown for Exercises 1–10 to plot each point with the given polar coordinates. Then find another representation (r, θ) of this point in which:

a. $r > 0, \quad 2\pi < \theta < 4\pi$
b. $r < 0, \quad 0 < \theta < 2\pi$
c. $r > 0, \quad -2\pi < \theta < 0$

21. $\left(5, \dfrac{\pi}{6}\right)$ **22.** $\left(8, \dfrac{\pi}{6}\right)$

23. $\left(10, \dfrac{3\pi}{4}\right)$ **24.** $\left(12, \dfrac{2\pi}{3}\right)$

25. $\left(4, \dfrac{\pi}{2}\right)$ **26.** $(6, \pi)$

In Exercises 27–32, select the representations that do not change the location of the given point.

27. $(7, 140°)$
  a. $(-7, 320°)$ **b.** $(-7, -40°)$
  c. $(-7, 220°)$ **d.** $(7, -220°)$

28. $(4, 120°)$
  a. $(-4, 300°)$ **b.** $(-4, -240°)$
  c. $(4, -240°)$ **d.** $(4, 480°)$

29. $\left(2, -\dfrac{3\pi}{4}\right)$
  a. $\left(2, -\dfrac{7\pi}{4}\right)$ **b.** $\left(2, \dfrac{5\pi}{4}\right)$
  c. $\left(-2, -\dfrac{\pi}{4}\right)$ **d.** $\left(-2, -\dfrac{7\pi}{4}\right)$

30. $\left(-2, \dfrac{7\pi}{6}\right)$
  a. $\left(-2, -\dfrac{5\pi}{6}\right)$ **b.** $\left(-2, -\dfrac{\pi}{6}\right)$
  c. $\left(2, -\dfrac{\pi}{6}\right)$ **d.** $\left(2, \dfrac{\pi}{6}\right)$

31. $\left(-5, -\dfrac{\pi}{4}\right)$
  a. $\left(-5, \dfrac{7\pi}{4}\right)$ **b.** $\left(5, -\dfrac{5\pi}{4}\right)$
  c. $\left(-5, \dfrac{11\pi}{4}\right)$ **d.** $\left(5, \dfrac{\pi}{4}\right)$

32. $(-6, 3\pi)$
  a. $(6, 2\pi)$ **b.** $(6, -\pi)$
  c. $(-6, \pi)$ **d.** $(-6, -2\pi)$

In Exercises 33–40, polar coordinates of a point are given. Find the rectangular coordinates of each point.

33. $(4, 90°)$ **34.** $(6, 180°)$

35. $\left(2, \dfrac{\pi}{3}\right)$ **36.** $\left(2, \dfrac{\pi}{6}\right)$

37. $\left(-4, \dfrac{\pi}{2}\right)$ **38.** $\left(-6, \dfrac{3\pi}{2}\right)$

39. $(7.4, 2.5)$ **40.** $(8.3, 4.6)$

In Exercises 41–48, the rectangular coordinates of a point are given. Find polar coordinates of each point.

41. $(-2, 2)$ **42.** $(2, -2)$

43. $(2, -2\sqrt{3})$ **44.** $(-2\sqrt{3}, 2)$

45. $(-\sqrt{3}, -1)$ **46.** $(-1, -\sqrt{3})$

47. $(5, 0)$ **48.** $(0, -6)$

In Exercises 49–58, convert each rectangular equation to a polar equation.

49. $3x + y = 7$ (Express r in terms of θ.)

50. $x + 5y = 8$ (Express r in terms of θ.)

51. $x = 7$ **52.** $y = 3$

53. $x^2 + y^2 = 9$ **54.** $x^2 + y^2 = 16$

55. $x^2 + y^2 = 4x$ **56.** $x^2 + y^2 = 6x$

57. $y^2 = 6x$ **58.** $x^2 = 6y$

In Exercises 59–72, convert each polar equation to a rectangular equation.

59. $r = 8$ **60.** $r = 10$

61. $\theta = \dfrac{\pi}{2}$ **62.** $\theta = \dfrac{\pi}{3}$

63. $r \sin \theta = 3$ **64.** $r \cos \theta = 7$

65. $r = 4 \csc \theta$ **66.** $r = 6 \sec \theta$

67. $r = \sin \theta$ **68.** $r = \cos \theta$

69. $r = 6 \cos \theta + 4 \sin \theta$ **70.** $r = 8 \cos \theta + 2 \sin \theta$

71. $r^2 \sin 2\theta = 2$ **72.** $r^2 \cos 2\theta = 2$

Application Exercises

Use the figure of the merry-go-round to solve Exercises 73–74. There are four circles of horses. Each circle is three feet from the next circle. The radius of the inner circle is 6 feet.

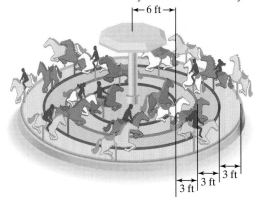

73. If a horse in the outer circle is $\frac{2}{3}$ of the way around the merry-go-round, give its polar coordinates.

74. If a horse in the inner circle is $\frac{5}{6}$ of the way around the merry-go-round, give its polar coordinates.

The wind is blowing at 10 knots. Sailboat racers look for a sailing angle to the 10-knot wind that produces maximum sailing speed. In this application, (r, θ) describes the sailing speed, r, in knots, at an angle θ to the 10-knot wind. Use this information to solve Exercises 75–77.

75. Interpret the polar coordinates: $(6.3, 50°)$.

76. Interpret the polar coordinates: $(7.4, 85°)$.

77. Four points in this 10-knot-wind situation are $(6.3, 50°)$, $(7.4, 85°)$, $(7.5, 105°)$, $(7.3, 135°)$. Based on these points,

which sailing angle to the 10-knot wind would you recommend to a serious sailboat racer? What sailing speed is achieved at this angle?

Writing in Mathematics

78. Explain how to plot (r, θ) if $r > 0$ and $\theta > 0$.

79. Explain how to plot (r, θ) if $r < 0$ and $\theta > 0$.

80. If you are given polar coordinates of a point, explain how to find two additional sets of polar coordinates for the point.

81. Explain how to convert a point from polar to rectangular coordinates. Provide an example with your explanation.

82. Explain how to convert a point from rectangular to polar coordinates. Provide an example with your explanation.

83. Explain how to convert from a rectangular equation to a polar equation.

84. In converting $r = 5$ from a polar equation to a rectangular equation, describe what should be done to both sides of the equation and why this should be done.

85. In converting $r = \sin \theta$ from a polar equation to a rectangular equation, describe what should be done to both sides of the equation and why this should be done.

86. Suppose that (r, θ) describes the sailing speed, r, in knots, at an angle θ to a wind blowing at 20 knots. You have a list of all ordered pairs (r, θ) for integral angles from $\theta = 0°$ to $\theta = 180°$. Describe a way to present this information so that a serious sailboat racer can visualize sailing speeds at different sailing angles to the wind.

Technology Exercises

In Exercises 87–89, polar coordinates of a point are given. Use a graphing utility to find the rectangular coordinates of each point to three decimal places.

87. $\left(4, \dfrac{2\pi}{3}\right)$ **88.** $(5.2, 1.7)$

89. $(-4, 1.088)$

In Exercises 90–92, the rectangular coordinates of a point are given. Use a graphing utility to find polar coordinates of each point to three decimal places.

90. $(-5, 2)$ **91.** $\left(\sqrt{5}, 2\right)$

92. $(-4.308, -7.529)$

Critical Thinking Exercises

93. Prove that the distance, d, between two points with polar coordinates (r_1, θ_1) and (r_2, θ_2) is
$$d = \sqrt{r_1^2 + r_2^2 - 2r_1 r_2 \cos(\theta_2 - \theta_1)}.$$

94. Use the formula in Exercise 93 to find the distance between $\left(2, \dfrac{5\pi}{6}\right)$ and $\left(4, \dfrac{\pi}{6}\right)$. Express the answer in simplified radical form.

95. Convert $r = 4 \cos \theta$ from a polar equation to a rectangular equation. Use the rectangular equation to give the center and the radius.

SECTION 2.4 *Complex Numbers in Polar Form; DeMoivre's Theorem*

Objectives

1. Plot complex numbers in the complex plane.
2. Find the absolute value of a complex number.
3. Write complex numbers in polar form.
4. Convert a complex number from polar to rectangular form.
5. Find products of complex numbers in polar form.
6. Find quotients of complex numbers in polar form.
7. Find powers of complex numbers in polar form.
8. Find roots of complex numbers in polar form.

A magnification of the Mandelbrot set

One of the new frontiers of mathematics suggests that there is an underlying order in things that appear to be random, such as the hiss and crackle of background noises as you tune a radio. Irregularities in the heartbeat, some of them severe enough to cause a heart attack, or irregularities in our sleeping patterns, such as insomnia, are examples of chaotic behavior. Chaos in the mathematical sense does not mean a complete lack of form or arrangement. In mathematics, chaos is used to describe something that appears to be random but is not actually random. The patterns of chaos appear in images like the one shown above, called the Mandelbrot set. Magnified portions of this image yield repetitions of the original structure, as well as new and unexpected patterns. The Mandelbrot set transforms the hidden structure of chaotic events into a source of wonder and inspiration.

The Mandelbrot set is made possible by opening up graphing to include complex numbers in the form $a + bi$, where $i = \sqrt{-1}$. In this section, you will learn how to graph complex numbers and write them in terms of trigonometric functions.

1 Plot complex numbers in the complex plane.

The Complex Plane

We know that a real number can be represented as a point on a number line. By contrast, a complex number $z = a + bi$ is represented as a point (a, b) in a coordinate plane, as shown in Figure 2.28. The horizontal axis of the coordinate plane is called the **real axis.** The vertical axis is called the **imaginary axis.** The coordinate system is called the **complex plane.** Every complex number corresponds to a point in the complex plane and every point in the complex plane corresponds to a complex number. When we represent a complex number as a point in the complex plane, we say that we are **plotting the complex number.**

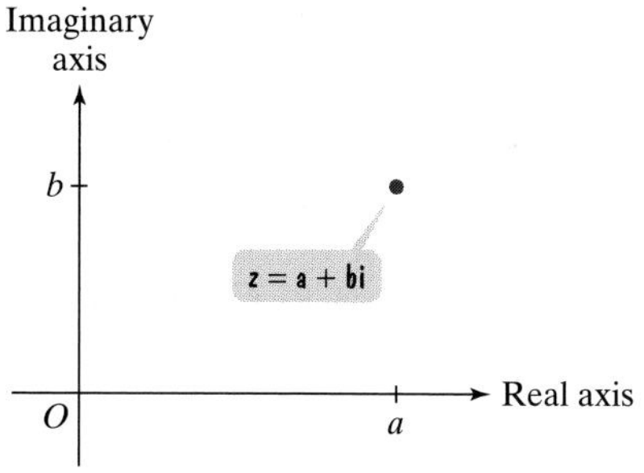

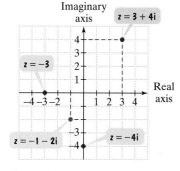

Figure 2.28
Plotting $z = a + bi$ in the complex plane

EXAMPLE 1 Plotting Complex Numbers

Plot each complex number in the complex plane:

a. $z = 3 + 4i$ **b.** $z = -1 - 2i$ **c.** $z = -3$ **d.** $z = -4i$.

Solution See Figure 2.29.

a. We plot the complex number $z = 3 + 4i$ the same way we plot $(3, 4)$ in the rectangular coordinate system. We move three units to the right on the real axis and four units up parallel to the imaginary axis.

b. The complex number $z = -1 - 2i$ corresponds to the point $(-1, -2)$ in the rectangular coordinate system. Plot the complex number by moving one unit to the left on the real axis and two units down parallel to the imaginary axis.

c. Because $z = -3 = -3 + 0i$, this complex number corresponds to the point $(-3, 0)$. We plot -3 by moving three units to the left on the real axis.

d. Because $z = -4i = 0 - 4i$, this number corresponds to the point $(0, -4)$. We plot the complex number by moving four units down on the imaginary axis.

Figure 2.29 Plotting complex numbers

Check Point 1 Plot each complex number in the complex plane:

a. $z = 2 + 3i$ **b.** $z = -3 - 5i$

c. $z = -4$ **d.** $z = -i$.

2 Find the absolute value of a complex number.

Recall that the absolute value of a real number is its distance from 0 on the number line. The **absolute value of the complex number $z = a + bi$,** denoted by $|z|$, is its distance from the origin in the complex plane.

The Absolute Value of a Complex Number

The **absolute value** of the complex number $a + bi$ is

$$|z| = |a + bi| = \sqrt{a^2 + b^2}.$$

EXAMPLE 2 Finding the Absolute Value of a Complex Number

Determine the absolute value of each of the following complex numbers:

a. $z = 3 + 4i$ **b.** $z = -1 - 2i$.

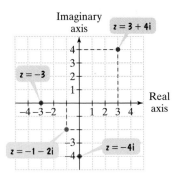

Figure 2.29, repeated

Solution

a. The absolute value of $z = 3 + 4i$ is found using $a = 3$ and $b = 4$.
$$|z| = \sqrt{3^2 + 4^2} = \sqrt{9 + 16} = \sqrt{25} = 5 \quad \text{Use } z = \sqrt{a^2 + b^2} \text{ with } a = 3 \text{ and } b = 4.$$

Thus, the distance from the origin to the point $z = 3 + 4i$, shown in quadrant I in Figure 2.36, is five units.

b. The absolute value of $z = -1 - 2i$ is found using $a = -1$ and $b = -2$.
$$|z| = \sqrt{(-1)^2 + (-2)^2} = \sqrt{1 + 4} = \sqrt{5} \quad \text{Use } z = \sqrt{a^2 + b^2} \text{ with } a = -1 \text{ and } b = -2.$$

Thus, the distance from the origin to the point $z = -1 - 2i$, shown in quadrant III in Figure 2.36, is $\sqrt{5}$ units.

Check Point 2 Determine the absolute value of each of the following complex numbers:

a. $z = 5 + 12i$ b. $2 - 3i$.

3 Write complex numbers in polar form.

Polar Form of a Complex Number

A complex number in the form $z = a + bi$ is said to be in **rectangular form.** Suppose that its absolute value is r. In Figure 2.30, we let θ be an angle in standard position whose terminal side passes through the point (a, b). From the figure, we see that
$$r = \sqrt{a^2 + b^2}.$$

Likewise, according to the definitions of the trigonometric functions,

$$\cos\theta = \frac{a}{r} \qquad \sin\theta = \frac{b}{r} \qquad \tan\theta = \frac{b}{a}.$$
$$a = r\cos\theta \qquad b = r\sin\theta$$

By substituting the expressions for a and b in $z = a + bi$, we write the complex number in terms of trigonometric functions.

$$z = a + bi = r\cos\theta + (r\sin\theta)i = r(\cos\theta + i\sin\theta)$$

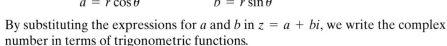

$a = r\cos\theta$ and $b = r\sin\theta$.   Factor out r from each of the two previous terms.

Figure 2.30

The expression $z = r(\cos\theta + i\sin\theta)$ is called the **polar form of a complex number.**

Polar Form of a Complex Number

The complex number $z = a + bi$ is written in **polar form** as
$$z = r(\cos\theta + i\sin\theta),$$
where $a = r\cos\theta$, $b = r\sin\theta$, $r = \sqrt{a^2 + b^2}$, and $\tan\theta = \dfrac{b}{a}$. The value of r is called the **modulus** (plural: moduli) of the complex number z, and the angle θ is called the **argument** of the complex number z, with $0 \le \theta < 2\pi$.

EXAMPLE 3 Writing a Complex Number in Polar Form

Plot $z = -2 - 2i$ in the complex plane. Then write z in polar form.

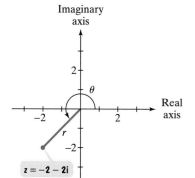

Figure 2.31 Plotting $z = -2 - 2i$ and writing the number in polar form

Solution The complex number $z = -2 - 2i$ is in rectangular form $z = a + bi$, with $a = -2$ and $b = -2$. We plot the number by moving two units to the left on the real axis and two units down parallel to the imaginary axis, as shown in Figure 2.31.

By definition, the polar form of z is $r(\cos \theta + i \sin \theta)$. We need to determine the value for r, the modulus, and the value for θ, the argument. Figure 2.31 shows r and θ. We use $r = \sqrt{a^2 + b^2}$ with $a = -2$ and $b = -2$ to find r.

$$r = \sqrt{a^2 + b^2} = \sqrt{(-2)^2 + (-2)^2} = \sqrt{4 + 4} = \sqrt{8} = \sqrt{4 \cdot 2} = 2\sqrt{2}$$

We use $\tan \theta = \dfrac{b}{a}$ with $a = -2$ and $b = -2$ to find θ.

$$\tan \theta = \frac{b}{a} = \frac{-2}{-2} = 1$$

We know that $\tan \dfrac{\pi}{4} = 1$. Figure 2.31 shows that the argument, θ, lies in quadrant III. Thus,

$$\theta = \pi + \frac{\pi}{4} = \frac{4\pi}{4} + \frac{\pi}{4} = \frac{5\pi}{4}.$$

We use $r = 2\sqrt{2}$ and $\theta = \dfrac{5\pi}{4}$ to write the polar form. The polar form of $z = -2 - 2i$ is

$$z = r(\cos \theta + i \sin \theta) = 2\sqrt{2}\left(\cos \frac{5\pi}{4} + i \sin \frac{5\pi}{4} \right).$$

Check Point 3 Plot $z = -1 - \sqrt{3}i$ in the complex plane. Then write z in polar form. Express the argument in radians.

4 Convert a complex number from polar to rectangular form.

EXAMPLE 4 Writing a Complex Number in Rectangular Form

Write $z = 2(\cos 60° + i \sin 60°)$ in rectangular form.

Solution The complex number $z = 2(\cos 60° + i \sin 60°)$ is in polar form, with $r = 2$ and $\theta = 60°$. We use exact values for $\cos 60°$ and $\sin 60°$ to write the number in rectangular form.

$$2(\cos 60° + i \sin 60°) = 2\left(\frac{1}{2} + i \frac{\sqrt{3}}{2} \right) = 1 + \sqrt{3}i$$

The rectangular form of $z = 2(\cos 60° + i \sin 60°)$ is

$$z = 1 + \sqrt{3}i.$$

Check Point 4 Write $z = 4(\cos 30° + i \sin 30°)$ in rectangular form.

5 Find products of complex numbers in polar form.

Products and Quotients in Polar Form

We can multiply and divide complex numbers fairly quickly if the numbers are expressed in polar form.

> ### Product of Two Complex Numbers in Polar Form
>
> Let $z_1 = r_1 (\cos \theta_1 + i \sin \theta_1)$ and $z_2 = r_2 (\cos \theta_2 + i \sin \theta_2)$ be two complex numbers in polar form. Their product, $z_1 z_2$, is
> $$z_1 z_2 = r_1 r_2 [\cos (\theta_1 + \theta_2) + i \sin (\theta_1 + \theta_2)].$$
> To multiply two complex numbers, multiply moduli and add arguments.

To prove this result, we begin by multiplying using the FOIL method. Then we simplify the product using the sum formulas for sine and cosine.

$$z_1 z_2 = [r_1(\cos \theta_1 + i \sin \theta_1)][r_2(\cos \theta_2 + i \sin \theta_2)]$$

$$= r_1 r_2 (\cos \theta_1 + i \sin \theta_1)(\cos \theta_2 + i \sin \theta_2) \qquad \text{Rearrange factors.}$$

$$= r_1 r_2 (\underset{F}{\cos \theta_1 \cos \theta_2} + \underset{O}{i \cos \theta_1 \sin \theta_2} + \underset{I}{i \sin \theta_1 \cos \theta_2} + \underset{L}{i^2 \sin \theta_1 \sin \theta_2}) \quad \text{Use the FOIL method.}$$

$$= r_1 r_2 [\cos \theta_1 \cos \theta_2 + i(\cos \theta_1 \sin \theta_2 + \sin \theta_1 \cos \theta_2) + i^2 \sin \theta_1 \sin \theta_2] \quad \text{Factor } i \text{ from the second and third terms.}$$

$$= r_1 r_2 [\cos \theta_1 \cos \theta_2 + i(\cos \theta_1 \sin \theta_2 + \sin \theta_1 \cos \theta_2) - \sin \theta_1 \sin \theta_2] \quad i^2 = -1$$

$$= r_1 r_2 [(\cos \theta_1 \cos \theta_2 - \sin \theta_1 \sin \theta_2) + i(\sin \theta_1 \cos \theta_2 + \cos \theta_1 \sin \theta_2)] \quad \text{Rearrange terms.}$$

This is $\cos (\theta_1 + \theta_2)$.   This is $\sin (\theta_1 + \theta_2)$.

$$= r_1 r_2 [\cos(\theta_1 + \theta_2) + i \sin(\theta_1 + \theta_2)]$$

This result gives a rule for finding the product of two complex numbers in polar form. The two parts to the rule are shown in the voice balloons below the product.

$$r_1 r_2 [\cos(\theta_1 + \theta_2) + i \sin(\theta_1 + \theta_2)]$$

Multiply moduli.   Add arguments.

EXAMPLE 5   Finding Products of Complex Numbers in Polar Form

Find the product of the complex numbers. Leave the answer in polar form.

$$z_1 = 4(\cos 50° + i \sin 50°) \qquad z_2 = 7(\cos 100° + i \sin 100°)$$

Solution

$z_1 z_2$

$= \left[4(\cos 50° + i \sin 50°) \right] \left[7(\cos 100° + i \sin 100°) \right]$ Form the product of the given numbers.

$= (4 \cdot 7) \left[\cos(50° + 100°) + i \sin(50° + 100°) \right]$ Multiply moduli and add arguments.

$= 28(\cos 150° + i \sin 150°)$ Simplify.

> **Check Point 5**   Find the product of the complex numbers. Leave the answer in polar form.
>
> $$z_1 = 6(\cos 40° + i \sin 40°) \qquad z_2 = 5(\cos 20° + i \sin 20°)$$

6   Find quotients of complex numbers in polar form.

Using algebraic methods for dividing complex numbers and the difference formulas for sine and cosine, we can obtain a rule for dividing complex numbers in polar form. The proof of this rule can be found in the appendix.

Quotient of Two Complex Numbers in Polar Form

Let $z_1 = r_1(\cos \theta_1 + i \sin \theta_1)$ and $z_2 = r_2(\cos \theta_2 + i \sin \theta_2)$ be two complex numbers in polar form. Their quotient, $\dfrac{z_1}{z_2}$, is

$$\frac{z_1}{z_2} = \frac{r_1}{r_2} \left[\cos(\theta_1 - \theta_2) + i \sin(\theta_1 - \theta_2) \right].$$

To divide two complex numbers, divide moduli and subtract arguments.

EXAMPLE 6   **Finding Quotients of Complex Numbers in Polar Form**

Find the quotient $\dfrac{z_1}{z_2}$ of the complex numbers. Leave the answer in polar form.

$$z_1 = 12\left(\cos \frac{3\pi}{4} + i \sin \frac{3\pi}{4} \right) \qquad z_2 = 4\left(\cos \frac{\pi}{4} + i \sin \frac{\pi}{4} \right)$$

Solution

$$\frac{z_1}{z_2} = \frac{12\left(\cos \dfrac{3\pi}{4} + i \sin \dfrac{3\pi}{4} \right)}{4\left(\cos \dfrac{\pi}{4} + i \sin \dfrac{\pi}{4} \right)}$$ Form the quotient of the given numbers.

$$= \frac{12}{4} \left[\cos\left(\frac{3\pi}{4} - \frac{\pi}{4} \right) + i \sin\left(\frac{3\pi}{4} - \frac{\pi}{4} \right) \right]$$ Divide moduli and subtract arguments.

$$= 3\left(\cos \frac{\pi}{2} + i \sin \frac{\pi}{2} \right)$$ Simplify: $\dfrac{3\pi}{4} - \dfrac{\pi}{4} = \dfrac{2\pi}{4} = \dfrac{\pi}{2}$.

Check Point 6 Find the quotient of the complex numbers. Leave the answer in polar form.

$$z_1 = 50\left(\cos\frac{4\pi}{3} + i\sin\frac{4\pi}{3}\right) \qquad z_2 = 5\left(\cos\frac{\pi}{3} + i\sin\frac{\pi}{3}\right)$$

7 Find powers of complex numbers in polar form.

Powers of Complex Numbers in Polar Form

We can use a formula to find powers of complex numbers if the complex numbers are expressed in polar form. This formula can be illustrated by repeatedly multiplying by $r(\cos\theta + i\sin\theta)$.

$z = r(\cos\theta + i\sin\theta)$	Start with z.
$z \cdot z = r(\cos\theta + i\sin\theta)r(\cos\theta + i\sin\theta)$	Multiply z by $z = r(\cos\theta + i\sin\theta)$.
$z^2 = r^2(\cos 2\theta + i\sin 2\theta)$	Multiply moduli: $r \cdot r = r^2$. Add arguments: $\theta + \theta = 2\theta$.
$z^2 \cdot z = r^2(\cos 2\theta + i\sin 2\theta)r(\cos\theta + i\sin\theta)$	Multiply z^2 by $z = r(\cos\theta + i\sin\theta)$.
$z^3 = r^3(\cos 3\theta + i\sin 3\theta)$	Multiply moduli: $r^2 \cdot r = r^3$. Add arguments: $2\theta + \theta = 3\theta$.
$z^3 \cdot z = r^3(\cos 3\theta + i\sin 3\theta)r(\cos\theta + i\sin\theta)$	Multiply z^3 by $z = r(\cos\theta + i\sin\theta)$.
$z^4 = r^4(\cos 4\theta + i\sin 4\theta)$	Multiply moduli: $r^3 \cdot r = r^4$. Add arguments: $3\theta + \theta = 4\theta$.

Do you see a pattern forming? If n is a positive integer, it appears that z^n is obtained by raising the modulus to the nth power and multiplying the argument by n. The formula for the nth power of a complex number is known as **DeMoivre's Theorem** in honor of the French mathematician Abraham DeMoivre (1667–1754).

> ### DeMoivre's Theorem
> Let $z = r(\cos\theta + i\sin\theta)$ be a complex number in polar form. If n is a positive integer, z to the nth power, z^n, is
> $$z^n = [r(\cos\theta + i\sin\theta)]^n = r^n(\cos n\theta + i\sin n\theta).$$

EXAMPLE 7   Finding the Power of a Complex Number

Find $[2(\cos 10° + i\sin 10°)]^6$. Write the answer in rectangular form, $a + bi$.

Solution   By DeMoivre's Theorem,

$[2(\cos 10° + i \sin 10°)]^6$

$= 2^6[\cos(6 \cdot 10°) + i \sin(6 \cdot 10°)]$ Raise the modulus to the 6th power and multiply the argument by 6.

$= 64(\cos 60° + i \sin 60°)$ Simplify.

$= 64\left(\dfrac{1}{2} + i\dfrac{\sqrt{3}}{2}\right)$ Write the answer in rectangular form.

$= 32 + 32\sqrt{3}i$ Multiply and express the answer in $a + bi$ form.

> **Check Point 7**   Find $[2(\cos 30° + i \sin 30°)]^5$. Write the answer in rectangular form.

EXAMPLE 8   Finding the Power of a Complex Number

Find $(1 + i)^8$ using DeMoivre's Theorem. Write the answer in rectangular form, $a + bi$.

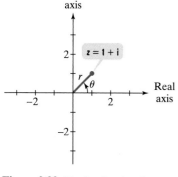

Figure 2.32 Plotting $1 + i$ and writing the number in polar form

Solution   DeMoivre's Theorem applies to complex numbers in polar form. Thus, we must first write $1 + i$ in $r(\cos\theta + i \sin\theta)$ form. Then we can use DeMoivre's Theorem. The complex number $1 + i$ is plotted in Figure 2.32. From the figure we obtain values for r and θ.

$$r = \sqrt{a^2 + b^2} = \sqrt{1^2 + 1^2} = \sqrt{2} \qquad \tan\theta = \dfrac{b}{a} = \dfrac{1}{1} = 1 \quad \text{and} \quad \theta = \dfrac{\pi}{4}$$

Using these values,

$$1 + i = r(\cos\theta + i\sin\theta) = \sqrt{2}\left(\cos\dfrac{\pi}{4} + i\sin\dfrac{\pi}{4}\right).$$

Now we use DeMoivre's Theorem to raise $1 + i$ to the 8th power.

$(1 + i)^8$

$= \left[\sqrt{2}\left(\cos\dfrac{\pi}{4} + i\sin\dfrac{\pi}{4}\right)\right]^8$ Work with the polar form of $1 + i$.

$= (\sqrt{2})^8\left[\cos\left(8 \cdot \dfrac{\pi}{4}\right) + i\sin\left(8 \cdot \dfrac{\pi}{4}\right)\right]$ Apply DeMoivre's Theorem. Raise the modulus to the 8th power and multiply the argument by 8.

$= 16(\cos 2\pi + i\sin 2\pi)$ Simplify: $(\sqrt{2})^8 = (2^{1/2})^8 = 2^4 = 16.$

$= 16(1 + 0i)$ $\cos 2\pi = 1$ and $\sin 2\pi = 0.$

$= 16$ Simplify.

> **Check Point 8**   Find $(1 + i)^4$ using DeMoivre's Theorem. Write the answer in rectangular form.

EXERCISE SET 2.4

Practice Exercises

In Exercises 1–10, plot each complex number and find its absolute value.

1. $z = 4i$ **2.** $z = 3i$

3. $z = 3$ **4.** $z = 4$

5. $z = 3 + 2i$ **6.** $z = 2 + 5i$

7. $z = 3 - i$ **8.** $z = 4 - i$

9. $z = -3 + 4i$ **10.** $z = -3 - 4i$

In Exercises 11–26, plot each complex number. Then write the complex number in polar form. You may express the argument in degrees or radians.

11. $2 + 2i$ **12.** $1 + \sqrt{3}i$ **13.** $-1 - i$

14. $2 - 2i$ **15.** $-4i$ **16.** $-3i$

17. $2\sqrt{3} - 2i$ **18.** $-2 + 2\sqrt{3}i$ **19.** -3

20. -4 **21.** $-3\sqrt{2} - 3\sqrt{3}i$ **22.** $3\sqrt{2} - 3\sqrt{2}i$

23. $-3 + 4i$ **24.** $-2 + 3i$

25. $2 - \sqrt{3}i$ **26.** $1 - \sqrt{5}i$

In Exercises 27–36, write each complex number in rectangular form. If necessary, round to the nearest tenth.

27. $6(\cos 30° + i \sin 30°)$ **28.** $12(\cos 60° + i \sin 60°)$

29. $4(\cos 240° + i \sin 240°)$ **30.** $10(\cos 210° + i \sin 210°)$

31. $8\left(\cos \dfrac{7\pi}{4} + i \sin \dfrac{7\pi}{4}\right)$ **32.** $4\left(\cos \dfrac{5\pi}{6} + i \sin \dfrac{5\pi}{6}\right)$

33. $5\left(\cos \dfrac{\pi}{2} + i \sin \dfrac{\pi}{2}\right)$ **34.** $7\left(\cos \dfrac{3\pi}{2} + i \sin \dfrac{3\pi}{2}\right)$

35. $20(\cos 205° + i \sin 205°)$ **36.** $30(\cos 2.3 + i \sin 2.3)$

In Exercises 37–44, find the product of the complex numbers. Leave answers in polar form.

37. $z_1 = 6(\cos 20° + i \sin 20°)$
$z_2 = 5(\cos 50° + i \sin 50°)$

38. $z_1 = 4(\cos 15° + i \sin 15°)$
$z_2 = 7(\cos 25° + i \sin 25°)$

39. $z_1 = 3\left(\cos \dfrac{\pi}{5} + i \sin \dfrac{\pi}{5}\right)$

$z_2 = 4\left(\cos \dfrac{\pi}{10} + i \sin \dfrac{\pi}{10}\right)$

40. $z_1 = 3\left(\cos \dfrac{5\pi}{8} + i \sin \dfrac{5\pi}{8}\right)$

$z_2 = 10\left(\cos \dfrac{\pi}{16} + i \sin \dfrac{\pi}{16}\right)$

41. $z_1 = \cos \dfrac{\pi}{4} + i \sin \dfrac{\pi}{4}$

$z_2 = \cos \dfrac{\pi}{3} + i \sin \dfrac{\pi}{3}$

42. $z_1 = \cos \dfrac{\pi}{6} + i \sin \dfrac{\pi}{6}$

$z_2 = \cos \dfrac{\pi}{4} + i \sin \dfrac{\pi}{4}$

43. $z_1 = 1 + i$ **44.** $z_1 = 1 + i$
$z_2 = -1 + i$ $z_2 = 2 + 2i$

In Exercises 45–52, find the quotient $\dfrac{z_1}{z_2}$ of the complex numbers. Leave answers in polar form. In Exercises 49–50, express the argument as an angle between $0°$ and $360°$.

45. $z_1 = 20(\cos 75° + i \sin 75°)$
$z_2 = 4(\cos 25° + i \sin 25°)$

46. $z_1 = 50(\cos 80° + i \sin 80°)$
$z_2 = 10(\cos 20° + i \sin 20°)$

47. $z_1 = 3\left(\cos \dfrac{\pi}{5} + i \sin \dfrac{\pi}{5}\right)$

$z_2 = 4\left(\cos \dfrac{\pi}{10} + i \sin \dfrac{\pi}{10}\right)$

48. $z_1 = 3\left(\cos \dfrac{5\pi}{18} + i \sin \dfrac{5\pi}{18}\right)$

$z_2 = 10\left(\cos \dfrac{\pi}{16} + i \sin \dfrac{\pi}{16}\right)$

49. $z_1 = \cos 80° + i \sin 80°$
$z_2 = \cos 200° + i \sin 200°$

50. $z_1 = \cos 70° + i \sin 70°$
$z_2 = \cos 230° + i \sin 230°$

51. $z_1 = 2 + 2i$ **52.** $z_1 = 2 - 2i$
$z_2 = 1 + i$ $z_2 = 1 - i$

In Exercises 53–64, use DeMoivre's Theorem to find the indicated power of the complex number. Write answers in rectangular form.

53. $[4(\cos 15° + i \sin 15°)]^3$

54. $[2(\cos 10° + i \sin 10°)]^3$

55. $[2(\cos 80° + i \sin 80°)]^3$

56. $[2(\cos 40° + i \sin 40°)]^3$

57. $\left[\dfrac{1}{2}\left(\cos \dfrac{\pi}{12} + i \sin \dfrac{\pi}{12}\right)\right]^6$

58. $\left[\dfrac{1}{2}\left(\cos \dfrac{\pi}{10} + i \sin \dfrac{\pi}{10}\right)\right]^5$

59. $\left[\sqrt{2}\left(\cos \dfrac{5\pi}{6} + i \sin \dfrac{5\pi}{6}\right)\right]^4$

60. $\left[\sqrt{3}\left(\cos \dfrac{5\pi}{18} + i \sin \dfrac{5\pi}{18}\right)\right]^6$

61. $(1 + i)^5$ **62.** $(1 - i)^5$

63. $(\sqrt{3} - i)^6$ **64.** $(\sqrt{2} - i)^4$

Writing in Mathematics

65. Explain how to plot a complex number in the complex plane. Provide an example with your explanation.

66. How do you determine the absolute value of a complex number?

67. What is the polar form of a complex number?

68. If you are given a complex number in rectangular form, how do you write it in polar form?

69. If you are given a complex number in polar form, how do you write it in rectangular form?

70. Explain how to find the product of two complex numbers in polar form.

71. Explain how to find the quotient of two complex numbers in polar form.

72. Explain how to find the power of a complex number in polar form.

Technology Exercises

73. Use the rectangular-to-polar feature on a graphing utility to verify any four of your answers in Exercises 11–26. Be aware that you may have to adjust the angle for the correct quadrant.

74. Use the polar-to-rectangular feature on a graphing utility to verify any four of your answers in Exercises 27–36.

Critical Thinking Exercise

75. Prove the rule for finding the quotient of two complex numbers in polar form. Begin the proof as follows, using the conjugate of the denominator:

$$\frac{r_1(\cos\theta_1 + i\sin\theta_1)}{r_2(\cos\theta_2 + i\sin\theta_2)} = \frac{r_1(\cos\theta_1 + i\sin\theta_1)}{r_2(\cos\theta_2 + i\sin\theta_2)} \cdot \frac{(\cos\theta_2 - i\sin\theta_2)}{(\cos\theta_2 - i\sin\theta_2)}.$$

Perform the indicated multiplications. Then use the difference formulas for sine and cosine.

SECTION 2.5 *Vectors*

Objectives

1. Use magnitude and direction to show vectors are equal.

2. Visualize scalar multiplication, vector addition, and vector subtraction as geometric vectors.

3. Represent vectors in the rectangular coordinate system.

4. Perform operations with vectors in terms of **i** and **j**.

5. Find the unit vector in the direction of **v**.

6. Write a vector in terms of its magnitude and direction.

7. Solve applied problems involving vectors.

8. Use a vector to represent a complex number.

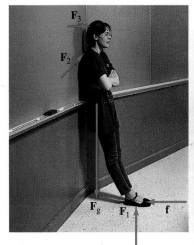

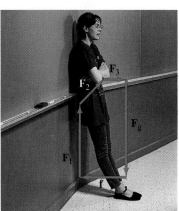

It's been a dynamic lecture, but now that it's over it's obvious that my professor is exhausted. She's slouching motionless against the board and—what's that? The forces acting against her body, including the pull of gravity, are appearing as arrows. I know that mathematics reveals the hidden patterns of the universe, but this is ridiculous. Does the arrangement of the arrows on the right have anything to do with the fact that my wiped-out professor is not sliding down the wall?

This sign shows a distance and direction for each city. Thus, the sign defines a vector for each destination.

Ours is a world of pushes and pulls. For example, suppose you are pulling a cart up a 30° incline, requiring an effort of 100 pounds. This quantity is described by giving its magnitude (a number indicating size, including a unit of measure) and also its direction. The magnitude is 100 pounds and the direction is 30° from the horizontal. Quantities that involve both a magnitude and a direction are called **vector quantities,** or **vectors** for short. Here is another example of a vector:

> You are driving due north at 50 miles per hour. The magnitude is the speed, 50 miles per hour. The direction of motion is due north.

Some quantities can be completely described by giving only their magnitude. For example, the temperature of the lecture room that you just left is 75°. This temperature has magnitude, 75°, but no direction. Quantities that involve magnitude, but no direction, are called **scalar quantities,** or **scalars** for short. Thus, a scalar has only a numerical value. Another example of a scalar is your professor's height, which you estimate to be 5.5 feet.

In the next two sections, we introduce the world of vectors, which literally surround your every move. Because vectors have both nonnegative magnitude and direction, we begin our discussion with directed line segments.

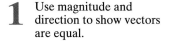

Figure 2.33 A directed line segment from P to Q

Directed Line Segments and Geometric Vectors

A line segment to which a direction has been assigned is called a **directed line segment.** Figure 2.33 shows a directed line segment from P to Q. We call P the **initial point** and Q the **terminal point.** We denote this directed line segment by

$$\overrightarrow{PQ}.$$

The **magnitude** of the directed line segment $\overrightarrow{PQ}$ is its length. We denote this by $\|\overrightarrow{PQ}\|$. Thus, $\|\overrightarrow{PQ}\|$ is the distance from point P to point Q. Because distance is nonnegative, vectors do not have negative magnitudes.

Geometrically, a **vector** is a directed line segment. Vectors are often denoted by boldface letters, such as **v**. If a vector **v** has the same magnitude and the same direction as the directed line segment $\overrightarrow{PQ}$, we write

$$\mathbf{v} = \overrightarrow{PQ}.$$

Because it is difficult to write boldface on paper, use an arrow over a single letter, such as $\vec{v}$, to denote **v**, the vector **v**.

Figure 2.34 shows four possible relationships between vectors **v** and **w**. In Figure 2.34 (a), the vectors have the same magnitude and the same direction, and are said to be *equal*. In general, vectors **v** and **w** are **equal** if they have the *same magnitude* and the *same direction*. We write this as **v** = **w**.

1 Use magnitude and direction to show vectors are equal.

(a) v = **w** because the vectors have the same magnitude and the same direction

(b) Vectors **v** and **w** have the same magnitude, but different directions

(c) Vectors **v** and **w** have the same magnitude, but opposite directions

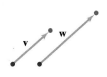

(d) Vectors **v** and **w** have the same direction, but different magnitudes

Figure 2.34 Relationships between vectors

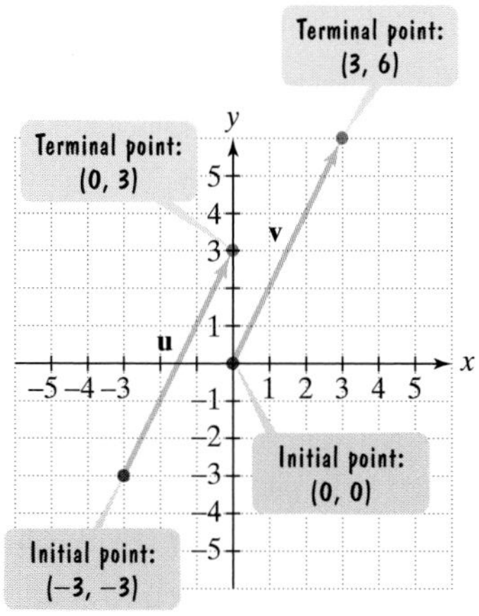

EXAMPLE 1   Showing That Two Vectors Are Equal

Use Figure 2.35 to show that **u** = **v**.

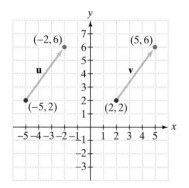

Terminal point:
(3, 6)

Terminal point:
(0, 3)

Initial point:
(0, 0)

Initial point:
(−3, −3)

Figure 2.35

Solution   Equal vectors have the same magnitude and the same direction. Use the distance formula to show that **u** and **v** have the same magnitude.

Magnitude of u

$$\|\mathbf{u}\| = \sqrt{(x_2 - x_1)^2 + (y_2 - y_1)^2} = \sqrt{[0 - (-3)]^2 + [3 - (-3)]^2}$$
$$= \sqrt{3^2 + 6^2} = \sqrt{9 + 36} = \sqrt{45} \quad (\text{or } 3\sqrt{5})$$

Magnitude of v

$$\|\mathbf{v}\| = \sqrt{(x_2 - x_1)^2 + (y_2 - y_1)^2} = \sqrt{(3 - 0)^2 + (6 - 0)^2}$$
$$= \sqrt{3^2 + 6^2} = \sqrt{9 + 36} = \sqrt{45} \quad (\text{or } 3\sqrt{5})$$

Thus, **u** and **v** have the same magnitude: $\|\mathbf{u}\| = \|\mathbf{v}\|$.

One way to show that **u** and **v** have the same direction is to find the slopes of the lines on which they lie.

Line on which u lies

$$m = \frac{y_2 - y_1}{x_2 - x_1} = \frac{3 - (-3)}{0 - (-3)} = \frac{6}{3} = 2$$

Line on which v lies

$$m = \frac{y_2 - y_1}{x_2 - x_1} = \frac{6 - 0}{3 - 0} = \frac{6}{3} = 2$$

Because **u** and **v** are both directed toward the upper right on lines having the same slope, 2, they have the same direction.

Thus, **u** and **v** have the same magnitude and direction, and **u** = **v**.

Check Point 1   Use Figure 2.36 to show that **u** = **v**.

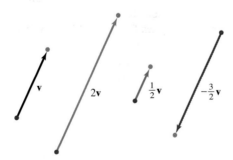

(−2, 6)   (5, 6)

u   **v**

(−5, 2)   (2, 2)

Figure 2.36

A vector can be multiplied by a real number. Figure 2.37 shows three such multiplications: $2\mathbf{v}, \frac{1}{2}\mathbf{v}$, and $-\frac{3}{2}\mathbf{v}$. **Multiplying a vector by any positive real number (except for 1) changes the magnitude of the vector, but not its direction.** This can be seen by the blue and green vectors in Figure 2.37. Compare the black and blue vectors. Can you see that $2\mathbf{v}$ has the same direction as **v** but is twice the magnitude of **v**? Now, compare the black and green vectors: $\frac{1}{2}\mathbf{v}$ has the same direction as **v** but is half the magnitude of **v**.

2   Visualize scalar multiplication, vector addition, and vector subtraction as geometric vectors.

v   **2v** $\frac{1}{2}$**v** $-\frac{3}{2}$**v**

Figure 2.37 Multiplying vector **v** by real numbers

Now compare the black and red vectors in Figure 2.37. **Multiplying a vector by a negative number reverses the direction of the vector.** Notice that $-\frac{3}{2}\mathbf{v}$ has the opposite direction as **v** and is $\frac{3}{2}$ the magnitude of **v**.

The multiplication of the real number, k, and the vector, **v**, is called **scalar multiplication.** We write this product as $k\mathbf{v}$.

Wiped Out, But Not Sliding Down the Wall

The figure shows the sum of five vectors:

$$\mathbf{F}_1 + \mathbf{F}_2 + \mathbf{F}_3 + \mathbf{F}_g + \mathbf{f}.$$

Notice how the terminal point of each vector coincides with the initial point of the vector that's being added to it. The vector sum, from the initial point of $\mathbf{F}_1$ to the terminal point of $\mathbf{f}$, is a single point. The magnitude of a single point is zero. These forces add up to a net force of zero, allowing the professor to be motionless.

3 Represent vectors in the rectangular coordinate system.

Scalar Multiplication

If k is a real number and $\mathbf{v}$ a vector, the vector $k\mathbf{v}$ is called a **scalar multiple** of the vector $\mathbf{v}$. The magnitude and direction of $k\mathbf{v}$ are given as follows:

The vector $k\mathbf{v}$ has a *magnitude* of $|k|\,\|\mathbf{v}\|$. We describe this as the absolute value of k times the magnitude of vector $\mathbf{v}$.

The vector $k\mathbf{v}$ has a *direction* that is:

- the same as the direction of $\mathbf{v}$ if $k > 0$, and
- opposite the direction of $\mathbf{v}$ if $k < 0$.

A geometric method for adding two vectors is shown in Figure 2.38. The sum of $\mathbf{u} + \mathbf{v}$ is called the **resultant vector.** Here is how we find this vector:

1. Position $\mathbf{u}$ and $\mathbf{v}$ so that the terminal point of $\mathbf{u}$ coincides with the initial point of $\mathbf{v}$.
2. The resultant vector, $\mathbf{u} + \mathbf{v}$, extends from the initial point of $\mathbf{u}$ to the terminal point of $\mathbf{v}$.

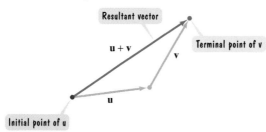

Figure 2.38 Vector addition $\mathbf{u} + \mathbf{v}$; the terminal point of $\mathbf{u}$ coincides with the initial point of $\mathbf{v}$.

The **difference of two vectors, $\mathbf{v} - \mathbf{u}$,** is defined as $\mathbf{v} - \mathbf{u} = \mathbf{v} + (-\mathbf{u})$, where $-\mathbf{u}$ is the scalar multiplication of $\mathbf{u}$ and -1: $-1\mathbf{u}$. The difference $\mathbf{v} - \mathbf{u}$ is shown geometrically in Figure 2.39.

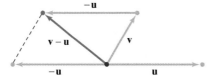

Figure 2.39 Vector subtraction $\mathbf{v} - \mathbf{u}$; the terminal point of $\mathbf{v}$ coincides with the initial point of $-\mathbf{u}$.

Vectors in the Rectangular Coordinate System

As you saw in Example 1, vectors can be shown in the rectangular coordinate system. Now let's see how we can use the rectangular coordinate system to represent vectors. We begin with two vectors that both have a magnitude of 1. Such vectors are called **unit vectors.**

The i and j Unit Vectors

Vector $\mathbf{i}$ is the unit vector whose direction is along the positive x-axis. Vector $\mathbf{j}$ is the unit vector whose direction is along the positive y-axis.

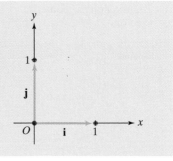

Why are the **i** and **j** unit vectors important? Vectors in the rectangular coordinate system can be represented in terms of **i** and **j**. For example, consider vector **v** with initial point at the origin, $(0, 0)$, and terminal point at $P = (a, b)$. The vector **v** is shown in Figure 2.40. We can represent **v** using **i** and **j** as $\mathbf{v} = a\mathbf{i} + b\mathbf{j}$.

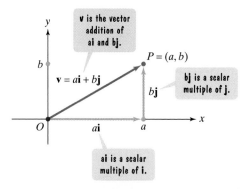

Figure 2.40 Using vector addition, vector **v** is represented as $\mathbf{v} = a\mathbf{i} + b\mathbf{j}$.

Representing Vectors in Rectangular Coordinates

Vector **v**, from $(0, 0)$ to (a, b), is represented as
$$\mathbf{v} = a\mathbf{i} + b\mathbf{j}.$$
The real numbers a and b are called the **scalar components** of **v**. Note that

- a is the **horizontal component** of **v**, and
- b is the **vertical component** of **v**.

The vector sum $a\mathbf{i} + b\mathbf{j}$ is called a **linear combination** of the vectors **i** and **j**. The magnitude of $\mathbf{v} = a\mathbf{i} + b\mathbf{j}$ is given by
$$\|\mathbf{v}\| = \sqrt{a^2 + b^2}.$$

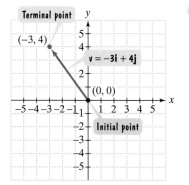

Figure 2.41 Sketching $\mathbf{v} = -3\mathbf{i} + 4\mathbf{j}$ in the rectangular coordinate system

EXAMPLE 2 **Representing a Vector in Rectangular Coordinates and Finding Its Magnitude**

Sketch the vector $\mathbf{v} = -3\mathbf{i} + 4\mathbf{j}$ and find its magnitude.

Solution For the given vector $\mathbf{v} = -3\mathbf{i} + 4\mathbf{j}$, $a = -3$ and $b = 4$. The vector can be represented with its initial point at the origin, $(0, 0)$, as shown in Figure 2.41. The vector's terminal point is then $(a, b) = (-3, 4)$. We sketch the vector by drawing an arrow from $(0, 0)$ to $(-3, 4)$. We determine the magnitude of the vector by using the distance formula. Thus, the magnitude is
$$\|\mathbf{v}\| = \sqrt{a^2 + b^2} = \sqrt{(-3)^2 + 4^2} = \sqrt{9 + 16} = \sqrt{25} = 5.$$

Check Point 2 Sketch the vector $\mathbf{v} = 3\mathbf{i} - 3\mathbf{j}$ and find its magnitude.

The vector in Example 2 was represented with its initial point at the origin. A vector whose initial point is at the origin is called a **position vector.** Any vector in rectangular coordinates whose initial point is not at the origin can be shown to be equal to a position vector. As shown in the following box, this gives us a way to represent vectors between any two points.

Representing Vectors in Rectangular Coordinates

Vector **v** with initial point $P_1 = (x_1, y_1)$ and terminal point $P_2 = (x_2, y_2)$ is equal to the position vector

$$\mathbf{v} = (x_2 - x_1)\mathbf{i} + (y_2 - y_1)\mathbf{j}.$$

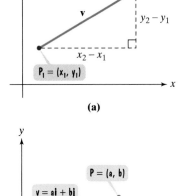

$P_2 = (x_2, y_2)$

v

$y_2 - y_1$

$x_2 - x_1$

$P_1 = (x_1, y_1)$

(a)

$P = (a, b)$

$\mathbf{v} = a\mathbf{i} + b\mathbf{j}$

v

b

a

$(0, 0)$

(b)

Figure 2.42

We can use congruent triangles to derive this formula. Begin with the right triangle in Figure 2.42(a). This triangle shows vector **v** from $P_1 = (x_1, y_1)$ to $P_2 = (x_2, y_2)$. In Figure 2.42(b), we move vector **v**, without changing its magnitude or its direction, so that its initial point is at the origin. Using this position vector in Figure 2.42 (b), we see that

$$\mathbf{v} = a\mathbf{i} + b\mathbf{j}.$$

The equal vectors and the right angles in the right triangles in Figures 2.42(a) and (b) result in congruent triangles. The corresponding sides of these congruent triangles are equal, so that $a = x_2 - x_1$ and $b = y_2 - y_1$. This means that **v** may be expressed as

$$\mathbf{v} = a\mathbf{i} + b\mathbf{j} = (x_2 - x_1)\mathbf{i} + (y_2 - y_1)\mathbf{j}.$$

Horizontal component: x-coordinate of terminal point minus x-coordinate of initial point

Vertical component: y-coordinate of terminal point minus y-coordinate of initial point

Thus, any vector between two points in rectangular coordinates can be expressed in terms of **i** and **j**. In rectangular coordinates, the term *vector* refers to the position vector expressed in terms of **i** and **j** that is equal to it.

EXAMPLE 3   Representing a Vector in Rectangular Coordinates

Let **v** be the vector from initial point $P_1 = (3, -1)$ to terminal point $P_2 = (-2, 5)$. Write **v** in terms of **i** and **j**.

Solution   We identify the values for the variables in the formula.

$$P_1 = (3, -1) \qquad P_2 = (-2, 5)$$

$x_1 \quad y_1 \qquad x_2 \quad y_2$

Using these values, we write **v** in terms of **i** and **j** as follows:

$$\mathbf{v} = (x_2 - x_1)\mathbf{i} + (y_2 - y_1)\mathbf{j} = (-2 - 3)\mathbf{i} + [5 - (-1)]\mathbf{j} = -5\mathbf{i} + 6\mathbf{j}$$

Figure 2.43 shows the vector from $P_1 = (3, -1)$ to $P_2 = (-2, 5)$ represented in terms of **i** and **j** and as a position vector.

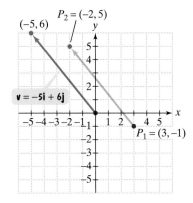

$P_2 = (-2, 5)$

$(-5, 6)$

$\mathbf{v} = -5\mathbf{i} + 6\mathbf{j}$

$P_1 = (3, -1)$

Figure 2.43 Representing the vector from $(3, -1)$ to $(-2, 5)$ as a position vector

Check Point 3   Let **v** be the vector from initial point $P_1 = (-1, 3)$ to $P_2 = (2, 7)$. Write **v** in terms of **i** and **j**.

4 Perform operations with vectors in terms of **i** and **j**.

Operations with Vectors in Terms of i and j

If vectors are expressed in terms of **i** and **j**, we can easily carry out operations such as vector addition, vector subtraction, and scalar multiplication. Recall the geometric definitions of these operations given earlier. Based on these ideas, we can add and subtract vectors using the following procedure:

Adding and Subtracting Vectors in Terms of i and j

If $\mathbf{v} = a_1\mathbf{i} + b_1\mathbf{j}$ and $\mathbf{w} = a_2\mathbf{i} + b_2\mathbf{j}$, then

$$\mathbf{v} + \mathbf{w} = (a_1 + a_2)\mathbf{i} + (b_1 + b_2)\mathbf{j}$$
$$\mathbf{v} - \mathbf{w} = (a_1 - a_2)\mathbf{i} + (b_1 - b_2)\mathbf{j}.$$

EXAMPLE 4   Adding and Subtracting Vectors

If $\mathbf{v} = 5\mathbf{i} + 4\mathbf{j}$ and $\mathbf{w} = 6\mathbf{i} - 9\mathbf{j}$, find:

a. $\mathbf{v} + \mathbf{w}$ **b.** $\mathbf{v} - \mathbf{w}$.

Solution

$$\begin{aligned}
\textbf{a. } \mathbf{v} + \mathbf{w} &= (5\mathbf{i} + 4\mathbf{j}) + (6\mathbf{i} - 9\mathbf{j}) && \text{These are the given vectors.}\\
&= (5 + 6)\mathbf{i} + \left[4 + (-9)\right]\mathbf{j} && \text{Add the horizontal components. Add the}\\
&&& \text{vertical components.}\\
&= 11\mathbf{i} - 5\mathbf{j} && \text{Simplify.}\\
\textbf{b. } \mathbf{v} - \mathbf{w} &= (5\mathbf{i} + 4\mathbf{j}) - (6\mathbf{i} - 9\mathbf{j}) && \text{These are the given vectors.}\\
&= (5 - 6)\mathbf{i} + \left[4 - (-9)\right]\mathbf{j} && \text{Subtract the horizontal components.}\\
&&& \text{Subtract the vertical components.}\\
&= -\mathbf{i} + 13\mathbf{j} && \text{Simplify.}
\end{aligned}$$

Check Point 4   If $\mathbf{v} = 7\mathbf{i} + 3\mathbf{j}$ and $\mathbf{w} = 4\mathbf{i} - 5\mathbf{j}$, find:
     a. $\mathbf{v} + \mathbf{w}$ **b.** $\mathbf{v} - \mathbf{w}$.

How do we perform scalar multiplication if vectors are expressed in terms of **i** and **j**? We use the following procedure to multiply the vector **v** by the scalar k:

Scalar Multiplication with a Vector in Terms of i and j

If $\mathbf{v} = a\mathbf{i} + b\mathbf{j}$ and k is a real number, then the scalar multiplication of the vector **v** and the scalar k is

$$k\mathbf{v} = (ka)\mathbf{i} + (kb)\mathbf{j}.$$

EXAMPLE 5   Scalar Multiplication

If $\mathbf{v} = 5\mathbf{i} + 4\mathbf{j}$, find:

a. $6\mathbf{v}$ **b.** $-3\mathbf{v}$.

Solution

a. $6\mathbf{v} = 6(5\mathbf{i} + 4\mathbf{j})$ *The scalar multiplication is expressed with the given vector.*

$= (6 \cdot 5)\mathbf{i} + (6 \cdot 4)\mathbf{j}$ *Multiply each component by 6.*

$= 30\mathbf{i} + 24\mathbf{j}$ *Simplify.*

b. $-3\mathbf{v} = -3(5\mathbf{i} + 4\mathbf{j})$ *The scalar multiplication is expressed with the given vector.*

$= (-3 \cdot 5)\mathbf{i} + (-3 \cdot 4)\mathbf{j}$ *Multiply each component by -3.*

$= -15\mathbf{i} - 12\mathbf{j}$ *Simplify.*

Check Point 5   If $\mathbf{v} = 7\mathbf{i} + 10\mathbf{j}$, find:

a. $8\mathbf{v}$ **b.** $-5\mathbf{v}$.

EXAMPLE 6   Vector Operations

If $\mathbf{v} = 5\mathbf{i} + 4\mathbf{j}$ and $\mathbf{w} = 6\mathbf{i} - 9\mathbf{j}$, find $4\mathbf{v} - 2\mathbf{w}$.

Solution

$4\mathbf{v} - 2\mathbf{w} = 4(5\mathbf{i} + 4\mathbf{j}) - 2(6\mathbf{i} - 9\mathbf{j})$ *Operations are expressed with the given vectors.*

$= 20\mathbf{i} + 16\mathbf{j} - 12\mathbf{i} + 18\mathbf{j}$ *Perform each scalar multiplication.*

$= (20 - 12)\mathbf{i} + (16 + 18)\mathbf{j}$ *Add horizontal and vertical components to perform the vector addition.*

$= 8\mathbf{i} + 34\mathbf{j}$ *Simplify.*

Check Point 6   If $\mathbf{v} = 7\mathbf{i} + 3\mathbf{j}$ and $\mathbf{w} = 4\mathbf{i} - 5\mathbf{j}$, find $6\mathbf{v} - 3\mathbf{w}$.

Properties involving vector operations resemble familiar properties of real numbers. For example, the order in which vectors are added makes no difference:

$$\mathbf{u} + \mathbf{v} = \mathbf{v} + \mathbf{u}.$$

Does this remind you of the commutative property $a + b = b + a$?

Just as 0 plays an important role in the properties of real numbers, the **zero vector 0** plays exactly the same role in the properties of vectors.

The Zero Vector

The vector whose magnitude is 0 is called the **zero vector, 0.** The zero vector is assigned no direction. It can be expressed in terms of $\mathbf{i}$ and $\mathbf{j}$ using

$$\mathbf{0} = 0\mathbf{i} + 0\mathbf{j}.$$

Properties of vector addition and scalar multiplication are given as follows:

Properties of Vector Addition and Scalar Multiplication

If $\mathbf{u}$, $\mathbf{v}$, and $\mathbf{w}$ are vectors, and c and d are scalars, then the following properties are true.

Vector Addition Properties

1. $\mathbf{u} + \mathbf{v} = \mathbf{v} + \mathbf{u}$ Commutative Property
2. $(\mathbf{u} + \mathbf{v}) + \mathbf{w} = \mathbf{u} + (\mathbf{v} + \mathbf{w})$ Associative Property
3. $\mathbf{u} + \mathbf{0} = \mathbf{0} + \mathbf{u} = \mathbf{u}$ Additive Identity
4. $\mathbf{u} + (-\mathbf{u}) = (-\mathbf{u}) + \mathbf{u} = \mathbf{0}$ Additive Inverse

Scalar Multiplication Properties

1. $(cd)\mathbf{u} = c(d\mathbf{u})$ Associative Property
2. $c(\mathbf{u} + \mathbf{v}) = c\mathbf{u} + c\mathbf{v}$ Distributive Property
3. $(c + d)\mathbf{u} = c\mathbf{u} + d\mathbf{u}$ Distributive Property
4. $1\mathbf{u} = \mathbf{u}$ Multiplicative Identity
5. $0\mathbf{u} = \mathbf{0}$ Multiplication Property
6. $\|c\mathbf{v}\| = |c|\,\|\mathbf{v}\|$

5 Find the unit vector in the direction of $\mathbf{v}$.

Unit Vectors

A unit vector is defined to be a vector whose magnitude is one. In many applications of vectors, it is helpful to find the unit vector that has the same direction as a given vector.

Discovery

To find out why the procedure in the box produces a unit vector, work Exercise 97 in Exercise Set 2.5.

Finding the Unit Vector that Has the Same Direction as a Given Nonzero Vector v

For any nonzero vector $\mathbf{v}$, the vector

$$\frac{\mathbf{v}}{\|\mathbf{v}\|}$$

is the unit vector that has the same direction as $\mathbf{v}$. To find this vector, divide $\mathbf{v}$ by its magnitude.

EXAMPLE 7   Finding a Unit Vector

Find the unit vector in the same direction as $\mathbf{v} = 5\mathbf{i} - 12\mathbf{j}$. Then verify that the vector has magnitude 1.

Solution   We find the unit vector in the same direction as $\mathbf{v}$ by dividing $\mathbf{v}$ by its magnitude. We first find the magnitude of $\mathbf{v}$.

$$\|\mathbf{v}\| = \sqrt{a^2 + b^2} = \sqrt{5^2 + (-12)^2} = \sqrt{25 + 144} = \sqrt{169} = 13$$

The unit vector in the same direction as **v** is

$$\frac{\mathbf{v}}{\|\mathbf{v}\|} = \frac{5\mathbf{i} - 12\mathbf{j}}{13} = \frac{5}{13}\mathbf{i} - \frac{12}{13}\mathbf{j}. \quad \text{This is the scalar multiplication of } \mathbf{v} \text{ and } \frac{1}{13}.$$

Now we must verify that the magnitude of this vector is 1. Recall that the magnitude of $a\mathbf{i} + b\mathbf{j}$ is $\sqrt{a^2 + b^2}$. Thus, the magnitude of $\frac{5}{13}\mathbf{i} - \frac{12}{13}\mathbf{j}$ is

$$\sqrt{\left(\frac{5}{13}\right)^2 + \left(-\frac{12}{13}\right)^2} = \sqrt{\frac{25}{169} + \frac{144}{169}} = \sqrt{\frac{169}{169}} = \sqrt{1} = 1.$$

Check Point 7 Find the unit vector in the same direction as $\mathbf{v} = 4\mathbf{i} - 3\mathbf{j}$. Then verify that the vector has magnitude 1.

6 Write a vector in terms of its magnitude and direction.

Writing a Vector in Terms of Its Magnitude and Direction

Consider the vector $\mathbf{v} = a\mathbf{i} + b\mathbf{j}$. The components a and b can be expressed in terms of the magnitude of **v** and the angle θ that **v** makes with the positive x-axis. This angle is called the **direction angle** of **v** and is shown in Figure 2.44. By the definitions of sine and cosine, we have

$$\cos \theta = \frac{a}{\|\mathbf{v}\|} \qquad \text{and} \qquad \sin \theta = \frac{b}{\|\mathbf{v}\|}$$

$$a = \|\mathbf{v}\| \cos \theta \qquad\qquad b = \|\mathbf{v}\| \sin \theta.$$

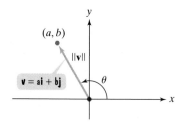

Figure 2.44 Expressing a vector in terms of its magnitude, $\|\mathbf{v}\|$, and its direction angle, θ

Thus,

$$\mathbf{v} = a\mathbf{i} + b\mathbf{j} = \|\mathbf{v}\| \cos \theta \mathbf{i} + \|\mathbf{v}\| \sin \theta \mathbf{j}.$$

Writing a Vector in Terms of Its Magnitude and Direction

Let **v** be a nonzero vector. If θ is the direction angle measured from the positive x-axis to **v**, then the vector can be expressed in terms of its magnitude and direction angle as

$$\mathbf{v} = \|\mathbf{v}\| \cos \theta \mathbf{i} + \|\mathbf{v}\| \sin \theta \mathbf{j}.$$

A vector that represents the direction and speed of an object in motion is called a **velocity vector.** In Example 8, we express a wind's velocity vector in terms of the wind's magnitude and direction.

EXAMPLE 8 Writing a Vector Whose Magnitude and Direction Are Given

The wind is blowing at 20 miles per hour in the direction N30°W. Express its velocity as a vector **v**.

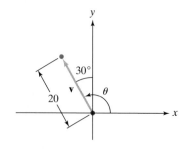

Figure 2.45 Vector **v** represents a wind blowing at 20 miles per hour in the direction N30°W.

Solution The vector **v** is shown in Figure 2.45. The vector's direction angle, from the positive x-axis to **v**, is

$$\theta = 90° + 30° = 120°.$$

Because the wind is blowing at 20 miles per hour, the magnitude of **v** is 20 miles per hour: $\|\mathbf{v}\| = 20$. Thus,

$$\mathbf{v} = \|\mathbf{v}\| \cos\theta\mathbf{i} + \|\mathbf{v}\| \sin\theta\mathbf{j} \qquad \textit{Use the formula for a vector in terms of magnitude and direction.}$$

$$= 20\cos 120°\mathbf{i} + 20\sin 120°\mathbf{j} \qquad \|\mathbf{v}\| = 20 \text{ and } \theta = 120°.$$

$$= 20\left(-\tfrac{1}{2}\right)\mathbf{i} + 20\left(\frac{\sqrt{3}}{2}\right)\mathbf{j} \qquad \cos 120° = -\frac{1}{2} \text{ and } \sin 120° = \frac{\sqrt{3}}{2}.$$

$$= -10\mathbf{i} + 10\sqrt{3}\mathbf{j} \qquad \textit{Simplify.}$$

The wind's velocity can be expressed in terms of **i** and **j** as $\mathbf{v} = -10\mathbf{i} + 10\sqrt{3}\mathbf{j}$.

Check Point 8   The jet stream is blowing at 60 miles per hour in the direction N45°E. Express its velocity as a vector **v** in terms of **i** and **j**.

7 Solve applied problems involving vectors.

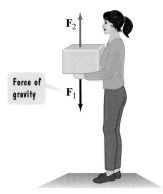

Force of gravity

Figure 2.46 Force vectors

Applications

Many physical concepts can be represented by vectors. A vector that represents a pull or push of some type is called a **force vector.** If you are holding a 10-pound package, two force vectors are involved. The force of gravity is exerting a force of magnitude 10 pounds directly downward. This force is shown by vector $\mathbf{F}_1$ in Figure 2.46. Assuming there is no upward or downward movement of the package, you are exerting a force of magnitude 10 pounds directly upward. This force is shown by vector $\mathbf{F}_2$ in Figure 2.46. It has the same magnitude as the force exerted on your package by gravity, but it acts in the opposite direction.

If $\mathbf{F}_1$ and $\mathbf{F}_2$ are two forces acting on an object, the net effect is the same as if just the resultant force, $\mathbf{F}_1 + \mathbf{F}_2$, acted on the object. If the object is not moving, as is the case with your 10-pound package, the vector sum of all forces is the zero vector.

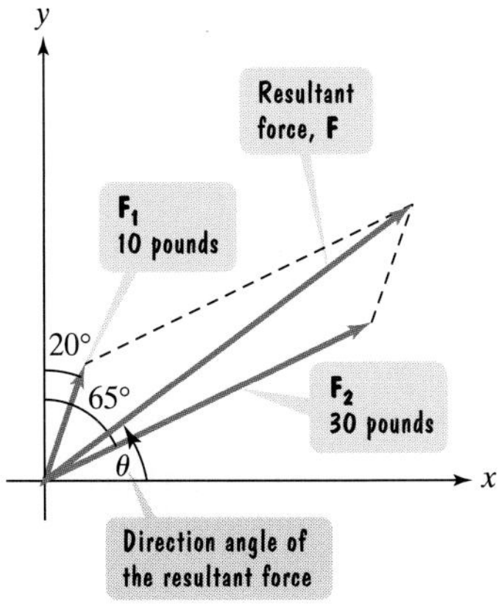

EXAMPLE 9   Finding the Resultant Force

Two forces, $\mathbf{F}_1$ and $\mathbf{F}_2$, of magnitude 10 and 30 pounds, respectively, act on an object. The direction of $\mathbf{F}_1$ is N20°E and the direction of $\mathbf{F}_2$ is N65°E. Find the magnitude and the direction of the resultant force. Express the direction angle to the nearest tenth of a degree.

Solution   The vectors $\mathbf{F}_1$ and $\mathbf{F}_2$ are shown in Figure 2.47. The direction angle for $\mathbf{F}_1$, from the positive x-axis to the vector, is 90°– 20°, or 70°. We express $\mathbf{F}_1$ using the formula for a vector in terms of its magnitude and direction.

$$\mathbf{F}_1 = \|\mathbf{F}_1\| \cos\theta\mathbf{i} + \|\mathbf{F}_1\| \sin\theta\mathbf{j}$$

$$= 10\cos 70°\mathbf{i} + 10\sin 70°\mathbf{j} \qquad \|\mathbf{F}_1\| = 10 \text{ and } \theta = 70°.$$

$$\approx 3.42\mathbf{i} + 9.40\mathbf{j} \qquad \textit{Use a calculator.}$$

Figure 2.47

Figure 2.47 illustrates that the direction angle for $\mathbf{F}_2$, from the positive x-axis to the vector, is $90° - 65°$, or $25°$. We express $\mathbf{F}_2$ using the formula for a vector in terms of its magnitude and direction.

$$\mathbf{F}_2 = \|\mathbf{F}_2\| \cos\theta\mathbf{i} + \|\mathbf{F}_2\| \sin\theta\mathbf{j}$$

$$= 30\cos 25°\mathbf{i} + 30\sin 25°\mathbf{j} \qquad \|\mathbf{F}_2\| = 30 \text{ and } \theta = 25°.$$

$$\approx 27.19\mathbf{i} + 12.68\mathbf{j} \qquad \text{Use a calculator.}$$

The resultant force, $\mathbf{F}$, is $\mathbf{F}_1 + \mathbf{F}_2$. Thus,

$$\mathbf{F} = \mathbf{F}_1 + \mathbf{F}_2$$

$$\approx (3.42\mathbf{i} + 9.40\mathbf{j}) + (27.19\mathbf{i} + 12.68\mathbf{j}) \quad \text{Use } \mathbf{F}_1 \text{ and } \mathbf{F}_2, \text{ found above.}$$

$$= (3.42 + 27.19)\mathbf{i} + (9.40 + 12.68)\mathbf{j} \quad \text{Add the horizontal components. Add the vertical components. Simplify.}$$

$$= 30.61\mathbf{i} + 22.08\mathbf{j}.$$

Now that we have the resultant force vector, $\mathbf{F}$, we can find its magnitude.

$$\|\mathbf{F}\| = \sqrt{a^2 + b^2} = \sqrt{(30.61)^2 + (22.08)^2} \approx 37.74$$

The magnitude of the resultant force is approximately 37.74 pounds.

To find θ, the direction angle of the resultant force, we can use

$$\cos\theta = \frac{a}{\|\mathbf{F}\|} \quad \text{or} \quad \sin\theta = \frac{b}{\|\mathbf{F}\|}.$$

Using the first formula, we obtain

$$\cos\theta = \frac{a}{\|\mathbf{F}\|} \approx \frac{30.61}{37.74}. \qquad \text{Recall that the resultant force is } \mathbf{F} = 30.61\mathbf{i} + 22.08\mathbf{j}.$$

Thus,

$$\theta = \cos^{-1}\left(\frac{30.61}{37.74}\right) \approx 35.8°. \qquad \text{Use a calculator.}$$

The direction angle of the resultant force is approximately $35.8°$.

In summary, the two given forces are equivalent to a single force of approximately 37.74 pounds with a direction angle of approximately $35.8°$.

Study Tip

If $\mathbf{F} = a\mathbf{i} + b\mathbf{j}$, the direction angle, θ, of $\mathbf{F}$ can also be found using

$$\tan\theta = \frac{b}{a}.$$

Check Point 9

Two forces, $\mathbf{F}_1$ and $\mathbf{F}_2$, of magnitude 30 and 60 pounds, respectively, act on an object. The direction of $\mathbf{F}_1$ is N10°E and the direction of $\mathbf{F}_2$ is N60°E. Find the magnitude, to the nearest hundredth of a pound, and the direction angle, to the nearest tenth of a degree, of the resultant force.

We have seen that velocity vectors represent the direction and speed of moving objects. Boats moving in currents and airplanes flying in winds are situations in which two velocity vectors act simultaneously. For example, suppose **v** represents the velocity of a plane in still air. Further suppose that **w** represents the velocity of the wind. The actual speed and direction of the plane is given by the vector **v** + **w**. This resultant vector describes the plane's speed and direction relative to the ground. Problems involving the resultant velocity of a boat or plane are solved using the same method that we used in Example 9 to find a single resultant force equivalent to two given forces.

8 Use a vector to represent a complex number

Using Vectors to Represent Complex Numbers

Because of the similarity in their component-wise additions,

Complex Numbers:	**Vectors:**
$z_1 = a_1 + b_1 i$	$\mathbf{v}_1 = a_1\mathbf{i} + b_1\mathbf{j}$
$z_2 = a_2 + b_2 i$	$\mathbf{v}_2 = a_2\mathbf{i} + b_2\mathbf{j}$
$z_1 + z_2 = (a_1 + a_2) + (b_1 + b_2)i$	$\mathbf{v}_1 + \mathbf{v}_2 = (a_1 + a_2)\mathbf{i} + (b_1 + b_2)\mathbf{j}$

Study Tip

It is important to remember that although vectors and complex numbers add in the same way, the methods by which we multiply and divide each of these mathematical entities is very different.

vectors are often used to represent complex numbers. When using this representation, the vector is drawn from the origin to the corresponding complex point and expressed in terms of the point's real and imaginary components as in Figure 2.48.

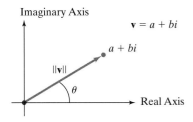

Figure 2.48

The length of the vector corresponds to the magnitude of the complex number that the vector represents:

Finding the Length of the Vector

$$\|\mathbf{v}\| = \sqrt{a^2 + b^2}$$

and the orientation (direction angle) of the vector is found from the real and imaginary components via

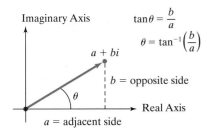

Figure 2.49

Finding the Orientation (Direction Angle) of the Vector

$$\theta = \tan^{-1}\left(\frac{b}{a}\right)$$

When using a vector to represent a complex number, the length and orientation of the vector are often used to express the vector as

$$\mathbf{v} = \|\mathbf{v}\| \angle \theta$$

EXAMPLE 10

Find the length and orientation of the vector that represents the complex number $3 + 4i$.

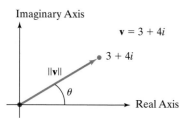

Figure 2.50

Solution We first find the length of the vector using the real and imaginary components of the complex number.

$$\|\mathbf{v}\| = \sqrt{a^2 + b^2}$$
$$\|\mathbf{v}\| = \sqrt{3^2 + 4^2}$$
$$\|\mathbf{v}\| = \sqrt{25}$$
$$\|\mathbf{v}\| = 5$$

Next we find the orientation of the vector:

$$\theta = \tan^{-1}\left(\frac{b}{a}\right)$$
$$\theta = \tan^{-1}\left(\frac{4}{3}\right)$$
$$\theta = 53.13°$$

Thus,

$$\mathbf{v} = 5\angle 53.13°$$

Check Point 10 Find the length and orientation of the vector that represents the complex number $1 + i$.

The real and imaginary components of the vector can be found using the magnitude and direction angle of the vector as we did on page 140.

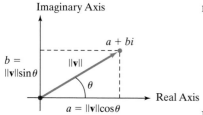

Figure 2.51

$$\cos\theta = \frac{a}{\|\mathbf{v}\|} \qquad \text{and} \qquad \sin\theta = \frac{b}{\|\mathbf{v}\|}$$
$$a = \|\mathbf{v}\|\cos\theta \qquad\qquad b = \|\mathbf{v}\|\sin\theta$$

Using these relations, the vector can be written as

$$\mathbf{v} = \|\mathbf{v}\|\cos\theta + (\|\mathbf{v}\|\sin\theta)i$$

EXAMPLE 11

Find the real and imaginary components of the complex number represented by the vector in Figure 2.52.

Solution Using the length of the vector, 2, and the orientation of the vector, 30°, the real and imaginary components become

$$a = \|\mathbf{v}\|\cos\theta \qquad\qquad b = \|\mathbf{v}\|\sin\theta$$
$$a = 2\cos30° \qquad \text{and} \qquad b = 2\sin30°$$
$$a = 1.73 \qquad\qquad b = 1.00$$

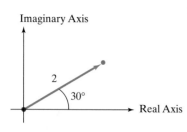

Figure 2.52

Check Point 11 Find the real and imaginary components of the complex number represented by a vector of length 4 oriented at 40°.

EXERCISE SET 2.5

Practice Exercises

In Exercises 1–4, **u** *and* **v** *have the same direction. In each exercise:* **a.** *Find* $\|\mathbf{u}\|$. **b.** *Find* $\|\mathbf{v}\|$. **c.** *Is* **u** = **v**? *Explain.*

1.

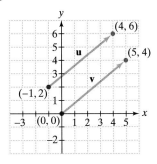

2.

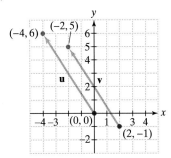

3.

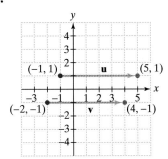

4.

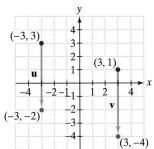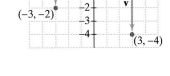

In Exercises 5–12, sketch each vector as a position vector and find its magnitude.

5. $\mathbf{v} = 3\mathbf{i} + \mathbf{j}$ **6.** $\mathbf{v} = 2\mathbf{i} + 3\mathbf{j}$
7. $\mathbf{v} = \mathbf{i} - \mathbf{j}$ **8.** $\mathbf{v} = -\mathbf{i} - \mathbf{j}$
9. $\mathbf{v} = -6\mathbf{i} - 2\mathbf{j}$ **10.** $\mathbf{v} = 5\mathbf{i} - 2\mathbf{j}$
11. $\mathbf{v} = -4\mathbf{i}$ **12.** $\mathbf{v} = -5\mathbf{j}$

In Exercises 13–20, let **v** *be the vector from initial point P_1 to terminal point P_2. Write* **v** *in terms of* **i** *and* **j**.

13. $P_1 = (-4, -4), P_2 = (6, 2)$
14. $P_1 = (2, -5), P_2 = (-6, 6)$
15. $P_1 = (-8, 6), P_2 = (-2, 3)$
16. $P_1 = (-7, -4), P_2 = (0, -2)$
17. $P_1 = (-1, 7), P_2 = (-7, -7)$
18. $P_1 = (-1, 6), P_2 = (7, -5)$
19. $P_1 = (-3, 4), P_2 = (6, 4)$
20. $P_1 = (4, -5), P_2 = (4, 3)$

In Exercises 21–38, let
$$\mathbf{u} = 2\mathbf{i} - 5\mathbf{j}, \mathbf{v} = -3\mathbf{i} + 7\mathbf{j}, \text{ and } \mathbf{w} = -\mathbf{i} - 6\mathbf{j}.$$

Find each specified vector or scalar.

21. $\mathbf{u} + \mathbf{v}$ **22.** $\mathbf{v} + \mathbf{w}$ **23.** $\mathbf{u} - \mathbf{v}$
24. $\mathbf{v} - \mathbf{w}$ **25.** $\mathbf{v} - \mathbf{u}$ **26.** $\mathbf{w} - \mathbf{v}$
27. $5\mathbf{v}$ **28.** $6\mathbf{v}$ **29.** $-4\mathbf{w}$
30. $-7\mathbf{w}$ **31.** $3\mathbf{w} + 2\mathbf{v}$ **32.** $3\mathbf{u} + 4\mathbf{v}$
33. $3\mathbf{v} - 4\mathbf{w}$ **34.** $4\mathbf{w} - 3\mathbf{v}$ **35.** $\|2\mathbf{u}\|$
36. $\|-2\mathbf{u}\|$ **37.** $\|\mathbf{w} - \mathbf{u}\|$ **38.** $\|\mathbf{u} - \mathbf{w}\|$

In Exercises 39–46, find the unit vector that has the same direction as the vector **v**.

39. $\mathbf{v} = 6\mathbf{i}$ **40.** $\mathbf{v} = -5\mathbf{j}$
41. $\mathbf{v} = 3\mathbf{i} - 4\mathbf{j}$ **42.** $\mathbf{v} = 8\mathbf{i} - 6\mathbf{j}$
43. $\mathbf{v} = 3\mathbf{i} - 2\mathbf{j}$ **44.** $\mathbf{v} = 4\mathbf{i} - 2\mathbf{j}$
45. $\mathbf{v} = \mathbf{i} + \mathbf{j}$ **46.** $\mathbf{v} = \mathbf{i} - \mathbf{j}$

In Exercises 47–52, write the vector **v** *in terms of* **i** *and* **j** *whose magnitude* $\|\mathbf{v}\|$ *and direction angle θ are given.*

47. $\|\mathbf{v}\| = 6, \quad \theta = 30°$ **48.** $\|\mathbf{v}\| = 8, \quad \theta = 45°$
49. $\|\mathbf{v}\| = 12, \quad \theta = 225°$ **50.** $\|\mathbf{v}\| = 10, \quad \theta = 330°$
51. $\|\mathbf{v}\| = \frac{1}{2}, \quad \theta = 113°$ **52.** $\|\mathbf{v}\| = \frac{1}{4}, \quad \theta = 200°$

In Exercises 53–56, find the length and direction angle for the vector that would represent each of the following complex numbers.

53. $1 + 2i$

54. $4i$

55. $-5i$

56. $2 + \sqrt{3}i$

In Exercises 57–60, find the real and imaginary components of the complex numbers represented by each of the vectors.

57. length: 5, direction angle: $45°$

58. length: 12, direction angle: $-30°$

59. $6\angle 50°$

60. $-4\angle -60°$

Application Exercises

In Exercises 61–64, a vector is described. Express the vector in terms of **i** *and* **j**. *If exact values are not possible, round components to the nearest tenth.*

61. A quarterback releases a football with a speed of 44 feet per second at an angle of $30°$ with the horizontal.

62. A child pulls a sled along level ground by exerting a force of 30 pounds on a handle that makes an angle of $45°$ with the ground.

63. A plane approaches a runway at 150 miles per hour at an angle of $8°$ with the runway.

64. A plane with an airspeed of 450 miles per hour is flying in the direction N35°W.

Vectors are used in computer graphics to determine lengths of shadows over flat surfaces. The length of the shadow for **v** *in the figure shown is the absolute value of the vector's horizontal component. In Exercises 65–66, the magnitude and direction angle of* **v** *are given. Write* **v** *in terms of* **i** *and* **j**. *Then find the length of the shadow to the nearest tenth of an inch.*

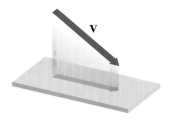

65. $\|\mathbf{v}\| = 1.5$ inches, $\theta = 25°$

66. $\|\mathbf{v}\| = 1.8$ inches, $\theta = 40°$

67. The magnitude and direction of two forces acting on an object are 70 pounds, S56°E, and 50 pounds, N72°E, respectively. Find the magnitude, to the nearest hundredth of a pound, and the direction angle, to the nearest tenth of a degree, of the resultant force.

68. The magnitude and direction exerted by two tugboats towing a ship are 4200 pounds, N65°E, and 3000 pounds, S58°E, respectively. Find the magnitude, to the nearest pound, and the direction angle, to the nearest tenth of a degree, of the resultant force.

The figure shows a box being pulled up a ramp inclined at $18°$ from the horizontal.

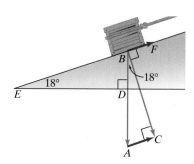

Use the following information to solve Exercises 69–70.

$$\overrightarrow{BA} = \text{force of gravity}$$
$$\|\overrightarrow{BA}\| = \text{weight of the box}$$
$$\|\overrightarrow{AC}\| = \text{magnitude of the force needed to pull the box up the ramp}$$
$$\|\overrightarrow{BC}\| = \text{magnitude of the force of the box against the ramp}$$

69. If the box weighs 100 pounds, find the magnitude of the force needed to pull it up the ramp.

70. If a force of 30 pounds is needed to pull the box up the ramp, find the weight of the box.

The forces $\mathbf{F}_1, \mathbf{F}_2, \mathbf{F}_3, \dots, \mathbf{F}_n$ *acting on an object are in* **equilibrium** *if the resultant force is the zero vector:*

$$\mathbf{F}_1 + \mathbf{F}_2 + \mathbf{F}_3 + \cdots + \mathbf{F}_n = \mathbf{0}.$$

In Exercises 71–79, the given forces are acting on an object.
  a. *Find the resultant force.*
  b. *What additional force is required for the given forces to be in equilibrium?*

71. $\mathbf{F}_1 = 3\mathbf{i} - 5\mathbf{j},\quad \mathbf{F}_2 = 6\mathbf{i} + 2\mathbf{j}$

72. $\mathbf{F}_1 = -2\mathbf{i} + 3\mathbf{j},\quad \mathbf{F}_2 = \mathbf{i} - \mathbf{j},\quad \mathbf{F}_3 = 5\mathbf{i} - 12\mathbf{j}$

73.

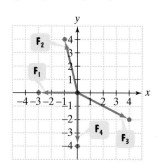

74.

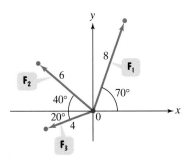

75. The figure shows a small plane flying at a speed of 180 miles per hour on a bearing of N50°E. The wind is blowing from west to east at 40 miles per hour. The figure indicates that **v** represents the velocity of the plane in still air and **w** represents the velocity of the wind.

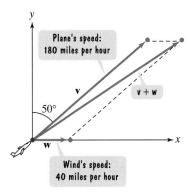

a. Express **v** and **w** in terms of their magnitudes and direction angles.

b. Find the resultant vector, **v** + **w**.

c. The magnitude of **v** + **w**, called the **ground speed** of the plane, gives its speed relative to the ground. Approximate the ground speed to the nearest mile per hour.

d. The direction angle of **v** + **w** gives the plane's true course relative to the ground. Approximate the true course to the nearest tenth of a degree. What is the plane's true bearing?

76. Use the procedure outlined in Exercise 67 to solve this exercise. A plane is flying at a speed of 400 miles per hour on a bearing of N50°W. The wind is blowing at 30 miles per hour on a bearing of N25°E.

a. Approximate the plane's ground speed to the nearest mile per hour.

b. Approximate the plane's true course to the nearest tenth of a degree. What is its true bearing?

77. A plane is flying at a speed of 320 miles per hour on a bearing of N70°E. Its ground speed is 370 miles per hour and its true course is 30°. Find the speed, to the nearest mile per hour, and the direction angle, to the nearest tenth of a degree, of the wind.

78. A plane is flying at a speed of 540 miles per hour on a bearing of S36°E. Its ground speed is 500 miles per hour and its true bearing is S44°E. Find the speed, to the nearest mile per hour, and the direction angle, to the nearest tenth of a degree, of the wind.

 Writing in Mathematics

79. What is a directed line segment?

80. What are equal vectors?

81. If vector **v** is represented by an arrow, how is −3**v** represented?

82. If vectors **u** and **v** are represented by arrows, describe how the vector sum **u** + **v** is represented.

83. What is the **i** vector?

84. What is the **j** vector?

85. What is a position vector? How is a position vector represented using **i** and **j**?

86. If **v** is a vector between any two points in the rectangular coordinate system, explain how to write **v** in terms of **i** and **j**.

87. If two vectors are expressed in terms of **i** and **j**, explain how to find their sum.

88. If two vectors are expressed in terms of **i** and **j**, explain how to find their difference.

89. If a vector is expressed in terms of **i** and **j**, explain how to find the scalar multiplication of the vector and a given scalar k.

90. What is the zero vector?

91. Describe one similarity between the zero vector and the number 0.

92. Explain how to find the unit vector in the direction of any given vector **v**.

93. Explain how to write a vector in terms of its magnitude and direction.

94. You are on an airplane. The pilot announces the plane's speed over the intercom. Which speed do you think is being reported: the speed of the plane in still air or the speed after the effect of the wind has been accounted for? Explain your answer.

95. Use vectors to explain why it is difficult to hold a heavy stack of books perfectly still for a long period of time. As you become exhausted, what eventually happens? What does this mean in terms of the forces acting on the books?

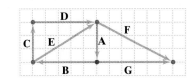 **Critical Thinking Exercises**

96. Use the figure shown to select a true statement.

a. **A** + **B** = **E**

b. **D** + **A** + **B** + **C** = **0**

c. **B** − **E** = **G** − **F**

d. ‖**A**‖ ≠ ‖**C**‖

97. Let **v** = a**i** + b**j**. Show that $\dfrac{\mathbf{v}}{\|\mathbf{v}\|}$ is a unit vector in the direction of **v**.

In Exercises 98–99, refer to the navigational compass shown in the figure. The compass is marked clockwise in degrees that start at north 0°.

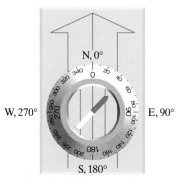

98. An airplane has an air speed of 240 miles per hour and a compass heading of 280°. A steady wind of 30 miles per hour is blowing in the direction of 265°. What is the plane's true speed relative to the ground? What is its compass heading relative to the ground?

99. Two tugboats are pulling on a large ship that has gone aground. One tug pulls with a force of 2500 pounds in a compass direction of 55°. The second tug pulls with a force of 2000 pounds in a compass direction of 95°. Find the magnitude and the compass direction of the resultant force.

100. You want to fly your small plane due north, but there is a 75 kilometer wind blowing from west to east.

a. Find the direction angle for where you should head the plane if your speed relative to the air is 310 kilometers per hour.

b. If you increase your air speed, should the direction angle in part (a) increase or decrease? Explain your answer.

SECTION 2.6 *The Dot Product*

Objectives

1. Find the dot product of two vectors.

2. Find the angle between two vectors.

Talk about hard work! I can see the weightlifter's muscles quivering from the exertion of holding the barbell in a stationary position above his head. Still, I'm not sure if he's doing as much work as I, sitting at my desk with my brain quivering from studying trigonometric functions and their applications.

Would it surprise you to know that neither you nor the weightlifter are doing any work at all? The definition of work in physics and mathematics is not the same as what we mean by "work" in everyday use. To understand what is involved in real work, we turn to a new vector operation called the dot product.

1 Find the dot product of two vectors.

The Dot Product of Two Vectors

The operations of vector addition and scalar multiplication result in vectors. By contrast, the *dot product* of two vectors results in a scalar (a real number), rather than a vector.

Definition of the Dot Product

If $\mathbf{v} = a_1\mathbf{i} + b_1\mathbf{j}$ and $\mathbf{w} = a_2\mathbf{i} + b_2\mathbf{j}$ are vectors, the **dot product** $\mathbf{v} \cdot \mathbf{w}$ is defined as

$$\mathbf{v} \cdot \mathbf{w} = a_1 a_2 + b_1 b_2.$$

The dot product of two vectors is the sum of the products of their horizontal and vertical components.

EXAMPLE 1 Finding Dot Products

If $\mathbf{v} = 5\mathbf{i} - 2\mathbf{j}$ and $\mathbf{w} = -3\mathbf{i} + 4\mathbf{j}$, find:

a. $\mathbf{v} \cdot \mathbf{w}$ **b.** $\mathbf{w} \cdot \mathbf{v}$ **c.** $\mathbf{v} \cdot \mathbf{v}$.

Solution   To find each dot product, multiply the two horizontal components, and then multiply the two vertical components. Finally, add the two products.

a. $\mathbf{v} \cdot \mathbf{w} = 5(-3) + (-2)(4) = -15 - 8 = -23$

Multiply the horizontal components and multiply the vertical components of
$\mathbf{v} = 5\mathbf{i} - 2\mathbf{j}$ and $\mathbf{w} = -3\mathbf{i} + 4\mathbf{j}$.

b. $\mathbf{w} \cdot \mathbf{v} = -3(5) + 4(-2) = -15 - 8 = -23$

Multiply the horizontal components and multiply the vertical components of
$\mathbf{w} = -3\mathbf{i} + 4\mathbf{j}$ and $\mathbf{v} = 5\mathbf{i} - 2\mathbf{j}$.

c. $\mathbf{v} \cdot \mathbf{v} = 5(5) + (-2)(-2) = 25 + 4 = 29$

Multiply the horizontal components and multiply the vertical components of
$\mathbf{v} = 5\mathbf{i} - 2\mathbf{j}$ and $\mathbf{v} = 5\mathbf{i} - 2\mathbf{j}$.

Check Point 1   If $\mathbf{v} = 7\mathbf{i} - 4\mathbf{j}$ and $\mathbf{w} = 2\mathbf{i} - \mathbf{j}$, find:

a. $\mathbf{v} \cdot \mathbf{w}$ **b.** $\mathbf{w} \cdot \mathbf{v}$ **c.** $\mathbf{w} \cdot \mathbf{w}$.

In Example 1 and Check Point 1, did you notice that $\mathbf{v} \cdot \mathbf{w}$ and $\mathbf{w} \cdot \mathbf{v}$ produced the same scalar? The fact that $\mathbf{v} \cdot \mathbf{w} = \mathbf{w} \cdot \mathbf{v}$ follows from the definition of the dot product. Properties of the dot product are given in the box at the top of the next page. Proofs for some of these properties are given in the appendix.

Properties of the Dot Product

If **u**, **v**, and **w** are vectors, and c is a scalar, then

1. $\mathbf{u} \cdot \mathbf{v} = \mathbf{v} \cdot \mathbf{u}$

2. $\mathbf{u} \cdot (\mathbf{v} + \mathbf{w}) = \mathbf{u} \cdot \mathbf{v} + \mathbf{u} \cdot \mathbf{w}$

3. $\mathbf{0} \cdot \mathbf{v} = 0$

4. $\mathbf{v} \cdot \mathbf{v} = \|\mathbf{v}\|^2$

5. $(c\mathbf{u}) \cdot \mathbf{v} = c(\mathbf{u} \cdot \mathbf{v}) = \mathbf{u} \cdot (c\mathbf{v})$

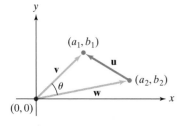

Figure 2.53

The Angle between Two Vectors

The Law of Cosines can be used to derive another formula for the dot product. This formula will give us a way to find the angle between two vectors.

Figure 2.53 shows vectors $\mathbf{v} = a_1\mathbf{i} + b_1\mathbf{j}$ and $\mathbf{w} = a_2\mathbf{i} + b_2\mathbf{j}$. By the definition of the dot product, we know that $\mathbf{v} \cdot \mathbf{w} = a_1a_2 + b_1b_2$. Our new formula for the dot product involves the angle between the vectors, shown as θ in the figure. Apply the Law of Cosines to the triangle shown in the figure.

$$\|\mathbf{u}\|^2 = \|\mathbf{v}\|^2 + \|\mathbf{w}\|^2 - 2\|\mathbf{v}\|\|\mathbf{w}\|\cos\theta$$ Use the Law of Cosines.

$$(a_1 - a_2)^2 + (b_1 - b_2)^2 = (a_1^2 + b_1^2) + (a_2^2 + b_2^2) - 2\|\mathbf{v}\|\|\mathbf{w}\|\cos\theta$$ Square the magnitudes of vectors **u**, **v**, and **w**.

$$a_1^2 - 2a_1a_2 + a_2^2 + b_1^2 - 2b_1b_2 + b_2^2 = a_1^2 + b_1^2 + a_2^2 + b_2^2 - 2\|\mathbf{v}\|\|\mathbf{w}\|\cos\theta$$ Square the binomials using $(A - B)^2 = A^2 - 2AB + B^2$.

$$-2a_1a_2 - 2b_1b_2 = -2\|\mathbf{v}\|\|\mathbf{w}\|\cos\theta$$ Subtract a_1^2, a_2^2, b_1^2, and b_2^2 from both sides of the equation.

$$a_1a_2 + b_1b_2 = \|\mathbf{v}\|\|\mathbf{w}\|\cos\theta$$ Divide both sides by -2.

By definition,
$\mathbf{v} \cdot \mathbf{w} = a_1a_2 + b_1b_2.$

$$\mathbf{v} \cdot \mathbf{w} = \|\mathbf{v}\|\|\mathbf{w}\|\cos\theta$$ Substitute $\mathbf{v} \cdot \mathbf{w}$ for the expression on the left side of the equation.

Alternative Formula for the Dot Product

If **v** and **w** are two nonzero vectors and θ is the smallest nonnegative angle between them, then

$$\mathbf{v} \cdot \mathbf{w} = \|\mathbf{v}\|\|\mathbf{w}\|\cos\theta.$$

2 Find the angle between two vectors.

Solving the formula in the box for $\cos\theta$ gives us a formula for finding the angle between vectors:

Formula for the Angle between Two Vectors

If **v** and **w** are two nonzero vectors and θ is the smallest nonnegative angle between **v** and **w**, then

$$\cos\theta = \frac{\mathbf{v} \cdot \mathbf{w}}{\|\mathbf{v}\|\|\mathbf{w}\|} \quad \text{and} \quad \theta = \cos^{-1}\left(\frac{\mathbf{v} \cdot \mathbf{w}}{\|\mathbf{v}\|\|\mathbf{w}\|}\right).$$

EXAMPLE 2 Finding the Angle between Two Vectors

Find the angle θ between the vectors $\mathbf{v} = 3\mathbf{i} - 2\mathbf{j}$ and $\mathbf{w} = -\mathbf{i} + 4\mathbf{j}$, shown in Figure 2.54. Round to the nearest tenth of a degree.

Solution Use the formula for the angle between two vectors.

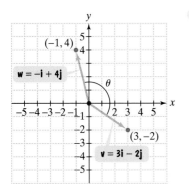

Figure 2.54 Finding the angle between two vectors

$$\cos\theta = \frac{\mathbf{v} \cdot \mathbf{w}}{\|\mathbf{v}\|\|\mathbf{w}\|}$$ This is the formula for the cosine of the angle between two vectors.

$$= \frac{(3\mathbf{i} - 2\mathbf{j}) \cdot (-\mathbf{i} + 4\mathbf{j})}{\sqrt{3^2 + (-2)^2}\sqrt{(-1)^2 + 4^2}}$$ Substitute the given vectors in the numerator. Find the magnitude of each vector in the denominator.

$$= \frac{3(-1) + (-2)(4)}{\sqrt{13}\sqrt{17}}$$ Find the dot product in the numerator. Simplify in the denominator.

$$= -\frac{11}{\sqrt{221}}$$ Perform the indicated operations.

The angle θ between the vectors is

$$\theta = \cos^{-1}\left(-\frac{11}{\sqrt{221}}\right) \approx 137.7°.$$ Use a calculator.

Check Point 2 Find the angle between the vectors $\mathbf{v} = 4\mathbf{i} - 3\mathbf{j}$ and $\mathbf{w} = \mathbf{i} + 2\mathbf{j}$. Round to the nearest tenth of a degree.

EXERCISE SET 2.6

Practice Exercises

*In Exercises 1–8, use the given vectors to find **a.** $\mathbf{v} \cdot \mathbf{w}$ and **b.** $\mathbf{v} \cdot \mathbf{v}$.*

1. $\mathbf{v} = 3\mathbf{i} + \mathbf{j}$, $\mathbf{w} = \mathbf{i} + 3\mathbf{j}$
2. $\mathbf{v} = 3\mathbf{i} + 3\mathbf{j}$, $\mathbf{w} = \mathbf{i} + 4\mathbf{j}$
3. $\mathbf{v} = 5\mathbf{i} - 4\mathbf{j}$, $\mathbf{w} = -2\mathbf{i} - \mathbf{j}$
4. $\mathbf{v} = 7\mathbf{i} - 2\mathbf{j}$, $\mathbf{w} = -3\mathbf{i} - \mathbf{j}$
5. $\mathbf{v} = -6\mathbf{i} - 5\mathbf{j}$, $\mathbf{w} = -10\mathbf{i} - 8\mathbf{j}$
6. $\mathbf{v} = -8\mathbf{i} - 3\mathbf{j}$, $\mathbf{w} = -10\mathbf{i} - 5\mathbf{j}$
7. $\mathbf{v} = 5\mathbf{i}$, $\mathbf{w} = \mathbf{j}$ 8. $\mathbf{v} = \mathbf{i}$, $\mathbf{w} = -5\mathbf{j}$

In Exercises 9–16, let

$$\mathbf{u} = 2\mathbf{i} - \mathbf{j}, \quad \mathbf{v} = 3\mathbf{i} + \mathbf{j}, \quad \text{and} \quad \mathbf{w} = \mathbf{i} + 4\mathbf{j}.$$

Find each specified scalar.

9. $\mathbf{u} \cdot (\mathbf{v} + \mathbf{w})$ 10. $\mathbf{v} \cdot (\mathbf{u} + \mathbf{w})$
11. $\mathbf{u} \cdot \mathbf{v} + \mathbf{u} \cdot \mathbf{w}$ 12. $\mathbf{v} \cdot \mathbf{u} + \mathbf{v} \cdot \mathbf{w}$
13. $(4\mathbf{u}) \cdot \mathbf{v}$ 14. $(5\mathbf{v}) \cdot \mathbf{w}$
15. $4(\mathbf{u} \cdot \mathbf{v})$ 16. $5(\mathbf{v} \cdot \mathbf{w})$

In Exercises 17–22, find the angle between $\mathbf{v}$ and $\mathbf{w}$. Round to the nearest tenth of a degree.

17. $\mathbf{v} = 2\mathbf{i} - \mathbf{j}$, $\mathbf{w} = 3\mathbf{i} + 4\mathbf{j}$
18. $\mathbf{v} = -2\mathbf{i} + 5\mathbf{j}$, $\mathbf{w} = 3\mathbf{i} + 6\mathbf{j}$
19. $\mathbf{v} = -3\mathbf{i} + 2\mathbf{j}$, $\mathbf{w} = 4\mathbf{i} - \mathbf{j}$
20. $\mathbf{v} = \mathbf{i} + 2\mathbf{j}$, $\mathbf{w} = 4\mathbf{i} - 3\mathbf{j}$
21. $\mathbf{v} = 6\mathbf{i}$, $\mathbf{w} = 5\mathbf{i} + 4\mathbf{j}$ 22. $\mathbf{v} = 3\mathbf{j}$, $\mathbf{w} = 4\mathbf{i} + 5\mathbf{j}$

Application Exercises

23. The components of $\mathbf{v} = 240\mathbf{i} + 300\mathbf{j}$ represent the respective number of gallons of regular and premium gas sold at a station on Monday. The components of $\mathbf{w} = 1.90\mathbf{i} + 2.07\mathbf{j}$ represent the respective prices per gallon for each kind of gas. Find $\mathbf{v} \cdot \mathbf{w}$ and describe what the answer means in practical terms.

24. The components of $\mathbf{v} = 180\mathbf{i} + 450\mathbf{j}$ represent the respective number of one-day and three-day videos rented from a video store on Monday. The components of $\mathbf{w} = 3\mathbf{i} + 2\mathbf{j}$ represent the prices to rent the one-day and three-day videos, respectively. Find $\mathbf{v} \cdot \mathbf{w}$ and describe what the answer means in practical terms.

Writing in Mathematics

25. Explain how to find the dot product of two vectors.

26. Using words and no symbols, describe how to find the dot product of two vectors with the alternative formula

$$\mathbf{v} \cdot \mathbf{w} = \|\mathbf{v}\| \|\mathbf{w}\| \cos \theta.$$

Critical Thinking Exercises

In Exercises 27–29, use the vectors

$$\mathbf{u} = a_1 \mathbf{i} + b_1 \mathbf{j}, \quad \mathbf{v} = a_2 \mathbf{i} + b_2 \mathbf{j}, \quad \text{and} \quad \mathbf{w} = a_3 \mathbf{i} + b_3 \mathbf{j},$$

to prove the given property.

27. $\mathbf{u} \cdot \mathbf{v} = \mathbf{v} \cdot \mathbf{u}$

28. $(c\mathbf{u}) \cdot \mathbf{v} = c(\mathbf{u} \cdot \mathbf{v})$

29. $\mathbf{u} \cdot (\mathbf{v} + \mathbf{w}) = \mathbf{u} \cdot \mathbf{v} + \mathbf{u} \cdot \mathbf{w}$

Group Exercise

30. Group members should research and present a report on unusual and interesting applications of vectors.

Chapter Summary, Review, and Test

Summary

DEFINITIONS AND CONCEPTS	EXAMPLES

2.1 and 2.2 The Law of Sines and the Law of Cosines

a. The Law of Sines

$$\frac{a}{\sin A} = \frac{b}{\sin B} = \frac{c}{\sin C}$$

Ex. 1, p. 92;
Ex. 2, p. 93;
Ex. 3, p. 95

b. The Law of Sines is used to solve SAA, ASA, and SSA (the ambiguous case) triangles. The ambiguous case may result in no triangle, one triangle, or two triangles; see the box on page 94.

Ex. 4, p. 96;
Ex. 5, p. 96

c. The area of a triangle equals one-half the product of the lengths of two sides times the sine of their included angle.

Ex. 6, p. 98

d. The Law of Cosines

$$a^2 = b^2 + c^2 - 2bc \cos A$$
$$b^2 = a^2 + c^2 - 2ac \cos B$$
$$c^2 = a^2 + b^2 - 2ab \cos C$$

e. The Law of Cosines is used to find the side opposite the given angle in an SAS triangle; see the box on page 104. The Law of Cosines is also used to find the angle opposite the longest side in an SSS triangle; see the box on page 105.

Ex. 1, p. 104;
Ex. 2, p. 106

f. Heron's Formula for the Area of a Triangle

The area of a triangle with sides $a, b,$ and c is

$$\sqrt{s(s - a)(s - b)(s - c)},$$

where s is one-half the perimeter:

$$s = \tfrac{1}{2}(a + b + c).$$

Ex. 4, p. 108

2.3 Polar Coordinates

a. A point P in the polar coordinate system is represented by (r, θ), where r is the directed distance of the point from the pole and θ is the angle from the polar axis to line segment OP. The elements of the ordered pair (r, θ) are called the polar coordinates of P. See Figure 2.19 on page 111. When r in (r, θ) is negative, a point is located $|r|$ units along the ray opposite the terminal side of θ. Important information about the sign of r and the location of the point (r, θ) is found in the box on page 112.

Ex. 1, p. 112

b. Multiple Representation of Points

If n is any integer, $(r, \theta) = (r, \theta + 2n\pi)$ or $(r, \theta) = (-r, \theta + \pi + 2n\pi)$.

Ex. 2, p. 114

c. Relations between Polar and Rectangular Coordinates

$$x = r \cos\theta, \quad y = r \sin\theta, \quad x^2 + y^2 = r^2, \quad \tan\theta = \frac{y}{x}$$

DEFINITIONS AND CONCEPTS	EXAMPLES

d. To convert a point from polar coordinates (r, θ) to rectangular coordinates (x, y), use $x = r \cos \theta$ and $y = r \sin \theta$.

Ex. 3, p. 115

e. To convert a point from rectangular coordinates (x, y) to polar coordinates (r, θ), use the procedure in the box on page 116.

Ex. 4, p.116;
Ex. 5, p. 117

2.4 Complex Numbers in Polar Form; DeMoivre's Theorem

a. The complex number $z = a + bi$ is represented as a point (a, b) in the complex plane, shown in Figure 2.28 on page 123.

Ex. 1, p. 123

b. The absolute value of $z = a + bi$ is $|z| = |a + bi| = \sqrt{a^2 + b^2}$.

Ex. 2, p. 123

c. The polar form of $z = a + bi$ is $z = r(\cos \theta + i \sin \theta)$,
where $a = r \cos \theta$, $b = r \sin \theta$, $r = \sqrt{a^2 + b^2}$, and $\tan \theta = \dfrac{b}{a}$. We call r the modulus and θ the argument of z, with $0 \le \theta < 2\pi$.

Ex. 3, p. 125;
Ex. 4, p. 125

d. Multiplying Complex Numbers in Polar Form: Multiply moduli and add arguments. See the box on page 126.

Ex. 5, p. 126

e. Dividing Complex Numbers in Polar Form: Divide moduli and subtract arguments. See the box on page 127.

Ex. 6, p. 127

f. DeMoivre's Theorem is used to find powers of complex numbers in polar form.

$$[r(\cos \theta + i \sin \theta)]^n = r^n(\cos n\theta + i \sin n\theta)$$

Ex. 7, p. 128;
Ex. 8, p. 129

2.5 Vectors

a. A vector is a directed line segment.

b. Equal vectors have the same magnitude and the same direction.

Ex. 1, p. 133

c. The vector $k\mathbf{v}$, the scalar multiple of the vector $\mathbf{v}$ and the scalar k, has magnitude $|k| \|\mathbf{v}\|$. The direction of $k\mathbf{v}$ is the same as that of $\mathbf{v}$ if $k > 0$ and opposite $\mathbf{v}$ if $k < 0$.

d. The sum $\mathbf{u} + \mathbf{v}$, called the resultant vector, can be expressed geometrically. Position $\mathbf{u}$ and $\mathbf{v}$ so that the terminal point of $\mathbf{u}$ coincides with the initial point of $\mathbf{v}$. The vector $\mathbf{u} + \mathbf{v}$ extends from the initial point of $\mathbf{u}$ to the terminal point of $\mathbf{v}$.

e. The difference of two vectors, $\mathbf{u} - \mathbf{v}$, is defined as $\mathbf{u} + (-\mathbf{v})$.

f. The vector $\mathbf{i}$ is the unit vector whose direction is along the positive x-axis. The vector $\mathbf{j}$ is the unit vector whose direction is along the positive y-axis.

g. Vector $\mathbf{v}$, from $(0, 0)$ to (a, b), called a position vector, is represented as $\mathbf{v} = a\mathbf{i} + b\mathbf{j}$, where a is the horizontal component and b is the vertical component. The magnitude of $\mathbf{v}$ is given by $\|\mathbf{v}\| = \sqrt{a^2 + b^2}$.

Ex. 2, p. 135

h. Vector $\mathbf{v}$ from (x_1, y_1) to (x_2, y_2) is equal to the position vector $\mathbf{v} = (x_2 - x_1)\mathbf{i} + (y_2 - y_1)\mathbf{j}$. In rectangular coordinates, the term "vector" refers to the position vector in terms of $\mathbf{i}$ and $\mathbf{j}$ that is equal to it.

Ex. 3, p. 136

i. Operations with Vectors in Terms of $\mathbf{i}$ and $\mathbf{j}$
If $\mathbf{v} = a_1\mathbf{i} + b_1\mathbf{j}$ and $\mathbf{w} = a_2\mathbf{i} + b_2\mathbf{j}$, then

1. $\mathbf{v} + \mathbf{w} = (a_1 + a_2)\mathbf{i} + (b_1 + b_2)\mathbf{j}$

2. $\mathbf{v} - \mathbf{w} = (a_1 - a_2)\mathbf{i} + (b_1 - b_2)\mathbf{j}$

3. $k\mathbf{v} = (ka_1)\mathbf{i} + (kb_1)\mathbf{j}$

Ex. 4, p. 137;
Ex. 5, p. 137;
Ex. 6, p. 138

j. The zero vector $\mathbf{0}$ is the vector whose magnitude is 0 and is assigned no direction. Many properties of vector addition and scalar multiplication involve the zero vector. Some of these properties are listed in the box on page 674.

DEFINITIONS AND CONCEPTS **EXAMPLES**

k. The vector $\dfrac{\mathbf{v}}{\|\mathbf{v}\|}$ is the unit vector that has the same direction as $\mathbf{v}$.   Ex. 7, p. 139

l. A vector with magnitude $\|\mathbf{v}\|$ and direction angle θ, the angle that $\mathbf{v}$ makes with the positive x-axis, can be expressed in terms of its magnitude and direction angle as   Ex. 8, p. 140; Ex. 9, p. 141

$$\mathbf{v} = \|\mathbf{v}\|\cos\theta\mathbf{i} + \|\mathbf{v}\|\sin\theta\mathbf{j}.$$

m. A vector can be used to represent a complex number $z = a + bi$. When using this representation, the vector is expressed as $\mathbf{v} = a + bi$ with length $\|\mathbf{v}\| = \sqrt{a^2 + b^2}$ and orientation (direction angle) $\theta = \tan^{-1}\left(\dfrac{b}{a}\right)$.   Ex. 10, p. 143;

n. The real and imaginary components of the vector are found using   Ex. 11, p. 144;

$$a = \|\mathbf{v}\|\cos\theta \text{ and } b = \|\mathbf{v}\|\sin\theta$$

2.6 The Dot Product

a. Definition of the Dot Product   Ex. 1, p. 149
If $\mathbf{v} = a_1\mathbf{i} + b_1\mathbf{j}$ and $\mathbf{w} = a_2\mathbf{i} + b_2\mathbf{j}$, the dot product of $\mathbf{v}$ and $\mathbf{w}$ is defined by $\mathbf{v} \cdot \mathbf{w} = a_1 a_2 + b_1 b_2$.

b. Alternative Formula for the Dot Product $\mathbf{v} \cdot \mathbf{w} = \|\mathbf{v}\|\|\mathbf{w}\|\cos\theta$, where θ is the smallest nonnegative angle between $\mathbf{v}$ and $\mathbf{w}$.

c. Angle between Two Vectors   Ex. 2, p. 151

$$\cos\theta = \frac{\mathbf{v}\cdot\mathbf{w}}{\|\mathbf{v}\|\|\mathbf{w}\|} \quad \text{and} \quad \theta = \cos^{-1}\left(\frac{\mathbf{v}\cdot\mathbf{w}}{\|\mathbf{v}\|\|\mathbf{w}\|}\right).$$

Review Exercises

2.1 and 2.2

In Exercises 1–12, solve each triangle. Round lengths to the nearest tenth and angle measures to the nearest degree. If no triangle exists, state "no triangle." If two triangles exist, solve each triangle.

1. $A = 70°, B = 55°, a = 12$

2. $B = 107°, C = 30°, c = 126$

3. $B = 66°, a = 17, c = 12$

4. $a = 117, b = 66, c = 142$

5. $A = 35°, B = 25°, c = 68$

6. $A = 39°, a = 20, b = 26$

7. $C = 50°, a = 3, c = 1$

8. $A = 162°, b = 11.2, c = 48.2$

9. $a = 26.1, b = 40.2, c = 36.5$

10. $A = 40°, a = 6, b = 4$

11. $B = 37°, a = 12.4, b = 8.7$

12. $A = 23°, a = 54.3, b = 22.1$

In Exercises 13–16, find the area of the triangle having the given measurements. Round to the nearest square unit.

13. $C = 42°, a = 4$ feet, $b = 6$ feet

14. $A = 22°, b = 4$ feet, $c = 5$ feet

15. $a = 2$ meters, $b = 4$ meters, $c = 5$ meters

16. $a = 2$ meters, $b = 2$ meters, $c = 2$ meters

17. The A-frame cabin shown in the next column is 35 feet wide. The roof of the cabin makes a 60° angle with the cabin's base. Find the length of one side of the roof from its ground level to the peak. Round to the nearest tenth of a foot.

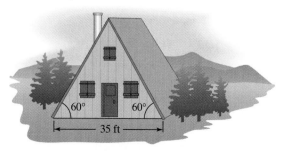

18. Two cars leave a city at the same time and travel along straight highways that differ in direction by 80°. One car averages 60 miles per hour and the other averages 50 miles per hour. How far apart will the cars be after 30 minutes? Round to the nearest tenth of a mile.

19. Two airplanes leave an airport at the same time on different runways. One flies on a bearing of N66.5°W at 325 miles per hour. The other airplane flies on a bearing of S26.5°W at 300 miles per hour. How far apart will the airplanes be after two hours?

20. The figure shows three roads that intersect to bound a triangular piece of land. Find the lengths of the other two sides of the land to the nearest foot.

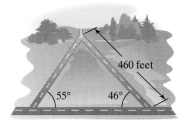

21. A commercial piece of real estate is priced at $5.25 per square foot. Find the cost, to the nearest dollar, of a triangular lot measuring 260 feet by 320 feet by 450 feet.

2.3

In Exercises 22–27, plot each point in polar coordinates and find its rectangular coordinates.

22. $(4, 60°)$

23. $(3, 150°)$

24. $\left(-4, \dfrac{4\pi}{3}\right)$

25. $\left(-2, \dfrac{5\pi}{4}\right)$

26. $\left(-4, -\dfrac{\pi}{2}\right)$

27. $\left(-2, -\dfrac{\pi}{4}\right)$

In Exercises 28–30, plot each point in polar coordinates. Then find another representation (r, θ) of this point in which:

a. $r > 0, \ 2\pi < \theta < 4\pi$.
b. $r < 0, \ 0 < \theta < 2\pi$.
c. $r > 0, -2\pi < \theta < 0$.

28. $\left(3, \dfrac{\pi}{6}\right)$

29. $\left(2, \dfrac{2\pi}{3}\right)$

30. $(3, \pi)$

In Exercises 31–36, the rectangular coordinates of a point are given. Find polar coordinates of each point.

31. $(-4, 4)$

32. $(3, -3)$

33. $(5, 12)$

34. $(-3, 4)$

35. $(0, -5)$

36. $(1, 0)$

2.4

In Exercises 37–40, plot each complex number. Then write the complex number in polar form. You may express the argument in degrees or radians.

37. $1 - i$

38. $-2\sqrt{3} + 2i$

39. $-3 - 4i$

40. $-5i$

In Exercises 41–44, write each complex number in rectangular form.

41. $8(\cos 60° + i \sin 60°)$

42. $4(\cos 210° + i \sin 210°)$

43. $6\left(\cos \dfrac{2\pi}{3} + i \sin \dfrac{2\pi}{3}\right)$

44. $0.6(\cos 100° + i \sin 100°)$

In Exercises 45–47, find the product of the complex numbers. Leave answers in polar form.

45. $z_1 = 3(\cos 40° + i \sin 40°)$
$z_2 = 5(\cos 70° + i \sin 70°)$

46. $z_1 = \cos 210° + i \sin 210°$
$z_2 = \cos 55° + i \sin 55°$

47. $z_1 = 4\left(\cos \dfrac{3\pi}{7} + i \sin \dfrac{3\pi}{7}\right)$
$z_2 = 10\left(\cos \dfrac{4\pi}{7} + i \sin \dfrac{4\pi}{7}\right)$

In Exercises 48–50, find the quotient $\dfrac{z_1}{z_2}$ of the complex numbers. Leave answers in polar form.

48. $z_1 = 10(\cos 10° + i \sin 10°)$
$z_2 = 5(\cos 5° + i \sin 5°)$

49. $z_1 = 5\left(\cos \dfrac{4\pi}{3} + i \sin \dfrac{4\pi}{3}\right)$
$z_2 = 10\left(\cos \dfrac{\pi}{3} + i \sin \dfrac{\pi}{3}\right)$

50. $z_1 = 2\left(\cos \dfrac{5\pi}{3} + i \sin \dfrac{5\pi}{3}\right)$
$z_2 = \cos \dfrac{\pi}{2} + i \sin \dfrac{\pi}{2}$

In Exercises 51–55, use DeMoivre's Theorem to find the indicated power of the complex number. Write answers in rectangular form.

51. $[2(\cos 20° + i \sin 20°)]^3$

52. $[4(\cos 50° + i \sin 50°)]^3$

53. $\left[\dfrac{1}{2}\left(\cos \dfrac{\pi}{14} + i \sin \dfrac{\pi}{14}\right)\right]^7$

54. $(1 - \sqrt{3}i)^7$

55. $(-2 - 2i)^5$

2.5

In Exercises 56–58, sketch each vector as a position vector and find its magnitude.

56. $\mathbf{v} = -3\mathbf{i} - 4\mathbf{j}$ **57.** $\mathbf{v} = 5\mathbf{i} - 2\mathbf{j}$

58. $\mathbf{v} = -3\mathbf{j}$

In Exercises 59–60, let $\mathbf{v}$ be the vector from initial point P_1 to terminal point P_2. Write $\mathbf{v}$ in terms of $\mathbf{i}$ and $\mathbf{j}$.

59. $P_1 = (2,-1), \quad P_2 = (5,-3)$

60. $P_1 = (-3,0), \quad P_2 = (-2,-2)$

In Exercises 61–64, let

$$\mathbf{v} = \mathbf{i} - 5\mathbf{j} \quad \text{and} \quad \mathbf{w} = -2\mathbf{i} + 7\mathbf{j}.$$

Find each specified vector or scalar.

61. $\mathbf{v} + \mathbf{w}$ **62.** $\mathbf{w} - \mathbf{v}$

63. $6\mathbf{v} - 3\mathbf{w}$ **64.** $\|-2\mathbf{v}\|$

In Exercises 65–66, find the unit vector that has the same direction as the vector $\mathbf{v}$.

65. $\mathbf{v} = 8\mathbf{i} - 6\mathbf{j}$ **66.** $\mathbf{v} = -\mathbf{i} + 2\mathbf{j}$

67. The magnitude and direction angle of $\mathbf{v}$ are $\|\mathbf{v}\| = 12$ and $\theta = 60°$. Express $\mathbf{v}$ in terms of $\mathbf{i}$ and $\mathbf{j}$.

68. The magnitude and direction of two forces acting on an object are 100 pounds, N25°E, and 200 pounds, N80°E, respectively. Find the magnitude, to the nearest pound, and the direction angle, to the nearest tenth of a degree, of the resultant force.

69. Your boat is moving at a speed of 15 miles per hour at an angle of $25°$ upstream on a river flowing at 4 miles per hour. The situation is illustrated in the figure at the top of the next column.

a. Find the vector representing your boat's velocity relative to the ground.

b. What is the speed of your boat, to the nearest mile per hour, relative to the ground?

c. What is the boat's direction angle, to the nearest tenth of a degree, relative to the ground?

In Exercises 70–71, find the length and direction angle for the vector that would represent each of the following complex numbers.

70. $3 + 5i$

71. $-7i$

In Exercises 72–73, find the real and imaginary components of the complex numbers represented by each of the vectors.

72. length: 8, direction angle: 35°

73. $3 \angle 20°$

2.6

74. If $\mathbf{u} = 5\mathbf{i} + 2\mathbf{j}, \mathbf{v} = \mathbf{i} - \mathbf{j}$, and $\mathbf{w} = 3\mathbf{i} - 7\mathbf{j}$, find $\mathbf{u} \cdot (\mathbf{v} + \mathbf{w})$.

In Exercises 75–77, find the dot product $\mathbf{v} \cdot \mathbf{w}$. Then find the angle between $\mathbf{v}$ and $\mathbf{w}$ to the nearest tenth of a degree.

75. $\mathbf{v} = 2\mathbf{i} + 3\mathbf{j}, \quad \mathbf{w} = 7\mathbf{i} - 4\mathbf{j}$

76. $\mathbf{v} = 2\mathbf{i} + 4\mathbf{j}, \quad \mathbf{w} = 6\mathbf{i} - 11\mathbf{j}$

77. $\mathbf{v} = 2\mathbf{i} + \mathbf{j}, \quad \mathbf{w} = \mathbf{i} - \mathbf{j}$

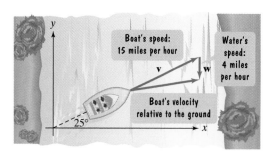

Chapter 2 Test

1. In oblique triangle ABC, $A = 34°, B = 68°$, and $a = 4.8$. Find b to the nearest tenth.

2. In oblique triangle ABC, $C = 68°, a = 5$, and $b = 6$. Find c to the nearest tenth.

3. In oblique triangle ABC, $a = 17$ inches, $b = 45$ inches, and $c = 32$ inches. Find the area of the triangle to the nearest square inch.

4. Plot $\left(4, \dfrac{5\pi}{4}\right)$ in the polar coordinate system. Then write two other ordered pairs (r, θ) that name this point.

5. If the rectangular coordinates of a point are $(1, -1)$, find polar coordinates of the point.

6. Write $-\sqrt{3} + i$ in polar form.

In Exercises 11–13, perform the indicated operation. Leave answers in polar form.

7. $5(\cos 15° + i \sin 15°) \cdot 10(\cos 5° + i \sin 5°)$

8. $\dfrac{2\left(\cos \dfrac{\pi}{2} + i \sin \dfrac{\pi}{2}\right)}{4\left(\cos \dfrac{\pi}{3} + i \sin \dfrac{\pi}{3}\right)}$

9. $[2(\cos 10° + i \sin 10°)]^5$

10. If $P_1 = (-2, 3)$, $P_2 = (-1, 5)$, and **v** is the vector from P_1 to P_2,

    a. Write **v** in terms of **i** and **j**.

    b. Find $\|\mathbf{v}\|$.

11. Find the real and complex components of the complex number represented by the vector $4 \angle 42°$

In Exercises 12–14, let
$$\mathbf{v} = -5\mathbf{i} + 2\mathbf{j} \quad \text{and} \quad \mathbf{w} = 2\mathbf{i} - 4\mathbf{j}.$$

Find the specified vector, scalar, or angle.

12. $3\mathbf{v} - 4\mathbf{w}$ **13.** $\mathbf{v} \cdot \mathbf{w}$.

14. the angle between **v** and **w**, to the nearest degree

Exponential and Logarithmic Functions

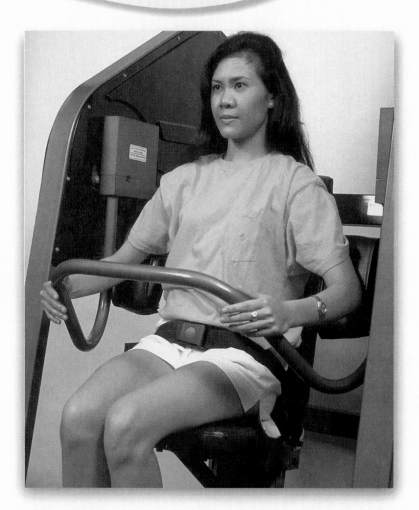

What went wrong on the space shuttle *Challenger*? Will population growth lead to a future without comfort or individual choice? Can I put aside a small amount of money and have millions for early retirement? Why did I feel I was walking too slowly on my visit to New York City? Why are people in California at far greater risk from drunk drivers than from earthquakes? What is the difference between earthquakes measuring 6 and 7 on the Richter scale? And what can I hope to accomplish in weightlifting?

The functions that you will be learning about in this chapter will provide you with the mathematics for answering these questions. You will see how these remarkable functions enable us to predict the future and rediscover the past.

You've recently taken up weightlifting, recording the maximum number of pounds you can lift at the end of each week. At first your weight limit increases rapidly, but now you notice that this growth is beginning to level off. You wonder about a function that would serve as a mathematical model to predict the number of pounds you can lift as you continue the sport.

SECTION 3.1 *Exponential Functions*

Objectives

1. Evaluate exponential functions.
2. Graph exponential functions.
3. Evaluate functions with base *e*.
4. Use compound interest formulas.

The space shuttle *Challenger* exploded approximately 73 seconds into flight on January 28, 1986. The tragedy involved damage to O-rings, which were used to seal the connections between different sections of the shuttle engines. The number of O-rings damaged increases dramatically as temperature falls.

The function

$$f(x) = 13.49(0.967)^x - 1$$

models the number of O-rings expected to fail when the temperature is $x°$F. Can you see how this function is different from polynomial functions? The variable x is in the exponent. Functions whose equations contain a variable in the exponent are called **exponential functions.** Many real-life situations, including population growth, growth of epidemics, radioactive decay, and other changes that involve rapid increase or decrease, can be described using exponential functions.

Definition of the Exponential Function

The **exponential function** f **with base** b is defined by

$$f(x) = b^x \quad \text{or} \quad y = b^x$$

where b is a positive constant other than $1 (b > 0$ and $b \neq 1)$ and x is any real number.

Here are some examples of exponential functions:

$$f(x) = 2^x \qquad g(x) = 10^x \qquad h(x) = 3^{x+1}.$$

Base is 2. Base is 10. Base is 3.

Each of these functions has a constant base and a variable exponent. By contrast, the following functions are not exponential:

$$F(x) = x^2 \qquad G(x) = 1^x \qquad H(x) = x^x.$$

Variable is the base and not the exponent. The base of an exponential function must be a positive constant other than 1. Variable is both the base and the exponent.

Why is $G(x) = 1^x$ not classified as an exponential function? The number 1 raised to any power is 1. Thus, the function G can be written as $G(x) = 1$, which is a constant function.

1 Evaluate exponential functions.

You will need a calculator to evaluate exponential expressions. Most scientific calculators have a $\boxed{y^x}$ key. Graphing calculators have a $\boxed{\wedge}$ key. To evaluate expressions of the form b^x, enter the base b, press $\boxed{y^x}$ or $\boxed{\wedge}$, enter the exponent x, and finally press $\boxed{=}$ or $\boxed{\text{ENTER}}$.

EXAMPLE 1 Evaluating an Exponential Function

The exponential function $f(x) = 13.49(0.967)^x - 1$ describes the number of O-rings expected to fail, $f(x)$, when the temperature is $x°$F. On the morning the *Challenger* was launched, the temperature was $31°$F, colder than any previous experience. Find the number of O-rings expected to fail at this temperature.

Solution Because the temperature was $31°$F, substitute 31 for x and evaluate the function.

$$f(x) = 13.49(0.967)^x - 1 \quad \text{This is the given function.}$$

$$f(31) = 13.49(0.967)^{31} - 1 \quad \text{Substitute 31 for x.}$$

Use a scientific or graphing calculator to evaluate $f(31)$. Press the following keys on your calculator to do this:

Scientific calculator: $13.49 \boxed{\times} .967 \boxed{y^x} 31 \boxed{-} 1 \boxed{=}$

Graphing calculator: $13.49 \boxed{\times} .967 \boxed{\wedge} 31 \boxed{-} 1 \boxed{\text{ENTER}}$.

The display should be approximately 3.7668627.

$$f(31) = 13.49(0.967)^{31} - 1 \approx 3.8 \approx 4$$

Thus, four O-rings are expected to fail at a temperature of $31°$F.

Check Point 1 Use the function in Example 1 to find the number of O-rings expected to fail at a temperature of $60°$F. Round to the nearest whole number.

2 Graph exponential functions.

Graphing Exponential Functions

We are familiar with expressions involving b^x, where x is a rational number. For example,

$$b^{1.7} = b^{17/10} = \sqrt[10]{b^{17}} \quad \text{and} \quad b^{1.73} = b^{173/100} = \sqrt[100]{b^{173}}.$$

However, note that the definition of $f(x) = b^x$ includes all real numbers for the domain x. You may wonder what b^x means when x is an irrational number, such as $b^{\sqrt{3}}$ or b^{π}. Using closer and closer approximations for $\sqrt{3}$ ($\sqrt{3} \approx 1.73205$), we can think of $b^{\sqrt{3}}$ as the value that has the successively closer approximations

$$b^{1.7}, b^{1.73}, b^{1.732}, b^{1.73205}, \ldots.$$

In this way, we can graph the exponential function with no holes, or points of discontinuity, at the irrational domain values.

EXAMPLE 2   Graphing an Exponential Function

Graph: $f(x) = 2^x$.

Solution   We begin by setting up a table of coordinates.

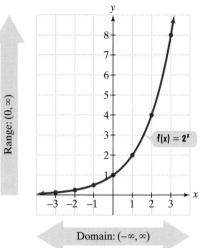

x	$f(x) = 2^x$
-3	$f(-3) = 2^{-3} = \frac{1}{8}$
-2	$f(-2) = 2^{-2} = \frac{1}{4}$
-1	$f(-1) = 2^{-1} = \frac{1}{2}$
0	$f(0) = 2^0 = 1$
1	$f(1) = 2^1 = 2$
2	$f(2) = 2^2 = 4$
3	$f(3) = 2^3 = 8$

Figure 3.1 The graph of $f(x) = 2^x$

We plot these points, connecting them with a continuous curve. Figure 3.1 shows the graph of $f(x) = 2^x$. Observe that the graph approaches, but never touches, the negative portion of the x-axis. Thus, the x-axis is a horizontal asymptote. The range is the set of all positive real numbers. Although we used integers for x in our table of coordinates, you can use a calculator to find additional points. For example, $f(0.3) = 2^{0.3} \approx 1.231$, $f(0.95) = 2^{0.95} \approx 1.932$. The points $(0.3, 1.231)$ and $(0.95, 1.932)$ approximately fit the graph.

Check Point 2   Graph: $f(x) = 3^x$.

Four exponential functions have been graphed in Figure 3.2. Compare the black and green graphs, where $b > 1$, to those in blue and red, where $b < 1$. When $b > 1$, the value of y increases as the value of x increases. When $b < 1$, the value of y decreases as the value of x increases. Notice that all four graphs pass through $(0, 1)$.

Study Tip

The graph of $y = (\frac{1}{2})^x$, meaning $y = 2^{-x}$, is the graph of $y = 2^x$ reflected about the y-axis.

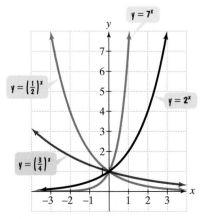

Figure 3.2 Graphs of four exponential functions

The graphs on the previous page illustrate the following general characteristics of exponential functions:

Characteristics of Exponential Functions of the Form $f(x) = b^x$

1. The domain of $f(x) = b^x$ consists of all real numbers. The range of $f(x) = b^x$ consists of all positive real numbers.
2. The graphs of all exponential functions of the form $f(x) = b^x$ pass through the point $(0, 1)$ because $f(0) = b^0 = 1 (b \neq 0)$. The y-intercept is 1.
3. If $b > 1, f(x) = b^x$ has a graph that goes up to the right and is an increasing function. The greater the value of b, the steeper the increase.
4. If $0 < b < 1, f(x) = b^x$ has a graph that goes down to the right and is a decreasing function. The smaller the value of b, the steeper the decrease.
5. $f(x) = b^x$ is one-to-one and has an inverse that is a function.
6. The graph of $f(x) = b^x$ approaches, but does not cross, the x-axis. The x-axis is a horizontal asymptote.

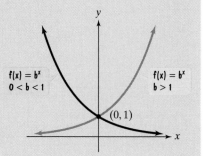

Transformations of Exponential Functions The graphs of exponential functions can be translated vertically or horizontally, reflected, stretched, or shrunk. We use the ideas summarized in Table 3.1 to do so.

Table 3.1   Transformations Involving Exponential Functions
In each case, c represents a positive real number.

Transformation	Equation	Description
Vertical translation	$g(x) = b^x + c$	• Shifts the graph of $f(x) = b^x$ upward c units.
	$g(x) = b^x - c$	• Shifts the graph of $f(x) = b^x$ downward c units.
Horizontal translation	$g(x) = b^{x+c}$	• Shifts the graph of $f(x) = b^x$ to the left c units.
	$g(x) = b^{x-c}$	• Shifts the graph of $f(x) = b^x$ to the right c units.
Reflecting	$g(x) = -b^x$	• Reflects the graph of $f(x) = b^x$ about the x-axis.
	$g(x) = b^{-x}$	• Reflects the graph of $f(x) = b^x$ about the y-axis.
Vertical stretching or shrinking	$g(x) = cb^x$	• Stretches the graph of $f(x) = b^x$ if $c > 1$. • Shrinks the graph of $f(x) = b^x$ if $0 < c < 1$.

Using the information in Table 3.1 and a table of coordinates, you will obtain relatively accurate graphs that can be verified using a graphing utility.

EXAMPLE 3 **Transformations Involving Exponential Functions**

Use the graph of $f(x) = 3^x$ to obtain the graph of $g(x) = 3^{x+1}$.

Solution Examine Table 3.1. Note that the function $g(x) = 3^{x+1}$ has the general form $g(x) = b^{x+c}$, where $c = 1$. Thus, we graph $g(x) = 3^{x+1}$ by shifting the graph of $f(x) = 3^x$ *one* unit to the *left*. We construct a table showing some of the coordinates for f and g, selecting integers from –2 to 2 for x. The graphs of f and g are shown in Figure 3.3.

x	$f(x) = 3^x$	$g(x) = 3^{x+1}$
–2	$f(-2) = 3^{-2} = \frac{1}{9}$	$g(-2) = 3^{-2+1} = 3^{-1} = \frac{1}{3}$
–1	$f(-1) = 3^{-1} = \frac{1}{3}$	$g(-1) = 3^{-1+1} = 3^0 = 1$
0	$f(0) = 3^0 = 1$	$g(0) = 3^{0+1} = 3^1 = 3$
1	$f(1) = 3^1 = 3$	$g(1) = 3^{1+1} = 3^2 = 9$
2	$f(2) = 3^2 = 9$	$g(2) = 3^{2+1} = 3^3 = 27$

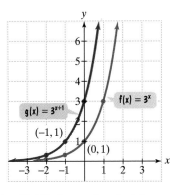

Figure 3.3 The graph of $g(x) = 3^{x+1}$ is the graph of $f(x) = 3^x$ shifted one unit to the left.

Check Point 3   Use the graph of $f(x) = 3^x$ to obtain the graph of $g(x) = 3^{x-1}$.

If an exponential function is translated upward or downward, the horizontal asymptote is shifted by the amount of the vertical shift.

EXAMPLE 4 **Transformations Involving Exponential Functions**

Use the graph of $f(x) = 2^x$ to obtain the graph of $g(x) = 2^x - 3$.

Solution The function $g(x) = 2^x - 3$ has the general form $g(x) = b^x - c$, where $c = 3$. Thus, we graph $g(x) = 2^x - 3$ by shifting the graph of $f(x) = 2^x$ *down three* units. We construct a table showing some of the coordinates for f and g, selecting integers from –2 to 2 for x.

The graphs of f and g are shown in Figure 3.4. Notice that the horizontal asymptote for f, the x-axis, is shifted down three units for the horizontal asymptote for g. As a result, $y = -3$ is the horizontal asymptote for g.

x	$f(x) = 2^x$	$g(x) = 2^x - 3$
-2	$f(-2) = 2^{-2} = \frac{1}{4}$	$g(-2) = 2^{-2} - 3 = \frac{1}{4} - 3 = -2\frac{3}{4}$
-1	$f(-1) = 2^{-1} = \frac{1}{2}$	$g(-1) = 2^{-1} - 3 = \frac{1}{2} - 3 = -2\frac{1}{2}$
0	$f(0) = 2^0 = 1$	$g(0) = 2^0 - 3 = 1 - 3 = -2$
1	$f(1) = 2^1 = 2$	$g(1) = 2^1 - 3 = 2 - 3 = -1$
2	$f(2) = 2^2 = 4$	$g(2) = 2^2 - 3 = 4 - 3 = 1$

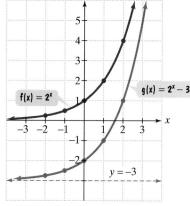

Figure 3.4 The graph of $g(x) = 2^x - 3$ is the graph of $f(x) = 2^x$ shifted down three units.

Check Point 4 Use the graph of $f(x) = 2^x$ to obtain the graph of $g(x) = 2^x + 1$.

3 Evaluate functions with base e.

The Natural Base e

An irrational number, symbolized by the letter e, appears as the base in many applied exponential functions. This irrational number is approximately equal to 2.72. More accurately,

$$e \approx 2.71828\ldots.$$

The number e is called the **natural base.** The function $f(x) = e^x$ is called the **natural exponential function.**

Use a scientific or graphing calculator with an $\boxed{e^x}$ key to evaluate e to various powers. For example, to find e^2, press the following keys on most calculators:

Scientific calculator: 2 $\boxed{e^x}$

Graphing calculator: $\boxed{e^x}$ 2 $\boxed{\text{ENTER}}$.

The display should be approximately 7.389.

$$e^2 \approx 7.389$$

The number e lies between 2 and 3. Because $2^2 = 4$ and $3^2 = 9$, it makes sense that e^2, approximately 7.389, lies between 4 and 9.

Because $2 < e < 3$, the graph of $y = e^x$ lies between the graphs of $y = 2^x$ and $y = 3^x$, shown in Figure 3.5.

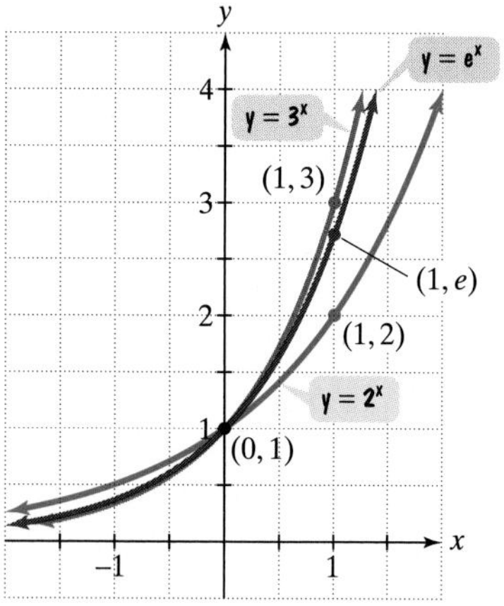

Figure 3.5 Graphs of three exponential functions

EXAMPLE 5 World Population

In a report entitled *Resources and Man*, the U.S. National Academy of Sciences concluded that a world population of 10 billion "is close to (if not above) the maximum that an intensely managed world might hope to support with some degree of comfort and individual choice." At the time the report was issued in 1969, world population was approximately 3.6 billion, with a growth rate of 2% per year. The function

$$f(x) = 3.6e^{0.02x}$$

describes world population, $f(x)$, in billions, x years after 1969. Use the function to find world population in the year 2020. Is there cause for alarm?

World Population, in Billions

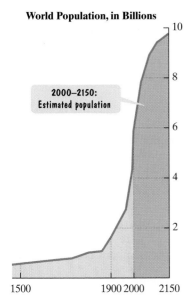

2000–2150:
Estimated population

1500   1900 2000   2150

Source: U.N. Population Division

Solution Because 2020 is 51 years after 1969, we substitute 51 for x in $f(x) = 3.6e^{0.02x}$:

$$f(51) = 3.6e^{0.02(51)}.$$

Perform this computation on your calculator.

Scientific calculator: 3.6 ×   (.02 × 51) e^x =

Graphing calculator: 3.6 × e^x (.02 × 51) ENTER

The display should be approximately 9.9835012. Thus,

$$f(51) = 3.6e^{0.02(51)} \approx 9.98.$$

This indicates that world population in the year 2020 will be approximately 9.98 billion. Because this number is quite close to 10 billion, the given function suggests that there may be cause for alarm.

World population in 2000 was approximately 6 billion, but the growth rate was no longer 2%. It had slowed down to 1.3%. Using this current growth rate, exponential functions now predict a world population of 7.8 billion in the year 2020. Experts think the population may stabilize at 10 billion after 2200 if the deceleration in growth rate continues.

Check Point 5 The function $f(x) = 6e^{0.013x}$ describes world population, $f(x)$, in billions, x years after 2000 subject to a growth rate of 1.3% annually. Use the function to find world population in 2050.

4 Use compound interest formulas.

Compound Interest

We all want a wonderful life with fulfilling work, good health, and loving relationships. And let's be honest: Financial security wouldn't hurt! Achieving this goal depends on understanding how money in savings accounts grows in remarkable ways as a result of *compound interest*. **Compound interest** is interest computed on your original investment as well as on any accumulated interest.

Suppose a sum of money, called the **principal**, P, is invested at an annual percentage rate r, in decimal form, compounded once per year. Because the interest is added to the principal at year's end, the accumulated value, A, is

$$A = P + Pr = P(1 + r).$$

The accumulated amount of money follows this pattern of multiplying the previous principal by $(1 + r)$ for each successive year, as indicated in Table 3.2.

Table 3.2

Time in Years	Accumulated Value after Each Compounding
0	$A = P$
1	$A = P(1 + r)$
2	$A = P(1 + r)(1 + r) = P(1 + r)^2$
3	$A = P(1 + r)^2(1 + r) = P(1 + r)^3$
4	$A = P(1 + r)^3(1 + r) = P(1 + r)^4$
⋮	⋮
t	$A = P(1 + r)^t$

This formula gives the balance, A, that a principal, P, is worth after t years at interest rate r, compounded once a year.

n	$\left(1 + \dfrac{1}{n}\right)^n$
1	2
2	2.25
5	2.48832
10	2.59374246
100	2.704813829
1000	2.716923932
10,000	2.718145927
100,000	2.718268237
1,000,000	2.718280469
1,000,000,000	2.718281827

As n takes on increasingly large values, the expression $\left(1 + \dfrac{1}{n}\right)^n$ approaches e.

Most savings institutions have plans in which interest is paid more than once a year. If compound interest is paid twice a year, the compounding period is six months. We say that the interest is **compounded semiannually.** When compound interest is paid four times a year, the compounding period is three months and the interest is said to be **compounded quarterly.** Some plans allow for monthly compounding or daily compounding.

In general, when compound interest is paid n times a year, we say that there are **n compounding periods per year.** The formula $A = P(1 + r)^t$ can be adjusted to take into account the number of compounding periods in a year. If there are n compounding periods per year, the formula becomes

$$A = P\left(1 + \frac{r}{n}\right)^{nt}.$$

Some banks use **continuous compounding,** where the number of compounding periods increases infinitely (compounding interest every trillionth of a second, every quadrillionth of a second, etc.). As n, the number of compounding periods in a year, increases without bound, the expression $\left(1 + \dfrac{1}{n}\right)^n$ approaches e. As a result, the formula for continuous compounding is $A = Pe^{rt}$. Although continuous compounding sounds terrific, it yields only a fraction of a percent more interest over a year than daily compounding.

Formulas for Compound Interest

After t years, the balance, A, in an account with principal P and annual interest rate r (in decimal form) is given by the following formulas:

1. For n compoundings per year: $A = P\left(1 + \dfrac{r}{n}\right)^{nt}$

2. For continuous compounding: $A = Pe^{rt}$.

EXAMPLE 6   Choosing between Investments

You want to invest $8000 for 6 years, and you have a choice between two accounts. The first pays 7% per year, compounded monthly. The second pays 6.85% per year, compounded continuously. Which is the better investment?

Solution The better investment is the one with the greater balance in the account after 6 years. Let's begin with the account with monthly compounding. We use the compound interest model with $P = 8000$, $r = 7\% = 0.07$, $n = 12$ (monthly compounding means 12 compoundings per year), and $t = 6$.

$$A = P\left(1 + \frac{r}{n}\right)^{nt} = 8000\left(1 + \frac{0.07}{12}\right)^{12 \cdot 6} \approx 12{,}160.84$$

The balance in this account after 6 years is $12,160.84. For the second investment option, we use the model for continuous compounding with $P = 8000$, $r = 6.85\% = 0.0685$, and $t = 6$.

$$A = Pe^{rt} = 8000e^{0.0685(6)} \approx 12{,}066.60$$

Technology

The graphs illustrate that as x increases, $\left(1 + \dfrac{1}{x}\right)^x$ approaches e.

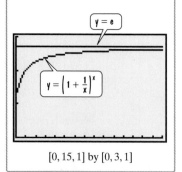

$y = e$

$y = \left(1 + \dfrac{1}{x}\right)^x$

[0, 15, 1] by [0, 3, 1]

The balance in this account after 6 years is $12,066.60, slightly less than the previous amount. Thus, the better investment is the 7% monthly compounding option.

Check Point 6

A sum of $10,000 is invested at an annual rate of 8%. Find the balance in the account after 5 years subject to **a.** quarterly compounding and **b.** continuous compounding.

EXERCISE SET 3.1

Practice Exercises

In Exercises 1–10, approximate each number using a calculator. Round your answer to three decimal places.

1. $2^{3.4}$ **2.** $3^{2.4}$ **3.** $3^{\sqrt{5}}$ **4.** $5^{\sqrt{3}}$ **5.** $4^{-1.5}$

6. $6^{-1.2}$ **7.** $e^{2.3}$ **8.** $e^{3.4}$ **9.** $e^{-0.95}$ **10.** $e^{-0.75}$

In Exercises 11–18, graph each function by making a table of coordinates. If applicable, use a graphing utility to confirm your hand-drawn graph.

11. $f(x) = 4^x$ **12.** $f(x) = 5^x$

13. $g(x) = \left(\frac{3}{2}\right)^x$ **14.** $g(x) = \left(\frac{4}{3}\right)^x$

15. $h(x) = \left(\frac{1}{2}\right)^x$ **16.** $h(x) = \left(\frac{1}{3}\right)^x$

17. $f(x) = (0.6)^x$ **18.** $f(x) = (0.8)^x$

In Exercises 19–24, the graph of an exponential function is given. Select the function for each graph from the following options:

$$f(x) = 3^x, g(x) = 3^{x-1}, h(x) = 3^x - 1,$$
$$F(x) = -3^x, G(x) = 3^{-x}, H(x) = -3^{-x}.$$

19.

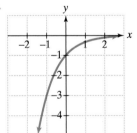

20.

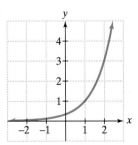

21.

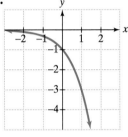

22.

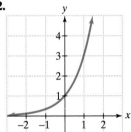

23.

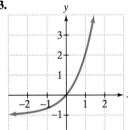

24.

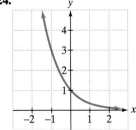

In Exercises 25–34, begin by graphing $f(x) = 2^x$. Then use transformations of this graph and a table of coordinates to graph the given function. If applicable, use a graphing utility to confirm your hand-drawn graphs.

25. $g(x) = 2^{x+1}$ **26.** $g(x) = 2^{x+2}$

27. $g(x) = 2^x - 1$ **28.** $g(x) = 2^x + 2$

29. $h(x) = 2^{x+1} - 1$ **30.** $h(x) = 2^{x+2} - 1$

31. $g(x) = -2^x$ **32.** $g(x) = 2^{-x}$

33. $g(x) = 2 \cdot 2^x$ **34.** $g(x) = \frac{1}{2} \cdot 2^x$

In Exercises 35–40, graph functions f and g in the same rectangular coordinate system. If applicable, use a graphing utility to confirm your hand-drawn graphs.

35. $f(x) = 3^x$ and $g(x) = 3^{-x}$

36. $f(x) = 3^x$ and $g(x) = -3^x$

37. $f(x) = 3^x$ and $g(x) = \frac{1}{3} \cdot 3^x$

38. $f(x) = 3^x$ and $g(x) = 3 \cdot 3^x$

39. $f(x) = (\frac{1}{2})^x$ and $g(x) = (\frac{1}{2})^{x-1} + 1$

40. $f(x) = (\frac{1}{2})^x$ and $g(x) = (\frac{1}{2})^{x-1} + 2$

Use the compound interest formulas $A = P\left(1 + \dfrac{r}{n}\right)^{nt}$ and $A = Pe^{rt}$ to solve Exercises 41–44. Round answers to the nearest cent.

41. Find the accumulated value of an investment of $10,000 for 5 years at an interest rate of 5.5% if the money is **a.** compounded semiannually; **b.** compounded quarterly; **c.** compounded monthly; **d.** compounded continuously.

42. Find the accumulated value of an investment of $5000 for 10 years at an interest rate of 6.5% if the money is **a.** compounded semiannually; **b.** compounded quarterly; **c.** compounded monthly; **d.** compounded continuously.

43. Suppose that you have $12,000 to invest. Which investment yields the greatest return over 3 years: 7% compounded monthly or 6.85% compounded continuously?

44. Suppose that you have $6000 to invest. Which investment yields the greatest return over 4 years: 8.25% compounded quarterly or 8.3% compounded semiannually?

Application Exercises

Use a calculator with a $\boxed{y^x}$ *key or a* $\boxed{\wedge}$ *key to solve Exercises 45–52.*

45. The exponential function $f(x) = 67.38(1.026)^x$ describes the population of Mexico, $f(x)$, in millions, x years after 1980.

a. Substitute 0 for x and, without using a calculator, find Mexico's population in 1980.

b. Substitute 27 for x and use your calculator to find Mexico's population in the year 2007 as predicted by this function.

c. Find Mexico's population in the year 2034 as predicted by this function.

d. Find Mexico's population in the year 2061 as predicted by this function.

e. What appears to be happening to Mexico's population every 27 years?

46. The 1986 explosion at the Chernobyl nuclear power plant in the former Soviet Union sent about 1000 kilograms of radioactive cesium-137 into the atmosphere. The function $f(x) = 1000(0.5)^{x/30}$ describes the amount, $f(x)$, in kilograms, of cesium-137 remaining in Chernobyl x years after 1986. If even 100 kilograms of cesium-137 remain in Chernobyl's atmosphere, the area is considered unsafe for human habitation. Find $f(80)$ and determine if Chernobyl will be safe for human habitation by 2066.

It is 8:00 P.M. and West Side Story *is scheduled to begin. When the curtain does not go up, a rumor begins to spread through the 400-member audience: The lead roles of Tony and Maria might be understudied by Anthony Hopkins and Jodie Foster. The function*

$$f(x) = \frac{400}{1 + 399(0.67)^x}$$

models the number of people in the audience, f (x), who have heard the rumor x minutes after 8:00. Use this function to solve Exercises 47–48.

47. Evaluate $f(10)$ and describe what this means in practical terms.

48. Evaluate $f(20)$ and describe what this means in practical terms.

The formula $S = C(1 + r)^t$ models inflation, where $C =$ the value today, $r =$ the annual inflation rate, and $S =$ the inflated value t years from now. Use this formula to solve Exercises 49–50.

49. If the inflation rate is 6%, how much will a house now worth $65,000 be worth in 10 years?

50. If the inflation rate is 3%, how much will a house now worth $110,000 be worth in 5 years?

51. A decimal approximation for $\sqrt{3}$ is 1.7320508. Use a calculator to find $2^{1.7}, 2^{1.73}, 2^{1.732}, 2^{1.73205}$, and $2^{1.7320508}$. Now find $2^{\sqrt{3}}$. What do you observe?

52. A decimal approximation for π is 3.141593. Use a calculator to find $2^3, 2^{3.1}, 2^{3.14}, 2^{3.141}, 2^{3.1415}, 2^{3.14159}$, and $2^{3.141593}$. Now find 2^{π}. What do you observe?

The graph on the next page shows the number of Americans enrolled in HMOs, in millions, from 1992 through 2000. The data can be modeled by the exponential function

$$f(x) = 36.1e^{0.113x},$$

which describes enrollment in HMOs, f (x), in millions, x years after 1992. Use this function to solve Exercises 53–54.

Enrollment in HMOs

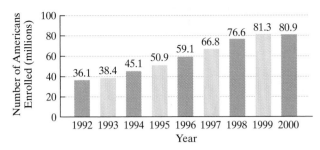

Source: Department of Health and Human Services

53. According to the model, how many Americans will be enrolled in HMOs in the year 2006? Round to the nearest tenth of a million.

54. According to the model, how many Americans will be enrolled in HMOs in the year 2008? Round to the nearest tenth of a million.

55. In college, we study large volumes of information—information that, unfortunately, we do not often retain for very long. The function

$$f(x) = 80e^{-0.5x} + 20$$

describes the percentage of information, $f(x)$, that a particular person remembers x weeks after learning the information.

  a. Substitute 0 for x and, without using a calculator, find the percentage of information remembered at the moment it is first learned.

  b. Substitute 1 for x and find the percentage of information that is remembered after 1 week.

  c. Find the percentage of information that is remembered after 4 weeks.

  d. Find the percentage of information that is remembered after one year (52 weeks).

56. In 1626, Peter Minuit convinced the Wappinger Indians to sell him Manhattan Island for $24. If the Native Americans had put the $24 into a bank account paying 5% interest, how much would the investment be worth in the year 2000 if interest were compounded
  a. monthly?   **b.** continuously?

57. The function

$$N(t) = \frac{30,000}{1 + 20e^{-1.5t}}$$

describes the number of people, $N(t)$, who become ill with influenza t weeks after its initial outbreak in a town with 30,000 inhabitants. The horizontal asymptote in the graph at the top of the next column indicates that there is a limit to the epidemic's growth.

  a. How many people became ill with the flu when the epidemic began? (When the epidemic began, $t = 0$.)

  b. How many people were ill by the end of the third week?

  c. Why can't the spread of an epidemic simply grow indefinitely? What does the horizontal asymptote shown in the graph indicate about the limiting size of the population that becomes ill?

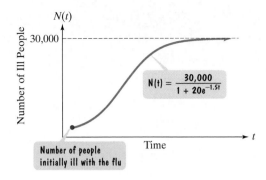

 Writing in Mathematics

58. What is an exponential function?

59. What is the natural exponential function?

60. Use a calculator to evaluate $\left(1 + \dfrac{1}{x}\right)^x$ for $x = 10, 100,$ 1000, 10,000, 100,000, and 1,000,000. Describe what happens to the expression as x increases.

61. Write an example similar to Example 6 on page 166 in which continuous compounding at a slightly lower yearly interest rate is a better investment than compounding n times per year.

62. Describe how you could use the graph of $f(x) = 2^x$ to obtain a decimal approximation for $\sqrt{2}$.

63. The exponential function $y = 2^x$ is one-to-one and has an inverse function. Try finding the inverse function by exchanging x and y and solving for y. Describe the difficulty that you encounter in this process. What is needed to overcome this problem?

64. In 2000, world population was approximately 6 billion with an annual growth rate of 1.3%. Discuss two factors that would cause this growth rate to slow down over the next ten years.

Technology Exercises

65. Graph $y = 13.49(0.967)^x - 1$, the function for the number of O-rings expected to fail at $x°$F, in a $[0, 90, 10]$ by $[0, 20, 5]$ viewing rectangle. If NASA engineers had used this function and its graph, is it likely they would have allowed the *Challenger* to be launched when the temperature was $31°$F? Explain.

66. You have $10,000 to invest. One bank pays 5% interest compounded quarterly and the other pays 4.5% interest compounded monthly.

  a. Use the formula for compound interest to write a function for the balance in each account at any time t.

  b. Use a graphing utility to graph both functions in an appropriate viewing rectangle. Based on the graphs, which bank offers the better return on your money?

67. a. Graph $y = e^x$ and $y = 1 + x + \dfrac{x^2}{2}$ in the same viewing rectangle.

  b. Graph $y = e^x$ and $y = 1 + x + \dfrac{x^2}{2} + \dfrac{x^3}{6}$ in the same viewing rectangle.

  c. Graph $y = e^x$ and $y = 1 + x + \dfrac{x^2}{2} + \dfrac{x^3}{6} + \dfrac{x^4}{24}$ in the same viewing rectangle.

  d. Describe what you observe in parts (a)–(c). Try generalizing this observation.

Critical Thinking Exercises

68. Which one of the following is true?

  a. As the number of compounding periods increases on a fixed investment, the amount of money in the account over a fixed interval of time will increase without bound.

  b. The functions $f(x) = 3^{-x}$ and $g(x) = -3^x$ have the same graph.

  c. $e = 2.718$

  d. The functions $f(x) = \left(\frac{1}{3}\right)^x$ and $g(x) = 3^{-x}$ have the same graph.

69. The graphs labeled (a)–(d) in the figure represent $y = 3^x$, $y = 5^x$, $y = \left(\frac{1}{3}\right)^x$, and $y = \left(\frac{1}{5}\right)^x$, but not necessarily in that order. Which is which? Describe the process that enables you to make this decision.

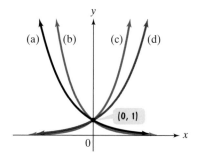

70. Graph $f(x) = 2^x$ and its inverse function in the same rectangular coordinate system.

71. The *hyperbolic cosine* and *hyperbolic sine* functions are defined by

$$\cosh x = \frac{e^x + e^{-x}}{2} \quad \text{and} \quad \sinh x = \frac{e^x - e^{-x}}{2}.$$

Prove that $(\cosh x)^2 - (\sinh x)^2 = 1$.

SECTION 3.2 *Logarithmic Functions*

Objectives

1. Change from logarithmic to exponential form.
2. Change from exponential to logarithmic form.
3. Evaluate logarithms.
4. Use basic logarithmic properties.
5. Graph logarithmic functions.
6. Find the domain of a logarithmic function.
7. Use common logarithms.
8. Use natural logarithms.

The earthquake that ripped through northern California on October 17, 1989, measured 7.1 on the Richter scale, killed more than 60 people, and injured more than 2400. Shown here is San Francisco's Marina district, where shock waves tossed houses off their foundations and into the street.

A higher measure on the Richter scale is more devastating than it seems because for each increase in one unit on the scale, there is a tenfold increase in the intensity of an earthquake. In this section, our focus is on the inverse of the exponential function, called the logarithmic function. The logarithmic function will help you to understand diverse phenomena, including earthquake intensity, human memory, and the pace of life in large cities.

The Definition of Logarithmic Functions

No horizontal line can be drawn that intersects the graph of an exponential function at more than one point. This means that the exponential function is one-to-one and has an inverse. The inverse function of the exponential function with base b is called the *logarithmic function with base b*.

> **Definition of the Logarithmic Function**
> For $x > 0$ and $b > 0, b \neq 1$,
> $$y = \log_b x \text{ is equivalent to } b^y = x.$$
> The function $f(x) = \log_b x$ is the **logarithmic function with base b**.

Study Tip

The inverse function of $y = b^x$ is $x = b^y$. Logarithms give us a way to express this inverse function for y in terms of x.

The equations

$$y = \log_b x \quad \text{and} \quad b^y = x$$

are different ways of expressing the same thing. The first equation is in **logarithmic form** and the second equivalent equation is in **exponential form.**

Notice that a **logarithm, y, is an exponent.** You should learn the location of the base and exponent in each form.

> **Location of Base and Exponent in Exponential and Logarithmic Forms**
>
> Logarithmic Form: $\;y = \log_b x\;$ (Exponent; Base)
> Exponential Form: $\;b^y = x\;$ (Exponent; Base)

1 Change from logarithmic to exponential form.

EXAMPLE 1 Changing from Logarithmic to Exponential Form

Write each equation in its equivalent exponential form:

a. $2 = \log_5 x$ **b.** $3 = \log_b 64$ **c.** $\log_3 7 = y$.

Solution We use the fact that $y = \log_b x$ means $b^y = x$.

a. $2 = \log_5 x$ means $5^2 = x$.   **b.** $3 = \log_b 64$ means $b^3 = 64$.

Logarithms are exponents.   Logarithms are exponents.

c. $\log_3 7 = y$ or $y = \log_3 7$ means $3^y = 7$.

Check Point 1 Write each equation in its equivalent exponential form:
a. $3 = \log_7 x$ **b.** $2 = \log_b 25$ **c.** $\log_4 26 = y$.

2 Change from exponential to logarithmic form.

EXAMPLE 2 Changing from Exponential to Logarithmic Form

Write each equation in its equivalent logarithmic form:

a. $12^2 = x$ **b.** $b^3 = 8$ **c.** $e^y = 9$.

Solution We use the fact that $b^y = x$ means $y = \log_b x$.

a. $12^2 = x$ means $2 = \log_{12} x$.   **b.** $b^3 = 8$ means $3 = \log_b 8$.

Exponents are logarithms.   Exponents are logarithms.

c. $e^y = 9$ means $y = \log_e 9$.

Check Point 2   Write each equation in its equivalent logarithmic form:

a. $2^5 = x$ **b.** $b^3 = 27$ **c.** $e^y = 33$.

3 Evaluate logarithms.

Remembering that logarithms are exponents makes it possible to evaluate some logarithms by inspection. The logarithm of x with base b, $\log_b x$, is the exponent to which b must be raised to get x. For example, suppose we want to evaluate $\log_2 32$. We ask, 2 to what power gives 32? Because $2^5 = 32$, $\log_2 32 = 5$.

EXAMPLE 3   Evaluating Logarithms

Evaluate:

a. $\log_2 16$ **b.** $\log_3 9$ **c.** $\log_{25} 5$.

Solution

Logarithmic Expression	Question Needed for Evaluation	Logarithmic Expression Evaluated
a. $\log_2 16$	2 to what power gives 16?	$\log_2 16 = 4$ because $2^4 = 16$.
b. $\log_3 9$	3 to what power gives 9?	$\log_3 9 = 2$ because $3^2 = 9$.
c. $\log_{25} 5$	25 to what power gives 5?	$\log_{25} 5 = \frac{1}{2}$ because $25^{1/2} = \sqrt{25} = 5$.

Check Point 3   Evaluate:

a. $\log_{10} 100$ **b.** $\log_3 3$ **c.** $\log_{36} 6$.

4 Use basic logarithmic properties.

Basic Logarithmic Properties

Because logarithms are exponents, they have properties that can be verified using properties of exponents.

Basic Logarithmic Properties Involving One

1. $\log_b b = 1$ because 1 is the exponent to which b must be raised to obtain b. $(b^1 = b)$

2. $\log_b 1 = 0$ because 0 is the exponent to which b must be raised to obtain 1. $(b^0 = 1)$

EXAMPLE 4 Using Properties of Logarithms

Evaluate:

a. $\log_7 7$ **b.** $\log_5 1$.

Solution

a. Because $\log_b b = 1$, we conclude $\log_7 7 = 1$.
b. Because $\log_b 1 = 0$, we conclude $\log_5 1 = 0$.

Check
Point
4

Evaluate:

a. $\log_9 9$ **b.** $\log_8 1$.

The inverse of the exponential function is the logarithmic function. Thus, if $f(x) = b^x$, then $f^{-1}(x) = \log_b x$. Inverse functions "undo" one another. In particular,

$$f(f^{-1}(x)) = x \text{ and } f^{-1}(f(x)) = x.$$

Applying these relationships to exponential and logarithmic functions, we obtain the following **inverse properties of logarithms:**

Inverse Properties of Logarithms

For $b > 0$ and $b \neq 1$,

$\log_b b^x = x$ The logarithm with base b of b raised to a power equals that power.

$b^{\log_b x} = x$ b raised to the logarithm with base b of a number equals that number.

EXAMPLE 5 Using Inverse Properties of Logarithms

Evaluate:

a. $\log_4 4^5$ **b.** $6^{\log_6 9}$.

Solution

a. Because $\log_b b^x = x$, we conclude $\log_4 4^5 = 5$.
b. Because $b^{\log_b x} = x$, we conclude $6^{\log_6 9} = 9$.

Check
Point
5

Evaluate:

a. $\log_7 7^8$ **b.** $3^{\log_3 17}$.

5 Graph logarithmic functions.

Graphs of Logarithmic Functions

How do we graph logarithmic functions? We use the fact that the logarithmic function is the inverse of the exponential function. This means that the logarithmic function reverses the coordinates of the exponential function. It also means that the graph of the logarithmic function is a reflection of the graph of the exponential function about the line $y = x$.

EXAMPLE 6 **Graphs of Exponential and Logarithmic Functions**

Graph $f(x) = 2^x$ and $g(x) = \log_2 x$ in the same rectangular coordinate system.

Solution We first set up a table of coordinates for $f(x) = 2^x$. Reversing, these coordinates gives the coordinates for the inverse function $g(x) = \log_2 x$.

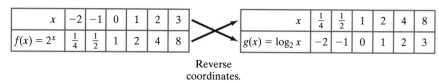

x	-2	-1	0	1	2	3
$f(x) = 2^x$	$\frac{1}{4}$	$\frac{1}{2}$	1	2	4	8

x	$\frac{1}{4}$	$\frac{1}{2}$	1	2	4	8
$g(x) = \log_2 x$	-2	-1	0	1	2	3

Reverse coordinates.

We now plot the ordered pairs in both tables, connecting them with smooth curves. Figure 3.6 shows the graphs of $f(x) = 2^x$ and its inverse function $g(x) = \log_2 x$. The graph of the inverse can also be drawn by reflecting the graph of $f(x) = 2^x$ about the line $y = x$.

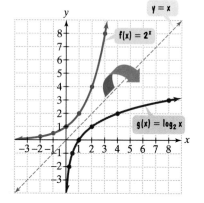

Figure 3.6 The graphs of $f(x) = 2^x$ and its inverse function

Check Point 6 Graph $f(x) = 3^x$ and $g(x) = \log_3 x$ in the same rectangular coordinate system.

Figure 3.7 illustrates the relationship between the graph of the exponential function, shown in blue, and its inverse, the logarithmic function, shown in red, for bases greater than 1 and for bases between 0 and 1.

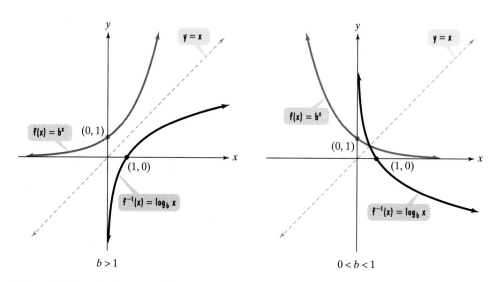

Figure 3.7 Graphs of exponential and logarithmic functions

Discovery

Verify each of the four characteristics in the box for the red graphs in Figure 3.7.

Characteristics of the Graphs of Logarithmic Functions of the Form $f(x) = \log_b x$

- The x-intercept is 1. There is no y-intercept.
- The y-axis is a vertical asymptote.
- If $b > 1$, the function is increasing. If $0 < b < 1$, the function is decreasing.
- The graph is smooth and continuous. It has no sharp corners or gaps.

The graphs of logarithmic functions can be translated vertically or horizontally, reflected, stretched, or shrunk. We use the ideas as summarized in Table 3.3 to do so.

Table 3.3   Transformations Involving Logarithmic Functions
In each case, c represents a positive real number.

Transformation	Equation	Description
Vertical translation	$g(x) = \log_b x + c$	• Shifts the graph of $f(x) = \log_b x$ upward c units.
	$g(x) = \log_b x - c$	• Shifts the graph of $f(x) = \log_b x$ downward c units.
Horizontal translation	$g(x) = \log_b (x + c)$	• Shifts the graph of $f(x) = \log_b x$ to the left c units. Vertical asymptote: $x = -c$.
	$g(x) = \log_b (x - c)$	• Shifts the graph of $f(x) = \log_b x$ to the right c units. Vertical asymptote: $x = c$.
Reflecting	$g(x) = -\log_b x$	• Reflects the graph of $f(x) = \log_b x$ about the x-axis.
	$g(x) = \log_b (-x)$	• Reflects the graph of $f(x) = \log_b x$ about the y-axis.
Vertical stretching or shrinking	$g(x) = c \log_b x$	• Stretches the graph of $f(x) = \log_b x$ if $c > 1$. • Shrinks the graph of $f(x) = \log_b x$ if $0 < c < 1$.

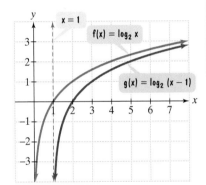

For example, Figure 3.8 illustrates that the graph of $g(x) = \log_2 (x - 1)$ is the graph of $f(x) = \log_2 x$ shifted one unit to the right. If a logarithmic function is translated to the left or to the right, both the x-intercept and the vertical asymptote are shifted by the amount of the horizontal shift. In Figure 3.8, the x-intercept of f is 1. Because g is shifted one unit to the right, its x-intercept is 2. Also observe that the vertical asymptote for f, the y-axis, is shifted one unit to the right for the vertical asymptote for g. Thus, $x = 1$ is the vertical asymptote for g.

Here are some other examples of transformations of graphs of logarithmic functions:

- The graph of $g(x) = 3 + \log_4 x$ is the graph of $f(x) = \log_4 x$ shifted up three units, shown in Figure 3.9.
- The graph of $h(x) = -\log_2 x$ is the graph of $f(x) = \log_2 x$ reflected about the x-axis, shown in Figure 3.10.
- The graph of $r(x) = \log_2 (-x)$ is the graph of $f(x) = \log_2 x$ reflected about the y-axis, shown in Figure 3.11.

Figure 3.8 Shifting $f(x) = \log_2 x$ one unit to the right

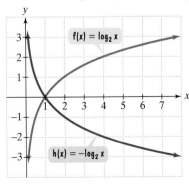

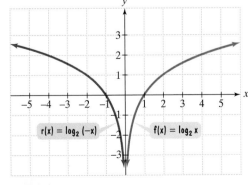

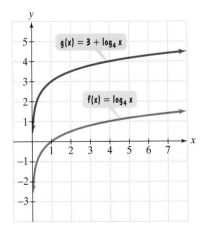

Figure 3.9 Shifting vertically up three units

Figure 3.10 Reflection about the x-axis

Figure 3.11 Reflection about the y-axis

6 Find the domain of a logarithmic function.

The Domain of a Logarithmic Function

In Section 3.1, we learned that the domain of an exponential function of the form $f(x) = b^x$ includes all real numbers and its range is the set of positive real numbers. Because the logarithmic function reverses the domain and the range of the exponential function, the **domain of a logarithmic function of the form $f(x) = \log_b x$ is the set of all positive real numbers.** Thus, $\log_2 8$ is defined because the value of x in the logarithmic expression, 8, is greater than zero and therefore is included in the domain of the logarithmic function $f(x) = \log_2 x$. However, $\log_2 0$ and $\log_2 (-8)$ are not defined because 0 and -8 are not positive real numbers and therefore are excluded from the domain of the logarithmic function $f(x) = \log_2 x$. In general, the domain of $f(x) = \log_b (x + c)$ consists of all x for which $x + c > 0$.

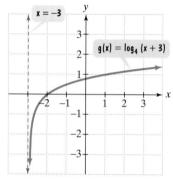

Figure 3.12 The domain of $g(x) = \log_4 (x + 3)$ is $(-3, \infty)$.

EXAMPLE 7   Finding the Domain of a Logarithmic Function

Find the domain of $g(x) = \log_4 (x + 3)$.

Solution   The domain of g consists of all x for which $x + 3 > 0$. Solving this inequality for x, we obtain $x > -3$. Thus, the domain of g is $(-3, \infty)$. This is illustrated in Figure 3.12. The vertical asymptote is $x = -3$, and all points on the graph of g have x-coordinates that are greater than -3.

Check Point 7   Find the domain of $h(x) = \log_4 (x - 5)$.

7 Use common logarithms.

Common Logarithms

The logarithmic function with base 10 is called the **common logarithmic function.** The function $f(x) = \log_{10} x$ is usually expressed as $f(x) = \log x$. A calculator with a $\boxed{\text{LOG}}$ key can be used to evaluate common logarithms. Here are some examples:

Logarithm	Most Scientific Calculator Keystrokes	Most Graphing Calculator Keystrokes	Display (or Approximate Display)
$\log 1000$	1000 $\boxed{\text{LOG}}$	$\boxed{\text{LOG}}$ 1000 $\boxed{\text{ENTER}}$	3
$\log \dfrac{5}{2}$	$\boxed{(}$ 5 $\boxed{\div}$ 2 $\boxed{)}$ $\boxed{\text{LOG}}$	$\boxed{\text{LOG}}$ $\boxed{(}$ 5 $\boxed{\div}$ 2 $\boxed{)}$ $\boxed{\text{ENTER}}$	0.39794
$\dfrac{\log 5}{\log 2}$	5 $\boxed{\text{LOG}}$ $\boxed{\div}$ 2 $\boxed{\text{LOG}}$ $\boxed{=}$	$\boxed{\text{LOG}}$ 5 $\boxed{\div}$ $\boxed{\text{LOG}}$ 2 $\boxed{\text{ENTER}}$	2.32193
$\log (-3)$	3 $\boxed{+/-}$ $\boxed{\text{LOG}}$	$\boxed{\text{LOG}}$ $\boxed{(-)}$ 3 $\boxed{\text{ENTER}}$	$\boxed{\text{ERROR}}$

The error message given by many calculators for $\log (-3)$ is a reminder that the domain of every logarithmic function, including the common logarithmic function, is the set of positive real numbers.

Many real-life phenomena start with rapid growth, and then the growth begins to level off. This type of behavior can be modeled by logarithmic functions.

EXAMPLE 8 Modeling Height of Children

The percentage of adult height attained by a boy who is x years old can be modeled by

$$f(x) = 29 + 48.8 \log (x + 1)$$

where x represents the boy's age and $f(x)$ represents the percentage of his adult height. Approximately what percent of his adult height is a boy at age eight?

Solution We substitute the boy's age, 8, for x and evaluate the function.

$$f(x) = 29 + 48.8 \log (x + 1) \quad \text{This is the given function.}$$
$$f(8) = 29 + 48.8 \log (8 + 1) \quad \text{Substitute 8 for } x.$$
$$= 29 + 48.8 \log 9 \quad \text{Graphing calculator keystrokes:}$$
$$\approx 76 \quad \boxed{29} \; \boxed{+} \; \boxed{48.8} \; \boxed{\text{LOG}} \; \boxed{9} \; \boxed{\text{ENTER}}$$

Thus, an 8-year-old boy is approximately 76% of his adult height.

> **Check Point 8** Use the function in Example 8 to answer this question: Approximately what percent of his adult height is a boy at age 10?

The basic properties of logarithms that were listed earlier in this section can be applied to common logarithms.

Properties of Common Logarithms	
General Properties	**Common Logarithm Properties**
1. $\log_b 1 = 0$	**1.** $\log 1 = 0$
2. $\log_b b = 1$	**2.** $\log 10 = 1$
3. $\log_b b^x = x$	**3.** $\log 10^x = x$
4. $b^{\log_b x} = x$	**4.** $10^{\log x} = x$

The property $\log 10^x = x$ can be used to evaluate common logarithms involving powers of 10. For example,

$$\log 100 = \log 10^2 = 2, \quad \log 1000 = \log 10^3 = 3, \quad \text{and} \quad \log 10^{7.1} = 7.1.$$

EXAMPLE 9 Earthquake Intensity

The magnitude, R, on the Richter scale of an earthquake of intensity I is given by

$$R = \log \frac{I}{I_0}$$

where I_0 is the intensity of a barely felt zero-level earthquake. The earthquake that destroyed San Francisco in 1906 was $10^{8.3}$ times as intense as a zero-level earthquake. What was its magnitude on the Richter scale?

Solution Because the earthquake was $10^{8.3}$ times as intense as a zero-level earthquake, the intensity, I, is $10^{8.3}I_0$.

$$R = \log \frac{I}{I_0} \qquad \text{This is the formula for magnitude on the Richter scale.}$$

$$R = \log \frac{10^{8.3}I_0}{I_0} \qquad \text{Substitute } 10^{8.3}I_0 \text{ for } I.$$

$$= \log 10^{8.3} \qquad \text{Simplify.}$$

$$= 8.3 \qquad \text{Use the property } \log 10^x = x.$$

San Francisco's 1906 earthquake registered 8.3 on the Richter scale.

Check Point 9 Use the formula in Example 9 to solve this problem. If an earthquake is 10,000 times as intense as a zero-level quake ($I = 10,000I_0$), what is its magnitude on the Richter scale?

8 Use natural logarithms.

Natural Logarithms

The logarithmic function with base e is called the **natural logarithmic function.** The function $f(x) = \log_e x$ is usually expressed as $f(x) = \ln x$, read "el en of x." A calculator with an $\boxed{\text{LN}}$ key can be used to evaluate natural logarithms.

Like the domain of all logarithmic functions, the domain of the natural logarithmic function is the set of all positive real numbers. Thus, the domain of $f(x) = \ln (x + c)$ consists of all x for which $x + c > 0$.

EXAMPLE 10 Finding Domains of Natural Logarithmic Functions

Find the domain of each function:
    a. $f(x) = \ln (3 - x)$ **b.** $g(x) = \ln (x - 3)^2$.

Solution

  a. The domain of f consists of all x for which $3 - x > 0$. Solving this inequality for x, we obtain $x < 3$. Thus, the domain of f is $\{x|x < 3\}$, or $(-\infty, 3)$. This is verified by the graph in Figure 3.13.

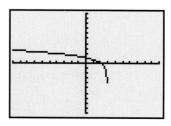

Figure 3.13 The domain of $f(x) = \ln (3 - x)$ is $(-\infty, 3)$.

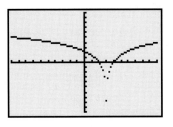

Figure 3.14 3 is excluded from the domain of $g(x) = \ln (x - 3)^2$.

b. The domain of g consists of all x for which $(x - 3)^2 > 0$. It follows that the domain of g is the set of all real numbers except 3. Thus, the domain of g is $\{x | x \neq 3\}$, or, in interval notation, $(-\infty, 3)$ or $(3, \infty)$. This is shown by the graph in Figure 3.14. To make it more obvious that 3 is excluded from the domain, we changed the $\boxed{\text{MODE}}$ to Dot.

Check Point 10   Find the domain of each function:

a. $f(x) = \ln (4 - x)$ **b.** $g(x) = \ln x^2$.

The basic properties of logarithms that were listed earlier in this section can be applied to natural logarithms.

Properties of Natural Logarithms

General Properties	Natural Logarithm Properties
1. $\log_b 1 = 0$	**1.** $\ln 1 = 0$
2. $\log_b b = 1$	**2.** $\ln e = 1$
3. $\log_b b^x = x$	**3.** $\ln e^x = x$
4. $b^{\log_b x} = x$	**4.** $e^{\ln x} = x$

The property $\ln e^x = x$ can be used to evaluate natural logarithms involving powers of e. For example,

$$\ln e^2 = 2, \quad \ln e^3 = 3, \quad \ln e^{7.1} = 7.1, \quad \text{and} \quad \ln \frac{1}{e} = \ln e^{-1} = -1.$$

EXAMPLE 11   Using Inverse Properties

Use inverse properties to simplify:

a. $\ln e^{7x}$ **b.** $e^{\ln 4x^2}$.

Solution

a. Because $\ln e^x = x$, we conclude that $\ln e^{7x} = 7x$.

b. Because $e^{\ln x} = x$, we conclude $e^{\ln 4x^2} = 4x^2$.

Check Point 11   Use inverse properties to simplify:

a. $\ln e^{25x}$ **b.** $e^{\ln \sqrt{x}}$.

EXAMPLE 12   Walking Speed and City Population

As the population of a city increases, the pace of life also increases. The formula

$$W = 0.35 \ln P + 2.74$$

models average walking speed, W, in feet per second, for a resident of a city whose population is P thousand. Find the average walking speed for people living in New York City with a population of 7323 thousand.

Solution   We use the formula and substitute 7323 for P, the population in thousands.

$$W = 0.35 \ln P + 2.74 \qquad \text{This is the given formula.}$$

$$W = 0.35 \ln 7323 + 2.74 \qquad \text{Substitute 7323 for } P.$$

$$\approx 5.9 \qquad\qquad \text{Graphing calculator keystrokes:}$$

$$0.35 \boxed{\text{LN}} \; 7323 \; \boxed{+} \; 2.74 \; \boxed{\text{ENTER}}.$$

The average walking speed in New York City is approximately 5.9 feet per second.

Check Point 12   Use the formula $W = 0.35 \ln P + 2.74$ to find the average walking speed in Jackson, Mississippi, with a population of 197 thousand.

EXERCISE SET 3.2

Practice Exercises

In Exercises 1–8, write each equation in its equivalent exponential form.

1. $4 = \log_2 16$

2. $6 = \log_2 64$

3. $2 = \log_3 x$

4. $2 = \log_9 x$

5. $5 = \log_b 32$

6. $3 = \log_b 27$

7. $\log_6 216 = y$

8. $\log_5 125 = y$

In Exercises 9–20, write each equation in its equivalent logarithmic form.

9. $2^3 = 8$

10. $5^4 = 625$

11. $2^{-4} = \frac{1}{16}$

12. $5^{-3} = \frac{1}{125}$

13. $\sqrt[3]{8} = 2$

14. $\sqrt[3]{64} = 4$

15. $13^2 = x$

16. $15^2 = x$

17. $b^3 = 1000$

18. $b^3 = 343$

19. $7^y = 200$

20. $8^y = 300$

In Exercises 21–38, evaluate each expression without using a calculator.

21. $\log_4 16$

22. $\log_7 49$

23. $\log_2 64$

24. $\log_3 27$

25. $\log_7 \sqrt{7}$

26. $\log_6 \sqrt{6}$

27. $\log_2 \frac{1}{8}$

28. $\log_3 \frac{1}{9}$

29. $\log_{64} 8$

30. $\log_{81} 9$

31. $\log_5 5$

32. $\log_{11} 11$

33. $\log_4 1$

34. $\log_6 1$

35. $\log_5 5^7$

36. $\log_4 4^6$

37. $8^{\log_8 19}$

38. $7^{\log_7 23}$

39. Graph $f(x) = 4^x$ and $g(x) = \log_4 x$ in the same rectangular coordinate system.

40. Graph $f(x) = 5^x$ and $g(x) = \log_5 x$ in the same rectangular coordinate system.

41. Graph $f(x) = \left(\frac{1}{2}\right)^x$ and $g(x) = \log_{1/2} x$ in the same rectangular coordinate system.

42. Graph $f(x) = \left(\frac{1}{4}\right)^x$ and $g(x) = \log_{1/4} x$ in the same rectangular coordinate system.

In Exercises 43–48, the graph of a logarithmic function is given. Select the function for each graph from the following options:

$$f(x) = \log_3 x, \; g(x) = \log_3 (x - 1), \; h(x) = \log_3 x - 1,$$

$$F(x) = -\log_3 x, \; G(x) = \log_3 (-x), \; H(x) = 1 - \log_3 x.$$

43.

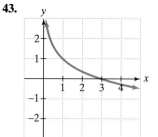

44.

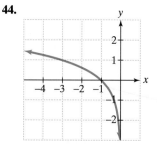

45.

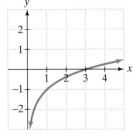

46.

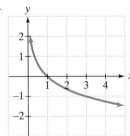

47.

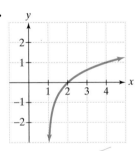

48.

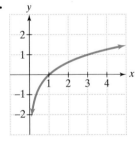

In Exercises 49–54, begin by graphing $f(x) = \log_2 x$. Then use transformations of this graph to graph the given function. What is the graph's x-intercept? What is the vertical asymptote?

49. $g(x) = \log_2 (x + 1)$ **50.** $g(x) = \log_2 (x + 2)$

51. $h(x) = 1 + \log_2 x$ **52.** $h(x) = 2 + \log_2 x$

53. $g(x) = \frac{1}{2} \log_2 x$ **54.** $g(x) = -2 \log_2 x$

In Exercises 55–60, find the domain of each logarithmic function.

55. $f(x) = \log_5 (x + 4)$ **56.** $f(x) = \log_5 (x + 6)$

57. $f(x) = \log (2 - x)$ **58.** $f(x) = \log (7 - x)$

59. $f(x) = \ln (x - 2)^2$ **60.** $f(x) = \ln (x - 7)^2$

In Exercises 61–74, evaluate each expression without using a calculator.

61. $\log 100$ **62.** $\log 1000$ **63.** $\log 10^7$

64. $\log 10^8$ **65.** $10^{\log 33}$ **66.** $10^{\log 53}$

67. $\ln 1$ **68.** $\ln e$ **69.** $\ln e^6$

70. $\ln e^7$ **71.** $\ln \dfrac{1}{e^6}$ **72.** $\ln \dfrac{1}{e^7}$

73. $e^{\ln 125}$ **74.** $e^{\ln 300}$

In Exercises 75–80, use inverse properties of logarithms to simplify each expression.

75. $\ln e^{9x}$ **76.** $\ln e^{13x}$ **77.** $e^{\ln 5x^2}$

78. $e^{\ln 7x^2}$ **79.** $10^{\log \sqrt{x}}$ **80.** $10^{\log \sqrt[3]{x}}$

Application Exercises

T he percentage of adult height attained by a girl who is x years old can be modeled by

$$f(x) = 62 + 35 \log (x - 4)$$

where x represents the girl's age (from 5 to 15) and $f(x)$ represents the percentage of her adult height. Use the function to solve Exercises 81–82.

81. Approximately what percent of her adult height is a girl at age 13?

82. Approximately what percent of her adult height is a girl at age ten?

83. The annual amount that we spend to attend sporting events can be modeled by

$$f(x) = 2.05 + 1.3 \ln x$$

where x represents the number of years after 1984 and $f(x)$ represents the total annual expenditures for admission to spectator sports, in billions of dollars. In 2000, approximately how much was spent on admission to spectator sports?

84. The percentage of U.S. households with cable television can be modeled by

$$f(x) = 18.32 + 15.94 \ln x$$

where x represents the number of years after 1979 and $f(x)$ represents the percentage of U.S. households with cable television. What percentage of U.S. households had cable television in 1990?

The loudness level of a sound, D, in decibels, is given by the formula

$$D = 10 \log (10^{12} I)$$

where I is the intensity of the sound, in watts per meter^2. Decibel levels range from 0, a barely audible sound, to 160, a sound resulting in a ruptured eardrum. Use the formula to solve Exercises 85–86.

85. The sound of a blue whale can be heard 500 miles away, reaching an intensity of 6.3×10^6 watts per meter^2. Determine the decibel level of this sound. At close range, can the sound of a blue whale rupture the human eardrum?

86. What is the decibel level of a normal conversation, 3.2×10^{-6} watt per meter^2?

87. Students in a psychology class took a final examination. As part of an experiment to see how much of the course content they remembered over time, they took equivalent forms of the exam in monthly intervals thereafter. The average score for the group, $f(t)$, after t months was modeled by the function

$$f(t) = 88 - 15 \ln (t + 1), \qquad 0 \le t \le 12.$$

a. What was the average score on the original exam?

b. What was the average score after 2 months? 4 months? 6 months? 8 months? 10 months? one year?

c. Sketch the graph of f (either by hand or with a graphing utility). Describe what the graph indicates in terms of the material retained by the students.

Writing in Mathematics

88. Describe the relationship between an equation in logarithmic form and an equivalent equation in exponential form.

89. What question can be asked to help evaluate $\log_3 81$?

90. Explain why the logarithm of 1 with base b is 0.

91. Describe the following property using words: $\log_b b^x = x$.

92. Explain how to use the graph of $f(x) = 2^x$ to obtain the graph of $g(x) = \log_2 x$.

93. Explain how to find the domain of a logarithmic function.

94. New York City is one of the world's great walking cities. Use the formula in Example 12 on page 179 to describe what frequently happens to tourists exploring the city by foot.

95. Logarithmic models are well suited to phenomena in which growth is initially rapid but then begins to level off. Describe something that is changing over time that can be modeled using a logarithmic function.

96. Suppose that a girl is 4′ 6″ at age 10. Explain how to use the function in Exercises 81–82 to determine how tall she can expect to be as an adult.

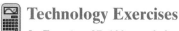

Technology Exercises

In Exercises 97–100, graph f and g in the same viewing rectangle. Then describe the relationship of the graph of g to the graph of f.

97. $f(x) = \ln x, g(x) = \ln (x + 3)$

98. $f(x) = \ln x, g(x) = \ln x + 3$

99. $f(x) = \log x, g(x) = -\log x$

100. $f(x) = \log x, g(x) = \log (x - 2) + 1$

101. Students in a mathematics class took a final examination. They took equivalent forms of the exam in monthly intervals thereafter. The average score, $f(t)$, for the group after t months was modeled by the human memory function $f(t) = 75 - 10 \log (t + 1)$, where $0 \le t \le 12$.

Use a graphing utility to graph the function. Then determine how many months will elapse before the average score falls below 65.

102. Graph f and g in the same viewing rectangle.

a. $f(x) = \ln (3x), g(x) = \ln 3 + \ln x$

b. $f(x) = \log (5x^2), g(x) = \log 5 + \log x^2$

c. $f(x) = \ln (2x^3), g(x) = \ln 2 + \ln x^3$

d. Describe what you observe in parts (a)–(c). Generalize this observation by writing an equivalent expression for $\log_b (MN)$, where $M > 0$ and $N > 0$.

e. Complete this statement: The logarithm of a product is equal to _____.

103. Graph each of the following functions in the same viewing rectangle and then place the functions in order from the one that increases most slowly to the one that increases most rapidly.

$$y = x, y = \sqrt{x}, y = e^x, y = \ln x, y = x^x, y = x^2$$

Critical Thinking Exercises

104. Which one of the following is true?

a. $\dfrac{\log_2 8}{\log_2 4} = \dfrac{8}{4}$

b. $\log (-100) = -2$

c. The domain of $f(x) = \log_2 x$ is $(-\infty, \infty)$.

d. $\log_b x$ is the exponent to which b must be raised to obtain x.

105. Without using a calculator, find the exact value of

$$\frac{\log_3 81 - \log_\pi 1}{\log_{2\sqrt{2}} 8 - \log 0.001}.$$

106. Solve for x: $\log_4[\log_3(\log_2 x)] = 0$.

107. Without using a calculator, determine which is the greater number: $\log_4 60$ or $\log_3 40$.

Group Exercise

108. This group exercise involves exploring the way we grow. Group members should create a graph for the function that models the percentage of adult height attained by a boy who is x years old, $f(x) = 29 + 48.8 \log (x + 1)$. Let $x = 1, 2, 3, \ldots, 12$, find function values, and connect the resulting points with a smooth curve. Then create a function that models the percentage of adult height attained by a girl who is x years old, $g(x) = 62 + 35 \log (x - 4)$. Let $x = 5, 6, 7, \ldots, 15$, find function values, and connect the resulting points with a smooth curve. Group members should then discuss similarities and differences in the growth patterns for boys and girls based on the graphs.

SECTION 3.3 *Properties of Logarithms*

Objectives

1. Use the product rule.
2. Use the quotient rule.
3. Use the power rule.
4. Expand logarithmic expressions.
5. Condense logarithmic expressions.
6. Use the change-of-base property.

We all learn new things in different ways. In this section, we consider important properties of logarithms. What would be the most effective way for you to learn about these properties? Would it be helpful to use your graphing utility and discover one of these properties for yourself? To do so, work Exercise 102 in Exercise Set 3.2 before continuing. Would the properties become more meaningful if you could see exactly where they come from? If so, you will find details of the proofs of many of these properties in the appendix. The remainder of our work in this chapter will be based on the properties of logarithms that you learn in this section.

1   Use the product rule.

The Product Rule

Properties of exponents correspond to properties of logarithms. For example, when we multiply with the same base, we add exponents:

$$b^m \cdot b^n = b^{m+n}.$$

This property of exponents, coupled with an awareness that a logarithm is an exponent, suggests the following property, called the **product rule:**

Discovery

We know that $\log 100{,}000 = 5$. Show that you get the same result by writing $100{,}000$ as $1000 \cdot 100$ and then using the product rule. Then verify the product rule by using other numbers whose logarithms are easy to find.

> ### The Product Rule
> Let b, M, and N be positive real numbers with $b \neq 1$.
> $$\log_b(MN) = \log_b M + \log_b N$$
> The logarithm of a product is the sum of the logarithms.

When we use the product rule to write a single logarithm as the sum of two logarithms, we say that we are **expanding a logarithmic expression.** For example, we can use the product rule to expand $\ln(4x)$:

$$\ln(7x) = \ln 7 + \ln x.$$

| The logarithm of a product | is | the sum of the logarithms. |

EXAMPLE 1 Using the Product Rule

Use the product rule to expand each logarithmic expression:

a. $\log_4 (7 \cdot 5)$ **b.** $\log (10x)$.

Solution

a. $\log_4 (7 \cdot 5) = \log_4 7 + \log_4 5$ — The logarithm of a product is the sum of the logarithms.

b. $\log (10x) = \log 10 + \log x$ — The logarithm of a product is the sum of the logarithms. These are common logarithms with base 10 understood.

$= 1 + \log x$ — Because $\log_b b = 1$, then $\log 10 = 1$.

Check Point 1 Use the product rule to expand each logarithmic expression:

a. $\log_6 (7 \cdot 11)$ **b.** $\log (100x)$.

2 Use the quotient rule.

The Quotient Rule

When we divide with the same base, we subtract exponents:

$$\frac{b^m}{b^n} = b^{m-n}.$$

This property suggests the following property of logarithms, called the **quotient rule:**

Discovery

We know that $\log_2 16 = 4$. Show that you get the same result by writing 16 as $\frac{32}{2}$ and then using the quotient rule. Then verify the quotient rule using other numbers whose logarithms are easy to find.

The Quotient Rule

Let b, M, and N be positive real numbers with $b \neq 1$.

$$\log_b \left(\frac{M}{N}\right) = \log_b M - \log_b N$$

Th1e logarithm of a quotient is the difference of the logarithms.

When we use the quotient rule to write a single logarithm as the difference of two logarithms, we say that we are **expanding a logarithmic expression.** For example, we can use the quotient rule to expand $\log \frac{x}{2}$:

$$\log \frac{x}{2} = \log x - \log 2.$$

The logarithm of a quotient | is | the difference of the logarithms.

EXAMPLE 2 Using the Quotient Rule

Use the quotient rule to expand each logarithmic expression:

a. $\log_7 \left(\frac{19}{x}\right)$ **b.** $\ln \left(\frac{e^3}{7}\right)$.

Solution

a. $\log_7\left(\dfrac{19}{x}\right) = \log_7 19 - \log_7 x$ The logarithm of a quotient is the difference of the logarithms.

b. $\ln\left(\dfrac{e^3}{7}\right) = \ln e^3 - \ln 7$ The logarithm of a quotient is the difference of the logarithms. These are natural logarithms with base e understood.

$$= 3 - \ln 7$$ Because $\ln e^x = x$, then $\ln e^3 = 3$.

> **Check Point 2**   Use the quotient rule to expand each logarithmic expression:
>
> **a.** $\log_8\left(\dfrac{23}{x}\right)$ **b.** $\ln\left(\dfrac{e^5}{11}\right)$.

3   Use the power rule.

The Power Rule

When an exponential expression is raised to a power, we multiply exponents:
$$\left(b^m\right)^n = b^{mn}.$$

This property suggests the following property of logarithms, called the **power rule:**

> **The Power Rule**
>
> Let b and M be positive real numbers with $b \neq 1$, and let p be any real number.
>
> $$\log_b M^p = p \log_b M$$
>
> The logarithm of a number with an exponent is the product of the exponent and the logarithm of that number.

When we use the power rule to "pull the exponent to the front," we say that we are **expanding a logarithmic expression.** For example, we can use the power rule to expand $\ln x^2$:

$$\ln x^2 = 2 \ln x.$$

The logarithm of a number with an exponent   is   the product of the exponent and the logarithm of that number.

Figure 3.15 shows the graphs of $y = \ln x^2$ and $y = 2 \ln x$. Are $\ln x^2$ and $2 \ln x$ the same? The graphs illustrate that $y = \ln x^2$ and $y = 2 \ln x$ have different domains. The graphs are only the same if $x > 0$. Thus, we should write

$$\ln x^2 = 2 \ln x \text{ for } x > 0.$$

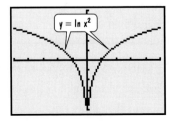

Domain: $(-\infty, 0)$ or $(0, \infty)$

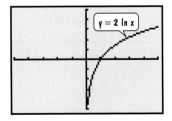

Domain: $(0, \infty)$

Figure 3.15 $\ln x^2$ and $2 \ln x$ have different domains.

The graphs show
$$y_1 = \ln (x + 3)$$
and
$$y_2 = \ln x + \ln 3.$$

The graphs are not the same. The graph of y_1 is the graph of the natural logarithmic function shifted 3 units to the left. By contrast, the graph of y_2 is the graph of the natural logarithmic function shifted upward by $\ln 3$, or about 1.1 units. Thus we see that
$$\ln (x + 3) \neq \ln x + \ln 3.$$
In general,
$$\log_b (M + N) \neq \log_b M + \log_b N.$$

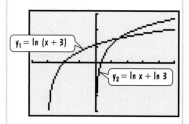

Try to avoid the following errors:

INCORRECT

$$\log_b (M + N) = \log_b M + \log_b N$$
$$\log_b (M - N) = \log_b M - \log_b N$$
$$\log_b (M \cdot N) = \log_b M \cdot \log_b N$$
$$\log_b \left(\frac{M}{N}\right) = \frac{\log_b M}{\log_b N}$$
$$\frac{\log_b M}{\log_b N} = \log_b M - \log_b N$$

4 Expand logarithmic expressions.

When expanding a logarithmic expression, you might want to determine whether the rewriting has changed the domain of the expression. For the rest of this section, assume that all variable and variable expressions represent positive numbers.

EXAMPLE 3 Using the Power Rule

Use the power rule to expand each logarithmic expression:

a. $\log_5 7^4$ **b.** $\ln \sqrt{x}$.

Solution

a. $\log_5 7^4 = 4 \log_5 7$ The logarithm of a number with an exponent is the exponent times the logarithm of the number.

b. $\ln \sqrt{x} = \ln x^{1/2}$ Rewrite the radical using a rational exponent.

$\qquad = \frac{1}{2} \ln x$ Use the power rule to bring the exponent to the front.

Check Point 3 Use the power rule to expand each logarithmic expression:

a. $\log_6 3^9$ **b.** $\ln \sqrt[3]{x}$.

Expanding Logarithmic Expressions

It is sometimes necessary to use more than one property of logarithms when you expand a logarithmic expression. Properties for expanding logarithmic expressions are as follows:

Properties for Expanding Logarithmic Expressions

For $M > 0$ and $N > 0$:

1. $\log_b (MN) = \log_b M + \log_b N$ Product rule

2. $\log_b \left(\frac{M}{N}\right) = \log_b M - \log_b N$ Quotient rule

3. $\log_b M^p = p \log_b M$ Power rule

EXAMPLE 4 Expanding Logarithmic Expressions

Use logarithmic properties to expand each expression as much as possible:

a. $\log_b (x^2 \sqrt{y})$ **b.** $\log_6 \left(\frac{\sqrt[3]{x}}{36y^4}\right)$.

Solution We will have to use two or more of the properties for expanding logarithms in each part of this example.

a. $\log_b (x^2 \sqrt{y}) = \log_b (x^2 y^{1/2})$ Use exponential notation.

$\qquad = \log_b x^2 + \log_b y^{1/2}$ Use the product rule.

$\qquad = 2 \log_b x + \frac{1}{2} \log_b y$ Use the power rule.

b. $\log_6\left(\dfrac{\sqrt[3]{x}}{36y^4}\right) = \log_6\left(\dfrac{x^{1/3}}{36y^4}\right)$ Use exponential notation.

$$= \log_6 x^{1/3} - \log_6(36y^4)$$ Use the quotient rule.

$$= \log_6 x^{1/3} - \left(\log_6 36 + \log_6 y^4\right)$$ Use the product rule on $\log_6(36y^4)$.

$$= \frac{1}{3}\log_6 x - \left(\log_6 36 + 4\log_6 y\right)$$ Use the power rule.

$$= \frac{1}{3}\log_6 x - \log_6 36 - 4\log_6 y$$ Apply the distributive property.

$$= \frac{1}{3}\log_6 x - 2 - 4\log_6 y$$ $\log_6 36 = 2$ because 2 is the power to which we must raise 6 to get 36. $(6^2 = 36)$

> **Check Point 4**   Use logarithmic properties to expand each expression as much as possible:
>
> **a.** $\log_b(x^4\sqrt[3]{y})$ **b.** $\log_5 \dfrac{\sqrt{x}}{25y^3}$.

5   Condense logarithmic expressions.

Condensing Logarithmic Expressions

To **condense a logarithmic expression,** we write the sum or difference of two or more logarithmic expressions as a single logarithmic expression. We use the properties of logarithms to do so.

Properties for Condensing Logarithmic Expressions

For $M > 0$ and $N > 0$:

1. $\log_b M + \log_b N = \log_b(MN)$ Product rule

2. $\log_b M - \log_b N = \log_b\left(\dfrac{M}{N}\right)$ Quotient rule

3. $p\log_b M = \log_b M^p$ Power rule

EXAMPLE 5   Condensing Logarithmic Expressions

Write as a single logarithm:

a. $\log_4 2 + \log_4 32$ **b.** $\log(4x - 3) - \log x.$

Solution

a. $\log_4 2 + \log_4 32 = \log_4(2 \cdot 32)$ Use the product rule.

$$= \log_4 64$$ We now have a single logarithm. However, we can simplify.

$$= 3$$ $\log_4 64 = 3$ because $4^3 = 64$.

b. $\log(4x - 3) - \log x = \log\left(\dfrac{4x - 3}{x}\right)$ Use the quotient rule.

Check Point 5   Write as a single logarithm:

    a. $\log 25 + \log 4$ **b.** $\log (7x + 6) - \log x$.

Coefficients of logarithms must be 1 before you can condense them using the product and quotient rules. For example, to condense

$$2 \ln x + \ln (x + 1),$$

the coefficient of the first term must be 1. We use the power rule to rewrite the coefficient as an exponent:

> 1. Use the power rule to make the number in front an exponent.

$$2 \ln x + \ln (x + 1) = \ln x^2 + \ln (x + 1) = \ln [x^2 (x + 1)].$$

> 2. Use the product rule. The sum of logarithms with coefficients 1 is the logarithm of the product.

EXAMPLE 6   Condensing Logarithmic Expressions

Write as a single logarithm:

  a. $\frac{1}{2} \log x + 4 \log(x - 1)$ **b.** $3 \ln (x + 7) - \ln x$

  c. $4 \log_b x - 2 \log_b 6 + \frac{1}{2} \log_b y$.

Solution

  a. $\frac{1}{2} \log x + 4 \log(x - 1)$

       $= \log x^{1/2} + \log (x - 1)^4$ Use the power rule so that all coefficients are 1.

       $= \log [x^{1/2} (x - 1)^4]$ Use the product rule. The condensation can be expressed as $\log [\sqrt{x} (x - 1)^4]$.

  b. $3 \ln (x + 7) - \ln x$

       $= \ln (x + 7)^3 - \ln x$ Use the power rule so that all coefficients are 1.

       $= \ln \left[\dfrac{(x + 7)^3}{x} \right]$ Use the quotient rule.

  c. $4 \log_b x - 2 \log_b 6 + \frac{1}{2} \log_b y$

       $= \log_b x^4 - \log_b 6^2 + \log_b y^{1/2}$ Use the power rule so that all coefficients are 1.

       $= (\log_b x^4 - \log_b 36) + \log_b y^{1/2}$ This optional step emphasizes the order of operations.

       $= \log_b \left(\dfrac{x^4}{36} \right) + \log_b y^{1/2}$ Use the quotient rule.

       $= \log_b \left(\dfrac{x^4}{36} \cdot y^{1/2} \right)$ or $\log \left(\dfrac{x^4 \sqrt{y}}{36} \right)$ Use the product rule.

Check Point 6   Write as a single logarithm:

    a. $2 \ln x + \frac{1}{3} \ln (x + 5)$ **b.** $2 \log (x - 3) - \log x$

    c. $\frac{1}{4} \log_b x - 2 \log_b 5 + 10 \log_b y$.

6 Use the change-of-base property.

The Change-of-Base Property

We have seen that calculators give the values of both common logarithms (base 10) and natural logarithms (base e). To find a logarithm with any other base, we can use the following change-of-base property:

The Change-of-Base Property

For any logarithmic bases a and b, and any positive number M,

$$\log_b M = \frac{\log_a M}{\log_a b}.$$

The logarithm of M with base b is equal to the logarithm of M with any new base divided by the logarithm of b with that new base.

In the change-of-base property, base b is the base of the original logarithm. Base a is a new base that we introduce. Thus, the change-of-base property allows us to change from base b to *any* new base a, as long as the newly introduced base is a positive number not equal to 1.

The change-of-base property is used to write a logarithm in terms of quantities that can be evaluated with a calculator. Because calculators contain keys for common (base 10) and natural (base e) logarithms, we will frequently introduce base 10 or base e.

Change-of-Base Property

$$\log_b M = \frac{\log_a M}{\log_a b}$$

a is the new introduced base.

Introducing Common Logarithms

$$\log_b M = \frac{\log_{10} M}{\log_{10} b}$$

10 is the new introduced base.

Introducing Natural Logarithms

$$\log_b M = \frac{\log_e M}{\log_e b}$$

e is the new introduced base.

Using the notations for common logarithms and natural logarithms, we have the following results:

The Change-of-Base Property: Introducing Common and Natural Logarithms

Introducing Common Logarithms

$$\log_b M = \frac{\log M}{\log b}$$

Introducing Natural Logarithms

$$\log_b M = \frac{\ln M}{\ln b}$$

EXAMPLE 7 Changing Base to Common Logarithms

Use common logarithms to evaluate $\log_5 140$.

Solution Because $\log_b M = \dfrac{\log M}{\log b}$,

$$\log_5 140 = \frac{\log 140}{\log 5}$$

$$\approx 3.07.$$

Use a calculator: 140 LOG ÷ 5 LOG = or LOG 140 ÷ LOG 5 ENTER.

This means that $\log_5 140 \approx 3.07$.

Discovery

Find a reasonable estimate of $\log_5 140$ to the nearest whole number. 5 to what power is 140? Compare your estimate to the value obtained in Example 7.

Check Point 7 Use common logarithms to evaluate $\log_7 2506$.

EXAMPLE 8 Changing Base to Natural Logarithms

Use natural logarithms to evaluate $\log_5 140$.

Solution Because $\log_b M = \dfrac{\ln M}{\ln b}$,

$$\log_5 140 = \frac{\ln 140}{\ln 5}$$

$$\approx 3.07. \qquad \text{Use a calculator: } 140 \boxed{\text{LN}} \boxed{\div} 5 \boxed{\text{LN}}$$

$$\boxed{=} \text{ or } \boxed{\text{LN}}\ 140 \boxed{\div}\ \boxed{\text{LN}}\ 5 \boxed{\text{ENTER}}.$$

We have again shown that $\log_5 140 \approx 3.07$.

Check Point 8 Use natural logarithms to evaluate $\log_7 2506$.

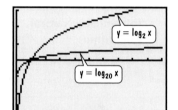

Figure 3.16 Using the change-of-base property to graph logarithmic functions

We can use the change-of-base property to graph logarithmic functions with bases other than 10 or e on a graphing utility. For example, Figure 3.16 shows the graphs of

$$y = \log_2 x \quad \text{and} \quad y = \log_{20} x$$

in a $[0, 10, 1]$ by $[-3, 3, 1]$ viewing rectangle. Because $\log_2 x = \dfrac{\ln x}{\ln 2}$ and $\log_{20} x = \dfrac{\ln x}{\ln 20}$, the functions can be entered as

$$y_1 = \boxed{\text{LN}}\ x \boxed{\div} \boxed{\text{LN}}\ 2$$

$$\text{and } y_2 = \boxed{\text{LN}}\ x \boxed{\div} \boxed{\text{LN}}\ 20.$$

EXERCISE SET 3.3

Practice Exercises

In Exercises 1–40, use properties of logarithms to expand each logarithmic expression as much as possible. Where possible, evaluate logarithmic expressions without using a calculator.

1. $\log_5 (7 \cdot 3)$

2. $\log_8 (13 \cdot 7)$

3. $\log_7 (7x)$

4. $\log_9 (9x)$

5. $\log (1000x)$

6. $\log (10{,}000x)$

7. $\log_7 \left(\dfrac{7}{x} \right)$

8. $\log_9 \left(\dfrac{9}{x} \right)$

9. $\log \left(\dfrac{x}{100} \right)$

10. $\log \left(\dfrac{x}{1000} \right)$

11. $\log_4 \left(\dfrac{64}{y} \right)$

12. $\log_5 \left(\dfrac{125}{y} \right)$

13. $\ln \left(\dfrac{e^2}{5} \right)$

14. $\ln \left(\dfrac{e^4}{8} \right)$

15. $\log_b x^3$

16. $\log_b x^7$

17. $\log N^{-6}$

18. $\log M^{-8}$

19. $\ln \sqrt[5]{x}$

20. $\ln \sqrt[7]{x}$

21. $\log_b (x^2 y)$

22. $\log_b (xy^3)$

23. $\log_4 \left(\dfrac{\sqrt{x}}{64} \right)$

24. $\log_5 \left(\dfrac{\sqrt{x}}{25} \right)$

25. $\log_6 \left(\dfrac{36}{\sqrt{x+1}} \right)$

26. $\log_8 \left(\dfrac{64}{\sqrt{x+1}} \right)$

27. $\log_b \left(\dfrac{x^2 y}{z^2} \right)$

28. $\log_b \left(\dfrac{x^3 y}{z^2} \right)$

29. $\log \sqrt{100x}$

30. $\ln \sqrt{ex}$

31. $\log \sqrt[3]{\dfrac{x}{y}}$

32. $\log \sqrt[5]{\dfrac{x}{y}}$

33. $\log_b\left(\dfrac{\sqrt{x}\,y^3}{z^3}\right)$

34. $\log_b\left(\dfrac{\sqrt[3]{x}\,y^4}{z^5}\right)$

35. $\log_5 \sqrt[3]{\dfrac{x^2 y}{25}}$

36. $\log_2 \sqrt[5]{\dfrac{x y^4}{16}}$

37. $\ln\left[\dfrac{x^3\sqrt{x^2+1}}{(x+1)^4}\right]$

38. $\ln\left[\dfrac{x^4\sqrt{x^2+3}}{(x+3)^5}\right]$

39. $\log\left[\dfrac{10x^2\sqrt[3]{1-x}}{7(x+1)^2}\right]$

40. $\log\left[\dfrac{100x^3\sqrt[3]{5-x}}{3(x+7)^2}\right]$

In Exercises 41–70, use properties of logarithms to condense each logarithmic expression. Write the expression as a single logarithm whose coefficient is 1. Where possible, evaluate logarithmic expressions.

41. $\log 5 + \log 2$

42. $\log 250 + \log 4$

43. $\ln x + \ln 7$

44. $\ln x + \ln 3$

45. $\log_2 96 - \log_2 3$

46. $\log_3 405 - \log_3 5$

47. $\log(2x+5) - \log x$

48. $\log(3x+7) - \log x$

49. $\log x + 3\log y$

50. $\log x + 7\log y$

51. $\frac{1}{2}\ln x + \ln y$

52. $\frac{1}{3}\ln x + \ln y$

53. $2\log_b x + 3\log_b y$

54. $5\log_b x + 6\log_b y$

55. $5\ln x - 2\ln y$

56. $7\ln x - 3\ln y$

57. $3\ln x - \frac{1}{3}\ln y$

58. $2\ln x - \frac{1}{2}\ln y$

59. $4\ln(x+6) - 3\ln x$

60. $8\ln(x+9) - 4\ln x$

61. $3\ln x + 5\ln y - 6\ln z$

62. $4\ln x + 7\ln y - 3\ln z$

63. $\frac{1}{2}(\log x + \log y)$

64. $\frac{1}{3}(\log_4 x - \log_4 y)$

65. $\frac{1}{2}(\log_5 x + \log_5 y) - 2\log_5(x+1)$

66. $\frac{1}{3}(\log_4 x - \log_4 y) + 2\log_4(x+1)$

67. $\frac{1}{3}\left[2\ln(x+5) - \ln x - \ln(x^2-4)\right]$

68. $\frac{1}{3}\left[5\ln(x+6) - \ln x - \ln(x^2-25)\right]$

69. $\log x + \log 7 + \log(x^2-1) - \log(x+1)$

70. $\log x + \log 15 + \log(x^2-4) - \log(x+2)$

In Exercises 71–78, use common logarithms or natural logarithms and a calculator to evaluate to four decimal places.

71. $\log_5 13$

72. $\log_6 17$

73. $\log_{14} 87.5$

74. $\log_{16} 57.2$

75. $\log_{0.1} 17$

76. $\log_{0.3} 19$

77. $\log_\pi 63$

78. $\log_\pi 400$

In Exercises 79–82, use a graphing utility and the change-of-base property to graph each function.

79. $y = \log_3 x$

80. $y = \log_{15} x$

81. $y = \log_2(x+2)$

82. $y = \log_3(x-2)$

Application Exercises

83. The loudness level of a sound can be expressed by comparing the sound's intensity to the intensity of a sound barely audible to the human ear. The formula

$$D = 10(\log I - \log I_0)$$

describes the loudness level of a sound, D, in decibels, where I is the intensity of the sound, in watts per meter^2, and I_0 is the intensity of a sound barely audible to the human ear.

  a. Express the formula so that the expression in parentheses is written as a single logarithm.

  b. Use the form of the formula from part (a) to answer this question: If a sound has an intensity 100 times the intensity of a softer sound, how much larger on the decibel scale is the loudness level of the more intense sound?

84. The formula

$$t = \frac{1}{c}\left[\ln A - \ln(A-N)\right]$$

describes the time, t, in weeks, that it takes to achieve mastery of a portion of a task, where A is the maximum learning possible, N is the portion of the learning that is to be achieved, and c is a constant used to measure an individual's learning style.

  a. Express the formula so that the expression in brackets is written as a single logarithm.

  b. The formula is also used to determine how long it will take chimpanzees and apes to master a task. For example, a typical chimpanzee learning sign language can master a maximum of 65 signs. Use the form of the formula from part (a) to answer this question: How many weeks will it take a chimpanzee to master 30 signs if c for that chimp is 0.03?

Writing in Mathematics

85. Describe the product rule for logarithms and give an example.

86. Describe the quotient rule for logarithms and give an example.

87. Describe the power rule for logarithms and give an example.

88. Without showing the details, explain how to condense $\ln x - 2\ln(x+1)$.

89. Describe the change-of-base property and give an example.

90. Explain how to use your calculator to find $\log_{14} 283$.

91. You overhear a student talking about a property of logarithms in which division becomes subtraction. Explain what the student means by this.

92. Find $\ln 2$ using a calculator. Then calculate each of the following: $1 - \frac{1}{2}$; $1 - \frac{1}{2} + \frac{1}{3}$; $1 - \frac{1}{2} + \frac{1}{3} - \frac{1}{4}$; $1 - \frac{1}{2} + \frac{1}{3} - \frac{1}{4} + \frac{1}{5}$; .... Describe what you observe.

Technology Exercises

93. a. Use a graphing utility (and the change-of-base property) to graph $y = \log_3 x$.

b. Graph $y = 2 + \log_3 x$, $y = \log_3 (x + 2)$, and $y = -\log_3 x$ in the same viewing rectangle as $y = \log_3 x$. Then describe the change or changes that need to be made to the graph of $y = \log_3 x$ to obtain each of these three graphs.

94. Graph $y = \log x$, $y = \log (10x)$, and $y = \log (0.1x)$ in the same viewing rectangle. Describe the relationship among the three graphs. What logarithmic property accounts for this relationship?

95. Use a graphing utility and the change-of-base property to graph $y = \log_3 x$, $y = \log_{25} x$, and $y = \log_{100} x$ in the same viewing rectangle.

a. Which graph is on the top in the interval $(0, 1)$? Which is on the bottom?

b. Which graph is on the top in the interval $(1, \infty)$? Which is on the bottom?

c. Generalize by writing a statement about which graph is on top, which is on the bottom, and in which intervals, using $y = \log_b x$ where $b > 1$.

Disprove each statement in Exercises 96–100 by
a. *letting y equal a positive constant of your choice.*
b. *using a graphing utility to graph the function on each side of the equal sign. The two functions should have different graphs, showing that the equation is not true in general.*

96. $\log(x + y) = \log x + \log y$ **97.** $\log \dfrac{x}{y} = \dfrac{\log x}{\log y}$

98. $\ln(x - y) = \ln x - \ln y$ **99.** $\ln(xy) = (\ln x)(\ln y)$

100. $\dfrac{\ln x}{\ln y} = \ln x - \ln y$

Critical Thinking Exercises

101. Which one of the following is true?

a. $\dfrac{\log_7 49}{\log_7 7} = \log_7 49 - \log_7 7$

b. $\log_b(x^3 + y^3) = 3 \log_b x + 3 \log_b y$

c. $\log_b(xy)^5 = (\log_b x + \log_b y)^5$

d. $\ln \sqrt{2} = \dfrac{\ln 2}{2}$

102. Use the change-of-base property to prove that
$$\log e = \frac{1}{\ln 10}.$$

103. If $\log 3 = A$ and $\log 7 = B$, find $\log_7 9$ in terms of A and B.

104. Write as a single term that does not contain a logarithm:
$$e^{\ln 8x^5 - \ln 2x^2}.$$

105. If $f(x) = \log_b x$, show that
$$\frac{f(x + h) - f(x)}{h} = \log_b \left(1 + \frac{h}{x}\right)^{1/h}, h \neq 0.$$

SECTION 3.4 *Exponential and Logarithmic Equations*

Objectives

1. Solve exponential equations.
2. Solve logarithmic equations.
3. Solve applied problems involving exponential and logarithmic equations.

Is an early retirement awaiting you?

You inherited $30,000. You'd like to put aside $25,000 and eventually have over half a million dollars for early retirement. Is this possible? In this section, you will see how techniques for solving equations with variable exponents provide an answer to the question.

1 Solve exponential equations.

Exponential Equations

An **exponential equation** is an equation containing a variable in an exponent. Examples of exponential equations include

$$3^x = 81, \quad 4^x = 15, \quad \text{and} \quad 40e^{0.6x} = 240.$$

Each side of the first equation can be expressed with the same base. Can you see that we can rewrite

$$3^x = 81 \quad \text{as} \quad 3^x = 3^4?$$

All exponential functions are one-to-one—that is, if b is a positive number other than 1 and $b^M = b^N$, then $M = N$. Because we have expressed $3^x = 81$ as $3^x = 3^4$, we conclude that $x = 4$. The equation's solution set is $\{4\}$.

Most exponential equations cannot be rewritten so that each side has the same base. Logarithms are extremely useful in solving such equations. The solution begins with isolating the exponential expression and taking the natural logarithm on both sides. Why can we do this? All logarithmic relations are functions. Thus, if M and N are positive real numbers and $M = N$, then $\log_b M = \log_b N$.

Using Natural Logarithms to Solve Exponential Equations

1. Isolate the exponential expression.
2. Take the natural logarithm on both sides of the equation.
3. Simplify using one of the following properties:

$$\ln b^x = x \ln b \quad \text{or} \quad \ln e^x = x.$$

4. Solve for the variable.

EXAMPLE 1 Solving an Exponential Equation

Solve: $4^x = 15$.

Solution Because the exponential expression, 4^x, is already isolated on the left, we begin by taking the natural logarithm on both sides of the equation.

$4^x = 15$ This is the given equation.

$\ln 4^x = \ln 15$ Take the natural logarithm on both sides.

$x \ln 4 = \ln 15$ Use the power rule and bring the variable exponent to the front: $\ln b^x = x \ln b$.

$x = \dfrac{\ln 15}{\ln 4}$ Solve for x by dividing both sides by $\ln 4$.

We now have an exact value for x. We use the exact value for x in the equation's solution set. Thus, the equation's solution is $\dfrac{\ln 15}{\ln 4}$ and the solution set is $\left\{ \dfrac{\ln 15}{\ln 4} \right\}$. We can obtain a decimal approximation by using a calculator: $x \approx 1.95$. Because $4^2 = 16$, it seems reasonable that the solution to $4^x = 15$ is approximately 1.95

Discovery

The base that is used when taking the logarithm on both sides of an equation can be any base at all. Solve $4^x = 15$ by taking the common logarithm on both sides. Solve again, this time taking the logarithm with base 4 on both sides. Use the change-of-base property to show that the solutions are the same as the one obtained in Example 1.

Check Point 1 Solve: $5^x = 134$. Find the solution set and then use a calculator to obtain a decimal approximation to two decimal places for the solution.

EXAMPLE 2 Solving an Exponential Equation

Solve: $40e^{0.6x} = 240$.

Solution   We begin by dividing both sides by 40 to isolate the exponential expression, $e^{0.6x}$. Then we take the natural logarithm on both sides of the equation.

$40e^{0.6x} = 240$	This is the given equation.
$e^{0.6x} = 6$	Isolate the exponential factor by dividing both sides by 40.
$\ln e^{0.6x} = \ln 6$	Take the natural logarithm on both sides.
$0.6x = \ln 6$	Use the inverse property $\ln e^x = x$ on the left.
$x = \dfrac{\ln 6}{0.6} \approx 2.99$	Divide both sides by 0.6.

Thus, the solution of the equation is $\dfrac{\ln 6}{0.6} \approx 2.99$. Try checking this approximate solution in the original equation to verify that $\left\{\dfrac{\ln 6}{0.6}\right\}$ is the solution set.

Check Point 2 Solve: $7e^{2x} = 63$. Find the solution set and then use a calculator to obtain a decimal approximation to two decimal places for the solution.

EXAMPLE 3 Solving an Exponential Equation

Solve: $5^{4x-7} - 3 = 10$

Solution   We begin by adding 3 to both sides to isolate the exponential expression, 5^{4x-7}. Then we take the natural logarithm on both sides of the equation.

$5^{4x-7} - 3 = 10$	This is the given equation.
$5^{4x-7} = 13$	Add 3 to both sides.
$\ln 5^{4x-7} = \ln 13$	Take the natural logarithm on both sides.
$(4x - 7)\ln 5 = \ln 13$	Use the power rule to bring the exponent to the front: $\ln M^p = p\ln M$.
$4x\ln 5 - 7\ln 5 = \ln 13$	Use the distributive property and distribute $\ln 5$ to both terms in parentheses.
$4x\ln 5 = \ln 13 + 7\ln 5$	Isolate the variable term by adding $7\ln 5$ to both sides.
$x = \dfrac{\ln 13 + 7\ln 5}{4\ln 5}$	Isolate x by dividing both sides by $4\ln 5$.

The solution set is $\left\{\dfrac{\ln 13 + 7\ln 5}{4\ln 5}\right\}$. The solution is approximately 2.15.

> **Check Point 3** Solve: $6^{3x-4} - 7 = 2081$. Find the solution set and then use a calculator to obtain a decimal approximation to two decimal places for the solution.

EXAMPLE 4 Solving an Exponential Equation

Solve: $e^{2x} - 4e^x + 3 = 0$.

Solution   The given equation is quadratic in form. If $t = e^x$, the equation can be expressed as $t^2 - 4t + 3 = 0$. Because this equation can be solved by factoring, we factor to isolate the exponential term.

Technology

Shown below is the graph of $y = e^{2x} - 4e^x + 3$. There are two x-intercepts, one at 0 and one at approximately 1.10. These intercepts verify our algebraic solution.

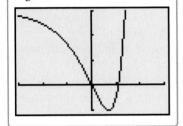

$e^{2x} - 4e^x + 3 = 0$	This is the given equation.
$(e^x - 3)(e^x - 1) = 0$	Factor on the left. Notice that if $t = e^x$, $t^2 - 4t + 3 = (t - 3)(t - 1)$.
$e^x - 3 = 0$ or $e^x - 1 = 0$	Set each factor equal to 0.
$e^x = 3$ $e^x = 1$	Solve for e^x.
$\ln e^x = \ln 3$ $x = 0$	Take the natural logarithm on both sides of the first equation. The equation on the right can be solved by inspection.
$x = \ln 3$	$\ln e^x = x$

The solution set is $\{0, \ln 3\}$. The solutions are 0 and approximately 1.10.

> **Check Point 4** Solve: $e^{2x} - 8e^x + 7 = 0$. Find the solution set and then use a calculator to obtain a decimal approximation to two decimal places, if necessary, for the solutions.

2 Solve logarithmic equations.

Logarithmic Equations

A **logarithmic equation** is an equation containing a variable in a logarithmic expression. Examples of logarithmic equations include

$$\log_4(x + 3) = 2 \quad \text{and} \quad \ln(2x) = 3.$$

If a logarithmic equation is in the form $\log_b x = c$, we can solve the equation by rewriting it in its equivalent exponential form $b^c = x$. Example 5 illustrates how this is done.

EXAMPLE 5 Solving a Logarithmic Equation

Solve: $\log_4(x + 3) = 2$.

Solution   We first rewrite the equation as an equivalent equation in exponential form using the fact that $\log_b x = c$ means $b^c = x$.

$$\log_4(x + 3) = 2 \quad \text{means} \quad 4^2 = x + 3$$

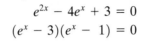

Logarithms are exponents.

Technology

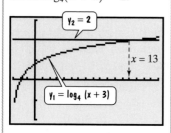

The graphs of
$y_1 = \log_4(x + 3)$ and $y_2 = 2$
have an intersection point
whose x-coordinate is 13. This
verifies that {13} is the solution
set for $\log_4(x + 3) = 2$.

$[-3, 17, 1]$ by $[-2, 3, 1]$

Note:
Because

$$\log_b x = \frac{\ln x}{\ln b}$$

(change-of-base property),
we entered y_1 using

$$y_1 = \frac{\ln(x + 3)}{\ln 4}.$$

Now we solve the equivalent equation for x.

$4^2 = x + 3$	This is the equation equivalent to $\log_4(x + 3) = 2$.
$16 = x + 3$	Square 4.
$13 = x$	Subtract 3 from both sides.

Check 13:

$\log_4(x + 3) = 2$	This is the given logarithmic equation.
$\log_4(13 + 3) \overset{?}{=} 2$	Substitute 13 for x.
$\log_4 16 \overset{?}{=} 2$	
$2 = 2 \checkmark$	$\log_4 16 = 2$ because $4^2 = 16$.

This true statement indicates that the solution set is {13}.

Check Point 5   Solve: $\log_2(x - 4) = 3$.

Logarithmic expressions are defined only for logarithms of positive real numbers. Always check proposed solutions of a logarithmic equation in the original equation. Exclude from the solution set any proposed solution that produces the logarithm of a negative number or the logarithm of 0.

To rewrite the logarithmic equation $\log_b x = c$ in the equivalent exponential form $b^c = x$, we need a single logarithm whose coefficient is one. It is sometimes necessary to use properties of logarithms to condense logarithms into a single logarithm. In the next example, we use the product rule for logarithms to obtain a single logarithmic expression on the left side.

EXAMPLE 6   Using the Product Rule to Solve a Logarithmic Equation

Solve: $\log_2 x + \log_2(x - 7) = 3$.

Solution

$\log_2 x + \log_2(x - 7) = 3$	This is the given equation.
$\log_2[x(x - 7)] = 3$	Use the product rule to obtain a single logarithm: $\log_b M + \log_b N = \log_b(MN)$.
$2^3 = x(x - 7)$	$\log_b x = c$ means $b^c = x$.
$8 = x^2 - 7x$	Apply the distributive property on the right and evaluate 2^3 on the left.
$0 = x^2 - 7x - 8$	Set the equation equal to 0.
$0 = (x - 8)(x + 1)$	Factor.
$x - 8 = 0$ or $x + 1 = 0$	Set each factor equal to 0.
$x = 8$ $x = -1$	Solve for x.

Check 8:

$\log_2 x + \log_2(x - 7) = 3$
$\log_2 8 + \log_2(8 - 7) \overset{?}{=} 3$
$\log_2 8 + \log_2 1 \overset{?}{=} 3$
$3 + 0 \overset{?}{=} 3$
$3 = 3 \checkmark$

The solution set is {8}.

Check −1:

$\log_2 x + \log_2(x - 7) = 3$
$\log_2(-1) + \log_2(-1 - 7) \overset{?}{=} 3$

The number −1 does not check.
Negative numbers do not have logarithms.

Check Point 6 Solve: $\log x + \log (x - 3) = 1$.

Equations involving natural logarithms can be solved using the inverse property $e^{\ln x} = x$. For example, to solve

$$\ln x = 5$$

we write both sides of the equation as exponents on base e:

$$e^{\ln x} = e^5.$$

This is called **exponentiating both sides** of the equation. Using the inverse property $e^{\ln x} = x$, we simplify the left side of the equation and obtain the solution:

$$x = e^5.$$

EXAMPLE 7 **Solving an Equation with a Natural Logarithm**

Solve: $3 \ln (2x) = 12$.

Solution

$3 \ln(2x) = 12$	This is the given equation.
$\ln (2x) = 4$	Divide both sides by 3.
$e^{\ln (2x)} = e^4$	Exponentiate both sides.
$2x = e^4$	Use the inverse property to simplify the left side: $e^{\ln x} = x$.
$x = \dfrac{e^4}{2} \approx 27.30$	Divide both sides by 2.

Check $\dfrac{e^4}{2}$:

$3 \ln (2x) = 12$	This is the given logarithmic equation.
$3 \ln \left[2\left(\dfrac{e^4}{2}\right)\right] \overset{?}{=} 12$	Substitute $\dfrac{e^4}{2}$ for x.
$3 \ln e^4 \overset{?}{=} 12$	Simplify: $\dfrac{2}{1} \cdot \dfrac{e^4}{2} = e^4$.
$3 \cdot 4 \overset{?}{=} 12$	Because $\ln e^x = x$, we conclude $\ln e^4 = 4$.
$12 = 12$ ✓	

This true statement indicates that the solution set is $\left\{\dfrac{e^4}{2}\right\}$.

Check Point 7 Solve: $4 \ln 3x = 8$.

3 Solve applied problems involving exponential and logarithmic equations.

Applications

Our first applied example provides a mathematical perspective on the old slogan "Alcohol and driving don't mix." In California, where 38% of fatal traffic crashes involve drinking drivers, it is illegal to drive with a blood alcohol concentration of 0.08 or higher. At these levels, drivers may be arrested and charged with driving under the influence.

EXAMPLE 8   Alcohol and Risk of a Car Accident

Medical research indicates that the risk of having a car accident increases exponentially as the concentration of alcohol in the blood increases. The risk is modeled by

$$R = 6e^{12.77x}$$

where x is the blood alcohol concentration and R, given as a percent, is the risk of having a car accident. What blood alcohol concentration corresponds to a 17% risk of a car accident?

Solution   For a risk of 17%, we let $R = 17$ in the equation and solve for x, the blood alcohol concentration.

$R = 6e^{12.77x}$	This is the given equation.
$6e^{12.77x} = 17$	Substitute 17 for R and (optional) reverse the two sides of the equation.
$e^{12.77x} = \dfrac{17}{6}$	Isolate the exponential factor by dividing both sides by 6.
$\ln e^{12.77x} = \ln\left(\dfrac{17}{6}\right)$	Take the natural logarithm on both sides.
$12.77x = \ln\left(\dfrac{17}{6}\right)$	Use the inverse property $\ln e^x = x$ on the left.
$x = \dfrac{\ln\left(\dfrac{17}{6}\right)}{12.77} \approx 0.08$	Divide both sides by 12.77.

For a blood alcohol concentration of 0.08, the risk of a car accident is 17%. In many states, it is illegal to drive at this blood alcohol concentration.

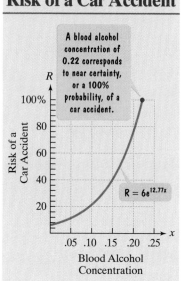

Visualizing the Relationship between Blood Alcohol Concentration and the Risk of a Car Accident

A blood alcohol concentration of 0.22 corresponds to near certainty, or a 100% probability, of a car accident.

$R = 6e^{12.77x}$

Risk of a Car Accident

Blood Alcohol Concentration

Check Point 8   Use the formula in Example 8 to answer this question: What blood alcohol concentration corresponds to a 7% risk of a car accident? (In many states, drivers under the age of 21 can lose their license for driving at this level.)

Suppose that you inherit $30,000. Is it possible to invest $25,000 and have over half a million dollars for early retirement? Our next example illustrates the power of compound interest.

EXAMPLE 9   Revisiting the Formula for Compound Interest

The formula

$$A = P\left(1 + \frac{r}{n}\right)^{nt}$$

describes the accumulated value, A, of a sum of money, P, the principal, after t years at annual percentage rate r (in decimal form) compounded n times a year. How long will it take $25,000 to grow to $500,000 at 9% annual interest compounded monthly?

Solution

$$A = P\left(1 + \frac{r}{n}\right)^{nt}$$

This is the given formula.

$$500{,}000 = 25{,}000\left(1 + \frac{0.09}{12}\right)^{12t}$$

A (the desired accumulated value) = $500,000,
P (the principal) = $25,000,
r (the interest rate) = 9% = 0.09, and n = 12
(monthly compounding).

Our goal is to solve the equation for t. Let's reverse the two sides of the equation and then simplify within parentheses.

$$25{,}000\left(1 + \frac{0.09}{12}\right)^{12t} = 500{,}000$$

Reverse the two sides of the previous equation.

$$25{,}000(1 + 0.0075)^{12t} = 500{,}000$$

Divide within parentheses: $\frac{0.09}{12} = 0.0075$.

$$25{,}000(1.0075)^{12t} = 500{,}000$$

Add within parentheses.

$$(1.0075)^{12t} = 20$$

Divide both sides by 25,000.

$$\ln(1.0075)^{12t} = \ln 20$$

Take the natural logarithm on both sides.

$$12t \ln(1.0075) = \ln 20$$

Use the power rule to bring the exponent to the front: $\ln M^p = p \ln M$.

$$t = \frac{\ln 20}{12 \ln 1.0075}$$

Solve for t, dividing both sides by 12 ln 1.0075.

$$\approx 33.4$$

Use a calculator.

After approximately 33.4 years, the $25,000 will grow to an accumulated value of $500,000. If you set aside the money at age 20, you can begin enjoying a life of leisure at about age 53.

Playing Doubles: Interest Rates and Doubling Time

One way to calculate what your savings will be worth at some point in the future is to consider doubling time. Shown below is how long it takes for your money to double at different annual interest rates subject to continuous compounding.

Annual Interest Rate	Years to Double
5%	13.9 *years*
7%	9.9 *years*
9%	7.7 *years*
11%	6.3 *years*

Of course, the first problem is collecting some money to invest. The second problem is finding a reasonably safe investment with a return of 9% or more.

Check Point 9 How long, to the nearest tenth of a year, will it take $1000 to grow to $3600 at 8% annual interest compounded quarterly?

Yogi Berra, catcher and renowned hitter for the New York Yankees (1946–1963), said it best: "Prediction is very hard, especially when it's about the future." At the start of the twenty-first century, we are plagued by questions about the environment. Will we run out of gas? How hot will it get? Will there be neighborhoods where the air is pristine? Can we make garbage disappear? Will there be any wilderness left? Which wild animals will become extinct? These concerns have led to the growth of the environmental industry in the United States.

EXAMPLE 10   The Growth of the Environmental Industry

The formula

$$N = 461.87 + 299.4 \ln x$$

models the thousands of workers, N, in the environmental industry in the United States x years after 1979. By which year will there be 1,500,000, or 1500 thousand, U.S. workers in the environmental industry?

Solution We substitute 1500 for N and solve for x, the number of years after 1979.

$$N = 461.87 + 299.4 \ln x \qquad \text{This is the given formula.}$$

$$461.87 + 299.4 \ln x = 1500 \qquad \text{Substitute 1500 for } N \text{ and reverse the} \\ \text{two sides of the equation.}$$

Our goal is to isolate $\ln x$. We can then find x by exponentiating both sides of the equation, using the inverse property $e^{\ln x} = x$.

$$299.4 \ln x = 1038.13 \qquad \text{Subtract 461.87 from both sides.}$$

$$\ln x = \frac{1038.13}{299.4} \qquad \text{Divide both sides by 299.4.}$$

$$e^{\ln x} = e^{1038.13/299.4} \qquad \text{Exponentiate both sides.}$$

$$x = e^{1038.13/299.4} \qquad e^{\ln x} = x$$

$$\approx 32 \qquad \text{Use a calculator.}$$

Approximately 32 years after 1979, in the year 2011, there will be 1.5 million U.S. workers in the environmental industry.

Check Point 10 Use the formula in Example 10 to find by which year there will be two million, or 2000 thousand, U.S. workers in the environmental industry.

EXERCISE SET 3.4

Practice Exercises

Solve each exponential equation in Exercises 1–26. Express the solution set in terms of natural logarithms. Then use a calculator to obtain a decimal approximation, correct to two decimal places, for the solution.

1. $10^x = 3.91$
2. $10^x = 8.07$
3. $e^x = 5.7$
4. $e^x = 0.83$
5. $5^x = 17$
6. $19^x = 143$
7. $5e^x = 23$
8. $9e^x = 107$
9. $3e^{5x} = 1977$
10. $4e^{7x} = 10{,}273$
11. $e^{1-5x} = 793$
12. $e^{1-8x} = 7957$
13. $e^{5x-3} - 2 = 10{,}476$
14. $e^{4x-5} - 7 = 11{,}243$
15. $7^{x+2} = 410$
16. $5^{x-3} = 137$
17. $7^{0.3x} = 813$
18. $3^{x/7} = 0.2$
19. $5^{2x+3} = 3^{x-1}$
20. $7^{2x+1} = 3^{x+2}$
21. $e^{2x} - 3e^x + 2 = 0$
22. $e^{2x} - 2e^x - 3 = 0$
23. $e^{4x} + 5e^{2x} - 24 = 0$
24. $e^{4x} - 3e^{2x} - 18 = 0$
25. $3^{2x} + 3^x - 2 = 0$
26. $2^{2x} + 2^x - 12 = 0$

Solve each logarithmic equation in Exercises 27–44. Be sure to reject any value of x that produces the logarithm of a negative number or the logarithm of 0.

27. $\log_3 x = 4$
28. $\log_5 x = 3$
29. $\log_4(x + 5) = 3$
30. $\log_5(x - 7) = 2$
31. $\log_3(x - 4) = -3$
32. $\log_7(x + 2) = -2$
33. $\log_4(3x + 2) = 3$
34. $\log_2(4x + 1) = 5$
35. $\log_5 x + \log_5(4x - 1) = 1$
36. $\log_6(x + 5) + \log_6 x = 2$
37. $\log_3(x - 5) + \log_3(x + 3) = 2$
38. $\log_2(x - 1) + \log_2(x + 1) = 3$
39. $\log_2(x + 2) - \log_2(x - 5) = 3$
40. $\log_4(x + 2) - \log_4(x - 1) = 1$
41. $2\log_3(x + 4) = \log_3 9 + 2$
42. $3\log_2(x - 1) = 5 - \log_2 4$
43. $\log_2(x - 6) + \log_2(x - 4) - \log_2 x = 2$
44. $\log_2(x - 3) + \log_2 x - \log_2(x + 2) = 2$

Exercises 45–52 involve equations with natural logarithms. Solve each equation by isolating the natural logarithm and exponentiating both sides. Express the answer in terms of e. Then use a calculator to obtain a decimal approximation, correct to two decimal places, for the solution.

45. $\ln x = 2$
46. $\ln x = 3$
47. $5\ln(2x) = 20$
48. $6\ln(2x) = 30$
49. $6 + 2\ln x = 5$
50. $7 + 3\ln x = 6$
51. $\ln \sqrt{x + 3} = 1$
52. $\ln \sqrt{x + 4} = 1$

Application Exercises

Use the formula $R = 6e^{12.77x}$, where x is the blood alcohol concentration and R, given as a percent, is the risk of having a car accident, to solve Exercises 53–54.

53. What blood alcohol concentration corresponds to a 25% risk of a car accident?

54. What blood alcohol concentration corresponds to a 50% risk of a car accident?

55. The formula $A = 18.9e^{0.0055t}$ models the population of New York State, A, in millions, t years after 2000.
   a. What was the population of New York in 2000?
   b. When will the population of New York reach 19.6 million?

56. The formula $A = 15.9e^{0.0235t}$ models the population of Florida, A, in millions, t years after 2000.
   a. What was the population of Florida in 2000?
   b. When will the population of Florida reach 17.5 million?

In Exercises 57–60, complete the table for a savings account subjected to n compoundings yearly $\left[A = P\left(1 + \dfrac{r}{n} \right)^{nt} \right]$. Round answers to one decimal place.

Amount Invested	Number of Compounding Periods	Annual Interest Rate	Accumulated Amount	Time t in Years
57. $12,500	4	5.75%	$20,000	
58. $7250	12	6.5%	$15,000	
59. $1000	360		$1400	2
60. $5000	360		$9000	4

In Exercises 61–64, complete the table for a savings account subjected to continuous compounding ($A = Pe^{rt}$). Round answers to one decimal place.

Amount Invested	Annual Interest Rate	Accumulated Amount	Time t in Years
61. $8000	8%	Double the amount invested	
62. $8000		$12,000	2
63. $2350		Triple the amount invested	7
64. $17,425	4.25%	$25,000	

65. The function $f(x) = 15,557 + 5259 \ln x$ models the average cost of a new car, $f(x)$, in dollars, x years after 1989. When was the average cost of a new car $25,000?

66. The function $f(x) = 68.41 + 1.75 \ln x$ models the life expectancy, $f(x)$, in years, for African-American females born x years after 1969. In which birth year was life expectancy 73.7 years? Round to the nearest year.

The function $P(x) = 95 - 30 \log_2 x$ models the percentage, $P(x)$, of students who could recall the important features of a classroom lecture as a function of time, where x represents the number of days that have elapsed since the lecture was given. The figure shows the graph of the function. Use this information to solve Exercises 67–68. Round answers to one decimal place.

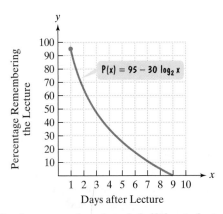

67. After how many days do only half the students recall the important features of the classroom lecture? (Let $P(x) = 50$ and solve for x.) Locate the point on the graph that conveys this information.

68. After how many days have all students forgotten the important features of the classroom lecture? (Let $P(x) = 0$ and solve for x.) Locate the point on the graph on the previous page that conveys this information.

The pH of a solution ranges from 0 to 14. An acid solution has a pH less than 7. Pure water is neutral and has a pH of 7. Normal, unpolluted rain has a pH of about 5.6. The pH of a solution is given by

$$\text{pH} = -\log x$$

where x represents the concentration of the hydrogen ions in the solution, in moles per liter. Use the formula to solve Exercises 69–70.

69. An environmental concern involves the destructive effects of acid rain. The most acidic rainfall ever had a pH of 2.4. What was the hydrogen ion concentration? Express the answer as a power of 10, and then round to the nearest thousandth.

70. The figure shows very acidic rain in the northeast United States. What is the hydrogen ion concentration of rainfall with a pH of 4.2? Express the answer as a power of 10, and then round to the nearest hundred-thousandth.

Acid Rain over Canada and the United States

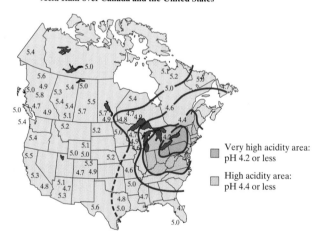

Very high acidity area: pH 4.2 or less

High acidity area: pH 4.4 or less

Source: National Atmospheric Program

 Writing in Mathematics

71. Explain how to solve an exponential equation. Use $3^x = 140$ in your explanation.

72. Explain how to solve a logarithmic equation. Use $\log_3(x - 1) = 4$ in your explanation.

73. In many states, a 17% risk of a car accident with a blood alcohol concentration of 0.08 is the lowest level for charging a motorist with driving under the influence. Do you agree with the 17% risk as a cutoff percentage, or do you feel that the percentage should be lower or higher?

Explain your answer. What blood alcohol concentration corresponds to what you believe is an appropriate percentage?

74. Have you purchased a new or used car recently? If so, describe if the function in Exercise 65 accurately models what you paid for your car. If there is a big difference between the figure given by the formula and the amount that you paid, how can you explain this difference?

Technology Exercises

In Exercises 75–82, use your graphing utility to graph each side of the equation in the same viewing rectangle. Then use the x-coordinate of the intersection point to find the equation's solution set. Verify this value by direct substitution into the equation.

75. $2^{x+1} = 8$ **76.** $3^{x+1} = 9$

77. $\log_3(4x - 7) = 2$ **78.** $\log_3(3x - 2) = 2$

79. $\log(x + 3) + \log x = 1$ **80.** $\log(x - 15) + \log x = 2$

81. $3^x = 2x + 3$ **82.** $5^x = 3x + 4$

Hurricanes are one of nature's most destructive forces. These low-pressure areas often have diameters of over 500 miles. The function $f(x) = 0.48 \ln(x + 1) + 27$ models the barometric air pressure, $f(x)$, in inches of mercury, at a distance of x miles from the eye of a hurricane. Use this function to solve Exercises 83–84.

83. Graph the function in a $[0, 500, 50]$ by $[27, 30, 1]$ viewing rectangle. What does the shape of the graph indicate about barometric air pressure as the distance from the eye increases?

84. Use an equation to answer this question: How far from the eye of a hurricane is the barometric air pressure 29 inches of mercury? Use the TRACE and ZOOM features or the intersect command of your graphing utility to verify your answer.

85. The function $P(t) = 145e^{-0.092t}$ models a runner's pulse, $P(t)$, in beats per minute, t minutes after a race, where $0 \le t \le 15$. Graph the function using a graphing utility. TRACE along the graph and determine after how many minutes the runner's pulse will be 70 beats per minute. Round to the nearest tenth of a minute. Verify your observation algebraically.

86. The function $W(t) = 2600(1 - 0.51e^{-0.075t})^3$ models the weight, $W(t)$, in kilograms, of a female African elephant at age t years. (1 kilogram $\approx$ 2.2 pounds) Use a graphing utility to graph the function. Then TRACE along the curve to estimate the age of an adult female elephant weighing 1800 kilograms.

Critical Thinking Exercises

87. Which one of the following is true?

a. If $\log(x + 3) = 2$, then $e^2 = x + 3$.

b. If $\log(7x + 3) - \log(2x + 5) = 4$, then in exponential form $10^4 = (7x + 3) - (2x + 5)$.

c. If $x = \dfrac{1}{k} \ln y$, then $y = e^{kx}$.

d. Examples of exponential equations include $10^x = 5.71$, $e^x = 0.72$, and $x^{10} = 5.71$.

88. If \$4000 is deposited into an account paying 3% interest compounded annually and at the same time \$2000 is deposited into an account paying 5% interest compounded annually, after how long will the two accounts have the same balance?

Solve each equation in Exercises 89–91. Check each proposed solution by direct substitution or with a graphing utility.

89. $(\ln x)^2 = \ln x^2$

90. $(\log x)(2 \log x + 1) = 6$

91. $\ln(\ln x) = 0$

Group Exercise

92. Research applications of logarithmic functions as mathematical models and plan a seminar based on your group's research. Each group member should research one of the following areas or any other area of interest: pH (acidity of solutions), intensity of sound (decibels), brightness of stars, consumption of natural resources, human memory, progress over time in a sport, profit over time. For the area that you select, explain how logarithmic functions are used and provide examples.

SECTION 3.5 Modeling with Exponential and Logarithmic Functions

Objectives

1. Model exponential growth and decay.
2. Use logistic growth models.
3. Model data with exponential and logarithmic functions.
4. Express an exponential model in base e.

The most casual cruise on the Internet shows how people disagree when it comes to making predictions about the effects of the world's growing population. Some argue that there is a recent slowdown in the growth rate, economies remain robust, and famines in Biafra and Ethiopia are aberrations rather than signs of the future. Others say that the 6 billion people on Earth is twice as many as can be supported in middle-class comfort, and the world is running out of arable land and fresh water. Debates about entities that are growing exponentially can be approached mathematically: We can create functions that model data and use these functions to make predictions. In this section we will show you how this is done.

1 Model exponential growth and decay.

Exponential Growth and Decay

One of algebra's many applications is to predict the behavior of variables. This can be done with *exponential growth* and *decay models*. With exponential growth or decay, quantities grow or decay at a rate directly proportional to their size. Populations that are growing exponentially grow extremely rapidly as they get larger because there are more adults to have offspring. For example, the **growth rate** for world population is 1.3%, or 0.013. This means that each year world population is 1.3% more than what it was in the previous year. In 2001, world population was approximately 6.2 billion. Thus, we compute the world population in 2002 as follows:

$$6.2 \text{ billion} + 1.3\% \text{ of } 6.2 \text{ billion} = 6.2 + (0.013)(6.2) = 6.2806.$$

This computation suggests that 6.2806 billion people will populate the world in 2002. The 0.0806 billion represents an increase of 80.6 million people from 2001 to 2002, the equivalent of the population of Germany. Using 1.3% as the annual growth rate, world population for 2003 is found in a similar manner:

$$6.2806 + 1.3\% \text{ of } 6.2806 = 6.2806 + (0.013)(6.2806) \approx 6.3622.$$

This computation suggests that approximately 6.3622 billion people will populate the world in 2003.

The explosive growth of world population may remind you of the growth of money in an account subject to compound interest. Just as the growth rate for world population is multiplied by the population plus any increase in the population, a compound interest rate is multiplied by your original investment plus any accumulated interest. The balance in an account subject to continuous compounding and world population are special cases of an *exponential growth model*.

Study Tip

You have seen the formula for exponential growth before, but with different letters. It is the formula for compound interest with continous compounding.

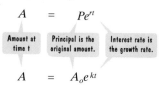

$$A = Pe^{rt}$$

| Amount at time t | Principal is the original amount. | Interest rate is the growth rate. |

$$A = A_o e^{kt}$$

Exponential Growth and Decay Models

The mathematical model for **exponential growth** or **decay** is given by

$$f(t) = A_0 e^{kt} \quad \text{or} \quad A = A_0 e^{kt}.$$

- **If $k > 0$, the function models the amount, or size, of a *growing* entity.** A_0 is the original amount, or size, of the growing entity at time $t = 0$, A is the amount at time t, and k is a constant representing the growth rate.

- **If $k < 0$, the function models the amount, or size, of a *decaying* entity.** A_0 is the original amount, or size, of the decaying entity at time $t = 0$, A is the amount at time t, and k is a constant representing the decay rate.

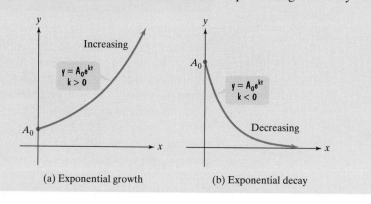

(a) Exponential growth   (b) Exponential decay

Sometimes we need to use given data to determine k, the rate of growth or decay. After we compute the value of k, we can use the formula $A = A_0 e^{kt}$ to make predictions. This idea is illustrated in our first two examples.

EXAMPLE 1   Modeling the Growth of the Minimum Wage

The graph in Figure 3.17 shows the growth of the minimum wage from 1970 through 2000. In 1970, the minimum wage was $1.60 per hour. By 2000, it had grown to $5.15 per hour.

Federal Minimum Wages, 1970–2000

Figure 3.17 *Source:* U.S. Employment Standards Administration

a. Find the exponential growth function that models the data for 1970 through 2000.

b. By which year will the minimum wage reach $7.50 per hour?

Solution

a. We use the exponential growth model

$$A = A_0 e^{kt}$$

in which t is the number of years after 1970. This means that 1970 corresponds to $t = 0$. At that time the minimum wage was $1.60, so we substitute 1.6 for A_0 in the growth model:

$$A = 1.6 e^{kt}.$$

We are given that $5.15 is the minimum wage in 2000. Because 2000 is 30 years after 1970, when $t = 30$ the value of A is 5.15. Substituting these numbers into the growth model will enable us to find k, the growth rate. We know that $k > 0$ because the problem involves growth.

$A = 1.6 e^{kt}$	Use the growth model, $A = A_0 e^{kt}$, with $A_0 = 1.6$.
$5.15 = 1.6 e^{k \cdot 30}$	When $t = 30$, $A = 5.15$. Substitute these numbers into the model.
$e^{30k} = \dfrac{5.15}{1.6}$	Isolate the exponential factor by dividing both sides by 1.6. We also reversed the sides.
$\ln e^{30k} = \ln \dfrac{5.15}{1.6}$	Take the natural logarithm on both sides.
$30k = \ln \dfrac{5.15}{1.6}$	Simplify the left side using $\ln e^x = x$.
$k = \dfrac{\ln \dfrac{5.15}{1.6}}{30} \approx 0.039$	Divide both sides by 30 and solve for k.

We substitute 0.039 for k in the growth model to obtain the exponential growth function for the minimum wage. It is

$$A = 1.6 e^{0.039t}$$

where t is measured in years after 1970.

b. To find the year in which the minimum wage will reach $7.50 per hour, we substitute 7.5 for A in the model from part (a) and solve for t.

$$A = 1.6e^{0.039t}$$ *This is the model from part (a).*

$$7.5 = 1.6e^{0.039t}$$ *Substitute 7.5 for A.*

$$e^{0.039t} = \frac{7.5}{1.6}$$ *Divide both sides by 1.6. We also reversed the sides.*

$$\ln e^{0.039t} = \ln \frac{7.5}{1.6}$$ *Take the natural logarithm on both sides.*

$$0.039t = \ln \frac{7.5}{1.6}$$ *Simplify on the left using $\ln e^x = x$.*

$$t = \frac{\ln \dfrac{7.5}{1.6}}{0.039} \approx 40$$ *Solve for t by dividing both sides by 0.039.*

Because 40 is the number of years after 1970, the model indicates that the minimum wage will reach $7.50 by 1970 + 40, or in the year 2010.

Check Point 1

In 1990, the population of Africa was 643 million and by 2000 it had grown to 813 million.
a. Use the exponential growth model $A = A_0e^{kt}$, in which t is the number of years after 1990, to find the exponential growth function that models the data.
b. By which year will Africa's population reach 2000 million, or two billion?

Lying with Statistics

Benjamin Disraeli, Queen Victoria's prime minister, stated that there are "lies, damned lies, and statistics." The problem is not that data lie, but rather that liars use data. For example, the data in Example 1 create the impression that wages are on the rise and workers are better off each year. The graph in Figure 3.18 is more effective in creating an accurate picture. Why? It is adjusted for inflation and measured in constant 1996 dollars. Something else to think about: In predicting a minimum wage of $7.50 by 2010, are we using the best possible model for the data? We return to this issue in the exercise set.

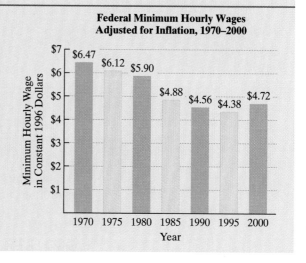

Federal Minimum Hourly Wages Adjusted for Inflation, 1970–2000

Figure 3.18
Source: U.S. Employment Standards Administration

Carbon Dating and Artistic Development

The artistic community was electrified by the discovery in 1995 of spectacular cave paintings in a limestone cavern in France. Carbon dating of the charcoal from the site showed that the images, created by artists of remarkable talent, were 30,000 years old, making them the oldest cave paintings ever found. The artists seemed to have used the cavern's natural contours to heighten a sense of perspective. The quality of the painting suggests that the art of early humans did not mature steadily from primitive to sophisticated in any simple linear fashion.

Our next example involves exponential decay and its use in determining the age of fossils and artifacts. The method is based on considering the percentage of carbon-14 remaining in the fossil or artifact. Carbon-14 decays exponentially with a *half-life* of approximately 5715 years. The **half-life** of a substance is the time required for half of a given sample to disintegrate. Thus, after 5715 years a given amount of carbon-14 will have decayed to half the original amount. Carbon dating is useful for artifacts or fossils up to 80,000 years old. Older objects do not have enough carbon-14 left to date age accurately.

EXAMPLE 2   Carbon-14 Dating: The Dead Sea Scrolls

a. Use the fact that after 5715 years a given amount of carbon-14 will have decayed to half the original amount to find the exponential decay model for carbon-14.

b. In 1947, earthenware jars containing what are known as the Dead Sea Scrolls were found by an Arab Bedouin herdsman. Analysis indicated that the scroll wrappings contained 76% of their original carbon-14. Estimate the age of the Dead Sea Scrolls.

Solution   We begin with the exponential decay model $A = A_0 e^{kt}$. We know that $k < 0$ because the problem involves the decay of carbon-14. After 5715 years ($t = 5715$), the amount of carbon-14 present, A, is half the original amount A_0. Thus, we can substitute $\dfrac{A_0}{2}$ for A in the exponential decay model. This will enable us to find k, the decay rate.

a. $A = A_0 e^{kt}$ Begin with the exponential decay model.

$\dfrac{A_0}{2} = A_0 e^{k \cdot 5715}$ After 5715 years ($t = 5715$), $A = \dfrac{A_0}{2}$ (because the amount present, A, is half the original amount, A_0).

$\dfrac{1}{2} = e^{5715k}$ Divide both sides of the equation by A_0.

$\ln \dfrac{1}{2} = \ln e^{5715k}$ Take the natural logarithm on both sides.

$\ln \dfrac{1}{2} = 5715k$ Simplify the right side using $\ln e^x = x$.

$k = \dfrac{\ln \dfrac{1}{2}}{5715} \approx -0.000121$ Divide both sides by 5715 and solve for k.

Substituting for k in the decay model, $A = A_0 e^{kt}$, the model for carbon-14 is

$$A = A_0 e^{-0.000121t}.$$

b. $A = A_0 e^{-0.000121t}$ This is the decay model for carbon-14.

$0.76A_0 = A_0 e^{-0.000121t}$ A, the amount present, is 76% of the original amount, so A = $0.76A_0$.

$0.76 = e^{-0.000121t}$ Divide both sides of the equation by A_0.

$\ln 0.76 = \ln e^{-0.000121t}$ Take the natural logarithm on both sides.

$$\ln 0.76 = \ln e^{-0.000121t}$$

We've repeated this equation from the bottom of the previous page.

$$\ln 0.76 = -0.000121t$$

Simplify the right side using $\ln e^x = x$.

$$t = \frac{\ln 0.76}{-0.000121} \approx 2268$$

Divide both sides by -0.000121 and solve for t.

The Dead Sea Scrolls are approximately 2268 years old plus the number of years between 1947 and the current year.

Check Point 2

Strontium-90 is a waste product from nuclear reactors. As a consequence of fallout from atmospheric nuclear tests, we all have a measurable amount of strontium-90 in our bones.

a. Use the fact that after 28 years a given amount of strontium-90 will have decayed to half the original amount to find the exponential decay model for strontium-90.

b. Suppose that a nuclear accident occurs and releases 60 grams of strontium-90 into the atmosphere. How long will it take for strontium-90 to decay to a level of 10 grams?

② Use logistic growth models.

Logistic Growth Models

From population growth to the spread of an epidemic, nothing on Earth can grow exponentially indefinitely. Growth is always limited. This is shown in Figure 3.19 by the horizontal asymptote. The **logistic growth model** is an exponential function used to model situations in which growth is limited.

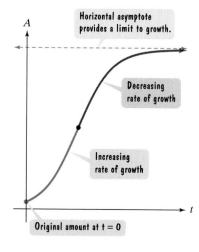

Figure 3.19 The logistic growth curve has a horizontal asymptote that limits the growth of A over time.

Logistic Growth Model

The mathematical model for limited logistic growth is given by

$$f(t) = \frac{c}{1 + ae^{-bt}} \quad \text{or} \quad A = \frac{c}{1 + ae^{-bt}}$$

where a, b, and c are constants, with $c > 0$ and $b > 0$.

As time increases $(t \to \infty)$, the expression ae^{-bt} in the model approaches 0, and A gets closer and closer to c. This means that $y = c$ is a horizontal asymptote for the graph of the function. Thus, the value of A can never exceed c and c represents the limiting size that A can attain.

EXAMPLE 3 Modeling the Spread of the Flu

The function

$$f(t) = \frac{30,000}{1 + 20e^{-1.5t}}$$

describes the number of people, $f(t)$, who have become ill with influenza t weeks after its initial outbreak in a town with 30,000 inhabitants.

a. How many people became ill with the flu when the epidemic began?

b. How many people were ill by the end of the fourth week?

c. What is the limiting size of $f(t)$, the population that becomes ill?

Solution

a. The time at the beginning of the flu epidemic is $t = 0$. Thus, we can find the number of people who were ill at the beginning of the epidemic by substituting 0 for t.

$$f(t) = \frac{30,000}{1 + 20e^{-1.5t}} \qquad \text{This is the given logistic growth function.}$$

$$f(0) = \frac{30,000}{1 + 20e^{-1.5(0)}} \qquad \text{When the epidemic began, } t = 0.$$

$$= \frac{30,000}{1 + 20} \qquad e^{-1.5(0)} = e^{0} = 1$$

$$\approx 1429$$

Approximately 1429 people were ill when the epidemic began.

b. We find the number of people who were ill at the end of the fourth week by substituting 4 for t in the logistic growth function.

$$f(t) = \frac{30,000}{1 + 20e^{-1.5t}} \qquad \text{Use the given logistic growth function.}$$

$$f(4) = \frac{30,000}{1 + 20e^{-1.5(4)}} \qquad \text{To find the number of people ill by the end of week four, let } t = 4.$$

$$= 28,583 \qquad \text{Use a calculator.}$$

Approximately 28,583 people were ill by the end of the fourth week. Compared with the number of people who were ill initially, 1429, this illustrates the virulence of the epidemic.

c. Recall that in the logistic growth model, $f(t) = \dfrac{c}{1 + ae^{-bt}}$, the constant c represents the limiting size that $f(t)$ can attain. Thus, the number in the numerator, 30,000, is the limiting size of the population that becomes ill.

Technology

The graph of the logistic growth function for the flu epidemic

$$y = \frac{30,000}{1 + 20e^{-1.5x}}$$

can be obtained using a graphing utility. We started x at 0 and ended at 10. This takes us to week 10. (In Example 3, we found that by week 4 approximately 28,583 people were ill.) We also know that 30,000 is the limiting size, so we took values of y up to 30,000. Using a $[0, 10, 1]$ by $[0, 30,000, 3000]$ viewing rectangle, the graph of the logistic growth function is shown below.

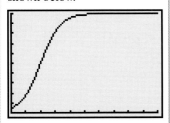

Check Point 3 In a learning theory project, psychologists discovered that

$$f(t) = \frac{0.8}{1 + e^{-0.2t}}$$

is a model for describing the proportion of correct responses, $f(t)$, after t learning trials.

Check
Point
3 **continued**

a. Find the proportion of correct responses prior to learning trials taking place.

b. Find the proportion of correct responses after 10 learning trials.

c. What is the limiting size of $f(t)$, the proportion of correct responses, as continued learning trials take place?

3 Model data with exponential and logarithmic functions.

The Art of Modeling

Throughout this chapter, we have been working with models that were given. However, we can create functions that model data by observing patterns in scatter plots. Figure 3.20 shows scatter plots for data that are exponential or logarithmic.

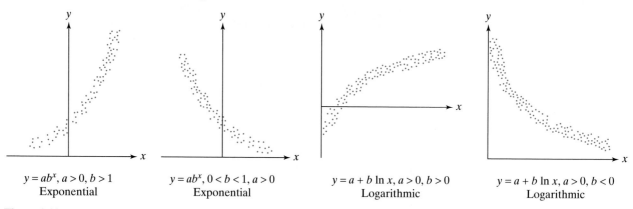

$y = ab^x, a > 0, b > 1$
Exponential

$y = ab^x, 0 < b < 1, a > 0$
Exponential

$y = a + b \ln x, a > 0, b > 0$
Logarithmic

$y = a + b \ln x, a > 0, b < 0$
Logarithmic

Figure 3.20 Scatter plots for exponential or logarithmic models

Graphing utilities can be used to find the equation of a function that is derived from data. For example, earlier in the chapter we encountered a function that modeled the size of a city and the average walking speed, in feet per second, of pedestrians. The function was derived from the data in Table 3.4. The scatter plot is shown in Figure 3.21.

Table 3.4

x, Population (thousands)	y, Walking Speed (feet per second)
5.5	3.3
14	3.7
71	4.3
138	4.4
342	4.8

Source: Mark and Helen Bornstein, "The Pace of Life"

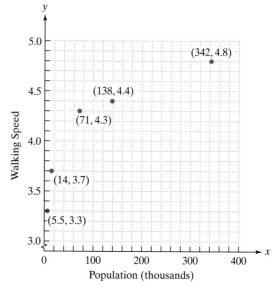

Figure 3.21 Scatter plot for data in Table 3.4

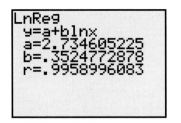

Figure 3.22 A logarithmic model for the data in Table 3.4

Because the data in this scatter plot increase rapidly at first and then begin to level off a bit, the shape suggests that a logarithmic model might be a good choice. A graphing utility fits the data in Table 3.4 to a logarithmic model of the form $y = a + b \ln x$ by using the Natural Logarithmic REGression (LnReg) option (see Figure 3.22). From the figure, we see that the logarithmic model of the data, with numbers rounded to three decimal places, is

$$y = 2.735 + 0.352 \ln x.$$

The number r that appears in Figure 3.22 is called the **correlation coefficient** and is a measure of how well the model fits the data. The value of r is such that $-1 \le r \le 1$. A positive r means that as the x-values increase, so do the y-values. A negative r means that as the x-values increase, the y-values decrease. **The closer that r is to -1 or 1, the better the model fits the data.** Because r is approximately 0.996, the model

$$y = 2.735 + 0.352 \ln x$$

fits the data very well.

Now let's look at data whose scatter plot suggests an exponential model. The data in Table 3.5 indicate world population for six years. The scatter plot is shown in Figure 3.23.

Table 3.5

x, Year	y, World Population (billions)
1950	2.6
1960	3.1
1970	3.7
1980	4.5
1989	5.3
2001	6.2

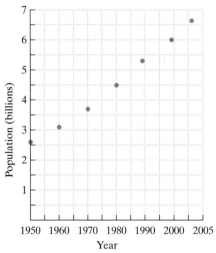

Figure 3.23 A scatter plot for data in Table 3.5

Because the data in this scatter plot have a rapidly increasing pattern, the shape suggests that an exponential model might be a good choice. (You might also want to try a linear model.) If you select the exponential option, you will use a graphing utility's Exponential REGression option. With this feature, a graphing utility fits the data to an exponential model of the form $y = ab^x$.

When computing an exponential model of the form $y = ab^x$, many graphing utilities rewrite the equation using logarithms. Because the domain of the logarithmic function is the set of positive numbers, **zero must not be a value for x** when using such utilities. What does this mean in terms of our data for world population that starts in the year 1950? We must start values of x after 0. Thus, we'll assign x to represent the number of years after 1949.

This gives us the data shown in Table 3.6. Using the Exponential REGression option, we obtain the equation in Figure 3.24.

Table 3.6

x, Numbers of Years after 1949		y, World Population (billions)
1	(1950)	2.6
11	(1960)	3.1
21	(1970)	3.7
31	(1980)	4.5
40	(1989)	5.3
52	(2001)	6.2

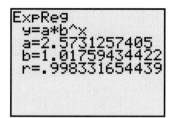

Figure 3.24 An exponential model for the data in Table 3.6

From Figure 3.24, we see that the exponential model of the data for world population, y, in billions, x years after 1949, with numbers rounded to three decimal places, is

$$y = 2.573(1.018)^x.$$

The correlation coefficient, r, is close to 1, indicating that the model fits the data very well.

Because $b = e^{\ln b}$, we can rewrite any model in the form $y = ab^x$ in terms of base e.

4 Express an exponential model in base e.

Expressing an Exponential Model in Base e

$y = ab^x$ is equivalent to $y = ae^{(\ln b) \cdot x}$.

EXAMPLE 4   **Rewriting an Exponential Model in Base e**

Rewrite $y = 2.573(1.018)^x$ in terms of base e.

Solution

$y = ab^x$ is equivalent to $y = ae^{(\ln b) \cdot x}$.

$y = 2.573(1.018)^x$ is equivalent to $y = 2.573e^{(\ln 1.018) \cdot x}$.

Using $\ln 1.018 \approx 0.018$, the exponential growth model for world population, y, in billions, x years after 1949 is

$$y = 2.573e^{0.018x}.$$

In Example 4, we can replace y with A and x with t so that the model has the same letters as those in the exponential growth model $A = A_0 e^{kt}$.

$A = A_0 e^{kt}$ This is the exponential growth model.

$A = 2.573e^{0.018t}$ This is the model for world population.

The value of k, 0.018, indicates a growth rate of 1.8%. Although this is an excellent model for the data, we must be careful about making projections about world population using this growth function. Why? World population growth rate is now 1.3%, not 1.8%, so our model will overestimate future populations.

Check Point 4 Rewrite $y = 4(7.8)^x$ in terms of base e. Express the answer in terms of a natural logarithm, and then round to three decimal places.

When using a graphing utility to model data, begin with a scatter plot, drawn either by hand or with the graphing utility, to obtain a general picture for the shape of the data. It might be difficult to determine which model best fits the data—linear, logarithmic, exponential, quadratic, or something else. If necessary, use your graphing utility to fit several models to the data. The best model is the one that yields the value r, the correlation coefficient, closest to 1 or -1. Finding a proper fit for data can be almost as much art as it is mathematics. In this era of technology, the process of creating models that best fit data is one that involves more decision making than computation.

EXERCISE SET 3.5

Practice and Application Exercises

The exponential growth model $A = 203e^{0.011t}$ describes the population of the United States, A, in millions, t years after 1970. Use this model to solve Exercises 1–4.

1. What was the population of the United States in 1970?
2. By what percentage is the population of the United States increasing each year?
3. When will the U.S. population be 300 million?
4. When will the U.S. population be 350 million?

India is currently one of the world's fastest-growing countries. By 2040, the population of India will be larger than the population of China; by 2050, nearly one-third of the world's population will live in these two countries alone. The exponential growth model $A = 574e^{0.026t}$ describes the population of India, A, in millions, t years after 1974. Use this model to solve Exercises 5–8.

5. By what percentage is the population of India increasing each year?
6. What was the population of India in 1974?
7. When will India's population be 1624 million?
8. When will India's population be 2732 million?
9. Low interest rates, easy credit, and strong demand from new immigrants have driven up the average sales price of new one-family houses in the United States. In 1995, the average sales price was $158,700 and by 2000 it had increased to $207,200.

   a. Use the exponential growth model $A = A_0 e^{kt}$, in which t is the number of years after 1995, to find the exponential growth function that models the data.

   b. According to your model, by which year will the average sales price of a new one-family house reach $300,000?

Average Sales Prices of New One-Family Houses

Source: U.S. Census Bureau

About the size of New Jersey, Israel has seen its population soar to more than 6 million since it was established. With the help of U.S. aid, the country now has a diversified economy rivaling those of other developed Western nations. By contrast, the Palestinians, living under Israeli occupation and a corrupt regime, endure bleak conditions. The graphs show that by 2050, Palestinians in the West Bank, Gaza Strip, and East Jerusalem will outnumber Israelis. Exercises 10–12 involve the projected growth of these two populations.

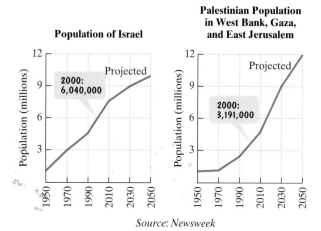

Population of Israel

2000: 6,040,000

Projected

Palestinian Population in West Bank, Gaza, and East Jerusalem

2000: 3,191,000

Projected

Source: Newsweek

10. In 2000, the population of the Palestinians in the West Bank, Gaza Strip, and East Jerusalem was approximately 3.2 million and by 2050 it is projected to grow to 12 million. Use the exponential growth model $A = A_0e^{kt}$, in which t is the number of years after 2000, to find the exponential growth function that models the data.

11. In 2000, the population of Israel was approximately 6.04 million and by 2050 it is projected to grow to 10 million. Use the exponential growth model $A = A_0e^{kt}$, in which t is the number of years after 2000, to find an exponential growth function that models the data.

12. Use the growth models in Exercises 10 and 11 to determine the year in which the two populations will be the same.

An artifact originally had 16 grams of carbon-14 present. The decay model $A = 16e^{-0.000121t}$ describes the amount of carbon-14 present, A, in grams, after t years. Use this model to solve Exercises 13–14.

13. How many grams of carbon-14 will be present after 5715 years?

14. How many grams of carbon-14 will be present after 11,430 years?

15. The half-life of the radioactive element krypton-91 is 10 seconds. If 16 grams of krypton-91 are initially present, how many grams are present after 10 seconds? 20 seconds? 30 seconds? 40 seconds? 50 seconds?

16. The half-life of the radioactive element plutonium-239 is 25,000 years. If 16 grams of plutonium-239 are initially present how many grams are present after 25,000 years? 50,000 years? 75,000 years? 100,000 years? 125,000 years?

Use the exponential decay model for carbon-14, $A = A_0e^{-0.000121t}$, to solve Exercises 17–18.

17. Prehistoric cave paintings were discovered in a cave in France. The paint contained 15% of the original carbon-14. Estimate the age of the paintings.

18. Skeletons were found at a construction site in San Francisco in 1989. The skeletons contained 88% of the expected amount of carbon-14 found in a living person. In 1989, how old were the skeletons?

19. The August 1978 issue of *National Geographic* described the 1964 find of dinosaur bones of a newly discovered dinosaur weighing 170 pounds, measuring 9 feet, with a 6-inch claw on one toe of each hind foot. The age of the dinosaur was estimated using potassium-40 dating of rocks surrounding the bones.

a. Potassium-40 decays exponentially with a half-life of approximately 1.31 billion years. Use the fact that after 1.31 billion years a given amount of potassium-40 will have decayed to half the original amount to show that the decay model for potassium-40 is given by $A = A_0e^{-0.52912t}$, where t is in billions of years.

b. Analysis of the rocks surrounding the dinosaur bones indicated that 94.5% of the original amount of potassium-40 was still present. Let $A = 0.945A_0$ in the model in part (a) and estimate the age of the bones of the dinosaur.

20. A bird species in danger of extinction has a population that is decreasing exponentially $(A = A_0e^{kt})$. Five years ago the population was at 1400 and today only 1000 of the birds are alive. Once the population drops below 100, the situation will be irreversible. When will this happen?

21. Use the exponential growth model, $A = A_0e^{kt}$, to show that the time it takes a population to double (to grow from A_0 to $2A_0$) is given by $t = \dfrac{\ln 2}{k}$.

22. Use the exponential growth model, $A = A_0e^{kt}$, to show that the time it takes a population to triple (to grow from A_0 to $3A_0$) is given by $t = \dfrac{\ln 3}{k}$.

Use the formula $t = \dfrac{\ln 2}{k}$ that gives the time for a population with a growth rate k to double to solve Exercises 23–24. Express each answer to the nearest whole year.

23. China is growing at a rate of 1.1% per year. How long will it take China to double its population?

24. Japan is growing at a rate of 0.3% per year. How long will it take Japan to double its population?

25. The logistic growth function
$$f(t) = \frac{100,000}{1 + 5000e^{-t}}$$
describes the number of people, $f(t)$, who have become ill with influenza t weeks after its initial outbreak in a particular community.

a. How many people became ill with the flu when the epidemic began?

b. How many people were ill by the end of the fourth week?

c. What is the limiting size of the population that becomes ill?

26. The logistic growth function
$$f(t) = \frac{500}{1 + 83.3e^{-0.162t}}$$
describes the population, $f(t)$, of an endangered species of birds t years after they are introduced to a nonthreatening habitat.

a. How many birds were initially introduced to the habitat?

b. How many birds are expected in the habitat after 10 years?

c. What is the limiting size of the bird population that the habitat will sustain?

The logistic growth function

$$P(x) = \frac{90}{1 + 271e^{-0.122x}}$$

models the percentage, $P(x)$, of Americans who are x years old with some coronary heart disease. Use the function to solve Exercises 27–30.

27. What percentage of 20-year-olds have some coronary heart disease?

28. What percentage of 80-year-olds have some coronary heart disease?

29. At what age is the percentage of some coronary heart disease 50%?

30. At what age is the percentage of some coronary heart disease 70%?

In Exercises 31–34, rewrite the equation in terms of base e. Express the answer in terms of a natural logarithm, and then round to three decimal places.

31. $y = 100(4.6)^x$ **32.** $y = 1000(7.3)^x$

33. $y = 2.5(0.7)^x$ **34.** $y = 4.5(0.6)^x$

 Writing in Mathematics

35. Nigeria has a growth rate of 0.031 or 3.1%. Describe what this means.

36 How can you tell if an exponential model describes exponential growth or exponential decay?

37. Suppose that a population that is growing exponentially increases from 800,000 people in 2003 to 1,000,000 people in 2006. Without showing the details, describe how to obtain the exponential growth function that models the data.

38. What is the half-life of a substance?

39. Describe a difference between exponential growth and logistic growth.

40. Describe the shape of a scatter plot that suggests modeling the data with an exponential function.

41. Based on the graphs in Exercises 10–12, for which population is an exponential growth function a better model? Explain your answer.

42. You take up weightlifting and record the maximum number of pounds you can lift at the end of each week. You start off with rapid growth in terms of the weight you can lift from week to week, but then the growth begins to level off. Describe how to obtain a function that models the number of pounds you can lift at the end of each week. How can you use this function to predict what might happen if you continue the sport?

43. Would you prefer that your salary be modeled exponentially or logarithmically? Explain your answer.

44. One problem with all exponential growth models is that nothing can grow exponentially forever. Describe factors that might limit the size of a population.

Technology Exercises

In Example 1 on page 420–421, we used two data points and an exponential function to model federal minimum wages that were not adjusted for inflation from 1970 through 2000. The data are shown again in the table. Use all seven data points to solve Exercises 45–49.

x, Number of Years after 1969	y, Federal Minimum Wage
1	1.60
6	2.10
11	3.10
16	3.35
21	3.80
26	4.25
31	5.15

45. Use your graphing utility's Exponential REGression option to obtain a model of the form $y = ab^x$ that fits the data. How well does the correlation coefficient, r, indicate that the model fits the data?

46. Use your graphing utility's Logarithmic REGression option to obtain a model of the form $y = a + b \ln x$ that fits the data. How well does the correlation coefficient, r, indicate that the model fits the data?

47. Use your graphing utility's Linear REGression option to obtain a model of the form $y = ax + b$ that fits the data. How well does the correlation coefficient, r, indicate that the model fits the data?

48. Use your graphing utility's Power REGression option to obtain a model of the form $y = ax^b$ that fits the data. How well does the correlation coefficient, r, indicate that the model fits the data?

49. Use the value of r in Exercises 45–48 to select the model of best fit. Use this model to predict by which year the minimum wage will reach $7.50. How does this answer compare to the year we found in Example 1, namely 2010? If you obtained a different year, how do you account for this difference?

50. In Exercises 27–30, you worked with the logistic growth function

$$P(x) = \frac{90}{1 + 271e^{-0.122x}}$$

which models the percentage, $P(x)$, of Americans who are x years old with some coronary heart disease. Use your graphing utility to graph the function in a $[0, 100, 10]$ by $[0, 100, 10]$ viewing rectangle. Describe as specifically as possible what the logistic curve indicates about aging and the percentage of Americans with coronary heart disease.

In Exercises 51–52, use a graphing utility to find the model that best fits the given data. Then use the model to make a reasonable prediction for a value that exceeds those shown on the graph's horizontal axis.

51.

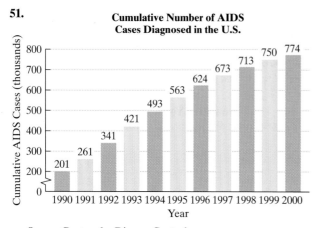

Cumulative Number of AIDS Cases Diagnosed in the U.S.

Source: Centers for Disease Control

52.

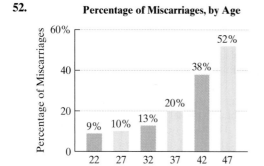

Percentage of Miscarriages, by Age

Source: Time

Critical Thinking Exercises

53. The World Health Organization makes predictions about the number of AIDS cases based on a compromise between a linear model and an exponential growth model. Explain why the World Health Organization does this.

54. Over a period of time, a hot object cools to the temperature of the surrounding air. This is described mathematically by

$$T = C + (T_0 - C)e^{-kt},$$

where t is the time it takes for an object to cool from temperature T_0 to temperature T, C is the surrounding air temperature, and k is a positive constant that is associated with the cooling object. A cake removed from the oven has a temperature of 210°F and is left to cool in a room that has a temperature of 70°F. After 30 minutes, the temperature of the cake is 140°F. What is the temperature of the cake after 40 minutes?

Group Exercise

55. This activity is intended for three or four people who would like to take up weightlifting. Each person in the group should record the maximum number of pounds that he or she can lift at the end of each week for the first 10 consecutive weeks. Use the Logarithmic REGression option of a graphing utility to obtain a model showing the amount of weight that group members can lift from week 1 through week 10. Graph each of the models in the same viewing rectangle to observe similarities and differences among weight-growth patterns of each member. Use the functions to predict the amount of weight that group members will be able to lift in the future. If the group continues to work out together, check the accuracy of these predictions.

56. Each group member should consult an almanac, newspaper, magazine, or the Internet to find data that can be modeled by exponential or logarithmic functions. Group members should select the two sets of data that are most interesting and relevant. For each data set selected, find a model that best fits the data. Each group member should make one prediction based on the model and then discuss a consequence of this prediction. What factors might change the accuracy of each prediction?

CHAPTER SUMMARY, REVIEW, AND TEST

Summary

DEFINITIONS AND CONCEPTS	EXAMPLES

3.1 Exponential Functions

a. The exponential function with base b is defined by $f(x) = b^x$, where $b > 0$ and $b \neq 1$. — Ex. 1, p. 160

b. Characteristics of exponential functions and graphs for $0 < b < 1$ and $b > 1$ are shown in the box on page 162. — Ex. 2, p. 161

c. Transformations involving exponential functions are summarized in Table 3.1 on page 162. — Exs. 3 & 4, p. 163

d. The natural exponential function $f(x) = e^x$. The irrational number e is called the natural base, where $e \approx 2.7183$. — Ex. 5, p. 164

e. Formulas for compound interest: After t years, the balance, A, in an account with principal P and annual interest rate r (in decimal form) is given by one of the following formulas: — Ex. 6, p. 166

   1. For n compoundings per year: $A = P\left(1 + \dfrac{r}{n}\right)^{nt}$

   2. For continuous compounding: $A = Pe^{rt}$

3.2 Logarithmic Functions

a. Definition of the logarithmic function: For $x > 0$ and $b > 0, b \neq 1$, $y = \log_b x$ is equivalent to $b^y = x$. The function $f(x) = \log_b x$ is the logarithmic function with base b. This function is the inverse function of the exponential function with base b. — Ex. 1, p. 171; Ex. 2, p. 171; Ex. 3, p. 172

b. Graphs of logarithmic functions for $b > 1$ and $0 < b < 1$ are shown in Figure 3.7 on page 174. Characteristics of the graphs are summarized in the box that follows the figure. — Ex. 6, p. 174

c. Transformations involving logarithmic functions are summarized in Table 3.3 on page 175.

d. The domain of a logarithmic function of the form $f(x) = \log_b x$ is the set of all positive real numbers. The domain of $f(x) = \log_b(x + c)$ consists of all x for which $x + c > 0$. — Ex. 7, p. 176; Ex. 10, p. 178

e. Common and natural logarithms: $f(x) = \log x$ means $f(x) = \log_{10} x$ and is the common logarithmic function. $f(x) = \ln x$ means $f(x) = \log_e x$ and is the natural logarithmic function. — Ex. 8, p. 177; Ex. 9, p. 177

f. Basic Logarithmic Properties

Base b ($b > 0, b \neq 1$)	Base 10 (Common Logarithms)	Base e (Natural Logarithms)	
$\log_b 1 = 0$	$\log 1 = 0$	$\ln 1 = 0$	Ex. 4, p. 173
$\log_b b = 1$	$\log 10 = 1$	$\ln e = 1$	Ex. 5, p. 173
$\log_b b^x = x$	$\log 10^x = 1$	$\ln e^x = x$	Ex. 11, p. 179
$b^{\log_b x} = x$	$10^{\log x} = x$	$e^{\ln x} = x$	Ex. 12, p. 179

3.3 Properties of Logarithms

a. *The Product Rule:* $\log_b(MN) = \log_b M + \log_b N$ — Ex. 1, p. 184

b. *The Quotient Rule:* $\log_b\left(\dfrac{M}{N}\right) = \log_b M - \log_b N$ — Ex. 2, p. 184

c. *The Power Rule:* $\log_b M^p = p \log_b M$ — Ex. 3, p. 186

d. *The Change-of-Base Property:*

The General Property	Introducing Common Logarithms	Introducing Natural Logarithms	
$\log_b M = \dfrac{\log_a M}{\log_a b}$	$\log_b M = \dfrac{\log M}{\log b}$	$\log_b M = \dfrac{\ln M}{\ln b}$	Ex. 7, p. 189; Ex. 8, p. 190

DEFINITIONS AND CONCEPTS	EXAMPLES

3.4 Exponential and Logarithmic Equations

a. An exponential equation is an equation containing a variable in an exponent. The solution procedure involves isolating the exponential expression and taking the natural logarithm on both sides. The box on page 408 provides the details.

Ex.1, p. 193;
Ex.2, p. 194;
Ex.3, p. 194;
Ex.4, p. 195

b. A logarithmic equation is an equation containing a variable in a logarithmic expression. Logarithmic equations in the form $\log_b x = c$ can be solved by rewriting as $b^c = x$.

Ex.5, p. 195

c. When checking logarithmic equations, reject proposed solutions that produce the logarithm of a negative number or the logarithm of 0 in the original equation.

Ex.6, p. 196

d. Equations involving natural logarithms are solved by isolating the natural logarithm with coefficient 1 on one side and exponentiating both sides. Simplify using $e^{\ln x} = x$.

Ex.7, p. 197

3.5 Modeling with Exponential and Logarithmic Functions

a. Exponential growth and decay models are given by $A = A_0 e^{kt}$ in which t represents time, A_0 is the amount present at $t = 0$, and A is the amount present at time t. If $k > 0$, the model describes growth and k is the growth rate. If $k < 0$, the model describes decay and k is the decay rate.

Ex.1, p. 204;
Ex.2, p. 207

b. The logistic growth model, given by $A = \dfrac{c}{1 + ae^{-bt}}$, describes situations in which growth is limited. $y = c$ is a horizontal asymptote for the graph, and growth, A, can never exceed c.

Ex.3, p. 209

c. Scatter plots for exponential and logarithmic models are shown in Figure 3.20 on page 210. When using a graphing utility to model data, the closer that the correlation coefficient, r, is to -1 or 1, the better the model fits the data.

d. Expressing an Exponential Model in Base e: $y = ab^x$ is equivalent to $y = ae^{(\ln b) \cdot x}$.

Ex.4, p. 212

Review Exercises

3.1

In Exercises 1–4, the graph of an exponential function is given. Select the function for each graph from the following options:

$$f(x) = 4^x, g(x) = 4^{-x},$$

$$h(x) = -4^{-x}, r(x) = -4^{-x} + 3.$$

1.

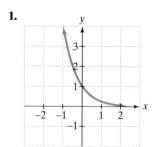

2.

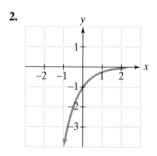

3.

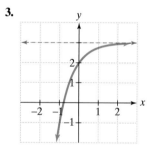

4.

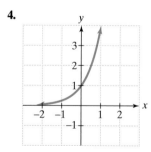

In Exercises 5–8, sketch by hand the graphs of the two functions in the same rectangular coordinate system. Use a table of coordinates to sketch the first function and transformations of this function with a table of coordinates to graph the second function.

5. $f(x) = 2^x$ and $g(x) = 2^{x-1}$

6. $f(x) = 3^x$ and $g(x) = 3^x - 1$

7. $f(x) = 3^x$ and $g(x) = -3^x$

8. $f(x) = \left(\frac{1}{2}\right)^x$ and $g(x) = \left(\frac{1}{2}\right)^{-x}$

Use the compound interest formulas to solve Exercises 9–10.

9. Suppose that you have $5000 to invest. Which investment yields the greater return over 5 years: 5.5% compounded semiannually or 5.25% compounded monthly?

10. Suppose that you have $14,000 to invest. Which investment yields the greater return over 10 years: 7% compounded monthly or 6.85% compounded continuously?

11. A cup of coffee is taken out of a microwave oven and placed in a room. The temperature, T, in degrees Fahrenheit, of the coffee after t minutes is modeled by the function $T = 70 + 130e^{-0.04855t}$. The graph of the function is shown in the figure.

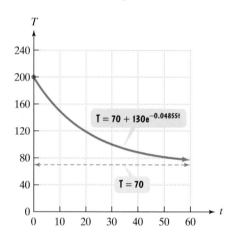

Use the graph to answer each of the following questions.

a. What was the temperature of the coffee when it was first taken out of the microwave?

b. What is a reasonable estimate of the temperature of the coffee after 20 minutes? Use your calculator to verify this estimate.

c. What is the limit of the temperature to which the coffee will cool? What does this tell you about the temperature of the room?

3.2

In Exercises 12–14, write each equation in its equivalent exponential form.

12. $\frac{1}{2} = \log_{49} 7$ **13.** $3 = \log_4 x$ **14.** $\log_3 81 = y$

In Exercises 15–17, write each equation in its equivalent logarithmic form.

15. $6^3 = 216$ **16.** $b^4 = 625$ **17.** $13^y = 874$

In Exercises 18–25, evaluate each expression without using a calculator. If evaluation is not possible, state the reason.

18. $\log_4 64$ **19.** $\log_5 \frac{1}{25}$ **20.** $\log_3(-9)$

21. $\log_{16} 4$ **22.** $\log_{17} 17$ **23.** $\log_3 3^8$

24. $\ln e^5$ **25.** $\log_3(\log_8 8)$

26. Graph $f(x) = 2^x$ and $g(x) = \log_2 x$ in the same rectangular coordinate system.

27. Graph $f(x) = \left(\frac{1}{3}\right)^x$ and $g(x) = \log_{1/3} x$ in the same rectangular coordinate system.

In Exercises 28–31, the graph of a logarithmic function is given. Select the function for each graph from the following options:

$$f(x) = \log x, g(x) = \log(-x),$$
$$h(x) = \log(2 - x), r(x) = 1 + \log(2 - x).$$

28.

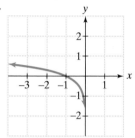

29.

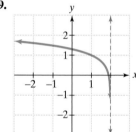

30.

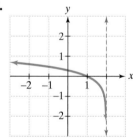

31.

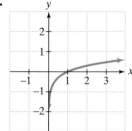

In Exercises 32–34, begin by graphing $f(x) = \log_2 x$. Then use transformations of this graph to graph the given function. What is the graph's x-intercept? What is the vertical asymptote?

32. $g(x) = \log_2(x - 2)$ **33.** $h(x) = -1 + \log_2 x$

34. $r(x) = \log_2(-x)$

In Exercises 35–37, find the domain of each logarithmic function.

35. $f(x) = \log_8(x + 5)$ **36.** $f(x) = \log(3 - x)$

37. $f(x) = \ln(x - 1)^2$

In Exercises 38–40, use inverse properties of logarithms to simplify each expression.

38. $\ln e^{6x}$ **39.** $e^{\ln \sqrt{x}}$ **40.** $10^{\log 4x^2}$

41. On the Richter scale, the magnitude, R, of an earthquake of intensity I is given by $R = \log \dfrac{I}{I_0}$, where I_0 is the intensity of a barely felt zero-level earthquake. If the intensity of an earthquake is $1000I_0$, what is its magnitude on the Richter scale?

42. Students in a psychology class took a final examination. As part of an experiment to see how much of the course content they remembered over time, they took equivalent forms of the exam in monthly intervals thereafter. The average score, $f(t)$, for the group after t months is modeled by the function $f(t) = 76 - 18 \log(t + 1)$, where $0 \le t \le 12$.

   a. What was the average score when the exam was first given?

   b. What was the average score after 2 months? 4 months? 6 months? 8 months? one year?

   c. Use the results from parts (a) and (b) to graph f. Describe what the shape of the graph indicates in terms of the material retained by the students.

43. The formula

$$t = \frac{1}{c} \ln\left(\frac{A}{A - N}\right)$$

describes the time, t, in weeks, that it takes to achieve mastery of a portion of a task. In the formula, A represents maximum learning possible, N is the portion of the learning that is to be achieved, and c is a constant used to measure an individual's learning style. A 50-year-old man decides to start running as a way to maintain good health. He feels that the maximum rate he could ever hope to achieve is 12 miles per hour. How many weeks will it take before the man can run 5 miles per hour if $c = 0.06$ for this person?

3.3

In Exercises 44–47, use properties of logarithms to expand each logarithmic expression as much as possible. Where possible, evaluate logarithmic expressions without using a calculator.

44. $\log_6(36x^3)$ **45.** $\log_4\left(\dfrac{\sqrt{x}}{64}\right)$

46. $\log_2\left(\dfrac{xy^2}{64}\right)$ **47.** $\ln\sqrt[3]{\dfrac{x}{e}}$

In Exercises 48–51, use properties of logarithms to condense each logarithmic expression. Write the expression as a single logarithm whose coefficient is 1.

48. $\log_b 7 + \log_b 3$ **49.** $\log 3 - 3\log x$

50. $3 \ln x + 4 \ln y$ **51.** $\frac{1}{2}\ln x - \ln y$

In Exercises 52–53, use common logarithms or natural logarithms and a calculator to evaluate to four decimal places.

52. $\log_6 72{,}348$ **53.** $\log_4 0.863$

3.4

Solve each exponential equation in Exercises 54–58. Express the answer in terms of natural logarithms. Then use a calculator to obtain a decimal approximation, correct to two decimal places, for the solution.

54. $8^x = 12{,}143$ **55.** $9e^{5x} = 1269$

56. $e^{12-5x} - 7 = 123$ **57.** $5^{4x+2} = 37{,}500$

58. $e^{2x} - e^x - 6 = 0$

Solve each logarithmic equation in Exercises 59–63.

59. $\log_4(3x - 5) = 3$

60. $\log_2(x + 3) + \log_2(x - 3) = 4$

61. $\log_3(x - 1) - \log_3(x + 2) = 2$

62. $\ln x = -1$ **63.** $3 + 4\ln(2x) = 15$

64. The formula $A = 10.1e^{0.005t}$ models the population of Los Angeles, California, A, in millions, t years after 1992. If the growth rate continues into the future, when will the population reach 13 million?

65. The amount of carbon dioxide in the atmosphere, measured in parts per million, has been increasing as a result of the burning of oil and coal. The buildup of gases and particles traps heat and raises the planet's temperature, a phenomenon called the *greenhouse effect*. Carbon dioxide accounts for about half of the warming. The function $f(t) = 364(1.005)^t$ projects carbon dioxide concentration, $f(t)$, in parts per million, t years after 2000. Using the projections given by the function, when will the carbon dioxide concentration be double the preindustrial level of 280 parts per million?

66. The formula $\overline{C}(x) = 15{,}557 + 5259 \ln x$ models the average cost of a new car, $\overline{C}(x)$, x years after 1989. When will the average cost of a new car reach \$30,000?

67. Use the formula for compound interest with n compoundings each year to solve this problem. How long, to the nearest tenth of a year, will it take \$12,500 to grow to \$20,000 at 6.5% annual interest compounded quarterly?

Use the formula for continuous compounding to solve Exercises 68–69.

68. How long, to the nearest tenth of a year, will it take \$50,000 to triple in value at 7.5% annual interest compounded continuously?

69. What interest rate is required for an investment subject to continuous compounding to triple in 5 years?

3.5

70. According to the U.S. Bureau of the Census, in 1990 there were 22.4 million residents of Hispanic origin living in the United States. By 2000, the number had increased to 35.3 million. The exponential growth function $A = 22.4e^{kt}$ describes the U.S. Hispanic population, A, in millions, t years after 1990.

   a. Find k, correct to three decimal places.

   b. Use the resulting model to project the Hispanic resident population in 2010.

   c. In which year will the Hispanic resident population reach 60 million?

71. Use the exponential decay model for carbon-14, $A = A_0 e^{-0.000121t}$, to solve this exercise. Prehistoric cave paintings were discovered in the Lascaux cave in France. The paint contained 15% of the original carbon-14. Estimate the age of the paintings at the time of the discovery.

72. The function

$$f(t) = \frac{500,000}{1 + 2499e^{-0.92t}}$$

models the number of people, $f(t)$, in a city who have become ill with influenza t weeks after its initial outbreak.

   a. How many people became ill with the flu when the epidemic began?

   b. How many people were ill by the end of the sixth week?

   c. What is the limiting size of $f(t)$, the population that becomes ill?

In Exercises 73–74, rewrite the equation in terms of base e. Express the answer in terms of a natural logarithm, and then round to three decimal places.

73. $y = 73(2.6)^x$ **74.** $y = 6.5(0.43)^x$

75. The figure shows world population projections through the year 2150. The data are from the United Nations Family Planning Program and are based on optimistic or pessimistic expectations for successful control of human population growth. Suppose that you are interested in modeling these data using exponential, logarithmic, linear, and quadratic functions. Which function would you use to model each of the projections? Explain your choices. For the choice corresponding to a quadratic model, would your formula involve one with a positive or negative leading coefficient? Explain.

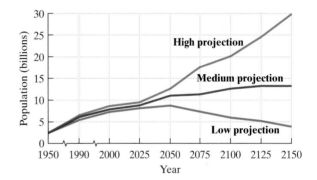

76. The figure shows the number of people in the United States age 65 and over, with projected figures for the year 2010 and beyond.

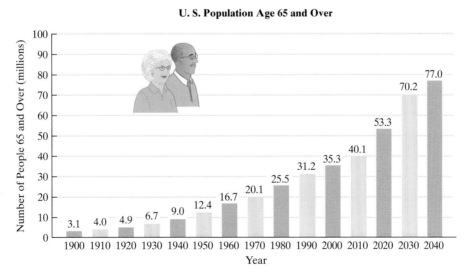

U. S. Population Age 65 and Over

Source: U.S. Bureau of the Census

Let x represent the number of years after 1899 and let y represent the U.S. population, in millions, age 65 and over. Use your graphing utility to find the model that best fits the data in the bar graph. Then use the model to find the projected U.S. population age 65 and over in 2050.

Chapter 3 Test

1. Graph $f(x) = 2^x$ and $g(x) = 2^{x+1}$ in the same rectangular coordinate system.

2. Graph $f(x) = \log_2 x$ and $g(x) = \log_2 (x - 1)$ in the same rectangular coordinate system.

3. Write in exponential form: $\log_5 125 = 3$.

4. Write in logarithmic form: $\sqrt{36} = 6$.

5. Find the domain of $f(x) = \ln (3 - x)$.

In Exercises 6–7, use properties of logarithms to expand each logarithmic expression as much as possible. Where possible, evaluate logarithmic expressions without using a calculator.

6. $\log_4 (64x^5)$

7. $\log_3 \left(\dfrac{\sqrt[3]{x}}{81} \right)$

In Exercises 8–9, write each expression as a single logarithm.

8. $6 \log x + 2 \log y$

9. $\ln 7 - 3 \ln x$

10. Use a calculator to evaluate $\log_{15} 71$ to four decimal places.

In Exercises 11–16, solve each equation.

11. $5^x = 1.4$

12. $400e^{0.005x} = 1600$

13. $e^{2x} - 6e^x + 5 = 0$

14. $\log_6 (4x - 1) = 3$

15. $\log x + \log (x + 15) = 2$

16. $2 \ln (3x) = 8$

17. Suppose you have \$3000 to invest. Which investment yields the greater return over 10 years: 6.5% compounded semiannually or 6% compounded continuously? How much more (to the nearest dollar) is yielded by the better investment?

18. On the decibel scale, the loudness of a sound, D, in decibels, is given by $D = 10 \log \dfrac{I}{I_0}$, where I is the intensity of the sound, in watts per meter^2, and I_0 is the intensity of a sound barely audible to the human ear. If the intensity of a sound is $10^{12} I_0$, what is its loudness in decibels? (Such a sound is potentially damaging to the ear.)

19. The function
$$P(t) = 89.18e^{-0.004t}$$
models the percentage, $P(t)$, of married men in the United States who were employed t years after 1959.

    a. What percentage of married men were employed in 1959?

    b. Is the percentage of married men who are employed increasing or decreasing? Explain.

    c. In what year were 77% of U.S. married men employed?

20. The 1990 population of Europe was 509 million; in 2000, it was 729 million. Write the exponential growth function that describes the population of Europe, in millions, t years after 1990.

21. Use the exponential decay model for carbon-14, $A = A_0 e^{-0.000121t}$, to solve this exercise. Bones of a prehistoric man were discovered and contained 5% of the original amount of carbon-14. How long ago did the man die?

22. The logistic growth function
$$f(t) = \dfrac{140}{1 + 9e^{-0.165t}}$$
describes the population, $f(t)$, of an endangered species of elk t years after they were introduced to a nonthreatening habitat.

    a. How many elk were initially introduced to the habitat?

    b. How many elk are expected in the habitat after 10 years?

    c. What is the limiting size of the elk population that the habitat will sustain?

Sequences and Probability

We often save for the future by investing small amounts at periodic intervals. To understand how our savings accumulate, we need to understand properties of lists of numbers that are related to each other by a rule. Such lists are called *sequences*. Learning about properties of sequences will show you how to make your financial goals a reality. Your knowledge of sequences will enable you to inform your college roommate of the best of the three appealing offers.

Something incredible has happened. Your college roommate, a gifted athlete, has been given a six-year contract with a professional baseball team. He will be playing against the likes of Barry Bonds and Sammy Sosa. Management offers him three options. One is a beginning salary of $1,700,000 with annual increases of $70,000 per year, starting in the second year. A second option is $1,700,000 the first year with an annual increase of 2% per year beginning in the second year. The third offer involves less money the first year—$1,500,000—but there is an annual increase of 9% yearly after that. Which option offers the most money over the six-year contract?

SECTION 4.1 *Sequences and Summation Notation*

Objectives

1. Find particular terms of a sequence from the general term.
2. Use recursion formulas.
3. Use factorial notation.
4. Use summation notation.

Sequences

Many creations in nature involve intricate mathematical designs, including a variety of spirals. For example, the arrangement of the individual florets in the head of a sunflower forms spirals. In some species, there are 21 spirals in the clockwise direction and 34 in the counterclockwise direction. The precise numbers depend on the species of sunflower: 21 and 34, or 34 and 55, or 55 and 89, or even 89 and 144.

This observation becomes even more interesting when we consider a sequence of numbers investigated by Leonardo of Pisa, also known as Fibonacci, an Italian mathematician of the thirteenth century. The **Fibonacci sequence** of numbers is an infinite sequence that begins as follows:

$$1, 1, 2, 3, 5, 8, 13, 21, 34, 55, 89, 144, 233 \ldots .$$

The first two terms are 1. Every term thereafter is the sum of the two preceding terms. For example, the third term, 2, is the sum of the first and second terms: $1 + 1 = 2$. The fourth term, 3, is the sum of the second and third terms: $1 + 2 = 3$, and so on. Did you know that the number of spirals in a daisy or a sunflower, 21 and 34, are two Fibonacci numbers? The number of spirals in a pine cone, 8 and 13, and a pineapple, 8 and 13, are also Fibonacci numbers.

We can think of the Fibonacci sequence as a function. The terms of the sequence

$$1, 1, 2, 3, 5, 8, 13, 21, 34, 55, 89, 144, 233 \ldots$$

are the range values for a function whose domain is the set of positive integers.

Domain:	1,	2,	3,	4,	5,	6,	7, ...
	↓	↓	↓	↓	↓	↓	↓
Range:	1,	1,	2,	3,	5,	8,	13, ...

Thus, $f(1) = 1$, $f(2) = 1$, $f(3) = 2$, $f(4) = 3$, $f(5) = 5$, $f(6) = 8$, $f(7) = 13$, and so on.

The letter a with a subscript is used to represent function values of a sequence, rather than the usual function notation. The subscripts make up the domain of the sequence, and they identify the location of a term. Thus, a_1 represents the first term of the sequence, a_2 represents the second term, a_3 the third term, and so on. This notation is shown for the first six terms of the Fibonacci sequence:

$$1, \quad 1, \quad 2, \quad 3, \quad 5, \quad 8.$$

$a_1 = 1$ $\quad$ $a_2 = 1$ $\quad$ $a_3 = 2$ $\quad$ $a_4 = 3$ $\quad$ $a_5 = 5$ $\quad$ $a_6 = 8$

Fibonacci Numbers on the Piano Keyboard

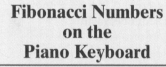

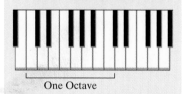

One Octave

Numbers in the Fibonacci sequence can be found in an octave on the piano keyboard. The octave contains 2 black keys in one cluster and 3 black keys in another cluster, for a total of 5 black keys. It also has 8 white keys, for a total of 13 keys. The numbers 2, 3, 5, 8, and 13 are the third through seventh terms of the Fibonacci sequence.

The notation a_n represents the nth term, or **general term,** of a sequence. The entire sequence is represented by $\{a_n\}$.

> **Definition of a Sequence**
> An **infinite sequence** $\{a_n\}$ is a function whose domain is the set of positive integers. The function values, or **terms,** of the sequence are represented by
>
> $$a_1, a_2, a_3, a_4, \dots, a_n, \dots.$$
>
> Sequences whose domains consist only of the first n positive integers are called **finite sequences.**

1 Find particular terms of a sequence from the general term.

EXAMPLE 1 **Writing Terms of a Sequence from the General Term**

Write the first four terms of the sequence whose nth term, or general term, is given:

a. $a_n = 3n + 4$ **b.** $a_n = \dfrac{(-1)^n}{3^n - 1}.$

Solution

a. We need to find the first four terms of the sequence whose general term is $a_n = 3n + 4$. To do so, we replace n in the formula with 1, 2, 3, and 4.

a_1, 1st term: $3 \cdot 1 + 4 = 3 + 4 = 7$ a_2, 2nd term: $3 \cdot 2 + 4 = 6 + 4 = 10$

a_3, 3rd term: $3 \cdot 3 + 4 = 9 + 4 = 13$ a_4, 4th term: $3 \cdot 4 + 4 = 12 + 4 = 16$

The first four terms are 7, 10, 13, and 16. The sequence defined by $a_n = 3n + 4$ can be written as

$$7, 10, 13, 16, \dots, 3n + 4, \dots.$$

b. We need to find the first four terms of the sequence whose general term is $a_n = \dfrac{(-1)^n}{3^n - 1}$. To do so, we replace each occurrence of n in the formula with 1, 2, 3, and 4.

a_1, 1st term: $\dfrac{(-1)^1}{3^1 - 1} = \dfrac{-1}{3 - 1} = -\dfrac{1}{2}$ a_2, 2nd term: $\dfrac{(-1)^2}{3^2 - 1} = \dfrac{1}{9 - 1} = \dfrac{1}{8}$

a_3, 3rd term: $\dfrac{(-1)^3}{3^3 - 1} = \dfrac{-1}{27 - 1} = -\dfrac{1}{26}$ a_4, 4th term: $\dfrac{(-1)^4}{3^4 - 1} = \dfrac{1}{81 - 1} = \dfrac{1}{80}$

The first four terms are $-\frac{1}{2}, \frac{1}{8}, -\frac{1}{26}$, and $\frac{1}{80}$. The sequence defined by $\dfrac{(-1)^n}{3^n - 1}$ can be written as

$$-\frac{1}{2}, \frac{1}{8}, -\frac{1}{26}, \frac{1}{80}, \dots, \frac{(-1)^n}{3^n - 1}, \dots.$$

Study Tip

The factor $(-1)^n$ in the general term of a sequence causes the signs of the terms to alternate between positive and negative, depending on whether n is even or odd.

Technology

Graphing utilities can write the terms of a sequence and graph them. For example, to find the first six terms of

$$\{a_n\} = \left\{\frac{1}{n}\right\}, \text{ enter}$$

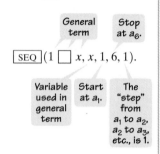

The first few terms of the sequence are shown in the viewing rectangle. By pressing the right arrow key to scroll right, you can see the remaining terms.

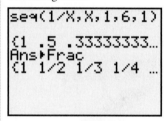

Check Point 1 Write the first four terms of the sequence whose nth term, or general term, is given:

a. $a_n = 2n + 5$ **b.** $a_n = \dfrac{(-1)^n}{2^n + 1}$.

Although sequences are usually named with the letter a, any lowercase letter can be used. For example, the first four terms of the sequence $\{b_n\} = \left\{\left(\frac{1}{2}\right)^n\right\}$ are $b_1 = \frac{1}{2}, b_2 = \frac{1}{4}, b_3 = \frac{1}{8}$, and $b_4 = \frac{1}{16}$.

Because a sequence is a function whose domain is the set of positive integers, the **graph of a sequence** is a set of discrete points. For example, consider the sequence whose general term is $a_n = \frac{1}{n}$. How does the graph of this sequence differ from the graph of the function $f(x) = \frac{1}{x}$? The graph of $f(x) = \frac{1}{x}$ is shown in Figure 4.1(a) for positive values of x. To obtain the graph of the sequence $\{a_n\} = \left\{\frac{1}{n}\right\}$, remove all the points from the graph of f except those whose x-coordinates are positive integers. Thus, we remove all points except $(1, 1), \left(2, \frac{1}{2}\right), \left(3, \frac{1}{3}\right), \left(4, \frac{1}{4}\right)$, and so on. The remaining points are the graph of the sequence $\{a_n\} = \left\{\frac{1}{n}\right\}$, shown in Figure 4.1(b). Notice that the horizontal axis is labeled n and the vertical axis a_n.

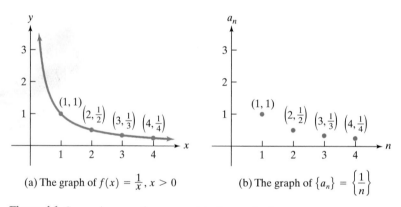

(a) The graph of $f(x) = \frac{1}{x}, x > 0$ (b) The graph of $\{a_n\} = \left\{\frac{1}{n}\right\}$

Figure 4.1 Comparing a continuous graph to the graph of a sequence

2 Use recursion formulas.

Recursion Formulas

In Example 1, the formulas used for the nth term of a sequence expressed the term as a function of n, the number of the term. Sequences can also be defined using **recursion formulas.** A recursion formula defines the nth term of a sequence as a function of the previous term. Our next example illustrates that if the first term of a sequence is known, then the recursion formula can be used to determine the remaining terms.

EXAMPLE 2   Using a Recursion Formula

Find the first four terms of the sequence in which $a_1 = 5$ and $a_n = 3a_{n-1} + 2$ for $n \geq 2$.

Solution

$$a_1 = 5 \qquad \text{This is the given first term.}$$
$$a_2 = 3a_1 + 2 \qquad \text{Use } a_n = 3a_{n-1} + 2, \text{ with } n = 2.$$
$$\qquad\qquad\qquad \text{Thus, } a_2 = 3a_{2-1} + 2 = 3a_1 + 2.$$
$$= 3(5) + 2 = 17 \qquad \text{Substitute 5 for } a_1.$$

$$a_3 = 3a_2 + 2$$

Again use $a_n = 3a_{n-1} + 2$, with $n = 3$.

$$= 3(17) + 2 = 53$$

Substitute 17 for a_2.

$$a_4 = 3a_3 + 2$$

Notice that a_4 is defined in terms of a_3.
We used $a_n = 3a_{n-1} + 2$, with $n = 4$.

$$= 3(53) + 2 = 161$$

Use the value of a_3, the third term, obtained from above.

The first four terms are 5, 17, 53, and 161.

Check Point 2 Find the first four terms of the sequence in which $a_1 = 3$ and $a_n = 2a_{n-1} + 5$ for $n \geq 2$.

3 Use factorial notation.

Factorial Notation

Products of consecutive positive integers occur quite often in sequences. These products can be expressed in a special notation, called **factorial notation.**

Factorial Notation

If n is a positive integer, the notation $n!$ (read "n factorial") is the product of all positive integers from n down through 1.

$$n! = n(n-1)(n-2)\ldots(3)(2)(1)$$

0! (zero factorial), by definition, is 1.

$$0! = 1$$

Factorials from 0 through 20

0!	1
1!	1
2!	2
3!	6
4!	24
5!	120
6!	720
7!	5040
8!	40,320
9!	362,880
10!	3,628,800
11!	39,916,800
12!	479,001,600
13!	6,227,020,800
14!	87,178,291,200
15!	1,307,674,368,000
16!	20,922,789,888,000
17!	355,687,428,096,000
18!	6,402,373,705,728,000
19!	121,645,100,408,832,000
20!	2,432,902,008,176,640,000

As n increases, $n!$ grows very rapidly. Factorial growth is more explosive than exponential growth discussed in Chapter 3.

The values of $n!$ for the first six positive integers are

$$1! = 1$$
$$2! = 2 \cdot 1 = 2$$
$$3! = 3 \cdot 2 \cdot 1 = 6$$
$$4! = 4 \cdot 3 \cdot 2 \cdot 1 = 24$$
$$5! = 5 \cdot 4 \cdot 3 \cdot 2 \cdot 1 = 120$$
$$6! = 6 \cdot 5 \cdot 4 \cdot 3 \cdot 2 \cdot 1 = 720.$$

Factorials affect only the number or variable that they follow unless grouping symbols appear. For example,

$$2 \cdot 3! = 2(3 \cdot 2 \cdot 1) = 2 \cdot 6 = 12$$

whereas

$$(2 \cdot 3)! = 6! = 6 \cdot 5 \cdot 4 \cdot 3 \cdot 2 \cdot 1 = 720.$$

In this sense, factorials are similar to exponents.

EXAMPLE 3 Finding Terms of a Sequence Involving Factorials

Write the first four terms of the sequence whose nth term is

$$a_n = \frac{2^n}{(n-1)!}.$$

Technology

Most calculators have factorial keys. To find 5!, many calculators use one of the following:

Scientific Calculators

$5 \boxed{x!}$

Graphing Calculators

$5 \boxed{!} \boxed{\text{ENTER}}$.

Because $n!$ becomes quite large as n increases, your calculator will display these larger values in scientific notation.

Solution We need to find the first four terms of the sequence. To do so, we replace each n in $\dfrac{2^n}{(n-1)!}$ with 1, 2, 3, and 4.

a_1, 1st term $\quad \dfrac{2^1}{(1-1)!} = \dfrac{2}{0!} = \dfrac{2}{1} = 2$

a_2, 2nd term $\quad \dfrac{2^2}{(2-1)!} = \dfrac{4}{1!} = \dfrac{4}{1} = 4$

a_3, 3rd term $\quad \dfrac{2^3}{(3-1)!} = \dfrac{8}{2!} = \dfrac{8}{2 \cdot 1} = 4$

a_4, 4th term $\quad \dfrac{2^4}{(4-1)!} = \dfrac{16}{3!} = \dfrac{16}{3 \cdot 2 \cdot 1} = \dfrac{16}{6} = \dfrac{8}{3}$

The first four terms are $2, 4, 4$, and $\frac{8}{3}$.

Check Point 3 Write the first four terms of the sequence whose nth term is
$$a_n = \dfrac{20}{(n+1)!}.$$

When evaluating fractions with factorials in the numerator and the denominator, try to reduce the fraction before performing the multiplications. For example, consider $\dfrac{26!}{21!}$. Rather than write out 26! as the product of all integers from 26 down to 1, we can express 26! as

$$26! = 26 \cdot 25 \cdot 24 \cdot 23 \cdot 22 \cdot 21!.$$

In this way, we can divide both the numerator and the denominator by the common factor, 21!.

$$\dfrac{26!}{21!} = \dfrac{26 \cdot 25 \cdot 24 \cdot 23 \cdot 22 \cdot \cancel{21!}}{\cancel{21!}} = 26 \cdot 25 \cdot 24 \cdot 23 \cdot 22 = 7{,}893{,}600$$

EXAMPLE 4 Evaluating Fractions with Factorials

Evaluate each factorial expression:

a. $\dfrac{10!}{2!8!}$ **b.** $\dfrac{(n+1)!}{n!}$.

Solution

a. $\dfrac{10!}{2!8!} = \dfrac{10 \cdot 9 \cdot \cancel{8!}}{2 \cdot 1 \cdot \cancel{8!}} = \dfrac{90}{2} = 45$

b. $\dfrac{(n+1)!}{n!} = \dfrac{(n+1) \cdot \cancel{n!}}{\cancel{n!}} = n+1$

Check Point 4 Evaluate each factorial expression:

a. $\dfrac{14!}{2!12!}$ **b.** $\dfrac{n!}{(n-1)!}$.

4 Use summation notation.

Summation Notation

It is sometimes useful to find the sum of the first n terms of a sequence. For example, consider the number of AIDS cases diagnosed in the United States for each year from 1991 through 2000, shown in Table 4.1.

Table 4.1   AIDS Cases Diagnosed in the United States, 1991–2000

Year	1991	1992	1993	1994	1995	1996	1997	1998	1999	2000
Cases Diagnosed	60,472	79,477	79,752	72,684	69,172	59,832	47,439	40,784	36,725	23,988

Source: U.S. Department of Health and Human Services

We can let a_n represent the number of AIDS cases diagnosed in year n, where $n = 1$ corresponds to 1991, $n = 2$ to 1992, $n = 3$ to 1993, and so on. The terms of the finite sequence in Table 4.1 are given as follows.

60,472 79,477 79,752 72,684 69,172 59,832 47,439 40,784 36,725 23,988

a_1 a_2 a_3 a_4 a_5 a_6 a_7 a_8 a_9 a_{10}

Why might we want to add the terms of this sequence? We do this to find the total number of AIDS cases diagnosed from 1991 through 2000. Thus,

$$a_1 + a_2 + a_3 + a_4 + a_5 + a_6 + a_7 + a_8 + a_9 + a_{10}$$

$$= 60,472 + 79,477, + 79,752, + 72,684, + 69,172, + 59,832, + 47,439 + 40,784 + 36,725 + 23,988$$

$$= 570,325.$$

We see that there were 570,325 AIDS cases diagnosed in the United States from 1991 through 2000.

There is a compact notation for expressing the sum of the first n terms of a sequence. For example, rather than write

$$a_1 + a_2 + a_3 + a_4 + a_5 + a_6 + a_7 + a_8 + a_9 + a_{10},$$

we can use **summation notation** to express the sum as

$$a_1 + a_2 + a_3 + a_4 + a_5 + a_6 + a_7 + a_8 + a_9 + a_{10} = \sum_{i=1}^{10} a_i.$$

We read the expression on the right as "the sum as i goes from 1 to 10 of a_i." The letter i is called the **index of summation** and is not related to the use of i to represent $\sqrt{-1}$.

You can think of the symbol Σ (the uppercase Greek letter sigma) as an instruction to add up terms of a sequence.

> ## Summation Notation
> The sum of the first n terms of a sequence is represented by the **summation notation**
> $$\sum_{i=1}^{n} a_i = a_1 + a_2 + a_3 + a_4 + \cdots + a_n$$
> where i is the **index of summation,** n is the **upper limit of summation,** and 1 is the **lower limit of summation.**

Any letter can be used for the index of summation. The letters i, j, and k are used commonly. Furthermore, the lower limit of summation can be an integer other than 1.

When we write out a sum that is given in summation notation, we are **expanding the summation notation.** Example 5 shows how to do this.

EXAMPLE 5   Using Summation Notation

Expand and evaluate the sum:

a. $\displaystyle\sum_{i=1}^{6} (i^2 + 1)$ b. $\displaystyle\sum_{k=4}^{7} [(-2)^k - 5]$ c. $\displaystyle\sum_{i=1}^{5} 3.$

Solution

a. We must replace i in the expression $i^2 + 1$ with all consecutive integers from 1 to 6 inclusive. Then we add.

$$\sum_{i=1}^{6} (i^2 + 1) = (1^2 + 1) + (2^2 + 1) + (3^2 + 1) + (4^2 + 1)$$
$$+ (5^2 + 1) + (6^2 + 1)$$
$$= 2 + 5 + 10 + 17 + 26 + 37$$
$$= 97$$

b. This time the index of summation is k. First we evaluate $(-2)^k - 5$ for all consecutive integers from 4 through 7 inclusive. Then we add.

$$\sum_{k=4}^{7} [(-2)^k - 5] = [(-2)^4 - 5] + [(-2)^5 - 5]$$
$$+ [(-2)^6 - 5] + [(-2)^7 - 5]$$
$$= (16 - 5) + (-32 - 5) + (64 - 5) + (-128 - 5)$$
$$= 11 + (-37) + 59 + (-133)$$
$$= -100$$

c. To find $\displaystyle\sum_{i=1}^{5} 3$, we observe that every term of the sum is 3. The notation $i = 1$ through 5 indicates that we must add the first five terms from a sequence in which every term is 3.

$$\sum_{i=1}^{5} 3 = 3 + 3 + 3 + 3 + 3 = 15$$

Technology

Graphing utilities can calculate the sum of a sequence. For example, to find the sum of the sequence in Example 5a, enter

$\boxed{\text{SUM}}$ $\boxed{\text{SEQ}}$ $(x^2 + 1, x, 1, 6, 1)$.

Then press $\boxed{\text{ENTER}}$; 97 should be displayed. Use this capability to verify Example 5b.

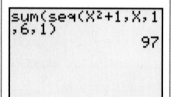

```
sum(seq(X²+1,X,1
,6,1)
            97
```

Check Point 5   Expand and evaluate the sum:

a. $\displaystyle\sum_{i=1}^{6} 2i^2$ b. $\displaystyle\sum_{k=3}^{5} (2^k - 3)$ c. $\displaystyle\sum_{i=1}^{5} 4.$

For a given sum, we can vary the upper and lower limits of summation, as well as the letter used for the index of summation. By doing so, we can produce different-looking summation notations for the same sum. For example, the sum of the squares of the first four integers, $1^2 + 2^2 + 3^2 + 4^2$, can be expressed in a number of equivalent ways:

$$\sum_{i=1}^{4} i^2 = 1^2 + 2^2 + 3^2 + 4^2 = 30$$

$$\sum_{i=0}^{3} (i + 1)^2 = (0 + 1)^2 + (1 + 1)^2 + (2 + 1)^2 + (3 + 1)^2$$

$$= 1^2 + 2^2 + 3^2 + 4^2 = 30$$

$$\sum_{k=2}^{5} (k - 1)^2 = (2 - 1)^2 + (3 - 1)^2 + (4 - 1)^2 + (5 - 1)^2$$

$$= 1^2 + 2^2 + 3^2 + 4^2 = 30.$$

EXAMPLE 6 Writing Sums in Summation Notation

Express each sum using summation notation:

a. $1^3 + 2^3 + 3^3 + \cdots + 7^3$ **b.** $1 + \dfrac{1}{3} + \dfrac{1}{9} + \dfrac{1}{27} + \cdots + \dfrac{1}{3^{n-1}}.$

Solution In each case, we will use 1 as the lower limit of summation and i for the index of summation.

a. The sum $1^3 + 2^3 + 3^3 + \cdots + 7^3$ has seven terms, each of the form i^3, starting at $i = 1$ and ending at $i = 7$. Thus,

$$1^3 + 2^3 + 3^3 + \cdots + 7^3 = \sum_{i=1}^{7} i^3.$$

b. The sum

$$1 + \frac{1}{3} + \frac{1}{9} + \frac{1}{27} + \cdots + \frac{1}{3^{n-1}}$$

has n terms, each of the form $\dfrac{1}{3^{i-1}}$, starting at $i = 1$ and ending at $i = n$. Thus,

$$1 + \frac{1}{3} + \frac{1}{9} + \frac{1}{27} + \cdots + \frac{1}{3^{n-1}} = \sum_{i=1}^{n} \frac{1}{3^{i-1}}.$$

Check Point 6 Express each sum using summation notation:

a. $1^2 + 2^2 + 3^2 + \cdots + 9^2$ **b.** $1 + \dfrac{1}{2} + \dfrac{1}{4} + \dfrac{1}{8} + \cdots + \dfrac{1}{2^{n-1}}.$

Table 4.2 contains some important properties of sums expressed in summation notation.

Table 4.2 Properties of Sums

Property	Example
1. $\sum\limits_{i=1}^{n} ca_i = c \sum\limits_{i=1}^{n} a_i$, c any real number	$\sum\limits_{i=1}^{4} 3i^2 = 3 \cdot 1^2 + 3 \cdot 2^2 + 3 \cdot 3^2 + 3 \cdot 4^2$ $3\sum\limits_{i=1}^{4} i^2 = 3(1^2 + 2^2 + 3^2 + 4^2) = 3 \cdot 1^2 + 3 \cdot 2^2 + 3 \cdot 3^2 + 3 \cdot 4^2$ Conclusion: $\sum\limits_{i=1}^{4} 3i^2 = 3\sum\limits_{i=1}^{4} i^2$
2. $\sum\limits_{i=1}^{n} (a_i + b_i) = \sum\limits_{i=1}^{n} a_i + \sum\limits_{i=1}^{n} b_i$	$\sum\limits_{i=1}^{4} (i + i^2) = (1 + 1^2) + (2 + 2^2) + (3 + 3^2) + (4 + 4^2)$ $\sum\limits_{i=1}^{4} i + \sum\limits_{i=1}^{4} i^2 = (1 + 2 + 3 + 4) + (1^2 + 2^2 + 3^2 + 4^2)$ $= (1 + 1^2) + (2 + 2^2) + (3 + 3^2) + (4 + 4^2)$ Conclusion: $\sum\limits_{i=1}^{4} (i + i^2) = \sum\limits_{i=1}^{4} i + \sum\limits_{i=1}^{4} i^2$
3. $\sum\limits_{i=1}^{n} (a_i - b_i) = \sum\limits_{i=1}^{n} a_i - \sum\limits_{i=1}^{n} b_i$	$\sum\limits_{i=3}^{5} (i^2 - i^3) = (3^2 - 3^3) + (4^2 - 4^3) + (5^2 - 5^3)$ $\sum\limits_{i=3}^{5} i^2 - \sum\limits_{i=3}^{5} i^3 = (3^2 + 4^2 + 5^2) - (3^3 + 4^3 + 5^3)$ $= (3^2 - 3^3) + (4^2 - 4^3) + (5^2 - 5^3)$ Conclusion: $\sum\limits_{i=3}^{5} (i^2 - i^3) = \sum\limits_{i=3}^{5} i^2 - \sum\limits_{i=3}^{5} i^3$

EXERCISE SET 4.1

Practice Exercises

In Exercises 1–12, write the first four terms of each sequence whose general term is given.

1. $a_n = 3n + 2$ **2.** $a_n = 4n - 1$

3. $a_n = 3^n$ **4.** $a_n = \left(\dfrac{1}{3}\right)^n$

5. $a_n = (-3)^n$ **6.** $a_n = \left(-\dfrac{1}{3}\right)^n$

7. $a_n = (-1)^n(n + 3)$ **8.** $a_n = (-1)^{n+1}(n + 4)$

9. $a_n = \dfrac{2n}{n + 4}$ **10.** $a_n = \dfrac{3n}{n + 5}$

11. $a_n = \dfrac{(-1)^{n+1}}{2^n - 1}$ **12.** $a_n = \dfrac{(-1)^{n+1}}{2^n + 1}$

The sequences in Exercises 13–18 are defined using recursion formulas. Write the first four terms of each sequence.

13. $a_1 = 7$ and $a_n = a_{n-1} + 5$ for $n \geq 2$

14. $a_1 = 12$ and $a_n = a_{n-1} + 4$ for $n \geq 2$

15. $a_1 = 3$ and $a_n = 4a_{n-1}$ for $n \geq 2$

16. $a_1 = 2$ and $a_n = 5a_{n-1}$ for $n \geq 2$

17. $a_1 = 4$ and $a_n = 2a_{n-1} + 3$ for $n \geq 2$

18. $a_1 = 5$ and $a_n = 3a_{n-1} - 1$ for $n \geq 2$

In Exercises 19–22, the general term of a sequence is given and involves a factorial. Write the first four terms of each sequence.

19. $a_n = \dfrac{n^2}{n!}$ **20.** $a_n = \dfrac{(n + 1)!}{n^2}$

21. $a_n = 2(n + 1)!$ **22.** $a_n = -2(n - 1)!$

In Exercises 23–28, evaluate each factorial expression.

23. $\dfrac{17!}{15!}$

24. $\dfrac{18!}{16!}$

25. $\dfrac{16!}{2!14!}$

26. $\dfrac{20!}{2!18!}$

27. $\dfrac{(n+2)!}{n!}$

28. $\dfrac{(2n+1)!}{(2n)!}$

In Exercises 29–42, find each indicated sum.

29. $\displaystyle\sum_{i=1}^{6} 5i$

30. $\displaystyle\sum_{i=1}^{6} 7i$

31. $\displaystyle\sum_{i=1}^{4} 2i^2$

32. $\displaystyle\sum_{i=1}^{5} i^3$

33. $\displaystyle\sum_{k=1}^{5} k(k+4)$

34. $\displaystyle\sum_{k=1}^{4} (k-3)(k+2)$

35. $\displaystyle\sum_{i=1}^{4} \left(-\dfrac{1}{2}\right)^i$

36. $\displaystyle\sum_{i=2}^{4} \left(-\dfrac{1}{3}\right)^i$

37. $\displaystyle\sum_{i=5}^{9} 11$

38. $\displaystyle\sum_{i=3}^{7} 12$

39. $\displaystyle\sum_{i=0}^{4} \dfrac{(-1)^i}{i!}$

40. $\displaystyle\sum_{i=0}^{4} \dfrac{(-1)^{i+1}}{(i+1)!}$

41. $\displaystyle\sum_{i=1}^{5} \dfrac{i!}{(i-1)!}$

42. $\displaystyle\sum_{i=1}^{5} \dfrac{(i+2)!}{i!}$

In Exercises 43–54, express each sum using summation notation. Use 1 as the lower limit of summation and i for the index of summation.

43. $1^2 + 2^2 + 3^2 + \cdots + 15^2$

44. $1^4 + 2^4 + 3^4 + \cdots + 12^4$

45. $2 + 2^2 + 2^3 + \cdots + 2^{11}$

46. $5 + 5^2 + 5^3 + \cdots + 5^{12}$

47. $1 + 2 + 3 + \cdots + 30$

48. $1 + 2 + 3 + \cdots + 40$

49. $\dfrac{1}{2} + \dfrac{2}{3} + \dfrac{3}{4} + \cdots + \dfrac{14}{14+1}$

50. $\dfrac{1}{3} + \dfrac{2}{4} + \dfrac{3}{5} + \cdots + \dfrac{16}{16+2}$

51. $4 + \dfrac{4^2}{2} + \dfrac{4^3}{3} + \cdots + \dfrac{4^n}{n}$

52. $\dfrac{1}{9} + \dfrac{2}{9^2} + \dfrac{3}{9^3} + \cdots + \dfrac{n}{9^n}$

53. $1 + 3 + 5 + \cdots + (2n-1)$

54. $a + ar + ar^2 + \cdots + ar^{n-1}$

In Exercises 55–60, express each sum using summation notation. Use a lower limit of summation of your choice and k for the index of summation.

55. $5 + 7 + 9 + 11 + \cdots + 31$

56. $6 + 8 + 10 + 12 + \cdots + 32$

57. $a + ar + ar^2 + \cdots + ar^{12}$

58. $a + ar + ar^2 + \cdots + ar^{14}$

59. $a + (a+d) + (a+2d) + \cdots + (a+nd)$

60. $(a+d) + (a+d^2) + \cdots + (a+d^n)$

Application Exercises

61. The bar graph shows the number of compact discs (CDs) sold in the United States. Let a_n represent the number of CDs sold, in millions, in year n, where $n = 1$ corresponds to 1991, $n = 2$ to 1992, and so on.

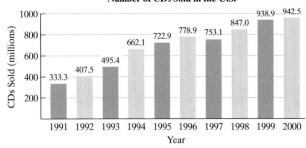

Number of CDs Sold in the U.S.

Source: Recording Industry Association of America

a. Find $\displaystyle\sum_{i=1}^{10} a_i$. What does this represent?

b. Find $\dfrac{1}{10} \displaystyle\sum_{i=1}^{10} a_i$. What does this represent?

62. The bar graph shows the number of vinyl long-playing records (LPs) sold in the United States. Let a_n represent the number of LPs sold, in millions, in year n, where $n =1$ corresponds to 1991, $n = 2$ to 1992, and so on.

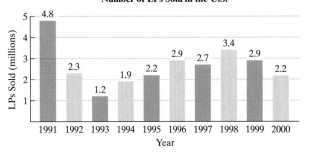

Number of LPs Sold in the U.S.

Source: Recording Industry Association of America

a. Find $\displaystyle\sum_{i=1}^{10} a_i$. What does this represent?

b. Find $\dfrac{1}{10} \displaystyle\sum_{i=1}^{10} a_i$. What does this represent?

The graph shows the millions of welfare recipients in the United States who received cash assistance from 1993 through 2000. In Exercises 63–64, consider a sequence whose general term, a_n, represents the millions of Americans receiving cash assistance n years after 1992.

Welfare Recipients in the U.S.

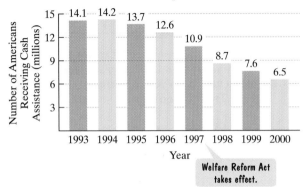

Number of Americans Receiving Cash Assistance (millions)

14.1 14.2 13.7 12.6 10.9 8.7 7.6 6.5

1993 1994 1995 1996 1997 1998 1999 2000

Year

Welfare Reform Act takes effect.

Source: Thomas R. Dye, *Politics in America,* Prentice Hall

63. a. Use the numbers given in the graph to find and interpret
$$\sum_{i=1}^{8} a_i.$$

  b. The finite sequence whose general term is $a_n = -1.23n + 16.55$, where $n = 1, 2, 3, \dots, 8$, models the millions of Americans receiving cash assistance, a_n, n years after 1992. Use the model to find $\sum_{i=1}^{8} a_i$. Does this seem reasonable in terms of the actual sum in part (a), or has model breakdown occurred?

64. a. Use the numbers given in the graph to find and interpret $\sum_{i=1}^{8} a_i.$

  b. The finite sequence whose general term is $a_n = -0.11n^2 - 0.22n + 14.88$, where $n = 1, 2, 3, \dots, 8$, models the millions of Americans receiving cash assistance, a_n, n years after 1992. Use the model to find $\sum_{i=1}^{8} a_i$. Does this seem reasonable in terms of the actual sum in part (a), or has model breakdown occurred?

65. A deposit of $6000 is made in an account that earns 6% interest compounded quarterly. The balance in the account after n quarters is given by the sequence
$$a_n = 6000\left(1 + \frac{0.06}{4}\right)^n, \qquad n = 1, 2, 3, \dots .$$

Find the balance in the account after five years. Round to the nearest cent.

66. A deposit of $10,000 is made in an account that earns 8% interest compounded quarterly. The balance in the account after n quarters is given by the sequence
$$a_n = 10,000\left(1 + \frac{0.08}{4}\right)^n, \qquad n = 1, 2, 3, \dots .$$

Find the balance in the account after six years. Round to the nearest cent.

 Writing in Mathematics

67. What is a sequence? Give an example with your description.

68. Explain how to write terms of a sequence if the formula for the general term is given.

69. What does the graph of a sequence look like? How is it obtained?

70. What is a recursion formula?

71. Explain how to find n! if n is a positive integer.

72. Explain the best way to evaluate $\frac{900!}{899!}$ without calculator.

73. What is the meaning of the symbol $\sum$? Give an example with your description.

74. You buy a new car for $24,000. At the end of n years, the value of your car is given by the sequence
$$a_n = 24{,}000\left(\frac{3}{4}\right)^n, \qquad n = 1, 2, 3, \dots .$$

Find a_5 and write a sentence explaining what this value represents. Describe the nth term of the sequence in terms of the value of your car at the end of each year.

75. It is estimated that 4 to 6 million people in the United States have overwhelming physical, psychological, and social problems that make it impossible for them to work. (*Source*: Thomas R. Dye, *Politics in America,* Prentice Hall) Describe what this means in terms of projecting the model in Exercise 63(b) into the first decade of the new millennium. In writing your answer, use the model and be as specific as possible.

 Technology Exercises

In Exercises 76–80, use a calculator's factorial key to evaluate each expression.

76. $\frac{200!}{198!}$

77. $\left(\frac{300}{20}\right)!$

78. $\frac{20!}{300}$

79. $\frac{20!}{(20-3)!}$

80. $\frac{54!}{(54-3)!\,3!}$

81. Use the $\boxed{\text{SEQ}}$ (sequence) capability of a graphing utility to verify the terms of the sequences you obtained for any five sequences from Exercises 1–12 or 19–22.

82. Use the $\boxed{\text{SUM}}$ $\boxed{\text{SEQ}}$ (sum of the sequence) capability of a graphing utility to verify any five of the sums you obtained in Exercises 29–42.

83. As n increases, the terms of the sequence
$$a_n = \left(1 + \frac{1}{n}\right)^n$$

get closer and closer to the number e (where $e \approx 2.7183$). Use a calculator to find $a_{10}, a_{100}, a_{1000}, a_{10,000}$, and $a_{100,000}$, comparing these terms to your calculator's decimal approximation for e.

Many graphing utilities have a sequence-graphing mode that plots the terms of a sequence as points on a rectangular coordinate system. Consult your manual; if your graphing utility has this capability, use it to graph each of the sequences in Exercises 84–87. What appears to be happening to the terms of each sequence as n gets larger?

84. $a_n = \dfrac{n}{n+1}$ $n:[0, 10, 1]$ by $a_n:[0, 1, 0.1]$

85. $a_n = \dfrac{100}{n}$ $n:[0, 1000, 100]$ by $a_n:[0, 1, 0.1]$

86. $a_n = \dfrac{2n^2 + 5n - 7}{n^3}$ $n:[0, 10, 1]$ by $a_n:[0, 2, 0.2]$

87. $a_n = \dfrac{3n^4 + n - 1}{5n^4 + 2n^2 + 1}$ $n:[0, 10, 1]$ by $a_n:[0, 1, 0.1]$

Critical Thinking Exercises

88. Which one of the following is true?

a. $\dfrac{n!}{(n-1)!} = \dfrac{1}{n-1}$

b. The Fibonacci sequence 1, 1, 2, 3, 5, 8, 13, 21, 34, 55, 89, 144, … can be defined recursively using $a_0 = 1, a_1 = 1$; $a_n = a_{n-2} + a_{n-1}$, where $n \geq 2$.

c. $\displaystyle\sum_{i=1}^{2} (-1)^i 2^i = 0$

d. $\displaystyle\sum_{i=1}^{2} a_i b_i = \sum_{i=1}^{2} a_i \sum_{i=1}^{2} b_i$

89. Write the first five terms of the sequence whose first term is 9 and whose general term is

$$a_n = \begin{cases} \dfrac{a_{n-1}}{2} & \text{if } a_{n-1} \text{ is even} \\ 3a_{n-1} + 5 & \text{if } a_{n-1} \text{ is odd.} \end{cases}$$

Group Exercise

90. Enough curiosities involving the Fibonacci sequence exist to warrant a flourishing Fibonacci Association, which publishes a quarterly journal. Do some research on the Fibonacci sequence by consulting the Internet or the research department of your library, and find one property that interests you. After doing this research, get together with your group to share these intriguing properties.

SECTION 4.2   Arithmetic Sequences

Objectives

1. Find the common difference for an arithmetic sequence.
2. Write terms of an arithmetic sequence.
3. Use the formula for the general term of an arithmetic sequence.
4. Use the formula for the sum of the first n terms of an arithmetic sequence.

Your grandmother and her financial counselor are looking at options in case nursing home care is needed in the future. The good news is that your grandmother's total assets are $350,000. The bad news is that yearly nursing home costs average $49,730, increasing by $1800 each year. In this section, we will see how sequences can be used to describe your grandmother's situation and help her to identify realistic options.

Arithmetic Sequences

A mathematical model for the average annual salaries of major league baseball players generates the following data:

Year	1996	1997	1998	1999	2000	2001	2002
Salary	1,076,865	1,304,152	1,531,439	1,758,726	1,986,013	2,213,300	2,440,587

From 1996 to 1997, salaries increased by \$1,304,152 − \$1,076,865 = \$227,287. From 1997 to 1998, salaries increased by \$1,531,439 − \$1,304,152 = \$227,287. If we make these computations for each year, we find that the yearly salary increase is \$227,287. The sequence of annual salaries shows that each term after the first, 1,076,865, differs from the preceding term by a constant amount, namely 227,287. The sequence of annual salaries

$$1,076,865, \ 1,304,152, \ 1,531,439, \ 1,758,726, \ 1,986,013,\ldots$$

is an example of an *arithmetic sequence*.

Definition of an Arithmetic Sequence

An **arithmetic sequence** is a sequence in which each term after the first differs from the preceding term by a constant amount. The difference between consecutive terms is called the **common difference** of the sequence.

1 Find the common difference of an arithmetic sequence.

The common difference, d, is found by subtracting any term from the term that directly follows it. In the following examples, the common difference is found by subtracting the first term from the second term: $a_2 - a_1$.

Arithmetic Sequence — **Common Difference**

$1,076,865, \ 1,304,152, \ 1,531,439, \ 1,758,726, \ldots$ — $d = 1,304,152 - 1,076,865 = 227,287$

$2, 6, 10, 14, 18, \ldots$ — $d = 6 - 2 = 4$

$-2, -7, -12, -17, \ldots$ — $d = -7 - (-2) = -5$

If the first term of an arithmetic sequence is a_1, each term after the first is obtained by adding d, the common difference, to the previous term. This can be expressed recursively as follows:

$$a_n = a_{n-1} + d.$$

Add d to the term in any position to get the next term.

To use this recursion formula, we must be given the first term.

2 Write the terms of an arithmetic sequence.

EXAMPLE 1 Writing the Terms of an Arithmetic Sequence Using the First Term and the Common Difference

The recursion formula $a_n = a_{n-1} - 0.67$ models the percentage of men working in the U.S. labor force, a_n, for each five-year period starting with 1980. Thus, $n = 1$ corresponds to 1980, $n = 2$ to 1985, $n = 3$ to 1990, and so on. In 1980, 77.4% of the U.S. men were working in the labor force. Find the first five terms of this arithmetic sequence in which $a_1 = 77.4$ and $a_n = a_{n-1} - 0.67$.

Men in the U.S. Labor Force

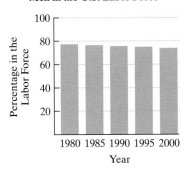

Women in the U.S. Labor Force

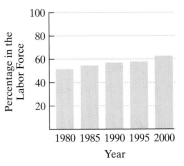

Source: U.S. Department of Labor

Solution The recursion formula $a_1 = 77.4$ and $a_n = a_{n-1} - 0.67$ indicates that each term after the first, 77.4, is obtained by adding -0.67 to the previous term. Thus, each five-year period the percentage of men in the labor force decreased by 0.67%.

$a_1 = 77.4$ *This is given.*

$a_2 = a_1 - 0.67 = 77.4 - 0.67 = 76.73$ *Use $a_n = a_{n-1} - 0.67$ with $n = 2$.*

$a_3 = a_2 - 0.67 = 76.73 - 0.67 = 76.06$ *Use $a_n = a_{n-1} - 0.67$ with $n = 3$.*

$a_4 = a_3 - 0.67 = 76.06 - 0.67 = 75.39$ *Use $a_n = a_{n-1} - 0.67$ with $n = 4$.*

$a_5 = a_4 - 0.67 = 75.39 - 0.67 = 74.72$ *Use $a_n = a_{n-1} - 0.67$ with $n = 5$.*

The first five terms are

$$77.4, 76.73, 76.06, 75.39, \text{ and } 74.72.$$

These numbers represent the percentage of men working in the U.S. labor force in 1980, 1985, 1990, 1995, and 2000, respectively, as given by the model.

Check Point 1 The recursion formula $a_n = a_{n-1} + 2.18$ models the percentage of women working in the U.S. labor force, a_n, for each five-year period starting with 1980. In 1980, 51.5% of U.S. women were working in the labor force. Find the first five terms of the arithmetic sequence in which $a_1 = 51.5$ and $a_n = a_{n-1} + 2.18$.

3 Use the formula for the general term of an arithmetic sequence.

The General Term of an Arithmetic Sequence

Consider an arithmetic sequence whose first term is a_1 and whose common difference is d. We are looking for a formula for the general term, a_n. Let's begin by writing the first six terms. The first term is a_1. The second term is $a_1 + d$. The third term is $a_1 + d + d$, or $a_1 + 2d$. Thus, we start with a_1 and add d to each successive term. The first six terms are

$$a_1, \quad a_1 + d, \quad a_1 + 2d, \quad a_1 + 3d, \quad a_1 + 4d, \quad a_1 + 5d.$$

a_1, first term a_2, second term a_3, third term a_4, fourth term a_5, fifth term a_6, sixth term

Compare the coefficient of d and the subscript of a denoting the term number. Can you see that the coefficient of d is 1 less than the subscript of a denoting the term number?

a_3: third term $= a_1 + 2d$ a_4: fourth term $= a_1 + 3d$

2 is one less than 3.   3 is one less than 4.

Thus, the formula for the nth term is

$$a_n: n\text{th term} = a_1 + (n - 1)d.$$

$n - 1$ is one less than n.

> **General Term of an Arithmetic Sequence**
>
> The nth term (the general term) of an arithmetic sequence with first term a_1 and common difference d is
>
> $$a_n = a_1 + (n - 1)d.$$

EXAMPLE 2 Using the Formula for the General Term of an Arithmetic Sequence

Find the eighth term of the arithmetic sequence whose first term is 4 and whose common difference is -7.

Solution To find the eighth term, a_8, we replace n in the formula with 8, a_1 with 4, and d with -7.

$$a_n = a_1 + (n - 1)d$$
$$a_8 = 4 + (8 - 1)(-7) = 4 + 7(-7) = 4 + (-49) = -45$$

The eighth term is -45. We can check this result by writing the first eight terms of the sequence:

$$4, -3, -10, -17, -24, -31, -38, -45.$$

Check Point 2 Find the ninth term of the arithmetic sequence whose first term is 6 and whose common difference is -5.

EXAMPLE 3 Using an Arithmetic Sequence to Model Teachers' Earnings

According to the National Education Association, teachers in the United States earned an average of $30,532 in 1990. This amount has increased by approximately $1472 per year.

a. Write a formula for the nth term of the arithmetic sequence that describes teachers' average earnings n years after 1989.

b. How much will U.S. teachers earn, on average, by the year 2010?

Solution

a. We can express teachers' earnings by the following arithmetic sequence:

30,532,   32,004,   33,476,   34,948,....

a_1: earnings in 1990, 1 year after 1989 | a_2: earnings in 1991, 2 years after 1989 | a_3: earnings in 1992, 3 years after 1989 | a_4: earnings in 1993, 4 years after 1989

In this sequence, a_1, the first term, represents the amount teachers earned in 1990. Each subsequent year this amount increases by $1472, so $d = 1472$. We use the formula for the general term of an arithmetic sequence to write the nth term of the sequence that describes teachers' earnings n years after 1989.

$$a_n = a_1 + (n - 1)d$$

This is the formula for the general term of an arithmetic sequence.

$$a_n = 30{,}532 + (n - 1)1472$$

$a_1 = 30{,}532$ and $d = 1472$.

$$a_n = 30{,}532 + 1472n - 1472 \quad \text{Distribute 1472 to each term in parentheses.}$$
$$a_n = 1472n + 29{,}060 \quad \text{Simplify.}$$

Thus, teachers' earnings n years after 1989 can be described by $a_n = 1472n + 29{,}060$.

b. Now we need to find teachers' earnings in 2010. The year 2010 is 21 years after 1989: That is, $2010 - 1989 = 21$. Thus, $n = 21$. We substitute 21 for n in $a_n = 1472n + 29{,}060$.

$$a_{21} = 1472 \cdot 21 + 29{,}060 = 59{,}972$$

The 22nd term of the sequence is 59,972. Therefore, U.S. teachers are predicted to earn an average of $59,972 by the year 2010.

> **Check Point 3** According to the U.S. Census Bureau, new one-family houses sold for an average of $159,000 in 1995. This average sales price has increased by approximately $9700 per year.
>
> **a.** Write a formula for the nth term of the arithmetic sequence that describes the average cost of new one-family houses n years after 1994.
>
> **b.** How much will new one-family houses cost, on average, by the year 2010?

4 Use the formula for the sum of the first n terms of an arithmetic sequence.

The Sum of the First n Terms of an Arithmetic Sequence

The sum of the first n terms of an arithmetic sequence, denoted by S_n, and called the **nth partial sum**, can be found without having to add up all the terms. Let

$$S_n = a_1 + a_2 + a_3 + \cdots + a_n$$

be the sum of the first n terms of an arithmetic sequence. Because d is the common difference between terms, S_n can be written forward and backward as follows.

Forward: Start with the first term. Keep adding d.

Backward: Start with the last term. Keep subtracting d.

$$S_n = a_1 \qquad\qquad + (a_1 + d) \ + (a_1 + 2d) + \cdots + a_n$$
$$S_n = a_n \qquad\qquad + (a_n - d) \ + (a_n - 2d) + \cdots + a_1$$
$$\overline{2S_n = (a_1 + a_n) + (a_1 + a_n) \ + (a_1 + a_n) \ + \cdots + (a_1 + a_n)} \quad \text{Add the two equations.}$$

Because there are n sums of $(a_1 + a_n)$ on the right side, we can express this side as $n(a_1 + a_n)$. Thus, the last equation can be simplified:

$$2S_n = n(a_1 + a_n)$$

$$S_n = \frac{n}{2}(a_1 + a_n). \quad \text{Solve for } S_n, \text{ dividing both sides by 2.}$$

We have proved the following result:

The Sum of the First n Terms of an Arithmetic Sequence

The sum, S_n, of the first n terms of an arithmetic sequence is given by

$$S_n = \frac{n}{2}(a_1 + a_n)$$

in which a_1 is the first term and a_n is the nth term.

To find the sum of the terms of an arithmetic sequence using $S_n = \dfrac{n}{2}(a_1 + a_n)$, we need to know the first term, a_1, the last te.rm, a_n, and the number of terms, n. The following examples illustrate how to use this formula.

EXAMPLE 4 Finding the Sum of n Terms of an Arithmetic Sequence

Find the sum of the first 100 terms of the arithmetic sequence: 1, 3, 5, 7, ...

Solution We are finding the sum of the first 100 odd numbers. To find the sum of the first 100 terms, S_{100}, we replace n in the formula with 100.

$$S_n = \frac{n}{2}(a_1 + a_n)$$

$$S_{100} = \frac{100}{2}(a_1 + a_{100})$$

The first term, a_1, is 1. We must find a_{100}, the 100th term.

We use the formula for the general term of an arithmetic sequence to find a_{100}. The common difference, d, of 1, 3, 5, 7, ..., is 2.

$a_n = a_1 + (n-1)d$ — This is the formula for the nth term of an arithmetic sequence. Use it to find the 100th term.

$a_{100} = 1 + (100-1) \cdot 2$ — Substitute 100 for n, 2 for d, and 1 (the first term) for a_1.

$= 1 + 99 \cdot 2$
$= 1 + 198 = 199$

Now we are ready to find the sum of the first 100 terms of 1, 3, 5, 7, ..., 199.

$S_n = \dfrac{n}{2}(a_1 + a_n)$ — Use the formula for the sum of the first n terms of an arithmetic sequence. Let $n = 100$, $a_1 = 1$, and $a_{100} = 199$.

$$S_{100} = \frac{100}{2}(1 + 199) = 50(200) = 10,000$$

The sum of the first 100 odd numbers is 10,000. Equivalently, the 100th partial sum of the sequence 1, 3, 5, 7, ... is 10,000.

Check Point 4 Find the sum of the first 15 terms of the arithmetic sequence: 3, 6, 9, 12, ...

EXAMPLE 5 Using S_n to Evaluate a Summation

Find the following sum: $\displaystyle\sum_{i=1}^{25}(5i - 9)$.

Solution

$$\sum_{i=1}^{25}(5i - 9) = (5 \cdot 1 - 9) + (5 \cdot 2 - 9) + (5 \cdot 3 - 9) + \cdots + (5 \cdot 25 - 9)$$

$$= -4 \qquad +1 \qquad +6 \qquad + \cdots + 116$$

By evaluating the first three terms and the last term, we see that $a_1 = -4$; d, the common difference, is $1 - (-4)$ or 5; and a_{25}, the last term, is 116.

Technology

To find

$$\sum_{i=1}^{25}(5i-9)$$

on a graphing utility, enter SUM
SEQ $(5x-9, x, 1, 25, 1)$.
Then press ENTER.

```
sum(seq(5X-9,X,1
,25,1)
           1400
```

$$S_n = \frac{n}{2}(a_1 + a_n)$$ Use the formula for the sum of the first n terms of an arithmetic sequence. Let n = 25, a₁ = −4, and a₂₅ = 116.

$$S_{25} = \frac{25}{2}(-4+116) = \frac{25}{2}(112) = 1400.$$

Thus,

$$\sum_{i=1}^{25}(5i-9) = 1400.$$

Check Point 5 Find the following sum: $\sum_{i=1}^{30}(6i-11)$.

EXAMPLE 6 Modeling Total Nursing Home Costs over a Six-Year Period

Your grandmother has assets of $350,000. One option that she is considering involves nursing home care for a six-year period beginning in 2001. The model

$$a_n = 1800n + 49{,}730$$

describes yearly nursing home costs n years after 2000. Does your grandmother have enough to pay for the facility?

Solution We must find the sum of an arithmetic sequence. The first term of the sequence corresponds to nursing home costs in the year 2001. The last term corresponds to nursing home costs in the year 2006. Because the model describes costs n years after 2000, n = 1 describes the year 2001 and n = 6 describes the year 2006.

$a_n = 1800n + 49{,}730$ This is the given formula for the general term of the sequence.

$a_1 = 1800 \cdot 1 + 49{,}730 = 51{,}530$ Find a₁ by replacing n with 1.

$a_6 = 1800 \cdot 6 + 49{,}730 = 60{,}530$ Find a₆ by replacing n with 6.

The first year the facility will cost $51,530. By year six, the facility will cost $60,530. Now we must find the sum of these costs for all six years. We focus on the sum of the first six terms of the arithmetic sequence

$$51{,}530, \quad 53{,}330, \quad \ldots, \quad 60{,}530.$$

We find this sum using the formula for the sum of the first n terms of an arithmetic sequence. We are adding 6 terms: n = 6. The first term is 51,530: a₁ = 51,530. The last term—that is, the sixth term—is 60,530: a₆ = 60,530.

$$S_n = \frac{n}{2}(a_1 + a_n)$$

$$S_6 = \frac{6}{2}(51{,}530 + 60{,}530) = 3(112{,}060) = 336{,}180$$

Total nursing home costs for your grandmother are predicted to be $336,180. Because your grandmother's assets are $350,000, she has enough to pay for the facility.

Check Point 6 In Example 6, how much would it cost for nursing home care for a ten-year period beginning in 2001?

EXERCISE SET 4.2

Practice Exercises

In Exercises 1–14, write the first six terms of each arithmetic sequence.

1. $a_1 = 200, d = 20$ **2.** $a_1 = 300, d = 50$

3. $a_1 = -7, d = 4$ **4.** $a_1 = -8, d = 5$

5. $a_1 = 300, d = -90$ **6.** $a_1 = 200, d = -60$

7. $a_1 = \frac{5}{2}, d = -\frac{1}{2}$ **8.** $a_1 = \frac{3}{4}, d = -\frac{1}{4}$

9. $a_n = a_{n-1} + 6, a_1 = -9$ **10.** $a_n = a_{n-1} + 4, a_1 = -7$

11. $a_n = a_{n-1} - 10, a_1 = 30$ **12.** $a_n = a_{n-1} - 20, a_1 = 50$

13. $a_n = a_{n-1} - 0.4, a_1 = 1.6$

14. $a_n = a_{n-1} - 0.3, a_1 = -1.7$

In Exercises 15–22, find the indicated term of the arithmetic sequence with first term, a_1, and common difference, d.

15. Find a_6 when $a_1 = 13, d = 4$.

16. Find a_{16} when $a_1 = 9, d = 2$.

17. Find a_{50} when $a_1 = 7, d = 5$.

18. Find a_{60} when $a_1 = 8, d = 6$.

19. Find a_{200} when $a_1 = -40, d = 5$.

20. Find a_{150} when $a_1 = -60, d = 5$.

21. Find a_{60} when $a_1 = 35, d = -3$.

22. Find a_{70} when $a_1 = -32, d = 4$.

In Exercises 23–34, write a formula for the general term (the nth term) of each arithmetic sequence. Do not use a recursion formula. Then use the formula for a_n to find a_{20}, the 20th term of the sequence.

23. $1, 5, 9, 13, \ldots$ **24.** $2, 7, 12, 17, \ldots$

25. $7, 3, -1, -5, \ldots$ **26.** $6, 1, -4, -9, \ldots$

27. $a_1 = 9, d = 2$ **28.** $a_1 = 6, d = 3$

29. $a_1 = -20, d = -4$ **30.** $a_1 = -70, d = -5$

31. $a_n = a_{n-1} + 3, a_1 = 4$ **32.** $a_n = a_{n-1} + 5, a_1 = 6$

33. $a_n = a_{n-1} - 10, a_1 = 30$ **34.** $a_n = a_{n-1} - 12, a_1 = 24$

35. Find the sum of the first 20 terms of the arithmetic sequence: $4, 10, 16, 22, \ldots$.

36. Find the sum of the first 25 terms of the arithmetic sequence: $7, 19, 31, 43, \ldots$.

37. Find the sum of the first 50 terms of the arithmetic sequence: $-10, -6, -2, 2, \ldots$.

38. Find the sum of the first 50 terms of the arithmetic sequence: $-15, -9, -3, 3, \ldots$.

39. Find $1 + 2 + 3 + 4 + \cdots + 100$, the sum of the first 100 natural numbers.

40. Find $2 + 4 + 6 + 8 + \cdots + 200$, the sum of the first 100 positive even integers.

41. Find the sum of the first 60 positive even integers.

42. Find the sum of the first 80 positive even integers.

43. Find the sum of the even integers between 21 and 45.

44. Find the sum of the odd integers between 30 and 54.

For Exercises 45–50, write out the first three terms and the last term. Then use the formula for the sum of the first n terms of an arithmetic sequence to find the indicated sum.

45. $\sum\limits_{i=1}^{17} (5i + 3)$ **46.** $\sum\limits_{i=1}^{20} (6i - 4)$

47. $\sum\limits_{i=1}^{30} (-3i + 5)$ **48.** $\sum\limits_{i=1}^{40} (-2i + 6)$

49. $\sum\limits_{i=1}^{100} 4i$ **50.** $\sum\limits_{i=1}^{50} -4i$

Application Exercises

The graph shows pounds of various food groups consumed per year by the average American. Exercises 51–54 involve developing arithmetic sequences that model the data. In Exercises 53–54, models will vary.

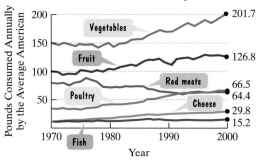

Per Capita Consumption of Various Food Groups

Source: U.S. Department of Agriculture

51. The graph shows that the average American consumed 150 pounds of vegetables in 1970. On average, this amount has increased by approximately 1.7 pounds per person per year.

    a. Write a formula for the *n*th term of the arithmetic sequence that describes pounds of vegetables consumed annually by the average American *n* years after 1969.

    b. How many pounds of vegetables will be consumed by the average American in 2006?

52. The graph shows that the average American consumed 100 pounds of fruit in 1970. On average, this amount has increased by approximately 0.9 pound per person per year.

  a. Write a formula for the nth term of the arithmetic sequence that describes pounds of fruit consumed annually by the average American n years after 1969.

  b. How many pounds of fruit will be consumed by the average American in 2006?

53. a. Use the data shown to write a formula for the *n*th term of the arithmetic sequence that describes pounds of cheese consumed annually by the average American *n* years after 1969.

  b. How many pounds of cheese will be consumed by the average American in 2006?

54. Use the data shown for fish, poultry, or red meats, and repeat both parts of Exercise 53.

55. Company A pays $24,000 yearly with raises of $1600 per year. Company B pays $28,000 yearly with raises of $1000 per year. Which company will pay more in year 10? How much more?

56. Company A pays $23,000 yearly with raises of $1200 per year. Company B pays $26,000 yearly with raises of $800 per year. Which company will pay more in year 10? How much more?

57. According to the Environmental Protection Agency, in 1960 the United States recovered 3.78 million tons of solid waste. Due primarily to recycling programs, this amount has increased by approximately 0.576 million ton per year.

  a. Write the general term for the arithmetic sequence modeling the amount of solid waste recovered in the United States *n* years after 1959.

  b. What is the total amount of solid waste recovered from 1960 through 2000?

58. According to the Environmental Protection Agency, in 1960 the United States generated 87.1 million tons of solid waste. This amount has increased by approximately 3.14 million tons per year.

  a. Write the general term for the arithmetic sequence modeling the amount of solid waste generated in the United States *n* years after 1959.

  b. What is the total amount of solid waste generated from 1960 through 2000?

59. A company offers a starting yearly salary of $33,000 with raises of $2500 per year. Find the total salary over a ten-year period.

60. You are considering two job offers. Company A will start you at $19,000 annually and guarantee a raise of $2600 per year. Company B will start you at a higher salary, $27,000 annually, but will only guarantee a raise of $1200 per year. Find the total salary that each company will pay you over a ten-year period. Which company pays the greater total amount?

61. A theater has 30 seats in the first row, 32 seats in the second row, increasing by 2 seats per row for a total of 26 rows. How many seats are there in the theater?

62. A section in a stadium has 20 seats in the first row, 23 seats in the second row, increasing by 3 seats per row for a total of 38 rows. How many seats are in this section of the stadium?

Writing in Mathematics

63. What is an arithmetic sequence? Give an example with your explanation.

64. What is the common difference in an arithmetic sequence?

65. Explain how to find the general term of an arithmetic sequence.

66. Explain how to find the sum of the first *n* terms of an arithmetic sequence without having to add up all the terms.

67. Teachers' earnings *n* years after 1989 can be described by $a_n = 1472n + 29{,}060$. According to this model, what will teachers earn in 2083? Describe two possible circumstances that would render this predicted salary incorrect.

Technology Exercises

68. Use the ⌈SEQ⌉ (sequence) capability of a graphing utility and the formula you obtained for a_n to verify the value you found for a_{20} in any five exercises from Exercises 23–34.

69. Use the capability of a graphing utility to calculate the sum of a sequence to verify any five of your answers to Exercises 45–50.

Critical Thinking Exercises

70. Give examples of two different arithmetic sequences whose fourth term, a_4, is 10.

71. In the sequence $21{,}700, 23{,}172, 24{,}644, 26{,}116, \ldots$, which term is 314,628?

72. A *degree-day* is a unit used to measure the fuel requirements of buildings. By definition, each degree that the average daily temperature is below 65°F is 1 degree-day. For example, a temperature of 42°F constitutes 23 degree-days. If the average temperature on January 1 was 42°F and fell 2°F for each subsequent day up to and including January 10, how many degree-days are included from January 1 to January 10?

73. Show that the sum of the first *n* positive odd integers,

$$1 + 3 + 5 + \cdots + (2n - 1),$$

is n^2.

Group Exercise

74. Members of your group have been hired by the Environmental Protection Agency to write a report on whether we are making significant progress in recovering solid waste. Use the models from Exercises 57 and 58 as the basis for your report. A graph of each model from 1960 through 2000 would be helpful. What percentage of solid waste generated is actually recovered on a year-to-year basis? Be as creative as you want in your report and then draw conclusions. The group should write up the report and perhaps even include suggestions as to how we might improve recycling progress.

SECTION 4.3   *Geometric Sequences*

Objectives

1. Find the common ratio of a geometric sequence.
2. Write terms of a geometric sequence.
3. Use the formula for the general term of a geometric sequence.
4. Use the formula for the sum of the first *n* terms of a geometric sequence.
5. Find the value of an annuity.
6. Use the formula for the sum of an infinite geometric series.

Here we are at the closing moments of a job interview. You're shaking hands with the manager. You managed to answer all the tough questions without losing your poise, and now you've been offered a job. As a matter of fact, your qualifications are so terrific that you've been offered two jobs—one just the day before, with a rival company in the same field! One company offers $30,000 the first year, with increases of 6% per year for four years after that. The other offers $32,000 the first year, with increases of 3% per year after that. Over a five-year period, which is the better offer?

If salary raises amount to a certain percent each year, the yearly salaries over time form a geometric sequence. In this section, we investigate geometric sequences and their properties. After studying the section, you will be in a position to decide which job offer to accept: you will know which company will pay you more over five years.

Geometric Sequences

Figure 4.2 shows a sequence in which the number of squares is increasing. From left to right, the number of squares is 1, 5, 25, 125, and 625. In this sequence, each term after the first, 1, is obtained by multiplying the preceding term by a constant amount, namely 5. This sequence of increasing number of squares is an example of a *geometric sequence*.

Figure 4.2 A geometric sequence of squares

Definition of a Geometric Sequence

A **geometric sequence** is a sequence in which each term after the first is obtained by multiplying the preceding term by a fixed nonzero constant. The amount by which we multiply each time is called the **common ratio** of the sequence.

1 Find the common ratio of a geometric sequence.

The common ratio, r, is found by dividing any term after the first term by the term that directly precedes it. In the following examples, the common ratio is found by dividing the second term by the first term: $\dfrac{a_2}{a_1}$.

Geometric sequence	Common ratio
$1, 5, 25, 125, 625, \ldots$	$r = \dfrac{5}{1} = 5$
$4, 8, 16, 32, 64, \ldots$	$r = \dfrac{8}{4} = 2$
$6, -12, 24, -48, 96, \ldots$	$r = \dfrac{-12}{6} = -2$
$9, -3, 1, -\dfrac{1}{3}, \dfrac{1}{9}, \ldots$	$r = \dfrac{-3}{9} = -\dfrac{1}{3}$

Study Tip

When the common ratio of a geometric sequence is negative, the signs of the terms alternate.

2 Write terms of a geometric sequence.

How do we find the terms of a geometric sequence when the first term and the common ratio are known? We multiply the first term by the common ratio to get the second term, multiply the second term by the common ratio to get the third term, and so on.

EXAMPLE 1 Writing the Terms of a Geometric Sequence

Write the first six terms of the geometric sequence with first term 6 and common ratio $\frac{1}{3}$.

Solution The first term is 6. The second term is $6 \cdot \frac{1}{3}$, or 2. The third term is $2 \cdot \frac{1}{3}$, or $\frac{2}{3}$. The fourth term is $\frac{2}{3} \cdot \frac{1}{3}$, or $\frac{2}{9}$, and so on. The first six terms are

$$6, 2, \tfrac{2}{3}, \tfrac{2}{9}, \tfrac{2}{27}, \text{ and } \tfrac{2}{81}.$$

Check Point 1 Write the first six terms of the geometric sequence with first term 12 and common ratio $\frac{1}{2}$.

3 Use the formula for the general term of a geometric sequence.

The General Term of a Geometric Sequence

Consider a geometric sequence whose first term is a_1 and whose common ratio is r. We are looking for a formula for the general term, a_n. Let's begin by writing the first six terms. The first term is a_1. The second term is $a_1 r$. The third term is $a_1 r \cdot r$, or $a_1 r^2$. The fourth term is $a_1 r^2 \cdot r$, or $a_1 r^3$, and so on. Starting with a_1 and multiplying each successive term by r, the first six terms are

$$a_1, \qquad a_1 r, \qquad a_1 r^2, \qquad a_1 r^3, \qquad a_1 r^4, \qquad a_1 r^5.$$

a_1, first term a_2, second term a_3, third term a_4, fourth term a_5, fifth term a_6, sixth term

Compare the exponent on r and the subscript of a denoting the term number. Can you see that the exponent on r is 1 less than the subscript of a denoting the term number?

$$a_3: \text{third term} = a_1 r^2 \qquad a_4: \text{fourth term} = a_1 r^3$$

2 is one less than 3.　　3 is one less than 4.

Thus, the formula for the nth term is

$$a_n = a_1 r^{n-1}.$$

$n-1$ is one less than n.

General Term of a Geometric Sequence

The nth term (the general term) of a geometric sequence with first term a_1 and common ratio r is

$$a_n = a_1 r^{n-1}$$ — common ratio

Term | First Term

EXAMPLE 2　Using the Formula for the General Term of a Geometric Sequence

Find the eighth term of the geometric sequence whose first term is -4 and whose common ratio is -2.

Solution　To find the eighth term, a_8, we replace n in the formula with 8, a_1 with -4, and r with -2.

$$a_n = a_1 r^{n-1}$$
$$a_8 = -4(-2)^{8-1} = -4(-2)^7 = -4(-128) = 512$$

The eighth term is 512. We can check this result by writing the first eight terms of the sequence:

$$-4, 8, -16, 32, -64, 128, -256, 512.$$

Study Tip

Be careful with the order of operations when evaluating

$$a_1 r^{n-1}.$$

First find r^{n-1}. Then multiply the result by a_1.

Check Point 2　Find the seventh term of the geometric sequence whose first term is 5 and whose common ratio is -3.

In Chapter 4, we studied exponential functions of the form $f(x) = b^x$ and the explosive exponential growth of world population. In our next example, we consider Florida's geometric population growth. Because **a geometric sequence is an exponential function whose domain is the set of positive integers,** geometric and exponential growth mean the same thing. (By contrast, an arithmetic sequence is a *linear function* whose domain is the set of positive integers.)

EXAMPLE 3　Geometric Population Growth

The population of Florida from 1990 through 1997 is shown in the following table:

Year	1990	1991	1992	1993	1994	1995	1996	1997
Population in millions	12.94	13.20	13.46	13.73	14.00	14.28	14.57	14.86

a. Show that the population is increasing geometrically.

b. Write the general term for the geometric sequence describing population growth for Florida n years after 1989.

c. Estimate Florida's population, in millions, for the year 2000.

Solution

a. First, we divide the population for each year by the population in the preceding year.

$$\frac{13.20}{12.94} \approx 1.02, \quad \frac{13.46}{13.20} \approx 1.02, \quad \frac{13.73}{13.46} \approx 1.02$$

Continuing in this manner, we will keep getting approximately 1.02. This means that the population is increasing geometrically with $r \approx 1.02$. In this situation, the common ratio is the growth rate, indicating that the population of Florida in any year shown in the table is approximately 1.02 times the population the year before.

b. The sequence of Florida's population growth is

$$12.94, 13.20, 13.46, 13.73, 14.00, 14.28, 14.57, 14.86, \dots.$$

Because the population is increasing geometrically, we can find the general term of this sequence using

$$a_n = a_1 r^{n-1}.$$

In this sequence, $a_1 = 12.94$ and [from part (a)] $r \approx 1.02$. We substitute these values into the formula for the general term. This gives the general term for the geometric sequence describing Florida's population n years after 1989.

$$a_n = 12.94(1.02)^{n-1}$$

c. We can use the formula for the general term, a_n, in part (b) to estimate Florida's population for the year 2000. The year 2000 is 11 years after 1989—that is, $2000 - 1989 = 11$. Thus, $n = 11$. We substitute 11 for n in $a_n = 12.94(1.02)^{n-1}$.

$$a_{11} = 12.94(1.02)^{11-1} = 12.94(1.02)^{10} \approx 15.77$$

The formula indicates that Florida had a population of approximately 15.77 million in the year 2000. According to the U.S. Census Bureau, Florida's population in 2000 was 15.98 million. Our geometric sequence models the actual population fairly well.

Geometric Population Growth

Economist Thomas Malthus (1766–1834) predicted that population growth would increase as a geometric sequence and food production would increase as an arithmetic sequence. He concluded that eventually population would exceed food production. If two sequences, one geometric and one arithmetic, are increasing, the geometric sequence will eventually overtake the arithmetic sequence, regardless of any head start that the arithmetic sequence might initially have.

Check Point 3 Write the general term for the geometric sequence

$$3, 6, 12, 24, 48, \dots.$$

Then use the formula for the general term to find the eighth term.

4 Use the formula for the sum of the first n terms of a geometric sequence.

The Sum of the First n Terms of a Geometric Sequence

The sum of the first n terms of a geometric sequence, denoted by S_n, and called the **nth partial sum,** can be found without having to add up all the terms. Recall that the first n terms of a geometric sequence are

$$a_1, a_1 r, a_1 r^2, \dots, a_1 r^{n-2}, a_1 r^{n-1}.$$

We proceed as follows:

$$S_n = a_1 + a_1r + a_1r^2 + \cdots + a_1r^{n-2} + a_1r^{n-1}$$ S_n is the sum of the first n terms of the sequence.

$$rS_n = a_1r + a_1r^2 + a_1r^3 + \cdots + a_1r^{n-1} + a_1r^n$$ Multiply both sides of the equation by r.

$$S_n - rS_n = a_1 - a_1r^n$$ Subtract the second equation from the first equation.

$$S_n(1 - r) = a_1(1 - r^n)$$ Factor out S_n on the left and a_1 on the right.

$$S_n = \frac{a_1(1 - r^n)}{1 - r}.$$ Solve for S_n by dividing both sides by $1 - r$ (assuming that $r \neq 1$).

We have proved the following result:

Study Tip

If the common ratio is 1, the geometric sequence is

$$a_1, a_1, a_1, a_1, \ldots.$$

The sum of the first n terms of this sequence is na_1:

$$S_n = \underbrace{a_1 + a_1 + a_1 + \cdots + a_1}_{\text{There are } n \text{ terms.}}$$

$$= na_1.$$

The Sum of the First n Terms of a Geometric Sequence

The sum, S_n, of the first n terms of a geometric sequence is given by

$$S_n = \frac{a_1(1 - r^n)}{1 - r}$$

in which a_1 is the first term and r is the common ratio ($r \neq 1$).

To find the sum of the terms of a geometric sequence, we need to know the first term, a_1, the common ratio, r, and the number of terms, n. The following examples illustrate how to use this formula.

EXAMPLE 4   Finding the Sum of the First n Terms of a Geometric Sequence

Find the sum of the first 18 terms of the geometric sequence: $2, -8, 32, -128, \ldots$.

Solution To find the sum of the first 18 terms, S_{18}, we replace n in the formula with 18.

$$S_n = \frac{a_1(1 - r^n)}{1 - r}$$

$$S_{18} = \frac{a_1(1 - r^{18})}{1 - r}$$

The first term, a_1, is 2.   We must find r, the common ratio.

We can find the common ratio by dividing the second term by the first term.

$$r = \frac{a_2}{a_1} = -\frac{8}{2} = -4$$

Now we are ready to find the sum of the first 18 terms of $2, -8, 32, -128, \ldots$.

$$S_n = \frac{a_1(1 - r^n)}{1 - r}$$ *Use the formula for the sum of the first n terms of a geometric sequence.*

$$S_{18} = \frac{2[1 - (-4)^{18}]}{1 - (-4)}$$ *a_1 (the first term) = 2, r = −4, and n = 18 because we want the sum of the first 18 terms.*

$$= -27{,}487{,}790{,}694$$ *Use a calculator.*

The sum of the first 18 terms is $-27{,}487{,}790{,}694$. Equivalently, this number is the 18th partial sum of the sequence $2, -8, 32, -128, \ldots$.

Check Point 4   Find the sum of the first nine terms of the geometric sequence: $2, -6, 18, -54, \ldots$.

Technology

To find

$$\sum_{i=1}^{10} 6 \cdot 2^i$$

on a graphing utility, enter

$\boxed{\text{SUM}}\ \boxed{\text{SEQ}}\ (6 \times 2^x, x, 1, 10, 1)$.

Then press $\boxed{\text{ENTER}}$.

```
sum(seq(6*2^X,X,
1,10,1)
           12276
```

EXAMPLE 5   Using S_n to Evaluate a Summation

Find the following sum: $\displaystyle\sum_{i=1}^{10} 6 \cdot 2^i$.

Solution   Let's write out a few terms in the sum.

$$\sum_{i=1}^{10} 6 \cdot 2^i = 6 \cdot 2 + 6 \cdot 2^2 + 6 \cdot 2^3 + \cdots + 6 \cdot 2^{10}$$

Can you see that each term after the first is obtained by multiplying the preceding term by 2? To find the sum of the 10 terms ($n = 10$), we need to know the first term, a_1, and the common ratio, r. The first term is $6 \cdot 2$ or 12: $a_1 = 12$. The common ratio is 2.

$$S_n = \frac{a_1(1 - r^n)}{1 - r}$$ *Use the formula for the sum of the first n terms of a geometric sequence.*

$$S_{10} = \frac{12(1 - 2^{10})}{1 - 2}$$ *a_1 (the first term) = 12, r = 2, and n = 10 because we are adding ten terms.*

$$= 12{,}276$$ *Use a calculator.*

Thus,

$$\sum_{i=1}^{10} 6 \cdot 2^i = 12{,}276$$

Check Point 5   Find the following sum: $\displaystyle\sum_{i=1}^{8} 2 \cdot 3^i$.

Some of the exercises in the previous exercise set involved situations in which salaries increase by a fixed amount each year. A more realistic situation is one in which salary raises increase by a certain percent each year. Example 6 shows how such a situation can be described using a geometric series.

EXAMPLE 6 Computing a Lifetime Salary

A union contract specifies that each worker will receive a 5% pay increase each year for the next 30 years. One worker is paid $20,000 the first year. What is this person's total lifetime salary over a 30-year period?

Solution The salary for the first year is $20,000. With a 5% raise, the second-year salary is computed as follows:

Salary for year $2 = 20{,}000 + 20{,}000(0.05) = 20{,}000(1 + 0.05) = 20{,}000(1.05)$.

Each year, the salary is 1.05 times what it was in the previous year. Thus, the salary for year 3 is 1.05 times $20{,}000(1.05)$, or $20{,}000(1.05)^2$. The salaries for the first five years are given in the table.

Yearly Salaries					
Year 1	**Year 2**	**Year 3**	**Year 4**	**Year 5**	...
20,000	$20{,}000(1.05)$	$20{,}000(1.05)^2$	$20{,}000(1.05)^3$	$20{,}000(1.05)^4$	...

The numbers in the second row form a geometric sequence with $a_1 = 20{,}000$ and $r = 1.05$. To find the total salary over 30 years, we use the formula for the sum of the first n terms of a geometric sequence, with $n = 30$.

$$S_n = \frac{a_1(1 - r^n)}{1 - r}$$

$$S_{30} = \frac{20{,}000[1 - (1.05)^{30}]}{1 - 1.05}$$

Total salary over 30 years

$$= \frac{20{,}000[1 - (1.05)^{30}]}{-0.05}$$

$$\approx 1{,}328{,}777 \qquad \text{Use a calculator.}$$

The total salary over the 30-year period is approximately $1,328,777.

Check Point 6 A job pays a salary of $30,000 the first year. During the next 29 years, the salary increases by 6% each year. What is the total lifetime salary over the 30-year period?

5 Find the value of an annuity.

Annuities

The compound interest formula

$$A = P(1 + r)^t$$

gives the future value, A, after t years, when a fixed amount of money, P, the principal, is deposited in an account that pays an annual interest rate r (in decimal form) compounded once a year. However, money is often invested in small amounts at periodic intervals. For example, to save for retirement, you might decide to place $1000 into an Individual Retirement Account (IRA) at the end of each year until you retire. An **annuity** is a sequence of equal payments made at equal time periods. An IRA is an example of an annuity.

Suppose P dollars is deposited into an account at the end of each year. The account pays an annual interest rate, r, compounded annually. At the end of the first year, the account contains P dollars. At the end of the second year, P dollars is deposited again. At the time of this deposit, the first deposit has received interest earned during the second year. The **value of the annuity** is the sum of all deposits made plus all interest paid. Thus, the value of the annuity after two years is

$$P + P(1 + r).$$

Deposit of P dollars at end of second year	First-year deposit of P dollars with interest earned for a year

The value of the annuity after three years is

$$P \quad + \quad P(1 + r) \quad + \quad P(1 + r)^2.$$

Deposit of P dollars at end of third year	Second-year deposit of P dollars with interest earned for a year	First-year deposit of P dollars with interest earned over two years

The value of the annuity after t years is

$$P + P(1 + r) + P(1 + r)^2 + P(1 + r)^3 + \cdots + P(1 + r)^{t-1}$$

Deposit of P dollars at end of year t	First-year deposit of P dollars with interest earned over t − 1 years

This is the sum of the terms of a geometric sequence with first term P and common ratio $1 + r$. We use the formula

$$S_n = \frac{a_1(1 - r^n)}{1 - r}$$

to find the sum of the terms:

$$S_n = \frac{P\left[1 - (1 + r)^t\right]}{1 - (1 + r)} = \frac{P\left[1 - (1 + r)^t\right]}{-r} = P\frac{(1 + r)^t - 1}{r}.$$

This formula gives the value of an annuity after t years if interest is compounded once a year. We can adjust the formula to find the value of an annuity if equal payments are made at the end of each of n compounding periods per year.

Value of an Annuity: Interest Compounded n Times per Year

If P is the deposit made at the end of each compounding period for an annuity at r percent annual interest compounded n times per year, the value, A, of the annuity after t years is

$$A = P\frac{\left(1 + \dfrac{r}{n}\right)^{nt} - 1}{\dfrac{r}{n}}.$$

EXAMPLE 7   Determining the Value of an Annuity

To save for retirement, you decide to deposit $1000 into an IRA at the end of each year for the next 30 years. If the interest rate is 10% per year compounded annually, find the value of the IRA after 30 years.

Solution   The annuity involves 30 year-end deposits of $P = \$1000$. The interest rate is 10%: $r = 0.10$. Because the deposits are made once a year and the interest is compounded once a year, $n = 1$. The number of years is 30: $t = 30$. We replace the variables in the formula for the value of an annuity with these numbers.

$$A = P\dfrac{\left(1 + \dfrac{r}{n}\right)^{nt} - 1}{\dfrac{r}{n}}$$

$$A = 1000\dfrac{\left(1 + \dfrac{0.10}{1}\right)^{1 \cdot 30} - 1}{\dfrac{0.10}{1}} \approx 164{,}494$$

The value of the IRA at the end of 30 years is approximately \$164,494.

> **Check Point 7**   If \$3000 is deposited into an IRA at the end of each year for 40 years and the interest rate is 10% per year compounded annually, find the value of the IRA after 40 years.

6 Use the formula for the sum of an infinite geometric series.

Geometric Series

An infinite sum of the form

$$a_1 + a_1 r + a_1 r^2 + a_1 r^3 + \cdots + a_1 r^{n-1} + \cdots$$

with first term a_1 and common ratio r is called an **infinite geometric series.** How can we determine which infinite geometric series have sums and which do not? We look at what happens to r^n as n gets larger in the formula for the sum of the first n terms of this series, namely

$$S_n = \frac{a_1(1 - r^n)}{1 - r}.$$

If r is any number between -1 and 1, that is, $-1 < r < 1$, the term r^n approaches 0 as n gets larger. For example, consider what happens to r^n for $r = \frac{1}{2}$:

$$\left(\tfrac{1}{2}\right)^1 = \tfrac{1}{2} \qquad \left(\tfrac{1}{2}\right)^2 = \tfrac{1}{4} \qquad \left(\tfrac{1}{2}\right)^3 = \tfrac{1}{8} \qquad \left(\tfrac{1}{2}\right)^4 = \tfrac{1}{16} \qquad \left(\tfrac{1}{2}\right)^5 = \tfrac{1}{32} \qquad \left(\tfrac{1}{2}\right)^6 = \tfrac{1}{64}.$$

> These numbers are approaching 0 as n gets larger.

Take another look at the formula for the sum of the first n terms of a geometric sequence.

$$S_n = \frac{a_1(1 - r^n)}{1 - r}$$

> If $-1 < r < 1$, r^n approaches 0 as n gets larger.

Let us replace r^n with 0 in the formula for S_n. This change gives us a formula for the sum of infinite geometric series with common ratios between -1 and 1.

The Sum of an Infinite Geometric Series

If $-1 < r < 1$ (equivalently, $|r| < 1$), then the sum of the infinite geometric series

$$a_1 + a_1 r + a_1 r^2 + a_1 r^3 + \cdots$$

in which a_1 is the first term and r is the common ratio is given by

$$S = \frac{a_1}{1 - r}.$$

If $|r| \geq 1$, the infinite series does not have a sum.

To use the formula for the sum of an infinite geometric series, we need to know the first term and the common ratio. For example, consider

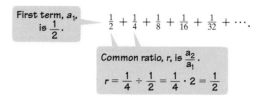

First term, a_1, is $\frac{1}{2}$.

$\frac{1}{2} + \frac{1}{4} + \frac{1}{8} + \frac{1}{16} + \frac{1}{32} + \cdots$.

Common ratio, r, is $\frac{a_2}{a_1}$.

$r = \frac{1}{4} \div \frac{1}{2} = \frac{1}{4} \cdot 2 = \frac{1}{2}$

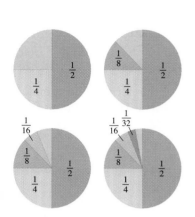

Figure 4.3 The sum $\frac{1}{2} + \frac{1}{4} + \frac{1}{8} + \frac{1}{16} + \frac{1}{32} + \cdots$ is approaching 1.

With $r = \frac{1}{2}$, the condition that $|r| < 1$ is met, so the infinite geometric series has a sum given by $S = \dfrac{a_1}{1 - r}$. The sum of the series is found as follows:

$$\frac{1}{2} + \frac{1}{4} + \frac{1}{8} + \frac{1}{16} + \frac{1}{32} + \cdots = \frac{a_1}{1-r} = \frac{\frac{1}{2}}{1 - \frac{1}{2}} = \frac{\frac{1}{2}}{\frac{1}{2}} = 1.$$

Thus, the sum of the infinite geometric series is 1. Notice how this is illustrated in Figure 4.3. As more terms are included, the sum is approaching the area of one complete circle.

EXAMPLE 8 Finding the Sum of an Infinite Geometric Series

Find the sum of the infinite geometric series: $\frac{3}{8} - \frac{3}{16} + \frac{3}{32} - \frac{3}{64} + \cdots$.

Solution Before finding the sum, we must find the common ratio.

$$r = \frac{a_2}{a_1} = \frac{-\frac{3}{16}}{\frac{3}{8}} = -\frac{3}{16} \cdot \frac{8}{3} = -\frac{1}{2}$$

Because $r = -\frac{1}{2}$, the condition that $|r| < 1$ is met. Thus, the infinite geometric series has a sum.

$$S = \frac{a_1}{1-r}$$

This is the formula for the sum of an infinite geometric series. Let $a_1 = \frac{3}{8}$ and $r = -\frac{1}{2}$.

$$= \frac{\frac{3}{8}}{1 - \left(-\frac{1}{2}\right)} = \frac{\frac{3}{8}}{\frac{3}{2}} = \frac{3}{8} \cdot \frac{2}{3} = \frac{1}{4}$$

Thus, the sum of this infinite geometric series is $\frac{1}{4}$. Put in an informal way, as we continue to add more and more terms, the sum approaches, and is approximately equal to, $\frac{1}{4}$.

Check Point 8 Find the sum of the infinite geometric series: $3 + 2 + \frac{4}{3} + \frac{8}{9} + \cdots$.

We can use the formula for the sum of an infinite series to express a repeating decimal as a fraction in lowest terms.

EXAMPLE 9   Writing a Repeating Decimal as a Fraction

Express $0.\overline{7}$ as a fraction in lowest terms.

Solution

$$0.\overline{7} = 0.7777\ldots = \frac{7}{10} + \frac{7}{100} + \frac{7}{1000} + \frac{7}{10,000} + \cdots$$

Observe that $0.\overline{7}$ is an infinite geometric series with first term $\frac{7}{10}$ and common ratio $\frac{1}{10}$. Because $r = \frac{1}{10}$, the condition that $|r| < 1$ is met. Thus, we can use our formula to find the sum. Therefore,

$$0.\overline{7} = \frac{a_1}{1 - r} = \frac{\frac{7}{10}}{1 - \frac{1}{10}} = \frac{\frac{7}{10}}{\frac{9}{10}} = \frac{7}{10} \cdot \frac{10}{9} = \frac{7}{9}.$$

An equivalent fraction for $0.\overline{7}$ is $\frac{7}{9}$.

Check Point 9   Express $0.\overline{9}$ as a fraction in lowest terms.

Infinite geometric series have many applications, as illustrated in Example 10.

EXAMPLE 10   Tax Rebates and the Multiplier Effect

A tax rebate that returns a certain amount of money to taxpayers can have a total effect on the economy that is many times this amount. In economics, this phenomenon is called the **multiplier effect.** Suppose, for example, that the government reduces taxes so that each consumer has $2000 more income. The government assumes that each person will spend 70% of this (= $1400). The individuals and businesses receiving this $1400 in turn spend 70% of it (= $980), creating extra income for other people to spend, and so on. Determine the total amount spent on consumer goods from the initial $2000 tax rebate.

Solution   The total amount spent is given by the infinite geometric series

$$1400 + 980 + 686 + \cdots.$$

70% of 1400   70% of 980

The first term is 1400: $a_1 = 1400$. The common ratio is 70%, or 0.7: $r = 0.7$. Because $r = 0.7$, the condition that $|r| < 1$ is met. Thus, we can use our formula to find the sum. Therefore,

$$1400 + 980 + 686 + \cdots = \frac{a_1}{1 - r} = \frac{1400}{1 - 0.7} \approx 4667.$$

This means that the total amount spent on consumer goods from the initial $2000 rebate is approximately $4667.

Check Point 10   Rework Example 10 and determine the total amount spent on consumer goods with a $1000 tax rebate and 80% spending down the line.

$1400

70% is spent.

$980

70% is spent.

$686

EXERCISE SET 4.3

Practice Exercises

In Exercises 1–8, write the first five terms of each geometric sequence.

1. $a_1 = 5, \quad r = 3$

2. $a_1 = 4, \quad r = 3$

3. $a_1 = 20, \quad r = \frac{1}{2}$

4. $a_1 = 24, \quad r = \frac{1}{3}$

5. $a_n = -4a_{n-1}, \quad a_1 = 10$

6. $a_n = -3a_{n-1}, \quad a_1 = 10$

7. $a_n = -5a_{n-1}, \quad a_1 = -6$

8. $a_n = -6a_{n-1}, \quad a_1 = -2$

In Exercises 9–16, use the formula for the general term (the nth term) of a geometric sequence to find the indicated term of each sequence with the given first term, a_1, and common ratio, r.

9. Find a_8 when $a_1 = 6, r = 2$.

10. Find a_8 when $a_1 = 5, r = 3$.

11. Find a_{12} when $a_1 = 5, r = -2$.

12. Find a_{12} when $a_1 = 4, r = -2$.

13. Find a_{40} when $a_1 = 1000, r = -\frac{1}{2}$.

14. Find a_{30} when $a_1 = 8000, r = -\frac{1}{2}$.

15. Find a_8 when $a_1 = 1{,}000{,}000, r = 0.1$.

16. Find a_8 when $a_1 = 40{,}000, r = 0.1$.

In Exercises 17–24, write a formula for the general term (the nth term) of each geometric sequence. Then use the formula for a_n to find a_7, the seventh term of the sequence.

17. $3, 12, 48, 192, \ldots$

18. $3, 15, 75, 375, \ldots$

19. $18, 6, 2, \frac{2}{3}, \ldots.$

20. $12, 6, 3, \frac{3}{2}, \ldots.$

21. $1.5, -3, 6, -12, \ldots$

22. $5, -1, \frac{1}{5}, -\frac{1}{25}, \ldots.$

23. $0.0004, -0.004, 0.04, -0.4, \ldots$

24. $0.0007, -0.007, 0.07, -0.7, \ldots$

Use the formula for the sum of the first n terms of a geometric sequence to solve Exercises 25–36.

25. Find the sum of the first 12 terms of the geometric sequence: $2, 6, 18, 54, \ldots.$

26. Find the sum of the first 12 terms of the geometric sequence: $3, 6, 12, 24, \ldots.$

27. Find the sum of the first 11 terms of the geometric sequence: $3, -6, 12, -24, \ldots.$

28. Find the sum of the first 11 terms of the geometric sequence: $4, -12, 36, -108, \ldots.$

29. Find the sum of the first 14 terms of the geometric sequence: $-\frac{3}{2}, 3, -6, 12, \ldots.$

30. Find the sum of the first 14 terms of the geometric sequence: $-\frac{1}{24}, \frac{1}{12}, -\frac{1}{6}, \frac{1}{3}, \ldots.$

In Exercises 31–36, find the indicated sum. Use the formula for the sum of the first n terms of a geometric sequence.

31. $\sum_{i=1}^{8} 3^i$

32. $\sum_{i=1}^{6} 4^i$

33. $\sum_{i=1}^{10} 5 \cdot 2^i$

34. $\sum_{i=1}^{7} 4(-3)^i$

35. $\sum_{i=1}^{6} \left(\frac{1}{2}\right)^{i+1}$

36. $\sum_{i=1}^{6} \left(\frac{1}{3}\right)^{i+1}$

In Exercises 37–44, find the sum of each infinite geometric series.

37. $1 + \frac{1}{3} + \frac{1}{9} + \frac{1}{27} + \cdots$

38. $1 + \frac{1}{4} + \frac{1}{16} + \frac{1}{64} + \cdots$

39. $3 + \frac{3}{4} + \frac{3}{4^2} + \frac{3}{4^3} + \cdots$

40. $5 + \frac{5}{6} + \frac{5}{6^2} + \frac{5}{6^3} + \cdots$

41. $1 - \frac{1}{2} + \frac{1}{4} - \frac{1}{8} + \cdots$

42. $3 - 1 + \frac{1}{3} - \frac{1}{9} + \cdots$

43. $\sum_{i=1}^{\infty} 8(-0.3)^{i-1}$

44. $\sum_{i=1}^{\infty} 12(-0.7)^{i-1}$

In Exercises 45–50, express each repeating decimal as a fraction in lowest terms.

45. $0.\overline{5} = \frac{5}{10} + \frac{5}{100} + \frac{5}{1000} + \frac{5}{10{,}000} + \cdots$

46. $0.\overline{1} = \frac{1}{10} + \frac{1}{100} + \frac{1}{1000} + \frac{1}{10{,}000} + \cdots$

47. $0.\overline{47} = \frac{47}{100} + \frac{47}{10{,}000} + \frac{47}{1{,}000{,}000} + \cdots$

48. $0.\overline{83} = \frac{83}{100} + \frac{83}{10{,}000} + \frac{83}{1{,}000{,}000} + \cdots$

49. $0.\overline{257}$

50. $0.\overline{529}$

In Exercises 51–56, the general term of a sequence is given. Determine whether the sequence is arithmetic, geometric, or neither. If the sequence is arithmetic, find the common difference; if it is geometric, find the common ratio.

51. $a_n = n + 5$

52. $a_n = n - 3$

53. $a_n = 2^n$

54. $a_n = \left(\frac{1}{2}\right)^n$

55. $a_n = n^2 + 5$

56. $a_n = n^2 - 3$

Application Exercises

Use the formula for the general term (the nth term) of a geometric sequence to solve Exercises 57–60.

In Exercises 57–58, suppose you save \$1 the first day of a month, \$2 the second day, \$4 the third day, and so on. That is, each day you save twice as much as you did the day before.

57. What will you put aside for savings on the fifteenth day of the month?

58. What will you put aside for savings on the thirtieth day of the month?

59. A professional baseball player signs a contract with a beginning salary of $3,000,000 for the first year and an annual increase of 4% per year beginning in the second year. That is, beginning in year 2, the athlete's salary will be 1.04 times what it was in the previous year. What is the athlete's salary for year 7 of the contract? Round to the nearest dollar.

60. You are offered a job that pays $30,000 for the first year with an annual increase of 5% per year beginning in the second year. That is, beginning in year 2, your salary will be 1.05 times what it was in the previous year. What can you expect to earn in your sixth year on the job?

61. The population of California from 1990 through 1997 is shown in the following table.

Year	1990	1991	1992	1993
Population in millions	29.76	30.15	30.54	30.94

Year	1994	1995	1996	1997
Population in millions	31.34	31.75	32.16	32.58

  a. Divide the population for each year by the population in the preceding year. Round to three decimal places and show that the population of California is increasing geometrically.

  b. Write the general term of the geometric sequence describing population growth for California n years after 1989.

  c. Estimate California's population, in millions, for the year 2000. According to the U.S. Census Bureau, California's population in 2000 was 33.87 million. How well does your geometric sequence model the actual population?

62. The population of Texas from 1990 through 1997 is shown in the following table.

Year	1990	1991	1992	1993
Population in millions	16.99	17.35	17.71	18.08

Year	1994	1995	1996	1997
Population in millions	18.46	18.85	19.25	19.65

  a. Divide the population for each year by the population in the preceding year. Round to three decimal places and show that the population of Texas is increasing geometrically.

  b. Write the general term of the geometric sequence describing population growth for Texas n years after 1989.

  c. Estimate Texas's population, in millions, for the year 2000. According to the U.S. Census Bureau, Texas's population in 2000 was 20.85 million. How well does your geometric sequence model the actual population?

Use the formula for the sum of the first n terms of a geometric sequence to solve Exercises 63–68.

In Exercises 63–64, you save $1 the first day of a month, $2 the second day, $4 the third day, continuing to double your savings each day.

63. What will your total savings be for the first 15 days?

64. What will your total savings be for the first 30 days?

65. A job pays a salary of $24,000 the first year. During the next 19 years, the salary increases by 5% each year. What is the total lifetime salary over the 20-year period? Round to the nearest dollar.

66. You are investigating two employment opportunities. Company A offers $30,000 the first year. During the next four years, the salary is guaranteed to increase by 6% per year. Company B offers $32,000 the first year, with guaranteed annual increases of 3% per year after that. Which company offers the better total salary for a five-year contract? By how much? Round to the nearest dollar.

67. A pendulum swings through an arc of 20 inches. On each successive swing, the length of the arc is 90% of the previous length.

$$20, \quad 0.9(20), \quad 0.9^2(20), \quad 0.9^3(20), \quad \dots$$

After 10 swings, what is the total length of the distance the pendulum has swung?

68. A pendulum swings through an arc of 16 inches. On each successive swing, the length of the arc is 96% of the previous length.

$$16, \quad 0.96(16), \quad (0.96)^2(16), \quad (0.96)^3(16), \quad \dots$$

After 10 swings, what is the total length of the distance the pendulum has swung?

Use the formula for the value of an annuity to solve Exercises 69–72. Round answers to the nearest dollar.

69. To save for retirement, you decide to deposit $2500 into an IRA at the end of each year for the next 40 years. If the interest rate is 9% per year compounded annually, find the value of the IRA after 40 years.

70. You decide to deposit $100 at the end of each month into an account paying 8% interest compounded monthly to save for your child's education. How much will you save over 16 years?

71. You contribute $600 at the end of each quarter to a Tax Sheltered Annuity (TSA) paying 8% annual interest compounded quarterly. Find the value of the TSA after 18 years.

72. To save for a new home, you invest $500 per month in a mutual fund with an annual rate of return of 10% compounded monthly. How much will you have saved after four years?

Use the formula for the sum of an infinite geometric series to solve Exercises 73–75.

73. A new factory in a small town has an annual payroll of $6 million. It is expected that 60% of this money will be spent in the town by factory personnel. The people in the town who receive this money are expected to spend 60% of what they receive in the town, and so on. What is the total of all this spending, called the *total economic impact* of the factory, on the town each year?

74. How much additional spending will be generated by a $10 billion tax rebate if 60% of all income is spent?

75. If the shading process shown in the figure is continued indefinitely, what fractional part of the largest square is eventually shaded?

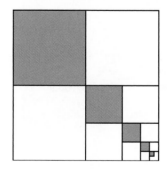

Writing in Mathematics

76. What is a geometric sequence? Give an example with your explanation.

77. What is the common ratio in a geometric sequence?

78. Explain how to find the general term of a geometric sequence.

79. Explain how to find the sum of the first n terms of a geometric sequence without having to add up all the terms.

80. What is an annuity?

81. What is the difference between a geometric sequence and an infinite geometric series?

82. How do you determine if an infinite geometric series has a sum? Explain how to find the sum of an infinite geometric series.

83. Would you rather have $10,000,000 and a brand new BMW or 1¢ today, 2¢ tomorrow, 4¢ on day 3, 8¢ on day 4, 16¢ on day 5, and so on, for 30 days? Explain.

84. For the first 30 days of a flu outbreak, the number of students on your campus who become ill is increasing. Which is worse: The number of students with the flu is increasing arithmetically or is increasing geometrically? Explain your answer.

Technology Exercises

85. Use the $\boxed{\text{SEQ}}$ (sequence) capability of a graphing utility and the formula you obtained for a_n to verify the value you found for a_7 in any three exercises from Exercises 17–24.

86. Use the capability of a graphing utility to calculate the sum of a sequence to verify any three of your answers to Exercises 31–36.

In Exercises 87–88, use a graphing utility to graph the function. Determine the horizontal asymptote for the graph of f and discuss its relationship to the sum of the given series.

Function

Series

87. $f(x) = \dfrac{2\left[1 - \left(\frac{1}{3}\right)^x\right]}{1 - \dfrac{1}{3}}$

$2 + 2\left(\frac{1}{3}\right) + 2\left(\frac{1}{3}\right)^2 + 2\left(\frac{1}{3}\right)^3 + \cdots$

88. $f(x) = \dfrac{4\left[1 - (0.6)^x\right]}{1 - 0.6}$

$4 + 4(0.6) + 4(0.6)^2 + 4(0.6)^3 + \cdots$

Critical Thinking Exercises

89. Which one of the following is true?
 a. The sequence 2, 6, 24, 120, ... is an example of a geometric sequence.
 b. The sum of the geometric series $\frac{1}{2} + \frac{1}{4} + \frac{1}{8} + \cdots + \frac{1}{512}$ can only be estimated without knowing precisely which terms occur between $\frac{1}{8}$ and $\frac{1}{512}$.
 c. $10 - 5 + \frac{5}{2} - \frac{5}{4} + \cdots = \dfrac{10}{1 - \frac{1}{2}}$
 d. If the nth term of a geometric sequence is $a_n = 3(0.5)^{n-1}$, the common ratio is $\frac{1}{2}$.

90. In a pest-eradication program, sterilized male flies are released into the general population each day. Ninety percent of those flies will survive a given day. How many flies should be released each day if the long-range goal of the program is to keep 20,000 sterilized flies in the population?

91. You are now 25 years old and would like to retire at age 55 with a retirement fund of $1,000,000. How much should you deposit at the end of each month for the next 30 years in an IRA paying 10% annual interest compounded monthly to achieve your goal? Round to the nearest dollar.

Group Exercise

92. Group members serve as a financial team analyzing the three options given to the professional baseball player described in the chapter opener on page 925. As a group, determine which option provides the most amount of money over the six-year contract and which provides the least. Describe one advantage and one disadvantage to each option.

SECTION 4.4   Counting Principles, Permutations, and Combinations

Objectives
1. Use the Fundamental Counting Principle.
2. Use the permutations formula.
3. Distinguish between permutation problems and combination problems.
4. Use the combinations formula.

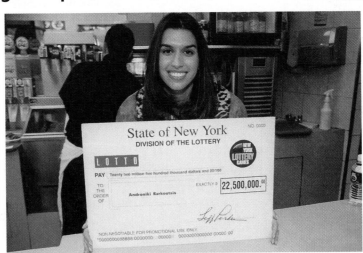

Have you ever imagined what your life would be like if you won the lottery? What changes would you make? Before you fantasize about becoming a person of leisure with a staff of obedient elves, think about this: The probability of winning top prize in the lottery is about the same as the probability of being struck by lightning. There are millions of possible number combinations in lottery games, and only one way of winning the grand prize. Determining the probability of winning involves calculating the chance of getting the winning combination from all possible outcomes. In this section, we begin preparing for the surprising world of probability by looking at methods for counting possible outcomes.

1 Use the Fundamental Counting Principle.

The Fundamental Counting Principle

It's early morning, you're groggy, and you have to select something to wear for your 8 A.M. class. (What *were* you thinking of when you signed up for a class at that hour?!) Fortunately, your "lecture wardrobe" is rather limited—just two pairs of jeans to choose from (one blue, one black), three T-shirts to choose from (one beige, one yellow, and one blue), and two pairs of sneakers to select from (one black, one red). Your possible outfits are shown in Figure 4.4.

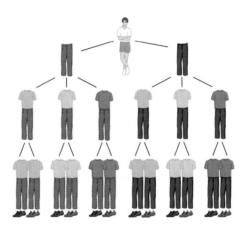

Figure 4.4 Selecting a wardrobe

The number of possible ways of playing the first four moves on each side in a game of chess is 318,979,564,000.

The **tree diagram**, so named because of its branches, shows that you can form 12 outfits from your two pairs of jeans, three T-shirts, and two pairs of sneakers. Notice that the number of outfits can be obtained by multiplying the number of choices for jeans, 2, the number of choices for T-shirts, 3, and the number of choices for sneakers, 2:

$$2 \cdot 3 \cdot 2 = 12.$$

We can generalize this idea to any two or more groups of items—not just jeans, T-shirts, and sneakers—with the **Fundamental Counting Principle:**

The Fundamental Counting Principle

The number of ways in which a series of successive things can occur is found by multiplying the number of ways in which each thing can occur.

For example, if you own 30 pairs of jeans, 20 T-shirts, and 12 pairs of sneakers, you have

$$30 \cdot 20 \cdot 12 = 7200$$

choices for your wardrobe!

EXAMPLE 1 Options in Planning a Course Schedule

Next semester you are planning to take three courses—math, English, and humanities. Based on time blocks and highly recommended professors, there are 8 sections of math, 5 of English, and 4 of humanities that you find suitable. Assuming no scheduling conflicts, how many different three-course schedules are possible?

Solution This situation involves making choices with three groups of items.

We use the Fundamental Counting Principle to find the number of three-course schedules. Multiply the number of choices for each of the three groups.

$$8 \cdot 5 \cdot 4 = 160$$

Thus, there are 160 different three-course schedules.

Check Point 1 A pizza can be ordered with three choices of size (small, medium, or large), four choices of crust (thin, thick, crispy, or regular), and six choices of toppings (ground beef, sausage, pepperoni, bacon, mushrooms, or onions). How many different one-topping pizzas can be ordered?

EXAMPLE 2 A Multiple-Choice Test

You are taking a multiple-choice test that has ten questions. Each of the questions has four answer choices, with one correct answer per question. If you select one of these four choices for each question and leave nothing blank, in how many ways can you answer the questions?

Solution We use the Fundamental Counting Principle to determine the number of ways you can answer the test. Multiply the number of choices, 4, for each of the ten questions.

$$4 \cdot 4 \cdot 4 \cdot 4 \cdot 4 \cdot 4 \cdot 4 \cdot 4 \cdot 4 \cdot 4 = 4^{10} = 1,048,576$$

Thus, you can answer the questions in 1,048,576 different ways.

Are you surprised that there are over one million ways of answering a ten-question multiple-choice test? Of course, there is only one way to answer the test and receive a perfect score. The probability of guessing your way into a perfect score involves calculating the chance of getting a perfect score, just one way, from all 1,048,576 possible outcomes. In short, prepare for the test and do not rely on guessing!

Check Point 2 You are taking a multiple-choice test that has six questions. Each of the questions has three answer choices, with one correct answer per question. If you select one of these three choices for each question and leave nothing blank, in how many ways can you answer the questions?

Permutations and Rubik's Cube

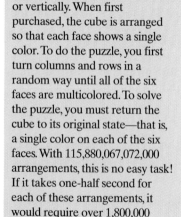

First developed in Hungary in the 1970s by Erno Rubik, a Rubik's cube contains 26 small cubes. The square faces of the cubes are colored in six different colors. The cubes can be twisted horizontally or vertically. When first purchased, the cube is arranged so that each face shows a single color. To do the puzzle, you first turn columns and rows in a random way until all of the six faces are multicolored. To solve the puzzle, you must return the cube to its original state—that is, a single color on each of the six faces. With 115,880,067,072,000 arrangements, this is no easy task! If it takes one-half second for each of these arrangements, it would require over 1,800,000 years to move the cube into all possible arrangements.

EXAMPLE 3   Telephone Numbers in the United States

Telephone numbers in the United States begin with three-digit area codes followed by seven-digit local telephone numbers. Area codes and local telephone numbers cannot begin with 0 or 1. How many different telephone numbers are possible?

Solution   This situation involves making choices with ten groups of items.

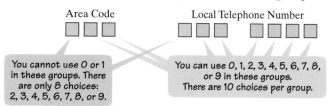

Area Code

Local Telephone Number

You cannot use 0 or 1 in these groups. There are only 8 choices: 2, 3, 4, 5, 6, 7, 8, or 9.

You can use 0, 1, 2, 3, 4, 5, 6, 7, 8, or 9 in these groups. There are 10 choices per group.

We use the Fundamental Counting Principle to determine the number of different telephone numbers that are possible. The total number of telephone numbers possible is

$$8 \cdot 10 \cdot 10 \cdot 8 \cdot 10 \cdot 10 \cdot 10 \cdot 10 \cdot 10 \cdot 10 = 6,400,000,000.$$

There are six billion four hundred million different telephone numbers that are possible.

> **Check Point 3**
>
> License plates in a particular state display two letters followed by three numbers, such as AT-887 or BB-013. How many different license plates can be manufactured?

2 Use the permutations formula.

Permutations

You are the coach of a little league baseball team. There are 13 players on the team (and lots of parents hovering in the background, dreaming of stardom for their little "Barry Bonds"). You need to choose a batting order having 9 players. The order makes a difference, because, for instance, if bases are loaded and "Little Barry" is fourth or fifth at bat, his possible home run will drive in three additional runs. How many batting orders can you form?

You can choose any of 13 players for the first person at bat. Then you will have 12 players from which to choose the second batter, then 11 from which to choose the third batter, and so on. The situation can be shown as follows:

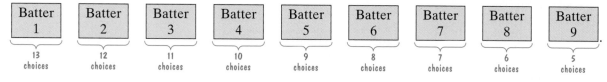

Batter 1	Batter 2	Batter 3	Batter 4	Batter 5	Batter 6	Batter 7	Batter 8	Batter 9
13 choices	12 choices	11 choices	10 choices	9 choices	8 choices	7 choices	6 choices	5 choices

We use the Fundamental Counting Principle to find the number of batting orders. The total number of batting orders is

$$13 \cdot 12 \cdot 11 \cdot 10 \cdot 9 \cdot 8 \cdot 7 \cdot 6 \cdot 5 = 259,459,200.$$

Nearly 260 million batting orders are possible for your 13-player little league team. Each batting order is called a *permutation* of 13 players taken 9 at a time. The number of permutations of 13 players taken 9 at a time is 259,459,200. A **permutation** is an ordered arrangement of items that occurs when

- No item is used more than once. (Each of the 9 players in the batting order bats exactly once.)
- The order of arrangement makes a difference.

We can obtain a formula for finding the number of permutations by rewriting our computation:

$$13 \cdot 12 \cdot 11 \cdot 10 \cdot 9 \cdot 8 \cdot 7 \cdot 6 \cdot 5$$

$$= \frac{13 \cdot 12 \cdot 11 \cdot 10 \cdot 9 \cdot 8 \cdot 7 \cdot 6 \cdot 5 \cdot \; 4 \cdot \boxed{3 \cdot 2 \cdot 1 \cdot 1}}{4 \cdot \boxed{3 \cdot 2 \cdot 1 \cdot 1}} = \frac{13!}{4!} = \frac{13!}{(13 - 9)!}.$$

Thus, the number of permutations of 13 things taken 9 at a time is $\frac{13!}{(13-9)!}$. The special notation $_{13}P_9$ is used to replace the phrase "the number of permutations of 13 things taken 9 at a time." Using this new notation, we can write

$$_{13}P_9 = \frac{13!}{(13 - 9)!}.$$

The numerator of this expression is the number of items, 13 team members, expressed as a factorial: 13! The denominator is also a factorial. It is the factorial of the difference between the number of items, 13, and the number of items in each permutation, 9 batters: $(13 - 9)!$.

The notation $_nP_r$ means the **number of permutations of n things taken r at a time.** We can generalize from the situation in which 9 batters were taken from 13 players. By generalizing, we obtain the following formula for the number of permuations if r items are taken from n items:

Permutations of n Things Taken r at a Time

The number of possible permutations if r items are taken from n items is

$$_nP_r = \frac{n!}{(n - r)!}.$$

Because all permutation problems are also Fundamental Counting problems, they can be solved using the formula for $_nP_r$, or using the Fundamental Counting Principle.

Technology

Graphing utilities have a menu item for calculating permutations, usually labeled $\boxed{_nP_r}$. For example, to find $_{20}P_3$, the keystrokes are:

20 $\boxed{_nP_r}$ 3 $\boxed{\text{ENTER}}$.

If you are using a scientific calculator, check your manual for the location of the menu item for calculating permutations and the required keystrokes.

EXAMPLE 4   Using the Formula for Permutations

You and 19 of your friends have decided to form an Internet marketing consulting firm. The group needs to choose three officers—a CEO, an operating manager, and a treasurer. In how many ways can those offices be filled?

Solution   Your group is choosing $r = 3$ officers from a group of $n = 20$ people (you and 19 friends). The order in which the officers are chosen matters because the CEO, the operating manager, and the treasurer each have different responsibilities. Thus, we are looking for the number of permutations of 20 things taken 3 at a time. We use the formula

$$_nP_r = \frac{n!}{(n - r)!}$$

with $n = 20$ and $r = 3$.

$$_{20}P_3 = \frac{20!}{(20 - 3)!} = \frac{20!}{17!} = \frac{20 \cdot 19 \cdot 18 \cdot 17!}{17!} = \frac{20 \cdot 19 \cdot 18 \cdot \cancel{17!}}{\cancel{17!}} = 20 \cdot 19 \cdot 18 = 6840$$

Thus, there are 6840 different ways of filling the three offices.

> **Check Point 4**
> A corporation has seven members on its board of directors. In how many different ways can it elect a president, vice-president, secretary, and treasurer?

EXAMPLE 5 Using the Formula for Permutations

You need to arrange seven of your favorite books along a small shelf. How many different ways can you arrange the books, assuming that the order of the books makes a difference to you?

Solution Because you are using all seven of your books in every possible arrangement, you are arranging $r = 7$ books from a group of $n = 7$ books. Thus, we are looking for the number of permutations of 7 things taken 7 at a time. We use the formula

$$_nP_r = \frac{n!}{(n-r)!}$$

with $n = 7$ and $r = 7$.

$$_7P_7 = \frac{7!}{(7-7)!} = \frac{7!}{0!} = \frac{7!}{1} = 5040$$

Thus, you can arrange the books in 5040 ways. There are 5040 different possible permutations.

> **Check Point 5**
> In how many ways can 6 books be lined up along a shelf?

3 Distinguish between permutation problems and combination problems.

Combinations

As the twentieth century drew to a close, *Time* magazine presented a series of special issues on the most influential people of the century. In their issue on heroes and icons (June 14, 1999), they discussed a number of people whose careers became more profitable after their tragic deaths, including Marilyn Monroe, James Dean, Jim Morrison, Kurt Cobain, and Selena.

Imagine that you ask your friends the following question: "Of these five people, which three would you select to be included in a documentary featuring the best of their work?" You are not asking your friends to rank their three favorite artists in any kind of order—they should merely select the three to be included in the documentary.

One friend answers, "Jim Morrison, Kurt Cobain, and Selena." Another responds, "Selena, Kurt Cobain, and Jim Morrison." These two people have the same artists in their group of selections, even if they are named in a different order. We are interested *in which artists are named, not the order in which they are named* for the documentary. Because the items are taken without regard to order, this is not a permutation problem. No ranking of any sort is involved.

Later on, you ask your roommate which three artists she would select for the documentary. She names Marilyn Monroe, James Dean, and Selena. Her selection is different from those of your two other friends because different entertainers are cited.

Marilyn Monroe, actress (1927–1962)

Selena, musician of Tejano music
(1971–1995)

Jim Morrison, musician and lead
singer of The Doors (1943–1971)

Kurt Cobain, musician and front man
for Nirvana (1967–1994)

James Dean, actor (1931–1955)

Mathematicians describe the group of artists given by your roommate as a *combination*. A **combination** of items occurs when

- The items are selected from the same group (the five stars who died young and tragically).
- No item is used more than once. (You may adore Selena, but your three selections cannot be Selena, Selena, and Selena).
- The order of items makes no difference. (Morrison, Cobain, Selena is the same group in the documentary as Selena, Cobain, Morrison.)

Do you see the difference between a permutation and a combination? A permutation is an ordered arrangement of a given group of items. A combination is a group of items taken without regard to their order. **Permutation** problems involve situations in which **order matters. Combination** problems involve situations in which the **order** of items **makes no difference.**

EXAMPLE 6 Distinguishing between Permutations and Combinations

For each of the following problems, explain whether the problem is one involving permutations or combinations. (It is not necessary to solve the problem.)

a. Six candidates are running for president, chief technology officer, and director of marketing of an Internet company. The candidate with the greatest number of votes becomes the president, the second biggest vote-getter becomes chief technology officer, and the candidate who gets the third largest number of votes will be director of marketing. How many different outcomes are possible for these three positions?

b. From the six candidates who desire to hold office in an Internet company, a three-person committee is formed to study ways of finding new investors. How many different committees could be formed?

Solution

   a. Voters are choosing three officers from six candidates. The order in which the officers are chosen makes a difference because each of the offices (president, chief technology officer, and director of marketing) is different. Order matters. This is a problem involving permutations. (How many permutations are possible if three candidates are elected from six candidates?)

   b. A three-person committee is to be formed from the six candidates. The order in which the three people are selected does not matter because they are not filling different roles on the committee. Because order makes no difference, this is a problem involving combinations. (How many different combinations of three people can be chosen from a group of six people?)

> **Check Point 6**
>
> For each of the following problems, explain whether the problem is one involving permutations or combinations. (It is not necessary to solve the problem.)
>
>   **a.** How many ways can you select 6 free videos from a list of 200 videos?
>
>   **b.** In a race in which there are 50 runners and no ties, in how many ways can the first three finishers come in?

4 Use the combinations formula.

   The notation $_nC_r$ means the **number of combinations of n things taken r at a time.** In general, there are $r!$ times as many permutations of n things taken r at a time as there are combinations of n things taken r at a time. Thus, we find the number of combinations of n things taken r at a time by dividing the number of permutations of n things taken r at a time by $r!$.

$$_nC_r = \frac{_nP_r}{r!} = \frac{\frac{n!}{(n-r)!}}{r!} = \frac{n!}{(n-r)!\,r!}$$

Combinations of n Things Taken r at a Time

The number of possible combinations if r items are taken from n items is

$$_nC_r = \frac{n!}{(n-r)!\,r!}.$$

   Notice that the formula for $_nC_r$ is the same as the formula for the binomial coefficient $\binom{n}{r}$.

   We cannot find the number of combinations if r items are taken from n items using the Fundamental Counting Principle. We must use the formula shown in the box to do so.

EXAMPLE 7   Using the Formula for Combinations

A three-person committee is needed to study ways of improving public transportation. How many committees could be formed from the eight people on the board of supervisors?

Solution   The order in which the three people are selected does not matter. This is a problem of selecting $r = 3$ people from a group of $n = 8$ people. We are looking for the number of combinations of eight things taken three at a time. We use the formula

$$_nC_r = \frac{n!}{(n-r)!\,r!}$$

with $n = 8$ and $r = 3$.

$$_8C_3 = \frac{8!}{(8-3)!\,3!} = \frac{8!}{5!\,3!} = \frac{8 \cdot 7 \cdot 6 \cdot 5!}{5! \cdot 3 \cdot 2 \cdot 1} = \frac{8 \cdot 7 \cdot 6 \cdot \cancel{5!}}{\cancel{5!} \cdot 3 \cdot 2 \cdot 1} = 56$$

Thus, 56 committees of three people each can be formed from the eight people on the board of supervisors.

Check Point 7   From a group of 10 physicians, in how many ways can four people be selected to attend a conference on acupuncture?

EXAMPLE 8   Using the Formula for Combinations

In poker, a person is dealt 5 cards from a standard 52-card deck. The order in which you are dealt the 5 cards does not matter. How many different 5-card poker hands are possible?

Solution   Because the order in which the 5 cards are dealt does not matter, this is a problem involving combinations. We are looking for the number of combinations of $n = 52$ cards drawn $r = 5$ at a time. We use the formula

$$_nC_r = \frac{n!}{(n-r)!\,r!}$$

with $n = 52$ and $r = 5$.

$$_{52}C_5 = \frac{52!}{(52-5)!\,5!} = \frac{52!}{47!\,5!} = \frac{52 \cdot 51 \cdot 50 \cdot 49 \cdot 48 \cdot \cancel{47!}}{\cancel{47!} \cdot 5 \cdot 4 \cdot 3 \cdot 2 \cdot 1} = 2{,}598{,}960$$

Thus, there are 2,598,960 different 5-card poker hands possible. It surprises many people that more than 2.5 million 5-card hands can be dealt from a mere 52 cards.

Figure 4.5 A royal flush

If you are a card player, it does not get any better than to be dealt the 5-card poker hand shown in Figure 4.5. This hand is called a *royal flush*. It consists of an ace, king, queen, jack, and 10, all of the same suit: all hearts, all diamonds, all clubs, or all spades. The probability of being dealt a royal flush involves calculating the number of ways of being dealt such a hand: just 4 of all 2,598,960 possible hands. In the next section, we move from counting possibilities to computing probabilities.

Check Point 8   How many different 4-card hands can be dealt from a deck that has 16 different cards?

EXERCISE SET 4.4

Practice Exercises

In Exercises 1–8, use the formula for $_nP_r$ to evaluate each expression.

1. $_9P_4$
2. $_7P_3$
3. $_8P_5$
4. $_{10}P_4$
5. $_6P_6$
6. $_9P_9$
7. $_8P_0$
8. $_6P_0$

In Exercises 9–16, use the formula for $_nC_r$ to evaluate each expression.

9. $_9C_5$
10. $_{10}C_6$
11. $_{11}C_4$
12. $_{12}C_5$
13. $_7C_7$
14. $_4C_4$
15. $_5C_0$
16. $_6C_0$

In Exercises 17–20, does the problem involve permutations or combinations? Explain your answer. (It is not necessary to solve the problem.)

17. A medical researcher needs 6 people to test the effectiveness of an experimental drug. If 13 people have volunteered for the test, in how many ways can 6 people be selected?   *Combination*

18. Fifty people purchase raffle tickets. Three winning tickets are selected at random. If first prize is $1000, second prize is $500, and third prize is $100, in how many different ways can the prizes be awarded?

19. How many different four-letter passwords can be formed from the letters A, B, C, D, E, F, and G if no repetition of letters is allowed?

20. Fifty people purchase raffle tickets. Three winning tickets are selected at random. If each prize is $500, in how many different ways can the prizes be awarded?

Application Exercises

Use the Fundamental Counting Principle to solve Exercises 21–32.

21. The model of the car you are thinking of buying is available in nine different colors and three different styles (hatchback, sedan, or station wagon). In how many ways can you order the car?

22. A popular brand of pen is available in three colors (red, green, or blue) and four writing tips (bold, medium, fine, or micro). How many different choices of pens do you have with this brand?

23. An ice cream store sells two drinks (sodas or milk shakes), in four sizes (small, medium, large, or jumbo), and five flavors (vanilla, strawberry, chocolate, coffee, or pistachio). In how many ways can a customer order a drink?

24. A restaurant offers the following lunch menu.

Main Course	Vegetables	Beverages	Desserts
Ham	Potatoes	Coffee	Cake
Chicken	Peas	Tea	Pie
Fish	Green beans	Milk	Ice cream
Beef		Soda	

$4(3)(4)(3) = 144$

If one item is selected from each of the four groups, in how many ways can a meal be ordered? Describe two such orders.

25. You are taking a multiple-choice test that has five questions. Each of the questions has three choices, with one correct choice per question. If you select one of these options per question and leave nothing blank, in how many ways can you answer the questions?

26. You are taking a multiple-choice test that has eight questions. Each of the questions has three answer choices, with one correct answer per question. If you select one of these three choices for each question and leave nothing blank, in how many ways can you answer the questions?

27. In the original plan for area codes in 1945, the first digit could be any number from 2 through 9, the second digit was either 0 or 1, and the third digit could be any number except 0. With this plan, how many different area codes were possible?

28. How many different four-letter radio station call letters can be formed if the first letter must be W or K?

29. Six performers are to present their comedy acts on a weekend evening at a comedy club. One of the performers insists on being the last stand-up comic of the evening. If this performer's request is granted, how many different ways are there to schedule the appearances?

30. Five singers are to perform at a night club. One of the singers insists on being the last performer of the evening. If this singer's request is granted, how many different ways are there to schedule the appearances?

31. In the *Cambridge Encyclopedia of Language* (Cambridge University Press, 1987), author David Crystal presents five sentences that make a reasonable paragraph regardless of their order. The sentences are

> Mark had told him about the foxes.
> John looked out the window.
> Could it be a fox?
> However, nobody had seen one for months.
> He thought he saw a shape in the bushes.

How many different five-sentence paragraphs can be formed if the paragraph begins with "He thought he saw a shape in the bushes" and ends with "John looked out of the window"?

32. A television programmer is arranging the order that five movies will be seen between the hours of 6 P.M. and 4 A.M. Two of the movies have a G rating, and they are to be shown in the first two time blocks. One of the movies is rated NC-17, and it is to be shown in the last of the time blocks, from 2 A.M. until 4 A.M. Given these restrictions, in how many ways can the five movies be arranged during the indicated time blocks?

Use the formula for $_nP_r$ to solve Exercises 33–40.

33. A club with ten members is to choose three officers— president, vice-president, and secretary-treasurer. If each office is to be held by one person and no person can hold more than one office, in how many ways can those offices be filled?

34. A corporation has ten members on its board of directors. In how many different ways can it elect a president, vice-president, secretary, and treasurer?

35. For a segment of a radio show, a disc jockey can play 7 records. If there are 13 records to select from, in how many ways can the program for this segment be arranged?

36. Suppose you are asked to list, in order of preference, the three best movies you have seen this year. If you saw 20 movies during the year, in how many ways can the three best be chosen and ranked?

37. In a race in which six automobiles are entered and there are no ties, in how many ways can the first three finishers come in?

38. In a production of *West Side Story*, eight actors are considered for the male roles of Tony, Riff, and Bernardo. In how many ways can the director cast the male roles?

39. Nine bands have volunteered to perform at a benefit concert, but there is only enough time for five of the bands to play. How many lineups are possible?

40. How many arrangements can be made using four of the letters of the word COMBINE if no letter is to be used more than once?

Use the formula for $_nC_r$ to solve Exercises 41–48.

41. An election ballot asks voters to select three city commissioners from a group of six candidates. In how many ways can this be done?

42. A four-person committee is to be elected from an organization's membership of 11 people. How many different committees are possible?

43. Of 12 possible books, you plan to take 4 with you on vacation. How many different collections of 4 books can you take?

44. There are 14 standbys who hope to get seats on a flight, but only 6 seats are available on the plane. How many different ways can the 6 people be selected?

45. You volunteer to help drive children at a charity event to the zoo, but you can fit only 8 of the 17 children present in your van. How many different groups of 8 children can you drive?

46. Of the 100 people in the U.S. Senate, 18 serve on the Foreign Relations Committee. How many ways are there to select Senate members for this committee (assuming party affiliation is not a factor in selection)?

47. To win at LOTTO in the state of Florida, one must correctly select 6 numbers from a collection of 53 numbers (1 through 53). The order in which the selection is made does not matter. How many different selections are possible?

48. To win in the New York State lottery, one must correctly select 6 numbers from 59 numbers. The order in which the selection is made does not matter. How many different selections are possible?

In Exercises 49–58, solve by the method of your choice.

49. In a race in which six automobiles are entered and there are no ties, in how many ways can the first four finishers come in?

50. A book club offers a choice of 8 books from a list of 40. In how many ways can a member make a selection?

51. A medical researcher needs 6 people to test the effectiveness of an experimental drug. If 13 people have volunteered for the test, in how many ways can 6 people be selected?

52. Fifty people purchase raffle tickets. Three winning tickets are selected at random. If first prize is $1000, second prize is $500, and third prize is $100, in how many different ways can the prizes be awarded?

53. From a club of 20 people, in how many ways can a group of three members be selected to attend a conference?

54. Fifty people purchase raffle tickets. Three winning tickets are selected at random. If each prize is $500, in how many different ways can the prizes be awarded?

55. How many different four-letter passwords can be formed from the letters A, B, C, D, E, F, and G if no repetition of letters is allowed?

56. Nine comedy acts will perform over two evenings. Five of the acts will perform on the first evening and the order in which the acts perform is important. How many ways can the schedule for the first evening be made?

57. Using 15 flavors of ice cream, how many cones with three different flavors can you create if it is important to you which flavor goes on the top, middle, and bottom?

58. Baskin-Robbins offers 31 different flavors of ice cream. One of their items is a bowl consisting of three scoops of ice cream, each a different flavor. How many such bowls are possible?

Writing in Mathematics

59. Explain the Fundamental Counting Principle.

60. Write an original problem that can be solved using the Fundamental Counting Principle. Then solve the problem.

61. What is a permutation?

62. Describe what $_nP_r$ represents.

63. Write a word problem that can be solved by evaluating $_7P_3$.

64. What is a combination?

65. Explain how to distinguish between permutation and combination problems.

66. Write a word problem that can be solved by evaluating $_7C_3$.

Technology Exercises

67. Use a graphing utility with an $\boxed{_nP_r}$ menu item to verify your answers in Exercises 1–8.

68. Use a graphing utility with an $\boxed{_nC_r}$ menu item to verify your answers in Exercises 9–16.

Critical Thinking Exercises

69. Which one of the following is true?
  a. The number of ways to choose four questions out of ten questions on an essay test is $_{10}P_4$.
  b. If $r > 1$, $_nP_r$ is less than $_nC_r$.
  c. $_7P_3 = 3!\,_7C_3$
  d. The number of ways to pick a winner and first runner-up in a piano recital with 20 contestants is $_{20}C_2$.

70. Five men and five women line up at a checkout counter in a store. In how many ways can they line up if the first person in line is a woman, and the people in line alternate woman, man, woman, man, and so on?

71. How many four-digit odd numbers less than 6000 can be formed using the digits 2, 4, 6, 7, 8, and 9? Digits may be repeated.

72. If a collection of n objects has n_1 identical objects of the same type, n_2 identical objects of a second kind, n_3 of a third kind, and so on for a total of $n = n_1 + n_2 + \cdots + n_k$ objects, the number of distinguishable permutations of the n objects is given by

$$\frac{n!}{n_1!\,n_2!\,n_3!\cdots n_k!}.$$

Use this formula to find the number of different signals consisting of eight flags that can be made using three white flags, four red flags and one blue flag.

Group Exercise

73. The group should select real-world situations where the Fundamental Counting Principle can be applied. These could involve the number of possible student ID numbers on your campus, the number of possible phone numbers in your community, the number of meal options at a local restaurant, the number of ways a person in the group can select outfits for class, the number of ways a condominium can be purchased in a nearby community, and so on. Once situations have been selected, group members should determine in how many ways each part of the task can be done. Group members will need to obtain menus, find out about telephone-digit requirements in the community, count shirts, pants, shoes in closets, visit condominium sales offices, and so on. Once the group reassembles, apply the Fundamental Counting Principle to determine the number of available options in each situation. Because these numbers may be quite large, use a calculator.

SECTION 4.5 *Probability*

Objectives

1. Compute empirical probability.
2. Compute theoretical probability.
3. Find the probability that an event will not occur.
4. Find the probability of one event or a second event occurring.
5. Find the probability of one event and a second event occurring.

Table 4.3   Number of Americans and the Hours of Sleep They Get on a Typical Night

Hours of Sleep	Number of Americans, in millions
4 or less	11.36
5	25.56
6	71
7	85.2
8	76.68
9	8.52
10 or more	5.68
	Total: 284

Source: Discovery Health Media

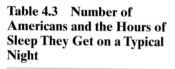

1 Compute empirical probability.

How many hours of sleep do you typically get each night? Table 11.3 indicates that 71 million out of 284 million Americans are getting six hours of sleep on a typical night. The *probability* of an American getting six hours of sleep on a typical night is $\frac{71}{284}$. This fraction can be reduced to $\frac{1}{4}$, or expressed as 0.25 or 25%. Thus, 25% of Americans get six hours of sleep each night.

We find a probability by dividing one number by another. Probabilities are assigned to an *event*, such as getting six hours of sleep on a typical night. Events that are certain to occur are assigned probabilities of 1, or 100%. For example, the probability that a given individual will eventually die is 1. Regrettably, taxes and death are always certain! By contrast, if an event cannot occur, its probability is 0. For example, the probability that Elvis will return from the dead and serenade us with one final reprise of "Heartbreak Hotel" is 0.

Probabilities of events are expressed as numbers ranging from 0 to 1, or 0% to 100%. The closer the probability of a given event is to 1, the more likely it is that the event will occur. The closer the probability of a given event is to 0, the less likely it is that the event will occur.

Empirical Probability

Empirical probability applies to situations in which we observe how frequently an event occurs. We use the following formula to compute the empirical probability of an event:

Computing Empirical Probability

The **empirical probability** of event E is

$$P(E) = \frac{\text{observed number of times } E \text{ occurs}}{\text{total number of observed occurrences}}.$$

EXAMPLE 1 Computing Empirical Probability

There are approximately 3 million Arab Americans in the United States. The circle graph in Figure 4.6 shows that the majority of Arab Americans are Christian. If an Arab American is selected at random, find the empirical probability of selecting a Catholic.

Solution The probability of selecting a Catholic is the observed number of Arab Americans who are Catholic, 1.26 (million), divided by the total number of Arab Americans, 3 (million).

P (selecting a Catholic from the Arab-American population)

$$= \frac{\text{number of Arab Americans who are Catholic}}{\text{total number of Arab Americans}} = \frac{1.26}{3.00} = \frac{126}{300} = 0.42$$

The empirical probability of selecting a Catholic from the Arab-American population is $\frac{126}{300}$, or 0.42. Equivalently, 42% of Arab Americans are Catholic.

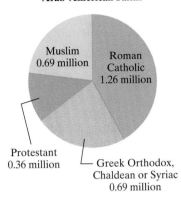

Arab-American Faiths

Muslim 0.69 million
Roman Catholic 1.26 million
Protestant 0.36 million
Greek Orthodox, Chaldean or Syriac 0.69 million

Figure 4.6
Source: Arab-American Institute

Check Point 1 If an Arab American is selected at random, find the empirical probability of selecting a Muslim.

Theoretical Probability

2 Compute theoretical probability.

You toss a coin. Although it is equally likely to land either heads up, denoted by H, or tails up, denoted by T, the actual outcome is uncertain. Any occurrence for which the outcome is uncertain is called an **experiment.** Thus, tossing a coin is an example of an experiment. The set of all possible outcomes of an experiment is the **sample space** of the experiment, denoted by S. The sample space for the coin-tossing experiment is

$$S = \{H, T\}.$$

Lands heads up   Lands tails up

We can define an event more formally using these concepts. An **event,** denoted by E, is any subcollection, or subset, of a sample space. For example, the subset $E = \{T\}$ is the event of landing tails up when a coin is tossed.

Theoretical probability applies to situations like this, in which the sample space only contains equally-likely outcomes, all of which are known. To calculate the theoretical probability of an event, we divide the number of outcomes resulting in the event by the total number of outcomes in the sample space.

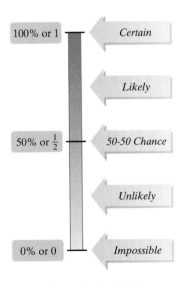

100% or 1 — Certain
Likely
50% or ½ — 50-50 Chance
Unlikely
0% or 0 — Impossible

Possible Values for Probabilities

Computing Theoretical Probability

If an event E has $n(E)$ equally-likely outcomes and its sample space S has $n(S)$ equally-likely outcomes, the theoretical probability of event E, denoted by $P(E)$, is

$$P(E) = \frac{\text{number of outcomes in event } E}{\text{number of outcomes in sample space } S} = \frac{n(E)}{n(S)}.$$

The sum of the theoretical probabilities of all possible outcomes in the sample space is 1.

How can we use this formula to compute the probability of a coin landing tails up? We use the following sets:

$$E = \{T\} \qquad S = \{H, T\}.$$

This is the event of landing tails up.

This is the sample space with all equally–likely outcomes.

The probability of a coin landing tails up is

$$P(E) = \frac{n(E)}{n(S)} = \frac{1}{2}.$$

Theoretical probability applies to many games of chance, including dice rolling, lotteries, card games, and roulette. The next example deals with the experiment of rolling a die. Figure 4.7 illustrates that when a die is rolled, there are six equally-likely outcomes. The sample space can be shown as

$$S = \{1, 2, 3, 4, 5, 6\}.$$

EXAMPLE 2 Computing Theoretical Probability

A die is rolled once. Find the probability of getting a number less than 5.

Solution   The sample space of equally-likely outcomes is $S = \{1, 2, 3, 4, 5, 6\}$. There are six outcomes in the sample space, so $n(S) = 6$.

We are interested in the probability of getting a number less than 5. The event of getting a number less than 5 can be represented by

$$E = \{1, 2, 3, 4\}.$$

There are four outcomes in this event, so $n(E) = 4$.

The probability of rolling a number less than 5 is

$$P(E) = \frac{n(E)}{n(S)} = \frac{4}{6} = \frac{2}{3}.$$

Check Point 2   A die is rolled once. Find the probability of getting a number greater than 4.

Figure 4.7 Outcomes when a die is rolled

EXAMPLE 3 Computing Theoretical Probability

Two ordinary six-sided dice are rolled. What is the probability of getting a sum of 8?

Solution   Each die has six equally-likely outcomes. By the Fundamental Counting Principle, there are $6 \cdot 6$, or 36, equally-likely outcomes in the sample space. That is, $n(S) = 36$. The 36 outcomes are shown below as ordered pairs. The five ways of rolling a sum of 8 appear in the green highlighted diagonal.

Surprising Probabilities

Imagine that one person is randomly selected from all 6 billion people on planet Earth. The following empirical probabilities, each rounded to two decimal places, might surprise you.

Probability of selecting

a woman	= 0.51
a non-white	= 0.7
a non-Christian	= 0.7
a person who cannot read	= 0.7
a person suffering from malnutrition	= 0.5
a person with a college education	= 0.01
a person who is near death	= 0.01

Source: United Nations

		Second Die					
		⚀	⚁	⚂	⚃	⚄	⚅
First Die	⚀	(1,1)	(1,2)	(1,3)	(1,4)	(1,5)	(1,6)
	⚁	(2,1)	(2,2)	(2,3)	(2,4)	(2,5)	(2,6)
	⚂	(3,1)	(3,2)	(3,3)	(3,4)	(3,5)	(3,6)
	⚃	(4,1)	(4,2)	(4,3)	(4,4)	(4,5)	(4,6)
	⚄	(5,1)	(5,2)	(5,3)	(5,4)	(5,5)	(5,6)
	⚅	(6,1)	(6,2)	(6,3)	(6,4)	(6,5)	(6,6)

$$S = \{(1,1), (1,2), (1,3), (1,4),$$
$$(1,5), (1,6), (2,1), (2,2),$$
$$(2,3), (2,4), (2,5), (2,6),$$
$$(3,1), (3,2), (3,3), (3,4),$$
$$(3,5), (3,6), (4,1), (4,2),$$
$$(4,3), (4,4), (4,5), (4,6),$$
$$(5,1), (5,2), (5,3), (5,4),$$
$$(5,5), (5,6), (6,1), (6,2),$$
$$(6,3), (6,4), (6,5), (6,6)\}$$

The phrase "getting a sum of 8" describes the event

$$E = \{(6,2), (5,3), (4,4), (3,5), (2,6)\}.$$

This event has 5 outcomes, so $n(E) = 5$. Thus, the probability of getting a sum of 8 is

$$P(E) = \frac{n(E)}{n(S)} = \frac{5}{36}.$$

Check Point 3 What is the probability of getting a sum of 5 when two six-sided dice are rolled?

Computing Theoretical Probability Without Listing an Event and the Sample Space

In some situations, we can compute theoretical probability without having to write out each event and each sample space. For example, suppose you are dealt one card from a standard 52-card deck, illustrated in Figure 4.8. The deck has four suits: Hearts and diamonds are red, and clubs and spades are black. Each suit has 13 different face values—A(ace), 2, 3, 4, 5, 6, 7, 8, 9, 10, J(jack), Q(queen), and K(king). Jacks, queens, and kings are called **picture cards** or **face cards.**

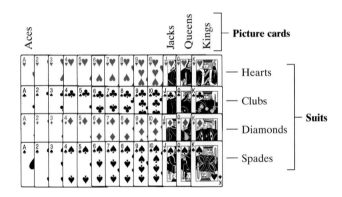

Figure 4.8 A standard 52-card bridge deck

EXAMPLE 4   Probability and a Deck of 52 Cards

You are dealt one card from a standard 52-card deck. Find the probability of being dealt a heart.

Solution Let E be the event of being dealt a heart. Because there are 13 hearts in the deck, the event of being dealt a heart can occur in 13 ways. The number of outcomes resulting in event E is 13: $n(E) = 13$. With 52 cards in the deck, the total number of possible ways of being dealt a single card is 52. The number of outcomes in the sample space is 52: $n(S) = 52$. The probability of being dealt a heart is

$$P(E) = \frac{n(E)}{n(S)} = \frac{13}{52} = \frac{1}{4}.$$

Check Point 4 If you are dealt one card from a standard 52-card deck, find the probability of being dealt a king.

State lotteries keep 50 cents on the dollar, resulting in $10 billion a year for public funding.

If your state has a lottery drawing each week, the probability that someone will win the top prize is relatively high. If there is no winner this week, it is virtually certain that eventually someone will be graced with millions of dollars. So how come you are unlucky compared to this undisclosed someone? In Example 5, we provide an answer to this question, using the counting principles discussed in Section 4.4.

EXAMPLE 5 **Probability and Combinations: Winning the Lottery**

Florida's lottery game, LOTTO, is set up so that each player chooses six different numbers from 1 to 53. If the six numbers chosen match the six numbers drawn randomly twice weekly, the player wins (or shares) the top cash prize. (As of this writing, the top cash prize has ranged from $7 million to $106.5 million.) With one LOTTO ticket, what is the probability of winning this prize?

Solution   Because the order of the six numbers does not matter, this is a situation involving combinations. Let E be the event of winning the lottery with one ticket. With one LOTTO ticket, there is only one way of winning. Thus, $n(E) = 1$. The sample space is the set of all possible six-number combinations. We can use the combinations formula

$$_nC_r = \frac{n!}{(n-r)!\,r!}$$

to find the total number of possible combinations. We are selecting $r = 6$ numbers from a collection of $n = 53$ numbers.

$$_{53}C_6 = \frac{53!}{(53-6)!\,6!} = \frac{53!}{47!\,6!} = \frac{53 \cdot 52 \cdot 51 \cdot 50 \cdot 49 \cdot 48 \cdot \cancel{47!}}{\cancel{47!} \cdot 6 \cdot 5 \cdot 4 \cdot 3 \cdot 2 \cdot 1} = 22{,}957{,}480$$

There are nearly 23 million number combinations possible in LOTTO. If a person buys one LOTTO ticket, the probability of winning is

$$P(E) = \frac{n(E)}{n(S)} = \frac{1}{22{,}957{,}480} \approx 0.0000000436.$$

The probability of winning the top prize with one LOTTO ticket is $\frac{1}{22{,}957{,}480}$, or about 1 in 23 million.

In 2001, Americans spent nearly 18 billion dollars on lotteries set up by revenue-hungry states. If a pigeon, er, person, buys, say 5000 different tickets in Florida's LOTTO, that person has selected 5000 different combinations of the six numbers. The probability of winning is

$$\frac{5000}{22{,}957{,}480} \approx 0.000218.$$

The chances of winning top prize are about 218 in a million. At $1 per LOTTO ticket, it is highly probable that Mr. or Ms. Pigeon will be $5000 poorer.

Comparing the Probability of Dying to the Probability of Winning Florida's LOTTO

As a healthy nonsmoking 30-year-old, your probability of dying this year is approximately 0.001. Divide this probability by the probability of winning LOTTO with one ticket:

$$\frac{0.001}{0.0000000436} \approx 22{,}936.$$

A healthy 30-year-old is nearly 23,000 times more likely to die this year than to win Florida's lottery.

Check Point 5   People lose interest when they do not win at games of chance, including Florida's LOTTO. With drawings twice weekly instead of once, the game described in Example 5 was brought in to bring back lost players and increase ticket sales. The original LOTTO was set up so that each player chose six different numbers from 1 to 49, rather than from 1 to 53, with a lottery drawing only once a week. With one LOTTO ticket, what was the probability of winning the top cash prize in Florida's original LOTTO? Express the answer as a fraction and as a decimal correct to ten places.

3 Find the probability that an event will not occur.

Probability of an Event Not Occurring

A survey (*source*: Penn, Schoen, and Berland) asked 500 Americans to rate their health. Of those surveyed, 270 rated their health as good/excellent. This means that $500 - 270$, or 230, people surveyed did not rate their health as good/excellent. Notice that

$$P(\text{good/excellent}) + P(\text{not good/excellent}) = \frac{270}{500} + \frac{230}{500} = \frac{500}{500} = 1.$$

In general, because the sum of the probabilities of all possible outcomes in any situation is 1,

$$P(E) + P(\text{not } E) = 1.$$

We now solve this equation for $P(\text{not } E)$, the probability that event E will not occur, by subtracting $P(E)$ from both sides. The resulting formula is given in the following box:

The Probability of an Event Not Occurring

The probability that an event E will not occur is equal to one minus the probability that it will occur.

$$P(\text{not } E) = 1 - P(E)$$

EXAMPLE 6   The Probability of Not Winning the Lottery

We have seen that the probability of winning Florida's LOTTO with one ticket is $\frac{1}{22,957,480}$. What is the probability of not winning?

Solution

$$P(\text{not winning}) = 1 - P(\text{winning}) = 1 - \frac{1}{22,957,480} = \frac{22,957,480}{22,957,480} - \frac{1}{22,957,480}$$

$$= \frac{22,957,479}{22,957,480} \approx 0.99999996$$

The probability of not winning is close to 1. It is almost certain that with one LOTTO ticket, a person will not win top prize.

> **Check Point 6** The essay on page 274 mentions that the probability of a 30-year-old dying this year is approximately $\frac{1}{1000}$. What is the probability of a 30-year-old not dying this year?

4 Find the probability of one event or a second event occurring.

Or Probabilities with Mutually Exclusive Events

Suppose that you randomly select one card from a deck of 52 cards. Let A be the event of selecting a king and B be the event of selecting a queen. Only one card is selected, so it is impossible to get both a king and a queen. The outcomes of selecting a king and a queen cannot occur simultaneously. They are called *mutually exclusive events*. If it is impossible for any two events, A and B, to occur simultaneously, they are said to be **mutually exclusive**. If A and B are mutually exclusive events, the probability that either A or B will occur is determined by adding their individual probabilities.

> **Or Probabilities with Mutually Exclusive Events**
>
> If A and B are mutually exclusive events, then
>
> $$P(A \text{ or } B) = P(A) + P(B).$$

EXAMPLE 7 **The Probability of Either of Two Mutually Exclusive Events Occurring**

If one card is randomly selected from a deck of cards, what is the probability of selecting a king or a queen?

Solution We find the probability that either of these mutually exclusive events will occur by adding their individual probabilities.

$$P(\text{king or queen}) = P(\text{king}) + P(\text{queen}) = \frac{4}{52} + \frac{4}{52} = \frac{8}{52} = \frac{2}{13}$$

The probability of selecting a king or a queen is $\frac{2}{13}$.

Check Point 7 If you roll a single, six-sided die, what is the probability of getting either a 4 or a 5?

13 Diamonds

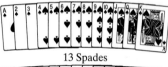

13 Hearts

13 Spades

13 Clubs

Figure 4.9 A deck of 52 cards

Or Probabilities with Events That Are Not Mutually Exclusive

Consider the deck of 52 cards shown in Figure 4.9. Suppose that these cards are shuffled and you randomly select one card from the deck. What is the probability of selecting a diamond or a picture card (jack, queen, king)? Begin by adding their individual probabilities:

$$P(\text{diamond}) + P(\text{picture card}) = \frac{13}{52} + \frac{12}{52}.$$

> There are 13 diamonds in the deck of 52 cards.

> There are 12 picture cards in the deck of 52 cards.

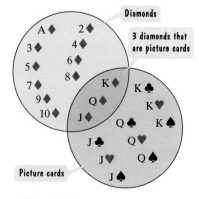

Figure 4.11

Figure 4.10 Three diamonds are picture cards.

However, this is not the probability of selecting a diamond or a picture card. The problem is that there are three cards that are simultaneously diamonds and picture cards, shown in Figure 4.10. The events of selecting a diamond and selecting a picture card are not mutually exclusive. It is possible to select a card that is both a diamond and a picture card.

The situation is illustrated in the diagram in Figure 4.11. Why can't we find the probability of selecting a diamond or a picture card by adding their individual probabilities? The diagram shows that three of the cards, the three diamonds that are picture cards, get counted twice when we add the individual probabilities. First the three cards get counted as diamonds, and then they get counted as picture cards. In order to avoid the error of counting the three cards twice, we need to subtract the probability of getting a diamond and a picture card, $\frac{3}{52}$, as follows:

P(diamond or picture card)

$$= P(\text{diamond}) + P(\text{picture card}) - P(\text{diamond and picture card})$$

$$= \frac{13}{52} + \frac{12}{52} - \frac{3}{52} = \frac{13 + 12 - 3}{52} = \frac{22}{52} = \frac{11}{26}.$$

Thus, the probability of selecting a diamond or a picture card is $\frac{11}{26}$.

In general, if A and B are events that are not mutually exclusive, the probability that A or B will occur is determined by adding their individual probabilities and then subtracting the probability that A and B occur simultaneously.

Or Probabilities with Events That Are Not Mutually Exclusive

If A and B are not mutually exclusive events, then

$$P(A \text{ or } B) = P(A) + P(B) - P(A \text{ and } B).$$

EXAMPLE 8 **An *Or* Probability with Events That Are Not Mutually Exclusive**

Figure 4.12 It is equally probable that the pointer will land on any one of the eight regions.

Figure 4.12 illustrates a spinner. It is equally probable that the pointer will land on any one of the eight regions, numbered 1 through 8. If the pointer lands on a borderline, spin again. Find the probability that the pointer will stop on an even number or on a number greater than 5.

Solution   It is possible for the pointer to land on a number that is both even and greater than 5. Two of the numbers, 6 and 8, are even and greater than 5. These events are not mutually exclusive. The probability of landing on a number that is even or greater than 5 is

$$P\left(\begin{array}{c}\text{even or}\\\text{greater than 5}\end{array}\right) = P(\text{even}) + P(\text{greater than 5}) - P\left(\begin{array}{c}\text{even and}\\\text{greater than 5}\end{array}\right)$$

$$= \frac{4}{8} + \frac{3}{8} - \frac{2}{8}$$

> Four of the eight numbers, 2, 4, 6, and 8, are even.

> Three of the eight numbers, 6, 7, and 8, are greater than 5.

> Two of the eight numbers, 6 and 8, are even and greater than 5.

$$= \frac{4 + 3 - 2}{8} = \frac{5}{8}.$$

The probability that the pointer will stop on an even number or on a number greater than 5 is $\frac{5}{8}$.

Check Point 8   Use Figure 4.12 to find the probability that the pointer will stop on an odd number or on a number less than 5.

EXAMPLE 9 An *Or* Probability with Events That Are Not Mutually Exclusive

A group of people is comprised of 15 U.S. men, 20 U.S. women, 10 Canadian men, and 5 Canadian women. If a person is selected at random from the group, find the probability that the selected person is a man or a Canadian.

Solution   The group is comprised of $15 + 20 + 10 + 5$, or 50 people. It is possible to select a man who is Canadian. We are given that there are 10 Canadian men, so these events are not mutually exclusive.

$$P(\text{man or Canadian}) = P(\text{man}) + P(\text{Canadian}) - P(\text{man and Canadian})$$

$$= \frac{25}{50} + \frac{15}{50} - \frac{10}{50}$$

Of the 50 people, 25 are men—15 U.S. men and 10 Canadian men.

Of the 50 people, 15 are Canadian—10 Canadian men and 5 Canadian women.

Of the 50 people, 10 are Canadian men.

$$= \frac{25 + 15 - 10}{50} = \frac{30}{50} = \frac{3}{5}$$

The probability of selecting a man or a Canadian is $\frac{3}{5}$.

Check Point 9   An interfaith group is comprised of 14 African-American Muslims, 12 African-American Christians, 6 Arab-American Muslims, and 8 Arab-American Christians. If one person is selected to attend a conference on shared ethical values in the faith community, find the probability that the selected person is Muslim or African American.

5 Find the probability of one event and a second event occurring.

And Probabilities with Independent Events

Suppose that you toss a fair coin two times in succession. The outcome of the first toss, heads or tails, does not affect what happens when you toss the coin a second time. For example, the occurrence of tails on the first toss does not make tails more likely or less likely to occur on the second toss. The repeated toss of a coin produces *independent events* because the outcome of one toss does not influence the outcome of others. Two events are **independent events** if the occurrence of either of them has no effect on the probability of the other.

If two events are independent, we can calculate the probability of the first occurring and the second occurring by multiplying their probabilities.

And Probabilities with Independent Events
If A and B are independent events, then
$$P(A \text{ and } B) = P(A) \cdot P(B).$$

Figure 4.13 A U.S. roulette wheel

EXAMPLE 10 Independent Events on a Roulette Wheel

Figure 4.13 shows a U.S. roulette wheel that has 38 numbered slots (1 through 36, 0, and 00). Of the 38 compartments, 18 are black, 18 are red, and two are green. A play has the dealer spin the wheel and a small ball in opposite directions. As the ball slows to a stop, it can land with equal probability on any one of the 38 numbered slots. Find the probability of red occurring on two consecutive plays.

Solution   The wheel has 38 equally-likely outcomes and 18 are red. Thus, the probability of red occurring on a play is $\frac{18}{38}$, or $\frac{9}{19}$. The result that occurs on each play is independent of all previous results. Thus,

$$P(\text{red and red}) = P(\text{red}) \cdot P(\text{red}) = \frac{9}{19} \cdot \frac{9}{19} = \frac{81}{361} \approx 0.224.$$

The probability of red occurring on two consecutive plays is $\frac{81}{361}$.

Some roulette players incorrectly believe that if red occurs on two consecutive plays, then another color is "due." Because the events are independent, the outcomes of previous spins have no effect on any other spins.

Check Point 10   Find the probability of green occurring on two consecutive plays on a roulette wheel.

The *and* rule for independent events can be extended to cover three or more events. Thus, if A, B, and C are independent events, then

$$P(A \text{ and } B \text{ and } C) = P(A) \cdot P(B) \cdot P(C).$$

EXAMPLE 11 Independent Events in a Family

The picture in the margin shows a family that has had nine girls in a row. Find the probability of this occurrence.

Solution   If two or more events are independent, we can find the probability of them all occurring by multiplying their probabilities. The probability of a baby girl is $\frac{1}{2}$, so the probability of nine girls in a row is $\frac{1}{2}$ used as a factor nine times.

$$P(\text{nine girls in a row}) = \frac{1}{2} \cdot \frac{1}{2} \cdot \frac{1}{2} \cdot \frac{1}{2} \cdot \frac{1}{2} \cdot \frac{1}{2} \cdot \frac{1}{2} \cdot \frac{1}{2} \cdot \frac{1}{2}$$

$$= \left(\frac{1}{2}\right)^9 = \frac{1}{512}$$

The probability of a run of nine girls in a row is $\frac{1}{512}$. (If another child is born into the family, this event is independent of the other nine, and the probability of a girl is still $\frac{1}{2}$.)

Check Point 11   Find the probability of a family having four boys in a row.

EXERCISE SET 4.5

Practice and Application Exercises

Exercises 1–8 involve empirical probability. Use the empirical probability formula to solve each exercise. Express answers as fractions. Then use a calculator to express probabilities as decimals, rounded to the nearest thousandth, if necessary.

Use the table showing the number of people who regularly participate in various forms of exercise, based on a survey of 2000 Americans, to solve Exercises 1–4.

Number of People Who Regularly Participate in Various Forms of Exercise in a Survey of 2000 People

Forms of Exercise	Number of People
Walking/hiking	1140
Weight training	320
Running/jogging	280
Biking	240
Aerobics	240
Exercise machines	220

Source: Discovery Health Media

Find the probability that a randomly selected American participates in:

1. weight training.
2. running/jogging.
3. biking.
4. walking/hiking.

Use the table showing world population by region to solve Exercises 5–8.

World Population, by Region

Region	Population
Africa	784,400,000
Asia	3,682,600,000
Europe	728,900,000
Latin America and the Caribbean	519,000,000
North America	309,600,000
Oceania	30,400,000

Total World Population: 6,054,900,000
Source: U.S. Bureau of the Census

If one person is randomly selected from all people on planet Earth, find the probability of selecting:

5. an African.
6. an Asian.
7. a North American.
8. a European.

Exercises 9–24 involve theoretical probability. Use the theoretical probability formula to solve each exercise. Express each probability as a fraction reduced to lowest terms.

In Exercises 9–14, a die is rolled. The sample space of equally likely outcomes is $\{1, 2, 3, 4, 5, 6\}$. Find the probability of getting:

9. a 4.
10. a 5.
11. an odd number.
12. a number greater than 3.
13. a number greater than 4.
14. a number greater than 7.

In Exercises 15–18, you are dealt one card from a standard 52 card deck. Find the probability of being dealt:

15. a queen.
16. a diamond.
17. a picture card.
18. a card greater than 3 and less than 7.

In Exercises 19–20, a fair coin is tossed two times in succession. The sample space of equally-likely outcomes is $\{HH, HT, TH, TT\}$. Find the probability of getting:

19. two heads.
20. the same outcome on each toss.

In Exercises 21–22, you select a family with three children. If M represents a male child and F a female child, the sample space of equally likely outcomes is $\{MMM, MMF, MFM, MFF, FMM, FMF, FFM, FFF\}$. Find the probability of selecting a family with:

21. at least one male child.
22. at least two female children.

In Exercises 23–24, a single die is rolled twice. The 36 equally likely outcomes are shown as follows:

	Second Roll					
	⚀	⚁	⚂	⚃	⚄	⚅
⚀	(1,1)	(1,2)	(1,3)	(1,4)	(1,5)	(1,6)
⚁	(2,1)	(2,2)	(2,3)	(2,4)	(2,5)	(2,6)
⚂	(3,1)	(3,2)	(3,3)	(3,4)	(3,5)	(3,6)
⚃	(4,1)	(4,2)	(4,3)	(4,4)	(4,5)	(4,6)
⚄	(5,1)	(5,2)	(5,3)	(5,4)	(5,5)	(5,6)
⚅	(6,1)	(6,2)	(6,3)	(6,4)	(6,5)	(6,6)

First Roll (row label)

Find the probability of getting:

23. two numbers whose sum is 4.
24. two numbers whose sum is 6.
25. To play the California lottery, a person has to correctly select 6 out of 51 numbers, paying $1 for each six-number selection. If the six numbers picked are the same as the ones drawn by the lottery, mountains of money are bestowed. What is the probability that a person with one combination of six numbers will win? What is the probability of winning if 100 different lottery tickets are purchased?
26. A state lottery is designed so that a player chooses six numbers from 1 to 30 on one lottery ticket. What is the probability that a player with one lottery ticket will win? What is the probability of winning if 100 different lottery tickets are purchased?

The table shows the probability of dying at any given age. Use the table and your answer from Exercise 25 to solve Exercises 27–28.

Probability of Dying at Any Given Age

Age	Probability of Male Death	Probability of Female Death
10	0.00013	0.00010
20	0.00140	0.00050
30	0.00153	0.00050
40	0.00193	0.00095
50	0.00567	0.00305
60	0.01299	0.00792
70	0.03473	0.01764
80	0.07644	0.03966
90	0.15787	0.11250
100	0.26876	0.23969
110	0.39770	0.39043

Source: George Shaffner, *The Arithmetic of Life and Death*

27. How many times more likely is a 20-year-old male to die this year than to win California's lottery with one lottery ticket?

28. How many times more likely is a 20-year-old female to die this year than to win California's lottery with one lottery ticket?

29. A poker hand consists of five cards.

    a. Find the total number of possible five-card poker hands that can be dealt from a deck of 52 cards.

    b. A diamond flush consists of a five-card hand containing all diamonds. Find the number of possible five-card diamond flushes.

    c. Find the probability of being dealt a diamond flush.

30. If you are dealt 4 cards from a shuffled deck of 52 cards, find the probability that all 4 are hearts.

The graph at the top of the next column shows the probability of cardiovascular disease, by age and gender. Use the information in the graph to solve Exercises 31–32. Express all probabilities as decimals, estimated to two decimal places.

31. a. What is the probability that a randomly selected man between the ages of 25 and 34 has cardiovascular disease?

    b. What is the probability that a randomly selected man between the ages 25 and 34 does not have cardiovascular disease?

32. a. What is the probability that a randomly selected woman, 75 or older, has cardiovascular disease?

    b. What is the probability that a randomly selected woman, 75 or older, does not have cardiovascular disease?

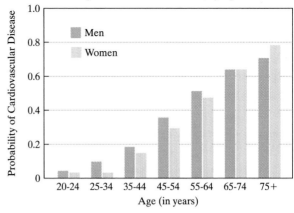

Probability of Cardiovascular Disease, by Age and Gender

Source: American Heart Association

Exercises 33–44 involve the probability of one event or a second event occurring. In order to use the correct probability formula, you will first need to determine whether or not the events are mutually exclusive.

In Exercises 33–36 you randomly select one card from a 52-card deck. Find the probability of selecting:

33. a 2 or a 3.   **34.** a 7 or an 8.

35. a red 2 or a black 3.   **36.** a red 7 or a black 8.

In Exercises 37–38, a single die is rolled. Find the probability of rolling:

37. an even number or a number less than 5.

38. an odd number or a number less than 4.

In Exercises 39–40, you are dealt one card from a 52-card deck. Find the probability that you are dealt:

39. a 7 or a red card.   **40.** a 5 or a black card.

In Exercises 41–42, it is equally probable that the pointer on the spinner shown will land on any one of the eight regions, numbered 1 through 8. If the pointer lands on a borderline, spin again.

Find the probability that the pointer will stop on:

41. an odd number or a number less than 6.

42. an odd number or a number greater than 3.

Use this information to solve Exercises 43–44. The mathematics department of a college has 8 male professors, 11 female professors, 14 male teaching assistants, and 7 female teaching assistants. If a person is selected at random from the group, find the probability that the selected person is:

43. a professor or a male.   **44.** a professor or a female.

Exercises 45–50 involve and probabilities with independent events.

In Exercises 45–48, a single die is rolled twice. Find the probability of getting:

45. a 2 the first time and a 3 the second time.

46. a 5 the first time and a 1 the second time.

47. an even number the first time and a number greater than 2 the second time.

48. an odd number the first time and a number less than 3 the second time.

49. If you toss a fair coin six times, what is the probability of getting all heads?

50. If you toss a fair coin seven times, what is the probability of getting all tails?

When making two or more selections from populations with large numbers, such as the population of Americans ages 45 to 65, we assume that each selection is independent of every other selection. The graph shows how Americans 45 to 65 rate their health. Use the information shown to solve Exercises 51–52.

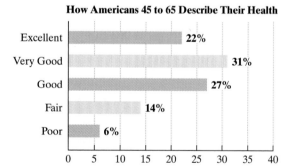

How Americans 45 to 65 Describe Their Health

Excellent 22%
Very Good 31%
Good 27%
Fair 14%
Poor 6%

Source: Newsweek

51. If four Americans ages 45 to 65 are selected at random, find the probability that all four rate their health as excellent.

52. If four Americans ages 45 to 65 are selected at random, find the probability that all four rate their health as poor.

53. The probability that South Florida will be hit by a major hurricane (category 4 or 5) in any single year is $\frac{1}{16}$. (*Source*: National Hurricane Center)
   a. What is the probability that South Florida will be hit by a major hurricane two years in a row?
   b. What is the probability that South Florida will be hit by a major hurricane in three consecutive years?

   c. What is the probability that South Florida will not be hit by a major hurricane in the next ten years?
   d. What is the probability that South Florida will be hit by a major hurricane at least once in the next ten years?

Writing in Mathematics

54. Describe the difference between theoretical probability and empirical probability.

55. Give an example of an event whose probability must be determined empirically rather than theoretically.

56. Write a probability word problem whose answer is one of the following fractions: $\frac{1}{6}$ or $\frac{1}{4}$ or $\frac{1}{3}$.

57. Explain how to find the probability of an event not occurring. Give an example.

58. What are mutually exclusive events? Give an example of two events that are mutually exclusive.

59. Explain how to find *or* probabilities with mutually exclusive events. Give an example.

60. Give an example of two events that are not mutually exclusive.

61. Explain how to find *or* probabilities with events that are not mutually exclusive. Give an example.

62. Explain how to find *and* probabilities with independent events. Give an example.

63. The president of a large company with 10,000 employees is considering mandatory cocaine testing for every employee. The test that would be used is 90% accurate, meaning that it will detect 90% of the cocaine users who are tested, and that 90% of the nonusers will test negative. This also means that the test gives 10% false positive. Suppose that 1% of the employees actually use cocaine. Find the probability that someone who tests positive for cocaine use is, indeed, a user.

Hint: Find the following probability fraction:

$$\frac{\text{the number of employees who test positive and are cocaine users}}{\text{the number of employees who test positive}}.$$

This fraction is given by

$$\frac{90\% \text{ of } 1\% \text{ of } 10,000}{\text{the number who test positive who actually use cocaine plus the number who test positive who do not use cocaine}}.$$

What does this probability indicate in terms of the percentage of employees who test positive who are not actually users? Discuss these numbers in terms of the issue of mandatory drug testing. Write a paper either in favor of or against mandatory drug testing, incorporating the actual percentage accuracy for such tests.

Critical Thinking Exercises

64. The target in the figure shown contains four squares. If a dart thrown at random hits the target, find the probability that it will land in a yellow region.

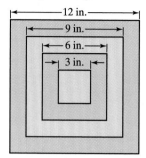

65. Suppose that it is a week in which the cash prize in Florida's LOTTO is promised to exceed $50 million. If a person purchases 22,957,480 tickets in LOTTO at $1 per ticket (all possible combinations), isn't this a guarantee of winning the lottery? Because the probability in this situation is 1, what's wrong with doing this?

66. a. If two people are selected at random, the probability that they do not have the same birthday (day and month) is $\frac{365}{365} \cdot \frac{364}{365}$. Explain why this is so. (Ignore leap years and assume 365 days in a year.)

b. If three people are selected at random, find the probability that they all have different birthdays.

c. If three people are selected at random, find the probability that at least two of them have the same birthday.

d. If 20 people are selected at random, find the probability that at least 2 of them have the same birthday.

e. How large a group is needed to give a 0.5 chance of at least two people having the same birthday?

Group Exercise

67. Research and present a group report on state lotteries. Include answers to some or all of the following questions: Which states do not have lotteries? Why not? How much is spent per capita on lotteries? What are some of the lottery games? What is the probability of winning top prize in these games? What income groups spend the greatest amount of money on lotteries? If your state has a lottery, what does it do with the money it makes? Is the way the money is spent what was promised when the lottery first began?

CHAPTER SUMMARY, REVIEW, AND TEST

Summary

DEFINITIONS AND CONCEPTS	EXAMPLES
4.1 Sequences and Summation Notation	
a. An infinite sequence $\{a_n\}$ is a function whose domain is the set of positive integers. The function values, or terms, are represented by $$a_1, a_2, a_3, a_4, \ldots, a_n, \ldots.$$	Ex. 1, p. 225
b. Sequences can be defined using recursion formulas that define the nth term as a function of the previous term.	Ex. 2, p. 226
c. Factorial Notation: $$n! = n(n-1)(n-2)\cdots(3)(2)(1) \quad \text{and} \quad 0! = 1$$	Ex. 3, p. 227; Ex. 4, p. 228
d. Summation Notation: $$\sum_{i=1}^{n} a_i = a_1 + a_2 + a_3 + a_4 + \cdots + a_n$$	Ex. 5, p. 230; Ex. 6, p. 231

DEFINITIONS AND CONCEPTS	EXAMPLES

4.2 Arithmetic Sequences

a. In an arithmetic sequence, each term after the first differs from the preceding term by a constant, the common difference. Subtract any term from the term that directly follows to find the common difference.

Ex. 1, p. 236

b. General term or nth term: $a_n = a_1 + (n-1)d$. The first term is a_1 and the common difference is d.

Ex. 2, p. 238;
Ex. 3, p. 238

c. Sum of the first n terms: $S_n = \dfrac{n}{2}(a_1 + a_n)$

Ex. 4, p. 240;
Ex. 5, p. 240;
Ex. 6, p. 241

4.3 Geometric Sequences

a. In a geometric sequence, each term after the first is obtained by multiplying the preceding term by a nonzero constant, the common ratio. Divide any term after the first by the term that directly precedes it to find the common ratio.

Ex. 1, p. 245

b. General term or nth term: $a_n = a_1 r^{n-1}$. The first term is a_1 and the common ratio is r.

Ex. 2, p. 246;
Ex. 3, p. 246

c. Sum of the first n terms: $S_n = \dfrac{a_1(1 - r^n)}{1 - r}, \quad r \neq 1$

Ex. 4, p. 248;
Ex. 5, p. 249;
Ex. 6, p. 250

d. An annuity is a sequence of equal payments made at equal time periods. The value of an annuity, A, is the sum of all deposits made plus all interest paid, given by

Ex. 7, p. 251

$$A = P \dfrac{\left(1 + \dfrac{r}{n}\right)^{nt} - 1}{\dfrac{r}{n}}.$$

The deposit made at the end of each period is P, the annual interest rate is r, compounded n times per year, and t is the number of years deposits have been made.

e. Sum of the infinite geometric series $a_1 + a_1 r + a_1 r^2 + a_1 r^3 + \cdots$ is $S = \dfrac{a_1}{1 - r}; |r| < 1$. If $|r| \geq 1$, the infinite series does not have a sum.

Ex. 8, p. 253;
Ex. 9, p. 254;
Ex. 10, p. 254

4.4 Counting Principles, Permutations, and Combinations

a. The Fundamental Counting Principle: The number of ways in which a series of successive things can occur is found by multiplying the number of ways in which each thing can occur.

Ex. 1, p. 260;
Ex. 2, p. 260;
Ex. 3, p. 261

b. A permutation from a group of items occurs when no item is used more than once and the order of arrangement makes a difference.

c. Permutations Formula: The number of possible permutations if r items are taken from n items is

Ex. 4, p. 262;
Ex. 5, p. 263

$$_nP_r = \dfrac{n!}{(n-r)!}.$$

d. A combination from a group of items occurs when no item is used more than once and the order of items makes no difference.

Ex. 6, p. 264

e. Combinations Formula: The number of possible combinations if r items are taken from n items is

Ex. 7, p. 265;
Ex. 8, p. 266

$$_nC_r = \dfrac{n!}{(n-r)!\,r!}.$$

DEFINITIONS AND CONCEPTS	EXAMPLES

4.5 Probability

a. Empirical probability applies to situations in which we observe the frequency of the occurrence of an event. The empirical probability of event E is

$$P(E) = \frac{\text{observed number of times } E \text{ occurs}}{\text{total number of observed occurrences}}.$$

Ex. 1, p. 271

b. Theoretical probability applies to situations in which the sample space of all equally likely outcomes is known. The theoretical probability of event E is

$$P(E) = \frac{\text{number of outcomes in event } E}{\text{number of outcomes in sample space } S} = \frac{n(E)}{n(S)}.$$

Ex. 2, p. 272;
Ex. 3, p. 272;
Ex. 4, p. 273;
Ex. 5, p. 274

c. Probability of an event not occurring: $P(\text{not } E) = 1 - P(E)$.

Ex. 6, p. 275

d. If it is impossible for events A and B to occur simultaneously, the events are mutually exclusive.

e. If A and B are mutually exclusive events, then $P(A \text{ or } B) = P(A) + P(B)$.

Ex. 7, p. 276

f. If A and B are not mutually exclusive events, then

$$P(A \text{ or } B) = P(A) + P(B) - P(A \text{ and } B).$$

Ex. 8, p. 277;
Ex. 9, p. 278

g. Two events are independent if the occurrence of either of them has no effect on the probability of the other.

h. If A and B are independent events, then

$$P(A \text{ and } B) = P(A) \cdot P(B).$$

Ex. 10, p. 279

i. The probability of a succession of independent events is the product of each of their probabilities.

Ex. 11, p. 279

Review Exercises

4.1

In Exercises 1–6, write the first four terms of each sequence whose general term is given.

1. $a_n = 7n - 4$

2. $a_n = (-1)^n \dfrac{n+2}{n+1}$

3. $a_n = \dfrac{1}{(n-1)!}$

4. $a_n = \dfrac{(-1)^{n+1}}{2^n}$

5. $a_1 = 9$ and $a_n = \dfrac{2}{3a_{n-1}}$ for $n \geq 2$

6. $a_1 = 4$ and $a_n = 2a_{n-1} + 3$ for $n \geq 2$

7. Evaluate: $\dfrac{40!}{4!38!}$.

In Exercises 8–9, find each indicated sum.

8. $\displaystyle\sum_{i=1}^{5}(2i^2 - 3)$

9. $\displaystyle\sum_{i=0}^{4}(-1)^{i+1}i!$

In Exercises 10–11, express each sum using summation notation. Use i for the index of summation.

10. $\dfrac{1}{3} + \dfrac{2}{4} + \dfrac{3}{5} + \cdots + \dfrac{15}{17}$

11. $4^3 + 5^3 + 6^3 + \cdots + 13^3$

4.2

In Exercises 12–15, write the first six terms of each arithmetic sequence.

12. $a_1 = 7, d = 4$

13. $a_1 = -4, d = -5$

14. $a_1 = \frac{3}{2}, d = -\frac{1}{2}$

15. $a_{n+1} = a_n + 5, a_1 = -2$

In Exercises 16–18, find the indicated term of the arithmetic sequence with first term, a_1, and common difference, d.

16. Find a_6 when $a_1 = 5, d = 3$.

17. Find a_{12} when $a_1 = -8, d = -2$.

18. Find a_{14} when $a_1 = 14, d = -4$.

In Exercises 19–21, write a formula for the general term (the nth term) of each arithmetic sequence. Do not use a recursion formula. Then use the formula for a_n to find a_{20}, the 20th term of the sequence.

19. $-7, -3, 1, 5, \ldots$

20. $a_1 = 200, d = -20$

21. $a_n = a_{n-1} - 5, a_1 = 3$

22. Find the sum of the first 22 terms of the arithmetic sequence: $5, 12, 19, 26, \ldots$.

23. Find the sum of the first 15 terms of the arithmetic sequence: $-6, -3, 0, 3, \ldots$.

24. Find $3 + 6 + 9 + \cdots + 300$, the sum of the first 100 positive multiples of 3.

In Exercises 25–27, use the formula for the sum of the first n terms of an arithmetic sequence to find the indicated sum.

25. $\displaystyle\sum_{i=1}^{16} (3i + 2)$

26. $\displaystyle\sum_{i=1}^{25} (-2i + 6)$

27. $\displaystyle\sum_{i=1}^{30} (-5i)$

28. The graph in the next column shows the changing pattern of work in the United States from 1900 through 2000.

In 1900, 20% of the total labor force was comprised of white-collar workers. On average, this increased by approximately 0.52% per year since then.

   a. Write a formula for the nth term of the arithmetic sequence that describes the percentage of white-collar workers in the labor force n years after 1899.

   b. Use the model to predict the percentage of white-collar workers in the labor force by the year 2010.

29. A company offers a starting salary of $31,500 with raises of $2300 per year. Find the total salary over a ten-year period.

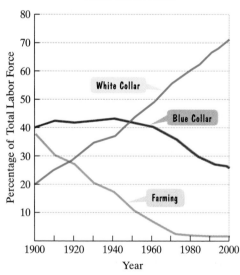

The Changing Pattern of Work in the United States

Source: U.S. Department of Labor

30. A theater has 25 seats in the first row and 35 rows in all. Each successive row contains one additional seat. How many seats are in the theater?

4.3

In Exercises 31–34, write the first five terms of each geometric sequence.

31. $a_1 = 3, r = 2$

32. $a_1 = \frac{1}{2}, r = \frac{1}{2}$

33. $a_1 = 16, r = -\frac{1}{2}$

34. $a_n = -5a_{n-1}, a_1 = -1$

In Exercises 35–37, use the formula for the general term (the nth term) of a geometric sequence to find the indicated term of each sequence.

35. Find a_7 when $a_1 = 2, r = 3$.

36. Find a_6 when $a_1 = 16, r = \frac{1}{2}$.

37. Find a_5 when $a_1 = -3, r = 2$.

In Exercises 38–40, write a formula for the general term (the nth term) of each geometric sequence. Then use the formula for a_n to find a_8, the eighth term of the sequence.

38. $1, 2, 4, 8, \ldots$

39. $100, 10, 1, \frac{1}{10}, \ldots$

40. $12, -4, \frac{4}{3}, -\frac{4}{9}, \ldots$

41. Find the sum of the first 15 terms of the geometric sequence: $5, -15, 45, -135, \ldots$.

42. Find the sum of the first 7 terms of the geometric sequence: $8, 4, 2, 1, \ldots$.

In Exercises 43–45, use the formula for the sum of the first n terms of a geometric sequence to find the indicated sum.

43. $\displaystyle\sum_{i=1}^{6} 5^i$

44. $\displaystyle\sum_{i=1}^{7} 3(-2)^i$

45. $\displaystyle\sum_{i=1}^{5} 2\left(\tfrac{1}{4}\right)^{i-1}$

In Exercises 46–49, find the sum of each infinite geometric series.

46. $9 + 3 + 1 + \dfrac{1}{3} + \cdots$

47. $2 - 1 + \dfrac{1}{2} - \dfrac{1}{4} + \cdots$

48. $-6 + 4 - \dfrac{8}{3} + \dfrac{16}{9} - \cdots$

49. $\displaystyle\sum_{i=1}^{\infty} 5(0.8)^i$

In Exercises 50–51, express each repeating decimal as a fraction in lowest terms.

50. $0.\overline{6}$

51. $0.\overline{47}$

52. The population of Iraq from 1998 through 2001 is shown in the following table.

Year	1998	1999	2000	2001
Population in Millions	19.96	20.72	21.51	22.33

Source: U.N. Population Division

   a. Show that Iraq's population is increasing geometrically.

   b. Write the general term of the geometric sequence describing population growth for Iraq n years after 1997.

   c. Estimate Iraq's population, in millions, for the year 2008.

53. A job pays \$32,000 for the first year with an annual increase of 6% per year beginning in the second year. What is the salary in the sixth year? What is the total salary paid over this six-year period? Round answers to the nearest dollar.

54. You decide to deposit \$200 at the end of each month into an account paying 10% interest compounded monthly to save for your child's education. How much will you save over 18 years?

55. A factory in an isolated town has an annual payroll of \$4 million. It is estimated that 70% of this money is spent within the town, that people in the town receiving this money will again spend 70% of what they receive in the town, and so on. What is the total of all this spending in the town each year?

4.4

In Exercises 56–59, evaluate each expression.

56. $_8P_3$
57. $_9P_5$
58. $_8C_3$
59. $_{13}C_{11}$

In Exercises 60–66, solve by the method of your choice.

60. A popular brand of pen comes in red, green, blue, or black ink. The writing tip can be chosen from extra bold, bold, regular, fine, or micro. How many different choices of pens do you have with this brand?

61. A stock can go up, go down, or stay unchanged. How many possibilities are there if you own five stocks?

62. A club with 15 members is to choose four officers—president, vice-president, secretary, and treasurer. In how many ways can these offices be filled?

63. How many different ways can a director select 4 actors from a group of 20 actors to attend a workshop on performing in rock musicals?

64. From the 20 CDs that you've bought during the past year, you plan to take 3 with you on vacation. How many different sets of three CDs can you take?

65. How many different ways can a director select from 20 male actors and cast the roles of Mark, Roger, Angel, and Collins in the musical *Rent*?

66. In how many ways can five airplanes line up for departure on a runway?

4.5

Exercises 67–68 involve empirical probabilities. Express each probability as a fraction. Then use a calculator to express the probability in decimal form, rounded to the nearest thousandth. The table on the next page shows the two states with the largest Hispanic populations. Find the probability that:

67. a person randomly selected from California is Hispanic.

68. a person randomly selected from Texas is Hispanic.

Largest Hispanic Population, 2000

State	Total Population	Hispanic Population
California	33,871,648	10,966,556
Texas	20,851,820	6,669,666

Source: Bureau of the Census

In Exercises 69–70, a die is rolled. Find the probability of:

69. getting a number less than 5.

70. getting a number less than 3 or greater than 4.

In Exercises 71–72, you are dealt one card from a 52-card deck. Find the probability of:

71. getting an ace or a king.

72. getting a queen or a red card.

In Exercises 73–74, it is equally probable that the pointer on the spinner shown will land on any one of the six regions, numbered 1 through 6, and colored as shown. If the pointer lands on a borderline, spin again. Find the probability of

73. not stopping on yellow.

74. stopping on red or a number greater than 3.

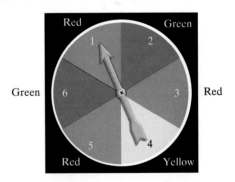

75. A lottery game is set up so that each player chooses five different numbers from 1 to 20. If the five numbers match the five numbers drawn in the lottery, the player wins (or shares) the top cash prize. What is the probability of winning the prize

a. with one lottery ticket?

b. with 100 different lottery tickets?

Use this information to solve Exercises 76–77. At a workshop on police work and the African-American community, there are 50 African-American male police officers, 20 African-American female police officers, 90 white male police officers, and 40 white female police officers. If one police officer is selected at random from the people at the workshop, find the probability that the selected person is:

76. African American or male.   **77.** female or white.

78. The bar graph shows five causes of death and the percentage of all deaths in the United States attributed to each cause. What is the probability that an American's death is caused by heart disease or cancer? Express the answer as a decimal to three decimal places.

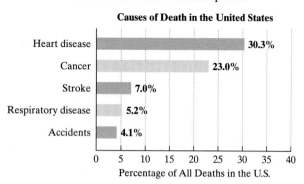

Causes of Death in the United States

Heart disease — 30.3%
Cancer — 23.0%
Stroke — 7.0%
Respiratory disease — 5.2%
Accidents — 4.1%

Percentage of All Deaths in the U.S.

Source: U.S. Department of Health and Human Services

79. What is the probability of a family having five boys born in a row?

80. The probability of a flood in any given year in a region prone to floods is 0.2.
  a. What is the probability of a flood two years in a row?
  b. What is the probability of a flood for three consecutive years?
  c. What is the probability of no flooding for four consecutive years?

Chapter 4 Test

1. Write the first five terms of the sequence whose general term is $a_n = \dfrac{(-1)^{n+1}}{n^2}$.

In Exercises 2–4, find each indicated sum.

2. $\sum_{i=1}^{5} (i^2 + 10)$ **3.** $\sum_{i=1}^{20} (3i - 4)$ **4.** $\sum_{i=1}^{15} (-2)^i$

In Exercises 5–7, evaluate each expression.

5. $\binom{9}{2}$ **6.** $_{10}P_3$ **7.** $_{10}C_3$

8. Express the sum using summation notation. Use i for the index of summation.
$$\frac{2}{3} + \frac{3}{4} + \frac{4}{5} + \cdots + \frac{21}{22}$$

In Exercises 9–10, write a formula for the general term (the nth term) of each sequence. Do not use a recursion formula. Then use the formula to find the twelfth term of the sequence.

9. 4, 9, 14, 19, … **10.** 16, 4, 1, $\frac{1}{4}$, …

In Exercises 11–12, use a formula to find the sum of the first ten terms of each sequence.

11. 7, −14, 28, −56, … **12.** −7, −14, −21, −28, …

13. Find the sum of the infinite geometric series:
$$4 + \frac{4}{2} + \frac{4}{2^2} + \frac{4}{2^3} + \cdots.$$

14. A job pays $30,000 for the first year with an annual increase of 4% per year beginning in the second year. What is the total salary paid over an eight-year period? Round to the nearest dollar.

15. A human resource manager has 11 applicants to fill three different positions. Assuming that all applicants are equally qualified for any of the three positions, in how many ways can this be done?

16. From the ten books that you've recently bought but not read, you plan to take four with you on vacation. How many different sets of four books can you take?

17. How many seven-digit local telephone numbers can be formed if the first three digits are 279?

18. A lottery game is set up so that each player chooses six different numbers from 1 to 15. If the six numbers match the six numbers drawn in the lottery, the player wins (or shares) the top cash prize. What is the probability of winning the prize with 50 different lottery tickets?

19. One card is randomly selected from a deck of 52 cards. Find the probability of selecting a black card or a picture card.

20. A group of students consists of 10 male freshmen, 15 female freshmen, 20 male sophomores, and 5 female sophomores. If one person is randomly selected from the group, find the probability of selecting a freshman or a female.

21. A quiz consisting of four multiple-choice questions has four available options (a, b, c, or d) for each question. If a person guesses at every question, what is the probability of answering all questions correctly?

22. If the spinner shown is spun twice, find the probability that the pointer lands on red on the first spin and blue on the second spin

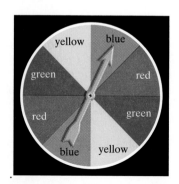

Answers to Selected Exercises

CHAPTER 1

Section 1.1

Check Point Exercises

1. a. 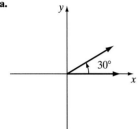 **b.** 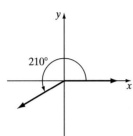 **c.** 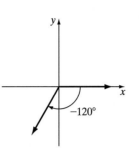 **d.**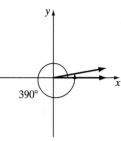

2. a. 40° **b.** 225° **3. a.** 12°; 102° **b.** no complementary angle; 30° **4.** 3.5 radians **5. a.** $\frac{\pi}{3}$ radians **b.** $\frac{3\pi}{2}$ radians

c. $-\frac{5\pi}{3}$ radians **6. a.** 45° **b.** −240° **c.** 343.8° **7.** $\frac{3\pi}{2}$ in. ≈ 4.71 in. **8.** 135π in./min ≈ 424 in./min

Exercise Set 1.1

1. quadrant II **3.** quadrant III **5.** quadrant I **7.** obtuse **9.** straight

11. 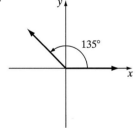 **13.** 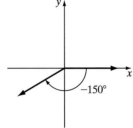 **15.** 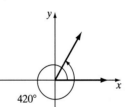 **17.**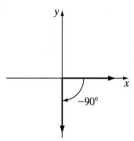

19. 35° **21.** 210° **23.** 315° **25.** 38°; 128° **27.** 52.6°; 142.6° **29.** no complement; 69° **31.** 4 radians **33.** $\frac{4}{3}$ radians

35. 4 radians **37.** $\frac{\pi}{4}$ radians **39.** $\frac{3\pi}{4}$ radians **41.** $\frac{5\pi}{3}$ radians **43.** $-\frac{5\pi}{4}$ radians **45.** 90° **47.** 120° **49.** 210° **51.** −540°

53. 0.31 radians **55.** −0.70 radians **57.** 3.49 radians **59.** 114.59° **61.** 13.85° **63.** −275.02° **65.** 3π in. ≈ 9.42 in.

67. 10π ft ≈ 31.42 ft. **69.** $\frac{12\pi \text{ radians}}{\text{second}}$ **71.** 60°; $\frac{\pi}{3}$ radians **73.** $\frac{8\pi}{3}$ in. ≈ 8.38 in. **75.** 12π in. ≈ 37.70 in. **77.** 2 radians; 114.59°

79. 2094 mi **81.** 1047 mph **83.** 1508 ft/min **97.** 30.25° **99.** 30°25′12″ **101.** smaller than a right angle **103.** 1815 mi

Section 1.2

Check Point Exercises

1. $\sin \theta = \frac{3}{5}$; $\cos \theta = \frac{4}{5}$; $\tan \theta = \frac{3}{4}$; $\csc \theta = \frac{5}{3}$; $\sec \theta = \frac{5}{4}$; $\cot \theta = \frac{4}{3}$ **2.** $\sqrt{2}$; $\sqrt{2}$; 1 **3.** $\sqrt{3}$; $\frac{\sqrt{3}}{3}$ **4.** $\tan \theta = \frac{2\sqrt{5}}{5}$; $\csc \theta = \frac{3}{2}$;

$\sec \theta = \frac{3\sqrt{5}}{5}$; $\cot \theta = \frac{\sqrt{5}}{2}$ **5.** $\frac{\sqrt{3}}{2}$ **6. a.** cos 44° **b.** $\tan \frac{5\pi}{12}$ **7. a.** 0.9553 **b.** 1.0025 **8.** 333.9 yd **9.** 54°

Exercise Set 1.2

1. 15; $\sin \theta = \dfrac{3}{5}$; $\cos \theta = \dfrac{4}{5}$; $\tan \theta = \dfrac{3}{4}$; $\csc \theta = \dfrac{5}{3}$; $\sec \theta = \dfrac{5}{4}$; $\cot \theta = \dfrac{4}{3}$ **3.** 20; $\sin \theta = \dfrac{20}{29}$; $\cos \theta = \dfrac{21}{29}$; $\tan \theta = \dfrac{20}{21}$; $\csc \theta = \dfrac{29}{20}$;

$\sec \theta = \dfrac{29}{21}$; $\cot \theta = \dfrac{21}{20}$ **5.** 24; $\sin \theta = \dfrac{5}{13}$; $\cos \theta = \dfrac{12}{13}$; $\tan \theta = \dfrac{5}{12}$; $\csc \theta = \dfrac{13}{5}$; $\sec \theta = \dfrac{13}{12}$; $\cot \theta = \dfrac{12}{5}$

7. 28; $\sin \theta = \dfrac{4}{5}$; $\cos \theta = \dfrac{3}{5}$; $\tan \theta = \dfrac{4}{3}$; $\csc \theta = \dfrac{5}{4}$; $\sec \theta = \dfrac{5}{3}$; $\cot \theta = \dfrac{3}{4}$ **9.** $\dfrac{\sqrt{3}}{2}$ **11.** $\sqrt{2}$ **13.** $\sqrt{3}$ **15.** 0

17. $\tan \theta = \dfrac{8}{15}$; $\csc \theta = \dfrac{17}{8}$; $\sec \theta = \dfrac{17}{15}$; $\cot \theta = \dfrac{15}{8}$ **19.** $\tan \theta = \dfrac{\sqrt{2}}{4}$; $\csc \theta = 3$; $\sec \theta = \dfrac{3\sqrt{2}}{4}$; $\cot \theta = 2\sqrt{2}$ **21.** $\dfrac{\sqrt{13}}{7}$

23. $\dfrac{5}{8}$ **25.** 1   **27.** 1   **29.** 1   **31.** $\cos 83°$ **33.** $\sec 65°$ **35.** $\cot \dfrac{7\pi}{18}$ **37.** $\sin \dfrac{\pi}{10}$ **39.** 0.6157   **41.** 0.6420   **43.** 3.4203

45. 0.9511   **47.** 3.7321   **49.** 188 cm   **51.** 182 in.   **53.** 41 m   **55.** 17°   **57.** 78°   **59.** 1.147 radians   **61.** 0.3950 radians

63. 529 yd   **65.** 36°   **67.** 2879 ft   **69.** 37°

83. 0.92106, −0.19735; 0.95534, −0.148878; 0.98007, −0.099667; 0.99500, −0.04996; 0.99995, −0.005; 0.9999995, −0.0005; 0.999999995,

−0.00005; 0.99999999995, −0.000005; $\dfrac{\cos \theta - 1}{\theta}$ approaches 0 as θ approaches 0.

85. In a right triangle, the hypotenuse is greater than either other side. Therefore, both $\dfrac{\text{opposite}}{\text{hypotenuse}}$ and $\dfrac{\text{adjacent}}{\text{hypotenuse}}$ must be less than 1 for an acute angle in a right triangle.

87. a. 357 ft   **b.** 394 ft

Section 1.3

Check Point Exercises

1. $\sin \theta = -\dfrac{3}{5}$; $\cos \theta = \dfrac{4}{5}$; $\tan \theta = -\dfrac{3}{4}$; $\csc \theta = -\dfrac{5}{3}$; $\sec \theta = \dfrac{5}{4}$; $\cot \theta = -\dfrac{4}{3}$ **2. a.** 1; undefined   **b.** 0; 1   **c.** −1; undefined

d. 0; −1   **3.** quadrant III   **4.** $\dfrac{\sqrt{10}}{10}$; $-\dfrac{\sqrt{10}}{3}$ **5. a.** 30°   **b.** $\dfrac{\pi}{4}$ **c.** 60°   **d.** 0.46   **6. a.** $-\dfrac{\sqrt{3}}{2}$ **b.** 1   **c.** $\dfrac{2\sqrt{3}}{3}$

Exercise Set 1.3

1. $\sin \theta = \dfrac{3}{5}$; $\cos \theta = -\dfrac{4}{5}$; $\tan \theta = -\dfrac{3}{4}$; $\csc \theta = \dfrac{5}{3}$; $\sec \theta = -\dfrac{5}{4}$; $\cot \theta = -\dfrac{4}{3}$ **3.** $\sin \theta = \dfrac{3\sqrt{13}}{13}$; $\cos \theta = \dfrac{2\sqrt{13}}{13}$; $\tan \theta = \dfrac{3}{2}$; $\csc \theta = \dfrac{\sqrt{13}}{3}$;

$\sec \theta = \dfrac{\sqrt{13}}{2}$; $\cot \theta = \dfrac{2}{3}$ **5.** $\sin \theta = -\dfrac{\sqrt{2}}{2}$; $\cos \theta = \dfrac{\sqrt{2}}{2}$; $\tan \theta = -1$; $\csc \theta = -\sqrt{2}$; $\sec \theta = \sqrt{2}$; $\cot \theta = -1$ **7.** $\sin \theta = -\dfrac{5\sqrt{29}}{29}$;

$\cos \theta = -\dfrac{2\sqrt{29}}{29}$; $\tan \theta = \dfrac{5}{2}$; $\csc \theta = -\dfrac{\sqrt{29}}{5}$; $\sec \theta = -\dfrac{\sqrt{29}}{2}$; $\cot \theta = \dfrac{2}{5}$ **9.** −1   **11.** −1   **13.** undefined   **15.** 0   **17.** quadrant I

19. quadrant III   **21.** quadrant II   **23.** $\sin \theta = -\dfrac{4}{5}$; $\tan \theta = \dfrac{4}{3}$; $\csc \theta = -\dfrac{5}{4}$; $\sec \theta = -\dfrac{5}{3}$; $\cot \theta = \dfrac{3}{4}$ **25.** $\cos \theta = -\dfrac{12}{13}$; $\tan \theta = -\dfrac{5}{12}$;

$\csc \theta = \dfrac{13}{5}$; $\sec \theta = -\dfrac{13}{12}$; $\cot \theta = -\dfrac{12}{5}$ **27.** $\sin \theta = -\dfrac{15}{17}$; $\tan \theta = -\dfrac{15}{8}$; $\csc \theta = -\dfrac{17}{15}$; $\sec \theta = \dfrac{17}{8}$; $\cot \theta = -\dfrac{8}{15}$ **29.** $\sin \theta = \dfrac{2\sqrt{13}}{13}$;

$\cos \theta = -\dfrac{3\sqrt{13}}{3}$; $\csc \theta = \dfrac{\sqrt{13}}{2}$; $\sec \theta = -\dfrac{\sqrt{13}}{3}$; $\cot \theta = -\dfrac{3}{2}$ **31.** $\sin \theta = -\dfrac{4}{5}$; $\cos \theta = -\dfrac{3}{5}$; $\csc \theta = -\dfrac{5}{4}$; $\sec \theta = -\dfrac{5}{3}$; $\cot \theta = \dfrac{3}{4}$

33. $\sin \theta = -\dfrac{2\sqrt{2}}{3}$; $\cos \theta = -\dfrac{1}{3}$; $\tan \theta = 2\sqrt{2}$; $\csc \theta = -\dfrac{3\sqrt{2}}{4}$; $\cot \theta = \dfrac{\sqrt{2}}{4}$ **35.** 20°   **37.** 25°   **39.** 5°   **41.** $\dfrac{\pi}{4}$ **43.** $\dfrac{\pi}{6}$ **45.** 30°

47. 25°   **49.** 1.56   **51.** $-\dfrac{\sqrt{2}}{2}$ **53.** $\dfrac{\sqrt{3}}{3}$ **55.** $\sqrt{3}$ **57.** $\dfrac{\sqrt{3}}{2}$ **59.** −2   **61.** 1   **63.** $\dfrac{\sqrt{3}}{2}$ **65.** −1

Section 1.4

Check Point Exercises

1. $\sin \pi = 0$; $\cos \pi = -1$; $\tan \pi = 0$; $\csc \pi$ is undefined; $\sec \pi = -1$; $\cot \pi$ is undefined   **2. a.** $\dfrac{1}{2}$ **b.** $-\dfrac{\sqrt{3}}{3}$ **3. a.** $\dfrac{\sqrt{2}}{2}$ **b.** $\sqrt{3}$

Exercise Set 1.4

1. $\sin t = \dfrac{8}{17}$; $\cos t = -\dfrac{15}{17}$; $\tan t = -\dfrac{8}{15}$; $\csc t = \dfrac{17}{8}$; $\sec t = -\dfrac{17}{15}$; $\cot t = -\dfrac{15}{8}$ **3.** $\sin\left(-\dfrac{\pi}{4}\right) = -\dfrac{\sqrt{2}}{2}$; $\cos\left(-\dfrac{\pi}{4}\right) = \dfrac{\sqrt{2}}{2}$;

$\tan\left(-\dfrac{\pi}{4}\right) = -1$; $\csc\left(-\dfrac{\pi}{4}\right) = -\sqrt{2}$; $\sec\left(-\dfrac{\pi}{4}\right) = \sqrt{2}$; $\cot\left(-\dfrac{\pi}{4}\right) = -1$ **5.** $-\dfrac{\sqrt{2}}{2}$ **7.** 2 **9.** $-\dfrac{\sqrt{2}}{2}$ **11.** $\dfrac{\sqrt{3}}{3}$ **13. a.** 12 hr

b. 20.3 hr **c.** 3.7 hr **15. a.** 1; 0; −1; 0; 1 **b.** 28 days **23.** 0 **25.** $-\dfrac{1}{4}$ **c.** 9.6hr

Section 1.5

Check Point Exercises

1.
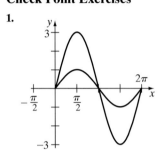

2.
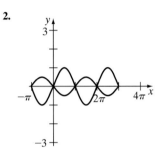

3.
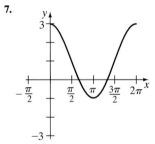

4.
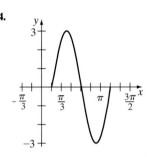

5.
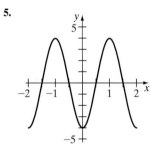

6.
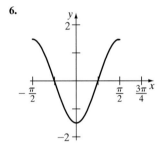

7.
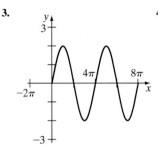

8. $y = 4\sin 4x$

9. $y = 2\sin\left(\dfrac{\pi}{6}x - \dfrac{\pi}{2}\right) + 12$

Exercise Set 1.5

1. 4 **3.** $\dfrac{1}{3}$ **5.** 3 **7.** 1; π

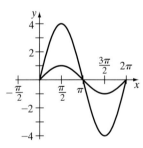
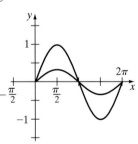
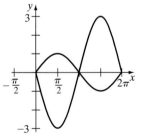
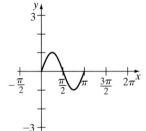

9. 3; 4π **11.** 4; 2 **13.** 3; 1 **15.** 1; 3π

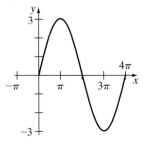
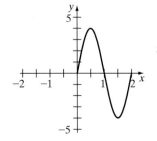
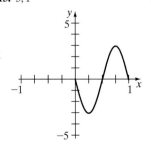
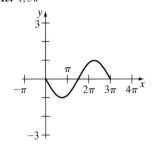

17. $1; 2\pi; \pi$

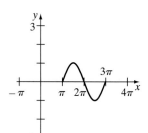

19. $1; \pi; \dfrac{\pi}{2}$

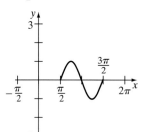

21. $3; \pi; \dfrac{\pi}{2}$

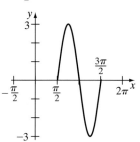

23. $\dfrac{1}{2}; 2\pi; -\dfrac{\pi}{2}$

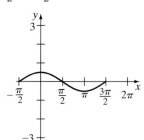

25. $2; \pi; -\dfrac{\pi}{4}$

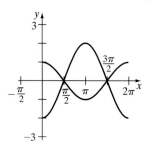

27. $3; 2; -\dfrac{2}{\pi}$

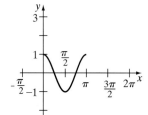

29. $2; 1; -2$

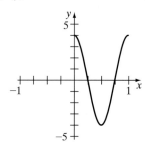

31. 2

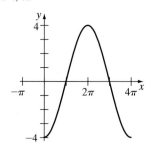

33. 2

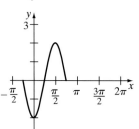

35. $1; \pi$

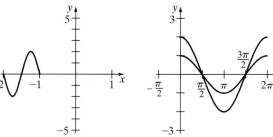

37. $4; 1$

39. $4; 4\pi$

41. $\dfrac{1}{2}; 6$

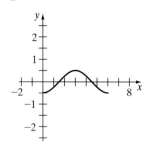

43. $3; \pi; \dfrac{\pi}{2}$

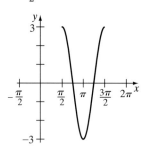

45. $\dfrac{1}{2}; \dfrac{2\pi}{3}; -\dfrac{\pi}{6}$

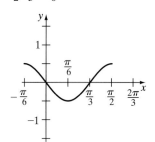

47. $3; \pi; \dfrac{\pi}{4}$

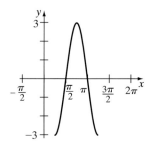

49. $2; 1; -4$

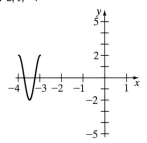

51.

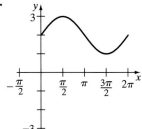

53.

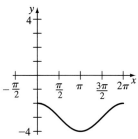

55.

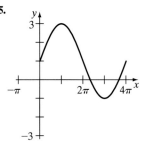

57.

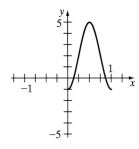

59. 33 days **61.** 23 days **63.** March 21 **65.** No

67.

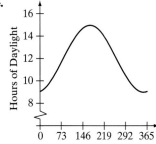

69. a. 3 **b.** 365 days **c.** 15 hours of daylight
d. 9 hours of daylight
e.

71. $y = 3 \cos \dfrac{\pi x}{6} + 9$ **73.** $4; \pi; \dfrac{\pi}{2}$

85.

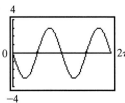

87.

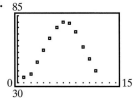

89.

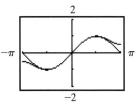

91.

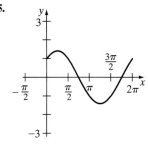

The graph is similar to $y = \sin x$,
except the amplitude is greater
and the curve is less smooth.

93. a.

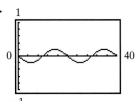

b. $y = 22.61 \sin(0.50x - 2.04) + 57.17$
c.

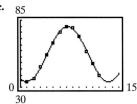

95.

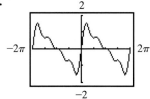

97. $y = 2 \cos(4x + \pi)$

Section 1.6

Check Point Exercises

1.
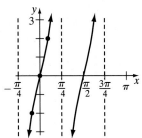

2.
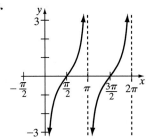

3.
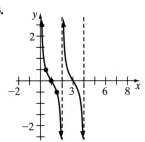

4.
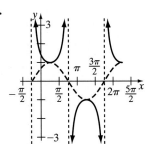

5.
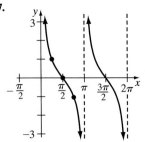

Exercise Set 1.6

1. $y = \tan(x + \pi)$ **3.** $y = -\tan\left(x - \dfrac{\pi}{2}\right)$

5.
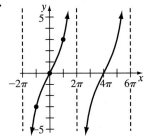

7.
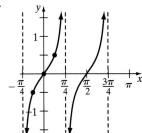

9.
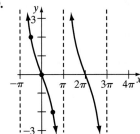

11.
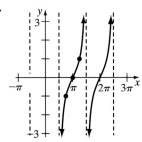

13. $y = -\cot x$ **15.** $y = \cot\left(x + \dfrac{\pi}{2}\right)$

17.
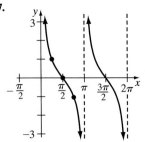

19.
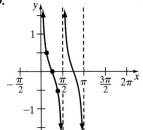

21.
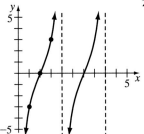

23.
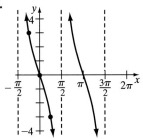

25. $y = -\frac{1}{2} \csc \frac{x}{2}$; **27.** $y = \frac{1}{2} \sec 2\pi x$;

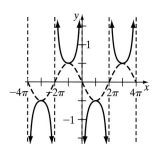

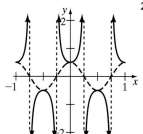

29.

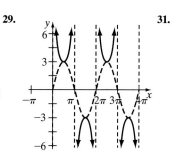

31.

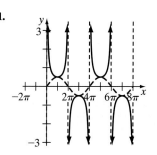

33.

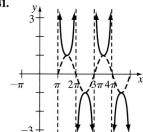

35.

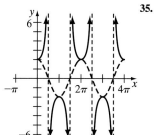

37.

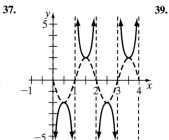

39.

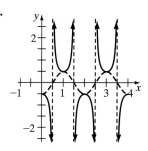

41.

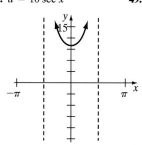

43.

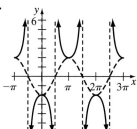

45. a.

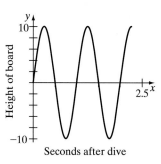

b. 0.25, 0.75, 1.25, 1.75;
The beacon is shining
parallel to the wall at
these times.

47. $d = 10 \sec x$ **49.**

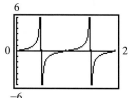

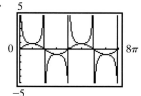

Seconds after dive

63.

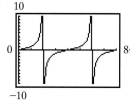

65.

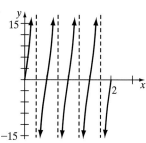

67.

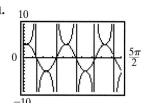

69.

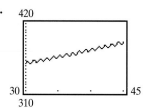

71.

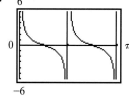

73.

75. $y = \cot \frac{3}{2} x$ **77.** 2^{-x} decreases the amplitude as x gets larger.

Chapter 1 Review Exercises

1.
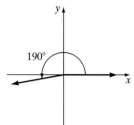

2.
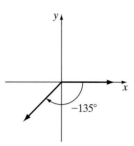

3.
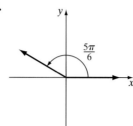

4.
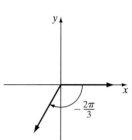

5. $40°$ **6.** $275°$ **7.** $17°; 107°$ **8.** no complement; $\dfrac{\pi}{3}$ radians **9.** 4.5 radians **10.** $\dfrac{\pi}{12}$ radians **11.** $\dfrac{2\pi}{3}$ radians **12.** $\dfrac{7\pi}{4}$ radians

13. $300°$ **14.** $252°$ **15.** $-150°$ **16.** $\dfrac{15\pi}{2}$ ft ≈ 23.56 ft **17.** 20.6π radians per min **18.** $42{,}412$ ft per min **19.** $\sin\theta = \dfrac{3}{5}$;

$\cos\theta = \dfrac{4}{5}$; $\tan\theta = \dfrac{3}{4}$; $\csc\theta = \dfrac{5}{3}$; $\sec\theta = \dfrac{5}{4}$; $\cot\theta = \dfrac{4}{3}$ **20.** $\sqrt{3}$ **21.** $\dfrac{\sqrt{2}}{2}$ **22.** $\dfrac{2\sqrt{3}}{3}$ **23.** 1 **24.** $\dfrac{\sqrt{21}}{7}$ **25.** $\cos 20°$

26. $\sin 0$ **27.** 42 mm **28.** 23 cm **29.** 37 in. **30.** 772 ft **31.** 31 m **32.** $56°$ **33.** $\sin\theta = -\dfrac{5\sqrt{26}}{26}$; $\cos\theta = -\dfrac{\sqrt{26}}{26}$; $\tan\theta = 5$;

$\csc\theta = -\dfrac{\sqrt{26}}{5}$; $\sec\theta = -\sqrt{26}$; $\cot\theta = \dfrac{1}{5}$ **34.** $\sin\theta = -1$; $\cos\theta = 0$; $\tan\theta$ is undefined; $\csc\theta = -1$; $\sec\theta$ is undefined; $\cot\theta = 0$

35. quadrant I **36.** quadrant III **37.** $\sin\theta = -\dfrac{\sqrt{21}}{5}$; $\tan\theta = -\dfrac{\sqrt{21}}{2}$; $\csc\theta = -\dfrac{5\sqrt{21}}{21}$; $\sec\theta = \dfrac{5}{2}$; $\cot\theta = -\dfrac{2\sqrt{21}}{21}$

38. $\sin\theta = \dfrac{\sqrt{10}}{10}$; $\cos\theta = -\dfrac{3\sqrt{10}}{10}$; $\csc\theta = \sqrt{10}$; $\sec\theta = -\dfrac{\sqrt{10}}{3}$; $\cot\theta = -3$ **39.** $85°$ **40.** $\dfrac{3\pi}{8}$ **41.** $50°$ **42.** $-\dfrac{\sqrt{3}}{2}$ **43.** $-\sqrt{3}$

44. $\sqrt{2}$ **45.** $\dfrac{\sqrt{3}}{2}$ **46.** $-\sqrt{3}$ **47.** $-\dfrac{2\sqrt{3}}{3}$ **48.** $-\dfrac{\sqrt{3}}{2}$ **49.** $\dfrac{\sqrt{2}}{2}$ **50.** 1

51.
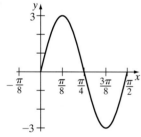

52.
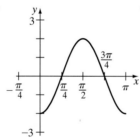

53.
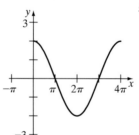

54.
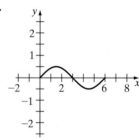

55.
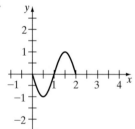

56.
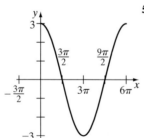

57.
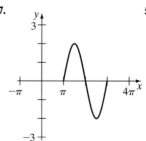

58.
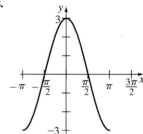

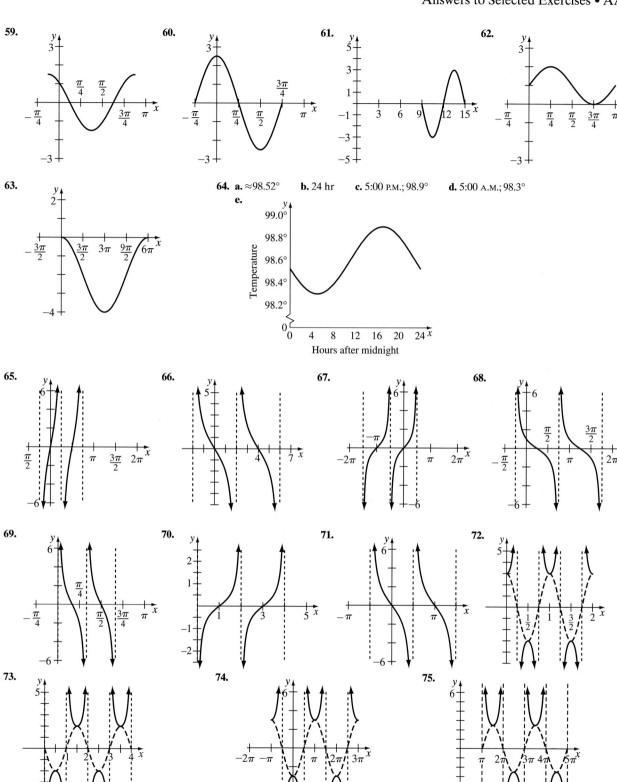

59.

60.

61.

62.

63.

64. a. ≈98.52°   **b.** 24 hr   **c.** 5:00 P.M.; 98.9°   **d.** 5:00 A.M.; 98.3°

e.

Hours after midnight

65.

66.

67.

68.

69.

70.

71.

72.

73.

74.

75.

Chapter 1 Test

1. $\dfrac{3\pi}{4}$ radians   **2.** $\dfrac{4\pi}{13}$ **3.** $\dfrac{25\pi}{3}$ ft ≈ 26.18 ft   **4.** $\sin\theta = \dfrac{5\sqrt{29}}{29}$; $\cos\theta = -\dfrac{2\sqrt{29}}{29}$; $\tan\theta = -\dfrac{5}{2}$; $\csc\theta = \dfrac{\sqrt{29}}{5}$; $\sec\theta = -\dfrac{\sqrt{29}}{2}$; $\cot\theta = -\dfrac{2}{5}$

5. quadrant III   **6.** $\sin\theta = -\dfrac{2\sqrt{2}}{3}$; $\tan\theta = -2\sqrt{2}$; $\csc\theta = -\dfrac{3\sqrt{2}}{4}$; $\sec\theta = 3$; $\cot\theta = -\dfrac{\sqrt{2}}{4}$ **7.** $\dfrac{\sqrt{3}}{6}$ **8.** $-\sqrt{3}$ **9.** $-\dfrac{\sqrt{2}}{2}$

10.
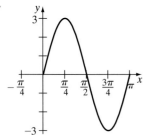

11.
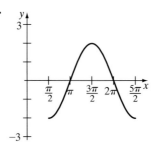

12.
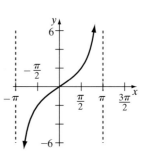

13.
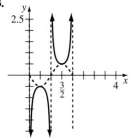

14. $-\sqrt{3}$ **15.** $B = 69°$; $a = 4.7$; $b = 12.1$ **16.** 23 yd   **17.** 36.1°

CHAPTER 2

Section 2.1

Check Point Exercises

1. $B = 34°$, $a \approx 13$ cm, $b \approx 8$ cm   **2.** $B = 117.5°$, $a \approx 9$, $c \approx 5$ **3.** one triangle; $C \approx 24°$, $b \approx 33°$, $b \approx 31$ **4.** no triangle
5. two triangles; $B_1 \approx 50°$, $C_1 \approx 95°$, $c_1 = 21$; $B_2 \approx 130°$, $C_2 \approx 15°$, $c_2 \approx 5$ **6.** approximately 34 sq m   **7.** approximately 11 mi

Exercise Set 2.1

1. $B = 42°$, $a \approx 8.1$, $b \approx 8.1$ **3.** $A = 44°$, $b \approx 18.6$, $c \approx 22.8$ **5.** $C = 95°$, $b \approx 81.0$, $c \approx 134.1$ **7.** $B = 40°$, $b \approx 20.9$, $c \approx 31.8$
9. $C = 111°$, $b \approx 7.3$, $c \approx 16.1$ **11.** $A = 80°$, $a \approx 39.5$, $c \approx 10.4$ **13.** $B = 30°$, $a \approx 316.0$, $b \approx 174.3$ **15.** $C = 50°$, $a \approx 7.1$, $b \approx 7.1$
17. one triangle; $B \approx 29°$, $c \approx 111°$, $c \approx 29.0$ **19.** one triangle; $C \approx 52°$, $B \approx 65°$, $b \approx 10.2$ **21.** one triangle; $C \approx 55°$, $B \approx 13°$, $b \approx 10.2$
23. no triangle   **25.** two triangles; $B_1 \approx 77°$, $C_1 \approx 43°$, $c_1 \approx 12.6$; $B_2 \approx 103°$, $C_2 \approx 17°$, $c_2 \approx 5.4$ **27.** two triangles; $B_1 \approx 54°$, $C_1 \approx 89°$,
$c_1 \approx 19.9$; $B_2 \approx 126°$, $C_2 \approx 17°$, $c_2 \approx 5.8$ **29.** two triangles; $C_1 \approx 68°$, $B_1 \approx 54°$, $b_1 \approx 21.0$; $C_2 \approx 112°$, $B_2 \approx 10°$, $b_2 \approx 4.5$
31. no triangle   **33.** 297 sq ft   **35.** 5 sq yd   **37.** 10 sq m   **39.** Station A is about 6 miles from the fire, station B is about 9 miles from
the fire.   **41.** The platform is about 3672 yards from one end of the beach and 3576 yards from the other.   **43.** about 184 ft
45. about 56 ft   **47.** about 30 ft   **49. a.** $a \approx 494$ ft   **b.** about 343 ft   **51.** either 9.9 mi or 2.4 mi   **63.** No   **65.** 41 ft

Section 2.2

Check Point Exercises

1. $a = 13$, $B \approx 28°$, $C \approx 32°$ **2.** $B \approx 97.9°$, $A \approx 52.4°$, $C \approx 29.7°$ **3.** approximately 917 mi apart   **4.** approximately 47 sq m

Exercise Set 2.2

1. $a \approx 6.0$, $B \approx 29°$, $C \approx 105°$ **3.** $c \approx 7.6$, $A \approx 52°$, $B \approx 32°$ **5.** $A \approx 44°$, $B \approx 68°$, $C \approx 68°$ **7.** $A \approx 117°$, $B \approx 36°$, $C \approx 27°$

9. $c \approx 4.7$, $A \approx 46°$, $B \approx 92°$ **11.** $a \approx 6.3$, $C \approx 28°$, $B \approx 50°$ **13.** $b \approx 4.7$, $C \approx 54°$, $A \approx 76°$ **15.** $b \approx 5.4$, $C \approx 22°$, $A \approx 68°$

17. $C \approx 112°$, $A \approx 28°$, $B \approx 40°$ **19.** $B \approx 100°$, $A \approx 19°$, $C \approx 61°$ **21.** $A = 60°$, $B = 60°$, $C = 60°$ **23.** no triangle   **25.** 4 sq ft

27. 22 sq m   **29.** 31 sq yd   **31.** about 61.7 mi apart   **33.** about 193 yd   **35.** N12°E   **37. a.** about 19.3 mi   **b.** S58°E

39. The guy wire anchored downhill is about 417.4 feet. The one anchored uphill is about 398.2 feet.   **41.** about 63.7 ft   **43.** $123,454

53. 153.4°

Section 2.3

Check Point Exercises

1. a.

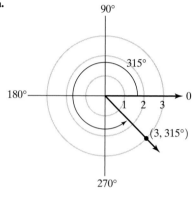

b.

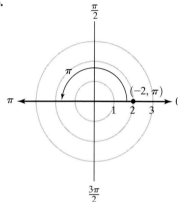

c.

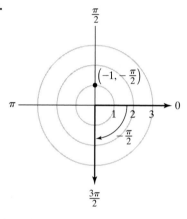

2. a. $\left(5, \dfrac{9\pi}{4}\right)$ **b.** $\left(-5, \dfrac{5\pi}{4}\right)$ **c.** $\left(5, -\dfrac{7\pi}{4}\right)$ **3. a.** $(-3, 0)$ **b.** $(-5\sqrt{3}, -5)$ **4.** $\left(2, \dfrac{5\pi}{3}\right)$ **5.** $\left(4, \dfrac{3\pi}{2}\right)$ **6.** $r = \dfrac{6}{3\cos\theta - \sin\theta}$

7. a. $x^2 + y^2 = 16$ **b.** $y = -x$ **c.** $x = 1$

Exercise Set 2.3

1. C **3.** A **5.** B **7.** C **9.** A **11.**

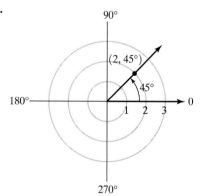

13.

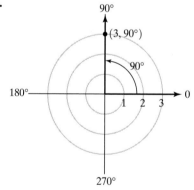

15.

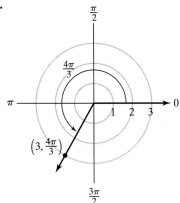

17.

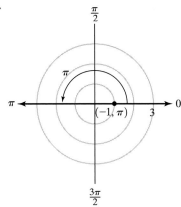

19.

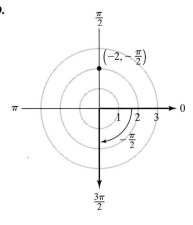

21.

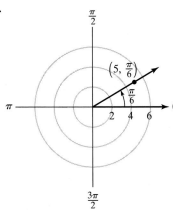

23.

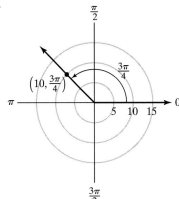

25.

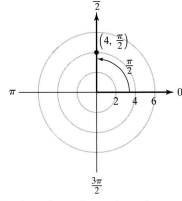

a. $\left(5, \dfrac{13\pi}{6}\right)$ **b.** $\left(-5, \dfrac{7\pi}{6}\right)$ **c.** $\left(5, -\dfrac{11\pi}{6}\right)$ **a.** $\left(10, \dfrac{11\pi}{4}\right)$ **b.** $\left(-10, \dfrac{7\pi}{4}\right)$ **c.** $\left(10, -\dfrac{5\pi}{4}\right)$ **a.** $\left(4, \dfrac{5\pi}{2}\right)$ **b.** $\left(-4, \dfrac{3\pi}{2}\right)$ **c.** $\left(4, -\dfrac{3\pi}{2}\right)$

27. a; b; d   **29. b, d**   **31. a, b**   **33.** $(0, 4)$ **35.** $(1, \sqrt{3})$ **37.** $(0, -4)$ **39.** approximately $(-5.9, 4.4)$ **41.** $\left(\sqrt{8}, \dfrac{3\pi}{4}\right)$

43. $\left(4, \dfrac{5\pi}{3}\right)$ **45.** $\left(2, \dfrac{7\pi}{6}\right)$ **47.** $(5, 0)$ **49.** $r = \dfrac{7}{3\cos\theta + \sin\theta}$ **51.** $r = \dfrac{7}{\cos\theta}$ **53.** $r = 3$ **55.** $r = 4\cos\theta$ **57.** $r = \dfrac{6\cos\theta}{\sin^2\theta}$

59. $x^2 + y^2 = 64$ **61.** $x = 0$ **63.** $y = 3$ **65.** $y = 4$ **67.** $x^2 + y^2 = y$ **69.** $x^2 + y^2 = 6x + 4y$ **71.** $y = \dfrac{1}{x}$ **73.** $\left(15, \dfrac{4\pi}{3}\right)$

75. 6.3 knots at an angle of 50° to the wind   **77.** Answers may vary.   **87.** $(-2, 3.464)$ **89.** $(-1.857, -3.543)$ **91.** $(3, 0.730)$

93. Answers may vary.   **95.** $x^2 + y^2 = 4x$; center: $(2, 0)$, radius: 2

Section 2.4

Check Point Exercises

1. a.

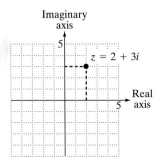

b.

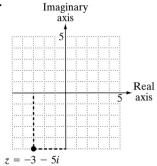

c.

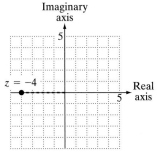

d.

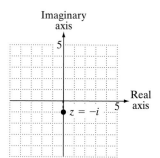

2. a. 13   **b.** $\sqrt{13}$ **3.**

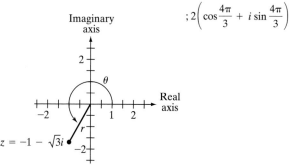

$; 2\left(\cos\dfrac{4\pi}{3} + i\sin\dfrac{4\pi}{3}\right)$

4. $z = 2\sqrt{3} + 2i$ **5.** $30(\cos 60° + i\sin 60°)$ **6.** $10(\cos\pi + i\sin\pi)$ **7.** $-16\sqrt{3} + 16i$ **8.** -4

9. $2(\cos 15° + i\sin 15°); 2(\cos 105° + i\sin 105°); 2(\cos 195° + i\sin 195°); 2(\cos 285° + i\sin 285°)$ **10.** $3; -\dfrac{3}{2} + \dfrac{3\sqrt{3}}{2}i; -\dfrac{3}{2} - \dfrac{3\sqrt{3}}{2}i$

Exercise Set 2.4

1.

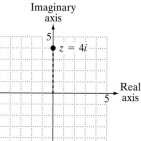

$; 4$ **3.**

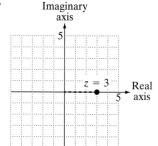

$; 3$ **5.**

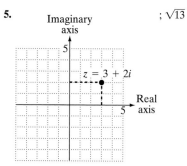

$; \sqrt{13}$

7.

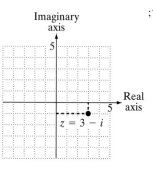

$; \sqrt{10}$ **9.**

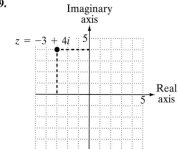

$; 5$ **11.**

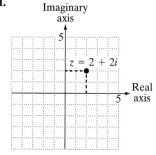

$2\sqrt{2}\left(\cos\dfrac{\pi}{4} + i\sin\dfrac{\pi}{4}\right)$ or $2\sqrt{2}(\cos 45° + i\sin 45°)$

13.

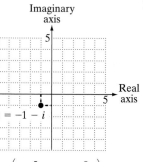

$\sqrt{2}\left(\cos\dfrac{5\pi}{4} + i\sin\dfrac{5\pi}{4}\right)$
or $\sqrt{2}(\cos 225° + i\sin 225°)$

15.

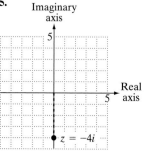

$4\left(\cos\dfrac{3\pi}{2} + i\sin\dfrac{3\pi}{2}\right)$
or $4(\cos 270° + i\sin 270°)$

17.

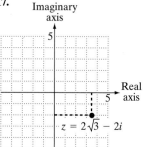

$4\left(\cos\dfrac{11\pi}{6} + i\sin\dfrac{11\pi}{6}\right)$
or $4(\cos 330° + i\sin 330°)$

19.

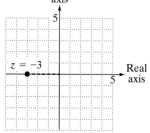

$3(\cos\pi + i\sin\pi)$
or $3(\cos 180° + i\sin 180°)$

21.

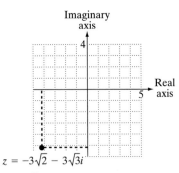

$z = -3\sqrt{2} - 3\sqrt{3}i$

$\approx 3\sqrt{5}(\cos 230.8° + i \sin 230.8°)$

23.

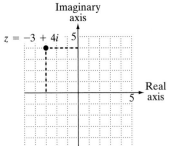

$z = -3 + 4i$

$\approx 5(\cos 126.9° + i \sin 126.9°)$

25.

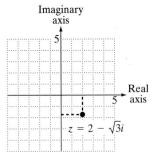

$z = 2 - \sqrt{3}i$

$\approx \sqrt{7}(\cos 319.1° + i \sin 319.1°)$

27. $3\sqrt{3} + 3i$ **29.** $-2 - 2\sqrt{3}i$ **31.** $4\sqrt{2} - 4\sqrt{2}i$ **33.** $5i$ **35.** $z \approx -18.1 - 8.5i$ **37.** $30(\cos 70° + i \sin 70°)$

39. $12\left(\cos\dfrac{3\pi}{10} + i \sin\dfrac{3\pi}{10}\right)$ **41.** $\cos\dfrac{7\pi}{12} + i \sin\dfrac{7\pi}{12}$ **43.** $2(\cos \pi + i \sin \pi)$ **45.** $5(\cos 50° + i \sin 50°)$ **47.** $\dfrac{3}{4}\left(\cos\dfrac{\pi}{10} + i \sin\dfrac{\pi}{10}\right)$

49. $\cos 240° + i \sin 240°$ **51.** $2(\cos 0° + i \sin 0°)$ **53.** $32\sqrt{2} + 32\sqrt{2}i$ **55.** $-4 - 4\sqrt{3}i$ **57.** $\dfrac{1}{64}i$ **59.** $-2 - 2\sqrt{3}i$

61. $-4 - 4i$ **63.** -64

Section 2.5

Check Point Exercises

1. $\|u\| = 5 = \|v\|$ and $m_u = \dfrac{4}{3} = m_v$

2.

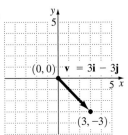

$(0,0)$ $v = 3i - 3j$

$(3, -3)$

$;\|v\| = 3\sqrt{2}$ **3.** $v = 3i + 4j$ **4. a.** $11i - 2j$ **b.** $3i + 8j$

5. a. $56i + 80j$ **b.** $-35i - 50j$ **6.** $30i + 33j$ **7.** $\dfrac{4}{5}i - \dfrac{3}{5}j$; $\sqrt{\left(\dfrac{4}{5}\right)^2 + \left(-\dfrac{3}{5}\right)^2} = \sqrt{\dfrac{16}{25} + \dfrac{9}{25}} = \sqrt{\dfrac{25}{25}} = 1$ **8.** $30\sqrt{2}i + 30\sqrt{2}j$

10. $\|v\| = \sqrt{2}, \theta = 45°$ **11.** $a = 3.1, b = 2.6$

Exercise Set 2.5

1. a. $\sqrt{41}$ **b.** $\sqrt{41}$ **c.** $u = v$ **3. a.** 6 **b.** 6 **c.** $u = v$

5.

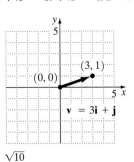

$(0,0)$ $(3, 1)$

$v = 3i + j$

$\sqrt{10}$

7.

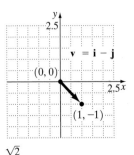

$v = i - j$

$(0,0)$

$(1, -1)$

$\sqrt{2}$

9.

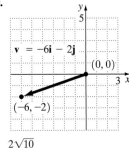

$v = -6i - 2j$

$(0,0)$

$(-6, -2)$

$2\sqrt{10}$

11.

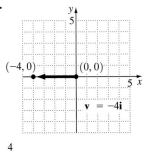

$(-4, 0)$ $(0,0)$

$v = -4i$

4

13. $10\mathbf{i} + 6\mathbf{j}$ **15.** $6\mathbf{i} - 3\mathbf{j}$ **17.** $-6\mathbf{i} - 14\mathbf{j}$ **19.** $9\mathbf{i}$ **21.** $-\mathbf{i} + 2\mathbf{j}$ **23.** $5\mathbf{i} - 12\mathbf{j}$ **25.** $-5\mathbf{i} + 12\mathbf{j}$ **27.** $-15\mathbf{i} + 35\mathbf{j}$ **29.** $4\mathbf{i} + 24\mathbf{j}$

31. $-9\mathbf{i} - 4\mathbf{j}$ **33.** $-5\mathbf{i} + 45\mathbf{j}$ **35.** $2\sqrt{29}$ **37.** $\sqrt{10}$ **39.** $\mathbf{i}$ **41.** $\dfrac{3}{5}\mathbf{i} - \dfrac{4}{5}\mathbf{j}$ **43.** $\dfrac{3\sqrt{13}}{13}\mathbf{i} - \dfrac{2\sqrt{13}}{3}\mathbf{j}$ **45.** $\dfrac{\sqrt{2}}{2}\mathbf{i} + \dfrac{\sqrt{2}}{2}\mathbf{j}$

47. $3\sqrt{3}\mathbf{i} + 3\mathbf{j}$ **49.** $-6\sqrt{2}\mathbf{i} - 6\sqrt{2}\mathbf{j}$ **51.** $\approx -0.20\mathbf{i} + 0.46\mathbf{j}$ **53.** $\|\mathbf{v}\| = \sqrt{5}$ $\theta = 63.4°$ **55.** $\|\mathbf{v}\| = 5$ $\theta = 270°$

57. $a = 3.5, b = 3.5$ **59.** $a = 3.9, b = 4.6$ **61.** $22\sqrt{3}\mathbf{i} + 22\mathbf{j}$ **63.** $148.5\mathbf{i} + 20.9\mathbf{j}$ **65.** $\approx 1.4\mathbf{i} + 0.6\mathbf{j}$; 1.4 in.

67. ≈ 108.21 lbs; S 77.4° E   **69.** ≈ 30.9 lbs   **71. a.** $\mathbf{F} = 9\mathbf{i} - 3\mathbf{j}$ **b.** $\mathbf{F}_3 = -9\mathbf{i} + 3\mathbf{j}$ **73. a.** $\mathbf{F} = -2\mathbf{j}$ **b.** $\mathbf{F}_5 = 2\mathbf{j}$

75. a. $\mathbf{v} = 180\cos 40°\mathbf{i} + 180\sin 40°\mathbf{j} \approx 137.89\mathbf{i} + 115.70\mathbf{j}$ $\mathbf{w} = 40\cos 0°\mathbf{i} + 40\sin 0°\mathbf{j} = 40\mathbf{i}$ **b.** $\mathbf{v} + \mathbf{w} \approx 177.89\mathbf{i} + 115.70\mathbf{j}$

c. 212 mph   **d.** 33.0°; N 57°E   **77.** 78 mph, 75.4°

Section 2.6

Check Point Exercises

1. a. 18   **b.** 18   **c.** 5   **2.** 100.3°   **3.** orthogonal   **4.** $\dfrac{7}{2}\mathbf{i} - \dfrac{7}{2}\mathbf{j}$ **5.** $\mathbf{v}_1 = \dfrac{7}{2}\mathbf{i} - \dfrac{7}{2}\mathbf{j}; \mathbf{v}_2 = -\dfrac{3}{2}\mathbf{i} - \dfrac{3}{2}\mathbf{j}$ **6.** approximately 2598 ft-lb

Exercise Set 2.6

1. a. 6   **b.** 10   **3. a.** -6 **b.** 41   **5. a.** 100   **b.** 61   **7. a.** 0   **b.** 25   **9.** 3   **11.** 3   **13.** 20   **15.** 20   **17.** 79.7°

19. 160.3°   **21.** 38.7°

23. 1077; $\mathbf{v} \cdot \mathbf{w} = 1077$ means \$1077 in revenue was generated on Monday by the sale of 240 gallons of regular gas at \$1.90 per gallon and 300 gallons of premium gas at \$2.07 per gallon.

27. $\mathbf{u} \cdot \mathbf{v} = (a_1\mathbf{i} + b_1\mathbf{j}) \cdot (a_2\mathbf{i} + b_2\mathbf{j})$
$= a_1a_2 + b_1b_2$
$= a_2a_1 + b_2b_1$
$= (a_2\mathbf{i} + b_2\mathbf{j}) \cdot (a_1\mathbf{i} + b_1\mathbf{j})$
$= \mathbf{v} \cdot \mathbf{u}$

29. $\mathbf{u} \cdot (\mathbf{v} + \mathbf{w}) = (a_1\mathbf{i} + b_1\mathbf{j}) \cdot [(a_2\mathbf{i} + b_2\mathbf{j}) + (a_3\mathbf{i} + b_3\mathbf{j})]$
$= (a_1\mathbf{i} + b_1\mathbf{j}) \cdot [(a_2 + a_3)\mathbf{i} + (b_2 + b_3)\mathbf{j}]$
$= a_1(a_2 + a_3) + b_1(b_2 + b_3)$
$= a_1a_2 + a_1a_3 + b_1b_2 + b_1b_3$
$= a_1a_2 + b_1b_2 + a_1a_3 + b_1b_3$
$= (a_1\mathbf{i} + b_1\mathbf{j}) \cdot (a_2\mathbf{i} + b_2\mathbf{j}) + (a_1\mathbf{i} + b_1\mathbf{j}) \cdot (a_3\mathbf{i} + b_3\mathbf{j})$
$= \mathbf{u} \cdot \mathbf{v} + \mathbf{u} \cdot \mathbf{w}$

Chapter 2 Review Exercises

1. $C = 55°, b \approx 10.5$, and $c \approx 10.5$ **2.** $A = 43°, a \approx 171.9$, and $b \approx 241.0$ **3.** $b \approx 16.3, A \approx 72°$, and $C \approx 42°$

4. $C \approx 98°, A \approx 55°$, and $B \approx 27°$ **5.** $C = 120°, a \approx 45.0$, and $b \approx 33.2$ **6.** two triangles; $B_1 \approx 55°, C_1 \approx 86°$, and $c_1 \approx 31.7$;

$B_2 \approx 125°, C_2 \approx 16°$, and $c_2 \approx 8.8$ **7.** no triangle   **8.** $a \approx 59.0, B \approx 3°$, and $C \approx 15°$ **9.** $B \approx 78°, A \approx 39°$, and $C \approx 63°$

10. $B \approx 25°, C \approx 115°$, and $c \approx 8.5$ **11.** two triangles; $A_1 \approx 59°, C_1 \approx 84°, c_1 \approx 14.4; A_2 \approx 121°, C_2 \approx 22°, c_2 \approx 5.4$

12. $B \approx 9°, C \approx 148°$, and $c \approx 73.6$ **13.** 8 sq ft   **14.** 4 sq ft   **15.** 4 sq m   **16.** 2 sq m   **17.** 35 ft   **18.** 35.6 mi   **19.** 861 mi

20. 404 ft; 551 ft   **21.** \$214,194

22.   **23.**   **24.**

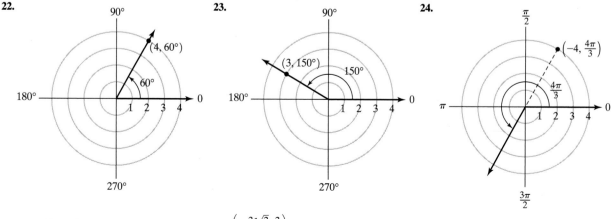

$(2, 2\sqrt{3})$ $\left(-\dfrac{3\sqrt{3}}{2}, \dfrac{3}{2}\right)$ $(2, 2\sqrt{3})$

25.

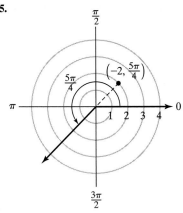

$(\sqrt{2}, \sqrt{2})$

26.

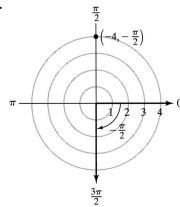

$(0, 4)$

27.

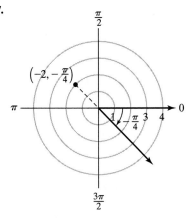

$(-\sqrt{2}, \sqrt{2})$

28.

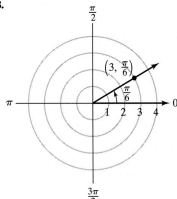

29.

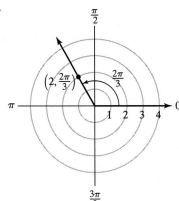

30.

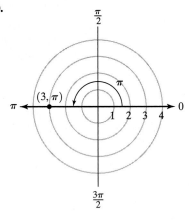

a. $\left(3, \dfrac{13\pi}{6}\right)$ **b.** $\left(-3, \dfrac{7\pi}{6}\right)$ **c.** $\left(3, -\dfrac{11\pi}{6}\right)$ **a.** $\left(2, \dfrac{8\pi}{3}\right)$ **b.** $\left(-2, \dfrac{5\pi}{3}\right)$ **c.** $\left(2, -\dfrac{4\pi}{3}\right)$ **a.** $(3, 3\pi)$ **b.** $(-3, 2\pi)$ **c.** $(3, -\pi)$

31. $\left(4\sqrt{2}, \dfrac{3\pi}{4}\right)$ **32.** $\left(3\sqrt{2}, \dfrac{7\pi}{4}\right)$ **33.** approximately $(13, 67°)$ **34.** approximately $(5, 127°)$ **35.** $\left(5, \dfrac{3\pi}{2}\right)$ **36.** $(1, 0)$

37.

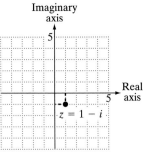

$\sqrt{2}\left(\cos\dfrac{7\pi}{4} + i\sin\dfrac{7\pi}{4}\right)$ or

$\sqrt{2}(\cos 315° + i\sin 315°)$

38.

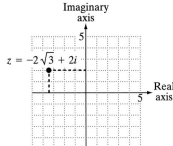

$4(\cos 150° + i\sin 150°)$ or

$4\left(\cos\dfrac{5\pi}{6} + i\sin\dfrac{5\pi}{6}\right)$

39.

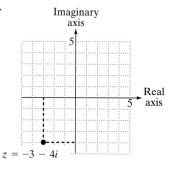

$z = -3 - 4i$

$z = -3 - 4i \approx 5(\cos 233° + i \sin 233°)$

40.

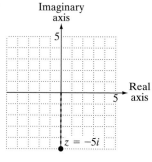

$z = -5i$

$5\left(\cos \dfrac{3\pi}{2} + i \sin \dfrac{3\pi}{2}\right)$ or $5(\cos 270° + i \sin 270°)$

41. $z = 4 + 4\sqrt{3}i$

42. $z = -2\sqrt{3} - 2i$

43. $z = -3 + 3\sqrt{3}i$

44. $z \approx -0.1 + 0.6i$

45. $15(\cos 110° + i \sin 110°)$

46. $\cos 265° + i \sin 265°$

47. $40(\cos \pi + i \sin \pi)$

48. $2(\cos 5° + i \sin 5°)$

49. $\dfrac{1}{2}(\cos \pi + i \sin \pi)$

50. $2\left(\cos \dfrac{7\pi}{6} + i \sin \dfrac{7\pi}{6}\right)$ **51.** $4 + 4\sqrt{3}i$ **52.** $-32\sqrt{3} + 32i$ **53.** $\dfrac{1}{128}i$ **54.** $64 - 64\sqrt{3}i$ **55.** $128 + 128i$

56. ; 5

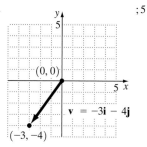

$(0, 0)$

$\mathbf{v} = -3\mathbf{i} - 4\mathbf{j}$

$(-3, -4)$

57. ; $\sqrt{29}$

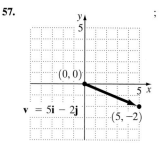

$(0, 0)$

$\mathbf{v} = 5\mathbf{i} - 2\mathbf{j}$

$(5, -2)$

58. ; 3

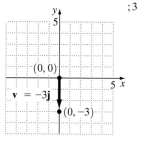

$(0, 0)$

$\mathbf{v} = -3\mathbf{j}$

$(0, -3)$

59. $3\mathbf{i} - 2\mathbf{j}$ **60.** $\mathbf{i} - 2\mathbf{j}$ **61.** $-\mathbf{i} + 2\mathbf{j}$ **62.** $-3\mathbf{i} + 12\mathbf{j}$ **63.** $12\mathbf{i} - 51\mathbf{j}$ **64.** $2\sqrt{26}$ **65.** $\dfrac{4}{5}\mathbf{i} - \dfrac{3}{5}\mathbf{j}$ **66.** $-\dfrac{1}{\sqrt{5}}\mathbf{i} + \dfrac{2}{\sqrt{5}}\mathbf{j}$

67. $6\mathbf{i} + 6\sqrt{3}\mathbf{j}$ **68.** 270 lb; 27.7° **69. a.** $13.59\mathbf{i} + 6.34\mathbf{j}$ **b.** 14.0 mph **c.** 13.9° **70.** $\sqrt{34}, 59°$ **71.** 7, 270°

72. $a = 6.55, b = 4.59$ **73.** $a = 2.82, b = 1.03$ **74.** 4 **75.** 2; 86.1° **76.** -32; 124.8° **77.** 1; 71.6°

Chapter 2 Test

1. 8.0 **2.** 6.2 **3.** 206 sq in.

4. ; Ordered pairs may vary.

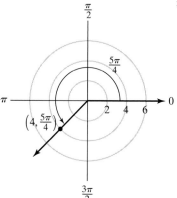

$\dfrac{\pi}{2}$

$\dfrac{5\pi}{4}$

π 0

2 4 6

$\left(4, \dfrac{5\pi}{4}\right)$

$\dfrac{3\pi}{2}$

5. $\left(\sqrt{2}, \dfrac{7\pi}{4}\right)$

6. $2(\cos 150° + i \sin 150°)$ or $2\left(\cos \dfrac{5\pi}{6} + i \sin \dfrac{5\pi}{6}\right)$ **7.** $50(\cos 20° + i \sin 20°)$ **8.** $\dfrac{1}{2}\left(\cos \dfrac{\pi}{6} + i \sin \dfrac{\pi}{6}\right)$

9. $32(\cos 50° + i \sin 50°)$ **10. a.** $\mathbf{i} + 2\mathbf{j}$ **b.** $\sqrt{5}$ **11.** $a = 2.97, b = 2.68$ **12.** $-23\mathbf{i} + 22\mathbf{j}$ **13.** -18 **14.** 138°

CHAPTER 3

Section 3.1

Check Point Exercises

1. 1 O-ring

2.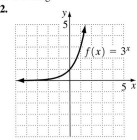

3.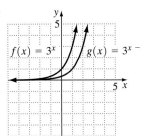

4.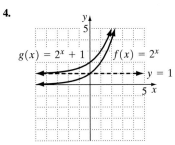

5. 11.49 billion

6. a. $14,859.47
   b. $14,918.25

Exercise Set 3.1

1. 10.556   **3.** 11.665   **5.** 0.125   **7.** 9.974   **9.** 0.387

11.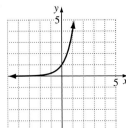

13.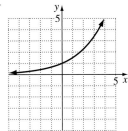

15.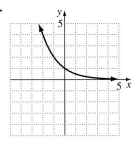

17.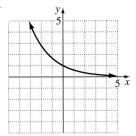

19. $H(x) = -3^{-x}$ **21.** $F(x) = -3^x$ **23.** $h(x) = 3^x - 1$

25.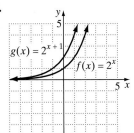

27.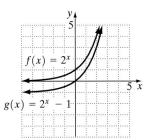

29.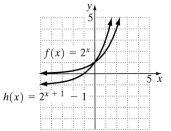

31.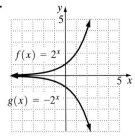

33.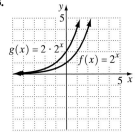

35.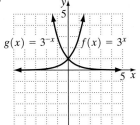

37.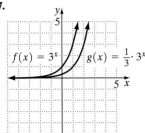

39.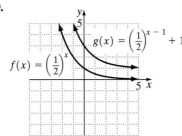

41. a. $13,116.51
b. $13,140.67
c. $13,157.04
d. $13,165.31

43. 7% compounded monthly

45. a. 67.38 million
b. about 134.74 million
c. about 269.46 million
d. 538.85 million
e. appears to double every 27 yr

47. $f(10) \approx 48$; 10 minutes after 8:00, 48 people have heard the rumor.　　**49.** $116,405.10

51. 3.249009585; 3.317278183; 3.321880096; 3.321995226; 3.321997068; $2^{\sqrt{3}} \approx 3.321997085$; The closer the exponent is to $\sqrt{3}$, the closer the value is to $2^{\sqrt{3}}$.　　**53.** 175.6　　**55. a.** 100%　　**b.** $\approx 68.5\%$　　**c.** $\approx 30.8\%$　　**d.** 20%

57. a. 1429　　**b.** 24,546　　**c.** Growth is limited by the population; The entire population will eventually become ill.

65.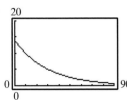

no; Nearly 4 O-rings are expected to fail.

67. a. 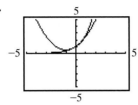　　**b.** 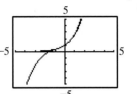　　**c.**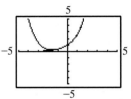

d. Answers may vary.

69. $y = 3^x$ is (d); $y = 5^x$ is (c); $y = \left(\dfrac{1}{3}\right)^x$ is (a); $y = \left(\dfrac{1}{5}\right)^x$ is (b).

71.
$$\left(\frac{e^x + e^{-x}}{2}\right)^2 - \left(\frac{e^x - e^{-x}}{2}\right)^2 \stackrel{?}{=} 1$$
$$\frac{e^{2x} + 2 + e^{-2x}}{4} - \frac{e^{2x} - 2 + e^{-2x}}{4} \stackrel{?}{=} 1$$
$$\frac{e^{2x} + 2 + e^{-2x} - e^{2x} + 2 - e^{-2x}}{4} \stackrel{?}{=} 1$$
$$\frac{4}{4} \stackrel{?}{=} 1$$
$$1 = 1$$

Section 3.2

Check Point Exercises

1. a. $7^3 = x$　　**b.** $b^2 = 25$　　**c.** $4^y = 26$　　**2. a.** $5 = \log_2 x$　　**b.** $3 = \log_b 27$　　**c.** $y = \log_e 33$　　**3. a.** 2　　**b.** 1　　**c.** $\dfrac{1}{2}$
4. a. 1　　**b.** 0　　**5. a.** 8　　**b.** 17　　**6.**

7. $(5, \infty)$
8. 80%
9. 4.0
10. a. $(-\infty, 4)$
b. $(-\infty, 0)$ or $(0, \infty)$
11. a. $25x$
b. $\sqrt{x}$
12. 4.6 ft per sec

Exercise Set 3.2

1. $2^4 = 16$　　**3.** $3^2 = x$　　**5.** $b^5 = 32$　　**7.** $6^y = 216$　　**9.** $\log_2 8 = 3$　　**11.** $\log_2 \dfrac{1}{16} = -4$　　**13.** $\log_8 2 = \dfrac{1}{3}$

15. $\log_{13} x = 2$　　**17.** $\log_b 1000 = 3$　　**19.** $\log_7 200 = y$　　**21.** 2　　**23.** 6　　**25.** $\dfrac{1}{2}$　　**27.** -3　　**29.** $\dfrac{1}{2}$　　**31.** 1

33. 0　　**35.** 7　　**37.** 19

39.

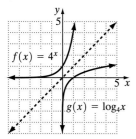

$f(x) = 4^x$

$g(x) = \log_4 x$

41.

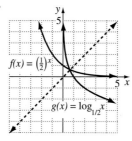

$f(x) = \left(\frac{1}{2}\right)^x$

$g(x) = \log_{1/2} x$

43. $H(x) = 1 - \log_3 x$
45. $h(x) = \log_3 x - 1$
47. $g(x) = \log_3(x - 1)$

49.

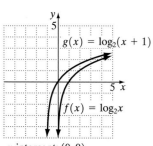

$g(x) = \log_2(x + 1)$

$f(x) = \log_2 x$

x-intercept: $(0, 0)$
vertical asymptote: $x = -1$

51.

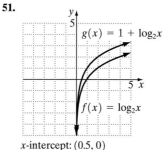

$g(x) = 1 + \log_2 x$

$f(x) = \log_2 x$

x-intercept: $(0.5, 0)$
vertical asymptote: $x = 0$

53.

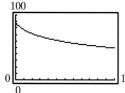

$f(x) = \log_2 x$

$g(x) = \frac{1}{2}\log_2 x$

x-intercept: $(1, 0)$
vertical asymptote: $x = 0$

55. $(-4, \infty)$ **57.** $(-\infty, 2)$ **59.** $(-\infty, 2)$ or $(2, \infty)$ **61.** 2   **63.** 7   **65.** 33   **67.** 0   **69.** 6   **71.** -6 **73.** 125

75. $9x$ **77.** $5x^2$ **79.** $\sqrt{x}$ **81.** 95.4%   **83.** \$5.65 billion   **85.** ≈ 188 db; yes

87. a. 88
b. 71.5; 63.9; 58.8; 55; 52; 49.5
c.

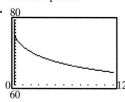

Material retention decreases
as time passes.

97.

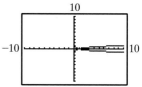

$g(x)$ is $f(x)$ shifted left 3 units left.

99.

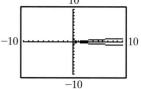

$g(x)$ is $f(x)$ reflected about the *x*-axis.

101.

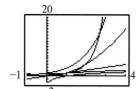

The score falls below 65 after 9 months.

103. $y = \ln x$, $y = \sqrt{x}$, $y = x$, $y = x^2$, $y = e^x$, $y = x^x$

105. $\dfrac{4}{5}$

107. $\log_3 40 > \log_4 60$

Section 3.3

Check Point Exercises

1. a. $\log_6 7 + \log_6 11$ **b.** $2 + \log x$ **2. a.** $\log_8 23 - \log_8 x$ **b.** $5 - \ln 11$ **3. a.** $9 \log_6 3$ **b.** $\dfrac{1}{3} \ln x$

4. a. $4 \log_b x + \dfrac{1}{3} \log_b y$ **b.** $\dfrac{1}{2} \log_5 x - 2 - 3 \log_5 y$ **5. a.** 2   **b.** $\log \dfrac{7x + 6}{x}$

6. a. $\ln x^2 \sqrt[3]{x + 5}$ **b.** $\log \dfrac{(x - 3)^2}{x}$ **c.** $\log_b \dfrac{\sqrt[4]{x}\, y^{10}}{25}$ **7.** 4.02   **8.** 4.02

Exercise Set 3.3

1. $\log_5 7 + \log_5 3$ **3.** $1 + \log_7 x$ **5.** $3 + \log x$ **7.** $1 - \log_7 x$ **9.** $\log x - 2$ **11.** $3 - \log_4 y$ **13.** $2 - \ln 5$

15. $3 \log_b x$ **17.** $-6 \log N$ **19.** $\dfrac{1}{5} \ln x$ **21.** $2 \log_b x + \log_b y$ **23.** $\dfrac{1}{2} \log_4 x - 3$ **25.** $2 - \dfrac{1}{2} \log_6(x + 1)$

27. $2\log_b x + \log_b y - 2\log_b z$ **29.** $1 + \dfrac{1}{2}\log x$ **31.** $\dfrac{1}{3}\log x - \dfrac{1}{3}\log y$ **33.** $\dfrac{1}{2}\log_b x + 3\log_b y - 3\log_b z$

35. $\dfrac{2}{3}\log_5 x + \dfrac{1}{3}\log_5 y - \dfrac{2}{3}$ **37.** $3\ln x + \dfrac{1}{2}\ln(x^2+1) - 4\ln(x+1)$ **39.** $\left(1 + 2\log x + \dfrac{1}{3}\log(1-x)\right) - (\log 7 + 2\log(x+1))$

41. 1   **43.** $\ln(7x)$ **45.** 5   **47.** $\log\left(\dfrac{2x+5}{x}\right)$ **49.** $\log(xy^3)$ **51.** $\ln(x^{1/2}y)$ or $\ln(y\sqrt{x})$ **53.** $\log_b(x^2y^3)$ **55.** $\ln\left(\dfrac{x^5}{y^2}\right)$

57. $\ln\left(\dfrac{x^3}{y^{1/3}}\right)$ or $\ln\left(\dfrac{x^3}{\sqrt[3]{y}}\right)$ **59.** $\ln\dfrac{(x+6)^4}{x^3}$ **61.** $\ln\left(\dfrac{x^3y^5}{z^6}\right)$ **63.** $\log\sqrt{xy}$ **65.** $\log_5\left(\dfrac{\sqrt{xy}}{(x+1)^2}\right)$ **67.** $\ln\sqrt[3]{\dfrac{(x+5)^2}{x(x^2-4)}}$

69. $\log\left(\dfrac{7x(x^2-1)}{x+1}\right)$ or $\log(7x(x-1))$ **71.** 1.5937   **73.** 1.6944   **75.** −1.2304   **77.** 3.6193

79. 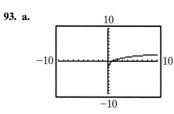   **81.** 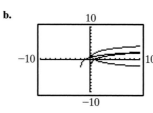   **83. a.** $D = 10\log\dfrac{I}{I_0}$ **b.** 20 decibels louder

93. a. 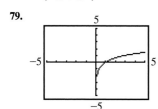   **b.** 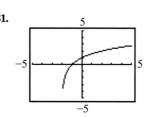 $y = 2 + \log_3 x$ shifts the graph of $y = \log_3 x$ two units upward; $y = \log_3(x+2)$ shifts the graph of $y = \log_3 x$ two units left; $y = -\log_3 x$ reflects the graph of $y = \log_3 x$ about the x-axis.

95. 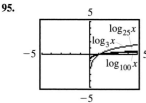   **a.** top graph: $y = \log_{100} x$; bottom graph: $y = \log_3 x$ **b.** top graph: $y = \log_3 x$; bottom graph: $y = \log_{100} x$ **c.** The graph of the equation with the largest b will be on the top in the interval $(0,1)$ and on the bottom in the interval $(1,\infty)$.

101. (d) is true.   **103.** $\dfrac{2A}{B}$ **105.** Answers may vary.

Section 3.4

Check Point Exercises

1. $\left\{\dfrac{\ln 134}{\ln 5}\right\}; \approx 3.04$ **2.** $\left\{\dfrac{\ln 9}{2}\right\}; \approx 1.10$ **3.** $\left\{\dfrac{\ln 2088 + 4\ln 6}{3\ln 6}\right\}; \approx 2.76$ **4.** $\{0, \ln 7\}; \ln 7 \approx 1.95$ **5.** $\{12\}$ **6.** $\{5\}$

7. $\left\{\dfrac{e^2}{3}\right\}$ **8.** 0.01   **9.** 16.2 yr   **10.** 2149

Exercise Set 3.4

1. $\left\{\dfrac{\ln 3.91}{\ln 10}\right\}; \approx 0.59$ **3.** $\{\ln 5.7\}; \approx 1.74$ **5.** $\left\{\dfrac{\ln 17}{\ln 5}\right\}; \approx 1.76$ **7.** $\left\{\ln\dfrac{23}{5}\right\}; \approx 1.53$ **9.** $\left\{\dfrac{\ln 659}{5}\right\}; \approx 1.30$

11. $\left\{\dfrac{\ln 793 - 1}{-5}\right\}; \approx -1.14$ **13.** $\left\{\dfrac{\ln 10{,}478 + 3}{5}\right\}; \approx 2.45$ **15.** $\left\{\dfrac{\ln 410}{\ln 7} - 2\right\}; \approx 1.09$ **17.** $\left\{\dfrac{\ln 813}{0.3\ln 7}\right\}; \approx 11.48$

19. $\left\{\dfrac{3\ln 5 + \ln 3}{\ln 3 - 2\ln 5}\right\}; \approx -2.80$ **21.** $\{0, \ln 2\}; \ln 2 \approx 0.69$ **23.** $\left\{\dfrac{\ln 3}{2}\right\}; \approx 0.55$ **25.** $\{0\}$ **27.** $\{81\}$ **29.** $\{59\}$ **31.** $\left\{\dfrac{109}{27}\right\}$

33. $\left\{\dfrac{62}{3}\right\}$ **35.** $\left\{\dfrac{5}{4}\right\}$ **37.** $\{6\}$ **39.** $\{6\}$ **41.** $\{5\}$ **43.** $\{2, 12\}$ **45.** $\{e^2\}; \approx 7.39$ **47.** $\left\{\dfrac{e^4}{2}\right\}; \approx 27.30$ **49.** $\{e^{-1/2}\}; \approx 0.61$

51. $\{e^2 - 3\}; \approx 4.39$ **53.** about 0.11   **55. a.** 18.9 million   **b.** ≈ 2006 **57.** 8.2 yr   **59.** 16.8%   **61.** 8.7 yr   **63.** 15.7%

65. 1995   **67.** 2.8 days; Yes, the point $(2.8, 50)$ appears to lie on the graph of P.   **69.** $10^{-2.4}$; 0.004 moles per liter

75. $\{2\}$ **77.** $\{4\}$ **79.** $\{2\}$ **81.** $\{-1.391606, 1.6855579\}$

83.

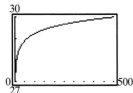

30

0
27
500

As distance from eye increases, barometric air pressure increases, leveling off at about 30 inches of mercury.

85.

150

Y1=145e^(-.092X)

0 X=7.92 ——— Y=69.971901 · 15
0

about 7.9 min

87. (c) is true.   **89.** $\{1, e^2\}, e^2 \approx 7.389$ **91.** $\{e\}, e \approx 2.718$

Section 3.5

Check Point Exercises

1. a. $A = 643\, e^{0.023t}$ **b.** 2039   **2. a.** $A = A_0 e^{-0.0248t}$ **b.** about 72 yr   **3. a.** 0.4 correct responses   **b.** 0.7 correct responses
c. 0.8 correct responses   **4.** $y = 4e^{(\ln 7.8)x}; y = 4e^{2.054x}$

Exercise Set 3.5

1. 203 million   **3.** 2005   **5.** 2.6%   **7.** 2014   **9. a.** $A = 158,700e^{0.053t}$ **b.** 2007   **11.** $A = 6.04e^{0.01t}$ **13.** 8.01 g
15. 8 g; 4 g; 2 g; 1 g; 0.5 g   **17.** 15,679 years old   **19. a.** $\frac{A_0}{2} = A_0 e^{k(1.31)}; \frac{1}{2} = e^{1.31k}; \ln\frac{1}{2} = \ln e^{1.31k}; \ln\frac{1}{2} = 1.31k; k = \dfrac{\ln\frac{1}{2}}{1.31} \approx -0.52912$
b. 107 million years   **21.** $2A_0 = A_0 e^{kt}; 2 = e^{kt}; \ln 2 = \ln e^{kt}; \ln 2 = kt; t = \dfrac{\ln 2}{k}$ **23.** 63 yr   **25. a.** about 20 people
b. about 1080 people   **c.** 100,000 people   **27.** about 3.7%   **29.** about 48 years old   **31.** $y = 100e^{(\ln 4.6)x}; y = 100e^{1.526x}$
33. $y = 2.5e^{(\ln 0.7)x}; y = 2.5e^{-0.357x}$ **45.** $y = 1.740(1.037)^x; r \approx 0.971$, a very good fit
47. $y = 0.112x + 1.547; r = 0.989$; a very good fit   **49.** The model of best fit is the linear model; 2022
51. The logarithmic model, $y = -905,231.353 + 119,204.060 \ln x$, best fits the data. Answers for prediction may vary.
53. Answers may vary.

Chapter 3 Review Exercises

1. $g(x) = 4^{-x}$ **2.** $h(x) = -4^{-x}$ **3.** $r(x) = -4^{-x} + 3$ **4.** $f(x) = 4^x$

5.

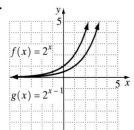

$f(x) = 2^x$
$g(x) = 2^{x-1}$

6.

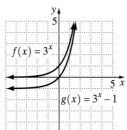

$f(x) = 3^x$
$g(x) = 3^x - 1$

7.

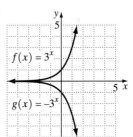

$f(x) = 3^x$
$g(x) = -3^x$

8.

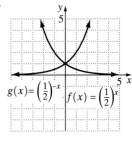

$g(x) = \left(\frac{1}{2}\right)^{-x}$
$f(x) = \left(\frac{1}{2}\right)^x$

9. 5.5% compounded semiannually   **10.** 7% compounded monthly
11. a. 200°   **b.** 120°; 119°   **c.** 70°; The temperature in the room is 70°.   **12.** $49^{1/2} = 7$ **13.** $4^3 = x$ **14.** $3^y = 81$
15. $\log_6 216 = 3$ **16.** $\log_b 625 = 4$ **17.** $\log_{13} 874 = y$ **18.** 3   **19.** -2 **20.** $\varnothing; \log_b x$ is defined only for $x > 0$.   **21.** $\frac{1}{2}$
22. 1   **23.** 8   **24.** 5   **25.** 0   **26.**   **27.**   **28.** $g(x) = \log(-x)$

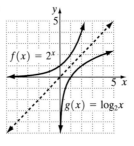

$f(x) = 2^x$
$g(x) = \log_2 x$

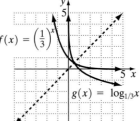

$f(x) = \left(\frac{1}{3}\right)^x$
$g(x) = \log_{1/3} x$

29. $r(x) = 1 + \log(2 - x)$ **30.** $h(x) = \log(2 - x)$ **31.** $f(x) = \log x$

32.

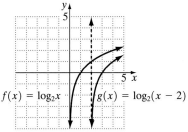

$f(x) = \log_2 x$ $g(x) = \log_2(x - 2)$

x-intercept: $(3, 0)$
vertical asymptote: $x = 2$

33.

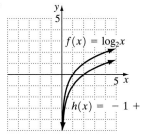

$f(x) = \log_2 x$

$h(x) = -1 + \log_2 x$

x-intercept: $(2, 0)$
vertical asymptote: $x = 0$

34.

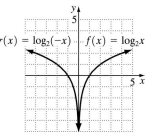

$r(x) = \log_2(-x)$ $f(x) = \log_2 x$

x-intercept: $(-1, 0)$
vertical asymptote: $x = 0$

35. $(-5, \infty)$ **36.** $(-\infty, 3)$ **37.** $(-\infty, 1)\cup(1, \infty)$ **38.** $6x$ **39.** $\sqrt{x}$ **40.** $4x^2$ **41.** 3.0

42. a. 76
b. $\approx 67, \approx 63, \approx 61, \approx 59, \approx 56$
c.

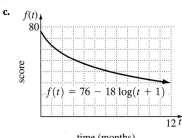

$f(t) = 76 - 18 \log(t + 1)$

time (months)

Retention decreases as time passes.

43. about 9 weeks **44.** $2 + 3 \log_6 x$ **45.** $\frac{1}{2} \log_4 x - 3$

46. $\log_2 x + 2 \log_2 y - 6$ **47.** $\frac{1}{3} \ln x - \frac{1}{3}$ **48.** $\log_b 21$ **49.** $\log \frac{3}{x^3}$

50. $\ln(x^3 y^4)$ **51.** $\ln \frac{\sqrt{x}}{y}$ **52.** 6.2448 **53.** -0.1063

54. $\left\{\frac{\ln 12{,}143}{\ln 8}\right\}; \approx 4.523$ **55.** $\left\{\frac{1}{5} \ln 141\right\}; \approx 0.990$

56. $\left\{\frac{12 - \ln 130}{5}\right\}; \approx 1.426$ **57.** $\left\{\frac{\ln 37{,}500 - 2 \ln 5}{4 \ln 5}\right\}; \approx 1.136$

58. $\{\ln 3\}; \approx 1.099$ **59.** $\{23\}$ **60.** $\{5\}$ **61.** $\varnothing$ **62.** $\left\{\frac{1}{e}\right\}$

63. $\left\{\frac{e^3}{2}\right\}$ **64.** 2042 **65.** 2086 **66.** 2005 **67.** 7.3 yr **68.** 14.6 yr **69.** about 21.97%

70. a. 0.045 **b.** 55.6 million **c.** 2012 **71.** about $15{,}679$ years old **72. a.** 200 people **b.** about $45{,}411$ people **c.** $500{,}000$ people
73. $y = 73e^{(\ln 2.6)x}; y = 73e^{0.956x}$ **74.** $y = 6.5e^{(\ln 0.43)x}; y = 6.5e^{-0.844x}$
75. high: exponential; medium: linear; low: quadratic; Explanations will vary; negative; The parabola opens downward.
76. The exponential model, $y = (3.460)(1.024)^x$, is the best fit; about 116 million

Chapter 3 Test

1.

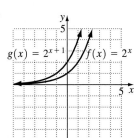

$g(x) = 2^{x+1}$ $f(x) = 2^x$

2.

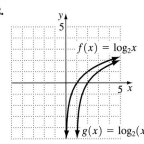

$f(x) = \log_2 x$

$g(x) = \log_2(x - 1)$

3. $5^3 = 125$ **4.** $\log_{36} 6 = \frac{1}{2}$ **5.** $(-\infty, 3)$

6. $3 + 5 \log_4 x$ **7.** $\frac{1}{3} \log_3 x - 4$ **8.** $\log(x^6 y^2)$

9. $\ln \frac{7}{x^3}$ **10.** 1.5741 **11.** $\left\{\frac{\ln 1.4}{\ln 5}\right\}$

12. $\left\{\frac{\ln 4}{0.005}\right\}$ **13.** $\{0, \ln 5\}$ **14.** $\{54.25\}$

15. $\{5\}$ **16.** $\left\{\frac{e^4}{3}\right\}$

17. 6.5% compounded semiannually; $\$221.15$ more **18.** 120 db **19. a.** about 89% **b.** decreasing; $k = -0.004 < 0$ **c.** 1995
20. 20. $A = 509e^{0.036t}$ **21.** about $24{,}758$ years ago **22. a.** 14 elk **b.** about 51 elk **c.** 140 elk

CHAPTER 4

Section 4.1

Check Point Exercises

1. a. $7, 9, 11, 13$ **b.** $-\dfrac{1}{3}, \dfrac{1}{5}, -\dfrac{1}{9}, \dfrac{1}{17}$ **2.** $3, 11, 27, 59$ **3.** $10, \dfrac{10}{3}, \dfrac{5}{6}, \dfrac{1}{6}$ **4. a.** 91 **b.** n **5. a.** 182 **b.** 47 **c.** 20

6. a. $\displaystyle\sum_{i=1}^{9} i^2$ **b.** $\displaystyle\sum_{i=1}^{n} \dfrac{1}{2^{i-1}}$

Exercise Set 4.1

1. $5, 8, 11, 14$ **3.** $3, 9, 27, 81$ **5.** $-3, 9, -27, 81$ **7.** $-4, 5, -6, 7$ **9.** $\dfrac{2}{5}, \dfrac{2}{3}, \dfrac{6}{7}, 1$ **11.** $1, -\dfrac{1}{3}, \dfrac{1}{7}, -\dfrac{1}{15}$ **13.** $7, 12, 17, 22$

15. $3, 12, 48, 192$ **17.** $4, 11, 25, 53$ **19.** $1, 2, \dfrac{3}{2}, \dfrac{2}{3}$ **21.** $4, 12, 48, 240$ **23.** 272 **25.** 120 **27.** $(n + 2)(n + 1)$ **29.** 105

31. 60 **33.** 115 **35.** $-\dfrac{5}{16}$ **37.** 55 **39.** $\dfrac{3}{8}$ **41.** 15 **43.** $\displaystyle\sum_{i=1}^{15} i^2$ **45.** $\displaystyle\sum_{i=1}^{11} 2^i$ **47.** $\displaystyle\sum_{i=1}^{30} i$ **49.** $\displaystyle\sum_{i=1}^{14} \dfrac{i}{i+1}$ **51.** $\displaystyle\sum_{i=1}^{n} \dfrac{4^i}{i}$

53. $\displaystyle\sum_{i=1}^{n} (2i - 1)$ **55.** $\displaystyle\sum_{k=1}^{14} (2k + 3)$ **57.** $\displaystyle\sum_{k=0}^{12} ar^k$ **59.** $\displaystyle\sum_{k=0}^{n} (a + kd)$ **61. a.** 6881.6; From 1991 through 2000, a total of 6881.6 million, CDs were sold.   **b.** 688.16; From 1991 through 2000, the average number of CDs sold each year was 688.16 million.

63. a. 88.3; From 1993 through 2000, a total of 88.3 million people received cash assistance.   **b.** 88.12; This is a reasonable model.

65. $\$8081.13$ **77.** $1,307,674,368,000$ **79.** 6840 **83.** $a_{10} = 2.5937$; $a_{100} = 2.7048$; $a_{1000} = 2.7169$; $a_{10,000} = 2.7181$; $a_{100,000} = 2.7183$; As n gets larger, a_n gets closer to $e \approx 2.7183$.

85.
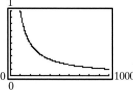
As n gets larger, a_n approaches 0.

87.
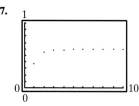
As n gets larger, a_n approaches $\dfrac{3}{5}$.

89. $9, 32, 16, 8, 4$

Section 4.2

Check Point Exercises

1. $51.5, 53.68, 55.86, 58.04, 60.22$ **2.** -34 **3. a.** $a_n = 9700n + 149,300$ **b.** $\$304,500$ **4.** 360 **5.** 2460 **6.** $\$596,300$

Exercise Set 4.2

1. $200, 220, 240, 260, 280, 300$ **3.** $-7, -3, 1, 5, 9, 13$ **5.** $300, 210, 120, 30, -60, -150$ **7.** $\dfrac{5}{2}, 2, \dfrac{3}{2}, 1, \dfrac{1}{2}, 0$ **9.** $-9, -3, 3, 9, 15, 21$

11. $30, 20, 10, 0, -10, -20$ **13.** $1.6, 1.2, 0.8, 0.4, 0, -0.4$ **15.** 33 **17.** 252 **19.** 955 **21.** -142 **23.** $a_n = 4n - 3$; $a_{20} = 77$

25. $a_n = 11 - 4n$; $a_{20} = -69$ **27.** $a_n = 7 + 2n$; $a_{20} = 47$ **29.** $a_n = -16 - 4n$; $a_{20} = -96$ **31.** $a_n = 1 + 3n$; $a_{20} = 61$

33. $a_n = 40 - 10n$; $a_{20} = -160$ **35.** 1220 **37.** 4400 **39.** 5050 **41.** 3660 **43.** 396 **45.** $8 + 13 + 18 + \cdots + 88$; 816

47. $2 - 1 - 4 - \cdots - 85$; -1245 **49.** $4 + 8 + 12 + \cdots + 400$; $20,200$ **51. a.** $a_n = 1.7n + 148.3$ **b.** 211.2 lbs

53. Answers may vary. One possibility is given.   **a.** $a_n = 0.5n + 14.5$ **b.** 33 lbs   **55.** Company A will pay $\$1400$ more.

57. a. $a_n = 3.204 + 0.576n$ **b.** 627.3 million tons   **59.** $\$442,500$ **61.** 1430 seats   **71.** the 200th term

73. $S_n = \dfrac{n}{2}(1 + 2n - 1) = \dfrac{n}{2}(2n) = n^2$

Section 4.3

Check Point Exercises

1. $12, 6, 3, \dfrac{3}{2}, \dfrac{3}{4}, \dfrac{3}{8}$ **2.** 3645 **3.** $a_n = 3(2)^{n-1}$; 384 **4.** 9842 **5.** $19,680$ **6.** $\$2,371,746$ **7.** $\$1,327,778$ **8.** 9 **9.** 1

10. $\$4000$

Exercise Set 4.3

1. $5, 15, 45, 135, 405$ **3.** $20, 10, 5, \dfrac{5}{2}, \dfrac{5}{4}$ **5.** $10, -40, 160, -640, 2560$ **7.** $-6, 30, -150, 750, -3750$ **9.** $a_8 = 768$

11. $a_{12} = -10{,}240$ **13.** $a_{40} \approx -0.000000002$ **15.** $a_8 = 0.1$ **17.** $a_n = 3(4)^{n-1}; a_7 = 12{,}288$ **19.** $a_n = 18\left(\dfrac{1}{3}\right)^{n-1}; a_7 = \dfrac{2}{81}$

21. $a_n = 1.5(-2)^{n-1}; a_7 = 96$ **23.** $a_n = 0.0004(-10)^{n-1}; a_7 = 400$ **25.** $531{,}440$ **27.** 2049 **29.** $\dfrac{16{,}383}{2}$ **31.** 9840

33. $10{,}230$ **35.** $\dfrac{63}{128}$ **37.** $\dfrac{3}{2}$ **39.** 4 **41.** $\dfrac{2}{3}$ **43.** $S_\infty \approx 6.15385$ **45.** $\dfrac{5}{9}$ **47.** $\dfrac{47}{99}$ **49.** $\dfrac{257}{999}$ **51.** arithmetic, $d = 1$
53. geometric, $r = 2$ **55.** neither   **57.** \$16,384   **59.** \$3,795,957   **61. a.** $1.013, 1.013, 1.013, 1.013, 1.013, 1.013, 1.013$; the population is increasing geometrically with $r \approx 1.013$ **b.** $a_n = 29.76(1.013)^{n-1}$ **c.** ≈ 33.86; very well   **63.** \$32,767

65. \$793,582.90   **67.** 130.26 in.   **69.** \$844,706.11   **71.** \$94,834.21   **73.** \$9 million   **75.** $\dfrac{1}{3}$

87.

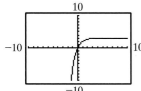

Horizontal asymptote at $y = 3$; $\displaystyle\sum_{n=0}^{\infty} 2\left(\dfrac{1}{3}\right)^n = 3$ **89.** (d) is true.   **91.** \$442.38

Section 4.4

Check Point Exercises

1. 72   **2.** 729   **3.** 676,000   **4.** 840   **5.** 720   **6. a.** combinations   **b.** permutations   **7.** 210   **8.** 1820

Exercise Set 4.4

1. 3024   **3.** 6720   **5.** 720   **7.** 1   **9.** 126   **11.** 330   **13.** 1   **15.** 1   **17.** combinations   **19.** permutations
21. 27 ways   **23.** 40 ways   **25.** 243 ways   **27.** 144 area codes   **29.** 120 ways   **31.** 6 paragraphs   **33.** 720 ways
35. 8,648,640 ways   **37.** 120 ways   **39.** 15,120 lineups   **41.** 20 ways   **43.** 495 collections   **45.** 24,310 groups
47. 22,957,480 selections   **49.** 360 ways   **51.** 1716 ways   **53.** 1140 ways   **55.** 840 passwords   **57.** 2730 cones
69. (c) is true.   **71.** 144 numbers

Section 4.5

Check Point Exercises

1. $\dfrac{0.69}{3.00} = 0.23$ **2.** $\dfrac{1}{3}$ **3.** $\dfrac{1}{9}$ **4.** $\dfrac{1}{13}$ **5.** $\dfrac{1}{13{,}983{,}816} \approx 0.0000000715$ **6.** $\dfrac{999}{1000} \approx 0.999$ **7.** $\dfrac{1}{3}$ **8.** $\dfrac{3}{4}$ **9.** $\dfrac{4}{5}$
10. $\dfrac{1}{361} \approx 0.003$ **11.** $\dfrac{1}{16}$

Exercise Set 4.5

1. $\dfrac{4}{25} \approx 0.16$ **3.** $\dfrac{3}{25} \approx 0.12$ **5.** $\dfrac{7844}{60{,}549} \approx 0.13$ **7.** $\dfrac{1032}{20{,}183} \approx 0.05$ **9.** $\dfrac{1}{6}$ **11.** $\dfrac{1}{2}$ **13.** $\dfrac{1}{3}$ **15.** $\dfrac{1}{13}$ **17.** $\dfrac{3}{13}$ **19.** $\dfrac{1}{4}$
21. $\dfrac{7}{8}$ **23.** $\dfrac{1}{12}$ **25.** $\dfrac{1}{18{,}009{,}460}; \dfrac{5}{900{,}473}$ **27.** $\approx 25{,}213$ **29. a.** 2,598,960   **b.** 1287   **c.** $\dfrac{1287}{2{,}598{,}960} \approx 0.0005$ **31. a.** ≈ 0.1
b. ≈ 0.9 **33.** $\dfrac{2}{13}$ **35.** $\dfrac{1}{13}$ **37.** $\dfrac{5}{6}$ **39.** $\dfrac{7}{13}$ **41.** $\dfrac{3}{4}$ **43.** $\dfrac{33}{40}$ **45.** $\dfrac{1}{36}$ **47.** $\dfrac{1}{3}$ **49.** $\dfrac{1}{64}$ **51.** 0.00234256
53. a. $\dfrac{1}{256}$ **b.** $\dfrac{1}{4096}$ **c.** $\left(\dfrac{15}{16}\right)^{10}$ **d.** $1 - \left(\dfrac{15}{16}\right)^{10}$ **65.** Answers may vary.

Chapter 4 Review Exercises

1. $a_1 = 3; a_2 = 10; a_3 = 17; a_4 = 24$ **2.** $a_1 = -\dfrac{3}{2}; a_2 = \dfrac{4}{3}; a_3 = -\dfrac{5}{4}; a_4 = \dfrac{6}{5}$ **3.** $a_1 = 1; a_2 = 1; a_3 = \dfrac{1}{2}; a_4: \dfrac{1}{6}$

4. $a_1 = \dfrac{1}{2}; a_2 = -\dfrac{1}{4}; a_3 = \dfrac{1}{8}; a_4 = -\dfrac{1}{16}$ **5.** $a_1 = 9; a_2 = \dfrac{2}{27}; a_3 = 9; a_4 = \dfrac{2}{27}$ **6.** $a_1 = 4; a_2 = 11; a_3 = 25; a_4 = 53$ **7.** 65   **8.** 95

9. -20 **10.** $\displaystyle\sum_{i=1}^{15} \dfrac{i}{i+2}$ **11.** $\displaystyle\sum_{i=1}^{10} (i+3)^3$ **12.** $7, 11, 15, 19, 23, 27$ **13.** $-4, -9, -14, -19, -24, -29$ **14.** $\dfrac{3}{2}, 1, \dfrac{1}{2}, 0, -\dfrac{1}{2}, -1$

15. $-2, 3, 8, 13, 18, 23$ **16.** $a_6 = 20$ **17.** $a_{12} = -30$ **18.** $a_{14} = -38$ **19.** $a_n = 4n - 11; a_{20} = 69$

20. $a_n = 220 - 20n; a_{20} = -180$ **21.** $a_n = 8 - 5n; a_{20} = -92$ **22.** 1727   **23.** 225   **24.** 15,150   **25.** 440   **26.** -500

27. -2325 **28. a.** $a_n = 0.52n + 19.48$ **b.** 77.2%   **29.** \$418,500   **30.** 1470 seats   **31.** $3, 6, 12, 24, 48$ **32.** $\dfrac{1}{2}, \dfrac{1}{4}, \dfrac{1}{8}, \dfrac{1}{16}, \dfrac{1}{32}$

33. $16, -8, 4, -2, 1$ **34.** $-1, 5, -25, 125, -625$ **35.** $a_7 = 1458$ **36.** $a_6 = \dfrac{1}{2}$ **37.** $a_5 = -48$ **38.** $a_n = 2^{n-1}; a_8 = 128$

39. $a_n = 100\left(\dfrac{1}{10}\right)^{n-1}; a_8 = \dfrac{1}{100,000}$ **40.** $a_n = 12\left(-\dfrac{1}{3}\right)^{n-1}; a_8 = -\dfrac{4}{729}$ **41.** 17,936,135   **42.** $\dfrac{127}{8}$ **43.** 19,530   **44.** -258

45. $\dfrac{341}{128}$ **46.** $\dfrac{27}{2}$ **47.** $\dfrac{4}{3}$ **48.** $-\dfrac{18}{5}$ **49.** 20   **50.** $\dfrac{2}{3}$ **51.** $\dfrac{47}{99}$ **52. a.** $\dfrac{20.72}{19.96} \approx 1.038, \dfrac{21.51}{20.72} \approx 1.038, \dfrac{22.33}{21.51} \approx 1.038;$

the population is increasing geometrically with $r \approx 1.038$.   **b.** $a_n = 19.96(1.038)^{n-1}$ **c.** ≈ 27.92 million people

53. \$42,823; \$223,210   **54.** \$120,112.64   **55.** $\$9\dfrac{1}{3}$ million   **56.** 336   **57.** 15,120   **58.** 56   **59.** 78   **60.** 20 choices

61. 243 possibilities   **62.** 32,760 ways   **63.** 4845 ways   **64.** 1140 sets   **65.** 116,280 ways

66. 120 ways   **67.** $\dfrac{10,966,556}{33,871,648} \approx 0.324$ **68.** $\dfrac{6,669,666}{20,851,820} \approx 0.320$ **69.** $\dfrac{2}{3}$ **70.** $\dfrac{2}{3}$ **71.** $\dfrac{2}{13}$ **72.** $\dfrac{7}{13}$ **73.** $\dfrac{5}{6}$ **74.** $\dfrac{5}{6}$

75. a. $\dfrac{1}{15,504}$ **b.** $\dfrac{25}{3876}$ **76.** $\dfrac{4}{5}$ **77.** $\dfrac{3}{4}$ **78.** ≈ 0.533 **79.** $\dfrac{1}{32}$ **80. a.** 0.04   b. 0.008   c. 0.4096

Chapter 4 Test

1. $a_1 = 1; a_2 = -\dfrac{1}{4}; a_3 = \dfrac{1}{9}; a_4 = -\dfrac{1}{16}; a_5 = \dfrac{1}{25}$ **2.** 105   **3.** 550   **4.** $-21,846$ **5.** 36   **6.** 720   **7.** 120   **8.** $\displaystyle\sum_{i=1}^{20} \dfrac{i+1}{i+2}$

9. $a_n = 5n - 1; a_{12} = 59$ **10.** $a_n = 16\left(\dfrac{1}{4}\right)^{n-1}; a_{12} = \dfrac{1}{262,144}$ **11.** -2387 **12.** -385 **13.** 8   **14.** \$276,426.79

15. 990 ways   **16.** 210 sets   **17.** $10^4 = 10,000$ **18.** $\dfrac{10}{1001}$ **19.** $\dfrac{8}{13}$ **20.** $\dfrac{3}{5}$ **21.** $\dfrac{1}{256}$ **22.** $\dfrac{1}{16}$

Subject Index

scalar multiplication with vectors in terms of, 137
Juneau, Alaska, 70

K
*k***v** (scalar multiple), 134

L
Labor force, 236–37
Lascaux cave, 207, 221
Law of Cosines, 103, 152
  applications, 107
  derivation, 103–4
  problem solving with, 107
  solving SAS triangles with, 104–6
Law of Sines, 91, 92, 152
  applications, 98–99
  derivation of, 91–92
  problem solving with, 98–99
  solving ASA triangles with, 93–94
  solving oblique triangles with, 92–94
  solving SAA triangles with, 92–93
  solving SSA triangles with (no solution), 96
  solving SSA triangles with (one solution), 95
  solving SSA triangles with (two solutions), 96–97
Leaning Tower of Pisa, 101
Learning trials, 209–10
Length
  of circular arc, 10–11
  of hypotenuse, 19
  of vectors, 143
Leonardo of Pisa, 224
Lifetime salary, 250
Line segments, directed, 132–36
Linear speed, 11–13
  definition of, 11
  example, 12–13
  in terms of angular speed, 12
LN key, 178
Log Key, 176
Logarithmic equations, 171, 195–97
  applications, 197–200
  changing from exponential equations to, 171–72
  changing to exponential form, 171, 197
  exponentiating both sides, 197
  location of base and exponent in, 171
  problem solving with, 197–200
  solving, 195–96
  solving with natural logarithms, 197
  solving with product rule, 196–97
Logarithmic expressions
  condensing, 187–88
  expanding, 183, 184, 185–86, 186–87
Logarithmic functions, 170–82
  with base *b*, 171
  common, 176–78
  definition of, 171–72
  domain of, 176
  of $f(x) = \log_b x$ form, 171, 174, 176
  graphing, 173–75, 190
  modeling with, 203–16
  natural, 178–80
  transformations of, 175
Logarithmic models
  example, 211
  scatter plots for, 210
Logarithms
  basic properties of, 172–73, 217
  changing base to common logarithms, 189–90
  changing base to natural logarithms, 190
  common, 176–78, 189
  evaluating, 172
  as exponents, 171
  inverse properties of, 173, 179
  natural, 178–80, 189, 197
  properties of, 173, 177, 183–203, 217
Logistic growth functions, 209
Logistic growth models, 208–10, 218
Los Angeles, California, 69

Lotteries, 258–59, 274, 275
LOTTO (Florida), 274, 275

M
Magnitude
  of directed line segments, 132
  of *k***v**, 134
  of vectors, 135
  writing vectors in terms of, 140–41
Major league baseball player salaries, 236
Malthus, Thomas, 247
Mandelbrot set, 122
Manhattan Island, 169
Map making, 28
Mathematical designs, 224
Men in U.S. labor force, 236–37
Mexico, 168
Minimum wage
  adjusted for inflation, 206
  modeling, 204–6
Minuit, Peter, 169
Miscarriages, 216
Mode, calculator, 24–25
Modeling
  with arithmetic sequences, 238–39
  art of, 210–13
  decay models, 203, 204
  examples, 67–68, 177, 204–6, 209–10, 241
  with exponential functions, 203–16
  exponential growth and decay models, 203–4
  with logarithmic functions, 203–16
  logistic growth models, 208–10, 218
  of periodic behavior, 66–68
Modulus, 124
Monroe, Marilyn, 263
Morrison, Jim, 263, 264
Mount Everest, 16
Muhammad, 16
Multiple-choice tests, 260
Multiples, scalar (*k***v**), 134
Multiplication
  scalar, 133, 134, 137–38, 139
  of vectors, 133
Multiplier effect, 254
Mutually exclusive events, 275
  or probabilities with, 275–76
  probability of either of two occurring, 276

N
n! (*n* factorial), 227
National Geographic, 28, 214
Natural base *e*, 164–65
  evaluating with calculators, 164
  expressing exponential models in, 212
  introducing, 189
  rewriting exponential models in, 212–13
Natural exponential function $f(x) = e^x$, 164
Natural logarithmic functions, 178–80
Natural Logarithmic REGression (LnReg) option, 211
Natural logarithms, 178–80
  and change-of-base property, 189
  changing base logarithms to, 190
  introducing, 189
  notation for, 189
  properties of, 179
  solving exponential equations with, 193
  solving logarithmic equations with, 197
$_nC_r$ (combination of *n* things taken *r* at a time), 265
Negative angles, 3
Negative numbers, multiplying vectors by, 133
Nigeria, 215
90° angles. See Right triangles
Notation
  a_n, 225
  for angles, 4

for common logarithms, 189
degree, minute, second (D°M'S"), 4
factorial, 227–28, 283
index of summation (*i*), 229
for natural logarithms, 189
$_nC_r$, 265
$_nP_r$, 262
summation, 229–32, 283
for vectors, 132
$_nP_r$ (permutations of *n* things *r* at a time), 262
*n*th partial sum (*Sn*), 239, 247, 284
*n*th term (general term), 225
  of arithmetic sequence, 237–39
  formula for, 238, 246
  of geometric sequence, 245–47
  writing terms of sequence from, 225–26
Numbers
  complex, 122–31, 143–44
  negative, 133
  real, 43–45, 133
Nursing home costs, 241

O
O-rings, 159
Oblique triangles, 91
  area of, 97–98
  solving, 92–94, 104–6
Obtuse angles, 3
Odd functions, 45–46, 86
One, basic logarithmic properties involving, 172
Operations with vectors, 138
  in terms of **i** and **j**, 137–39, 153–54
Or probabilities
  with events not mutually exclusive, 276–77, 278
  with mutually exclusive events, 275–76
Orientation (direction angle) of vectors, 143

P
Pairs of coterminal angles, 5
Palestinian population, 213–14
Partial sums, *n*th (S_n), 239, 247, 284
Period, 46, 55
  of $y = A \cos Bx$, 61
  of $y = A \sin x$, 55
  of $y = \cot x$, 76
  of $y = \csc x$, 77
  of $y = \sec x$, 78
  of $y = \tan x$, 73
Periodic behavior, modeling, 66–68
Periodic functions, 46–48
Periodic properties
  finding exact values with, 47
  of sine and cosine functions, 47
  of tangent and cotangent functions, 47
Permutations, 261–63
  calculating with graphing utilities, 262
  distinguishing between combinations and, 264–65
  formula for, 262–63, 284
  of *n* things *r* at a time ($_nP_r$), 262
  and Rubik's cube, 260
Phase shift, 57, 63
Piano keyboard, 224
Picture cards, 273
Plotting complex numbers, 122, 123
Plotting points in polar coordinate system, 111–13
Point Reyes National Seashore, 91
Points
  initial, 132
  multiple representation of, 113–14, 152
  plotting, 111–13
  polar coordinates for, 112, 114
  polar-to-rectangular conversion, 115–16
  rectangular-to-polar conversion, 116–18
  terminal, 132
Poker, 266
Polar axis, 111

Polar coordinate system, 111
  multiple representation of points in, 113–14, 152
  plotting points in, 111–13
  and rectangular coordinate system, 114
Polar coordinates, 111
  conversion from rectangular coordinates to, 116–18
  conversion to rectangular coordinates from, 115–16, 118–19
  finding, 114
  locating points in, 112
  multiple sets for given points, 113–14
  rectangular coordinates and, 114, 152
  sign of *r* and point's location in, 112
Polar equations, 117, 118
Polar form
  of complex numbers, 124–26, 125
  powers of complex numbers in, 128–29
  product of complex numbers in, 126–28
  quotients of complex numbers in, 127–28
Pole, 111
Pole distance (*r*), 112
Population
  Africa, 206
  age 65 and over, 221
  China and India, 213
  city, 179–80
  Florida, 246
  Israel, 213–14
  Mexico, 168
  world, 164–65, 203–4, 211, 212
Population growth, 203, 210
  Florida, 246, 247
  geometric, 246–47
Position vector, 135
Positive angles, 3
Power rule, 185–86, 217
Powers of complex numbers, 128–29
Prediction, 199
Principal (*P*), 165
Probability, 258–59, 270–83
  and, 278–79
  and combinations, 274
  and deck of cards, 273
  of either of two mutually exclusive events occurring, 276
  empirical, 270–71, 285
  of events not occurring, 275
  of not winning lottery, 275
  or, 275–76, 276–77, 278
  possible values for, 271
  theoretical, 271–73, 285
Problem solving
  with angle of elevation, 26–27
  with exponential equations, 197–200
  with Law of Cosines, 107
  with Law of Sines, 98–99
  with logarithmic equations, 197–200
  with right triangle trigonometry, 26–28
  with vectors, 141–43
Product rule, 183–84, 217
  example use, 184
  solving logarithmic equations with, 196–97
Products of complex numbers in polar form, 126–28
Pythagorean identities, 23, 85
Pythagorean Theorem, 19, 22

Q
Quadrantal angles, 3
  trigonometric functions of, 34–36
Quadrants, 37
Quarterly compounding, 165
Quotient identities, 21, 22, 85
Quotient rule, 184–85, 217
Quotients of complex numbers in polar form, 127–28

R
r (common ratio), 245
r (distance from pole), 112

Photo Credits

About the Author   Robert F. Blitzer

CHAPTER 1   Peter Langone/ImageState/International Stock Photography Ltd.   **p2** San Francisco MOMA/Olivier Laude/Getty Images, Inc.—Liaison   **p11** Pictor/Image-State/International Stock Photography Ltd.   **p16** Chris Noble/Getty Images Inc.—Stone **p28** Janet Foster/Masterfile Corporation   **p31** Hugh Sitton/Getty Images Inc.—Stone **p32** Gary Kufner/Corbis Sharpshooters   **p42** Nature Source/Raphael Macia/Photo Researchers, Inc.   **p50** Jon Feingersh/Corbis/Stock Market   **p72** Mehau Kulyk/Science Photo Library/Photo Researchers, Inc.

CHAPTER 2   Jim Cummins/Getty Images, Inc.   **p91** Frank Clarkson/Getty Images, Inc.—Liaison   **p103** Bob Dammerich/Stock Boston   **p122** R.F. Voss "29-Fold M-set Sea-horse" computer-generated image. ©1990 R.F. Voss/IBM Research.   **p131** Tom Cogill/Stephen T. Thornton   **p132** Jeff Greenberg/Photo Researchers, Inc.   **p134** Tom Cogill/Stephen T. Thornton   **p148** Karl Heinz Kreifelts/AP/Wide World Photos   **p156** Robert E. Daemmrich/Getty Images Inc.—Stone; Mimmo Jodice/CORBIS

CHAPTER 3   Anthony Neste   **p159** Bruce Weaver/AP/Wide World Photos   **p170** David Weintraub/Photo Researchers, Inc.   **p183** Ron Chapple/Getty Images, Inc.—Taxi **p192** KEN CHERNUS/Getty Images, Inc.—Taxi   **p203** Bullit Marquez/AP/Wide World Photos   **p207** Jean-Marie Chauvet/Corbis/Sygma

CHAPTER 4   REUTERS/Colin Braley/CORBIS   **p224** Dick Morton   **p235** David Young-Wolff/PhotoEdit   **p244** SuperStock, Inc.   **p247** Richard Lord/The Image Works **p250** U.S. Bureau of Engraving and Printing   **p258** L. Schwartzwald/Corbis/Sygma   **p259** SuperStock, Inc.   **p260** Sue Klemen/Stock Boston   **p263** Picture Desk, Inc./Kobal Collection   **p264** Imapress/Globe Photos, Inc.; Michael Ochs Archives Ltd.; SIN/CORBIS; AP/Wide World Photos   **p270** SuperStock, Inc.   **p274** Karen Furth   **p279** UPI/CORBIS